GOD, TSAR, AND PEOPLE

A volume in the NIU Series in Slavic, East European,
and Eurasian Studies
Edited by Christine D. Worobec

For a list of books in the series, visit our website at cornellpress.cornell.edu.

GOD, TSAR, AND PEOPLE

THE POLITICAL CULTURE OF EARLY MODERN RUSSIA

Daniel B. Rowland

NORTHERN ILLINOIS UNIVERSITY PRESS
AN IMPRINT OF CORNELL UNIVERSITY PRESS
Ithaca and London

Copyright © 2020 by Cornell University

All rights reserved. Except for brief quotations in a review, this book, or parts thereof, must not be reproduced in any form without permission in writing from the publisher. For information, address Cornell University Press, Sage House, 512 East State Street, Ithaca, New York 14850. Visit our website at cornellpress.cornell.edu.

First published 2020 by Cornell University Press

Library of Congress Cataloging-in-Publication Data

Names: Rowland, Daniel B. (Daniel Bruce), 1941–author.
Title: God, Tsar, and people : the political culture of early modern Russia / Daniel B. Rowland.
Description: Ithaca [New York] : Cornell University Press, 2020. | Series: NIU series in Slavic, East European, and Eurasian studies | Includes bibliographical references and index.
Identifiers: LCCN 2020011767 (print) | LCCN 2020011768 (ebook) | ISBN 9781501752094 (cloth) | ISBN 9781501753725 (paperback) | ISBN 9781501752100 (epub) | ISBN 9781501752117 (pdf)
Subjects: LCSH: Political culture—Russia. | Russia—Intellectual life. | Moscow (Russia)—Kings and rulers.
Classification: LCC DK32.7 .R69 2020 (print) | LCC DK32.7 (ebook) | DDC 306.20947/09031—dc23
LC record available at https://lccn.loc.gov/2020011767
LC ebook record available at https://lccn.loc.gov/2020011768

To Wendy

Contents

Acknowledgments   ix

A Brief Note on Transliteration and Our Editorial Policy   xiii

Foreword: Pathbreaking and Paradigm-Shifting by Russell E. Martin   xv

The Textual: Breaking the Code

1. Kurbskii and the Historians   3
2. Toward an Understanding of the Political Ideas in Ivan Timofeev's *Vremennik*   23
3. The Problem of Advice in Muscovite Tales about the Time of Troubles   54
4. Did Muscovite Literary Ideology Place Limits on the Power of the Tsar (1540s–1660s)?   82
5. The Memory of Saint Sergius in Sixteenth-Century Russia   115

Adding the Visual: Investigating Art and Architecture

6. Biblical Military Imagery in the Political Culture of Early Modern Russia: The Blessed Host of the Heavenly Tsar   127
7. Moscow—The Third Rome or the New Israel?   155

8. Architecture and Dynasty: Boris Godunov's Uses of Architecture, 1584–1606 — 188

9. Two Cultures, One Throne Room: Secular Courtiers and Orthodox Culture in the Golden Hall of the Moscow Kremlin — 211

10. Architecture, Image, and Ritual in the Throne Rooms of Muscovite Russia — 234

11. Advice, Advisers, and Courtiers: Decision Making and Advice in the Royal Book Volume of the Illustrated Chronicle Compilation — 259

12. Ivan the Terrible as a Carolingian Renaissance Prince — 299

Summing Up: What Our Work Means

13. Autocracy — 315

14. Muscovy — 319

15. God, Tsar, and People: Some Further Thoughts — 358

Index 389

Acknowledgments

Any scholar who has been active over a period of almost five decades would have accumulated major debts to his or her colleagues in the field. But in my case, my colleagues in the field of Muscovite history have had an unusual degree of influence over my work. Over these decades, we have puzzled together over the same or similar problems, starting with what to make of the picture of Muscovite culture and politics that we inherited from earlier generations. Each of us charted his or her own course, examined different types of evidence, and came to separate conclusions. But, as we presented our research and commented on each other's papers yearly at the conferences of the American Association for the Advancement of Slavic Studies, now renamed the Association for Slavic, Eastern European, and Eurasian Studies, and in numerous other venues, both formal and informal, we felt part of a common undertaking: the creation of a new paradigm in our understanding of that time and place. In that extraordinarily fertile and long-lasting environment, it is hard for me to say where my own ideas end and those of my colleagues begin. So my first acknowledgment is to all of my colleagues in early modern Russian history without whose work virtually none of these essays would be the same.

Among this scholarly family, I am indebted particularly to a small handful of friends and colleagues who have been of special help, and whose influence on these essays is particularly great. The last essay in this volume explores this influence in substantive terms, but I can here express my personal gratitude to these friends. First, to Bob Crummey and Ned Keenan, whose guidance was essential to my formation as a historian of Muscovy. My longest-lasting friendship in the field is with Don Ostrowski. He put me up on his floor or couch during my earliest visits to Harvard, and we have discussed intensely and at length both issues in early modern history and problems we encountered in our teaching of the history of various places and periods.

As I wrote in the final essay here, Nancy Shields Kollmann, Russ Martin, Valerie Kivelson, and Michael Flier have had direct and continuing influence on my thinking. Together these scholars have reimagined many, even most aspects of Muscovite history. Their work has been a model for me of hard academic work, of rigorous and careful scholarship, and of bold and often revolutionary interpretations. I am also indebted to Isolde Thyret, an accomplished scholar both in art history and the medieval Christian culture of the West whose insights and use of visual evidence have been highly influential on all members of our merry band. Daniel Waugh trained me in manuscript studies while we were both on an exchange in Leningrad in 1972 and has since been an inspiration both of modesty and of extraordinary knowledge.

Among Russian scholars, I am particularly indebted to Engelina Sergeevna Smirnova. Engelina Sergeevna possesses a knowledge both of Byzantine and of Russian art history beyond the capabilities of any of us in the West. She has been a model of patience and generosity in sharing this knowledge, which has greatly enriched my own understanding as I worked on many of the essays here. Nina Klvidze and Andrei Batalov have also been a major influence, both in personal contacts and in their published works. Finally Mikhail Krom has been a wonderful interlocutor in recent years as I've struggled to put together the various pieces of the Muscovite puzzle as interpreted by my colleagues, both in Russia and in the West. In particular, his command of the comparative histories of early modern states all over Europe has been exceptionally useful.

My academic home over these decades has been the Department of History at the University of Kentucky. I am most grateful to all of my colleagues there for creating a vibrant culture of inquiry and scholarship, as expressed in numberless discussions and papers on many subjects. My greatest debt is to my beloved colleague Karen Petrone, whose extraordinary human qualities of generosity and humor have matched her now widely recognized scholarly achievements. Bruce Eastwood was an early supporter and a vigorous questioner of my early ideas. His rigorous mind has been a model for me. I also want to thank Gerald Janecek of the Department of Modern and Classical Languages at the University of Kentucky for both wonderful advice and unfailing moral support of my work in a field far removed from his own.

My experience with the Yale Russian Chorus has also been crucial for my work, giving me repeated intense experiences of the emotional impact of Russian music, particularly Russian liturgical music, over many decades, from 1966 to the present. This experience has helped me imagine the way Muscovites experienced both church services and even secular events.

I owe a major debt to the Hilandar Research Library of The Ohio State University and its director Mary-Allen ("Pasha") Johnson. The Hilandar Room has repeatedly welcomed me (and many other colleagues) to do research in its remarkable collection and has especially helped with the images in chapter 11.

ACKNOWLEDGMENTS

In the creation of this book, my greatest debt is to Ryan Voogt, former graduate student at Kentucky and now an impressive scholar in his own right. Ryan has been crucial at every stage of production, from digitizing the original texts to corralling many public domain images to illustrate those texts. It is no exaggeration to say that, without Ryan, this book would not exist. I am also deeply grateful to Russell Martin, not only for his generous introductory essay but also for his painstaking and very useful editing of my final essay. Amy Farranto of Northern Illinois University Press has been a wonderful and supportive editor, whose confidence in this project over several years has kept my spirits up and my computer busy.

Finally, and most importantly, my greatest debt is to my wife Wendy, without whose love and support this book would not exist, and its author's life would be much poorer.

I would also like here to acknowledge with gratitude the generosity of the publishers of most of the essays in this volume, and many of its images. Publishers of texts have not only given cheerful permission to republish their material without payment but have also wished me hearty good luck in this project. I am grateful, therefore, to *The Slavonic and East European Review, The Russian Review,* and *Harvard Ukrainian Studies,* plus Slavica Publishers, Holy Trinity Publications, the University of California Press, Pennsylvania State University Press, Brill, and Yale University Press (London). I also want to thank Kharis Mustafin of AKTEON for his encouragement for authors to use and publish images from his wonderful edition of the *Litsevoi letopisnyi svod,* to the staff of the Beinecke Library of Yale University for help with the Olearius image, and Rikard Nordstrom for permission to use the image of the icon of the Apocalypse in the collection of the National Museum in Stockholm.

A Brief Note on Transliteration and Our Editorial Policy

My editors at Cornell and Northern Illinois University Presses and I have decided against a "pure" recreation of the previously published essays in this volume in order to maintain consistent editorial conventions. Nevertheless, I have resisted the temptation to revise my earlier essays to update any new opinions that I may have. Issues of consistency were particularly pressing in chapters 2 and 13, which were originally published in Great Britain. Therefore, we have made small alterations to conform those texts with American editorial and spelling conventions. We have also changed all passages transliterated from Russian to conform to the most widely accepted transliteration system in the United States—the Library of Congress system.

Foreword

Pathbreaking and Paradigm-Shifting

In his earnest defense of the academic article over the academic book, Robert Schneider, editor of the *American Historical Review*, laid out several reasons why today is the "golden age of the scholarly article." Articles are, he lists, "accessible and durable," digitized and therefore "searchable," and a willing format for "highly specialized material." But it is Schneider's last reason that rings especially true for our purposes here. Articles are, as a genre, "well-suited for the kind of essay-length historical arguments that can have pathbreaking and paradigm-shifting effects. We all can cite the names of historians who have had their primary impact in our fields through essays."[1] Schneider then goes on to cite two such pathbreaking articles: Frederick Jackson Turner's "The Significance of the Frontier in American History" and Joan Scott's "Gender: A Useful Category of Historical Analysis."[2] Were he a Russian historian, Schneider might have cited a few others, such as Gregory Freeze's "The Soslovie (Estate) Paradigm and Russian Social History," Leopold Haimson's "The Problem of Social Stability in Urban Russia, 1905–1917," Marc Raeff's "The Well-Ordered Police State and the Development of Modernity in Seventeenth- and Eighteenth-Century Europe," or Edward Keenan's "Muscovite Political Folkways."[3] Still other seminal articles in the field of Russian history come, of course, quickly to mind, as well. Historians have, as Schneider says, used the academic article, more often than the book, as the main vehicle to "impact their field"—especially now, in these days of crisis in academic book publishing. To be sure, an influential, pathbreaking article on a CV has launched or lengthened more than one or two academic careers.

But usually only one per historian per career. "Pathbreaking" and "paradigm-shifting" articles are, to be sure, few and far between: and rightly so. They express moments of insight and imagination that come to the seasoned historian (and sometimes to the prodigy) once in a lifetime, if that. What is truly remarkable about the pages that follow is that they contain a sizeable set of articles and book chapters that are genuinely pathbreaking in their impact, influence, and originality, and, furthermore, all emerged from the pen of one

xv

scholar: Daniel Rowland. Collected here are works that emulate what Schneider thought was the very definition of the seminal article: "a means of engaging with large questions, presenting bold interpretations, or perhaps thinking out loud about what direction we want our fields to take."[4]

"Engaging large questions, presenting bold interpretations," and "thinking aloud" are things Daniel Rowland has been doing his entire career. Looking at the collection of works in this volume, one might be justifiably struck at Dan's rare ability to dig deep into a topic and yet pull back and trace connections to larger historiographical trends and questions. To do so with such frequency and success on such a range of topics is what makes Dan a central figure in the study of Muscovy. As the editors of the Festschrift published in his honor wrote: "Not constrained by received wisdom or canonical conventions of the field, he continually questions and challenges traditional frameworks and offers creative ways to reconceptualize the premises from which we approach Russian history."[5] It is his willingness to question and challenge that has been the secret to Dan's scholarly success; it is his fresh approaches to the old and familiar that have made so many of his works essential reading.

The range of topics treated herein is, indeed, impressive. Among the most important articles and book chapters that Dan has produced (so far!) are those that have grappled with the nature of Muscovite monarchy—particularly the question of advice from boyars and courtiers, and the customary forms of restraint on monarchical power. Here Dan has not been tempted, as many have, to explore this question by focusing on institutions that did or did not develop in Russia and that might have curtailed the tsar's power—a path that invariably leads to pondering such futile questions as, Was Russia backward? Or Is Russia part of the West? Instead, Dan chose to explore the way informal, notional ideas of "good" and "bad" rulership existed in Muscovy in the fifteenth through seventeenth centuries, and how those ideas were represented by and to the tsar—who was, to be sure, ever in need of being reminded of them—to the court, to middle- and lower-ranking servitors, secretaries, and scribes, and even merchants of various ranks. Few articles deserve the appellation "seminal" more than Dan's "The Problem of Advice in Muscovite Tales about the Time of Troubles" (1979) or his "Did Muscovite Literary Ideology Place Limits on the Power of the Tsar (1540s–1660s)?" (1990). These two mainstays can now, thanks to this collection, be read next to his most recent word on the subject—"Advice, Advisers, and Courtiers: Decision Making and Advice in the Royal Book of the Illustrated Chronicle Compilation" (2017)—which both supports and supplements the ideas he laid out decades earlier.

If the numerical distribution of his articles indicate anything, Dan's major thrust has been in the realm of architecture and art. Dan has emerged as one of the most sensitive readers of Russian primary sources of his generation, and he has modeled ways of thinking about space and decoration as primary sources as well—"documents" that can be "read" and interpreted as much as words in ink on paper or vellum. His studies of architecture in particular have been pathbreaking: studies of the Kremlin's palace and church spaces date back a century or more, but Dan's modern studies of these and other important architectural monuments have blended traditional archival (documentary) research with detailed examinations of the layouts of physical spaces, yielding genuinely new findings about the way these spaces were used to convey messages about power, monarchy, dynasty, and religious piety in the early modern period. Dan's "Biblical Military Imagery in the Political Culture of Early Modern Russia: The Blessed Host of the Heavenly Tsar" (1994) was a major contribution to a paradigm shift in how we think of architectural spaces and the artwork that fills them, being one of Dan's most cited essays. Dan's masterful follow-up articles to this early piece (and his co-edited book) have only cemented his place as the premier authority on political imagery and architectural messaging in Muscovy.[6] Readers can now read in sequence his first study of the "Blessed Host" alongside "Architecture and Dynasty: Boris Godunov's Uses of Architecture, 1584–1605" (2003), "Two Cultures, One Throne Room: Secular Courtiers and Orthodox Culture in the Golden Hall of the Moscow Kremlin" (2003), and "Architecture, Image, and Ritual in the Throne Rooms of Muscovy, 1550–1650" (2008)—all of which move forward the idea that power, space, and image were integrated in Muscovy in ways not unlike that elsewhere in Christian Europe, though in an unmistakable Orthodox visual register.

Dan's interest in architecture and art brings him very close to the Russian Orthodox world, which relied on imagery to articulate everything from complex theological concepts to the dynastic legitimacy of the ruling houses. This collection reveals, perhaps better than anywhere else, Dan's deep interest and respect for Russian Orthodoxy. It is a theme that runs through his work and takes center stage in his masterful "Moscow—The Third Rome or the New Israel?" (1996), which broke new ground in linking texts and motifs in Muscovy to Old Testamental themes, even in preference to early Christian or Byzantine motifs—a thesis that most at the time accepted with a near audible "aha!," as if someone had finally pointed out for the first time an idea that had been hiding in plain sight. Russian Orthodoxy was not a blueprint for Muscovite society, but it was an indispensable element of it, and therefore serves as a vital lens through which historians today can understand early modern Russian culture. Without being known principally as a historian of the Church or of Orthodox theology and liturgics, Dan is one of the most important scholars of these things. Readers of this collection will bump into Dan's sensitive, appreciative treatment of Russian Orthodoxy again and again on the pages that follow. They will see it dazzlingly on display in "Toward an Understanding of the Political Ideas in Ivan Timofeyev's *Vremennik*" (1984).

Finally, this collection includes a piece that is a favorite of many of Dan's colleagues: "Ivan the Terrible as a Carolingian Renaissance Prince" (1995). It is a luxurious essay, comparing the textual and political cultures of Muscovy and the Carolingian kingdom. And it has no footnotes. It is the kind of piece that only the seasoned practitioner of the historian's craft dare write and publish. It rests on experience, not the footnote; and it conveys a sense of things rather than—to borrow Carlyle's phrase—"Dryasdust" results of "torpedo Histories."[7] It is an essay modeled, in form if not content, on Keenan's "Muscovite Political Folkways"—one of the great seminal articles of early Russian history mentioned at the outset, which also has few footnotes. "Ivan the Terrible as a Carolingian Renaissance Prince" originally appeared in the Festschrift for Ned, and its format was envisioned as itself a tribute to Keenan, for whom Dan has the highest possible respect and affection. It is fitting and useful, then, to have this piece in this collection: a place where many of Dan's varied arguments appear, synthetically, under one title.

Readers will likely bounce from article to article as they encounter this book. This is probably not a book to be read in sequence from page one forward to the end. One might want to have their first pass through it that way, but readers will want later to return to this collection and rearrange for themselves its rich contents: reading it thematically and chronologically (that is, by date of publication), so that Dan's thinking can be apprehended as it evolved over time. Readers may want to trace sequentially the themes of power, advice, and monarchy; architecture and dynastic imagery; art and power; and religion and culture. But readers will, however the book is read and reread, return to its pages to read these articles and book chapters, because they will certainly remain useful and instructive for as far ahead as we can see. Which is in the nature of those works that have earned the appellation "pathbreaking" and "paradigm-shifting."

Russell E. Martin
Westminster College
New Wilmington, PA

Notes

1. Robert A. Schneider, "The Golden Age of the Scholarly Article Is Now," *Perspectives on History*, September 1, 2006, 39–40.

2. Frederick Jackson Turner, "The Significance of the Frontier in American History," *The Annual Report of the American Historical Association for the Year 1893* (1894): 197–227; Joan Scott, "Gender: A Useful Category of Historical Analysis," *American Historical Review* 91, no. 5 (December 1986): 1053–1075.

3. Gregory Freeze, "The Soslovie (Estate) Paradigm and Russian Social History," *American Historian Review* 91, no. 1 (February 1986): 11–36; Leopold Haimson, "The Problem of Social Stability in Urban Russia, 1905–1917 (Part One)," *Slavic Review* 23, no. 4 (December 1964): 619–642; Leopold Haimson, "The Problem of Social Stability in Urban Russia, 1905–1917 (Part Two)," *Slavic Review* 24, no. 1 (March 1965): 1–22; Marc Raeff, "The Well-Ordered Police State and the Development of Modernity in Seventeenth- and Eighteenth-Century Europe: An Attempt at a Comparative Approach," *American Historical Review* 80, no. 5 (December 1975): 1221–1243; Edward L. Keenan Jr., "Muscovite Political Folkways," *Russian Review* 45 (1986): 115–181.

4. Schneider, "The Golden Age of the Scholarly Article Is Now," 39.

5. Valerie Kivelson, Karen Petrone, Nancy Shields Kollmann, and Michael S. Flier, "Daniel Rowland and Muscovite Cultural History," in Valerie Kivelson et al., eds., *The New Muscovite Cultural History: A Collection in Honor of Daniel B. Rowland* (Bloomington, IL: Slavica, 2009), 3–8 (quote at 3).

6. See James Cracraft and Daniel B. Rowland, eds., *Architectures of Russian Identity: 1500 to the Present* (Ithaca, NY: Cornell University Press, 2003).

7. S. C. Lomas, ed., *The Letters and Speeches of Oliver Cromwell with Elucidations by Thomas Carlyle*, with an introduction by C. H. Firth, 3 vols. (London: Methuen & Co., 1904), 1:1–10, at 3.

GOD, TSAR, AND PEOPLE

The Textual
Breaking the Code

CHAPTER 1

Kurbskii and the Historians

If there is a *Russkaia Sloboda* in heaven as there was a *Nemetskaia Sloboda* in Muscovy, its unruly inhabitants must often have been amused at the roles in which they have been cast by succeeding generations of their countrymen. And few could have been more amused, amazed, and even, I think, horrified, than Prince Andrei Mikhailovich Kurbskii. Indeed one wonders if the poor prince, in the ages of ages left to him, will ever succeed in disentangling the various interpretations given to his life and works by historians and in reconciling the historians' opinions with his own recollections.

Although the volume of opinion about Kurbskii is considerable, the information about his life prior to his desertion to Poland-Lithuania on April 30,

---

This littler essay was written almost entirely in the spring of 1969, toward the end of my second official year in graduate school at Yale. I wrote it for my own wise adviser, Robert Crummey, who had assigned a topic entirely different from this one. (I did complete the original assignment.) I include it here not because it is a great work of scholarship, but because it shows me trying to work on a problem that has preoccupied me ever since: How can modern historians more accurately interpret cultural evidence from Muscovite Russia? Edward Keenan's major book (*The Kurbskii-Groznyi Apocrypha*) questioning the authenticity of both Kurbskii's *Correspondence* with Ivan IV and his *History* was published in 1971 by Harvard University Press, and has occasioned much debate, both pro and con. I am a firm supporter of Keenan's hypothesis, and so for me this essay relates more to historiography—how three seminal historians of Russia interpreted a famous set of texts—than to what that evidence tells us about Russia. But the significance of the Kurbskii corpus remains, only now the evidence applies to seventeenth-century, rather then sixteenth-century, Muscovy, a discussion now well under way.

1564, is slight.¹ He was descended from the princes of Yaroslavl´, although he belonged to a cadet branch of that family. He was remotely connected to the family of the Tsaritsa Anastasia, and had closer connections with the important families of Bel´skii and Tuchkov.² A pupil and perhaps a friend of Maksim the Greek, he almost certainly had a better-than-average education for a Russian nobleman of his time.³ He seems to have thought he did.⁴ According to Iasinskii and Andreyev, he became a *stol´nik* (gentleman of the table) at the age of twenty-one.⁵ He then began a successful military career, serving in both sieges of Kazan´ and later in the Livonian war in increasingly important positions until about a year before his flight, when the service lists stop mentioning him altogether.⁶ This career is well documented both by his own accounts, chiefly in his *History of Ivan IV*, and by references in other sources. The main conclusion that may be drawn is that Kurbskii's military services were in such demand that he spent very little time at home or at court in Moscow, but, as he wrote in his first letter to Ivan "always in far-distant towns have I stood in arms against your foes."⁷

The exact nature of his relationship with Ivan remains unclear. His military duties must have prevented him from taking an active role in day-to-day governmental decisions, but the tsar seems to have felt well disposed toward him in the 1550s at least. During the succession crisis of March 1553, Kurbskii claims to have supported Ivan's son Dmitrii against the claims of Prince Vladimir Andreievich Staritskii,⁸ and the tsar does not deny this. Shortly thereafter, Ivan took Kurbskii, along with Aleksei Adashev and several others who had sworn allegiance to Dmitrii, on a pilgrimage to the Holy Trinity and Kirillo-Belozerskii Monasteries.⁹ In 1560, Ivan used "exceedingly loving words" with Kurbskii before sending him to Derpt.¹⁰

This career is not particularly remarkable, and Kurbskii would have attracted little interest had he not been the alleged author of five polemical letters to Ivan and a history of the latter's reign.¹¹ Since, as we shall see, many assumptions not only about Ivan's reign but about the whole nature of politics in sixteenth-century Muscovy are based largely on these materials, it would be of some interest to compare the views of several of those historians whose work contributed to the acceptance of these assumptions with the documents themselves.

This essay, then, deals with historiography more than with history. Indeed its main concerns are very detailed, even esoteric matters. I don't propose to enter into the about-to-be-created discussions on whether Kurbskii was or was not the author of these documents, nor to reinterpret Kurbskii's role in Russian history. Rather I shall examine the interpretations given to these documents by three of the most influential Russian historians. I don't even propose to show that any of these historians grossly misinterpreted this source—Karamzin, Solov´ev, and Kliuchevskii were all too skillful as historians and the source was too readily available for them to have attributed to Kurbskii statements completely at variance with what he said. Rather we shall explore fine points of interpretation, small increments of meaning that several of these historians, in my opinion, laid over or injected into the words of the documents. These subtle shifts in meaning had effects that were not small, for they collectively created the impression that Kurbskii's work, together with Ivan's letters to him, "constituted the most complete summing-up of that conflict between the autocratic ideals of the Muscovite grand princes and the conservative opposition of the boyars which characterized the political life of the Muscovite state in the sixteenth century."[12] By the time of the Revolution, interpretations of this source by succeeding generations of historians had played a vital part in creating the general understanding implicit in almost all historical writing about the period that the interplay between the centralizing autocracy and the conservative, centrifugal *boyarstvo* constituted the basis of Muscovite politics during the sixteenth century.

Now one of the things that differentiate sixteenth-century Muscovite history from the history of Western European countries of the same period is the relative lack of sources. Fires and other acts of God and man succeeded in destroying much of the comparatively small amount that was originally written down. The result has been that the discovery of new sources has had a fairly small importance in altering the historian's major assumptions about Muscovy before the Troubles. Many of the most important sources were known by the beginning of the nineteenth century; most were known by the middle of that century. Changes in interpretation were therefore due not so much to what historians read, but to how they interpreted what they read. Since no historian dealing with the period could afford to ignore Kurbskii's work, each had to find what he needed in it, and in this task, it would not be unkind to say, these historians succeeded very well.

Before dealing with the historians, we should first get some feel for how Kurbskii operates as a historian and writer, some idea of his general style. We shall therefore begin by some simple, even obvious, observations drawn specifically from the first section of the *History* in which Kurbskii describes Vasilii's second marriage to Elena Glinskii. I select this passage because it is a self-contained little section that has no great importance in itself but well illustrates Kurbskii's style of argument.[13]

The main point of this passage is stated at the outset, that "evil ends with evil"—that is that Vasilii's evil second marriage ended with the conception of

Ivan IV. Kurbskii very quickly sketches out the two sides involved in the struggle over the marriage. On the one side we have Vasilii himself, "the great (especially in pride and ferocity) prince"; Elena, whom Kurbskii has already called one of the "evil and sorcerous wives," whom the devil used to corrupt the clan of Russian princes; and, finally, "the most wicked Josephians." On the other side we see Solomonia, Vasilii's "holy and innocent" wife; a number of "holy and reverend men" who opposed the marriage and were persecuted by Grand Prince Vasilii; Prince Semen Kurbskii; Vasilii/Vassian Patrikeev; Maksim the Greek; and, somewhat to the side, "that eminent man" Herberstein, imperial ambassador to Moscow. There is no middle ground between these camps; except for ancestors mentioned in passing, everyone is put firmly into one camp or the other. Not surprisingly, we have here a good old-fashioned struggle between good and evil, told with no embarrassment and no apologies. The same struggle is the main focus of attention in the rest of Kurbskii's work. On one side are the "holy," the "righteous," the "wise," the "brave"; on the other, with the devil prompting them, are the "evil flatterers," the "children of darkness," the "priests of Cronus."

Given this view of history, Kurbskii's main task is to assign his characters to a given side, but after he has accomplished that, he relaxes a little. Once he has placed a figure in one category or the other, his concern for distinctions within each category is small. It wouldn't matter very much, for example, if one were to call Vasilii "most wicked" or the Josephians "great in pride and ferocity,"[14] and Semen Kurbskii's "holy way of life" could have been ascribed equally to Maksim or Vassian. In the same way, there is very little to differentiate Ivan's "wicked flatterers" from his "companions of the table," or "the accursed ones" from "the strong and great satanic host." The important thing about these figures is that they were evil, inspired by the devil. There is more precise meaning in the epithets applied to the other side, the good side, but not a great deal: "glorious in virtue, and brilliant in birth," "truly great in courage and bravery," "select [*izbrannyi*] in birth," and "a man of great bravery and intellect . . . versed in the holy scriptures."[15]

This loose use of descriptions does not seem to be due so much to carelessness or even polemical exaggeration, but to a very primitive view of psychology. For Kurbskii, a figure either works for the devil or for Christ. Middle positions, difficult moral choices, psychological strains are all foreign to this view. Ivan himself is one of the very few figures who changes sides, so to speak, at first appearing as debauched, then as righteous under the spiritual guidance of Syl'vestr and Adashev, and finally as a "foul beast" surrounded by his "children of darkness." But the interesting thing is that, although these changes in Ivan are the focus of Kurbskii's attention, we learn almost nothing about

Ivan's character or the way he felt at any moment. His debauchery and his reform are both described in general terms with no real connection with a personality.[16] And when he falls again into the devil's hands, Kurbskii calls him "the beast newly appeared" (*novoiavlennyi zver'*).[17] Thus "men, created gentle by God according to nature, change by their own self-will [*samovlastno voleiu*] to ferocity and inhumanity."[18]

Another thing that strikes the modern reader is that Kurbskii's logic is not very logical. Again let us go back to the passage we have been examining. It seems strange that although he mainly seems interested in establishing the evil nature of Vasilii's marriage, Kurbskii devotes over four times as much space to describing the "holy and reverent men" who opposed the marriage as he does to the marriage itself. Moreover, he never cites any scriptural or patristic authority as to why the marriage was "against the law of God," but mentions rather the attendant circumstances, the forcible tonsure and incarceration of Solomonia and the disapproval of the "holy" men. In short, he does not argue with logical or legal precision.

There is, however, an important method of argument operating here, one that underlies almost all of the *History* and much of the *Correspondence*. It stems directly from Kurbskii's strictly dualistic view of the world and operates by association and opposition. When he gratuitously mentions Vasilii's "many evil deeds committed against the law of God" the implication is that if Vasilii had committed many evil deeds, he was likely to commit more. He used evil monks, "those most wicked Josephians," to carry out the execution of Vassian. Vasilii and his second marriage are also condemned by the fact that holy and reverent men opposed the marriage and Vasilii cruelly persecuted them. In other words, because good men opposed it, the marriage was bad; because he persecuted good men, Vasilii was bad. One suspects that Solomonia, like many of Ivan's victims described in the sixth and seventh chapters of the *History*, was "holy and innocent" at least in part because she suffered at the hands of an evil tsar. Thus the picture of the court as divided sharply into "holy" and "foul" camps is not only the end product of Kurbskii's writing but an important part of his argument as well.

Since the welfare of the realm depended on the actions of the tsar, and since the actions of the tsar depended on his spiritual health, Kurbskii's description of the reign falls into three periods according to Ivan's spiritual condition. In the earliest period, Ivan was brought up "in every enjoyment and lust" by the "great proud . . . boyars." The young prince, surrounded by evil men, became a cruel murderer both of dumb beasts and of his own servants. God punished Ivan and the land with the Moscow fire and Tatar invasions.[19] The second phase begins with the appearance of Syl'vestr and Adashev. Their "main good deed," according to Kurbskii, was the strengthening of the tsar, his spiritual regeneration. As part of that task, they separated him from his evil advisers and surrounded him with "advisers [*sovetniki*], men of understanding and perfection."[20] As a result, the country was well governed and prevailed against her enemies, principally Kazan′. After the victory over Kazan′, the devil began to tempt Ivan, shooting him like an arrow to Bishop Vassian Toporkov, who advised him not to keep about him advisers wiser than himself.[21] Ivan listened, and thereupon disasters again began to recur: the death of Dmitrii Ivanovich and defeat at the hands of the Tatars. This latter defeat frightened the tsar, so that "then it seemed as though he once again repented, and he ruled well for some years."[22]

"Flatterers" and "comrades of the table" persuaded Ivan not to strike a final blow at the Tatars in 1558, which Kurbskii felt would have been successful.[23] But, in general, the second phase, the phase of good government, lasted until the disgrace of Syl′vestr and Adashev, when Ivan again opened "his ears to those wicked flatterers, than whom, as I have already said many times, not a single deathly boil can be more pestilential in the tsardom. . . . Thus, with countless other tissues of lies, in agreement with their father the devil . . . they deceived their man with flattering words and overthrew the soul of the Christian tsar, who was living righteously and in penitence, and thus they broke that bond which was woven by God for spiritual love . . . and those accursed ones drove him away from the vicinity of God."[24] Thus began the final disastrous epoch of the reign marked by the slaughter of holy and innocent men and Russia's defeat at the hands of her enemies.

Kurbskii's interpretation is transparently clear. When the tsar surrounded himself with holy men, then he lived righteously, the *tsarstvo* prospered, and its enemies were defeated. When "flatterers" and "comrades of the table" replaced "holy men" in the tsar's confidence, then his spiritual health declined, justice was perverted, and Russia's enemies prevailed. This message is repeated over and over again.

The first historian to use the *Correspondence* and the *History* extensively was N. M. Karamzin.[25] Their impact on him was great: a glance at the footnotes in volumes 8 and 9 of his *History of the Russian State* reveal the extent of his debt to Kurbskii. Karamzin relied on Kurbskii not only for details of various historical events such as the siege of Kazan′ but also for the interpretative framework of Ivan's reign as a whole. He adopted Kurbskii's general scheme of three phases based on Ivan's moral progress. Ivan, after a debauched childhood, was suddenly and forcefully converted into a virtuous ruler by the stern admonitions of Syl′vestr, who for Ivan's reform played upon the fear that the recent Moscow fire had inspired in the young tsar.[26] The priest was seconded in his efforts by Ivan's virtuous first wife Anastasia and by the young tsar's friend Aleksei Adashev, "a handsome young man described as an angel on earth whose soul was pure and delicate, whose morals were excellent, and whose mind was as agreeable and substantial as it was strong."[27] Karamzin asserts, "These friends of the fatherland and of piety were able to touch, to smite his heart using its own salutary terror."[28] The result of this moral conversion was the good government of the late 1540s and 1550s.

However, the soul of the tsar was not firm enough to remain on its path of virtue. First, seeds of distrust for Syl'vestr were planted in Ivan's mind when Sil'vestr was reluctant to swear an oath to Ivan's son and "perhaps secretly supported" Vladimir Andreevich Staritskii, the tsar's cousin.[29] Virtue triumphed, however, and, after his recovery, Ivan showed the greatest clemency to those who had supported Vladimir. The real blow to Ivan and to the realm was Anastasia's death in 1560. "It is at this point," wrote Karamzin darkly at the end of volume 8, "that the fortunate days of Ivan and of Russia ended, because, at the same time that he lost his wife, he abandoned the path of virtue."[30] In the first pages of volume 9,[31] Karamzin describes the changes that took place in Ivan's heart and in his court, his bitterness over Anastasia's death, his resentment of Syl'vestr and Adashev's domination, the trial of these former favorites, and the emergence of an evil group of counselors—"debauchers" (*razvrashniki*)[32] as Karamzin calls them—who corrupt the tsar's soul. Corruption having entered the heart of the ruler, the government of the realm is corrupted, the innocent are punished, evil flatterers are rewarded, the *oprichnina* begins.[33]

Certainly there are differences between Kurbskii's account and Karamzin's. Kurbskii's strictly Orthodox idea of piety and Karamzin's sentimental idea of virtue are different.[34] Kurbskii everywhere sees the direct intervention of God, "for our sins," while Karamzin goes further into the psychology of the tsar. Karamzin, for example, makes much of the role of Anastasia and of the influence of Ivan's family life for the ruler and the realm, while Kurbskii hardly mentions Ivan's first wife.[35] "Even the family of the monarch," writes Karamzin of the situation after the appearance of Syl'vestr and Adashev, "where coldness, envy and hatred had formerly reigned, now offered to Russia an example both of peace and of perfect union. Ivan was better able to appreciate the good qualities of his wife since he knew the happiness which flows from virtue. Strengthened by the beautiful Anastasia in good intentions, given to noble sentiments, he became a good prince, a good relative."[36]

Yet this difference amounts to little compared with the overall similarity of points of view. Both Karamzin and Kurbskii pose the same question: How was it that a tsar formerly so excellent had now become a cruel and heartless ruler?[37] Both answer the question by describing the moral progress, or rather regress, of the tsar, surrounded first by virtuous advisers and then by debauchers. For both authors, the moving force of the realm was the tsar's will, and therefore the most important causes were to be sought inside the tsar, in the forces that operated on his mind and soul.[38] The emphasis in both accounts is therefore thoroughly moral, and indeed moralistic. Both writers were essentially telling a story and not given to analysis of this or that "factor," this or that class.[39] Both spend much of their time describing battles, praising the valor of warriors, roundly condemning those characters they disliked, all occupations generally avoided by their modern descendants. And yet, Karamzin at the least did manage to give an accurate rendering of this particular source, which is more than can be said of most of the later historians who dealt with it.

Before we leave Karamzin, it might be worth noting how that historian regarded Kurbskii himself, since Kurbskii's own historical role (imagined or real) was soon to play a considerable part in determining what historians saw in his writings. Up until his flight to Lithuania, Kurbskii is only mentioned in passing as a "sensitive contemporary" whose opinion should be trusted, as a glorious warrior.[40] While describing Kurbskii's flight, Karamzin devotes a good deal of space to Kurbskii and his correspondence with Ivan.[41] The whole of this discussion is devoted to answering the question of whether Kurbskii's flight was justified. Nothing is said about Kurbskii as a representative of this or that class of Russian society, or about his ideology.

S. M. Solov'ev had a different view of Ivan's reign than did Karamzin, and asked different questions of his sources. Karamzin and Kurbskii concentrated their attention on the moral struggle taking place within Ivan, a struggle closely connected with the moral qualities of those surrounding the tsar. Solov'ev, although he mentions this moral struggle, prefers to concentrate on a social and political clash:

> But around these princes [of Moscow], collected under the guise of servants of the new state the descendants of princes and appanage princes, deprived of their *otchinas* by the descendants of Kalita. . . . Around the Muscovite grand prince, the representative of the new order whose main interest lay in the consolidation and growth of that order, around this prince gathered people who lived in the past with all of their own best memories, who could not sympathize with the new, for whom even their prominent position, their title itself, reminded them of a more brilliant

position, a greater importance in the not distant past, a past well known to all. A clash [*stolknovenie*] was inevitable given such a confrontation between two principles [*dvukh nachal*], one of which was striving toward continuing growth, while the other wished to hold it back from this striving, to hold it back in the name of old relationships now vanished.[42]

It is not hard to guess where Kurbskii fits into this general scheme.

Solov'ev begins his discussion of the role of advisers in Kurbskii's work with the following: "We saw that the main reason for the displeasure of the princes and the descendants of the old *druzhina* with the new order of things was that the Muscovite rulers stopped observing the old custom of doing nothing without the advice of the *druzhina*."[43] He then goes on to describe Kurbskii's condemnation of Vassian Toporkov's advice: "to do the same," that is, apparently, to rule without the advice of the *druzhina*. By implication, Kurbskii is connected with "the princes and the descendents of the old *druzhina*." Moreover, already a slight distortion has crept in, since Toporkov's advice was not to rule without any advisers at all, but to rule without advisers "wiser than yourself."[44] When he translates Kurbskii's condemnation of this advice into modern Russian, he makes a further slight alteration. Kurbskii cites the biblical example of David's failure to take the advice of his counselors about counting the people of Israel.[45] But where Kurbskii refers to "counselors" (*singlity svoimi*), Solov'ev translates this as "grandees" (*svoimi vel'mozhami*).[46] He ignores the fact that in the next example brought forward by Kurbskii, that of Rehoboam (1 Kings 12), difficulty arose not by consulting no advisers but by consulting the wrong advisers, by preferring the advice of young men to the counsel of old men. In neither case was the criterion for a good adviser noble birth; in the case of Rehoboam, the criterion was age, and in the case of David, military rank. (In the Church Slavic version of the Bible, he consulted with the "leaders of the forces.")

Solov'ev then proceeds to argue that, "in the mind of Kurbskii the work of Ivan was seen as the completion of the work of his father and grandfather, the conclusion of the struggle of the Muscovite rulers with the princes of the same family."[47] What are the words from which this observation is "evident"? "Already you have killed with various forms of death not only princes of your family, and [you have robbed] [not only] their movable and immovable possessions, such as your grandfather did not plunder; but also—I may speak with boldness according to the word of the Gospel—our last shirts have we not forbidden your haughty and royal [*tsar'skomu*] majesty to take."[48]

There is a close but by no means exact correspondence between Kurbskii's words and Solov'ev's interpretation of them. In the first place, Solov'ev's remarks, taken in the context of his overall views, carry a wide meaning that is absent from Kurbskii's statement. Solov'ev's words evoke the "confrontation of two principles" and all the political and social ideas that went along with them. Kurbskii is only talking of murder and plunder, with no principles involved. More important, Solov'ev injects a new element into Kurbskii's statement, an element Kurbskii did not mention, the element of struggle. The idea of a "struggle," "confrontation," or "clash" recurs again and again in Solov'ev and is crucial to his picture of Muscovite politics. Kurbskii mentions no struggle but on the contrary states that, obeying the injunction of the Gospel, the princes did not refuse their last shirts. The passage to which Kurbskii refers is as follows: "Love your enemies, do good to them that hate you, Bless them that curse you, and pray for them which despitefully use you. And unto him that smiteth thee on the one cheek offer also the other; and him that taketh away thy cloak forbid not to take thy coat also" (Luke 6). If this sufferance was indeed the model that the aristocracy set for itself in its dealings with the Muscovite rulers, then what of the image of struggle and conflict that Solov'ev and virtually all later historians use to describe the politics of this period?

Solov'ev ascribes to Kurbskii opposition to two specific innovations undertaken by the Muscovite rulers: the abrogation of the right of departure and the increasing use of "new men" (*liudi novye*), that is, *d'iaki*, in government.[49] Here again, Solov'ev is close to the truth but does not tell the whole story. Kurbskii argues that oaths exacted under force are not binding, but the fact remains that he never mentions the right of departure, and indeed doesn't mention the argument about the invalidity of forced oaths until his third letter to Ivan after the latter has specifically accused him of breaking such an oath.[50] Now, since the right of departure was a prominent feature of the "old order of things" for which Kurbskii and the other aristocrats allegedly hankered, and since Kurbskii found himself in the embarrassing situation of having fled Muscovy, it is surprising that he hasn't made more of this right of departure, which after all would have justified his flight and silenced one of Ivan's most powerful arguments against him. What is notable is not that in this one instance Kurbskii obliquely referred to the right of departure, but that in the bulk of his polemics with Ivan, he made so little use of this right.

As evidence for Kurbskii's opposition to "new men," Solov'ev cites Kurbskii's reference to "our Russian clerks [*pisari*], whom the grand prince puts great faith in—he chooses them, not from noble or high born stock but rather from priests' sons or from the rank and file [*ot prostago vsenarodstva*]."[51]

Against this quotation, we could place another, cited a few pages earlier by Solov'ev himself. "Now a tsar, if he is honored by his realm but has not received certain gifts from God, must seek good and useful counsel not only from his advisers, but also from all kinds of men [*no i u vsenarodnykh chelovek*]."⁵² On the basis of the *Correspondence* and the *History*, Kurbskii can be made into a hater or a lover of "new men."

However, taking these documents as a whole, Kurbskii seems to be more often an opponent than a supporter of "new men," especially in the military, as when he describes the vagabonds (*kaliki*) who served as *voevodas* (generals or provincial governors) under the *oprichnina*.⁵³ But I don't think this proves much. In general, Kurbskii considers one of the signs of a good government to be the just promotion of worthy men, and among the attributes of these deserving men is an eminent family. But there are many other qualities he ascribes to men deserving of high positions, such as wisdom, old age, piety, and skill in civil and military affairs.⁵⁴ There is evidence that Kurbskii, like most aristocrats of any time or place, felt a certain resentment against upstarts; Solov'ev's main error was not in pointing out this feeling, but in exaggerating its importance until it became a major preoccupation. The resentment was Kurbskii's, the preoccupation, Solov'ev's.

There is also a short circuit in Solov'ev's logic here. According to his own account, Ivan turned to the Syl'vestr and Adashev group, of which Kurbskii was an alleged member, as a way of freeing himself from that same conservative aristocratic opposition with a hankering after "the old order of things" that Kurbskii is supposed to represent.⁵⁵ Kurbskii thus finds himself on both sides of the "struggle."

In fact, Kurbskii makes a poor champion of the boyar class. It is boyars who are responsible for the depravity of Ivan's youth: "After a few years his mother died too; then the great proud pans, or boyars in their tongue, brought him up—to their own misfortune and to the misfortune of their children—quarrelling with each other, flattering him, and pleasing him in every enjoyment and lust."⁵⁶

This is a strange way for Kurbskii to refer to his allies in the "clash" with the princes of Moscow. The boyars continue to be the main agents of Ivan's corruption. It is boyars who seduce the tsar away from the saintly life into which Syl'vestr and Adashev, men of comparatively low birth, have led him. Just after the successful conquest of Kazan, for example, Ivan leaves for Moscow. His wise and judicious counselors advise him against this move, but he is persuaded to remain not by *d'iaki* or even by boyar children, but by his two brothers-in-law Daniil and Nikita Romanovich Yur'ev-Zakhar'in and "other flatterers" (*drugi laskateli*).⁵⁷

Solov'ev steadily pushes his evidence in a certain direction, in the direction of imputing to Kurbskii views that are more secular and political than the evidence warrants. And if the distortions in each case are small, the overall effect of them is not. For Solov'ev leaves us with the impression that Kurbskii's main preoccupation was resentment that the boyars had lost their old rights: the right to be consulted, the right to depart, the right to fill the main positions in the government and army without competition from "new men." Since these sentiments, or some approximation of them, are present in the evidence, one is at first inclined to agree with Solov'ev. But even these opinions, as we have seen, are not quite what they seem to be. More important, with the possible exception of the role of advisers, these opinions are not major preoccupations by any means. Kurbskii spends most of his time discussing the moral condition of Ivan at various points in his reign. He describes Ivan's spiritual progress and not unreasonably relates the condition of the tsardom to the condition of the tsar. To transform this account into a kind of manifesto for the political aspirations of the declining boyar class demands not only the small misreadings of the sources but a major shift of emphasis from the moral to the political, and the exclusion of the bulk of the evidence.

V. O. Kliuchevskii took over his teacher's idea that the struggle between the Muscovite rulers and the boyars was the basis for sixteenth-century Muscovite politics. But whereas Solov'ev's mind flew immediately to a conflict between two principles, Kliuchevskii connected each side with a particular kind of constitutional arrangement. The tsar aimed at autocracy, the boyars at a kind of constitutional monarchy with the tsar ruling through the Boyar Duma. The chief spokesman for the latter camp was, not surprisingly, Prince A. M. Kurbskii. Having just concluded his discussion of the boyar rule during Ivan's minority with the observation that "the reason for its [the *boyarstvo*'s] disagreement with the ruler was not made clear at this time," Kliuchevskii continues, "In the reign of Ivan the Terrible when the clash [*stolknovenie*] renewed itself, both sides in the dispute had a chance to express their political opinions more clearly, and to clarify the reasons for their mutual dislike. In 1564 the boyar Prince A. M. Kurbskii . . ."[58]

The implication here, even more clearly than in Solov'ev's work, is that Kurbskii is the mouthpiece for the boyar class, and that, at last, we can hear what the boyars (and Ivan as well) had to say for themselves. Throughout his discussion of Kurbskii's writings, Kliuchevskii proceeds on this assumption; he never makes a distinction between Kurbskii's private opinions and the opinions of the mass of boyars whom he is taken to represent. It is especially in the *History*, according to Kliuchevskii, that "he expresses the political opinions of his boyar brothers." Kliuchevskii then goes on to make some revealing remarks:

Since both sides as it were confessed to each other, one would expect that they would express fully and frankly their political opinions [*svoi politicheskie vozreniia*], that is, the causes for their mutual hostility. But even in this polemic, carried out by both sides with great ardor and talent, we do not find a straightforward and clear answer about these causes: the polemic therefore does not relieve the reader of his perplexity. The letters of Kurbskii are all filled mainly with individual or class [*soslovnymi*] reproaches and political grievances [*politicheskimi zhalobami*], but in the *History*, he expresses several political and historical judgments of a general nature [*obshchikh politicheskikh i istoricheskikh suzhdenii*].[59]

The first point of interest about these remarks is the admission that the polemic "does not relieve the reader of his perplexity" about the question at issue, which appears to be the question of Kurbskii's and Ivan's "political opinions." If this observation is true, is it not strange that when Kurbskii, spokesman for the boyars, took the trouble to correspond at such length with the tsar, neither side should include their "political opinions?" Kliuchevskii gives us no answer to this puzzling question.

Part of the confusion here stems from Kliuchevskii's use of the term "political opinions" (*politicheskie vozreniia*). In the first sentence of the passage quoted above, he equates the phrases "their political opinions" and "the reasons for their mutual hostility." Yet he does not seem to mean this, for both the *Correspondence* and the *History* abound in causes given by Kurbskii for his dislike of Ivan. Indeed, Kurbskii's letters contain little else. Ivan is personally corrupt, surrounded by corrupt friends. He drinks, swears, massacres innocents, treats his friends badly, and is a sodomist to boot. One hardly needs more causes for Kurbskii's hostility toward Ivan. But these reasons, religious and moral, are not what Kliuchevskii is searching for. The last sentence of the passage modifies his definition. There he implies that he is not looking for "individual or class reproaches" or even "political grievances" but for "political and historical opinions of a general nature."

These are exceptionally hard to find in Kurbskii's writings, as Kliuchevskii or anyone else who has read them will attest. The great bulk of these writings are devoted to demonstrating the religious and moral corruption that characterizes the tsar, his family, and his government. By the way in which he frames his question, therefore, Kliuchevskii refuses to consider most of the evidence at his disposal, that is the great majority of Kurbskii's writing that concerns "personal or class reproaches" or "political grievances." His desire to see Kurbskii as a constitutional or political thinker prevents him from listening to precisely those considerations on which Kurbskii, for whatever reasons, lavished most of his attention.⁶⁰

In fact, Kliuchevskii seems to have been looking for nothing less than a constitutional theory, a "plan for the political organization of the land."⁶¹ To understand the way in which he extracted this plan, the reader must bear with an even longer quotation.

> In Kurbskii we even come across political judgments similar to principles, to theory. He regards as normal only that governmental organization that is based not on the individual judgment of the autocracy, but on the participation of a *sinklit*, or boyar council [*boiarskogo soveta*] in the government. In order to carry out governmental affairs successfully and in good order [*blagochinno*] the ruler must get advice from the boyars [*sovetovat'sia s boiarami*]. The tsar should be the head and should love his wise advisers [*sovetnikov*] "like his own limbs": thus Kurbskii expresses the just and seemly relations of the tsar with the boyars. His entire *History* is built on one thought, the beneficent activity of the boyar council. The tsar ruled wisely and gloriously when he was surrounded by "well-born and just advisers." Therefore the tsar ought to confide in his royal dumas and not in individual well-born and truthful counselors. Prince Kurbskii allows even for popular participation in government; he stands for both the advantage and the necessity of the *zemskii sobor*. In his *History*, he relates just such a political thesis: "Now a tsar, if he is honored by his realm but has not received certain gifts from God, must seek good and useful counsel [*sovet*] not only from his advisers but also from men of all ranks [*ne tol'ko u sovetnikov no i u vsenarodnykh chelovek*], for the gift of the spirit is granted not according to worldly wealth and the strength of the realm, but according to righteousness of soul." By this "men of all ranks," Kurbskii could only have understood an assembly of people summoned for advice from the different estates, from all the land: *in camera* consultation with separate individuals was hardly to his taste. Here are almost all of Kurbskii's political opinions. The prince stands for the governmental significance of the boyar council and the participation in government of the *zemskii sobor*.⁶²

Let's begin with the end of the argument. Kliuchevskii claims on the basis of the passage cited that Kurbskii envisioned a *zemskii sobor* as a regular part of government. This jump from "all ranks of men" to a constitutional body, the *zemskii sobor*, is the most obvious weakness in the exposition. It is not at all clear that Kurbskii "could only have understood" a *zemskii sobor* in this instance, and Kliuchevskii's statement doesn't make it any clearer. What is clear is Kliuchevskii's imposition of a constitutional or institutional interpretation on words the plain sense of which points in a very different direction.

I think Kliuchevskii is guilty of the same reification or institutionalization in the case of the boyar council, although the Russian word *sovet* makes the transitions in meaning more difficult to detect. This word encompasses a spectrum of meanings from "advice" or "counsel" through a "loose group of advisers or council" to "a constitutional body with a corporate identity and a fixed membership." And whereas when Kurbskii used the word, he intended a looser, more general meaning, Kliuchevskii used it in a sense with definite constitutional implications. In considering the passage directly quoted from Kurbskii, Kliuchevskii changes Kurbskii's statement that the tsar should "seek good and useful advice . . . from his advisers" to "the governmental significance of the boyar council [*boiarsago soveta*]." That boyar council or even Boyar Council was meant in this case and not "the advice of the boyars" is evident in the next page when he says "The Boyar Council [*boiarskii sovet*] and the *zemskii sobor* were already at that time political facts."[63] The institutional sense with which Kliuchevskii invested the term *sovet* is also evident a little earlier in the argument where he states that, in Kurbskii's opinion, "the tsar ought to confide in his royal dumas and not in individual well-born and just advisers." The use of the word "duma" has a more clearly constitutional sense than *sovet*—the royal dumas are evidently the Boyar Council and the *zemskii sobor*. Thus in the first part of the argument Kliuchevskii moves from the "wise advisers" of Kurbskii's body metaphor to "boyar council" to "royal dumas," constitutional bodies that by implication prevent the tsar from taking advice from an individual adviser or friend. Such ideas are common enough in English constitutional history (for example, the fear of Fox and the Rockingham Whigs that King George III was being influenced by a "minister behind the drapes"), but how far do they apply to a sixteenth-century Muscovite boyar? This imposition of a constitutional relationship to the tsar, this assumption that Kurbskii did not want the tsar to consult with individual well-born and truthful advisers, is Kliuchevskii's and not Kurbskii's.

It is ironic that the clearest statement of Kurbskii's view of advice and advice givers is contained in the very passage of Kurbskii's that Kliuchevskii quotes. The point of this passage is not darkly expressed nor difficult to understand. Good counsel or wisdom is a gift of God. If a tsar has not been granted this gift, then he must seek advice from counselors. The qualification for counselorship is not rank or wealth, not membership in one or another constitutional body, but "righteousness of soul" (*po pravosti duchevnoi*). Kurbskii had just spent a good deal of time explaining that, according to Saint John Chrysostom, the gift of counsel was a gift of God, a gift of the spirit. He cites the example of Moses, a powerful and glorious ruler "who conversed with god, who divided the sea, who destroyed the god of Pharaoh and the mighty Amalekites, who worked most wondrous miracles, and yet who did not possess the gift of counsel." And whom did Moses consult? Not a man of noble birth, not a member of some council or other, but his father-in-law.[64]

Kurbskii does not consider all *sovets*, *radas*, and dumas good in themselves. Arrogant counselors (*siglitove*) urge Ivan to greater ferocity in his youth.[65] The advisers of the khan of Kazan´ are all referred to as "senators" (*senaty*).[66] We even are told of "the first duma of men-pleasers."[67]

When describing Ivan's final fall from righteousness just before the trial of Syl´vestr and Adashev, Kurbskii movingly states: "And thus, with countless other tissues of lies, in agreement with their father the devil . . . they deceived their man with flattering words and overthrew the soul of the Christian tsar, and thus they broke that bond which was woven by God in spiritual love [*sitse rasterzaiut plenitsu onuiu, Bogom sopletenuiu v liubov´ dukhovnuiu*]."[68] There, it seems to me, is the heart of Kurbskii's "theory" of good counselors. God's favor and wisdom are the essential attributes of a good counselor, and the relationship between him and the tsar is woven by God in spiritual love.

To be fair to Kliuchevskii, we must admit that he felt considerable misgivings about his own conclusions. The chapters of both the *Kurs* and the *Boiarskaia Duma* begin with gusto and end in perplexity. In the *Kurs*, Kliuchevskii finally decides that there isn't so much difference between Ivan's and Kurbskii's views, since they both support the existing order of things. In the *Boiarskaia Duma*, he notes with surprise that the sixteenth-century boyars failed to use three potentially useful weapons to defend their threatened position: *mestnichestvo* (the Muscovite precedence system), the Duma, and their bastion of local power, the *gubnoi* elderships. He explains how important each of these was. And yet they were never used. Kurbskii never mentions either the first or the last, and never refers by name to the Duma: "The observer who is acquainted with the tactics of ruling classes in other countries and at other times will be struck by the lack of political foresight or the excess of political light-heartedness of the Muscovite *boiarstvo* of the sixteenth century."[69]

It seems to me that if Kliuchevskii had listened more carefully to what Kurbskii or "Kurbskii" was saying, at least some of the reasons for this apparent lack of foresight would have become clear. For by finding in Kurbskii's work a social, political, and constitutional awareness that was in fact absent, Kliuchevskii was able then to project this awareness on to the rest of the sixteenth-century Muscovite *boiarstvo*, thus creating an opposition party with its own ideology that "clashed" or "struggled" with the autocracy. But if we take into account our own conclusions about these documents, that their vocabulary and logic are loose, that their arguments have a religious basis, that political and social views are very hard to find in them, then perhaps we should change our views about this boyar opposition and about the nature of Muscovite politics as a whole.

What lesson can we learn from this little historiographical excursion? We should stand warned against a particular kind of error in the use of sources. This kind of error arises not from illegible manuscripts, "dark places" where the meaning is unclear, or from later interpolations in earlier texts. It arises from a misunderstanding between the historian and his source, when each uses the same words but means different things. In this case, two very eminent historians imposed their own meanings on the words of a given source, consistently pushing them in a secular, political direction, investing them with a social or constitutional meaning that their author did not put in them. In order to understand sources from a culture as remote from ours as sixteenth-century Muscovy we must at least try to get some notion as to how the people who wrote these documents thought, especially about politics. This is what I propose to do.

Notes

Although the format of the notes has been modernized, I am presenting the essay pretty much exactly as it was written almost fifty years ago, though I must have added the references to Nebel and to Grabovsky slightly later. I have therefore resisted the temptation to delete the cheeky last sentence and other youthfully overconfident passages. I have relied on John Fennell's translations for the Kurbskii texts, but the translations of texts from Karamzin, Solov´ev, and Kliuchevskii are mine.

1. The best easily available source in English about Kurbskii's early life is in N. Andreyev, "Kurbsky's Letters to Vas´yan Muromtsev," *Slavonic and East European Review* 33, no. 81 (1955): 414–436, on which most of this very short account is based on.

2. For Anastasia, see the genealogy in A. M. Kurbskii, *Skazaniia kniazia Kurbskago*, ed. N. G. Ustrialov (Saint Petersburg: Tipografiia Imperatorskoi Akademii Nauk, 1868), end of vol. 1. For Bel´skii and Tuchkov, see A. N. Iasinskii, *Sochineniia kniazia Kurbskogo kak istoricheskii material* (Kiev: Tip. Imp. Universiteta sv. Vladimira, 1889), 26–27, cited in Andreyev, "Kurbsky's Letters," 419.

3. See Kurbskii's preface to his edition of the *Novyi Margarit*, ed. Ustrialov, 273–274, and his remark in his *History* that Maksim trusted him along with several others to remonstrate with Ivan IV about his decision to go to the Kyrillo-Belozerskii Monastery, cited in J. L. I. Fennell, ed. and trans., *Prince A. M. Kurbsky's History of Ivan IV* (Cambridge: Cambridge University Press, 1965), 80–81, hereafter cited as *History*.

4. See Kurbskii's disparaging remarks about Muscovy, "that land which was, I say, indeed ungrateful and unworthy to receive learned men . . . the land of fierce barbarians." Fennell, *History*, 212–213. Except where noted, I use Fennell's excellent and elegant translations.

5. Iasinskii, *Sochineniia*, 27; Andreyev, "Kurbsky's Lettters," 419.

6. V. I. Buganov, ed., *Razriadnaia kniga 1475–1598 gg* (Moscow: Izd. Nauka, 1966), citations listed under Kurbskii's name in index.

7. J. L. I. Fennell, ed. and trans., *The Correspondence between Prince A. M. Kurbsky and Tsar Ivan IV of Russia 1564–1579* (Cambridge: Cambridge University Press, 1963), 6–7 (hereafter cited as *Correspondence*).

8. Fennell, *Correspondence*, 210–213.

9. Fennell, *History*, 74–91.

10. Fennell, *History*, 136–137, Fennell translates *liubovnymi* as "amiable."

11. Edward Keenan at Harvard apparently doubts that Kurbskii was indeed the author of these works. Since his work has not been published, and also for stylistic reasons, I continue to refer to Kurbskii as the author, avoiding such awkward devices as encircling Kurbskii's name in quotation marks, or perhaps referring to him as "pseudo-Kurbskii." Since the main argument of this essay is historiographical rather than historical, however, Keenan's conclusions, if they are true, should not interfere too much.

12. Fennell, *Correspondence*, ix.

13. Fennell, *History*, 2–9.

14. Indeed, Metropolitan Daniil, the leading Josephian during Vasilii's reign, is called "that most proud and fierce man" later. Fennell, *History*, 76–77.

15. A. N. Grobovsky, *The "Chosen Council" of Ivan IV: A Reinterpretation* (Brooklyn, NY: Gaus, 1969) very skillfully points out the misunderstandings that resulted from this imprecision in the use of adjectives in the case of the phrase *izbrannaia rada* (chosen council). Needless to say, I am a great admirer of Grobovsky's work.

16. Fennell, *History*, 16–23, 78–90, 152–157.

17. Fennell, *History*, 176–177.

18. Fennell, *History*, 238–241. Kurbskii varies in his ascription of responsibility for the corruption of human nature between free human will, as in this passage and the little section we have been examining at the beginning of the history, and the devil himself. For example, "Consider now with attentiveness what our implacable enemy the devil devises" (80–81).

19. Fennell, *History*, 8–17.

20. Fennell, *History*, 18–21.

21. Fennell, *History*, 80–83.

22. Fennell, *History*, 102–103.

23. Fennell, *History*, 122–127.

24. Fennell, *History*, 152–155.

25. N. M. Karamzin, *Istoriia Gosudarstva Rossiiskago*, 3rd. ed., vols. 8 and 9 (Saint Peterburg: Tip. A. Pliushara, 1830–1831).

26. See Karamzin, *Istoriia*, 8:98–120, for this conversion and its results.

27. Karamzin, *Istoriia*, 8:114.

28. Karamzin, *Istoriia*, 9:4.

29. Karamzin, *Istoriia*, 8:241. See 8:234–247 for the succession crisis.

30. Karamzin, *Istoriia*, 8:362.

31. Karamzin, *Istoriia*, 9:1–25.
32. Karamzin, *Istoriia*, 9:19.
33. Karamzin, *Istoriia*, 9:81–91.
34. H. M. Nebel, *N. M. Karamzin, A Russian Sentimentalist* (The Hague: Mouton, 1967).
35. Ivan's references in his letters to Kurbskii indicate that Anastasia's death powerfully affected him (Fennell, *Correspondence*, 190–193) and that Kurbskii, Syl'vestr, and Adashev were all antagonistic to her (Fennell, *Correspondence*, 94–99, 136–137, and 148–149).
36. Karamzin, *Istoriia*, 8:121.
37. Karamzin, *Istoriia*, 9:4; Fennell, *History*, 2–3.
38. Karamzin, *Istoriia*, 9:4.
39. For a very interesting and provocative essay about "storytelling" and "factors" as they relate to early modern European history, see J. H. Hexter, "'Factors' in Modern History," *Reappraisals in History* (Evanston, IL: Northwestern University Press, 1961), 26–44.
40. Karamzin, *Istoriia*, 8:114, 104.
41. Karamzin, *Istoriia*, 9:64–75.
42. S. M. Solov'ev, *Istoriia Rossii s Drevneishikh Vremen*, vol. 6 (Moscow: Izd-vo sotsialno-ekonomicheskoi lit-ry, 1962), 438. For a devastating critique of Solov'ev's view of Ivan's reign, see Grobovsky, *Chosen Council of Ivan IV*, 15–23.
43. Solov'ev, *Istoriia Rossii*, 544.
44. Fennell, *History*, 82–83.
45. II Samuel XXIV; Fennell, *History*, 84–85.
46. Solov'ev, *Istoriia Rossii*, 544.
47. Solov'ev, *Istoriia Rossii*, 545.
48. Fennell, *Correspondence*, 182–193.
49. Solov'ev, *Istoriia Rossii*, 545–547.
50. Fennell, *Correspondence*, 206–207.
51. Solov'ev, *Istoriia Rossii*, 546; Fennell, *History*, 96–97.
52. Solov'ev, *Istoriia Rossii*, 544; Fennell, *History*, 86–87.
53. Fennell, *Correspondence*, 212–215.
54. This list comes from Kurbskii's description of the advisers Syl'vestr and Adashev placed around Ivan. Fennell, *History*, 20–21.
55. Solov'ev, *Istoriia Rossii*, 435–439.
56. Fennell, *History*, 8–9.
57. Fennell, *History*, 72–75.
58. V. O. Kliuchevskii, *Kurs Russkoi Istorii*, 3rd ed., vol. 2 (Petrograd: Gosudarsvennoe Izd, 1918), 202. It may seem unfair to rely on the *Kurs* for Kliuchevskii's treatment of Kurbskii, but the discussion in the more scholarly *Boiarskaia Duma drevnei Rusi*, 2nd ed. (Moscow: Izd. T. Malinskago i A Ivanova, 1883), 285–306, deals with several sixteenth-century writers at once, and it is often unclear which conclusions relate to Kurbskii and which to other authors. The basic approach and the general conclusions about Kurbskii are the same in each book.
59. Kliuchevskii, *Kurs*, 203.
60. Kliuchevskii is dealing here with ideas fraught with semantic difficulty. He seems to have felt that the term "political" did not apply to most of Kurbskii's work. But where

do "individual or class reproaches" end and "political opinions" begin? Kliuchevskii never sorted this out.

61. Kliuchevskii, *Boiarskaia Duma*, 294.
62. Kliuchevskii, *Kurs*, 204.
63. Kliuchevskii, *Kurs*, 205.
64. Fennell, *History*, 86–87.
65. Fennell, *History*, 10–11.
66. Fennell, *History*, 56–57.
67. Fennell, *History*, 74–75.
68. Fennell, *History*, 154–155.
69. Kliuchevskii, *Boiarskai Duma*, 5th ed. (Saint Petersburg: Izd. Narodnogo Komissariata po Prosvshcheniiu, 1919), 281–289, quotation on 283.

CHAPTER 2

Toward an Understanding of the Political Ideas in Ivan Timofeev's *Vremennik*

In the last twenty years or so there has been a transformation in the way that historians of Western political thought have approached their sources. As summarized by J. G. A. Pocock,[1] one of the chief agents of this transformation, the essence of the change has lain in a greater effort to understand any past statement about politics not as if it constituted part of a logically coherent system of thought, the elaboration and explication of which became the task of the historian, but as it was understood by contemporaries at the time (or at some specified later time). A determined concentration on the meanings, denotative and connotative, attached to particular phrases and groups of ideas in particular historical contexts has been the chief instrument for achieving this apparently obvious goal, and has led to important advances in our understanding of early modern European texts as well as to a fairly sophisticated philosophy and methodology.[2]

For several reasons, historians of Muscovite political ideas have generally not taken part in this reorientation. Among those reasons has been a recent, fully justified concern with the problem of authenticating texts, their authorship, and their probable date of composition. Obviously this problem claims

---

This essay originally appeared in *The Slavonic and East European Review* 62 (July 1984): 371–399. The author gratefully acknowledges the publisher for permission to reprint this essay. For this edition, we have adopted American, rather than British, usage, both in English and in the transliteration system.

priority, since we cannot be sure even of the text, to say nothing of the audience of readers, without careful textological work, which alone can deal with the questions of forgeries, later insertions in the text, and so on. But where we have a text whose history can be fairly clearly traced, where the likelihood of redating or reattribution is small, we are in a position to move on to the second stage, to try as best we can to establish the meaning of the text as it was understood by the author and by his contemporaries before proceeding to the third stage, that is, to ask the meaning of the text within our (i.e., historians') present ideas of early seventeenth-century Muscovy. This second stage, which has received scant attention, may well prove to be as crucial as the first in arriving at the general level of understanding implied by the third.[3]

Introduction

This essay attempts to examine what I believe is such a text, the *Vremennik* of Ivan Timofeev,[4] on this second-stage level.

It is odd that more attention in recent years has not been paid to the various historical accounts associated with the so-called Time of Troubles (*smutnoe vremia*) in Muscovy (1598–1613), and in particular to the *Vremennik* of Ivan Timofeev. The disasters that then engulfed Muscovite Rus'—famine, civil war, foreign intervention—stimulated historical thought as perhaps no other period had.[5] The writers who set themselves the difficult task of integrating these disturbing events, particularly the virtual collapse of the "God-established *tsarstvo*," with the earlier history of Rus' were both numerous and very able. They included some of the most prominent cultural figures of the time—Avraamy Palitsyn, Semen Shakhovskoi, and Ivan Khvorostinin, among others. In this distinguished company, Ivan Timofeev's *Vremennik* stands out as the most-sustained effort to understand these events that has come down to us. It was Timofeev who wrestled longest (the unique surviving manuscript has 312 written folios) and hardest with the historiographical problems posed by the Troubles, and it is therefore his *Vremennik* that is probably the single-best source for investigating how early seventeenth-century Muscovites thought about their own history and politics.

Another advantage of the *Vremennik* from the point of view of understanding Muscovite ideas is that Timofeev, like a number of other *smuta* tale authors, was not writing primarily to promote either a particular political point of view or a particular set of ideas.[6] As both the structure of the work and the remarks Timofeev makes in it reveal, the *Vremennik* is closer to a diary than a polemical work. A highly personal document, it was composed over a long period of time, and, although the author certainly had his own political opinions, the work as a whole is remarkably untendentious. Instead, Timofeev concentrated his attention on the problem of the causes of the Troubles, returning to it again and again in the course of his narrative, repeatedly questioning the role played both by the rulers and the people. In the process, we can see how the various ideas in the political vocabulary of Muscovy were marshalled not so much as ends in themselves, as tended to be the case with ideological works of the sixteenth century, but as means to the end of understanding the causes and meaning of the very disturbing events between the death of Fedor Ivanovich and the election of Mikhail Romanov.

The meager material that had served as the basis for all biographical work on Timofeev has recently been dramatically increased by Soviet scholarship.[7] His family was from "the petty service people around Moscow,"[8] and in particular from the region around Maloiaroslavets, a town about seventy miles southwest of Moscow. He exchanged his original surname, Semenov, for Timofeev, a name based on his patronymic, at an early stage in his career. He seems to have developed close connections both with the young Mikhail Skopin-Shuyskii and with the Vorotynskii clan. His career began and advanced rapidly while Boris Godunov dominated affairs. His rank appears for the first time, as *pod'iachii*, around 1590, and by 1598 he had become a *d'iak* in the Artillery Chancery. By 1604 his competence had been widened to include financial affairs,[9] although he continued his military duties as well. The advent of Prince Vasilii Shuiskii to the throne in 1606 signaled a reversal for Timofeev, for by 1607 he had been sent to Novgorod, an apparent demotion. There he allied himself with a group that supported Skopin-Shuiskii and opposed the growing Swedish influence in the city. As a result, his fortunes fell even further when Sweden occupied Novgorod in 1611, and, in spite of several efforts to return to Moscow, he was forced to remain in Novgorod until the end of the occupation in 1617. He then resumed his service career, but remained in the provinces (Yaroslavl', Nizhniy Novgorod) until the last years of his life. Several years before his death, early in 1631, he seems to have come under the personal patronage of Patriarch Filaret, probably because of the efforts of his adopted son, the *duma d'iak* I. K. Gryazev, and may have finished the editing of his *Vremennik* as a part of the general historical activity that surrounded Filaret in the years around 1630.[10]

In spite of the new biographical material, it is hard to penetrate to the character of this writer-bureaucrat. His rapid rise under Boris Godunov and the scorn evident in the *Vremennik* for improperly trained bureaucrats would indicate that he was a competent administrator whose later misfortunes were due more to court politics than to his own weaknesses.[11] The impression of unusual ability is confirmed by the style and content of the *Vremennik*. The language of the *Vremennik*, though often obscure and pedantic, is a highly original creation; Timofeev frequently makes up his own words and creates fantastic grammatical constructions, possibly in imitation of Greek. He refers not only to biblical but to Byzantine and early East Slav history. In short, the author appears to have been widely conversant with the literary as well as the bureaucratic cultures of the day.

The *Vremennik* is not a unified work; it consists of a number of short articles and segments that have been joined together, in some cases carefully, in other cases in a purely mechanical way. Timofeev himself gave the best description of the disjointed structure of his work and the reasons for it:

> The work put together by my humble intelligence was never unified; the parts were entirely separate one from the other . . . like pieces of a garment just cut out but not yet sewn together, or having fallen apart with age. These parts were not corrected or united in proper order because of fear, because I was held in the city [of Novgorod] as a prisoner, because my stay there was unfree and terrifying, and because both paper and [what I needed for] bodily sustenance were scarce and insufficient.

The passage goes on to describe how worried he was that his writing might get him into trouble, how in terror he hid his manuscripts, moving them from place to place:

> I carefully concealed and preserved [my secret writing] in deserted, solitary places, and often moved it from place to place in fear of my enemies and in expectation of death. I even feared those dark silent places themselves where I hid my work, as if they were alive and able to speak. I worried lest they speak out, lest they inform someone about my work.[12]

The manuscript has preserved reasonably clear evidence of the separate parts or pieces to which Timofeev referred. The text consists of some sixty-two separate sections set off from each other by a variety of devices: indentation, use of capital or cinnabar letters, lines left blank, decorative figures at the ends of the passage, and so on.[13]

I. I. Polosin, the scholar who has done by far the most careful work on the structure and dating of Timofeev's text, after textual analysis added two more sections, making a total of sixty-four.[14] He considered these fragments (*otryvki*) the basic units of the *Vremennik*. Polosin believed that these units were written at various times between 1598 and the 1620s; the last sections seem to have been written around 1630. The bulk of the writing was done in the period

1606–1617 when Timofeev was in Novgorod, much of it after 1610, and therefore during the Swedish occupation. Conditions at that time explain not only the fragmentary nature of Timofeev's work but also his reluctance to use proper names in the text and the obviously erroneous title of chapter 5, part 9: "The oath on the cross to the Crown Prince Wladislaw"—the section in fact deals with Novgorod-Swedish relations. Thus when Timofeev at last emerged from Novgorod in 1617, his "personal archive," as Polosin repeatedly calls the *Vremennik*, consisted of a number of loosely related sketches.[15] He then resumed a full-service career and probably had little time to edit and combine what he had written. In any case, the coherence of the text deteriorates as one progresses: the first part (chapters 1–4) is fairly smoothly put together, the middle part (chapter 5) is less so, and the final part (*Letopisets vkratse*) is in almost complete disorder.

The manuscript contains evidence that the fragments were grouped together in a variety of ways. The three parts just mentioned constitute the largest divisions, as the dirty leaves at the ends of these sections show. Gathering numbers reveal six shorter units within these three (chapters 1; II and III; IV; V, part 1; V, part 2; and the *Letopisets vkratse*). Finally there are the chapters and headings themselves, as shown in the table of contents. It is thus an open question whether the *Vremennik* with all its divisions and subdivisions should be considered a single work, or several.[16]

The manuscript as we have it now was written in several stages; Timofeev almost certainly took no part in the first stage and could not have taken part in any later stages. At some time in the second quarter of the seventeenth century a number of scribes made a complete copy of the *Vremennik* from an already-existing copy (not scraps of paper). It is not known if this original copy was by Timofeev himself. In the course of time, sheets and whole gatherings of the manuscript were lost. Around the 1670s, these missing pages were replaced, presumably copied from another manuscript, and at about the same time another scribe added the table of contents, a number of chapter headings, and other marginal notations. The work of this scribe, whom Polosin seems to have taken for Timofeev himself, is of doubtful authenticity. Finally, near the end of the century, the manuscript was bound in its present form.

Was Ivan Timofeev indeed the author of the *Vremennik*, as we have assumed? Although some questions remain,[17] and although some new evidence may well come to light, the preponderance of currently available evidence favors the traditional attribution. Scholars have long pointed to the parallels between Timofeev's life and the narrative of the *Vremennik*.[18] Timofeev seems to have analyzed and discussed in detail precisely those events or those subjects that, so external documentary evidence tells us, he either knew at firsthand or understood particularly well because of his professional expertise. Recent Soviet research has more than doubled the biographical information we had on Timofeev twenty years ago, and this new evidence is as consistent with the *Vremennik* as is the old.[19] Moreover, even though the history of the manuscript is complex, watermark evidence suggests that most of the text was copied shortly after Timofeev's final work on the *Vremennik*.[20] Finally, an independent source interested in finding a copy of the *Vremennik* for the government in 1658, and presumably anxious to name the correct author, confirms that Timofeev was indeed the author and searched for a copy among members of the same family, the Vorotynskiis, with whom Timofeev had had close service and social contacts at the beginning of the century.[21]

Timofeev's Methods as a Historian

One historian has described the *Vremennik* as representing "an original combination" of "artistocratic-reactionary tendencies" with "the principle of theocratic-democratic absolutism."[22] The logical absurdity in this conclusion derives not from the author's ignorance of the *Vremennik* but from his application to it of categories—absolutism, democracy, theocracy—that are borrowed from political philosophy, that is from discussion of politics carried out within the bounds of logical philosophical inquiry. Timofeev clearly believed in a strong ruler, in the ultimate authority of God, and, under some conditions, in an important role for the righteous among the people. But to describe these views as absolutism, theocracy, and democracy is to bring well-developed consistent political theories into a discussion where they drive the investigator to ridiculous and contradictory conclusions.

Discarding this Western philosophical framework is more difficult than it might appear, since its assumptions are embedded in a great deal of the vocabulary we normally use to discuss political ideas (including the term "political"). Perhaps the best strategy is to begin by making some preliminary observations on the ways in which Timofeev approached the task of writing history, his goals, his methods, and the "rules" under which he operated. We can then proceed to discuss some of his main ideas, keeping these characteristics in mind.

Timofeev was obviously not a consistent political philosopher. His culture had neither an Aristotelian nor a scholastic tradition; he was writing as an historian, so that his political ideas are revealed in his commentaries on passing events rather than in abstract statements of principle. Timofeev seems to have retained a number of ambiguous or even contradictory assumptions in the varied collection of ideas he used to explain individual events. Any analysis must make ample provision for describing multiple perspectives, and avoid trying to force Timofeev's ideas into a logically consistent pattern.

Perhaps the most obvious characteristic of Timofeev's writing is the role he ascribes to God, the transcendental element, one might say, in Timofeev's thought. As I have argued elsewhere,[23] the *smuta* tales, including the *Vremennik*, rest on assumptions that are "God-dependent" rather than "independent," that is, they assume that God intervenes constantly in worldly events, and often make His actions an indispensable element in understanding those events. When the role of God is removed, the remaining secular philosophy is not coherent by itself. This mental attitude, I would argue, is one of the main reasons why the authors of the *smuta* tales never worked out a coherent secular solution to the pressing problem of legitimacy but stuck with the traditional doctrine that the only legitimate tsar was one chosen by God.[24] The modern historian is tempted to dismiss Timofeev's historical accounts as naive, primitive, and even foolish on that account; yet it was precisely his connection of passing events with a transcendent reality, the discovery of the eternal patterns of divine retribution and salvation in the confusing ebb and flow of Muscovite history, that gave Timofeev's work significance and power.

The chief vehicle for establishing this connection in the *Vremennik* is the frequent use of references to historical, largely biblical, events.[25] For example, when he describes the alleged murder of the Tsarevich Dmitrii by Boris Godunov, Timofeev mentions a number of historical parallels in which innocent victims are slaughtered by wicked murderers: Abel's murder by Cain (Gen. 4:1–15), Herod's slaughter of the Innocents (Matt. 2:16), and Sviatopolk's murder of Gleb (Boris is omitted, probably because he had the same name as Boris Godunov).[26] Closer examination reveals that the list is not haphazard; the references bring with them interpretative ideas that relate directly to Timofeev's overall portrait of Boris as a skillful administrator who nevertheless let his ambition and his intelligence overcome his faith (65). Cain and Abel both offered sacrifices to God, but only Abel's was accepted because he alone had faith. Compare Paul's interpretation of this story (Heb. 9:4) with Timofeev's account of Boris's vainglorious building of churches (64–66; see also 59–61). Herod not only slew the Innocents, he was the symbol of a man who "exalteth himself (and) shall be abased," of "the kings of the earth" who persecuted Jesus. He finally was killed by an angel of the Lord because "he gave not God the glory."[27] The reference to Gleb adds the theme of legitimacy (or illegitimacy), a theme also implicit in the Cain and Abel story,[28] to complete the picture of Boris as a worldly wise but overly ambitious usurper whose lack of faith and righteousness led him to murder a (by implication) holy victim. This example illustrates several characteristics of Timofeev's history writing. First, he uses analogy to establish the interpretation of an event. By citing references from the Bible and the earlier history of Rus´, Timofeev established a context within which contemporary events could be understood; superficial similarities led to more fundamental interpretative parallels. In other words, this past provided a fund of events, together with their interpretations, which could be drawn on by analogy to create an interpretation of recent events. Naturally this device had a rhetorical side. Timofeev obviously could and did select his references carefully in order to bolster his own interpretations. Yet the device was effective because people believed both in the truth of that to which reference was being made and in the appropriateness of the method by which the two elements, new information and accepted truth, were connected.

It follows that Timofeev considered his own history, the history of Rus´, as analogous to biblical history, his own time as continuous with biblical time, governed by the same forces and understood by the same criteria. When Timofeev called Muscovy "the New Israel" as he did in the title to his work and frequently elsewhere (10, 78–79, 136, 150), he was only making explicit what was implicit already in his historical method. Biblical, especially Old Testament references, far outnumber other references.[29] Ivan IV and Boris are compared to David (the latter unfavorably) (14, 65); Fedor to Solomon, Job, John the Baptist, and David (24–26, 151, 164); the Lithuanian army to the Egyptian army that drowned in the Red Sea (90); Sigismund III of Poland to the Pharoah (121); Vasilii Shuiskii to Saul (136); Mikhail Romanov and Prince Mikhail Skopin-Shuiskii to Moses (136, 149); and so on. These references helped to provide Timofeev and his readers with the meaning of recent events in terms of the relationship of God to His people.

Indeed, this interpretative framework was the major point of writing in the first place. Many of the *smuta* tales were written either after the Troubles were over or, like the *Vremennik,* had for other reasons little or no polemical value. They are not rich in detailed historical information. The chief reason for their composition, and an important cause of their continuing popularity in seventeenth-century manuscript miscellanies, is that they helped to heal the mental wounds opened by the Troubles; they all attempted to provide some answer to the difficult but all-important question of why God so harshly punished His people, "the New Israel," and almost destroyed the "God-created" *tsarstvo.* In this situation it is obvious that scriptural references bore a heavier meaning than, say, a modern scholar's comparison of the Russian and French Revolutions, in that the authority of the source was absolute, and served to provide a divinely revealed way to see God's will as it manifested itself in day-to-day Muscovite events. In that sense, Timofeev as an historian functioned like an icon painter whose task was "to uncover" (*raskryvat'*) what exists but cannot be seen, to reveal the eternal theological essence expressed in an historical event, be it the nativity of Christ or the conquest of Kazan'.[30] Likewise the function of a historian was to depict the "real" meaning of the events he describes, a meaning that needs to be "uncovered" by revealing the eternal patterns, God's intentions as shown in sacred history, beneath accidental day-to-day events. For that reason, events or characters may be distorted to conform to the pattern: in the case of the murder of Dmitrii cited above, Boris, whose governmental skills Timofeev obviously admired (and under whom his own career steadily advanced) is cast as a cruel tyrant, while Dmitrii, who, according to Giles Fletcher, was a sadistic brat who apparently slaughtered helpless animals for pleasure, emerges as a pure and innocent little boy.[31]

This characteristic of Timofeev's thought, his connection of day-to-day events with eternal truths as expressed in sacred writing, presents a particularly difficult problem of translation to modern historians. Since modern historians acting in their professional capacity seldom or never seek to explain events by reference to Divine Providence, they have been inclined simply to exclude the theological elements in these tales and to try to make sense out of what is left. Thus the role of godly, wise advisers, a prominent feature of Muscovite thought in general and of the *Vremennik* in particular, is either transformed into the constitutional rule of the will of the people as expressed by the Boyar Duma or the *zemskii sobor*, or it is dismissed altogether because it lacks "real" political machinery.[32]

But even if one leaves aside this upper religious or mythic level in Timofeev's thought, a formidable difference of approach remains between Timofeev and almost any modern historian. Both study social and political events, but each seeks to explain the causes for those events in a different way. While modern historians often find social causes for social or political events, Timofeev consistently searched for (and found) the causes of events, in this case the Troubles themselves, on the personal, spiritual level, whether he was considering the ruler or the ruled. Thus the disasters of Ivan's reign, his bloody sack of Novgorod, his cruel treatment of his relatives—disasters that Timofeev describes with powerfully felt horror—are attributed not to any social, economic, or even political factors, but again and again to the personal *gnev* (anger) or *liutost'* (fierceness) of Ivan himself and to the moral depravity (and foreignness) of his advisers (10–24). In a typical passage, Timofeev describes how Ivan's cousin, Vladimir Andreyevich of Staritsa, the last Muscovite appanage prince, was slandered by his own servants, and Ivan, "ablaze with fierceness," believed the slanderers and failed to recognize in their evil advice the teaching of the devil. He thereupon ordered the death of Vladimir and his entire family

(23). One might have expected some comment on the end of appanages and the decay of the aristocracy, but Timofeev treats the whole affair in terms of slander, fierceness, and family relations. Similarly, when Timofeev blamed the Troubles on the "wordless silence" of the people, their failure to restrain Boris from killing "those most well-born after the Tsar," he blamed the social sin of silence directly on the personal sins of the people concerned, their greed, gluttony, lack of brotherly love, pride, fornication, envy, and so on (92).[33] This inclination to moral interpretation was naturally reinforced by the strong Old Testament–style emphasis on the role of God mentioned above. The sins of individuals, rulers or ruled, could not only lead by themselves to evil events, they could also anger God, who then would send political and military disaster.

Now this "personalism" of Timofeev, his regular tendency to seek the causes (and remedies) for events on the primary level of the individual behavior of each person rather than in the institutions and customs that govern the behavior of groups of people, poses a difficult problem for historians, who are fond of searching for political parties and/or social groupings behind the moral categories of Muscovite authors.[34] Such a procedure is inherently dangerous, since it implies that the author really meant something quite different from what he said. It also begs the question of whether political parties or social groupings (beyond the peasant-landowner conflict) played an important part at all in Muscovite affairs. In any case, it is difficult to find in the *Vremennik* any traces of what we would call a political party, that is a group joined together in defense of a common set of ideas, apart from the patriotic "party" that struggled for the reestablishment of a Muscovite Orthodox state against various forces, foreign, evil, or both.

Timofeev and Corruption in the Political World

With at least some idea of Timofeev's methods in mind, we are in a better position to discuss his views about tsar and people in such a way that all of his major ideas can be brought into view. Since many of these ideas have been explored partially or thoroughly elsewhere,[35] I shall concentrate on their interrelationships rather than on an elaboration of the ideas themselves.

A natural focus for such a discussion is the section of the *Vremennik* (109–113) that comes closer than any other to being an abstract treatment of the nature of the Muscovite state and the causes of the Troubles, a section unrelated textually and distinct codicologically from the rest of the *Vremennik*. I have discussed some aspects of the beginning of this section elsewhere,[36] but since, as I believe, it provides a key to understanding both the structure of thought and the meaning of the *Vremennik*, it is worth returning to again. The first part of the section is an analogy between the Genesis creation story and the political life of Muscovy.[37]

> Our ancestors, the first couple Adam and Eve, were created in ancient times by the hand of God—he from dust and she from his rib. God appointed him to be as it were the all-powerful tsar [*tsar' samovlasten*][38] over everything that existed, over all creation; the birds, the beasts, and reptiles all fearfully placed themselves in submission to him as if he were their creator, master of all, and lord. And until the first-created [Adam] was tempted by the Destroyer and Enemy of all to break the first commandment, all the speechless [animals] trembled at the command of that creature [Adam], even those that now terrify us. When the serpent whispered temptation into the ears of Eve, and she, instructed by it, tempted her own husband, immediately after that the newly created tsar of all the world himself became terrified of those animals. And from that time to the present because of this disobedience we are all partakers of the fall.
>
> And as all the wild animals were in everything obedient to Adam until his transgression, so in the same way in recent times our own autocrats [*nasha samoderzhavnii*] in their realms ruled over everyone, their servants from time immemorial, while they themselves kept the commandments given by God, as long as up to the end they did not sin before Him. In the passing of many centuries up to now we did not oppose them, as according to the scriptures a servant should obey his master in all services. We were obedient to them not only to [the spilling of] blood, but even to death itself; as a beast cannot oppose the man who leads him to slaughter, we were answerless before them like voiceless fish; with great care we bore the yoke of servitude, obeying them with such fear that out of fear we showed them honor nearly equal to [that we showed] God.

After this emphatic description of Edenic autocracy, Timofeev then goes on to describe the introduction of corruption into this perfect world:

> When the years came to an end, the more our rulers changed our old lawful regulations [*blagoustavlenniia zakonnaia*] passed on by our fathers, and changed the good customs into new opposing customs, the more in their obeying servants the natural fear and submission to masters began to diminish, to die out. . . . Those in power wanted eagerly

to incline their ears to the false words of whisperers as in the Old [Testament] the ancestress of all, Eve, listened with attention to the tempter-snake [because of which they were expelled from Eden]. . . . This disease of lies [*lzhevnyi nedug*] spread through the entire tsardom like bitter tares and thorns [in a wheat field].[39] . . . Thus these people killed those who listened lovingly to them with their tongues, as if with a sword. . . .

Many who had been obedient servants became fainthearted [*samoslabostni*] and fearful by nature and habit, changeable at every moment, easily changing their word, firm in absolutely nothing, inconstant in word and deed, turning in everything like a wheel. . . .

Once this corruption had been introduced into Eden, other evils followed. Foreign merchants noted this change in "our nature," "they found no courage of any kind in any one of us," and set up false usurpers. The natural hierarchies of age and society were overturned. The old, instead of being wise, were feeble minded, the middle aged, ambitious, and the young instructed the old. "All began in everything to be done against the laws established by previous tsars, the small overcame the great, the young the old, the dishonorable the honorable, the slaves their masters." Those who used to rule are now ruled, the foot is crowned while the head is humbled. Thus, instead of "God-given tsars" our present rulers are "God-opposing enemies." "And all this occurred because of the small indulgence [*popolznovenie*] [in sin] by those in power, like Adam's softness [*umiakchenie*] to sin, and by the great sins of servants—in general because of the failure of both [rulers and ruled] to carry out our virtuous obligations to God."

This passage is remarkable not only because it mentions almost all of the main themes in the *Vremennik* as a whole but because, by bringing these themes together in a small space, it shows the structure by which Timofeev connected them to produce a coherent interpretation of the Troubles. The most obvious point to emerge is the strong duality in Timofeev's thought, a tension between the Edenic and the post-Edenic political worlds: a perfect world of purely autocratic rulers and subjects as voiceless as fish on the one hand, and a corrupt world of sinful tsars and weak and wavering subjects on the other. The same tension between these two visions of politics is expressed in a slightly different and less elaborate way in the famous passage from the sixth-century Byzantine writer Agapetus's *Hortatory Chapters* to which Timofeev refers in this section and that he quotes directly elsewhere: "If the tsar is a man by nature, in the sufficiency of his power he approaches God" (107). As Ihor Sevcenko has shown, the short Agapetus text (of which this sentence is the kernel) formed by far the most important literary source for Muscovite ideology.[40] Muscovites may well have found this text as appealing as they did, not because it advanced their political thinking (Sevcenko tells us it served almost as a substitute for such thinking), but because it stated in brief form (but did not resolve) what seems to have been the chief paradox of Muscovite ideology.[41] The tsar, as the divinely appointed ruler of Rus', transmitted and interpreted God's will for the earthly political life of His people; in order to perform this ritual function, the tsar needed two attributes: a pure soul through which the divine will could be transparently reflected,[42] and pure autocracy, so that all the people would perfectly obey God's will as transmitted by the tsar. Such a scheme depended completely on the purity of the ruler's soul, but purity of soul was not always a characteristic of the tsars whom Timofeev described. The problem of the human corruptibility of the tsar, referred to in the first phrase of the Agapetus quotation above, was solved neither by Agapetus nor by Timofeev. Indeed, one could say that the purpose of the *Vremennik* was to explore this theme, to resolve somehow the paradox of a theoretically perfect tsardom manned by very corruptible tsars.

It is not surprising, therefore, that when in the above passage Timofeev explained the causes of the Troubles, he should choose as an analogy the biblical creation story, itself the classic story about how a perfect Creator produced a creation in which evil and sin had a place. In so doing, he "uncovered" for the reader the "real" cause of the Troubles: human corruption. By using this analogy, however, Timofeev expands Agapetus's theme of the human (and therefore potentially sinful) nature of the tsar to the more general theme of the corruptibility of mankind, thus widening the blame for the Troubles from the corruption of the tsars to that of their "slaves" as well. This reflects a wider notion of responsibility that was typical not only of Timofeev but of many *smuta* tale writers.[43] This passage, then, provides a clue to the entire work; in it Timofeev reveals that the ultimate cause of the Troubles is the corruption of tsar and man in Rus', the theme that dominates the entire *Vremennik*, a theme that is revealed in various guises as events unfold, and that, as we have seen, lies at the end of every causal chain.[44]

Since Michael Cherniavsky has adequately described Timofeev's views on the autocratic power of the tsar, there is no need to elaborate this theme in detail.[45] Timofeev's theoretical views on the relationship between ruler and ruled are expressed in the passage above where he refers to the latter as "servants," "voiceless fish," and beasts being led to slaughter. Christian authors have a long record of depicting their own vision of a perfect society as what occurred in Eden, and there is no doubt that for Timofeev this vision was neither egalitarian nor democratic, but purely autocratic. Yet this autocracy did not mean that the tsar could do whatever he wanted. The analogy to the Genesis creation story shows that the contrary is the case. The tsar was bound to obey "the commandments given by God" just as surely as Adam was, even though there obviously was no constitutional organ to force him to do so.

What did Timofeev mean when he talked of these "commandments given by God"? The creation story passage does not tell us specifically, but it does offer important hints, which can then be amplified by reference to the rest of the *Vremennik*. The first and most important obligation is for the tsar to maintain and nourish his own piety and righteousness. It was the tsars' "softness" on sin that first led to disaster in the creation story passage. The classic example of a thoroughly pious tsar for Timofeev, as for the authors of the other *smuta* tales, was Fedor Ivanovich:

> The oldest of them [Ivan's remaining sons] received the name meaning "gift of God" [Fedor], and by the Grace given to him was extremely pious, flourishing after his ancestors both in bodily and even more in spiritual nobility; he perceived his original [purity] and imitated his mother's virtues in all ways.... By his prayers to God, my tsar protected this entire place [*tu vsiudu*] unharmed from enemy machinations. He was by nature meek [*krotok*], very merciful to all, chaste, and, like Job, he preserved himself from any sort of evil in everything he did, loving above all else piety, the grandeur of the church, and, after the regular clergy, the order of monks even down to the last of our brothers in Christ, blessed by our Lord himself in the Gospels. To put it simply, he gave all of himself to Christ; he passed all of his holy and revered [*prepodobnogo*] reign not bloodthirstily, but like a monk in fasting; in prayers and supplications on his knees day and night, he exhausted himself all his life in spiritual feats. (24–25)

Timofeev goes on to compare Fedor with Josaphat, the hero of a tale based on the life of Buddha that had long circulated in Muscovy (25).[46] If we omit Mikhail Fedorovich Romanov, whose reign fell mostly outside the period Timofeev discussed, Fedor's image was by far the most positive among the rulers Timofeev described.

The tsar also had the duty to preserve the purity of the Orthodox faith. Timofeev complimented Ivan IV on this: "After his ancestors until his very death, he preserved like a pastor the true faith in Christ firm and unshakeable, especially reverence for the Three-in-One and One-in-Three" (16). Conversely, the First False Dmitrii who, according to Timofeev, wanted to eradicate Orthodoxy, is likened to Julian the Apostate and Antichrist (83–84). After the obviously evil False Dmitrii, the problem of a tsar destroying Orthodoxy does not come up again, but the preservation of the faith is clearly an important duty of the tsar.

One might suspect that the "commandments given by God" would end with these religious duties. In the same passage, however, Timofeev seems to identify the "commandments given by God" with the "old lawful regulations" and good customs passed on from earlier reigns. These in turn are directly linked to the destruction of the traditional social hierarchy. Elsewhere in the *Vremennik* the words "law" (*zakon*) and "custom" (*obychai*) and their derivatives are used by Timofeev either to refer specifically to the social hierarchy or more generally to the moral and the religious order. In all cases, references to specific laws or customs are lacking; nevertheless, the tsars are shown to have a very clear obligation to preserve the religion and the social structure of Muscovite Rus'. In line with this, the most detailed favorable description of the actual administration of a tsar, that of Boris Godunov, stresses the function of the tsar as the preserver and regulator of an essentially static society (65).[47]

The fact that Timofeev's favorite tsar was poor Fedor Ivanovich, "the bellringer," also sheds an odd light on the exalted autocracy in which Timofeev allegedly believed. Although Fedor took virtually no part in secular affairs and was anything but an autocrat in practice, his piety enabled him perfectly to fulfill the ritual role of linking the earthly *tsarstvo* to the heavenly Tsar, the political community of Muscovite Rus' to the power and will of God, who Himself, with the Virgin, protects Muscovy and subdues its enemies because of Fedor's piety and purity.[48] Fedor served this ritual function perfectly, but the actual giving of orders was carried out in his name by others, namely Boris Godunov. This in no way means that Timofeev thought that the power of the state should be weak.[49] It means only that the autocratic power of the tsar could be exercised by one or more persons around the tsar acting in the tsar's name.[50]

Thus, while Timofeev made many autocratic-sounding theoretical statements, he spent much of his time in the *Vremennik* describing rulers who were far from the theoretical perfection he required in his abstract statements. Far from criticizing his fellow Muscovites for not being "voiceless fish," he constantly upbraided them for not having restrained the rulers from their evil deeds.

It is tempting to follow Cherniavsky in explaining this irritating duality by reference to the issue of legitimacy. By this theory, Timofeev included all fully legitimate tsars in his theoretical "absolutist" statements and cast all those of doubtful legitimacy—all claimants to the throne between the death of Fedor and the election of Mikhail Romanov—as upstart usurpers for whom the normal theoretical rules were suspended or even reversed. Thus the duality neatly disappears, for the interregnum rulers were not really tsars at all.[51]

There are a number of statements in the *Vremennik* that indicate that Timofeev did indeed believe that all the rulers between Fedor and Mikhail were not legitimate. Near the end of the work, for example, Timofeev tells us that just as the lawful power of the tsar was extinguished when there were no princes in Judah, so the present line was extinguished with Fedor Ivanovich, but is renewed in "Mikhail, whom God raised up after the well-beloved Fedor" (160; see also 26, 75, 112, 164). Yet this apparent consistency breaks down under closer scrutiny. The First False Dmitrii and Sidorka are clearly beyond the pale: Timofeev refers to the first as "the Antichrist" and the second as the "tormentor-false-tsar" (*muchitel'-lzhetsar'*) (83, 84, 88, 124, 127, 129). But Prince Vasilii Shuiskii was treated ambiguously. Timofeev refers to him as "tsar" and to his local officials as "established by the tsar from God" (113, 157). Yet in another passage he is called a "self-elected, so-called tsar" (100). "He cannot be called a tsar in truth," we are told, "because he held power like a tormentor and not like a tsar" (102). In yet another passage, there is a reference to Shuiskii's "cross-violating power" (153). Boris Godunov is generally portrayed as a usurper, a "slave" who "impudently accomplished this jumping up to the highest power" (56–57), but Timofeev tells us explicitly that his son, Fedor Borisovich, could have been a perfectly legitimate tsar if he had only been anointed (85).

There is perhaps another reason why Timofeev did not see the legitimacy/illegitimacy issue as a black-and-white one. Under a complete usurper like Sidorka, all the political rules were suspended; since there was absolutely no connection between such a ruler and the will of God, political life lost all meaning, and Timofeev had no rules by which he could describe political events. The admission of some degree of legitimacy rectified this problem and in addition permitted Timofeev to describe the good qualities of the rulers concerned while escaping from the awkward restrictions of the Edenic model autocracy.

If the line between legitimacy and illegitimacy were the boundary between perfect autocrats and corrupt pretenders, then all legitimate rulers should have been portrayed as perfect. This indeed is the picture Cherniavsky gives us. He argues that during this period (the "age of Ivan the Terrible" and the Time of Troubles) the tsar was by nature above human judgment, that "the human nature of the Prince was as exalted as his divine office."[52] After drawing some rather one-sided conclusions from sources allegedly dating to Ivan's own time,[53] he describes the *smuta* tales in general and the *Vremennik* in particular as exemplifying the victory of the tsar's autocratic power over his human weakness, or rather, the exaltation of both the tsar's power and his personality, and thus the destruction of the tension in Agapetus's formulation discussed earlier.

The legacy of the Troubles, therefore, was the "exaggeration of the absolute and sacred character of the tsar's office," which was justified by God from above and by his "exalted humanity" from below. For Timofeev, Cherniavsky tells us, "all the actions of a true tsar are, by definition, proper."[54]

We have already discussed one of the two rulers in the small class of "true" tsars, Fedor Ivanovich, and have remarked on his unlikely qualifications as an ideal autocratic monarch.[55] When we turn to his father, Ivan, we do find formal encomiums on the piety of the tsar, disclaimers that an ordinary person should not criticize a true tsar (17, 33–34), and even the extravagant statement that "even the whole world cannot compare in value with only one hair of the tsar's head" (64). Yet the concrete descriptions of what Ivan did are horrifying. In direct contradiction to Cherniavsky's assertion, Timofeev tells us that Ivan "was moved to fury as much by [his] nature as by anger" (*Zane k iarosti udob podvizhen be kupno po estestvu i za gnev*) (11). Ivan was moved by a mighty fierceness against his own slaves (subjects); he hated all the towns of his kingdom (11); he humiliated himself like a slave before the Tatar Semen Bekbulatovich, whom he had set up in his own place, "thus playing with God's people" (11). His actions, especially the *oprichnina*, angered God and foreshadowed (*proobrazuia*) the Troubles themselves (12). As a result of his plunder of Novgorod, Ivan "filled [Novgorod's] land with blood and tormented all [its] people with various tortures, not only covering the land but thickening the water with blood." There were so many corpses that the wild animals were full and could eat no more (13–14). He forced his own cousin and all of his cousin's family to drink poison, and killed his own son (19, 23–24). If this was exalted humanity, one wonders what depraved humanity would be like.[56]

The tension between the divine power and the human nature of the tsar, far from disappearing, becomes particularly acute in the portrait of Ivan. Timofeev's rhetorical glorifications of the tsar who was descended from his royal family as the morning light comes from the sun (10–11) stand in stark contrast to his actual reporting of the acts of the ruler. An examination of the language Timofeev used in describing Ivan reveals how far he was prepared to go in condemning the tsar, and furnishes at least a hint, "in covered words," as he put it (23), as to how he justified that criticism in his own mind. Timofeev describes Ivan's character with words like *iarost'* (rage), *gnev* (anger), *liutost'* (ferocity)—words usually associated with evil deeds or people, but used with approval to describe the tsarevich Ivan Ivanovich (19). However, when he chose the adverb *nechestivno* (godlessly, unrighteously) to describe Ivan's invasion of Novgorod (13), he crossed the boundary into a vocabulary that was completely inappropriate for any "real," that is, uncorrupted tsar. The same is true of the words *mirogubitel'* (peace-destroyer), possibly a contrast to the "peacemakers" (*mirotvortsy*) of the Sermon on the Mount (Matt. 9) and *rabogubitel'* (slave/subject killer) (14). Ivan's destruction of Novgorod is described in phrases taken from the beginning of Psalm 78 (79). Timofeev draws the attention of the reader directly to the analogy with Psalms 78 and 79 (79 and 80), an analogy that was justified in his mind by the fact that the events described took place in the "seventy-eighth year," the year 7078 by the Muscovite system (14).[57] The first of these psalms is a call to God to revenge "the blood of thy servants" and the second is a prayer that God restore His people to His favor. Although the major burden of the analogy is a call on God's mercy, an obvious and important implication is that Ivan is identified with the godless enemies of Israel.[58] After describing Ivan's murder both of his son and his cousin, Timofeev concludes (23) that "their blood will cry out to him forever like [the blood] of Abel against Cain."[59] The implications of the Cain analogy have already been discussed.

In his description of the *oprichnina* (11–13), Timofeev carries this process even further. This institution not only angered God but foreshadowed the Troubles. The *oprichniki* are described as wearing badges "like darkness" (*tmoobrazny*); they were dressed by Ivan from head to foot in black. Their appearance before the terrified populace was "like the dark night." A notation in the margin adds that, in every way, Ivan made all of his warriors like demonic servants (*iako besopodobny slugi*).[60] Lest the reader miss this clear connection of Ivan with the devil and perhaps even with the Antichrist, Timofeev concludes his description thus: "Those reading this will understand from the description of the thing its basic nature."[61]

Timofeev thus felt impelled to move in contradictory directions. If anything, he intensified the earlier Muscovite emphasis on the exalted nature of the tsar, as Cherniavsky correctly observed. But at the same time, he felt he had to describe the sins of rulers, and to connect those sins causally with the disasters that engulfed the country. In describing a tsar like Ivan IV, where the theoretical escape of illegitimacy was closed, Timofeev used language that connected the tsar certainly with the forces of evil, and perhaps with the Antichrist and the end of the world. The creation story analogy has the similar implication that the corruption of the tsardom was an irreversible process.[62] Yet Timofeev was concerned above all *not* to undermine the ideal of a God-chosen ruler and thus was forced to describe Ivan as at once perfect and gravely flawed.

Timofeev did not adopt the interpretation, based on the Old Testament it would seem, that good and bad rulers may succeed each other, calling forth God's reward or punishment but not threatening the institution of rulership, nor did he use the idea of the "king's two bodies" by means of which the medieval West gradually worked out a solution to this conundrum.[63] Because of this theoretical impasse, political reversals and apparently evil rulers produced extreme tension in a system of political thought that derived all authority from God, with the purity of the tsars as the essential link with the Divine. As the tide of violence rose during the Troubles (and Timofeev's biography indicates that his experience was far from pleasant), belief in a sacred political order embodied in a God-chosen tsar, seen nostalgically as having exercised in the past complete power over subjects silent as fish, must have seemed the best, if not the only, defense against the constantly confronted alternative of chaos. Hence the greater the problems of the actual ruler, the greater the need to assert his perfection. The only two escapes from this brittle paradox were to ignore the faults of the ruler, or to abandon faith in the God-created tsardom altogether and slide into apocalypticism.

The only major element in Timofeev's political thought that remains undiscussed is the element of advice.[64] Advice for Timofeev served as a corrective, an alternate channel by which God's will can reach a corrupted tsar. Every tsar, legitimate or not, had the obligation to surround himself with good advisers. Most of Ivan's disastrous policies were traced to his listening to evil advice either of slanderers (13, 23) or of foreigners (12). Timofeev equated Ivan's trust in foreigners with putting his head in the mouth of an asp (12). The theme of evil advice maintains its importance throughout the *Vremennik*. Under the interregnum rulers, Timofeev believed that the righteous among the "slaves" should themselves have taken the initiative to object to the evil policies of various rulers, and blames their "wordless silence" (92) for many of the calamities of the period. This obligation of the subjects to correct, on their own initiative, the sins of the rulers seems to have been present only under tsars of questionable legitimacy; none of Ivan's subjects are blamed for their wordless silence.[65] The duty to give this advice was reserved to the righteous, the "strong in Israel," and was not confined either to a social class or to a political party. Eve's role in the creation story passage shows that evil advice was worse than no advice at all.

The relationship of these ideas can fairly easily be put in the form of a diagram (figure 2.1). Although we must bear in mind that it conveys the impression of more precise boundaries and more consistent definitions than Timofeev had in mind, it is nevertheless a useful tool to visualize the structure of Timofeev's thought.

The goal of the whole arrangement is for the people to obey the will of God. On the left, the mirrorlike souls of righteous tsars transmit this will to the people, who obey because of the tsar's perfect autocracy. On the right, "fallen" tsars and people have to work out another arrangement. This

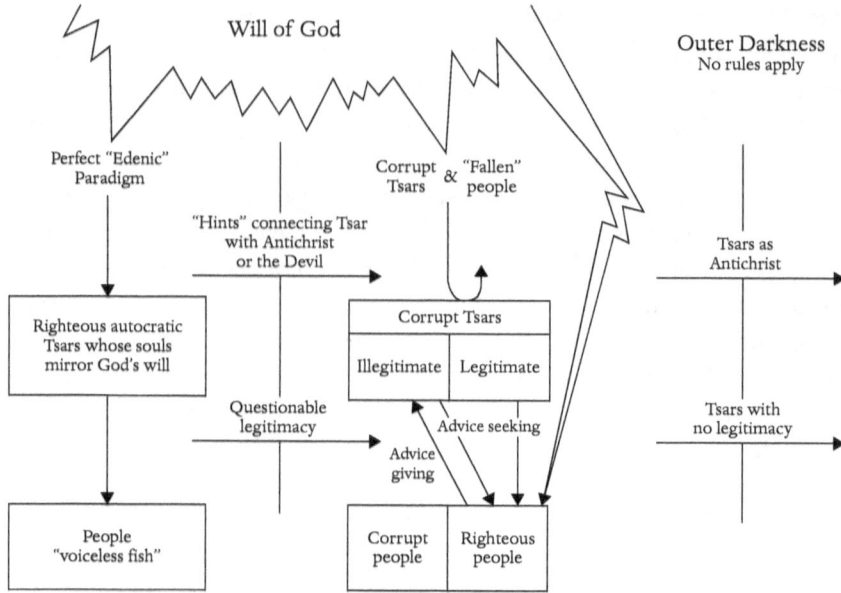

FIGURE 2.1. Diagram of the structure of Ivan Timofeev's political thought. Drawn by author's wife, Wendy Bolton Rowland, for which he feels great gratitude.

arrangement, because it is imperfect, receives no theoretical discussion and has no theoretical justification. Corrupt tsars must seek advice from wise counselors, while shunning advice from slanderers, foreigners, and so on. In the case of the interregnum rulers, these wise advisers have the duty to render advice whether it is asked for or not. If the ruler is of questionable legitimacy or is linked by use of language to the Antichrist, or the devil, the observer (historian) considers him in the corrupt right-hand paradigm. If he is clearly identified as the Antichrist or is completely illegitimate, he has no authority at all and is out of the system.

Some Conclusions

I do not wish to claim that this discussion, which has focused in detail on only two segments of the *Vremennik*, does justice to the richness and complexity of the ideas in that work. Nevertheless, the evidence accumulated so far makes some tentative conclusions and suggestions possible.

First, the evidence of the *Vremennik* and the knowledge of biblical and other literature that it reveals throw some doubt on Edward Keenan's thesis that "a rather sharp contrast between secular and religious cultures" existed in mid-sixteenth-century Muscovy.[66] We can be fairly sure from the biographical evidence we have now that Timofeev received his education in the 1580s or earlier. His service career connects him firmly to the secular bureaucracy. It is possible that the contrast of cultures had largely disappeared by the 1580s or that Timofeev acquired his knowledge of religious culture during the long period he spent in Novgorod, but otherwise the *Vremennik* would seem to be evidence against the two-culture hypothesis.

Whether or not that is true, it is clear that Timofeev's thought about tsar and people was largely traditional and that the language he used to describe the tsar with his advisers—all the material that we would call "political"— derives from the ecclesiastical culture, has strong bases in the Bible, and contains no important political ideas from outside that culture.

The theoretical statements that Timofeev made all stress, and for ritual reasons had to stress, the exalted nature and the perfect autocracy of the tsar, since both were necessary to give meaning to political life. Yet few if any of the rulers that he actually described fit the pattern, and so he found himself in an awkward position. He needed to be in two places at once on figure 2.1: he needed to be on the left, perfect side, because only that side could really legitimize and give meaning to political life; he needed to be on the right, corrupted side, because only there, as a historian, could he describe what was going on. The tension between these two sides, the same tension as that in the Agapetus formula and in the creation story analogy, is not resolved by any logical means, and, in the description of Ivan, reaches a very high pitch. Only a little further pressure would be necessary to break the two sides apart completely; the Old Believers, using the same imagery of the Antichrist as Timofeev, did exactly that. For them, the tsar's destruction of Orthodoxy made it impossible for them to believe in him as a ritual link with God, and therefore both his position and all other political forms lost their meaning.

Short of such a radical step, however, the perfect autocracy paradigm could not be changed. It was as absolute as the multiplication table or a theorem in geometry. In spite of, or perhaps because of, this characteristic, allegiance to this paradigm proved remarkably durable. That Timofeev could emerge from 312 folios of discussion of the unusual characters, savory and unsavory, who reigned in Muscovy from 1547 to 1613 with this allegiance firmly intact was no mean achievement. Such temporary expedients as the governing of the country by a (vaguely) representative assembly or even the election of a tsar by the *zemskii sobor* remained just that—temporary expedients operating in the gray area to the right in figure 2.1. They could not be brought over to the left side without fatally polluting its theoretical perfection, and thus inducing a collapse of the whole structure.

To approach the problem from a more historical point of view, we could say that the concepts Timofeev inherited from Byzantium left him no middle ground between the mutually exclusive concepts of a pious autocratic *basileus* (Slavic *tsar'*) on the one hand and a God-opposing *tyrannos* (Slavic *muchitel'*) on the other. The crux of Timofeev's dilemma was that he had no theoretical way to describe the faults of a fully legitimate ruler such as Ivan IV without stating explicitly, or at least implicitly, that he was a *tyrannos*, an admission he most emphatically did not want to make.

I would like to end with an admittedly highly speculative question. If we accept the hypothesis that Timofeev was typical of politically active Muscovites of the sixteenth and early seventeenth centuries, what sort of "politics" would we imagine such men carried on? Our own conception of politics, based on our own nineteenth- and twentieth-century experience, presupposes two characteristics of the people taking part: (1) the ability to conceptualize one's own interest in various policy options under debate and to develop a position on the options consistent with those interests; and (2) the ability to join with others who share those interests in defense of a common set of ideas, now formulated as the "ideology" of a "party." Both activities can be carried on only within the framework of the language and concepts available. The language and concepts found in the *Vremennik*, I think it is fair to say, would have inhibited both of these processes. Timofeev describes events less by conceptualizing the secular advantages or disadvantages, causes or results, of a policy than by judging a policy by analogy to sacred texts, by reference to the perfect autocracy paradigm, by establishing the righteousness (or lack thereof) of the policy concerned.

Now historians are trained to be a trifle cynical about such things. I am not arguing that Muscovites never either perceived or pursued their own interests, but the evidence of the *Vremennik* seems to suggest that people who thought the way Timofeev apparently did would be less likely to go through the steps above, and would go through them less often, on a narrower range of issues, than nineteenth- or twentieth-century Europeans. If this idea is correct, it would help to explain why the historical record has so few traces of the aristocratic opposition to the crown that historians, on the basis of their own political perceptions, have assumed must have existed as the expanding powers of the monarchy gradually eroded the independence of that class. It would help to explain why the boyars failed to set up permanent institutional restraints on the tsar's power even in periods when that power was weak or nonexistent, such as the minority of Ivan IV, the reign of Fedor, or the Time of Troubles. It might even help to explain the variety of ideological alignments that have been ascribed by various historians to various "parties" or individuals in the succession crisis under Ivan III.

Notes

1. J. G. A. Pocock, "Languages and Their Implications: The Transformation of the Study of Political Thought," *Politics, Language, and Time* (New York: Atheneum, 1973), 3–41. For a different statement of the same problems, discerned in a much wider historiographical context, see J. H. Hexter, "Personal Retrospect and Historical Postscripts," in his *Reappraisals in History* (Evanston, IL: Northwestern University Press, 1961), 202–210.

2. See, for example, Pocock, "Languages and Their Implications," 13–41, esp. 26–27; and J. H. Hexter, *The Vision of Politics on the Eve of the Reformation* (New York: Basic Books, 1973). For references to further theoretical statements by Pocock, Quentin Skinner, and John Dunn, as well as a critique of their ideas, see Charles Tarlton, "Historicity, Meaning, and Revisionism in the Study of Political Thought," *History and Theory* 12, no. 3 (1973): 307–328. The questions I ask of the *Vremennik* in this essay may seem unsophisticated by the standards of Pocock and his colleagues. I assume, for example, that the paradigms or clusters of political ideas with which Timofeev attempted to explain events, and the verbal expressions of those ideas, were meant and understood almost solely in a religious, specifically Orthodox Christian context, a context that I believe continued to dominate Muscovite "high culture" well into the seventeenth century. I doubt, therefore, that the "language" (to use Pocock's term), the general framework of ideas that Timofeev and his contemporaries used to understand political events, was the kind of "complex plural language" that Pocock found in Western European sources of roughly the same period. I suspect that the reason is that Muscovite society and culture themselves were both remarkably unified by Western European standards. There is, however, one serious obstacle to a "Pocockian" examination of the *Vremennik* (or any other early seventeenth-century text): the doubts that exist about the authenticity and dating of many sixteenth-century sources make it difficult to establish the "language" or the "paradigms" (clusters of ideas within a language) that Timofeev inherited from the previous generation, or to ascertain the changes he wrought in that language.

3. I emphatically do not mean to imply that such "second-level" inquiry begins with this essay, or, even worse, that I have met and solved all the problems this inquiry involves, even with respect to the *Vremennik*. I here would only like to focus attention on the problem and the continuing need for careful attention to it. The reluctance of historians of Muscovy to render this attention can be seen in the lukewarm reception given to Antony N. Grobovsky's *The "Chosen Council" of Ivan IV: A Reinterpretation* (Brooklyn, NY: Gaus, 1969), an intensive "second-level" investigation of the meaning of the term *izbrannaia rada* and the misinterpretations that the term has suffered at the hands of succeeding generations of historians. Two of the reviewers complained that Grobovsky's book did not address the "basic" questions of the character of the reforms carried out in the early part of Ivan's reign or the "political party" behind these reforms. They ignored the implication that if Grobovsky is right (none of the reviewers

challenged any of his careful and exhaustive documentation), if it is impossible to interpret *izbrannaia rada* either as a constitutional body or as a political party with an ideology and a definable membership, then we must ask ourselves how far the concepts of "constitutional bodies" or "political parties," concepts largely imported from Western nineteenth- and twentieth-century history and absent from all contemporary sources, can be applied to sixteenth-century Muscovy without doing unacceptable violence to the evidence. See the reviews by Joel Raba, in *Canadian-American Slavic Studies* 6, no. 3 (1972): 496–497; and by V. Vodoff in *Le Moyen Age* 77 (1972): 167–171. These reviews are among the most careful and the most favorable the book received.

For an effective critique of the several sets of assumptions on which almost all studies of Muscovite ideology and its connection with Muscovite society are based, especially the "ideological struggle" interpretation of Muscovite political thought, see Clifford Geertz, "Ideology as a Culture System," in *Ideology and Discontent*, ed. D. Apter (Glencoe, I: Glencoe Free Press, a Division of the Macmillan Company, 1964), 47–56, reprinted in Geertz's *The Interpretation of Cultures* (New York: Basic Books, 1973), 193–223. "Both interest theory [for explaining cultural statements] and strain theory go directly from source analysis to consequence analysis without ever seriously examining ideologies as systems of interacting symbols, as patterns of interworking meanings. Themes are outlined, of course. . . . But they are referred for elucidation not to other themes nor to any sort of semantic theory, but either backward to the effect they presumably mirror or forward to the social reality they presumably distort" (207).

4. The edition of the *Vremennik* used here is found in O. A. Derzhavina, ed., *Vremennik Ivana Timofeeva* (Moscow-Leningrad: Izdatel´stvo Akademii nauka, 1951), 9–168, to which the page numbers in the text refer. For a full list and critical evaluation of various published versions of the text, see Helmut Keipert, *Beitriige zur Textgeschichte und Nominalmorphologie des Vremennik Ivana Timofeeva* (Dissertation; Bonn: Reinische-Friedrich-Universitet, 1968), 8–20. Keipert considered that the best editions were the Soviet one by Derzhavina and one found in the second edition of *Russkaia istoricheskiya biblioteka* (henceforth *RIB*), vol. 13 (Saint Petersburg, 1909). In difficult places, I have checked the published text with a not always clear microfilm of the text. The most complete discussion of works about Timofeev published before 1949 can be found in I. I. Polosin, "'Ivan Timofeev—russkii myslitel´, istorik i d´iak XVII veka," *Uchenye zapiski Moskovskogo pedagogicheskogo instituta im. V.I. Lenina*, LX, kafedra istorii SSSR, part 2 (1949): 135–149. Since Polosin's time, most of the specialized historical work on Timofeev has been biographical (see below, note 6), except O. A. Derzhavina's long article "D´iak Ivan Timofeev i ego 'Vremennik,'" *Vremennik*, 351–409, and a recent article by V. I. Koretsky on the textual history of the *Vremennik*, "Ob osnovnom letopisnom istochnike 'Vremennika' Ivana Timofeeva," *Letopisi i khroniki* (1976), 113–141.

5. The most complete study of historical works describing the Time of Troubles is S. F. Platonov, *Drevnerusskie skazaniia i povesti o smutnom vremeni XVII veka, kak istoricheskii istochnik* (Saint Petersburg: Tip. V.S. Balasheva, 1888). For some revisions of Platonov's conclusions in the light of later scholarship and of additional manuscript study, see Daniel Rowland, "Muscovite Political Attitudes as Reflected in Early Seventeenth-Century Tales about the Time of Troubles" (PhD diss., Yale University, 1976), 13–118, 230–70.

6. A minor exception to this statement may be Timofeev's remarks about the *d'iak* E. Telepnev. See V. I. Koretskii, "Novye materialy o d'iake Ivane Timofeeve, istorike i publitsiste XVII v.," *Arkheograficheskii ezhegodnik za 1974 god* (1975), 164.

7. The two main sources of biographical information about Timofeev were Platonov, *Drevnerusskie skazaniia*, 163–166, 448–449n10; and N. P. Likhachev, *Razriadnye d'iaki XVI veka. Opyt istoricheskogo issledovaniia* (Saint Petersburg: Tip. V. S. Balasheva, 1888), 197–199. Later biographers gleaned virtually all their information from these sources: P. G. Vasenko, "D'iak Ivan Timofeev, avtor 'Vremennika,'" *Zhurnal Ministerstva narodnogo prosveshcheniia*, part 14, N. S. (Saint Petersburg, 1908), 102–103; Derzhavina, "D'iak Ivan Timofeev." Later on, L. V. Cherepnin unearthed materials connected with the Novgorod phase of Timofeev's career: "Novye materialy o d'iake Ivane Timofeeve-avtore 'Vremennika,'" *Istoricheskii arkhiv* 6, part 4, (1960): 162–177; and "Materialy po istorii russkoi kultury i russko-shvedskikh kulturnykh sviazey XVII v. v arkhivakh Shvetsii," *Trudy Otdela drevnerusskoy literautry* 17 (1961): 454–470; V. B. Kobrin, using cadastral material from the Vereia district, discovered that Timofeev's original last name was Semenov: "Novoe o d'iake Ivane Timofeeve," *Istoricheskii arkhiv* 8, part 1 (1962): 246. V. I. Koretskii ("Novye materialy," 145–167) confirmed Kobrin's suggestion, added a great deal of new information, mostly from archival sources, and combined all this data with the material in the *Vremennik* itself into a substantial biographical sketch. Although a few minor questions remain, and a number of Koretskii's conclusions remain probabilities rather than certainties (the statement that he came from near Maloiaroslavets is based on the evidence that most of his lands were located there and his second wife came from there, for example), the outlines of Timofeev's life now seem clear.

8. Koretskii, "Novye materialy," 148.

9. In that year he is listed as a *d'iak* in the Chancery of the Great Receipt (*Prikaz bol'shogo prikhoda*).

10. See below, note 22.

11. Timofeev seems to have had two lapses. First, the evidence indicates that he conspired to steal from the estate of his enemy M. I. Tatishchev, though probably for political rather than personal motives. See Cherepnin, "Materialy po istorii russkoi kultury," 456–467. Second, Koretskii feels he rendered a false judgment clearly against the evidence in order to curry favor with Filaret. See Koretskii, "Novye materialy," 164–165.

12. *Vremennik*, 118–119.

13. For a full description of the manuscript (Gosudarstvennaya biblioteka imeni Lenina, Moscow, Museum Collection, no. 10692) see Rowland, "Muscovite Political Attitudes," 237–242. This description includes a table listing the hand, paper, and contents found in each gathering and notes a number of watermarks not previously observed.

14. See Polosin, "'Ivan Timofeev—russkii myslitel,'" 157–191, for a description of these fragments and an analysis of the chronological information contained in each fragment. This article represents the first part of a much longer work on Timofeev that Polosin had ready for the press as early as 1949. Most of the rest of this work, including the chapters "Facts and Ideas," "Language and Style," and "Conclusion," was published in a posthumous collection of Polosin's work: I. I. Polosin, "Ivan Timofeev—

russkii myslitel′, istorik i d′iak XVII v.," *Sotsial′no-politicheskaia istoriia Rossii* (Moscow: Akademiia Nauk, 1963), 263–347. This article contains a number of helpful suggestions on the meaning of Timofeev's difficult prose. Polosin's comments on Derzhavina's modern Russian translation in *Vremennik*, 171–346, are also very useful: I. I. Polosin, "Retsenziia, *Vremennik Ivana Timofeeva*, podgotovka k pechati, perevod, i komentarii O. A. Derzhavinoi," *Izvestiia AN SSSR: Otdelenie literatury i iazyka* 2 (1952): 85–89.

15. Polosin, "Ivan Timofeev—russkii myslitel′" (both 1949 and 1963). Polosin pushes this point too far, for though Timofeev wrote the fragments at different times, he seems to have written them with the intention of uniting them into one work (*Vremennik*, 118). They were not completely random fragments, but sketches for a work that was only partially completed.

16. It was repeatedly referred to in the plural in the middle of the seventeenth century when the government was looking for a copy of it. See S. A. Belokurov, *Iz dukhovnoi zhizni moskovskogo obshchestva XVII v.* (Moscow: n.p., 1903), 62–63.

17. For example, I feel uneasy about the authenticity of those passages, especially marginal passages, written in hand 6, according to the numbering of Derzhavina (*Vremennik*, 415–33). More generally, Edward L. Keenan has questioned in conversations with the author whether a native-born early seventeenth-century d′iak could have written in the pedantic convoluted style of the *Vremennik*.

18. See, for example, Platonov, *Drevnerusskie skazaniia*, 163–166.

19. See the excellent summary of the parallels based on evidence up to and including Cherepnin's discoveries, in Keipert, *Beitriige zur Textgeschichte*, 61–65. Koretskii, in "Novye materialy," incorporates both his new documentary evidence and the evidence from the *Vremennik* into one convincing, chronological narrative.

20. If Koretskii is right ("Ob osnovnom istochnike," 141) that the *Vremennik* and the *Novyi letopisets* used a common source, the "Istoriia o razorenii Moskovskom" of Patriarch Iov's *keleinik* Iosif, a tale now lost, it seems likely that the final work on the *Vremennik* was done at the end of Timofeev's life, when he developed a close connection with Filaret, who might well have had a copy of Iosif's tale in his library and who was also closely connected with the compilation of the *Novyi letopisets*. See also L. V. Cherepnin, "'Smuta' i istoriografiia XVII veka," *Istoricheskie zapiski* 14 (1945): 82–97. According to Koretskii, in "Novye materialy," 161–164, Timofeev composed the "panegyric" to Filaret in the *Vremennik* (165–166) in 1629–1630. His evidence is far from conclusive, but it seems likely that Timofeev finished his editorial work in the period between the end of his service career (1628) and his death (1631). The watermark evidence, though ambiguous, suggests the early 1630s as the most likely date of the earliest parts of the manuscript. See Rowland, "Muscovite Political Attitudes," 238–242.

21. Belokurov, *Iz dukhovnoi zhizni moskovskogo*, 62–63; Koretskii, "Novye materialy," 155–156.

22. Vasenko, "D′iak Ivan Timofeev, avtor 'Vremennika,'" 102–103.

23. See Daniel Rowland, "The Problem of Advice in Early Seventeenth-Century Tales about the Time of Troubles," *Russian History* 6, no. 1 (1979): 259–283 (chapter 3 of this volume).

24. D. J. Bennet Jr., "The Idea of Kingship in Seventeenth-Century Russia" (PhD diss., Harvard University, 1967), 1–69; see also Rowland, "Muscovite Political Attitudes," 200–218.

25. An important article by Riccardo Picchio has recently shown how these biblical references are crucial for understanding the meaning of a number of texts in several genres of Old Slavic literature: "The Function of Biblical Thematic Clues in the Literary Code of 'Slavia Orthodoxa,'" *Slavica Hierosolymitana* 1 (1977): 1–32. I agree wholeheartedly with Picchio, but I should point out one important limitation that he neglects to mention: we do not know precisely which texts of what is now the Bible were available to Timofeev or to earlier writers. Since a rigorous textual comparison is impossible at the moment, I have contented myself by following Picchio's example of giving the King James Version of the relevant texts.

26. *Vremennik*, 29–30. Subsequent in-text page citations reference this source.

27. Luke 8:32; Acts 4:26–27; 12:21–23.

28. After God had discovered Cain's crime, He drove the latter out and condemned him to be a "fugitive and wanderer" (Gen. 4:16).

29. I have not tried to count scriptural references because I suspect I have found only the most obvious of them, where a biblical figure is specifically mentioned by name, or when a phrase happened to strike my ear. I am sure that readers more familiar with biblical and other sacred texts (and surely Timofeev and his readers fall into this category) would "hear" many more. This problem is stated very clearly by Horace Lunt, in the introduction to *Concise Dictionary of Old Russian (11th–17th Centuries)* (Munich: Wilhelm Fink Verlag, 1970), vi.

I also believe that to oppose biblical to other historical references (or to other religious texts) is to draw a largely false dichotomy. The preponderance of biblical references presumably reflects a greater acquaintance and preoccupation with biblical events and their interpretations than with Byzantine or pre-Muscovite East Slavic events, though these, as the example of Gleb shows, are also mentioned, and are apparently equally authoritative.

30. As Pavel Florensky wrote, "The artist does not compose the image from his own conception, but merely removes the covers from the already existing and unique image. He does not superimpose the paint on the canvas, but, as it were, clears away its extraneous coatings, the incrustations concealing its spiritual reality." Quoted in Boris A. Uspensky, *The Semiotics of the Russian Icon*, ed. Stephen Rudy and trans. P. A. Reed (Lisse; Peter de Ridder Press, 1976), 50. For further explanation and details, see also 16, 27–29, and notes 50–52.

For an excellent (twentieth-century) explanation of the icon's ability to reveal a wonderfully complex and integrated theological message through the portrayal of an historical event, see the discussion of nativity icons in Leonid Ouspensky and Vladimir Lossky, *The Meaning of Icons* (Boston: Boston Book and Art Shop, 1952), 159–163.

A clear example of Muscovy's belief in the continuity of present, past, and biblical time, and of Muscovites' inclination to see eternal themes and forces in contemporary events is the famous *Church Militant* icon now in the Tret´iakov Gallery in Moscow. The icon depicts the triumphant forces of Rus´, the New Israel; the warriors, led by the Archangel Michael, include among many others St Demetrius of Salonika, St Vladimir, Vladimir Monomakh, Boris, Gleb, and Ivan IV. On the right is the burning city of Sodom, presumably symbolizing the newly conquered Kazan´, and on the left is Jerusalem/Moscow where the Virgin and Child hand out martyrs' crowns which are carried by angels towards the warriors. See V. I. Antonova and N. E. Mneva, eds., *Gosudarstvennaia Tret´yakovskiya gallereia: Katalog drevnerusskoi zhivopisi, XI–nachala*

XVIII v.v., 2 vols. (Moscow: Iskusstvo, 1963), 2:128–134, for extensive documentation on the meaning of the icon and the identification of the figures. The section containing "Kazan" was painted in the eighteenth century. See 130–131 for references to similar icons from the end of the sixteenth century.

Note the similarity between these icons and the passage in the *Vremennik* (20) in which Ivan IV's son Ivan Ivanovich goes to heaven to join forces with Saints Constantine, Boris, and Gleb "in the defense of the fatherland [*otechestva*]."

31. Fletcher's account is found in Lloyd E. Berry and Robert O. Crummey, eds., *Rude and Barbarous Kingdom: Russia in the Accounts of Sixteenth-Century English Voyagers* (Madison, WI: University of Wisconsin Press, 1968), 128–129. Konrad Bussow tells of Dmitrii's habit of decapitating snowman effigies of various courtiers, especially Boris Godunov. Konrad Bussov, *Moskovskaia khronika 1584–1613* (Moscow-Leningrad: Izdatel´stvo Akadamii Nsuk,1961), 204.

From the time of Dmitrii's canonization in 1606, the pure and innocent interpretation was formally adopted by the church as the true one. The evidence of the *Vremennik* indicates that, even if Timofeev felt uneasy portraying Godunov as totally evil and included his good as well as his evil deeds, he nevertheless accepted this view. Had he cynically adopted the official position while secretly disagreeing with it, he would not have agonized over Boris Godunov the way he did.

32. On constitutional rule, see chapter 3. On lack of political machinery, see, for example, Marc Raeff, "An Early Theorist of Absolutism: Joseph of Volokolamsk," *American Slavic and East European Review* 8 (1949): 86–88.

33. It would be a distortion of Timofeev's meaning to overemphasize the distinction between social and personal sins, a distinction Timofeev did not seem to draw himself.

34. Derzhavina (*Vremennik*, 381) states that Timofeev expressed the opinion of the "boyar party" about Boris Godunov. Why an author who was a service bureaucrat par excellence would agree with the "boyar party" is not explained. For further discussion, see chapter 3 (Rowland, "The Problem with Advice," 280–282).

35. The most thorough and penetrating discussion of the contents of the *Vremennik* is in Polosin, "Ivan Timofeev—russkii myslitel´" (1963). Derzhavina's essay (in *Vremennik*, 351–409) gives an extensive account. V. E. Val´denberg, *Drevnerusskiye ucheniia o predelakh tsarskoi vlasti* (Petrograd: Izd. dom Territoriia budushchego, 1916), 366–367, argues that Timofeev (and the other *smuta* tale authors) "understood the tsar's power as limited by law." An opposite point of view, that for Timofeev, "the tsar is all power and glory, far above humanity and its judgements," is argued by Michael Cherniavsky, *Tsar and People: Studies in Russian Myths*, 2nd ed. (New York: Random House, 1969), 53–59.

36. Rowland, "The Problem of Advice," 265–267, chap. 3.

37. This passage includes two of Polosin's *otryvki*, numbers one and two by his count. Polosin, "Ivan Timofeev—russkii myslitel´" (1949), 157.

38. According to I. I. Sreznevskii, the word *samovlasten* carried the two related meanings of "all-powerful" and "having free will." (*Materialy dlia slovaria drevnerusskago iazyka* [Saint Petersburg: Otdelenie russkago iazyka i slovesnosti Imp. Akademii nauk, 1893–1906], 3:247).

39. See Matthew 13:1–30. In two parables Jesus explains how thorns and tares choked out the newly planted seed, symbolizing the word of God; see also Genesis 3:18–19.

40. Ihor Sevcenko, "A Neglected Byzantine Source of Muscovite Political Ideology," *Harvard Slavic Studies* 11 (1954): 141–179, reprinted in *The Structure of Russian History*, ed. Michael Cherniavsky (New York: Random House, 1970), 80–107. Further references are to the reprint.

41. Sevcenko, "A Neglected Byzantine Source," 99.

42. See Agapetus, chap. 9, discussed in Sevcenko, "A Neglected Byzantine Source," 91.

43. A. Iakovlev, "Bezumnoe molchanie," *Sbornik staei posviashchennykh V. O. Kliuchevskomu* (Moscow: S. P. Iakovlev, 1909), 651–678.

44. It is natural that Timofeev should feel that the best remedy for the Troubles lay in moral reform rather than in political action. D. S. Likhachev has pointed out that Timofeev was a pioneer within Muscovy in overcoming the old habit of treating human character in strictly binary terms, as an agent either of good or evil. Both in his portrait of Boris Godunov, and in his description of Ivan IV, Timofeev depicted the positive and the negative sides of his subjects' characters and did his best to understand the relation between the two. See D. S. Likhachev, *Chelovek v literature drevnei Rusi* (Moscow-Leningrad: Nauka, 1958), 7–26, esp. 17–24. While Likhachev's point is both true and important in regard to these royal portraits, ordinary subjects and other rulers continued to be treated in the old binary fashion. With the exception of the mixed portraits mentioned by Likhachev, both the type of classification and even many of the terms used are remarkably similar to those found in the works attributed to Prince A. M. Kurbskii. For an excellent discussion of this "psychomachic" vocabulary, see Grobovsky, *The "Chosen Council" of Ivan IV*, 95–139. For a description of the binary opposition of Muscovite and Tatar characteristics in the work of Metropolitan Makarii, see Jaroslaw Pelenski, *Russia and Kazan: Conquest and Imperial Ideology (1438–1560)* (The Hague: Mouton, 1974), 302–303.

45. See Cherniavsky, *Tsar and People*, 57–59.

46. For the tale about Varlaam and Josaphat, see A. Orlov, *Perevodnye povesti feodal'noi Rusi i Moskovskogo gosudarstva XII-XVII vv.* (Leningrad: n.p., 1934), 69–77.

47. I hope to explore this theme more fully in a forthcoming article (chapter 4 of this volume) on the question of whether the *smuta* tales in particular and Muscovite ideology in general should be called "absolutist."

48. By "ritual role" I mean the means by which an individual or a community located in time and space is linked to a divine or mythic truth outside time and space. See Lord Raglan, "Ritual and Myth," *Journal of American Folklore* 68 (1955): 454–468. Neither Timofeev nor any other Muscovite could give up at least the ideal of this theoretically perfect autocracy, for without it political life would be deprived of meaning. Timofeev called Fedor a "prayerful horn of strength" (the horn is the biblical symbol for strength and military power, see Deut. 33:17; Dan. 8:20–21), who preserves his kingdom from the enemy with his prayers "as if with a sword." *Vremennik*, 151; see also 22–25, 35–37.

49. "The evil accomplished by such people [bad servants] was permitted by the silence of those in power who did not prevent them by fear" (*Vremennik*, 77).

50. This interpretation derives ultimately from a suggestion made in a letter of November 1976 from Edward L. Keenan to the author suggesting that perhaps the Muscovite tsar should be seen as a "(nominal) despot." Naturally I bear full responsibility for any interpretation of Timofeev.

51. Cherniavsky, *Tsar and People*, 54–57.

52. Cherniavsky, *Tsar and People*, 49–59, esp. 52.

53. Cherniavsky assumes (*Tsar and People*, 49–52) that everyone would have sided with Ivan IV in his arguments with Metropolitan Filipp and in his alleged correspondence with Kurbskii, and that no one would have accepted the latter's stress on the corruptibility and responsibility of the tsar. The sole evidence for this assumption seems to be the habit of tsars from Vasilii III's time of having themselves tonsured on their deathbeds and thus gaining remission for their sins. This ceremony accomplished "the destruction of the tension between the prince's two natures" (48). Was this ceremony seen by both tsar and people as relieving the former completely of his responsibilities before God?

54. Cherniavaky, *Tsar and People*, 55.

55. I again omit Mikhail Romanov from consideration as a "true tsar," partly because Timofeev described only his election rather than his reign, and partly because Timofeev was hardly free, since he completed the version of the *Vremennik* that we now have during that reign, to say anything other than that Mikhail was a perfect, holy ruler.

56. In order to emphasize the difference Timofeev saw between the nature of a tsar and the nature of everybody else, Cherniavsky reasonably cites the statement that Mariia Nagaia's nature in her sorrow at the death of her son, the holy martyr Dmitry, differs from the nature of "we the lowly . . . as a droplet of rain from the whole great depth of the sea" (Timofeev, *Vremennik*, 14; Cherniavsky, *Tsar and People*, 57). But does Timofeev really have Agapetus and his two royal natures in mind? Does the theory of the exalted nature of the ruler extend to cover the whole family of the tsar, including even his seventh, and therefore uncanonical, wife? May not Mariia's special nature spring from her connection with her martyr son as well as from her connection with the tsar? And does not Timofeev's strong feeling for the social hierarchy play a role here as well? Cherniavsky briefly mentions Timofeev's description of Ivan's sins, but claims that a single comparison of Ivan with King David "provided a solution to the problem" (*Tsar and People*, 56–57).

57. "Tozhdestvo chisla . . . krepost' glagolom vo ispolnenie dast" ["The identity of the numbers (of the years with the numbers of Psalms) provides confirmation of these words"]. Timofeev, *Vremennik*, 14.

58. See also Timofeev's statement (13) that Ivan divided the possessions of the people of Novgorod among his servants by lot. Compare with Matthew 27:35; Mark 15:24.

59. See Kurbskii's first letter to Ivan in J. L. I. Fennell, ed. and trans., *The Correspondence between Prince Kurbsky and Tsar Ivan IV of Russia, 1564–1579* (Cambridge: Cambridge University Press, 1963), 4; see also Genesis 4:10.

60. This notation, in hand 6 by Derzhavina's numbering, is of questionable authenticity. Polosin's assertion that the original copyist omitted it and that it was restored by someone later is simply a guess. Polosin, "Ivan Timofeev—russkii myslitel'" (1963), 270. It is consistent with the rest of the text, but slightly more specific.

61. See also the title (9), which announces itself as a description of the first years of the eighth millennium of the creation of the world. For an excellent discussion of this apocalyptic theme and of Timofeev's "number mysticism," see Polosin, "Ivan Timofeev—russkii myslitel'" (1963), 310–315.

62. Only in the descriptions of Sidorka or the First False Dmitii are these implications made entirely explicit, but the direction in which Timofeev's rhetoric was lead-

ing him is surely clear from the description of Ivan discussed above. Polosin was convinced on the basis of his study of the "fragments" of which the *Vremennik* consists and their probable date of composition that Timofeev for a while believed that the end of the world had come and that Ivan was connected with the Antichrist. Polosin, "Ivan Timofeyev—russkii myslitel'" (1963), 310–315.

63. See E. Kantorowicz, *The King's Two Bodies* (Princeton, NJ: Princeton University Press, 1957). In one passage, Timofeev does suggest that the throne itself can remain pure (*neporochen*) whatever the sins of its occupant, but this idea is not developed further (107).

64. I discuss the theme in detail in Rowland, "The Problem of Advice" (chapter 3 of this volume) and only summarize it here.

65. There is only one possible exception: Timofeev seems to blame the clergy for being afraid to stand up to Ivan when he attempted to alter Orthodoxy (12). Timofeev also reports a rumor that Ivan killed his son because the latter tried to restrain him from an evil deed. In his description of the alleged murder of Ivan by Boris Godunov and others, he in no way blames the regicides but states that God permitted the murder to occur (15).

66. E. L. Keenan, *The Kurbskii-Groznyi Apocrypha: The Seventeenth-Century Genesis of the "Correspondence" Attributed to Prince A. M. Kurbskii and Tsar Ivan IV* (Cambridge, MA: Harvard University Press, 1971), 53–54.

CHAPTER 3

The Problem of Advice in Muscovite Tales about the Time of Troubles

In a review in 1890 of S. F. Platonov's *Drevnerusskie skazaniia i povesti o smutnom vremeni XVII veka* (*Old Russian tales and stories about the time of troubles of the seventeenth century*), the celebrated Russian historian V. O. Kliuchevskii complained that, in spite of his excellent textological work, Platonov had virtually ignored a significant aspect of these tales, namely their political ideas. These ideas illustrated "the awakening and development of political thought under the influence of the Troubles." A systematic treatment of this theme, according to Kliuchevskii, would have unified and vastly improved Platonov's work.[1] So far, no such systematic study has been undertaken.

Kliuchevskii himself returned to this theme in his famous *Course in Russian History*, where he commented extensively on these new ideas and cast them into a constitutional framework. He noted that the weakness or even nonexistence of the royal power during this period had thrust the people into a completely novel political role. "The community had been more than once called upon to decide important questions of state policy" and had become accustomed to electing the tsar. From this he concluded that the community had at last seen that "the politically accidental element in the state was not the people

---

This article originally appeared in *Russian History/Histoire Russe* 6, no. 2 (1979): 359–383. The author gratefully acknowledges the publisher for permission to reprint this essay.

but the dynasty," and that "the people should take an active and organized part in public affairs." In sum, the beginning of the century witnessed "strenuous efforts by the ruling classes to establish fundamental laws and a constitutional government."[2]

These conclusions, however, were drawn almost wholly from the study of political events. The tales themselves (which Kliuchevskii obviously knew well, having quoted from them or paraphrased them extensively in his account of the Troubles) were discussed only briefly, in order to show that they provided a negative reinforcement of the constitutional ideas found elsewhere. After arguing that "the tsar's will was often supported, and sometimes replaced, by another political power—the will of the people," Kliuchevskii continued,

> Similar conclusions were drawn from another, negative point of view by contemporary publicists who wrote about the Time of Troubles—Avraamii Palitsyn, Ivan Timofeev, and others who have not left their names. They thought that at the root of the calamity was the lack of manly courage in the community, the people's inability jointly to oppose vested authorities when they violated law and order. When Boris Godunov was "behaving lawlessly" and "destroying great pillars which adorned the country, all the noblest turned dumb, were mute as fishes; no strong man was found in Israel, no one dared to tell the truth to the ruler." It was for this social connivance, for "the foolish silence [*bezumnoe molchanie*] of the whole community," as Avraamii Palitsyn put it, that the country was punished.

Kliuchevskii clearly took this emphasis on the failure to give good advice as an endorsement of the sovereign power of representative institutions. This attitude is shown in his next paragraph, where he equated the "retrograde" insistence of the Assembly of the Land of 1613 that Michael Romanov was born tsar rather than elected with "a return to the old tradition, to the foolish silence of the whole community."[3]

I here suggest that the reason Kliuchevskii failed to produce positive evidence from the tales themselves in support of his position is that they simply do not reflect the kind of constitutional sentiment he claimed to find in other historical sources. The legal-institutional approach that he brought to the problem led him to treat the tales as a negative echo of ideas he had found elsewhere, and so to miss two important points. First, the tales contain a fairly simple and consistent positive philosophy about political advice, one that is not amenable to institutional or constitutional analysis. Second, because Kliuchevskii assumed that the tales contained constitutional ideas that in fact are conspicuously absent in them, he failed to see the lag between popular political thinking and political practice. This lag surely is one important reason for the gradual disappearance of whatever constitutional institutions may have existed at the beginning of the century.

A closer look at the political ideas contained in the tales would help us answer another question, one also raised by Kliuchevskii in connection with the Troubles and their intellectual legacy. Kliuchevskii, like Platonov, saw a struggle for dominance taking place in sixteenth- and seventeenth-century Muscovy between the old aristocracy and the emerging new service class. This struggle also had an ideological dimension, since "the new men [*novye litsa*], free of governmental traditions, became the bearers and champions of the new political ideas that had penetrated into Muscovite minds during the Time of Troubles." Soviet historians agree that there was an intra-class struggle between service people and aristocrats and that this struggle was the basis for the superstructure of ideological debate.[4]

The tales about the Time of Troubles (or *smuta* tales), obviously tell us only indirectly about the aspirations and ideals of the important political actors of the period, none of whom wrote about what he did. They also give little evidence one way or the other about the alleged service people–aristocracy conflict. Yet without bothering to trace the various ideological opinions different historians have ascribed to each side in this conflict, we can ask a fairly simple question about the tales. The authors represent virtually all segments of literate Muscovite society, and include representatives of both the service people and the aristocracy. Do we find one or several sets of ideas here as to what the *tsarstvo* was and how it should have been run? In fact, did the political struggles that raged at the time have an ideological dimension?

The surviving *smuta* tales have number of advantages as sources on which to base answers to these questions. First, by Muscovite standards, they are plentiful, about eighteen separate and independent items by my count. Second, many were composed at a time when the central government was weak, and these may be presumed to be franker than many earlier sources, especially those from the long reign of Ivan IV. Third, the diversity of the authors' social backgrounds gives us as great an assurance as we can hope for that their views are representative of literate Muscovite society as a whole (excluding, obviously, the illiterate classes, who made up the vast majority of the population). Fourth, none of these authors was content simply to list events in chronicle fashion; all of them attempted to cast events in a historical framework, to understand why and how they occurred. This process is, of course, crucial from our point of view. Last, but by no means least, a careful examination of the manuscript tradition indicates that any radical redating of these sources is unlikely.[5] Thus briefly, and in rough order of composition, the tales are identified as follows: Patriarch Iov's tale about Fedor Ivanovich;[6] five separate tales that together were sources for the so-called *Inoe Skazanie*;[7] the "Skazanie . . . o Grishke Otrep'eve";[8] four short tales from the interregnum (the "Novaia povest";[9] the "Plach o plenenii";[10] the "Povest' o nekoei brani";[11] and the so-called Kazanskoe skazanie[12]); the *Vremennik* of Ivan Timofeev;[13] the *Skazanie* of Avraamii Palitsyn (both redactions);[14] I. A. Khvorostinin's "Slovesa dnei i tsarei";[15] and S. I. Shakhovskoi's historical accounts.[16]

The *smuta* tales, then, constitute a fairly reliable body of evidence on the political attitudes of literate Muscovy in the early seventeenth century. But how should we use this evidence? The traditional approach of intellectual historians in analyzing pre-Petrine materials has been a thematic one, the tracing of a theme or a series of themes (e.g., the divine and human nature of the ruler, the saintly prince and the princely saint) through many centuries of development in Kievan and/or Muscovite literature. This method is entirely legitimate and has yielded rich results, revealing to us many, probably most, of the main ideas in the political vocabulary of Muscovites. The large volume of literary political writings that suddenly appeared after 1600, however, suggests a "horizontal" rather than a "vertical" approach, one aimed not at tracing one or more themes through time but at understanding how these ideas were used in practice by fairly ordinary literate men to explain a very troubling set of events. The questions raised by this approach are more basic (What are the attributes of a good tsar? How should the subject behave? What is the role of advisers in the state?) than those that have been raised by the thematic method. In addition, rather than tracing a few themes in many sources, I have traced a larger number of themes in a few sources. This method makes it easier to keep in mind the context of each individual source and thus to avoid some of the distortions that result when the historian's spotlight is focused too narrowly on just a few passages of a given text.[17]

The Function of the Tsar and the Problem of Getting Advice

The Time of Troubles witnessed the arrival and departure of many rulers. Which were admired and why? By far the most important characteristic of a tsar was his piety or righteousness, his internal condition, his spiritual health, so to speak. Ivan the Terrible's son Fedor, whom modern historians generally regard as feebleminded, and who, as the authors of the tales themselves observed, took virtually no part in any kind of governmental activity, nevertheless was universally admired by every single author who mentioned him. They especially admired his piety, which was so great, in our authors' opinion, that God Himself became the protector of the Russian land and the preserver of domestic peace. Patriarch Iov goes so far as to refer to the Virgin as Fedor's *voevoda*. Boris Godunov, on the other hand, again by the admission of these authors themselves, possessed the very government skills that Fedor lacked, yet he is universally condemned by them because he acted out of pride and ambition. Ivan IV is a kind of middle case. Generally they regard the early part of his reign as successful and the latter part as disastrous in many respects. The change, though nowhere explained fully, is seen by all the authors who comment upon it as the result of a spiritual decline from the righteousness of his early years to the "fierceness" (*liutost'*) and "anger" (*gnev*) that dominated the end of his reign.[18]

At least two observations may be made regarding these literary portraits. The first is that the actions of a ruler, the direction of his policies, are seen to spring from his moral character, and thus it was often in the heart or soul of a tsar that the ultimate causes of historical events were sought. For that reason, Ivan Timofeev felt as Pushkin and Musorgskii did later, that it was Godunov's conscience that finally brought him low, not the strength of the First Pretender's armies.[19] But this is not merely a primitive, seventeenth-century version of psycho-history. If we assume our authors meant what they said, the example of Fedor shows that their view of what qualities a tsar should possess are "God-dependent" rather than "independent." By this expression I mean that without an assumption of God's constant and direct intervention in the world, the view of Fedor as the most admired tsar of the period does not make sense. It is not an "independent" view, that is, it is simply not coherent in purely secular terms.

How should a tsar run the *tsarstvo*? As mentioned, Boris Godunov is the ruler whose administration of the realm is most admired. The various descriptions of his deeds reveal how traditional was the view of these authors in regard to the functions of a tsar. He is admired because he was a just judge, the defender of the poor against the rich, the enemy of bribery and corruption, and the protector of the church. These descriptions reveal that the function of the tsar was a conservative one, in the sense that his duty was to conserve or preserve the existing order in church and state.[20] There is little trace here of the more rational, even manipulative approach found in the works traditionally attributed to Ivan IV and Ivan Peresvetov, where, although the ultimate aim of the state remains religious, a given administrative structure—a strong monarch with weak nobles and advisers—is often seen as a means to attain a particular goal, the growth or maintenance of the state's power. The idea of the tsar as a preserver of the old order in state and church is common to all the tales, but it is most strikingly expressed in the section of Timofeev's *Vremennik* that now stands at the beginning of the unique surviving manuscript but that actually belongs, as both the paper and the handwriting indicate, to the second part of the text.[21] It is thus clearly not a clumsy imitation of the biblical creation story stuck on to the beginning of the *Vremennik* in imitation of the chronicle writers, as has usually been thought, but a revealing and thoughtful examination of that story as an analogue of political life.

> Our ancestors, the first couple Adam and Eve, were created in ancient times by the hand of God—he from dirt and she from his rib. God, out of all that existed, appointed him to be as it were the autocratic tsar [*tsar' samovlasten*] of all creation; the birds, the beasts and reptiles all obeyed him with submission as their creator, master of all, and lord. And until the first-created [Adam] was tempted by the Destroyer and Enemy of all to break the first commandment, all the speechless [animals] trembled at the command of that creature [Adam], even those which now terrify us. When the serpent whispered temptation into the ears of Eve, and Eve, instructed by it, tempted her own husband, immediately after that, the newly-created tsar of all the world himself became terrified of those animals....
>
> And as all the wild animals were in everything obedient to Adam until his transgression, so in the same way in recent times our own autocrats in their states ruled over us, their age-old servants, while they themselves kept the commandments given by God up to the end, as long as they did not sin before Him. In the passing of many centuries up to now we did not oppose them, as according to the scriptures a servant should obey his master. In all services we were obedient to them not only to [the spilling of] blood, but even to death itself; as a beast cannot oppose the man who leads him to slaughter, we were answerless before them like voiceless fish; with great care we bore the yoke of servitude, obeying them with such fear that out of fear we showed them honor nearly equal to [that we showed] God.[22]

This small section contains a cluster of ideas that is central to Timofeev's thought. In the first place, we find a picture of what Timofeev considered to be the natural relation between tsar and subject. The tsar is thoroughly autocratic, while the subject is abjectly obedient. The image of the beast being led to slaughter is striking. The subject obeys out of natural fear and honors the tsar almost as God. Elsewhere Timofeev repeats the passage from Agapetus, which by then was a commonplace in Muscovite ideology: "If the tsar is a man by nature, in the sufficiency of his power he approaches God."[23] The other metaphor Timofeev uses frequently is that of master and servant. But clearly, neither the metaphor of God and man nor that of master and servant suggests any idea of a constitutionally limited power or any notion of the rights of the subject. On the contrary, the relation is seen in personal terms, based not on reason but on will, power, even force. As in Byzantine thought, the state is both modeled on and justified by the relationship of God to his creation; it is not seen as a rationally organized set of arrangements to promote certain ends, be they the strength of the country or the happiness of its subjects. And just as the original relationship between Adam and the other creatures depends upon the keeping of the Lord's commandments, so does the proper relationship between ruler and subject depend on the preservation of the "laws and customs" of the land. When these old "laws" are altered, the subjects lose their natural obedience, and corruption creeps into the political order.

Timofeev continues almost from where we left off: "When the years came to an end, the more our rulers changed the old lawful regulations [*blagoustavleniia zakonnaia*] passed on by our fathers, and changed the good customs into new opposing customs, the more in their obeying servants the natural fear of obedience to a master began to diminish."[24]

Now in seventeenth-century English sources, the accusation that the ruler had ignored old laws and changed old customs might well mean that the writer had specific laws and customs in mind. Tradition was for Englishmen a source of authority independent of the will of the king. The English used law and custom, the common law, and parliamentary precedent as a counterpoise to the royal will, as a means with which they could defend what they saw as their rights. Such appeals to the past were possible because they were specific: Edward Coke and his associates were able to cite particular cases, particular precedents to prove their points. Without these citations, their arguments would have had little effect. But what of the case before us? How similar is the Muscovite view of the law?

This is not the place to discuss in detail what Timofeev and our other authors meant by the law.[25] Briefly, their references to the law were remarkably unspecific; the meaning of the law for these authors was much closer to the early medieval concept, where "the law" encompassed divine or moral law and unwritten custom, which might or might not be reflected in written positive law, than it was, say, to the much more precise way in which the law was understood by Edward Coke and other early seventeenth-century English common lawyers.[26]

Very often the term "lawless" (*bezzakonnyi*) is used in the sources under review with a sense very similar to "unseemly" (*nedostoinnyi*) or "improper" (*nelepyi*), that is, simply to refer to a violation of the good order, especially the social order, of the realm and of the traditional way of doing things in it. The tales are full of examples of people being promoted "beyond their nature" (*pache estestva*), a practice for which the rulers of the time were soundly condemned. As part of his version of the creation story, Timofeev tells us that, as a result of the corruption of the Russian *tsarstvo*, "all began in every way to be done against the laws established by previous tsars. The small overcame the great, the young, the old, the dishonorable, the honorable, the servants, their masters.... [Those who used to rule are now ruled;] the foot is crowned while the head is humbled."[27] The author of the first redaction of Palitsyn's *Skazanie* similarly rails against the disruption of the social order: "Everyone began to want to climb higher than his own rank to which he was called; servants wanted to be masters, the unfree leapt for freedom, and military servitors began to behave like boyars [*voinstvennyi zhe chin boliarstvovate nachinakhu*]."[28] It was the duty of the ruler to prevent this from happening, in the first place by being a firm ruler, and, in the second, by promoting only worthy people, "worthy" usually (but not always) meaning "from the appropriate social class."[29]

The problem of promoting worthy people leads directly to the problem of how the tsar should obtain advice. The most pernicious consequence of the promotion of unworthy people was the admission of evil men into the tsar's confidence and his consequent heeding of bad advice. The reader will recall that in Timofeev's version of the creation story, evil began by the "whispering" of the serpent to Eve—in other words, by bad advice. This expression is not accidental. A little further in the same passage, Timofeev elaborates on this theme, drawing his usual parallel between the moral corruption of Eden and the political corruption of Muscovy. He has just finished describing how "after the years came to an end" Russian tsars began to change the old laws and customs. "Our rulers wanted gladly to incline their ears to false whispered words just as in the Old [Testament] Eve, the ancestress of all, attentively inclined her ear to the tempter snake."[30] He then goes on to show how this evil, this false advice and flattery, spread through the kingdom like weeds in a wheat field and now is the "mother of all evil." Thus, evil advisers "killed with their tongues, as if with swords, those who lovingly listened to them."[31] We should note Timofeev's great emphasis on the importance of the advice-taking function of the tsar. The failure of tsars to obtain good advice—or, more accurately, their willingness to listen to evil advisers as a result of their own corruption—led to the fall of the Russian *tsarstvo* just as surely as Eve's inclination to listen to evil led to the fall of man.

The other authors of the *smuta* tales agree with Timofeev in assigning a crucial role to good or bad advice. Throughout the tales, the theme of evil advice as the cause of disastrous royal decisions appears over and over again. Perhaps the most obvious case is the secret and false denunciation of the innocent, which leads to their unjust punishment. According to Shakhovskoi, Tsar Vasilii Shuiskii (1606–1610) "greeted those lies which were whispered into his ears against people with a happy face, and wanted to listen to them sweetly."[32] Khvorostinin accuses him of accepting "the false whispering of the ignorant," of being "attentive to those who came to him in the spirit of deceit and with the teaching of the devil."[33] The author of *Skazanie I* reports that Boris Godunov was prepared to listen to denunciations of masters by their own servants, and on their false advice killed many good men so that "the wise, though innocent, were eliminated from his palace and those strong in judgment were driven far away."[34]

We should note the flavor of the language our authors use here. The notion of secrecy, of "whispered" words, is important, the implication being that wise counselors speak openly. The advice of evil counselors is consciously false, and represents their own self-interest and the influence of the devil. And, as the last quotation shows, these false advisers not only caused the tsar to punish the innocent and thus to fail in his duty as a just judge; they also deceived him into making major decisions the consequences of which nearly ruined the country. The influence of evil counselors is blamed for the sack of Novgorod by Ivan IV, Godunov's murder of the Tsarevich Dmitrii, his persecution of the Shuiskiis and of the Romanovs, the plans of the First Pretender to execute Shuiskii and to "kill the boyars, the gentry, the merchants and all Orthodox Christians," as well as his brutal murder of Boris Godunov's son and wife.[35] Patriarch Germogen warned Shuiskii when the latter was tsar that he was falling into sin because of evil counselors, and tried to curb the influence of those counselors.[36]

There is no doubt, then, that evil advice plays a crucial rule in the *smuta* tales. The importance of whispering advisers is not only that they could create bad policies but, by corrupting the tsar himself, they could poison the very spring from which all his actions flowed. Bad policies were the result of sin: the sin of the tsar, which inclined him to listen to evil advisers, and the sin of the advisers, which made their advice evil. All of these elements—the moral failure of tsars, the disruption of the good order of the realm, evil advice—are drawn together in a moving passage of the "Plach o plenenii," where the author gives his interpretation of the cause of the Troubles:

For this reason Russia the most high was brought low and such a firm column [of piety] was destroyed: instead of following the ladder of saving words leading up to God that come from dogmas found in books, the tsars living in [Russia] adopted devilish cunning tricks [*besovskie kozni*], witchcraft and charms. And instead of spiritual men and the sons of light, they loved the children of Satan, those who lead away from God and from the pure light into darkness. They did not allow a place in their intelligent minds for just words, but obviously listened to slander of the well-born inspired by hatred, and as a result they poured out the blood of many people like a river. Instead of the unconquerable rod of God-imitating meekness [*krotost'*] they loved pride and malice, and on that account [Russia], which previously was so brilliant, like the morning star, fell from highest heaven.[37]

The Duties of the Subject

When we turn from the mission of the tsar to the duties of his subjects, and to the particular problem of advice giving, we find a fairly simple set of ideas that are complementary to those that we have just discussed. The word for "subject"—*poddannyi*, an abstract legal term—does not appear at all in our sources. The word commonly used to denote a person subject to the tsar is *rab*, which means "servant" or "slave," as in *rab bozhii*, "the servant/slave of God." The meaning of the term for a seventeenth-century Muscovite was probably closer to the latter than the former. The long passage cited from Timofeev gives an accurate and representative picture of what our writers considered the normal relationship between a righteous tsar and his servants: the former commanded and the latter obeyed, mainly out of fear.

Yet our authors do not see the period of the Troubles as normal in that sense. A number of the tsars are regarded as unrighteous at best and imposters at worst. Under these special conditions, as Kliuchevskii correctly remarked, our authors feel that certain servants should speak up, and speak up forcefully. Their failure to do so, their "foolish silence" (*bezumnoe molchanie*), is seen as a main cause of the disasters that engulfed the country, as Kliuchevskii also correctly observed. But this advice was not to be given by just anyone, nor is there evidence that it was to be given "jointly" or in an organized fashion, as Kliuchevskii stated. This difference of view, though apparently small, is of considerable importance.

First, who should give advice? The reader will recall that Kliuchevskii implied that it was up to the people as a community to do so—the people who now feel a new sense of their own power as a result of their experience running their affairs without a tsar. But Timofeev regards such a situation with horror; without the fear of a strong tsar to inspire them, subjects "expelled all fear from themselves, both of God and the tsar; they clothed themselves willfully in fearlessness and kept within themselves only one wish, [one] rooted [in them] from their parents' loins, [namely] the skill mercilessly to ravage their rulers' treasure like a foreigner and to fill their insatiable purses shamelessly, or rather fearlessly."[38] Thus, the people are seen as evil, or at least weak, by nature, and are only restrained from selfish greedy acts by the iron rule of the tsar. All classes are condemned: merchants for their greed, aristocrats for fickle behavior during the Tushino period, the service people for their pretensions, and all landowning classes for their treatment of peasants. The words typically associated with people in this deplorable condition are "weakness" (*slabost'*), "vacillation" (*kolebanie*), and the like.[39]

Not everybody was weak, wavering, and greedy, however. Admirable figures who do in fact take an active part in affairs appear in the tales. Probably the most universally admired of these is Patriarch Germogen, the fiery inspirer of the national revival against the boyar government and the Polish dominance of Muscovy.[40] His image is the exact opposite of that of the weak subject discussed above. The *Kazanskoe skazanie* describes him as "a hard diamond and unwavering column" (his standard epithet, especially in the interregnum tales); "like a column [he] stands firmly . . . and he alone stands against them all like a giant without arms . . . holding only his teachings, like a club."[41] A striking image indeed. Similarly admired are the defenders of Smolensk and Chernigov, and Patriarch Filaret.

Thus subjects, like rulers, fall into two categories: the weak, vacillating and unrighteous; and the strong, firm and righteous. And just as the spiritual condition of the ruler was the source of his actions, good or bad, so the spiritual condition of the people had a strong influence on the fate of the realm. The evidence of the *smuta* tales does suggest, as Kliuchevskii and other historians have argued, that the experience of the Troubles strengthened the idea that the people were responsible to a considerable extent for what happened to the *tsarstvo*. But this responsibility was taken in a moral sense. If the subject allows himself to be corrupted, to become weak and vacillating, seeking his own advantage, then he becomes the pliant tool of foreigners, pretenders, or other evil men, and the country falls into chaos. If, on the contrary, he remains firm in his faith and unwavering in his loyalty, then Russia will be able to overcome all of her unrighteous enemies, both internal and external. The best and most eloquent example of this view is the "Novaia povest'," which is nothing but a long and moving plea to follow the firm and unshakable examples of Germogen and the defenders of Smolensk in the second of these alternative paths and so to bring an end to the disasters incurred as a result of following the first. Thus, subjects are seen as responsible for what happened, partly because they angered God, and God punished them, but partly because their own behavior allowed them to be exploited by the ungodly. This second mode of responsibility, in which the actions of the people directly influence the fate of the realm without any mention of God's intervention, finds its clearest and most eloquent expression at the end of the *Vremennik*, where Timofeev complains bitterly about the fear and lack of brotherly love that prevented the Russians from uniting against their common enemies. He has already put forth a multitude of examples of how greed or ambition on the part of subjects led to disaster. "Foreigners are not the ravagers of our land," he finally exclaims, "we ourselves are its destroyers."[42]

This responsibility was not merely passive, however. As the phrase "foolish silence" quoted above by Kliuchevskii implies, subjects were obliged not only to be firm and unshakable, but to speak out.[43] The crucial passage occurs in the first redaction of Palitsyn's *Skazanie*. The author has just discussed Godunov's persecution of the Romanovs and members of the royal family, and then accuses Godunov of encouraging servants to denounce their masters. He goes on:

> Only with great danger could the father speak with his son or a brother with a brother, or a friend with a friend; after the conversation, they bound themselves with fearsome oaths not to reveal what had been said about matters great or small. . . . But about this everyone was very sorry: that the wise, though innocent, were eliminated from his [Godunov's] palace and those strong in judgment [*silnii v razsuzhenii*] were driven far away.

About the Beginning of Trouble in All Russia

And as it were for the sake of [the persecution of] these Nikitich-Iur'evs [i.e., Romanovs] and because of foolish silence of the whole community when no-one dared to speak the truth to the tsar about the destruction of the guiltless ones, the Lord darkened the sky with clouds, and such a rain poured forth that all men were terrified [and the Troubles began].[44]

A remarkably similar passage, also mentioned by Kliuchevskii, can be found in Timofeev's *Vremennik*. In a long series of historical arguments, Timofeev traces the cause of the Troubles directly back to the failure of the people to prevent Godunov from purging his aristocratic enemies in the reign of Fedor:

"And if in fact we had not been silent, and had not permitted Godunov to kill all those most well-born after the tsar, the great pillars [of the realm] who strengthened all our land, and had we not permitted him step by step to rule over all," then Godunov would not have dared to kill the Tsarevich Dmitrii, to burn Moscow, and so forth.[45]

These two passages, especially the first, show the obvious connection between advice-getting and "foolish silence." The tsar should have had the wisdom to heed good advice, while the subjects should have had the courage ("no-one dared") to give it. In this form, the idea is not only found in the *Vremennik* and the first redaction of Palityn's *Skazanie*, but is shared by most of our authors.[46] If we count passages praising good advice as well as passages condemning cowardly silence, then in addition to these two works the idea finds expression in the works of Shakhovskoi and Khvorostinin, the *Khronograf of 1617*, the "Povest' kako," the "Novaia povest'," and the "Kazanskoe Skazanie."[47]

The authors of the tales generally seem to have assumed that the wealthier, more aristocratic members of society are the most natural advisers, though this is by no means always the case.[48] Germogen himself was hardly a great magnate and was considerably lower by birth than most of the nobles surrounding Tsar Vasilii Shuiskii; yet he provided much-admired advice, while they failed to do so. Kuzma Minin is an even clearer example. The *Khronograf of 1617* describes him thus: "But God is near to all those who call upon him. . . . He raised up a certain man from the Christian people, not from a glorious family but wise in thought, whose name was Kozma Minin, a meat merchant by trade."[49] As one might expect from what we have already said, good advisers are described as wise, firm, the "strong in Israel," not "those of fiendish descent." A lexical examination of the phrases used—one by Timofeev (*bezslovesnoe molchanie*, literally "wordless silence") and the other by the author of the first redaction of Palityn's *Skazanie* (*bezumnoe molchanie*) reveals that each adjective is used by the author in question to mean "ungodly" or "evil" as well as "wordless" or "foolish."[50] Thus giving advice is a responsibility of the righteous, not of a particular social class.

How are these good advisers to be heard? If Kliuchevskii was right, that the will of the people was seen as having been increasingly important during this period, then one would expect, as Kliuchevskii did, that our tales would assign a good deal of importance to the two apparently constitutional organs that had at least the potential of representing that will, the Boyar Duma and the Assembly of the Land. Yet one of the most remarkable features of the *smuta* tales is that they assign a much smaller role to these bodies than they in fact played. Take the example of the Duma, or *sinklit*, as our sources often call it. With all the emphasis on the importance of good advice, one would think that this organization, traditionally entrusted with advising the tsar, would occupy an important place. The opposite is true. If one examines the contexts in which the word *sinklit* or its derivatives are found, it is almost never found playing an active role. In the overwhelming majority of cases, the word *sinklit* is used only as a designation of rank: so-and-so became a member of the *sinklit*, so-and-so was one of the most important counselors of the *sinklit*. In over a thousand columns of text, it seldom occurs as the subject of a sentence. The need to get good advice, the obligation to heed the advice of the Duma—these two ideas, which might seem related to us, were not seen as such by the authors of the *smuta* tales.

Nor is the Assembly of the Land given an important place in our tales. With the exception of its role in electing tsars, it is hardly mentioned, despite the important role it actually played in events. Passed by in silence are the activities of organizing the government and collecting taxes carried out by popular assemblies from 1611 to the election of Michael Romanov.[51] Equally remarkable is the obvious desire of the authors of these tales to describe the elections of tsars as a result purely of God's will, and to disregard the role of politics in the Assembly of the Land as much as possible. Avraamii Palitsyn, for example, argues that God chose Michael Romanov to be tsar when he was still in his mother's womb, and that his unanimous election (which was far from unanimous at first) was only a result of that fact.[52]

In the tales, advice giving is described in very different terms. Khvorostinin best characterized the process when he said that Germogen spoke "like a prophet."[53] Indeed, an Old Testament prophet is precisely the image that comes to mind when one reads the many descriptions of his activities. (One might argue that Germogen, being Patriarch, might have been expected to speak in this fashion, yet even secular advisers are shown using the same approach, as Khvorostinin's portrait of his own [probably fictitious] advice to the First Pretender illustrates.)[54] There is no mention here or elsewhere of constitutional machinery of any kind; the acceptance of advice depends on the moral force of the adviser. This is natural, since a corrupt tsar *wants* to take bad advice; the wise adviser must first restore the spiritual health of the tsar so that he will listen to the wise advice that is being proffered.

All of these ideas can be summed up fairly simply: The ideal tsar is linked to God by his own righteousness and piety; the acts of a righteous tsar are seen as representing the will of God. Advisers become important only when this crucial link is broken. The wise adviser serves as an alternate channel by which God's will can penetrate the state until such time as the tsar, under the influence of his good counselors, can re-establish the original channel by setting his footsteps back on "the path of the righteous," as the Psalmist put it. The adviser therefore has two functions: He not only gives his opinion on matters of policy, on questions of how the *tsarstvo* should be run; he is also responsible for restoring the piety of the tsar himself so that the connection between the acts of the tsar and the will of God can be re-established. None of our authors considered the possibility of abolishing the monarchy altogether and setting up the direct rule of wise advisers; errors of policy were not seen as the result of faulty rational calculation but as the result of sin and moral corruption. It follows, therefore, that the restorative function of an adviser is the more important. For this reason, most of the advice given in our tales has what we would call a "moral" rather than a "political" character.

This notion of the adviser as a prophet also explains why the chief qualification for an adviser is his own righteousness. The authority of a figure like Germogen, like the authority of an Old Testament prophet, derives from the fact that he was seen as the mouthpiece of God. In order to act as an alternative channel of God's will, he had to have the righteousness that the tsar lacked. And since righteousness was not the exclusive preserve of either the clergy or of any one social class, any man had at least the potential of being a wise adviser.

Why is it, one wonders, that Kliuchevskii (and other historians) have paid so little attention to these fairly simple ideas? Subtly, perhaps unconsciously, by the addition of a few words here and there ("the people's inability *jointly* to oppose vested authorities," "the idea that the people should take an active *and organized* part in public affairs" [my italics]), Kliuchevskii created the impression that these authors were talking about "fundamental laws and a constitutional government," when they certainly were not. The idea that *certain righteous* people had a *duty* to play an active part in affairs was translated to mean *the people* (as an entity) had a *right* to play that part. Kliuchevskii discussed these questions in abstract, legal, and constitutional terms: "rights, fundamental laws, sovereignty." The authors of our tales regarded the state not as a neutral abstraction, a collection of constitutionally balanced forces, but as a personal force, a force with its own will and power, the will and power of the tsar. It was as good or bad as the person of the tsar was good or bad.

The fundamental problem, it seems to me, is that Kliuchevskii was asking questions of his sources that they could not answer. His predilection for constitutional arrangements led him to supply his own answers to the questions of how and by whom advice should be given. By concentrating on the negative aspect of advice giving, on the complaints *against* the "foolish silence" of the people, Kliuchevskii was able to ignore the answers supplied by the authors of the tales themselves. He thus was able to substitute legal and constitutional ideas for the concept of the righteous prophet as an adviser that is pretty clearly implied in our tales, a concept that in its own terms neither needed nor produced procedures and guarantees of a constitutional kind. What "constitutional" arrangement did Timofeev or Shakhovskoi favor? It is hard to say. Did one favor the Duma and the boyar class while the other supported the Assembly of the Land and the service people? These categories simply do not relate to the categories that, to judge from their texts, the authors themselves had in mind.

But historians, one might argue, should be more interested in politics than in prophecy. Can our authors' categories be transformed into the kind of categories Kliuchevskii and most other modern historians are interested in? Without reading these tales very carefully, one might suppose that they could. All the talk of God and righteousness could be disregarded, for example, if the tales consistently said that the decisions of the Duma represented the will of God. In that case we would have a theory of the state that was coherent in purely secular terms—the tsar should obey the decisions of the Duma—and the role of God could be dispensed with. But such is not the case in the *smuta* tales. Once we remove God and His relationship with tsar and subject, we are left without any coherent set of ideas at all. How can one tell a good from an evil counselor? A good counselor does not have to be a member of a constitutional body or a representative of one or another social class. In Muscovy as in the Old Testament, as the examples of David and Saul show, political power is seen to come from God alone, to have been independent alike of constitutional mechanics and social distinctions.[55] Nor does the law, at least in the sense in which it was used by our authors, provide an institutional framework for the state.

The power of the tsar is clearly not seen as unlimited. Tsars could and did make serious errors for which all Russia suffered. The subjects should have restrained them from committing these errors. But how? By this question *we* mean, "How could the tsar be constrained to accept or act on the advice of the people?" Our authors not only never answered this question; they seem never to have felt the need to ask it. Their notion of the adviser as a prophet, if taken seriously, makes the question ridiculous. One might as well ask whether Jeremiah, if he were reborn in New York City today, would run for Congress. A wise adviser was a spokesman for God, not the people. Our authors' version of the question of how the tsar should be restrained is "How can the tsar be kept on the path of righteousness?" Toward the beginning of every vigil service in the Orthodox Church, a service heard thousands of times in the lifetime of a devout Orthodox believer, the congregation hears or sings the first Psalm of David, which begins, *"Blazhen muzh izhe ne ide na sovet nechestivykh* [*Blessed is the man who walketh not in the counsel, under the influence of the ungodly*]." The tsar should be such a man. *Sovet* here, as in the *smuta* tales, obviously has no constitutional meaning but refers to moral influence,[56] but in contemporary usage means "council" as is the intent in the title Soviet Union.

This theory of the state, then, is God-dependent rather than independent. Without God, it makes no sense. It is religious and prophetic rather than secular and constitutional. The role of the opposition, which is admitted under certain circumstances, is not constitutionally defined. If we were to imagine an opposition movement comprising people who shared the political attitudes of our authors, we would see a movement based on righteousness and the preservation of the old order in church and state. We would expect such a movement not to work through constitutional channels but to depend on the prophetic force of its own rhetoric on the righteousness of its advocates. Such a movement would resemble the Old Believers of the seventeenth century to a remarkable degree, and would have little in common with the sort of opposition, constitutional and progressive, that Kliuchevskii envisioned. These tales enable us to make one further observation about the way Muscovites perceived political events: The ideological assumptions of all of our authors are remarkably homogeneous. This is true even when the political point of view is quite different. The *Khronograf of 1617* and the "*Povest' kako*," for example, are very sympathetic to Shuiskii: Palitsyn and the author of the first redaction of Palitsyn's *Skazanie* are not. Yet the criteria that all four tales use in dealing with the various questions we have been considering—how a tsar or subject should or should not behave—are essentially the same. The "*Povest' kako*" and the first redaction of Palitsyn's *Skazanie* might disagree over whether Shuiskii was a good tsar, but they agree over the question of how a good tsar should act.

It follows from the above that I must disagree with the efforts of many investigators, especially Soviet investigators, to pin a class label on each of the various tales.[57] According to one Soviet investigator, these tales "formulate the political demands of various social groups, the aristocracy, the gentry [*dvorianstvo*], the third estate."[58] And since these classes are generally seen to have been "struggling" against each other, one would expect to find a number of conflicting sets of political assumptions. But do the ideas of those authors who pretty clearly belonged to the gentry class—Timofeev, Palitsyn, the authors of the first redaction of Palitsyn's *Skazanie,* the "*Novaia povest'*," and the "*Povest' o nekoei brani*"—differ in any significant respect from the ideas of the aristocrats Shakhovskoi and Khvorostinin? I think not.

Take the example of the first redaction of Palitsyn's *Skazanie*. The author is a consistently stern critic of the social pretensions of the *dvorianstvo*; in fact, he invents a word, *boiarstvovati*, "to behave like a boyar," to describe these pretensions.[59] The awkward problem is that, of the two possible authors, at least as far as we know at the moment, Dionisii Zobninovskii and Avraamii Palitsyn, both were *dvoriane* and certainly not boyars. One could suggest, as Derzhavina does, that the author was attached to "boyar circles" and thus explain his antigentry passages. But the fiery author of this tale does not restrict his criticism to the gentry. He also denounces the boyars who flitted back and forth between Tushino and Moscow, changing their allegiance in return for larger and larger land grants or increased privileges, and roundly condemns all classes for their greed.[60] Moreover, we are entitled to ask who the gentry authors are who do *not* belong to boyar circles. Virtually all of our authors, including especially Timofeev, condemn the appointment of people "beyond their suitability." The most obvious case in point is the anti-aristocratic policies of Boris Godunov. Godunov is shown in the *smuta* tales to have purged the greatest aristocratic families from the government. This policy should have benefitted the gentry and is in general referred to in Soviet historical literature as pro-gentry. Yet every author who discusses Godunov's rule at any length (except, for obvious reasons, Iov) mentions this policy and condemns it.[61] The unanimity is remarkable. Timofeev and the author of the first redaction of Palitsyn's *Skazanie*, both gentry writers, saw in this persecution the beginning of the Troubles. If there are no gentry tales, in spite of the fact that there are a number of gentry authors, one might conclude that all of these authors were part of one or another "boyar circle," a suggestion that implies that the political divisions of the country were vertical as much as horizontal, that these divisions consisted of groups each comprising some members of all politically active classes, with an aristocratic family or two at the top, rather than one class struggling against another. In sociological terms, this arrangement might be described as a web system of group relationships that cut across class lines and served to strengthen the social system by blurring class antagonisms.[62]

Whether or not that is true, the best explanation of this evidence is that, in spite of often sharp political differences, the politically active segments of Muscovite society shared a common set of political ideals. On the issue of social divisions, they believed, as we have seen, that the social fabric should be preserved, that people should be appointed according to their social standing, that aristocrats should be aristocrats and gentry, gentry. The evidence indicates that ideological struggles, such as those that devastated a number of European states in the sixteenth and seventeenth centuries, once the Reformation was well under way, were not possible among the upper levels of Muscovite society. However sharp the political struggles may have been, they were carried on by people with the same basic political assumptions.⁶³

The political ideas with which Muscovites emerged from the Time of Troubles were not only homogeneous, they were also traditional. Although as far as I know no one has attempted a systematic investigation of Polish or other Western influences on these tales, I think it is safe to say that the Time of Troubles, with its kaleidoscopic political changes and its massive intrusion of foreigners, did not cause important innovations in the political ideas of Muscovy. The picture of an ideal tsar or a good subject, the criteria of legitimacy—these ideas had their roots for the most part in the Old Testament and had been traditional in Russia for some time. Although the political events of the period offered excellent possibilities for developing new theories that the tsar should be elected by the people, or that the ruler should rule by the consent of the governed, the authors of the *smuta* tales decisively rejected these ideas. On the contrary, the Troubles seem to have caused a sharp reaction: Our writers, recoiling from ideological innovations, clung to the traditional Russian and Orthodox visions of society. It was the rupture of this traditional order, they argued, that was an important cause of the Troubles, and the way to restore the political health of Muscovy was to restore that order. This argument is strengthened by lexical evidence. Whereas the *smuta* tales employ contemporary language when they describe local customs, trade, or finance, the language used to describe the tsar, his power, and his relationship with his subjects is archaic, with a very strong Church Slavic influence.⁶⁴ This implies that the authors, in language as well as in ideology, clung to sacred images from the Russian past.

If reaction was the historical legacy of the Troubles, what do our tales tell us about the general nature of Muscovite politics? They suggest (and the narrow base of evidence makes it definitely no more than a suggestion) that there was no substantial disagreement within literate Russian society over the nature of the state and how it should be run. In particular, as we have just seen, there are no important differences between the assumptions of gentry and aristocratic writers. If there was a dialogue, it was between conservative subjects and innovative tsars. In the discussion of Ivan IV's *oprichnina* and other policies, for example, we find several authors who condemn these policies, but none who support them.⁶⁵ The same is true of Godunov's persecution of the upper aristocracy. The evidence of these tales suggests that these policies were resented by all of the literate sections of Russian society, at least to a degree, and not merely by a narrow circle of conservative boyars, as has often been thought.

Why was this resentment not translated into a more effective opposition? Here I think the evidence of the tales is more useful. One reason is that the "lawful customs and regulations," "the laws of God" against which the tsars' behavior was judged, were too vague to be used as instruments for limiting the royal power. The obligation of the wise and righteous subject to advise the tsar, an obligation recognized by most of our authors, might under other circumstances have led to a real limitation. But this potentially important notion was completely lacking in political machinery. There was definitely no assumption that a constitutional body would fulfill this function, which in our tales is always carried out by individuals. Moreover, righteousness, the essential qualification for giving advice, was not recognizable from a political point of view. It is a characteristic knowable by God, but debatable by man.

Were these terms, then, simply rhetorical insults that one side in a factional struggle could hurl against the other? I think they were more than that. The unanimity of opinion on Ivan IV's and Godunov's policies shows that the assumptions of our authors could and did provide criteria by which a ruler could be judged. Yet because these assumptions were God-dependent, because they lacked the very constitutional implications that Kliuchevskii wanted to find in them, they seem to have provided an inadequate basis for any effective and sustained opposition movement of the type found in contemporary Western Europe.[66] As in the Old Testament, the causes and therefore the solutions for social and political problems were not sought where historians themselves (Kliuchevskii included) almost always search for them—on the social and political levels, the political structure of the state, the position of various classes, and so on—but in the personal spiritual well-being of each person in society. Muscovite Rus' was perceived fundamentally as a sacred community normally connected to the will of God by the tsar, and not as a collection of classes or even of interest groups; ideology, therefore, instead of providing a means by which these groups could have conceptualized their differences, served rather to blur whatever differences may have existed.

Notes

Both the history and the texts of these tales, based on my work in Soviet archives, are explored more fully in my unpublished PhD dissertation, "Muscovite Political Attitudes as Reflected in Early Seventeenth Century Tales about the Time of Troubles" (Yale University, 1976), 13–118, 230–70. In this article I argue against the legal-institutional interpretation of these tales and of Muscovite ideology in general as represented in the work of V. O. Kliuchevskii. I am currently at work on a complementary article (chapter 4 of this volume) that will show that the other main interpretation of these tales, the absolutist interpretation, is equally invalid. I am indebted to the International Research and Exchanges Board for enabling me to work in the Soviet Union in 1972; to the courteous help of the staffs of the manuscript departments of the Lenin Library, the State Historical Museum, the State Public Library, and the Library of the Academy of Sciences; and to Daniel Waugh, University of Washington, for generous help both in Leningrad and in the United States. The article has also benefitted from the suggestions and ideas of Robert Crummey, University of California at Davis; Edward Keenan, Harvard University; and Bruce Eastwood, University of Kentucky. A preliminary version of this article was presented at the Seminar for Ukrainian Studies, the Ukrainian Research Institute, and Harvard University, where I also received a number of helpful suggestions.

1. V. O. Kliuchevskii, *Sochineniia*, 8 vols. (Moscow: Gos. izd-vo polit. lit-ry, 1956–1959), 7:440–441.

2. Kliuchevskii, *Sochineniia*, 3:66–70, 88. The section of Kliuchevskii's *Course in Russian History* dealing with the seventeenth century has been translated by Natalie Duddington in *A Course in Russian History: The Seventeenth Century* (Chicago: Quandrangle Press, 1968), 69–74, 88.

3. Kliuchevskii, *Sochineniia*, 3:69; Duddington, *Course in Russian History*, 7.

4. Kliuchevskii saw the enmity between a centralizing monarchy and a conservative high aristocracy as one of the basic features of the sixteenth century. The ultimate solution to the problem, the replacement of the upper aristocracy by a middle class of service people, though hinted at already in the sixteenth century, was not actually worked out until the seventeenth century. Ivan Peresvetov and Prince A. M. Kurbskii are presented as the rival ideologues of middle service class and aristocracy. See Kliuchevskii, *Sochineniia*, 2:157–171, 181–183; 3:7, 37–45, 56–58, 70–74; Duddington, *Course in Russian History*, 4, 36–45, 56–59, 74–78.

Platonov stated the thesis of a class struggle even more pointedly. He believed that Ivan IV's *oprichnina* dealt a severe blow to the aristocracy and that the Troubles effectively ended its influence. S. F. Platonov, *Ocherki po istorii smuty v Moskovskom gosudarstve X VI–X VI/vv.* (Saint Petersburg: Tipografiia I. N. Skorokhodova, 1899), 565–571. Later, in a more popular version of his account of the Troubles, Platonov added that at the same time "the ancient patrimonial state order yielded place to a new higher and more complex one—the nation-state." S. F. Platonov, *The Time of Troubles*, trans. John T. Alexander (Lawrence, KS: University Press of Kansas, 1970), 172. For Soviet views, see, in addition to the works cited in notes 63 and 64 below, I. U. Budovnits, *Russkaia publitsistika XVI veka* (Moscow: Izd-vo Akademii nauk SSSR, 1947), 40–41.

There is a strong similarity between this general view of Muscovite politics, especially as expressed by Platonov, and the cluster of features ascribed by A. F. Pollard and others to the "New Monarchs" of sixteenth-century Western Europe who finally replaced the old medieval feudal states dominated by the aristocracy with new bureaucratic modern governments. In this task they relied heavily on the support of the "middle class" to replace the aristocracy. A. F. Pollard, *Factors in Modern History* (London: A. Constable, 1907). Although there is still debate on a number of the points Pollard raised, the thesis of a rising middle class (whether landed or bourgeois) and a declining aristocracy as the major feature of the social landscape and the explanation for most political events between 1500 and 1640 has come under heavy fire, especially by J. H. Hexter in his *Reappraisals in History* (New York: Harper and Row, 1963), 26–44, 71–162. A great deal of the recent scholarship about Muscovite history from the succession crisis under Ivan III to the *oprichnina* under Ivan IV can be seen as revisions of Platonov's general scheme. Particularly pertinent here is Robert O. Crummey's convincing argument that the Time of Troubles produced no dramatic influx of parvenu families into the Boyar Duma. See Robert O. Crummey, "Crown and Boiars under Fedor Ivanovich and Michael Romanov," *Canadian-American Slavic Studies* 6, no. 4 (1972): 549–574; Crummey, "The Reconstruction of the Boiar Aristocracy, 1613–1645," *Forschungen zur osteuropiiischen Geschichte* 18 (1973): 187–220.

   5. See S. F. Platonov, *Drevnerusskie skazaniia i povesti o smutnom vremeni XVII veka*, 2nd rev. ed. (Saint Petersburg: Tip. M. Z. Aleksandrova, 1912), chaps. 1–4.

   6. *Polnoe sobranie russkikh letopisei* (hereafter, *PSRL*), 34 vols. (Moscow-Saint Petersburg-Leningrad, 1846–1978), vol. 14, part 1 (1910), 1–22 (hereafter Iov).

   7. The "Povest' kako voskhiti nepravdoiu tsarskii prestol Boris Godunov," *Russkaia istoricheskaia biblioteka* [hereafter *RIB*], 2nd ed., 39 vols. (Saint Petersburg-Leningrad: Arkheograficheskaia Kommissliia, 1872–1927), vol. 13 (1909), cols. 145–176; the life ("Zhitie") and account of the translation of the relics of the Tsarevich Dmitrii from the Tulupov Menologue (*RIB*, vol. 13, cols. 877–898); the "Izvet Varlaama" (the oldest text is found in *Akty, sobrannye v bibliotekakh i arkhivakh Rossiikoi imperii Arkheograficheskoiu ekspeditsieiu Jmperatorskoi Akademii nauk*, 4 vols. [Saint Petersburg: Tip. II Otdeleniia Sobstvennoi E. I. V. Kantseliarii, 1836], 2:141–144, following the variants at the foot of the page); the "Povest' o videnii nekoemu m uzhu dukhovnu" (*RIB*, vol. 13, cols. 101–105); and the articles about the Time of Troubles found in the *Khronograf of 1617* (*RIB*, vol. 13, cols. 1273–1322).

   8. *RIB*, vol. 13, cols. 713–754, following the alternate readings designated in the text by the letter B.

   9. *Novaia povest' o preslavnom Rossiiskom tsarstve i sovremennaia ei agitatsionnaia patrioticheskaia pis'mennost'*, ed. N. E. Droblenkova (Moscow-Leningrad: Izd-vo Akademii nauk SSSR, 1960), 189–209.

   10. "Plach o plenenii i o konechnom razorenii . . . Moskovskago gosudarstva," *RIB*, vol. 13, cols. 219–234.

   11. For the best available text and a convincing identification of its author with the scribe Evstratii, see O. A. Belobrova, "K izucheniiu 'Povesti o nekoei brani' i ee avtora Evstratiia," *Trudy Otdela drevnerusskoi literatury* 25 (1970): 150–161.

   12. M. N. Tikhomirov, "Novyi istochnik po istorii vosstaniia Bolotnikova," *Istoricheskii arkhiv* 6 (1954): 96–101, 115–127; henceforth "Kaz skaz."

   13. *Vremennik Ivana Timofeeva*, ed. O. A. Derzhavina (Moscow-Leningrad: Izd-vo Akademii nauk SSSR, 1951), 9–168.

   14. *Skazanie Avraamiia Palitsyna*, ed. O. A. Derzhavina and E. V. Kolosova (Moscow-Leningrad: Izd-vo Akademii nauk SSSR, 1955), gives the texts of both the short, first redaction (250–279, hereafter Sk I) and the much longer second redaction (95–249, hereafter Sk II). I am inclined to agree with Derzhavina's suggestion (*Skazanie Avraamiia Palitsyna*, 29–43) that Dionisii Zobninovskii, Abbot of the Holy Trinity Monastery, rather than Palitsyn, was the author of the first redaction. See Daniel Rowland, "Muscovite Political Attitudes as Reflected in Early Seventeenth-Century Tales about the Time of Troubles" (PhD diss., Yale University, 1976), 87–94.

   15. *RIB*, vol. 13, cols. 525–558 (hereafter Khv).

   16. The most important and interesting is the "Povest' knigi sea" previously ascribed to I. M. Katyrev-Rostovskii. *RIB*, vol. 13, cols. 559–624 (hereafter Sh I). His other two historical tales are much more ecclesiastical in tone and content: the "Tale about the

Murder of the Tsarevich Dmitrii" (*RIB*, vol. 13, cols. 837–858; hereafter Sh II) and the "Tale about a Certain Monk" (*RIB*, vol. 13, cols. 859–876, hereafter Sh III).

17. I refer chiefly here to the work of Michael Cherniavsky, especially his *Tsar and People: Studies in Russian Myths* (New Haven, CT: Yale University Press, 1961) and his "Khan or Basileus: An Aspect of Russian Mediaeval Political Theory," *Journal of the History of Ideas* 20 (October–December 1959): 459–476. The most careful study using the thematic approach is Igor Sevcenko, "A Neglected Source of Muscovite Political Ideology," *Harvard Slavic Studies* 2 (1954): 141–179.

18. A detailed discussion of the criteria used to judge various tsars can be found in Rowland, "Muscovite Political Attitudes," 119–162.

19. *Vremennik Ivana Timofeeva*, 83.

20. For example, see the description of Boris Godunov's administration in *Vremennik Ivana Timofeeva*, 65; "Plach o plenenii," *RIB*, vol. 13, col. 224; Khv, *RIB*, vol. 13, col. 532; *Khronograf 1617*, *RIB*, vol. 13, cols. 1282–1283; Sk I, *Skazanie Avraamiia Palitsyna*, 252; Iov, *PSRL*, vol. 14, pt. 1, 6–7.

21. O. A. Derzhavina, "Arkheograficheskii komentarii," *Vremennik Ivana Timofeeva*, 425–426, points out the problem. However, her two suggestions that the section originally belonged either between folios 207 and 208 (*Vremennik Ivana Timofeeva*, 108–113) or between folios 191 and 192 (see O. A. Derzhavina, "Vremennik Ivana Timofeeva," *Gosudarstvennaia ordena Lenina biblioteka SSSR imeni V.I. Lenina. Zapiski Otdela rukopisei* 2 [1950]: 75–76) are both unlikely on paleographic grounds. My opinion is that the section may either have existed as a separate entity or have come between folios 234 and 235 (see Rowland, "Muscovite Political Attitudes," 235–242, esp. 241–242).

22. *Vremennik Ivana Timofeeva*, 109.

23. *Vremennik Ivana Timofeeva*, 107. On the Agapetus text and its importance, see Sevcenko, "A Neglected Byzantine Source."

24. *Vremennik Ivana Timofeeva*, 110.

25. For other interesting passages using *zakon* (law) and its derivatives, see Khv, *RIB*, vol. 13, cols. 536, 540, 552; *Novaia povest'*, 192; *Vremennik Ivana Timofeeva*, 89, 101. See also V. E. Val'denberg, *Drevnerusskie ucheniia o predelakh tsarskoi vlasti* (Petrograd: n.p., 1916), 366–367, who argues on the basis of passages from these tales that their authors "understood the tsar's power as limited by the law" (367). This is true if "the law" is understood primarily as a nonwritten, noninstitutionalized moral force. See Rowland, "Muscovite Political Attitudes," 149–156, and what follows here.

26. My authority for the early medieval view of the law is Fritz Kern, *Kingship and Law in the Middle Ages*, trans. S. B. Chrimes (Oxford: B. Blackwell, 1939), esp. 149–205. The meaning and significance of the law in Muscovite and earlier literary sources need further investigation.

27. *Vremennik Ivana Timofeeva*, 111–112. See also 45.

28. Sk I, *Skazanie Avraamiia Palitsyna*, 269; see also 258–259. Perhaps an even more revealing passage is that in which Timofeev condemns the troops who suddenly and without an order left Novgorod in 1609 on the pretext of trying to get help from Sweden: "Such an affair is foreign to the nature [*ustroenie*] of servants who are afraid, and such impudence goes beyond the laws of the tsars' customs.... According to the laws of our previous rulers it is not fitting [*ne dostoino*] to entrust such a wide jurisdiction in government to them" (*Vremennik Ivana Timofeeva*, 133; see also 127).

29. "Our true tsars before them [those who ruled during the Troubles] knew what honor to give to what family for what reason and [did] not [give honors] to those of low birth" (*Vremennik Ivana Timofeeva*, 104). See also 75, 87, 101, or, more obviously, the numerous disparaging references to the low birth of the First Pretender as when he is called "a dog jumping onto the royal throne." *Vremennik Ivana Timofeeva*, 89; Sh I, *RIB*, vol. 13, col. 580.

30. *Vremennik Ivana Timofeeva*, 110.

31. *Vremennik Ivana Timofeeva*, 110.

32. *RIB*, vol. 13, col. 622.

33. *RIB*, vol. 13, cols. 544–545.

34. Sk 1, *Skazanie Avraamiia Palitsyna*, 252; see also Sh I and *Khronograf 1617*, *RIB*, vol. 13, cols. 563, 1283–1284.

35. *Vremennik Ivana Timofeeva*, 13; "Povest' kako voskhiti," *RIB*, vol. 13, col. 151; Sk I, *Skazanie Avraamiia Palitsyna*, 251; *Khronograf 1617*, *RIB*, vol. 13, cols. 1279, 1284; Sk I, *Skazanie Avraamiia Palitsyna*, 253; "Povest' kako voskhiti," *RIB*, vol. 13, cols. 160, 165; Khv, *RIB*, vol. 13, cols. 534–535.

36. *Khronograf 1617*, *RIB*, vol. 13, col. 1314. This passage is absent from version A as represented by GBL Ms, Egorov Collection, no. 220, and is probably a later addition.

37. *RIB*, vol. 13, cols. 224–225.

38. *Vremennik Ivana Timofeeva*, 75–76.

39. See, for example, Sh I, *RIB*, vol. 13, cols 575, 577, where the weakness of the subjects is described by the word *kolebanie* (literally, "trembling") or its derivatives. The most eloquent description of subjects weakened by corruption and the changing of the old laws is in Timofeev's creation story analogy: "Many [people] who had been obedient became faint-hearted [*samoslabostni*] and fearful by nature, easily breaking their word, convinced of nothing, inconstant [*nestoiatel'ni*] in word and deed, turning in everything like a wheel." This constituted a change of "our nature" (*nashego estestva*). Foreign diplomats "found no courage of any kind in any one of us, since because of our sins, we acquired a weakness [*slabost'*], which inclined us to temptation. This led to our utter fall and ruinous susceptibility to false tsars which they [the foreigners] set up for us." *Vremennik Ivana Timofeeva*, 110–111; see also 161.

40. The exception is the *Khronograf of 1617* (*RIB*, vol. 13, cols. 1310–1312). The author admits that Germogen was very learned in the scriptures and in church law, but accuses him of being rude in morals and lenient to those falling into temptation. He himself, according to the author, fell under the influence of flatterers and evil men, believed slander about Shuiskii, and spoke "perfidiously" (*stroptivno*) when he gave advice to Shuiskii. There then follows a defense of Germogen apparently composed by the copyist of one of the manuscripts on which the *RIB* text is based (*RIB*, vol. 13, cols. 1312–1315). This passage is significant, although it is not part of the original *Khronograf* text. Germogen did not quarrel with Shuiskii, its author states, but with his evil advisers. He saw that Shuiskii was falling into sin on account of his evil advisers and therefore begged (*moliashe*) the tsar "that the advice of those near him was not good." Although the tsar persisted in his errors, Germogen, "the godly wise pastor, constantly comforted him [Shuiskii] in everything lovingly and meekly." The evil advisers (who seemed to have all been clerics) he instructed (*nakaza*) by the Holy Scripture, by prayers, or by prohibitions. The rest of the description emphasizes Germogen's patience (*terpenie*) and charity (*milostynia*). For more information on these portraits, see P. G.

Vasenko, "Novye dannye dlia kharakteristiki patr. Germogena," *Zhurnal Ministerstva narodnago prosveshcheniia* (July 1901), sec. 2, 140–142.

41. "Kaz skaz," Tikhomirov, "Novyi istochnik," 129; *Novaia povest'*, 195. "Hard diamond" and "unwavering column" were standard epithets for Germogen.

42. *Vremennik Ivana Timofeeva*, 163. A. Iakovlev puts great stress on the shift to the second of these two types of responsibility in which the social behavior of the people is seen directly to influence events (people-events) from the first, the type in which the sins of the people anger God, who then sends a punishment on his people (people-God-events). A. Iakovlev, "Bezumnoe molchanie," *Sbornik statei posviashchennykh V. O. Kliuchevskomu* (Moscow: Pechatnia S. P. Iakovleva, 1909), 651–678. The point is a good one, that during the Troubles the "people-events" type of explanation became more common, but I think Iakovlev takes it a little too far. In the first place, the idea already existed both in the Bible (see Matthew 12:25, for example), and in Old Russian Literature. See *Slovo o polku Igoreve*, ed. V. Adrianova-Peretts (Moscow-Leningrad: Izd-vo Akademii nauk SSSR, 1950), 17–18, 25. Moreover, Iakovlev connects this "new" type of social responsibility directly with the idea of *bezumnoe molchanie*, the duty of a subject to speak out against evil policies, which I discuss below. This connection is not clear, for in the crucial passage from Sk I in which the phrase *bezumnoe molchanie* occurs (Sk I, *Skazanie Avraamiia Palitsyna*, 252), the result of the silence (*molchanie*) of the people was that God was angry with this sinful silence and sent rain, an obvious example of people-God-event causality. Yet the same author is capable of a very penetrating secular analysis of a particular situation, as his explanation of the desertion to Poland of the southwest border cities shows. Sk I, *Skazanie Avraamiia Palitsyna*, 254–255. The conclusion to be drawn, I think, is that to distinguish between these two types of causation rigorously is difficult or impossible. All of our authors used both types without feeling any contradiction between the two.

This discussion is an excellent illustration of the difficulties encountered when modern analytical categories are applied to a premodern culture. The conflict between divine and secular causality exists in our minds but does not seem to have bothered the authors of the *smuta* tales. For a stimulating explanation of this problem in connection with the cultures of the ancient Near East, see Henri Frankfort et al., *The Intellectual Adventure of Ancient Man* (Chicago, 1946; repr. ed. with revised bibliographies, Chicago: University of Chicago Press, 1977), 13, 15–20. See also John A. Wilson's remarks on Egyptian cosmology in this same volume, 44 and on. Ancient man apparently felt perfectly content with several explanations or descriptions of the same phenomena, even though the explanations seem to us quite different or even contradictory.

43. On the significance of this phrase, see Iakovlev, "Bezumnoe molchanie"; and D. J. Bennet Jr., "The Idea of Kingship in Seventeenth Century Russia" (PhD diss., Harvard University, 1967), 106–109.

44. *Skazanie Avraamiia Palitsyna*, 252–253. The context is vital here. The chapter begins with the conjunction "and" (I); the connection across the chapter heading between the failure to get good advice and *bezumnoe molchanie* is clear. This passage was deprived of its original sense when Palitsyn (re-) edited the first six chapters for inclusion in his longer tale (105).

45. *Vremennik Ivana Timofeeva*, 94 and on.

46. See also *Vremennik Ivana Timofeeva*, 66, 71, 87, 108, 133–134; Sk I, *Skazanie Avraamiia Palitsyna*, 262.

47. For passages condemning the silence of the people, see "Povest' kako voskhiti," *RIB*, vol. 13, cols. 152, 153; "Plach o plenenii," *RIB*, vol. 13, col. 226; Sh I, *RIB*, vol. 13, col. 565; Sh II, *RIB*, vol. 13, col. 853: Sh III, *RIB*, vol. 13, col. 865. For passages praising good advice, see "Plach o plenenii," *RIB*, vol. 13, col. 230; Khv, *RIB*, vol. 13, cols. 537–554; *Khronograf 1617*, *RIB*, vol. 13, col. 1319; *Novaia povest'*, 200–202; "Kaz skaz," Tikhomirov, "Novyi istochnik," 96. These examples deal mostly with advice to a tsar but occasionally concern advice to other subjects or even to a foreign monarch; the qualities admired in the subject—courage, firmness, righteousness—are the same in every case. See also the discussion above of Germogen as an advice giver.

48. See, for example, Timofeev's condemnation of the wealthier Novgorodians' failure to guide discussion in that city after Skopin-Shuiskii had left the city with no effective garrison. *Vremennik Ivana Timofeeva*, 133–134, and note 29 above.

49. *RIB*, vol. 13, col. 1317.

50. The author of *Skazanie I* refers to *bezumnoe molchanie*, which means "senseless" or "foolish" silence. But the author of *Skazanie I* usually uses the word in a special sense, meaning not so much "unintelligent" or "ungifted," but "foolish" or even "deliberately wrong-headed" (see Psalm 5:5). After the overthrow of the First Pretender, for example, the people got drunk rather than thanking God for their salvation. This action is twice attributed to the *bezumstvo* of the people. *Skazanie Avraamiia Palitsyna*, 265. With a similarly strong moral and religious connotation, the author tells us that "the foolish [*bezumnye*] are allowed to puff themselves up endlessly by building houses more sumptuous than churches" (259–260). See also 262. Timofeev refers to the *bezslovesnoe molchanie* (*Vremennik Ivana Timofeeva*, 92) of the people as a chief cause of the Troubles. He is making a typical and peculiar pun here. Elsewhere in the tales, the phrase *slovesnye ovtsi* means not "garrulous sheep" but "sheep of the Word," that is, true Christians. By using the word *bezslovesnoe* here, Timofeev implies that the silence of the people is "ungodly" (*RIB*, vol. 13, col. 173; John 10:9–14). Timofeev himself explains that the cowardly silence of the people was caused by their sins in general, which Timofeev lists in considerable detail, and in particular by their sinful failure to fulfill God's will. *Vremennik Ivana Timofeeva*, 92–94.

51. See Platonov, *Ocherki*, 487–565, esp. 499–502, 546–552.

52. Bennet ("Idea of Kingship," 38–62) gives an excellent analysis of this election and its successive reflections in various sources. See *Skazanie Avraamiia Palitsyna*, 231–233, 235, 238; Sh I, *RIB*, vol. 13, col. 618; *Khronograf 1617 RIB*, vol. 13, col. 1319; *Vremennik Ivana Timofeeva*, 165; see also Rowland, "Muscovite Political Attitudes," 212–218.

53. *RIB*, vol. 13, col. 548.

54. *RIB*, vol. 13, col. 537–538. The beginning of this section of the text has gaps in all known copies. See col. 537; Gosudarstvennaia publichnaia biblioteka SSSR imeni V. I. Lenina, Vifanskii Collection, ms. no. 34, f. 680v; Gosudarstvennyi istoricheskii muzei, Zabelin Collection, ms. no. 474, f. 8.

55. It is striking how often our authors saw events of their own time in the context of the Old Testament. The standard structure of Old Russian chronicles, in which the history of the East Slavs follows after the story of the creation, the history of the ancient Israelites, and Byzantine history, implies that the history of Rus' was seen as a direct continuation of Old Testament history, the dealing of God with His people. (For

a highly condensed example of this form, see Khv, *RIB*, vol. 13, cols. 525–530.) A number of authors refer to Russia specifically as the "New Israel." "Povest' o videnii," *RIB*, vol. 13, col. 183; "Plach," *RIB*, vol. 13, col. 224; Khv, *RIB*, vol. 13, col. 540; *Vremennik Ivana Timofeeva*, 136, 150; *Novaia povest'*, 198. For a number of Old Testament historical parallels, see Iov, *PSRL*, vol. 14, pt. 1, 11–13. Others call Muscovites the "people of the Lord" and Muscovy "the Lord's inheritance." *Khronograf 1617*, *RIB*, vol. 13, col. 1317; "Povest' o videnii," *RIB*, vol. 13, cols. 179, 181; Iov, *PSRL*, vol. 14, pt. 1, 11. Still other expressions are used that indicate that Russia has a special relationship to God, the explanation usually being that she is the last Christian nation left. Iov, *PSRL*, vol. 14, pt. 1, 5; "Povest' o nekoei brani," Belobrova, "Kizucheniiu," 115; *Khronograf 1617*, *RIB*, vol. 13, col. 1320; "Plach o plenenii," *RIB*, vol. 13, cols. 219–221, 224, 234. Timofeev alone compares Sigismund III to Pharaoh, Skopin-Shuiskii to Moses, Boris Godunov (unfavorably) to David, and Lithuanian troops to the Egyptian army that drowned in the Red Sea. *Vremennik Ivana Timofeeva*, 121, 136, 65, 90. These references are not mere literary window dressing. Our authors really did think of Russia as the New Israel, her people as God's chosen people, whom He punished or rewarded according to their sins. Religious and moral regeneration had to come first, both temporally and logically. The political results—alterations in the structure of the state—were of secondary importance; these authors paid little attention to them, assuming that they would follow naturally from the increased godliness of the subject or, more likely, be unnecessary, since righteous subjects would normally be abjectly obedient to a righteous tsar.

56. "By the counsel of the ungodly (*sovetom nechestivym*)," Khvorostinin tells us, "the tsar chose [the path of] lawlessness" (*RIB*, vol. 13, cols. 534–535). For other references to this psalm, see also *Khronograf 1617*, *RIB*, vol. 13, cols. 1283, 1385; Sh II, *RIB*, vol. 13, col. 869. *Sovet* can also mean "plan."

57. See, for example, the remarks of Derzhavina, *Skazanie Avraamiia Palitsyna*, 22–24. For a discussion of the alleged class bias of the "Novaia povest'," see Rowland, "Muscovite Political Attitudes," 223–224.

58. A. I. Filatova, "Cherty novogo v istoricheskoi povesti 20-kh godov XVII veka" (PhD diss., Ural'skii Gosudarstvennyi universitet, Sverdlovsk, 1949), 1–2.

59. For a blistering denunciation of these pretensions, see *Skazanie Avraamiia Palitsyna*, 258–260. Other social groups are also included in the condemnation, but the "rising gentry" seem to bear the main brunt of the attack. See also 269.

60. *Skazanie Avraamiia Palitsyna*, 262, 269–270, 276–278.

61. See "Povest' kako voskhiti," *RIB*, vol. 13, col. 150; Sh I, *RIB*, vol. 13, cols. 567, 580; Khv, *RIB*, vol. 13, col. 532; *Khronograf 1617 RIB*, vol. 13, col. 1279; *Vremennik Ivana Timofeeva*, 56. Sk I singles out the Romanovs and the royal family as the victims: *Skazanie Avraamiia Palitsyna*, 252–253.

62. For the importance of multiclass groups clustered around aristocratic families in medieval Western Europe, especially in cities, see two books by Jacques Heers: *Le clan familial au Mayen Age: etude sur les structures politiques et sociales des milieux urbains* (Paris: Presses universitaires de France, 1974), and *L'Occident aux XIVe et XVe siecles: Aspects economiques et sociaux* (Paris: Presses universitaires de France, 1963). The first has been translated into English as *Family Clans in the Middle Ages: A Study of Political and Social Structures in Urban Areas*, trans. Barry Herbert, vol. 4, *Europe in the Middle Ages: Selected Studies* (Amsterdam: Elsevier, 1977). These groups encompassed "great landed, military and political lords [*seigneurs*], rich merchants or bankers, small trad-

ers, men of little substance, liberated slaves and even paupers," and thus cut across class boundaries (*Le clan familial*, 263–264). Surely Heers's approach could throw some light on the history of Muscovy. See also Hexter, *Reappraisals of History*, 32: "In brief it seems to me that the historical researches of the last five decades have revealed the sixteenth century to be an era during which the lines of class interest and national interest were traversed and frequently—perhaps more frequently than not—dominated by other lines of allegiance and action." For a list of these "lines of allegiance and action" found useful by historians of sixteenth-century Europe, see 34–37.

63. I must stress the fact that these ideas most emphatically do *not* apply to the peasantry, whose entry into the political arena during the Troubles greatly embittered and lengthened the unrest.

64. See L. L. Kutina, "Leksika istoricheskikh povestei o smutnom vremeni" (PhD diss., Institut iazykoznaniia Akademii nauk SSSR, Leningrad, 1953), 445–528. This dissertation is very useful; it is a pity it is not more widely available.

65. "And he [Ivan] began to destroy many of his own family and also many of the grandees of his *sinklit*" (*Khronograf 1617*, *RIB*, vol. 13, col. 1275). Of the other two serious discussions of Ivan, both of which mention his persecution of his subjects in general, neither mentions the nobility in particular: Sh I, *RIB*, vol. 13, cols. 561–562, 620; *Vremennik Ivana Timofeeva*, 10–18.

66. The Old Believers, of course, certainly constituted a sustained if not effective opposition movement. As we might expect from reading the *smuta* tales, they depended on the moral force of their rhetoric as righteous advisers to save the day. When this failed, they did not turn to constitutional means to enforce their views, and had no alternative but to withdraw from an unrighteous society.

CHAPTER 4

Did Muscovite Literary Ideology Place Limits on the Power of the Tsar (1540s–1660s)?

In 1974, Richard Pipes of Harvard published a sweeping and influential reinterpretation of pre-Soviet Russian political culture. His central idea was that Muscovite Rus´ was a patrimonial state; the tsar, or great prince, exercised power over his subjects "comparable to that of the possessor of *dominium* in Roman law, a power defined as 'absolute ownership excluding all other appropriation and involving the right to use, to abuse, and to destroy at will.'"[1] In addition to tracing the growth of the actual power of the monarch and the gradual narrowing of the boundaries of possible action for all classes, Pipes undertook to show why no class or social group was able to limit this excessive growth of royal power. The clergy, far from limiting this power, actually did the opposite: "The entire ideology of royal absolutism in Russia was worked out by clergymen who felt that the interests of religion and church were best served by a monarchy with no limits to its power." The Russian church, in particular Joseph of Volokolamsk and his followers, threw "its weight . . . fully behind royal absolutism" partly to save its own landed property against the threat posed by the nonpossessors.[2]

This essay originally appeared in *The Russian Review* 49 (April 1990): 125–155. The author gratefully acknowledges the publisher for permission to reprint this essay. I would like to thank the Russian Research Center, Harvard University, where much of this text was written and revised, and Donald Ostrowski, James Cracraft, and Samuel Baron, each of whom offered both constructive criticism and encouragement at critical moments.

I shall leave aside Pipes's emphasis on Muscovy as a patrimonial regime. I have no quarrel with the term, but it may be misleading, because in Muscovy the *paterfamilias* was limited in what he could do with a family patrimony, or *votchina*.³ Pipes's view of the church as the creator of an "ideology" supporting unlimited or "absolutist" royal power represents an intelligent reading of the available secondary literature by a well-informed nonspecialist in Muscovite affairs.⁴ Nevertheless, several recent students have suggested that Muscovy's image of its political authority was more collegial than autocratic.⁵ Before the Russian Revolution of 1917, several Russian scholars worked out what might be called a liberal interpretation of Muscovite ideology, investing it with constitutional overtones, but no general study since the Revolution has addressed the question of what limits, if any, Muscovite authors put upon the power of the tsar.⁶

I argue that Muscovite literary ideology (the political ideas found in literary, or high-style, texts) placed ill-defined but important limits on the power of the tsar and that these limits were understood and accepted by most literate people. In approaching this problem, however, a troublesome methodological problem arises: the proliferation in the texts of seemingly contradictory views. The traditional way to explain these contradictions has been to assign the seemingly opposed ideas found in the sources to different groups, or "parties," thus projecting on the society of Muscovy the contradictions perceived in the ideology. Certainly some figures, such as Maksim the Greek or Vassian Patrikeev, in the early sixteenth century emphasized the limits of royal power more often than its prerogatives, whereas Joseph of Volokolamsk did the opposite. Pipes, with ample evidence, calls Joseph "an extravagant apologist of royal absolutism."⁷ However, the same Joseph was capable of calling on the Muscovite people to refuse obedience to an unrighteous tsar, a "tsar tormentor" who consistently violated God's will: "Such a tsar is not a servant of God but a devil, not a tsar but a tormentor [*muchitel'*]. Our Lord Jesus Christ did not call such a person a tsar but a fox; you should not heed such a person who leads you into dishonor and cunning."⁸

The contradictory statements in the works of the same author reveal why the "parties" approach has not proved productive. In Joseph's case, Ia. S. Lur'e and other scholars have carefully dated his writings and have connected the varying images of the ruler in his writings to his changing real-life relationship to the grand prince and to the official church.⁹ This detailed biographical approach has revolutionized the old view of Joseph as expressed by Pipes, but it retains the conception that the changes in Joseph's writings corresponded to shifts in his ideological affiliation. This view continues to obscure the fact that Joseph drew on an existing fund of political ideas and images for *both* of his positions. Further, since Joseph placed the above and other similar passages alongside encomiums to the power of a God-chosen prince when he compiled the *Enlightener* in 1514 (well after his alleged conversion into a monarchist ideologue), it seems fair to assume that his "ideology" still included both images of a ruler. He had neither forgotten nor rejected the image of the ruler as a devil. Instead, it was his perception of a given ruler or a particular situation that determined the choice of which image was appropriate. In the case of Joseph, as for many other writers, it is simpler and safer to assume that there was one "ideology" that provided a number of alternate ruler images than to assume that each of these writers flip-flopped from one "ideological camp" to another every time they used a different image to describe a ruler of Muscovy. An examination of a group of texts by various authors on a single theme fails to reveal evidence of different ideological groupings even during the chaotic Time of Troubles, when we would most expect to see them.[10]

If we turn from the texts themselves to what we are learning about Muscovite society, the "ideological struggle" model also seems inappropriate. Two recent and careful discussions of Kremlin court politics have shown that ideological or even policy disputes played little role in court groupings, especially when compared with factors such as marriage ties and clan alliances.[11] V. B. Kobrin has forcefully argued that the social struggle between the *boiarstvo* and the *dvorianstvo* (which Soviet historiography traditionally viewed as underlying the ideological struggle between opponents and proponents of an unlimited monarchical power) is a myth. Donald Ostrowski has cast grave doubt on the importance of that political and ideological split between the "Possessors" and the "Non-possessors" that historians have used as the linchpin for their descriptions of sixteenth-century politics. Supposedly, Joseph of Volokolamsk led the "Possessors," who were dedicated to the defense of church landholding and to the magnification of the power of the tsar, while the "Non-possessors" allegedly argued that monasteries should not hold land and that the tsar's power should be limited in some way. Ostrowski has shown that the dispute over church landholding in particular was much more limited in both time and political importance than historians have thought.[12] I argue in parallel that there was little real dispute over ideology. In sum, both the internal evidence of the texts themselves and the external evidence of what we are learning about the society from which the texts sprang lead us to question the "ideological struggle" approach to the interpretation of these texts.

If we are not to distort the views of such a thinker as Joseph, therefore, we must devise a scheme that can encompass *both* types of image of the ruler—

the autocrat and the tormentor; citing one while ignoring the other will not do. A term that inclines us to choose inadvertently this latter course is the word "ideology." Taken in the commonly used sense in which Pipes uses it—that is, as a deliberate concoction of available ideas to justify a (usually nefarious) political cause, as in "Nazi ideology"—the word disposes us to search for a political message and then to focus on the evidence that supports the message. It thus acts as a kind of verbal filter, selecting out those elements that are not consistent with the assumed political purpose. A more useful way to understand Joseph's ideology is to think of it not so much as a deliberate creation bent toward amplifying (or limiting) the tsar's power, but as a system of symbols through which he could conceptualize and therefore understand the relationship of ruler to subject. As with any language, this system of symbols had its own grammar, its own rhetorical rules, which governed the deployment and use of its symbols and thus defined (and restricted) political thought in important ways.[13] In this modified sense, Joseph's ideology not only reflected his interests and changing relations to his ruler but also governed his perception of those interests and his conduct of those relations.[14] This definition enables us to take all elements of political discourse, even contradictory ones, into account and to look for the rhetorical rules that would enable an author like Joseph to move from an imperial autocratic image to the image of the ruler as a devil.

The term "absolute" and its derivatives hide another danger in Pipes's formulation. This word typically has both a general and a specific meaning. Both seem suitable to the Muscovite context at first glance but turn out on closer inspection to be misleading. In its general meaning, "absolute" denotes both perfection and complete freedom from any restriction. There are plenty of encomiums to the power of the tsar in Muscovite texts. Indeed, readers get the impression that Muscovite authors wanted desperately to believe that their rulers were perfect and therefore should be free of all restrictions, particularly when these authors are discussing the tsardom in a general context. Ivan Timofeev, for example, refers in a striking metaphor to a golden age when the ruler was a pure autocrat (*tsar' samovlasten*) and subjects were "as voiceless as fish."[15] Problems arose, however, as soon as the ideology was put to work to describe actual rulers who were often far from perfect. If the perfection of the ruler implied by the word "absolute" were spoiled, then so was his independence, since, as we shall see, erring monarchs needed to be corrected by wise advisers, deposed, or even killed. The term "absolute" consequently inclines us to filter out just those elements omitted through the conventional use of the term "ideology."

Pipes was probably using the word in its specific sense, however, as it refers to the absolute monarchs of seventeenth-century Europe of whom Louis

XIV was the archetype. The difference between Muscovite political ideas and Western European absolutist philosophy is a tricky but a crucial one. Again there is a tempting similarity. After all, the power of the monarch in both is derived from God above, not from the people below. Yet there are important differences visible from the evolution of each form. Western absolutist theory—like its contemporary rival, the theory of popular sovereignty—sprang from the imprecisely articulated but powerful Byzantine idea of a divinely appointed monarch, adopted by Western thinkers in the Early Middle Ages. This idea contained many unanswered questions, among them the problem of what to do about a bad king, one who contravened God's law or another generally accepted norm of political behavior. For almost a millennium, from the eighth to the seventeenth centuries, generations of polemicists and scholars labored in universities as well as in royal and papal chancelleries to resolve this question. They used Aristotelian logic to defend the claims of the Papacy against the various monarchs of Europe, or vice versa. None of these elements—neither the institutions nor the scholars nor the political rivalries between church and state nor even the Aristotelian logic—was present in Kievan or Muscovite Rus' before the seventeenth century.

As a result, Western absolutist theory was articulated quite differently from its Muscovite counterpart. Formed in an atmosphere of intense attention to political philosophy, it was cast in a logically coherent form to remove the ambiguities that had led to so much confusion in the Middle Ages. It used concepts such as "sovereignty" and "reason of state" that were entirely foreign to the Muscovite political vocabulary. In ninth-century Europe as in sixteenth-century Muscovy, the role of God and the ruler's responsibility to Him were taken with great seriousness as active political questions: Political theory permitted and indeed encouraged the overthrow of a monarch who violated his obligations, however vaguely defined. By the seventeenth century, absolutist theorists like Bossuet, in response to republican and other popular-based political theories, had reduced the role of God in a functional sense to a rhetorical device for giving the system legitimacy without any popular participation. The emphasis in the formula "the King is responsible to God alone" was on the last word.[16] As Robert Crummey recently observed, the remark of James I of England that kings "even by God are . . . called gods" would have "sounded a note of unimaginable blasphemy" within the Muscovite context.[17]

If we are to escape from these difficulties of terminology, then, we need to redefine our problem. Instead of seeking some "ideology" in the conventional sense, we will try to develop a sense of the political images that Muscovite writers used to describe the power of the ruler under varying circumstances, to see Muscovite ideology at work passing judgment on current events. A particularly useful source for such an undertaking is the remarkable set of historical accounts written during or shortly after the Time of Troubles.[18] Although they have received relatively little attention from historians, these tales are valuable precisely because they lack any particular ideological program. Furthermore, they were written by a wide variety of people, from bureaucrat to prince. The events of the Troubles, including the virtual disappearance of the God-established tsardom, violent social strife, and massive foreign intervention, were so traumatic that they forced writers to search deeply in their stock of received ideas for some sort of explanation. The first part of this essay therefore uses these tales to answer the question of what limits, if any, were placed on the power of the tsar.

Our definition of ideology as a symbolic language expressing political relations leads us to an important observation. Whereas this symbolic language was obviously not created by Joseph or any other Muscovite "ideologue" but was inherited from Byzantium via Kiev, the political relationships described by that language were a distinctly Muscovite creation largely based on Tatar precedent.[19] With political practice and political theory coming from quite different sources, the question arises of what connection the literary texts that form the basis of our discussion had with the world of political action. The second part attempts to trace a few such connections. In so doing, we widen our focus slightly to include some selectively chosen sources from the reign of Ivan IV and some of the writings of Avvakum. A final section suggests some hypotheses about the overall importance of Muscovite ideology and the limits it placed on the power of the tsar.

Limits to the Power of the Tsar in Tales About the "Time of Troubles"

What do the language and concepts in the tales about the Time of Troubles tell us about the power and obligations of the tsar? Are there criteria by which royal acts can be judged, or are all of the actions of a tsar considered by definition "proper"? As in the case of Joseph's writings, we must be aware of some important contradictions. In particular, we find that in most of the tales, a tension exists between theoretical statements about the pious nature and autocratic power of the tsar, on one hand, and, on the other, the actual reportage of events, reportage that is often explicitly critical of the rulers concerned. In fact, the portraits of Ivan IV to be discussed shortly suggest that the worse the actions of a ruler were, the more it was necessary to praise his theoretical perfection. This makes sense if we take seriously the tsar's role as the transmitter of God's will: Only a perfect tsar can perform the ritual function of connecting Muscovite politics to God's will and thus legitimize government. To admit the rulers' faults was to cast into doubt the very basis of governmental authority. Given these assumptions, as well as a very pessimistic view of the sinful nature of ordinary people, the tsar had to be endowed with and to use great power.

The experience of living through an extended and painful period of violent anarchy and civil war undoubtedly also contributed to the value placed on a firm and powerful ruler. Weakness or irresolution on the part of a ruler was swiftly condemned. The *Khronograf of 1617* sneeringly reports that "by such insurrections, those evil rebels shook the heart of Tsar Vasilii [Shuiskii] like many rough waves shaking a boat," while I. A. Khvorostinin condemns Shuiskii for having an insatiable desire to fulfill the people's wishes, motivated by his aspiration to be elected tsar rather than to serve God. The remedy for the dangerous moral and political vacillation of the people is a strong ruler.[20] Ivan Timofeev clearly sees the value of a firm hand: "The evil accomplished by such people [rebellious subjects] was permitted by the silence of those in power who did not restrain them with fear."[21] Semen Shakhovskoi, the writer who, together with Khvorostinin, had the closest connections with the West, obviously admires the period of Boris Godunov's rule when Godunov's "hand was strengthened over the whole Russian [*russkii*] state, and great fear and trembling [*strakh i trepet velii*] fell upon all people, and they began truly to serve him from the unimportant even to the very great."[22] Clearly, Muscovites—at least these Muscovites—liked a strong ruler.

But that is not all there is to the question. The role of the tsar as a mediator between God's will and the people's actions depended upon the righteousness and piety of the tsar himself. Without these qualities he could not receive, to say nothing of transmit, God's will. And as Ivan IV (or whoever wrote the first letter to "Kurbskii" usually attributed to him) said (echoing Agapetus), "For even if I wear the purple, none the less I know this, that like unto all men, I am altogether clothed with frailty by nature."[23] The authors of the tales about the Time of Troubles agreed with this judgment. Indeed, their picture of Ivan is remarkably similar in general outline to that found in the famous "correspondence" traditionally ascribed to him and to Prince A. M. Kurbskii.[24]

These portraits of Ivan are important because, unlike most of the rulers described in the tales, Ivan was fully legitimate, clearly a "God-chosen" tsar. They not only give us some idea of the public reaction to Ivan's reign, but they also reveal the criteria by which an unquestionably true tsar could be judged. The three authors who discuss Ivan's reign at any length—Ivan Timofeev, Semen Shakhovskoi, and the author of the *Khronograf of 1617*—all see the cause for Ivan's evil actions in his moral decline. Timofeev tells us that Ivan's character varied, but that "he was moved to evil as much by [his] nature as by anger." His various assaults on his subjects are usually ascribed to his fierceness and anger as well as to the evil influence of the foreigners with whom he surrounded himself. He later informs us that Ivan had a homosexual love for Bogdan Bel'skii.[25] Shakhovskoi (like "Kurbskii") divides Ivan's reign into two parts, a good early part when God raised him up above even his ancestors and widened his state, and an evil second part: "Thus for our sins he showed himself to be the opposite [of the righteous tsar he had been]; he was filled with anger and fierceness, and began to persecute his servants evilly and mercilessly."[26] A similar interpretation is given by the author of the *Khronograf*, who implies that the death of Ivan's first wife, Anastasia, who had influenced Ivan to lead a virtuous life, was central to the change. Among the virtues of the "early Ivan" are his courage, military skill, his conquest of foreigners, his intelligence and oratorical eloquence, and his piety.[27]

Although the amount of detail in each source varies, all sources agree in blaming Ivan for his persecution of his own subjects, including his murder of his own family. "[He] began evilly and mercilessly to persecute his servants who were in his power and to spill their blood" and to murder "his *voevody* given to him by God," Shakhovskoi tells us.[28] Similarly, the *Khronograf* blames him for destroying "his own family and also many of the grandees of his *sinklit* [council]."[29] Timofeev does not particularly mention grandees or *voevody*, but he gives a truly horrifying picture of Ivan's atrocities, his sack of Novgorod, his murder of his own son, of his cousin Prince Vladimir of Staritskii, and of Vladimir's entire family. He also describes the *oprichnina*—an institution specifically condemned by all three authors: "He divided one people into two separate halves, creating as it were two faiths [*iako dvoeverny*]"; he "humiliated himself like a bondsman [before Semen Bekbulatovich], kept only a small portion of his inheritance, and after a short time took everything back, thus playing with God's people."[30] These words by Timofeev imply that Ivan violated a divine trust. The people he was "playing" with were not his, but God's. The *oprichnina* was bad because it threatened the unity of Orthodox Christianity, or so Timofeev seems to imply. Both other sources also specifically condemn the *oprichnina*. Shakhovskoi sees it also as a violation of God's trust: "He divided his *tsarstvo*, given to him by God, into two pieces . . . and he ordered [those in] the other part to rape and murder [those in] that part."[31] Timofeev goes the furthest, however. The language he uses in his description of the *oprichniki* seems clearly to link them with the forces of Antichrist.[32] After reporting the rumor that Ivan was murdered by Boris Godunov, Bogdan Bel'skii, and one other, Timofeev tells us that God would have permitted such a murder.³³ All of the authors saw the *tsarstvo* as a trust given by God; many of Ivan's actions—especially the *oprichnina* and his destruction of his own subjects and family—were seen as violations of that trust.

The description of Fedor Ivanovich, Ivan's son who ruled from 1584 through 1598, is even more puzzling in the context of the question of "absolutist" ideology that we have been considering. Fedor, nicknamed "the Bell Ringer" because of his constant attendance at church services, was feebleminded and took virtually no part in government at all. Nevertheless, he is the most admired ruler of the whole period. Every single author who mentions him, regardless of that author's other political opinions, praises him and his reign, and, especially, his piety. These authors realized Fedor's severe mental limitations, but if they meant what they said, they believed that his piety made God Himself the protector of Muscovy, and thus rendered Fedor's secular administrative abilities, or his lack of them, irrelevant.³⁴ Although several authors made descriptions of Fedor's piety the occasion for considerable literary elaboration, Patriarch Iov created the most ornate description in his "Tale" of Fedor's life. He argued that God Himself or the Mother of God (who, in an echo of the *Akathistos* hymn is described several times as Fedor's *voevoda*) protected Muscovy as the result of Fedor's prayers.³⁵

> For this cross-bearing tsar was very pious, merciful to all, meek [*krotok*], gentle [*nezlobiv*], and compassionate [*miloserd*]; he loved the humble and accepted suffering, and moreover was generous to widows and orphans, had mercy on all who grieved and helped those in misfortune. . . . He conquered all the neighboring countries of unbelieving nations that rebelled against the pious Christian faith and his God-preserved royal state—not with military troops or with the sharpness of a sword, but with the all-night vigil and ceaseless prayers to God did he finally conquer them.³⁶

Here and in other descriptions of Fedor we see a set of characteristics—meekness, mercy, acceptance of suffering—which stands in marked contrast to the traditional image of the haughty merciless ruler implied by the reigning historiography and stated in several other royal portraits in our tales.³⁷ These portraits illustrate the point that Muscovite ideology contained within itself at least two images of an ideal ruler, one of which emphasized strength and power, while another stressed meekness and humility. We also see in these portraits that one of the tsar's greatest public responsibilities was to maintain his own personal piety, because that piety alone could link his acts to God's will, and could enable him to serve as a conduit for God's protection. As the example of Fedor shows, a pious tsar can do no wrong, regardless of his skill as an administrator.

Perhaps a more important, because a more definable, obligation of the ruler was to preserve the Orthodox faith. Most of the rulers are described in the tales as having fulfilled this obligation. According to Iov's account, when Patriarch Jeremiah returned to Constantinople from Muscovy after setting up the Muscovite patriarchate, he told the people of Constantinople of the "miraculous embellishment of the pious Christian churches of the Greek faith, the extraordinary royal piety [of Fedor Ivanovich], and the following [*ispravlenie*] of all the divine Orthodox dogmas."[38] Timofeev compliments Ivan IV: "After his ancestors until his very death, he preserved like a pastor the true faith in Christ firm and unshakable, especially reverence for the Unity in Trinity."[39] This idea of the tsar as a pastor, the spiritual as well as the temporal guardian of his people, is developed further by the author of the "Tale of How Boris Godunov Unjustly Seized the Throne" in his description of Shuiskii as "the true intercessor and pastor of his Christian flock."[40] "And now he observes the true Orthodox faith . . . and corrects us, and sets each [of us] on the path of salvation that after his departure, all would be inheritors of the paradise of life; he does not lead us into evil but goodness, and, again I say, turns [us] from the path of perdition."[41]

However, where a ruler violated this obligation, and threatened to change or destroy Orthodoxy, he was not only condemned, he was not regarded as a tsar at all. The First Pretender is the classic example. Most of our authors thought he had the intention of converting Russia to Catholicism. This opinion, together with the assumption that he was an imposter who was simply pretending to be Ivan's son Dmitrii, was sufficient to deprive him of all claims to power. Timofeev tells us that after the Pretender had seated himself on the royal throne in the Dormition Cathedral, now full of his heretical followers, "he was nothing less than the Antichrist to those looking on, improperly sitting on the throne, and not a tsar."[42] The grace of God was withdrawn at that point. The author of the first redaction of the first six chapters of Palitsyn's *Skazanie* tells of two "new martyrs" who were executed for daring to state that the Pretender was "the image of Antichrist" and was sent by Satan.[43] The author of the "Tale of How Boris Godunov Unjustly Seized the Throne" states that he was neither a tsar, nor the son of a tsar, "but an actual new lawbreaker/apostate" (*zakonoprestupnik*—the epithet traditionally used for Julian the Apostate), the "forerunner of Satan" (*sotonin predotecha*), and compares him with Julian the Apostate, Phocas "the Tormentor," and Constantine V (a fierce iconoclast).[44] The "Orison on the Conquest and Final Destruction . . . of the Muscovite State" calls the Pretender "the forerunner of Antichrist who battles against God."⁴⁵ The *Khronograf of 1617* compares the Pretender to Julian the Apostate, calls him an "ungodly tormentor" (*nechestivyi muchitel'*) because he fiercely persecuted Orthodox Christianity, and states that those who revealed his true identity and were tortured "were crowned [with martyrdom]."⁴⁶

Here is a third image of the ruler, derived, as the examples conveniently reveal, from Byzantine terms worked out many centuries earlier to describe emperors like Julian the Apostate, who attempted to destroy Orthodox Christianity. (The Slavic word for "tormentor" [*muchitel'*] is a translation of the Greek *tyrannos*.) Muscovite and Kievan history offered few historical parallels to these evil native rulers, but this image of an anti-tsar, the mirror image of a true tsar, remained an important part of the literary heritage and was ready to apply to anyone who threatened Orthodoxy.⁴⁷ This image (which is also notably neglected in the conventional picture of Muscovite ideology) encouraged the removal of any ruler who fell within its bounds; it was, of course, the one drawn upon by Joseph in the passage referred to at the beginning of this essay.

Princes Semen Shakhovskoi and Ivan Khvorostinin each use the regimes of Boris Godunov and the Pretender as a pretext for generalizing about the responsibilities of the tsar to God. Shakhovskoi begins with the familiar idea that "the tsar is nothing other than the living image of God, and is chosen by God." If the tsar rules according to God's wish, then he flourishes, but those, like Saul, who abandon God's will, are thrown down from their high position. "If he who has received power from God governs in a praiseworthy way and well, if he strengthens himself in piety and dwells in the fear of the Lord and in His law," he will flourish "like a tree planted by a river" (Ps. 1:2). "And he who gets power from the devil does not stand in truth and does not preserve piety; his end is destruction and death." When the people hear that the Pretender is an apostate (*bogootstupnik*) who wants to destroy Orthodoxy, they will destroy him.⁴⁸ These passages are amply furnished with biblical references describing God's punishment of unjust rulers. Khvorostinin draws a relevant (even if fictitious) picture of himself upbraiding the First Pretender, whom he had already called a "lawbreaker" and a "lawless tormentor." "But I will not honor you more than God," he tells the Pretender, "since a tsar is a man. No evil can tear me away from thy mercy, independent ruler [*samoderzhets*], except the throwing down of God's law."⁴⁹ Clearly there were limits to the power of the tsar.

One objection, of course, is that neither Boris Godunov nor the First Pretender was a fully legitimate monarch, and that therefore statements about them do not apply to true tsars. This argument is only partly valid. For one thing, our authors failed both as individuals and as a group to decide exactly what (aside from God's will) constituted true legitimacy. God's will was assumed to be plain if the claimant were the eldest son of a recently deceased tsar (thus working in a distinctly patrimonial way). After the death of Fedor Ivanovich, however, no one enjoyed that distinction; in spite of the coronations of many tsars or would-be tsars, no coherent theory of legitimacy was worked out. Thus, not only between tales but within the same tale, we find the same ruler, Vasilii Shuiskii, called in one passage a "tsar" whose local officials were "established by the tsar from God" and, in another, "a self-elected so-called tsar."[50] Michael Romanov and Boris Godunov each came to the throne by the same path, election by an Assembly of the Land, but one came to be regarded as legitimate while the other did not. The answer to the question of legitimacy would often determine the answers to all other questions about a ruler; but just as often a ruler's legitimacy was itself determined by other issues—in Godunov's case his alleged murder of the Tsarevich Dmitrii and the overthrow of his regime by the First Pretender. Undoubtedly, had Michael Romanov sought to abolish the Orthodox faith in Muscovy, he would have been regarded as illegitimate for that reason. The reasoning of these authors works cumulatively rather than in a legally precise way: the First Pretender is a false tsar because he wanted to destroy Orthodoxy; because he was an imposter; and because he brought a lot of foreign troops into Muscovy. No one reason is singled out as sufficient. Similarly, his debauchery and lack of piety are not separated from his hostility to Orthodoxy. All these qualities are naturally combined together to create the image not of a tsar but of an antitsar, a "tormentor" who should be overthrown rather than obeyed.

There is a third obligation of the tsar, as imprecisely defined as the first two and perhaps less important because more secular: the duty to preserve the general order of the *tsarstvo* and the hierarchical order of people and things within it.[51] The evidence within the tales about the Time of Troubles indicates that Muscovites were deeply conservative about most matters that we would term political, and were offended by any radical change. The unanimous condemnation of Ivan's *oprichnina*, which we have just discussed, is perhaps the clearest example. The author of the *Novaia povest'* argues that Wladislaw, the king of Poland's son, should become tsar and that, among other good deeds, "he would in no way destroy our law and regulation [*zakona by nashego i ustava nichem ni razoriati*]."[52] Out of context, this sounds temptingly close to a constitutional view, but we must remember first that Wladislaw was a foreigner and a Catholic and may not have been seen in the same light as a "true," native tsar. Second, neither in the *Novaia povest'* nor anywhere else was there mention of any mechanism of enforcement, so that, if there is a constitutional meaning in these words, it is a constitutionalism of a pre–Magna Carta type. Indeed, as we read the tales, the similarity of the concepts of "law" found in them and in documents from the early Middle Ages is striking. As in many traditional societies, there was a reverence both for what was perceived to be old and for what was perceived to be good (that is, according to the will of God), and a tendency to equate the two.[53]

Timofeev sees the violation of this traditional order as one of the principal causes of the Troubles: "When the years came to an end the more our rulers changed the old lawful regulations [*blagoustavlenniia zakonnaia*] passed on by [their] fathers, the more in their slaves the natural fear and obedience to a master began to diminish."[54] The terminology is revealing here. Clearly the ruler was not responsible to his "slaves" for the fulfillment of the law, but, just as clearly, Timofeev regarded the preservation of "the old lawful regulations" as a crucial obligation. It is hard to nail down the exact meaning Timofeev gave to "the law." Although his extensive experience as a *d'iak* would have given him ample acquaintance with administrative and judicial affairs, he does not ever seem to have referred to the "law" in a legally precise way, that is, by citing a particular law that had been broken. He tells us, for example, that Vasilii Shuiskii governed "lawlessly, being in all ways ungodly and like a beast, in fornication and in drunkenness."[55] A more precise meaning is implied in a passage in which Timofeev describes the sudden desertion of Novgorod by the troops appointed to guard over it, leaving the city completely at the mercy of its enemies: "For such an affair [the desertion of the troops] is foreign to the nature [*ustroenie*] of slaves who are afraid, and such impudence goes beyond the regulations of the laws of the royal customs. . . . According to the laws of our previous despots, it is not suitable [*ne dostoit*] to entrust such a wide jurisdiction to them."[56] Here the meaning of the law appears to center on the preservation of the social hierarchy, and the avoidance of promoting unsuitable people to important positions. This sentiment is encountered again and again throughout the tales.[57]

These authors, then, had a strong feeling for the natural order of the realm, and an equally strong feeling that the tsar should not violate this order. Timofeev tells us that Afanasii Vlasov, favorite of the First Pretender, was appointed "beyond his suitability" (*pache dostoianiia svoego*), while the lowborn Mikhail Tatishchev, who was promoted under Godunov and Shuiskii, was brought into the Duma not "meetly" (*dostoine*), but because of some ungodly service to Godunov. "Our true tsars before them [those who ruled during the Troubles] knew what honor to give to what family for what reason and [did] not [give honors] to those of low birth."⁵⁸ It is important to note here that Timofeev was not a member of an old aristocratic clan but a parvenu bureaucrat. Nowhere in his writings do we find the suggestion that the social hierarchy should be in any way changed. Indeed Avraamii Palitsyn's *Skazanie* calls Godunov's touching coronation promise that he would abolish poverty and divide his last cloak with his subjects "loathsome to God."⁵⁹

It seems clear, then, that our authors regarded the power of the tsar as a means by which the Muscovite people could be forced to obey a higher, divinely established order perceived on earth as an ill-defined mixture of divine law and social custom. The tsar did not create this order, but was a creation of it—indeed he was the chief means of its preservation. Particularly important was the tsar's generosity and defense of the weak.⁶⁰

But how was his adherence to this natural order to be enforced? If the tsar violated any of those obligations, his subjects had not so much the right as the duty to tell him so, to become "wise advisers" who could, by the moral force of their advice, restore the tsar's piety and reestablish his obedience to God's will. This need for advisers was one of the main preoccupations of these authors, and appears again and again in the tales.⁶¹ The failure of the people to provide wise advice was blamed far more often than any other social factor for the disasters that overtook Muscovy. However, the function of giving advice was not specifically entrusted to any institution or social class; in theory anyone could be a wise adviser. This idea of an erring monarch corrected by wise advisers constitutes yet another image of the ruler.

So far we have seen that the tsar's rule was a means to a divine end; that he had certain vital, although often ill-defined, obligations; that he was to be corrected by wise advisers when he erred; and that the vocabulary of Muscovite political thought included terms to describe meek and merciful rulers as well as fierce and mighty ones, "tormentors" as well as true tsars.

All of the ruler images we have discussed—the powerful and mighty prince, the meek and merciful spiritual *podvizhnik* (spiritual hero), the erring monarch corrected by wise advisers, even the evil and ungodly tormentor—were so common as to be tropes in the literary culture Muscovites inherited from their Byzantine and Kievan forebears. The evidence of the tales about the Time of Troubles indicates that each of these images remained an active part of the Muscovite political vocabulary, ready to use as occasion demanded. During the Time of Troubles the literary culture provided intellectual support both to the critics and to the supporters of a threatened regime. Indeed, almost every author was both a critic and a supporter at one time or another.

Limits to Royal Power Seen in a Wider Variety of Sources

The ambiguity caused by the multiple images of a ruler can be found in texts throughout the reign of Ivan IV as well as the Time of Troubles. Authors felt that there were significant, though vaguely defined, limits to a tsar's power, and that these limits, set by a literary culture a millennium in the building, had important consequences in the relatively new rough-and-tumble world of Muscovite political practice. All that was required was an appropriate occasion to question the behavior of a tsar. Such occasions were unfortunately common.

As we have seen, Ivan's reign, particularly the *oprichnina*, provided such an occasion for authors writing about the Time of Troubles. It similarly stimulated the author of the letters conventionally attributed to Prince A. M. Kurbskii in his correspondence with Ivan. Pipes pointed out that the "Kurbskii" letters "assailed the entire notion of the state as *votchina*," but he dismissed them because their sixteenth-century origins had been called into question by Edward L. Keenan.[62] The question of the authenticity of the correspondence does not negate its usefulness as a document of Muscovite ideology. Were it to be proven to be the work of Ivan IV and Prince Kurbskii, it reflects the ideology of major political actors. If Keenan is right (and I believe the evidence favors his view), the correspondence was produced by a talented layman, Prince Semen Shakhovskoi, during the first third of the seventeenth century. Drawing on the resources of the Patriarchal library (surely the ideal repository of the literary culture we are discussing), he concocted two entirely believable historical but fictitious *personae* to express fully blown defenses of opposite "ideological" positions. What could better illustrate the diversity and ambiguity of the political messages embedded in Muscovite literary culture in the early 1600s? Indeed, if we accept Keenan's hypothesis, Shakhovskoi was the first writer self-consciously to recognize, expand, and develop in virtuoso fashion the contradiction that has caused such difficulty in the interpretation of Joseph's *Enlightener*, the contradiction with which we began our discussion.

Metropolitan Filipp's encounter with Ivan provided another occasion to question Ivan's behavior. Pipes repeats Maksim the Greek's question (framed in typical Old Testament analogies) of why there were in Russia "no Samuels to stand up to Saul and no Nathans to tell the truth to erring David."[63] Filipp seems to have played this role, not only in the mind of his hagiographer(s) but also in real political life. The sources do not agree on how often Filipp upbraided Ivan IV, or what he said.[64] Apparently, even before he became metropolitan, he had demanded the abolition of the *oprichnina*. Although Ivan refused to allow Filipp to meddle in his affairs, he nevertheless did guarantee the metropolitan the right "to give advice" (*sovetoval by*) to the tsar as the metropolitan had done under Ivan's father and grandfather.[65] After his elevation to the metropolitan throne on July 25, 1566, Filipp, according to his *Vita*, continued to criticize the tsar. The dramatic climax of the affair occurred in the Dormition Cathedral in the Kremlin on March 22, 1568, when Filipp accused the tsar of spilling the blood of innocent Christians. He plainly stated that the tsar is a mortal like any other man, who will suffer at the judgment of Christ for his deeds, which in his case were unrighteous (*ne pravednaia dela tvorishi*).[66] If we believe the second redaction of the *Vita*, we find in a speech given to Ivan earlier and in private many of the themes already discussed relative to the *smuta* tales. The tsar is told that he, like the church, must care for the "piety and salvation of all Orthodox Christianity." "Observe the law given to you from God," Filipp is reported to have said. "Rule lawfully and in peace."[67] According to the *Vita*, he repeatedly harped on the need to listen to wise advisers, and to avoid the influence of flatterers.[68] In the Dormition Cathedral speech, he told the tsar, "Master, I cannot obey your command more than [the command of] God."[69] Filipp later apparently went so far as to say that an *oprichnik* who came to church with Ivan looked "as if [he came] from the Satanic host" (*slovno ot lika sataninskago*).[70]

The information about the Dormition Cathedral speech from Filipp's *Vita* is remarkably corroborated by the testimony of two foreign observers, Taube and Kruse, who presumably had little or no access to the literary culture that produced the *Vita*. Both the first redaction of the *Vita* and the foreigners' account agree that Filipp's speech had three common themes: reproaches for the spilling of blood, the reminder that the tsar is mortal and that he is responsible for his deeds before God, and, finally, the attempt to direct the actions of the tsar into the channel of justice and the laws.[71] Thus, the literary ideology provided both criteria by which Filipp could judge the tsar and ample role models for his courageous and ultimately fatal opposition. Indeed, one wonders whether Filipp may have found his spiritual strength from that tradition, especially from the very biblical examples of Samuel and Nathan cited by Maksim and Pipes.

Filipp was not an isolated example. German Polev, who had been chosen as metropolitan before Filipp, also was dismissed for objecting to the *oprichnina* and was eventually executed for his support of Filipp. When we take into account that the metropolitan before Polev, Afanasii Protopopov, had lost his position apparently for objecting to Ivan's policies, and that in connection with the affair of Filipp or soon after, Ivan purged the entire hierarchy except Bishop Kornnilii of Rostov, we can see that these objections had serious political consequences indeed.[72]

The church was not the only source of serious objections to the *oprichnina* however. Not long before Filipp's speech in the Dormition Cathedral, a group of notables who had just served in the *zemskii sobor* of 1566 approached Ivan to petition him to abolish the *oprichnina*. One source lists the number present at three hundred; clearly this was meant and perceived as a serious challenge.[73] Two years earlier, a smaller but similar group, including Filipp's predecessor Metropolitan Afanasii, had lodged a similar protest against Ivan's executions. Albert Schlichting, a Pomeranian observer of Muscovy, describes the situation again in terms that recall what we know of Filipp's words to Ivan:

> Horrified by the savagery of this deed [the execution of Prince Dmitrii Ovchinin Telepnev-Obolenskii], certain noblemen, including the Metropolitan, decided it was their duty to restrain the tyrant from brutally destroying his subjects, who were clearly innocent of wrong-doing. They told him that no Christian ruler had the right to treat human beings like animals; instead he should fear the righteous dooms of God, who avenges the blood of innocents unto the third generation. Ivan was considerably taken aback by these representations and particularly embarrassed by the Metropolitan, nor could he justify his behavior.[74]

Again, the account of the protest by Schlichting, who was a foreigner like Taube and Kruse, with little access to Muscovite literary culture, stresses Ivan's spilling of innocent blood and responsibility to God; note also that, according to Schlichting, Ivan had no suitable reply. There is thus clear evidence that when Ivan tried to treat his state in a "patrimonial" way—"to use, abuse, or destroy as he saw fit"—the existing ideology provided firm grounds for objection. Ivan was opposed by both church and secular figures. Indeed, R. G. Skrynnikov (probably the most thorough investigator of the *oprichnina*) believed that Ivan saw in these events such a threat that he thenceforth resorted to a policy of intensified executions to eliminate opposition to him. Thus, only brute force enabled him to act in contradiction to the prevailing ideological norms.[75] Although the evidence remains incomplete, it suggests a strong similarity between the tenor of contemporary protests against Ivan and the reasons for condemning him in the tales about the Time of Troubles. These events show unequivocally that a number of Muscovites took political values from the literary culture seriously enough to risk their lives to act as wise advisers trying to restrain Ivan from his evil deeds. Ideology had meaning in the real world of politics.

A much more faithfully preserved example of "wise advice" can be found from the beginning of Ivan's reign. The document is a long defense of church property, and the author (either directly or indirectly) is Metropolitan Makarii, the person who probably has the best claim to being called the creator of official Muscovite ideology, the cleric under whom "the Josephite party attained the apogee of its influence," according to Pipes.[76]

This document, the "Reply of Makarii," quotes or paraphrases a number of authorities—among them the "Donation of Constantine"—to prove the point. The inclusion of this source, an ecclesiastical forgery long used by the church in the West to strengthen its political authority against secular rulers, would not imply that the author envisioned a church meekly subservient to the state. Although the explicit issue in the "Reply," church property, does not directly concern us here, the author assumed throughout that tsars could not simply do as they wished, but were bound to obey the laws of God, as revealed in the writings of the Church Fathers, the decisions of the Seven Ecumenical Councils, and so forth. Near the beginning, we find the explicit statement: "Since the priesthood [*sviashchennicheskoe nachalo*] and the power and the glory of Christian piety were established by the Heavenly Tsar, it is unrighteous [*nepravedno est'*] for an earthly tsar to rule over [the church]."[77] At the end of the "Reply," the author warns Ivan directly: "Even if I am constrained by the tsar himself or by his grandees, if they order me to do something contrary to divine rules [*krome Bozhestvennykh pravil*], I will not obey them—even if they threaten me with death, I will not obey them in any way."[78] A number of sections of the "Reply," including a shorter version of the "Donation," were included among the decisions of the Stoglav Council, and thus became official church doctrine.[79] The coronation service of Ivan IV, probably also composed by Makarii and his circle, again emphasizes the divine source of the tsar's power and his responsibility to return to God what he had received from God.[80] The metropolitan in his admonition asks the new tsar to imagine the Last Judgment, when he will render an account of the task God gave him: "Here, Lord, are Thy people of Thy great Russian kingdom, whom Thou gavest to me."[81] The very verbs used in the service to describe what the tsar does to the *tsarstvo*—*bliusti, sokhraniti, sobliusti*, all meaning "to care for," "keep," "preserve"—reinforce the idea of the tsar as a steward who will be held accountable for preserving what he holds in trust.

This theme is also found in another remarkable example of "wise advice" preserved as a letter to Ivan IV from about the same period, a copy of which is found in a manuscript miscellany that once belonged to the priest Sil'vestr.[82] The author was trying to persuade Ivan to persecute fiercely those in his kingdom guilty of various sins, especially sodomy. To emphasize the tsar's responsibility, the author mentions the parable of the talents, the image of the tsar as pastor of his flock who is ready to lay down his soul (*dushu polozhiti*) for his charges, and the scriptural admonition: "For unto whomsoever much is given, of him shall much be required" (Luke 12:48).⁸³ Ivan is told that if he roots out sin—and the suggested tortures are clearly described—he will not only be saved, seemingly by this one act alone, but that "by God's grace . . . all your enemies will fall beneath your feet and will be unable to arise."⁸⁴ Indeed, in this letter we find most of the ideas we have been discussing—the need to seek good advice and avoid evil advice, the primary responsibility of the tsar to preserve both his own righteousness (Ivan is told that God chose David to rule Israel because the latter was "gentle, simple, meek and wise") and that of this subjects, and the use of words like *bezumie* and *bezzakonie* to describe violations of the unwritten moral law.⁸⁵ Richly endowed with scriptural and other quotations, the letter repeatedly calls on Ivan to carry out God's law and to follow the example of David, Saint Vladimir, and other righteous rulers. There is no idea of limiting the power of the tsar on earth. On the contrary, great power and harsh punishment are needed to root out sinful behavior, but such power is always a means and never an end in itself. The whole message of the letter is summed up in a quotation from the eighty-first (eighty-second) Psalm: "Oh, that my people had hearkened unto me, and Israel had walked in my ways. I should soon have subdued their enemies and turned my hand against their adversaries."⁸⁶

Although there are numerous other sources, a clear pattern has emerged from these texts. In every source we find the same set of assumptions: the responsibility of the tsar before God to maintain his own piety, to strengthen Orthodoxy, and to preserve the good order of his realm; the role of wise advisers in correcting a sinful and therefore erring monarch; and the strongly felt belief in autocracy, in the power (*vlast'*) of the tsar. The "Possessors" seem not to have held significantly different views from the "Non-possessors" on the subject. The opinions of Metropolitan Makarii, a man with alleged "Possessor" credentials, and those of Sil'vestr, a "Non-possessor," judging by his connections, and the most likely author of the "Letter to Ivan," share a common set of ideological principles.⁸⁷ According to A. A. Zimin, Metropolitan Filipp was a "Non-possessor," while his immediate predecessor, German Polev, had "Possessor" connections (he copied out Joseph of Volokolamsk's *Prosvetitel'* himself).⁸⁸ Yet both apparently objected to Ivan's *oprichnina*, and both were eventually executed. If there were indeed two church "parties" with rival ideologies concerning the nature of the tsar's power, as is often assumed, they should have been apparent in the texts we have examined. The tales about the Time of Troubles similarly fail to provide any convincing evidence of an ideological split.

If our hypothesis is correct that most literate Muscovites held a common ideology that called for *both* a very strong ruler *and* traditional but vaguely defined limits to his power, then these limits should have had political effects. They did. We have seen that two metropolitans and two separate groups of laymen objected to Ivan's policies using justifications drawn from this ideology, and that their opposition may well have forced Ivan to a systematic use of terror to oppose them. (Metropolitan German Polev also objected, although we do not know the grounds.) The priest Sil'vestr, who had no office or position on which to base his power, may well have attained whatever influence he had over Ivan by his ability to step into the well-defined literary role of a prophetic wise adviser.[89] The "holy fools" may have enjoyed their influence for the same reason.[90]

The full implications of these ideas were not revealed until the second half of the next century, however, when many Old Believers, constituting numerically the largest and most long-lived dissident movement in Russian history, withdrew from the state and refused to acknowledge the authority of the tsar, all the while relying on the same assumptions we have been discussing. Once one believed, as a high proportion of devout Muscovites did, that Nikon had introduced heresy into the church by changing the sacred rituals, and that Tsar Aleksei Mikhailovich, however great his personal piety, was supporting the Nikonian heresy and destroying Orthodoxy, then it was not only possible but necessary to withdraw from him the obedience owed to a "God-chosen" tsar.

We can see the path by which this conclusion was reached if we examine Avvakum's five petitions to the tsar. The reader is struck by how long it took him finally to abandon his belief in a godly tsar. As late as the third petition, written in 1664, he calls Tsar Aleksei "equal-to-the-apostles [*ravnoapostol' nyi*]," an expression usually reserved for Great Prince Vladimir and the Emperor Constantine and one that surely equaled the most extravagant claims of contemporary royal apologists.[91] He seems to have seen himself as fulfilling the traditional role of a wise adviser modeled on the Old Testament prophets, since he compared Aleksei to David and King Uzziah and himself to Nathan and Azariah (2 Sam. 11–12; 2 Chr. 26:16–21).[92] Nikon he compares to Julian the Apostate, and refers to his innovations as "new lawless laws [*novykh zakonov bezzakonnykh*]," using language and imagery similar to that used in the tales about the Time of Troubles to describe the First Pretender.[93] As in the "Letter to Ivan," Ivan IV's coronation service, and the *Vita* of Metropolitan Filipp, Avvakum in the fifth petition forcefully reminds the tsar of his responsibility at the Last Judgment. "Bear in mind, Lord, with what justice you wish to stand at the Last Judgment of Christ, before the angelic host."[94] Avvakum also envisions the tsar's evil advisers, those "who fawn on and flatter you," being judged by Christ and His saints as the flatterers themselves judged Avvakum.[95] Shortly before he had very roughly paraphrased two chapters of

Agapetus, the classical source for Muscovite ideology, in order to remind Aleksei that, although as tsar he rules over all men, yet with all men he is God's slave.[96]

Now there is no doubt that occasionally Avvakum goes far beyond these traditional ideas. In the same fifth petition, he relates to Aleksei a vision he had in which his body grew until "God cast into me heaven and earth, and all creation." As a result, "you [Aleksei] rule on your own [na svobode] only the Russian land, while the Son of God entrusted to me . . . heaven and earth."[97] Such statements were highly idiosyncratic, however, and were unnecessary for Avvakum to make his point. Under the assumptions of Muscovite ideology, Avvakum had to oppose a tsar who was destroying Orthodoxy. Unless Avvakum were to agree to the legitimacy of the Nikonian reforms, he ultimately had to abandon his belief in the perfectly autocratic "God-chosen" tsar, and to consider Aleksei as an anti-tsar rather than a true tsar. Moreover, traditional Muscovite thought provided him with the language and images he needed to describe the change. When he associated the Muscovite tsar with the devil and the Antichrist, Avvakum was using the same language, but in a more explicit form, that both Filipp's *Vita* and Ivan Timofeev (and "Kurbskii") used to describe Ivan IV.[98] His language was less explicit and less derogatory than that used by many writers to describe the First Pretender. But in all cases, the general line of argument is the same: an evil tsar, one who breaks God's law, is a servant of the Antichrist, part of the "Satanic host," and so on. Thus Avvakum, far from introducing "reformist" or "revolutionary" changes into traditional Muscovite political thought, as Michael Chemiavsky has argued, was able to justify his position fully within the bounds of that thought. Indeed, the basic tenets of that thought forced him to oppose the tsar.[99]

Some Conclusions

Our survey of some significant sources concerning Muscovite ideology over a 120-year period permits several conclusions. Most important, Muscovite writers relied not on one but on several images of the tsar, each deeply embedded in a long literary history stretching back to Byzantium. Like those old picture postcards where the picture changes when you move your head slightly, what you see depends on your point of view. Each of these ruler images takes its place in the ideology as a whole, and served a function in Muscovite court society.

Recent studies of Muscovite court politics have emphasized the stability of court life and the absence of ideological or even political factions in the nineteenth-century sense.[100] Nancy Shields Kollmann argues persuasively that "the pursuit of static harmony" was the chief goal of politics, protecting the fragile state order from the chaos that would result from unrestrained boyar competition, the ever-present dangers of foreign enemies abroad, and a fragile economy at home. Political chaos, as during a disputed succession or under an incapacitated monarch, was more to be feared than any other domestic evil. As Kollmann has argued, several of the images of the ruler were useful in maintaining this fragile stability and were thus accepted by the boyars as well as by the churchmen who were the natural keepers of the literary tradition.[101]

The most valuable image was that of the all-powerful ruler whose autocratic commands were seen as mirroring God's will. This commonplace image of Christian rulership, as important in the West as in the East, was carefully burnished in programmatic statements about the power of the tsar. It was used as the chief public description of royal power; it was reflected in elaborate court ceremonies stressing the magnificence of the ruler. It lay behind the conception of disgrace, where absence from the ruler's presence was equated with political nonexistence. It elicited horror from foreign observers such as Olearius in the seventeenth century, who described the debasement of the great men of the realm who "call themselves slaves and are treated as such."[102] Sigismund Freiherr von Herberstein, in the sixteenth century, testifies to the acceptance of this image when he reports that "the people openly confess that the will of the prince is the will of God and that whatever the prince does, he does by the will of God."[103] This image is the linchpin of the ideology, for at a stroke it legitimizes and sanctifies the political order. Muscovite court society found it useful in promoting stability because it concealed all factional struggles behind a myth of autocracy. Its transcendental focus left unmentioned most issues of importance at court—clan rivalries, marriages, domestic governance—and therefore kept those issues safe from public ideological discussion. It provided no role for the people, who were regarded as sinful and thus rightly excluded from government. At the same time, it allowed conceptual space for the growth of the bureaucracy, characterized as agents of the tsar's will. It also made the rhetorical cost of questioning a ruler very high, since the legitimacy of the whole system collapsed once the ruler's policies were cut off from God's will.

Yet, in spite of these compelling advantages, the autocratic image had a liability from the court's point of view. The tsar's power derived from his position as the agent of God's will, and therefore his responsibilities to obey that will grew together with his power. This linking of power to responsibility may explain why the state was so reluctant to accept church-generated formulations like the famous Third Rome theory (see chapter 7). This theory certainly magnified the power of the ruler, but only in order to stress his obligations, as the head of the last universal empire, to root out heresy and protect the church. A grand prince and his boyars who thought of the state as their patrimony might very sensibly have seen such a theory as a step backward.

The seemingly contrary list of characteristics stressing humility and mercy, which observers used in describing Fedor Ivanovich, provides a useful supplement to the image of the mighty fierce autocrat. Within the rhetoric of the ideology, the obvious piety of such a ruler suits him ideally to the ritual function of linking the commands of the state to the will of God. In practice, these characteristics assured legitimacy to rulers who were not great warriors, decisive rulers, or even competent human beings. Thus, stability was assured even if the tsar, who in theory was responsible for doing everything, was a minor or a mere figurehead who did almost nothing at all.

A third image was that of an erring or even a "good" monarch who might be either corrected by wise advisers or led astray by flatterers.[104] Since this image blurs the clarity of the autocratic image, it did not appear in programmatic statements about the power of the tsar. It was essential, however, in narrative sources describing and judging various rulers, where it was used to justify the role of actual critics of the regime. From the point of view of the court, this layer was also useful, although it placed more emphasis on the obligations of the tsar than the autocratic image did. Since it depicted the relationship between the tsar and his advisers as personal and moral rather than institutional or constitutional, it well described in inherited symbolic language the informal, personal consensus politics of the Kremlin. By giving the boyars a literarily defined role to fill as junior colleagues of the ruler, it complemented court ceremonies emphasizing the corporate responsibility of tsar and boyars together.[105] This informal, much less public, image of the tsar and his advisers was as well adapted to describe relationships within the court as the autocratic image was to describe the relationships between the court and the people as a whole.

The idea of a tsar corrected by his advisers was potentially more dangerous to the goal of court stability than the autocratic image. It suggests political factions at court trying to persuade the tsar to adopt a "righteous" policy and reject an "evil" one. Several characteristics of the development of this idea in Muscovite sources, however, prevented it from encouraging faction. First, advice was seen in moral, not political, terms. Second, the obligations of the ruler were described in terms so vague that it was hard to prove exactly when a ruler had failed to meet them. Third, the identity of potential advisers was similarly left vague; no constitutional body, if such a term fits either the Boyar

Duma or the Assembly of the Land, was specifically endowed in our sources with an advisory function. This exclusive emphasis on the moral quality of advice and advisers, together with the necessarily informal status of advice giving, was surely an important factor in preventing the constitutional experiments of the last years of the Troubles from becoming permanent.

Of the tsar's obligations to preserve his own piety, the purity of Orthodoxy, and the traditional order of the realm, the first was purely personal, while the last benefitted a court society whose aim was the maintenance of stability. Most courtiers had their own good reasons to object to the innovations of the *oprichnina*, for example. Moreover, these obligations did not touch on most issues of domestic or foreign policy. This separation of ideology from most important governmental issues resulted in the isolation of the latter from public ideological debate. Further, it must have had a powerful dampening effect on political divisions at court. Finally, two basic features of all literary political discourse—the insistent emphasis on political life as a means to a divine end and an idea of history in which divine will prevailed over secular causation—would have similarly inhibited people from identifying their own interests in a given policy debate and from then acting in concert with those with a similar interest.[106]

If these features of Muscovite political thought prevented the images of the ruler from leading to political divisions and factions at court, one image remained a dangerous liability—that of a false tsar, a tsar tormentor, a tyrant. For a society seeking political stability, this image was disastrous, since it destroyed all political authority without providing any alternative. A political embodiment of this image occurred in the Time of Troubles when political authority in fact disintegrated and when several rulers were described as tormentors. The political costs of this disappearance of legitimate government were obvious. The rhetorical costs were also high, since a tsar tormentor on the throne destroyed not only the authority of the monarch but also the holy mission of the state, the meaning of history, and, according to the Third Rome doctrine, even history itself. Nobody wanted this situation. Yet the ideal of a divinely appointed autocracy brought with it the inescapable corollary: rulers who disobeyed God's will could be removed from power.

The vagueness of the obligations of the tsar did not mean that those obligations did not exist. The failure of a tsar to fulfill these obligations drove Muscovite authors from the autocratic to the erring monarch image. If the failure was obvious and long-lasting enough, the tsar came to be seen as a tormentor, and opposition to him became the obligation of all righteous people. If, from the court's point of view, the function of ideology was to compel the allegiance of all subjects and maintain stability, the Old Believer schism demonstrated that Muscovite ideology had failed. In the next generation it had to be substantially altered, grafted onto the Western European ideas of absolutism and "the well-ordered police state"—self-contained systems of thought that did away with the troublesome alternate images of wise advisers and erring monarchs, to say nothing of the image of an anti-tsar.[107] Under the new dispensation, the ruler was the sole judge alike of God's will and the public good; to advocate putting God's law above the law of the state became an act of treason.

The question of whether Muscovite ideology placed any limits on the power of the tsar thus requires a complicated answer. It depends on which of these various ruler images was in view at a given time. If we take all of the images together as a dynamic system, we see that the power of the ruler changed as the ruler was seen to violate (or not to violate) certain vague but strongly felt norms of governance. Since his power decreased as the norms were violated, from a functional point of view the ideology did place important limits on the power of the tsar throughout the period. It thus created a considerable conflict with (instead of reinforcing) the "patrimonial" attitude Pipes ascribed to the secular culture of the tsar and his court. In spite of the great usefulness of several of these images to the court as we now imagine it, the idea of a tsar tormentor could and did cause great trouble. The evidence now suggests that real political actors, both clerical and lay, took these literary ideas seriously enough to act on them, producing significant political consequences.

Notes

1. Richard Pipes, *Russia under the Old Regime* (New York: Charles Scribner's Sons, 1974), 64.

2. Pipes, *Russia under the Old Regime*, chap. 9, esp. 229–234.

3. Recent research has shown that *"votchina* by its nature was never owned individually and [that] prospective heirs had to be consulted in its disposal outside the family." Sandra Levy, "Women and the Control of Property in Sixteenth-Century Muscovy," *Russian History/Histoire Russe* 10, no. 2 (1983): 201–212, quotation on 203. Eve Levin similarly found that in medieval Novgorod, the *paterfamilias* was obliged to consult all heirs and claimants before disposing of a *votchina*. "Women and Property in Medieval Novgorod: Dependence and Independence," *Russian History/Histoire Russe* 10, no. 2 (1983): 154–179.

4. In particular, Michael Chemiavsky, *Tsar and People*, 2nd ed. (New York: Random House, 1969), 45–71, argues that during the sixteenth and seventeenth centuries, the Muscovite image of both the human nature and the divine power of the tsar became so exalted that he was largely above criticism. For a detailed discussion of Chemiavsky's views on Ivan Timofeev and earlier sources, see my "Towards an Understanding of the Political Ideas in Ivan Timofeyev's *Vremennik*," *Slavonic and East European Review* 62,

no. 3 (July 1984): 391–395 (chapter 2 of this volume). Even Ihor Sevcenko called Timofeev "a staunch defender of absolute power" in "A Neglected Byzantine Source of Muscovite Political Ideology," *Harvard Slavic Studies* 2 (1954) reprinted in *The Structure of Russian History*, ed. Michael Cherniavsky (New York: Random House, 1970), 106. For general views of Muscovite ideology along the lines outlined by Pipes, see Bjarne Nørretranders, *The Shaping of Czardom under Ivan Groznyj* (Copenhagen: Munksgaard, 1964), 42–56, 135; Joel Raba, "The Authority of the Muscovite Ruler at the Dawn of the Modern Age," *Jahrbucher fur Geschichte Osteuropas* 24, no. 2 (1976): 321–344, esp. 323–326. Francis Dvornik seems to subscribe to this general view, but he warns that Muscovy's secular rulers did not understand these "literary" notions all that well. See Dvornik, *The Slavs in European History and Civilization* (New Brunswick, NJ: Rutgers University Press, 1962), 378. Ideology in the period we are discussing has not figured prominently in recent historical scholarship either in the Soviet Union or in the West.

5. See Robert O. Crummey, "Court Spectacles in Seventeenth-Century Russia: Illusion and Reality," *Essays in Honor of A. A. Zimin* (Columbus, OH: Slavica, 1985), 130–158; Nancy Shields Kollmann, *Kinship and Politics: The Making of the Muscovite Political System, 1345–1547* (Stanford, CA: Stanford University Press, 1987), 148–150; Paul Bushkovitch, "The Formation of a National Consciousness in Early Modern Russia," *Harvard Ukrainian Studies* 10, nos. 3–4 (December 1986): 355–376; Daniel Rowland, "The Problem of Advice in Muscovite Tales about the Time of Troubles," *Russian History* 6, no. 2 (1979): 259–283 (chapter 3 in this volume). See also Hans-Joachim Torke, *Die Staatsbedingte Gesellschaft im Moskauer Reich* (Leiden: E. J. Brill, 1974) for further references.

6. For sound prerevolutionary surveys of this subject, see V. Val'denberg, *Drevnerusskie ucheniia o predelakh tsarskoi vlasti* (Petrograd: n.p., 1916); M. D'iakonov, *Vlast' Moskovskikh gosudarei* (Saint Petersburg: Tip. I. N. Skorokhodova, 1889). Val'denberg's book provides additional information on many of the points discussed below. See also his "Poniatie o tirane v drevnerusskoi literature v sravnenii s zapadnoi," *Akademiia Nauk SSSR. Izvestiia po russkomy iazyku i slovestnosti* 2 (1929): 214–236.

7. Pipes, *Old Regime*, 232. See also Marc Raeff, "An Early Theorist of Absolutism: Joseph of Volokolamsk," *American Slavic and East European Review* 8 (1949): 77–89.

8. Iosif Volotskii, *Prosvetitel'*, ed. A. Volkov (Kazan': Tipo-Litografiia Imp. Universiteta, 1896), 287.

9. See especially Ia. S. Lur'e, *Ideologicheskaia bor'ba v russkoi publitsistike kontsa XV–nachala XVI veka* (Moscow-Leningrad: Akademiia nauk, 1960), 204–284, 426–481. Marc Szeftel has judiciously surveyed this literature and attempted to come to grips with the apparent contradictions in Joseph's views: "Joseph Volotsky's Political Ideas," *Jahrbiicher fur Geschichte Osteuropas, Neue Folge* 13 (Munich, 1965): 19–29, reprinted in his *Russian Institutions and Culture up to Peter the Great* (London: Variorum1975). I hope the present article will serve as a continuation and expansion of Szeftel's work.

10. Rowland, "Problem of Advice."

11. Robert O. Crummey, *Aristocrats and Servitors: The Boyar Elite in Russia, 1613–1689* (Princeton, NJ: Princeton University Press, 1983), 81–106, 167; Kollmann, *Kinship and Politics*, chap. 5.

12. V. B. Kobrin, *Vlast' i sobstvennost' v srednevekovoi Rossii (XV-XVI vv.)* (Moscow: Mysl', 1985); Donald Ostrowski, "Church Polemics and Monastic Land Acquisition in Sixteenth-Century Muscovy," *Slavonic and East European Review* 64 (1986): 355–379.

13. This definition of ideology is an admittedly simplified condensation of the version offered by Clifford Geertz in "Ideology as a Culture System," in his *The Interpretation of Cultures* (New York: Basic Books, 1973), 193–229.

14. For an innovative and convincing discussion of the importance of an ideology and its rhetorical rules on the political events of the French Revolution, see Lynn Hunt, *Politics, Culture, and Class in the French Revolution* (Berkeley: University of California Press, 1984).

15. *Vremennik Ivana Timofeeva*, ed. O. A. Derzhavina (Moscow-Leningrad, 1951), 109. The context suggests this modern meaning of the word *samovlasten*. See below, note 49.

16. I have been unable to discover a better discussion of the differences between early medieval and early modern political theory than Fritz Kern's in his *Kingship and Law in the Middle Ages*, trans. S. B. Chrimes (Oxford: Basil Blackwell, 1939), 12ff.

17. Crummey, "Court Spectacles," 135.

18. The classic description of these texts is S. F. Platonov's *Drevnerusskie skazaniia i povesti o smutnom vremeni XVII veka kak istoricheskii istochnik* (Saint Petersburg: Tip. V. S. Balasheva, 1888). For a revision of some of Platonov's conclusions in the light of later scholarship and a reexamination of many manuscripts, see my dissertation, Daniel Rowland, "Muscovite Political Attitudes as Reflected in Early Seventeenth Century Tales about the Time of Troubles" (PhD diss., Yale University, 1976), 13–118, 230–270.

19. Donald Ostrowski argues that almost all of the Muscovite governmental apparatus derived from Kipchak administration. "The Mongol Origins of Muscovite Political Institutions," *Slavic Review* 49, no. 4 (1990): 525–542.

20. *Russkaia istoricheskaia biblioteka* (henceforth *RIB*), vol. 13, 2nd ed. (Saint Petersburg, 1909), cols. 1303, 541–542, 547.

21. *Vremennik Ivana Timofeeva*, 77.

22. *RIB*, vol. 13, col. 567. Patriarch Iov expressed the same opinion in his "Tale about the Honorable Life of . . . Fedor Ivanovich," in *Polnoe sobraine russkikh letopisei* (hereafter *PSRL*), vol. 14, part 1 (Saint Petersburg, 1910; photo reprint: Moscow, 1965), 2.

23. J. L. I. Fennell, ed. and trans., *The Correspondence between Prince A. M. Kurbsky and Tsar Ivan IV of Russia* (Cambridge: Cambridge University Press, 1963), 122–123; see also 110–111. For the comparison to Agapetus, see Sevcenko, "A Neglected Byzantine Source," 92.

24. The political ideas found in the *smuta* tales and in the *Correspondence* seem to me to be remarkably similar. I do not believe alleged differences in ideological content are convincing grounds for establishing (or denying) the authenticity of the *Correspondence*, as Inge Auerbach has suggested in "Further Findings on Kurbskii's Life and Work," in *Russian and Slavic History*, ed. D. K. Rowney and G. E. Orchard (Columbus, OH: Slavica Publishers, 1977), 242–245. In particular, her statement that "[seventeenth-century] writers were no longer concerned with the reasons for [Ivan's] terror" (243) is wrong. As we shall see below, several *smuta* tale authors, especially Timofeev, devoted considerable attention to this problem and came up with conclusions very similar to those of "Kurbskii." Shakhovskoi's statements are particularly similar.

25. *Vremennik Ivana Timofeeva*, 11, 46.

26. *RIB*, vol. 13, col. 561.

27. *RIB*, vol. 13, col. 1275.

28. *RIB*, vol. 13, col. 561.

29. *RIB*, vol. 13, 1275.

30. *Vremennik Ivana Timofeeva*, 11.

31. *RIB*, vol. 13, cols. 561, 1275–1276.

32. For a closer analysis of the language Timofeev used in describing Ivan and his *oprichnina*, see Rowland, "Towards an Understanding," 392–395 (chapter 2 of this volume).

33. *Vremennik Ivana Timofeeva*, 15.

34. Timofeev admits that Muscovites thought Fedor ill-suited to govern (*Vremennik Ivana Timofeeva*, 19, 22), while Shakhovskoi called him "divinely foolish" (*blagoiurodiv*) (*RIB*, vol. 13, col. 564).

35. *PSRL*, vol. 14, pt. 1, 11–12.

36. *PSRL*, vol. 14, pt. 1, 116.

37. For descriptions of Fedor, see, for example, *PSRL*, vol. 14, part 1, 3; the *Khronograf of 1617* (*RIB*, vol. 13, cols. 1277–1278); Shakhovskoi's historical tales (*RIB*, vol. 13, cols. 620, 852–853); and the first redaction of Palitsyn's *Skazanie* (*Skazanie Avraamiia Palitsyna*, ed. O. A. Derzhavina and E. V. Kolosova (Moscow-Leningrad: Akademiia nauk, 1955), 250. The most striking positive portrait of a mighty prince is Timofeev's description of the tsarevich Ivan Ivanovich, son of Ivan the Terrible, in *Vremennik Ivana Timofeeva*, 19–23.

38. *PSRL*, vol. 14, part 1, 5.

39. *Vremennik Ivana Timofeeva*, 16–17.

40. Literally, "sheep of the Word": see John 10:9–14. None of our authors appears to have felt that this royal obligation posed a threat to the power of the patriarch (or metropolitan). It was assumed that both secular and ecclesiastical authorities would cooperate in protecting both the church and its dogma. In practice, of course, the threat came from the secular side.

41. *RIB*, vol. 13, col. 173.

42. *Vremennik Ivana Timofeeva*, 88.

43. *Skazanie Avraamiia Palitsyna*, 260. A little further on (264), the author refers to demons as "the Pretender's friends."

44. *RIB*, vol. 13, cols. 162, 163, 165.

45. *RIB*, vol. 13, col. 225.

46. *RIB*, vol. 13, cols. 1291–1293.

47. The compilers of Kievan chronicle compendia jettisoned almost all secular Byzantine history from their Byzantine sources except material on church councils and heresies (which would have contained the most information on tsar-tormentors): Simon Franklin, "The Empire of the *Romaioi* as Viewed from Kievan Russia," *Byzantion* 53, no. 2 (1983): 117. See O. V. Tvorogov, *Drevnerusskie khronografy* (Leningrad: Izd. Nauka, 1975), 55, 221–223, for the inclusion of passages relating to the iconoclast emperors and Julian the Apostate, respectively.

48. *RIB*, vol. 13, cols. 857–858, 869, 581.

49. *RIB*, vol. 13, cols. 534–538. The *Khronograf of 1617* says of Godunov: "And he did not remember the saying that the Lord raises up and throws down, and gives the kingdom to whom he wishes" (*RIB*, vol. 13, col. 1294). Timofeev quotes a similar passage to explain the end of the ruling dynasty: "'I gave you a king [*tsar'*] in my anger,' saith the Lord, 'and I take him away in my fierceness'" (*Vremennik Ivana Timofeeva*, 33; Hosea 13:11). As in the Old Testament, the compact between God and the ruler remains

an open question. On this meaning of *samoderzhets*, as opposed to the modern concept of autocrat as a ruler without limits to his power, see Marc Szeftel, "The Title of the Muscovite Monarch," *Canadian-American Slavic Studies* 13, nos. 1–2 (1979): 65–69.

50. *Vremennik Ivana Timofeeva*, 113, 127, 100. For further discussion on the role of legitimacy in Timofeev's thought, see Rowland, "Towards an Understanding," 391–393 (chapter 2 of this volume).

51. Georges Florovsky has written eloquently about the Muscovite preoccupation with "established order" and its stifling effect on culture in "The Problem of Old Russian Culture," *Slavic Review* 21, no. 1 (March 1962): 11–15.

52. *Novaia povest' o preslavnom Rossiiskom tsarstve i sovremennaia ei agitatsionnaia patrioticheskaia pis'mennost'*, ed. N. F. Droblenkova (Moscow-Leningrad: Izd-vo Akademii nauk, 1960) (hereafter *Novaia povest'*), 192.

53. Kern (*Kingship and Law*, 149–180) describes the early medieval Western European view of the law in terms that are close to the concept of the law that emerges from the tales about the Time of Troubles.

54. *Vremennik Ivana Timofeeva*, 110. The apocalyptic theme, which became so important in Old Believer political statements, is already hinted at here in the phrase "when the years came to an end." Elsewhere Timofeev equates the *oprichniki* with evil, and possibly with the devil (see Rowland, "Toward an Understanding," 394 [chapter 2 in this volume]).

55. *Vremennik Ivana Timofeeva*, 101. See also his description of the First Pretender, at 89.

56. *Vremennik Ivana Timofeeva*, 133.

57. See, for example, the strong statement against a rupture of the social order by the author of the first redaction of Palitsyn's *Skazanie* (*Skazanie Avraamia Palitsyna*, 269): "Everyone began to want to climb higher than his own rank to which he was called; servants wanted to be masters, the unfree leapt for freedom, and military servitors began to behave like boayrs [*voinstvennyi zhe chin boliarstvovati nachinakhu*]." For other references, see Rowland, "The Problem of Advice," 267–268 (chapter 3 in this volume).

58. *Vremennik Ivana Timofeeva*, 75, 87, 101, 104.

59. *Skazanie Avraamiia Palitsyna*, 252. This opinion did not prevent the author from condemning Muscovites for failing to help the poor (276–277) or from bitterly denouncing the way noble masters treated their servants (255–256).

60. It follows that the descriptions of the actual administration of Boris Godunov, the ruler most admired for his administrative skills, should emphasize in traditional fashion the role of the tsar as a preserver and corrector of an already-established state order. Timofeev provides the best example:

> In the beginning of his life he was virtuous in every way. First, he did good deeds above all for God and not for people; he was an ardent zealot for piety and a diligent guardian of the ancient ecclesiastical order [*po drevnikh o tserkvakh s chinmi*]; he was a generous donor to those in need, and meekly inclined [his ear] to the people's petitions about everything, was sweet in his answers to all who showed grace to their offenders, and a speedy avenger of the helpless and widows. He took great trouble over the government of the land and was an unbribable lover of justice and a frank eliminator of any kind of injustice . . . [he beautified the cities with buildings]. In his time the domestic life of all proceeded quietly, without offense, even until the beginning of anarchy [*samobeznachal'stvo*]

in the land after him. He turned with anger on those who ravished the powerless, unless he did not hear about it, and was a strong defender of those offended by the hand of the strong; in general, he showed abundant concern for the strengthening of the whole land when he was not preoccupied with ambition. He everywhere rooted out with punishments the extreme habit of drunkenness, which was loathsome to God, and mercilessly punished any bribe-taking by the great with death, for it was hateful to him . . . , but in all of this he deceived all of Russia. (*Vremennik Ivana Timofeeva*, 65)

Parallel passages in our other sources praise essentially the same qualities in Godunov: his hatred of corruption, his generosity to the poor, his construction of churches and other buildings, and, especially, his protection of the weak against the depredations of the mighty. The *Khronograf* calls him "a sea of gifts, a lake of nourishment [to the poor]." See the "Orison on the Capture and final Destruction . . . of the Muscovite State" (*RIB*, vol. 13, col. 224); Khvorostinin (*RIB*, vol. 13, col. 532); the *Khronograf of 1617* (*RIB*, vol. 13, cols. 1282–1283); *Skazanie Avraamiia Palitsyna*, 252; Iov, *PSRL*, vol. 14, pt. 1, 6–7. This image of the tsar as a protector of the poor is also at variance with the usual view of Muscovite ideology.

61. See Rowland, "The Problem of Advice" (chapter 3 in this volume).

62. Pipes, *Old Regime*, 66; Edward L. Keenan, *The Kurbskii-Groznyi Apocrypha: The Seventeenth-Century Genesis of the "Correspondence" Attributed to Prince A. M. Kurbskii and Tsar Ivan IV* (Cambridge, MA: Harvard University Press, 1971).

63. Pipes, *Old Regime*, 230.

64. R. G. Skrynnikov, *Nachalo oprichniny* (Leningrad: Izd. Leningradskogo universiteta, 1966), 384. The exact content of Filipp's speech (or speeches) cannot be determined without manuscript work, since the chief source, his *Vita*, which exists in two redactions, has not yet been published. The work of most scholars is based on the second, later, redaction, which contains lengthy additions to Filipp's speeches drawn from Agapetus. G. G. Latysheva's article, "Publisisticheskii istochnik po istorii oprichniny (K voprosu o datirovanii)," *Voprosy istoriografii i istochnikovedeniia otechestvennoi istorii* (1974), 30–62, provides excerpts from the first redaction. G. P. Fedotov's *Sviatoi Filipp, metropolit moskovskii* (Paris, 1928) provides a lengthy, easily available paraphrase of the second redaction of the *Vita*. An English translation of Fedotov's monograph is *Saint Filipp, Metropolitan of Moscow—Encounter with Ivan the Terrible*, vol. 1 of *Collected Works*, trans. Richard Haugh and Nicholas Lupinin (Belmont, MA: Nordland, 1978).

65. *Sobranie gosudarstvennykh gramot i dogovorov, khraniashchikhsia v Gosudarstvennoi kolegii innostrannykh del*, 5 vols. (Moscow, 1813–1894), 1:557–58.

66. Latysheva, "Publitsisticheskii istochnik," 58.

67. Fedotov, *Sviatoi Filipp*, 142.

68. Fedotov, *Sviatoi Filipp*, 144, 147.

69. Fedotov, *Sviatoi Filipp*, 148.

70. Fedotov, *Sviatoi Filipp*, 152.

71. Latysheva, "Publitsisticheskii istochnik," 57–58.

72. The best discussion of this entire episode is chapter 5 of A. A. Zimin's *Oprichnina Ivana Groznogo* (Moscow: Mysl´, 1964), a discussion that includes a careful analysis of the family and service connections of the individuals involved. Zimin sees the

affair as a crucial part of the necessary liquidation of the church as "a state within a state," a process finally completed by Peter the Great.

73. On this episode, see Zimin, *Oprichnina*, 202–210, and Skrynnikov, *Nachalo oprichniny*, 308–352. Albert Schlichting says that "300 noble members of the tyrant's court" were present. Albert Schlichting, "'A Brief Account of the Character and Brutal Rule of Vasil'evich, Tyrant of Muscovy' (Albert Schlichting on Ivan Groznyi)," ed. and trans. Hugh F. Graham, *Canadian-American Slavic Studies* 9, no. 2 (Summer 1975): 248–249. The *Piskarevskii letopisets* describes the meeting thus: "And there was hatred for the tsar from all the people [in the *zemskii sobor*] and they petitioned him orally and handed him a signed petition saying it was *improper* [*ne dostoin*] for such a thing as the *oprichnina* to exist" (my italics). O. A. Iakovleva, ed., *Materialy po istorii SSSR* 2 (1955): 76.

74. Schlichting, "A Brief Account," 217.

75. The account of these events in the *Piskarevskii letopisets* gives the same impression. For citations to both Skrynnikov and the *Piskarevskii letopisets*, see above, note 73.

76. Pipes, *Old Regime*, 232.

77. I use the text provided by Donald G. Ostrowski in "A 'Fontological' Investigation of the Muscovite Church Council of 1503" (PhD diss., Pennsylvania State University, 1977), 416–491, based on *Gosudarstvennaia publichnaia biblioteka*, Ms. Q. I. 214, fols. 464–468. This passage occurs at p. 426 of the thesis. Two of the manuscript copies add "or to judge such things." For the stemma indicating the relationship of the various manuscripts of the "Reply," see 143. Ostrowski convincingly refutes the contention by G. N. Moiseeva that the "Reply" represents a later version of an earlier "Message" (*pisanie*) (133–139).

78. Ostrowski, "A 'Fontological' Investigation," 489. See also 486.

79. For a comparison of the contents of the "Reply," the "Message," and the Stoglav chapters, as well as further textological remarks, see Jack E. Kollmann Jr., "The Moscow *Stoglav* (Hundred Chapters) Church Council of 1551" (PhD diss., University of Michigan, 1978), 95–99. Val'denberg (*Drevnerusskie ucheniia*, 282–287) discusses at some length those sections of the Stoglav decisions that limit the tsar's power.

80. For two apparently contemporary versions of the service, see E. V. Barsov, *Drevnerusskie pamiatniki sviashchennago venchaniia tsarei na tsarstvo* (Moscow: Moskovskii universitet, 1883; repr., Paris: Mouton, 1969), 42–90. I rely chiefly on the admonition (*pouchenie*) given by the metropolitan to the tsar (56–60, 80–84). The speech of the tsar (48, 73–74) is much terser, and stresses the hereditary rather than the divine source of his authority. The source thus well illustrates the tension between the patrimonial and the Christian concepts of rulership. The alternate readings given by Barsov for the metropolitan's admonition expand on the ideas in the basic text, but do not alter its sense.

81. Barsov, *Drevnerusskie pamiatniki*, 184. David Miller has pointed out that Makarii in his other works emphasized the responsibilities of the tsar to obey God's will as well as his great power in "The Velikie Minei Chetii and the Stepennaia Kniga of Metropolitan Makarii and the Origins of Russian National Consciousness," *Forschungen zur osteuropäische Geschichte* 20 (1973): 277 and so on.

82. The letter is printed in D. P. Golokhvastov and [Archimandrite] Leonid, "Blagoveshchenskii ierei Sil'vestr i ego pisaniia," *Chtenie v Imperatorskom Obshchestve istorii i drevnostei rossiskikh pri Moskovskom universitete* (1874), bk. 1, sec. 1, 231–257. The authorship of the letter remains to be established beyond a doubt (see Kollmann, "The Mos-

cow *Stoglav*," 106–107), although Sil'vestr seems the most likely candidate. For information on Sil'vestr, see A. A. Zimin, *Peresvetov i ego sovremenniki* (Moscow: Izd. Akademii nauk, 1958), 41–53; and I. I. Smirnov, *Ocherki politicheskoi istorii russkogo gosudarstva 30–50kh godov XVI veka* (Moscow-Leningrad: Izd. Akademii nauk, 1958), 202–263.

83. Golokhvastov and Leonid, "Blagoveshchenskii ierei Sil'vestr," 73, 77, 82.

84. Golokhvastov and Leonid, "Blagoveshchenskii ierei Sil'vestr," 82.

85. Golokhvastov and Leonid, "Blagoveshchenskii ierei Sil'vestr," 77, 80, 73–74, 72, and passim.

86. Golokhvastov and Leonid, "Blagoveshchenskii ierei Sil'vestr," 72 and passim.

87. For Makarii's and Sil'vestr's "party affiliations," see Zimin, *Peresvetov*, 42–44, 72–73. Zimin provides rather little evidence for Sil'vestr's pre-1550 Non-possessor connections, but repeatedly refers to "Sil'vestr and his non-acquisitor circle" (47, 48). His arguments that Sil'vestr is the most likely author for the "Letter to Ivan" (50–53) are persuasive, if not conclusive. For an effective critique of those who exaggerate the mutual differences and internal cohesion of these two church "parties," see Kollmann, "The Moscow *Stoglav*," 87–92, and Ostrowski, "Church Polemics."

88. Zimin, *Oprichnina*, 240–243, 237–239.

89. Indeed, the entire image of Sil'vestr usually held by historians may be the result of later literary fictions. For a brief summary of the literature on this problem, see Kollmann, *Kinship and Politics*, 179–180, 264nn161–164.

90. On the political activities of holy fools, see Giles Fletcher, *Rude and Barbarous Kingdom*, ed. Lloyd E. Berry and Robert O. Crummey (Madison: University of Wisconsin Press, 1968), 218–220; and G. P. Fedotov, *The Russian Religious Mind*, vol. 2 (Cambridge, MA: Harvard University Press, 1966), 338–342. Fedotov calls holy foolishness "a form of prophetic service, in the ancient Jewish sense." Fletcher reports that the holy fools "note their great men's faults that no-one else dare speak of." The best-documented example of a holy fool who influenced Ivan is Nikola, a holy fool from Pskov, who apparently persuaded Ivan either partially or wholly to abandon his destruction of that city. For the sources mentioning this event, see Zimin, *Oprichnina*, 302nnl, 2.

91. *RIB*, vol. 39 (Leningrad, 1927), col. 753. See also the same expression in the second petition (col. 752).

92. These comparisons occur not in the petitions, but in Avvakum's "Book of Interpretation and Moral Teachings" (*RIB*, vol. 39, cols. 473–475, 479).

93. *RIB*, vol. 39, col. 728.

94. *RIB*, vol. 39, col. 758.

95. *RIB*, vol. 39, col. 760.

96. *RIB*, vol. 39, col. 757. The Agapetus chapters are 21 and 18; see Sevcenko, "A Neglected Byzantine Source," 83, 91.

97. *RIB*, vol. 39, col. 763–764.

98. "Kurbskii" calls Ivan a "newly appeared beast" and the *oprichnina* "a strong and great satanic host" in J. L. I. Fennell, *Kurbsky's History of Ivan IV* (Cambridge: Cambridge University Press, 1965), 176–177, 156–157. I. I. Polosin, the scholar who has probably expended more thought and energy on Timofeev's *Vremennik* than anyone else, was of the opinion that Timofeev at different times may have considered both Ivan IV and Godunov as Antichrists. See I. I. Polosin, "Ivan Timofeev-russkii myslitel',

istorik, i d′iak XVII v.," an article printed in a posthumous collection of his essays, *Sotsial′ no-politicheskaia istoriia Rossii* (Moscow: Izd. Akademii nauk, 1963), 313.

99. This point is crucial for our argument since, if Michael Cherniavsky is right that "toward both Church and state, the Old Believer, Avvakumian positions appear far more consistently revolutionary and 'reformist' than has generally been thought," the Old Believers were acting outside of, rather than within, the bounds of traditional Muscovite thought, and the schism cannot be explained in terms of that thought. Michael Cherniavsky, "The Old Believers and the New Religion," *Slavic Review* 25, no. 1 (March 1966): 1–19. I do not deny that the Old Believers and Avvakum were creative thinkers, or even that the "apocalyptic mood of the mid-seventeenth century" (16) had an influence on apocalypticism among Old Believers. Nevertheless, apocalypticism was a part of the tsar-tormentor image at least from the Time of Troubles, as we have seen by the language used to describe Ivan IV and the First Pretender. Traditional Muscovite political thought provided the basic vocabulary of political ideas within which the Old Believers operated, whether or not these were reinforced by other influences.

100. Crummey, *Aristocrats and Servitors*; Kollmann, *Kinship and Politics*.

101. Kollmann, *Kinship and Politics*, 146–151.

102. Kollmann, *Kinship and Politics*, 147–148.

103. Sigismund Freiherr von Herberstein, *Notes upon Russia*, trans. R. H. Major, 2 vols. (London: Hakluyt Society, 1851–1852), 1:32.

104. Paul Bushkovitch ("The Formation of a National Consciousness," esp. 363–374) has recently shown that the image of a "good" tsar included the important element of harmony between the tsar and his boyars, and argues that this harmony was "the essence of the Russian polity" (368). The sources we have considered do not contain much evidence on this point (since they describe potentially or actually sinful monarchs), but Bushkovitch's evidence is persuasive. A pious tsar is united in will and purpose to pious wise advisers since both are following the will of God. Of course, as Bushkovitch points out, consultation or even harmony between tsar and elite do not guarantee anything, since evil rulers can exist in evil harmony with evil flatterers, as was seen to have happened during the Time of Troubles. Still, the point that a righteous tsar was supposed to live in harmony with his boyars is an important one, and shows that the collegial image of tsar and boyars applied to righteous as well as to sinful rulers.

105. Robert Crummey has studied this phenomenon in seventeenth-century court rituals, see "Court Spectacles," 136–138.

106. See Rowland, "Towards an Understanding," 398–399 (chapter 2 in this volume).

107. The best recent account of the change in ideology under Peter from religious to absolutist is James Cracraft, "Empire vs. Nation: Russian Political Theory under Peter I," *Harvard Ukrainian Studies* 10, nos. 3–4 (December 1986): 524–533. On the "well-ordered police state" in its peculiar Russian manifestation, see Marc Raeff, *The Well-Ordered Police State: Social and Institutional Change through Law in the Germanies and Russia (1600–1800)* (New Haven, CT: Yale University Press, 1983), 181–250.

CHAPTER 5

The Memory of Saint Sergius in Sixteenth-Century Russia

According to the *Kazanskaia istoriia*, one of the most important texts describing Russia's conquest of the Khanate of Kazan' in 1552 by Ivan the Terrible, Saint Sergius appeared in a number of omens and dreams connected with the conquest. During the siege of Kazan', Russian soldiers experienced visions of the saint sweeping the places of worship, streets, and squares of Kazan', presumably cleansing them allegorically of their Muslim associations on the eve of the conquest. When a boy asked him the reason for his work, Sergius replied that he was expecting guests in the city. After the conquest, native Tatars allegedly confirmed the saint's appearance in the town before it was taken. He was seen blessing Kazan' with a cross, and sweeping it clean.[1] In a chapter about omens foretelling the founding of the city of Sviiazhsk, a new town set up near Kazan' to more easily control the newly conquered territory, Sergius is reported to have glorified the town with his blessed signs and miracles.[2] Monks from the Holy Trinity Monastery brought an icon of the Trinity with the Mother of God and two apostles to Ivan just before the storming of the city.[3] Before the conquest, Ivan prayed to Sergius, asking his help against Kazan', as he had earlier helped "our ancestor [Dmitrii Donskoi]

This essay originally appeared in *The Trinity-Sergius Lavra in Russian History and Culture*, ed. Vladimir Tsurikov (Jordanville, NY: Holy Trinity Seminary Press, 2005), 56–69. The author gratefully acknowledges the publisher for permission to reprint this essay.

on the Don River against the infidel Mamai."[4] Other sources confirm this last event, and name one of the representatives of the monastery, *sobornoi starets* (senior monk and member of the monastic council) Andrei Angelov.[5]

These visions and stories testify to the remarkable place that Saint Sergius held in the memories of Muscovites in the sixteenth and seventeenth centuries, in this case, a century and a half and more after the death of the saint.[6] In this short essay, I try to show some of the many ways in which Sergius and his monastery were memorialized during this period. This evidence, which is meant only to indicate some dimensions of a very large subject, will show some of the means that Muscovites used to maintain the memory of Saint Sergius, and to create new memories of him. I argue that the memory of Saint Sergius and his monastery constituted a major part of the identity of the Muscovite state and its imagined connection to God's plans for the salvation of mankind. Since the connection between God's will and the will of the ruler was the main theoretical justification for the Muscovite state, this memory had an important legitimizing function.

There has been a lot of recent scholarship and theorizing about memory. The connection between identity and memory has long been recognized, since without memory an individual human being has no sense of his or her past, and thus no sense of personal identity.[7] The social aspects of memory, how groups of people (states, tribes, other groups) make memories and then conserve them, have been discussed at some length by many authors.[8] Reacting to a perceived "memory crisis" that overtook Western Europe in the nineteenth century, Pierre Nora created the notion of a "memory site" (*lieu de memoire*), a very elastic concept that included particular places (the literal meaning of *lieu*) as well as a vast array of concepts, organizations, and artifacts, including cemeteries, museums, anniversaries; intellectual notions of lineage, generation, and local memory; property law and landscape painting; Tablets of the Law in Jewish culture; statues and monuments or whole ensembles of art and architecture such as Chartres Cathedral or the Palace of Versailles; veterans associations; and "dictionaries, testaments and memoranda drafted by heads of families in the early modern period for the edification of their descendants."[9] This multiplicity of types of memory sites, which of course suggests an almost infinite variety of other types, makes one aware of the many ways in which the physical and cultural world can be saturated with memory and can thus serve for the creation and preservation of individual and collective memories. The whole perceived world, it would almost seem, can be activated into a series of memory sites that provide identities for individuals, families, regions, and nations.

A recent catalog of Luba memory objects provides a wonderful example of this multiplicity of memory sites. (Even though many of these objects date from the twentieth century, the Luba culture described in the catalog seems to have been little affected by the European memory crisis. Neither was the culture of Muscovite Russia, obviously.) The catalog describes a society of historians (*mbudye*) who interpret Luba history according to "memory boards" (*lukasas*), the symbols of which serve as prompts to sacred places, people, and concepts of the Luba past. These symbols (nails, cowry shells, beads arranged in patterns on the flat surface of the wooden *lukasa*) allow ideas about the past to be continuously reinterpreted and reshaped by *mbudye* members in the present in order to provide advice and guidance for the solution of present political or even economic problems (see figure 10.1). The variety of memory devices in Luba culture is dazzling—from architecture, wall painting, and sites in the landscape to body scarification, thrones, and other sacred objects.[10]

Early modern Russian society was similarly saturated with memory and memory sites. Even an abbreviated list would exceed the bounds of this essay, but here we might mention: icons of all types, which memorialized the specifically Christian past, both Slavic and non-Slavic; mural programs in churches and throne rooms alike; the great range of chronicles and other historical texts, to which Muscovites devoted so much of their literary attention; the *Lives* of saints, together with associated miracle stories, and, importantly, their tombs, relics, and other artifacts of remembrance; church building, which memorialized a person or event in Christian history and often also a more recent event in Rus' history as well; secular buildings such as the Kremlin, which was itself such a locus of state memories that it was depicted in the famous icon of Simon Ushakov as the ground from which the tree of the Russian state sprang; and so on.

The story with which we began our discussion allows us some insight into the creation of memory relative to the conquest of Kazan' and the role that the memory of Saint Sergius played in it. In the *Kazanskaia istoriia* and in other related texts such as the *Stepennaia kniga* (*Book of degrees*), the Christian conquest of Kazan' was forecasted by other omens and miracles, including appearances by Saint Nicholas and the Apostles Peter and Paul, and the miraculous ringing of church bells. In this context, Sergius's sweeping signifies the necessary destruction of the many Muslim memories intimately connected with Kazan' and their replacement by new, Christian memories, signifying a new era in the history of the town. His appearance in Sviiazshk, blessing the new town with signs and miracles, provided a foundation set of memories for the future urban center. The mention of monks from the Holy Trinity Monastery magnified this role. They acted as Saint Sergius's representatives in the sixteenth-century present. The icon they brought, the life-giving Trinity, including the Mother of God and the Apostles, echoed visions the saint had, as reflected in his *Vita* written a century and a half earlier by Epiphanius the Wise. This icon, and the invocation of Sergius by none other than Ivan IV himself, brought the saint into the very heart of the narrative of the conquest. In this way, both Kazan´ and, perhaps even more, the new town of Sviiazhsk, became new memory sites for Sergius and his monastery. According to the *Kazanskaia istoriia*, a church was established in Sviiazhsk in Sergius's honor at the very founding of the town, and many healing miracles followed, attributed to the icon of Saint Sergius. The author then recounts Ivan's determination to make his new town as splendid as possible by building beautiful structures and endowing them with sumptuous gifts. "Thus also our Blessed Father Sergius the Miracle-worker," the author continues, "beautified and glorified *his* new town [*novyi grad svoi*] with his signs and miracles, so that all would know from that time that [Sergius] wished to live there without leaving, and [wished] to preserve his town and all the people living in it under his protection from the barbarians forever. And before us all he was the joyful, truthful herald [*vestnik*], [telling us] about the final great destruction of the Kazanians."[11]

In keeping with this idea, Ivan IV, already in 1553, the year after the conquest, granted the Holy Trinity Monastery special privileges in the Kazan´ area, including permission to obtain land in the city of Kazan´ and certain trading privileges.

These references to Sergius make sense, of course. As Ivan himself remarked, Sergius, as depicted in his *Vita* and in later texts, urged Dmitrii Donskoi to attack Mamai before the Battle of Kulikovo Field, and supported him in prayer during the battle itself, so that, through Sergius's intercession, God gave victory to Dmitrii. By 1552, Sergius had become a potent anti-Tatar force in the minds of Rus´ warriors, or at least in the minds of anti-Tatar propagandists. A story about a miracle by Saint Sergius was included, for example, in narratives of the defeat of Muscovite forces at the battle of Belev in 1438 in both the Second Sophia and the L´vov Chronicles, showing that the association of the saint with victory over steppe Muslims (apart from his role in the battle of Kulikovo Field) dates back at least to the fifteenth century.[12]

In Orthodox culture, icons provide one of the most powerful tools of memory. Their sacred character, the close theological connection that they depend on between the image and its original, and the ability to transport and create copies of an icon—all these features make icons exceptionally powerful *lieux de memoire*. Let us return for a moment to the story of the conquest of Ka-

THE MEMORY OF SAINT SERGIUS IN SIXTEENTH-CENTURY RUSSIA 119

zan', when monks from Sergius's Holy Trinity Monastery brought an icon of Sergius to Ivan IV as he was besieging the city: At one level, the icon of Sergius brought the saint symbolically into Ivan's presence, since Sergius was seen as present in some degree in his icon. This presence, justified by the Orthodox theology of the icon, is graphically illustrated by Ivan's prayer to Sergius before the icon. Thus an icon as a memory device could not only create and preserve the memory of a sacred personage, but could make that person symbolically present centuries after his or her death, capable of acting in this case in the sixteenth-century world and causing important changes in the personal and political events of the time. The *Kazanskaia istoriia* tells us that Ivan and his troops were transformed by the appearance of the icon in their camp, and strongly implies that, from that moment on, the victory over the Kazanians was assured.[13] Thus the memory of Sergius, activated by his icon, achieved a prodigious effect indeed, at least in this one text.

A closer examination of this icon will allow us to make this memory and the way it worked a little more precise. The *Kazanskaia istoriia* describes the Sergius icon as "a holy icon on which was painted the image of the Life-giving Trinity and the Most Pure Mother of God with two apostles, the vision [*videnie*] of Sergius the Miracle-worker."[14] This vision is recounted in Epiphanius's *Life of Sergius*. The saint and one of his disciples went from Sergius's cell into the adjoining passage,

> and suddenly a great light spread over the saint, greater than the shining sun, and he then saw the Most Pure [Mother of God] Herself, with two Apostles, Peter and John. The Mother of God then said to Sergius, "Do not be terrified my chosen one; I came to visit you. Your prayer for your disciples for whom you prayed and for your abode [*obitel'*] was heard. You should not worry any more, for from now on there will be everything in abundance, and not only as long as you live, but even after your departure to the Lord, I will never leave your refuge, providing all necessities and protecting the donors."[15]

One can conclude from this vision that it was the Mother of God's promise of protection and sustenance to Sergius and his followers that was invoked by the icon. As the other passages in the text that we have discussed make clear, both Sviiazhsk and Kazan' after its conquest were seen as the "abodes" of Sergius. Thus the creation of these two towns as loci for the memory of Sergius was seen as bringing to the towns and their inhabitants the benefits announced in Sergius's vision. This message of course resonates with the messages of the other sections of the text dealing with Sergius, promising the saint's intercession in battle and his protection of the towns after the conquest.

What did the icon referred to look like? I have not been able to find a sixteenth-century icon of this configuration, but there are some clues. The depiction of the Holy Trinity probably was of the Old Testament Trinity shown in a semicircle, possibly "painted in the Rublev style" as in a sixteenth-century icon of Saint Sergius now in the collection of the Tretiakov Gallery.[16] Below an image of the Old Testament Trinity, the saint appears accompanied by the Mother of God and the two apostles who appeared in Sergius's vision, Peter and John. Jenn Spock, a scholar of the history of the Solevetsky Monastery now teaching at Eastern Kentucky University, recently compiled a list of icons held by that monastery based on manuscript inventories compiled in the sixteenth and early seventeenth centuries. According to an inventory compiled in 1613 by Igumen Irinarkh, there were six icons of Saint Sergius in the Transfiguration Cathedral at Solovki, and three in the Dormition Cathedral.[17] This number is surprisingly large, and, while not approaching the number of icons of Saint Nicholas (the patron saint of sailors and fishermen), for example, or Zosima and Savatii, the founders of the Solovetsky Monastery, it attests also to the importance of the memory of Saint Sergius even in this remote place. More interesting, five of the six icons in the Transfiguration Cathedral and one of the three in the Dormition Cathedral were not of Saint Sergius alone, but were titled "The Vision of Sergius." According to the inventory, the icons included the Mother of God "with Apostles." These icons surely represent the same icon type that was allegedly brought by monks of the Holy Trinity Monastery to Ivan IV before the conquest of Kazan'. If so, then the protection and sustenance offered by the Mother of God to Sergius, his "abode," and his followers must have resonated with a remote monastic community not founded by Sergius, and not directly connected to his monastery. Here again, icons of the saint served as preservers and creators of his memory far from the Holy Trinity Monastery itself. In this case, the memory would be renewed annually on Sergius's feast day, when the monks would pray to him and remember his vision and the promises contained in it.

If icons of the saint and monks from his monastery could promote his memory far from Sergius's own monastery the monastery itself remained perhaps the most potent reminder of the saint's importance. This strengthening of his memory was accomplished in many ways, including the increasingly elaborate buildings of the architectural ensemble constructed within the monastery walls, and the walls themselves, which, by the end of the sixteenth century, made the monastery one of the most heavily fortified sites in Russia. As a visitor progressed through the massive gates of the monastery and past the impressive cathedrals, churches, and other monastic buildings, the institutional strength and physical wealth of the monastery would have been obvious, and would have created for the visitor, especially for a pilgrim, new memories of Saint Sergius and his hoped-for intervention in his or her personal life. (Even today, when our eye for architectural scale has been transformed by seeing vast urban panoramas filled with competing skyscrapers, a visit to the monastery remains a treasured memory for all who visit it.) At the heart of this experience, the final destination of a trip that might have lasted hundreds or even a thousand miles, lay the tomb of the saint, even then decorated in the most sumptuous fashion, and the ongoing prayers sung to the saint by the monks. Here the pilgrim could bring before the saint his or her most urgent and personal needs and prayers.

Pilgrimage was thus another important means of creating and maintaining memories of the saint. From a political point of view, the most important pilgrims were members of the royal family and the court, and their frequent sixteenth-century pilgrimages to the Holy Trinity Monastery made the memory of Sergius something close to an official state requirement. In 1994, Nancy Shields Kollmann published a wonderful article on royal pilgrimages (and hunting trips) in sixteenth-century Russia.[18] Her findings show that the Holy Trinity Monastery was overwhelmingly the main pilgrimage site for rulers and the court. Starting in a trip that Ivan III made to the monastery in 1503 with his son "Grand Prince Vasilii Ivanovich" (his newly announced heir), Muscovite rulers visited the monastery with amazing regularity throughout the century. Kollmann's account details these trips. Although ruler and court visited many other monasteries, and also participated in hunting trips, the Holy Trinity Monastery is by far the most frequently mentioned destination in chronicle accounts of these travels. Autumn trips to coincide with the Feast of Saint Sergius became regular events for the court, but other pilgrimage times and occasions were also common. Vasilii III brought his firstborn (and long-awaited) son, the future Ivan IV, to the monastery for christening in August of 1530, a trip that, as Kollmann observes, "displayed the much-needed male heir to the elite and to the Muscovite populace." Vasilii may well have believed that the birth of Ivan was made possible at least in part by the intercession of the saint, since he had visited the monastery so frequently in the preceding years. Note also the close connection between the cult of the memory of the saint and some of the most important aspects of political life in the Muscovite kingdom. Shortly after the christening, Vasilii, in September 1530, took his wife and infant son back to monastery, in spite of the strain on both mother and son that such traveling must have involved. Two years later, he was back, again with his wife and young son. Vasilii's last pilgrimage, in 1533, just before his death, was also to the Trinity Monastery.[19]

Kollmann describes a similar pattern of pilgrimages throughout the century. Ivan IV in particular went on numerous occasions to the Trinity Monastery. To take only his childhood years, he visited the monastery as a six-year-old in 1536, and then again in the company of changing groups of boyars, in September 1537, September 1538, May and September 1539, June and September 1540, September 1541, May and September 1542, the autumn of 1543, March 1544, and in May and September 1545. In the autumn of 1546 he spent three months on extended pilgrimage to northern monasteries, including the Trinity Monastery. These pilgrimages continued after Ivan's coronation as tsar in 1547, including humble trips on foot by both the young tsar and his wife Anastasia, onward into the 1550s and 1560s.[20] These pilgrimages were significant for several reasons. First, the chronicles mention that many courtiers accompanied the ruler and his family on these trips, thus making the devotions to Sergius at his monastery court functions, not merely private royal prayers. Second, the pilgrimages, especially if they included other monastic destinations, took long periods of time, sometimes two to three months. This was an enormous investment of scarce time and money by the court, and shows the great importance accorded to these pilgrimages, especially of course to those to the Sergius Trinity Monastery.

There are several explanations for this importance. First, pilgrimages displayed for audiences all along the pilgrimage route from the capital to the monastery the personal piety of the ruler, a crucial ingredient in creating the image of a God-chosen legitimate ruler, as I have argued elsewhere. But these extraordinarily frequent pilgrimages may be read in a different sense. The memory of Saint Sergius (and other important saints of Rus') was crucial to the official image of the Muscovite state as a divinely chosen instrument of God's will. The fact that the land of Rus' was blessed by the lives and holy works of these saints was read as a supremely important sign of God's favor. Pilgrimages kept Sergius's life and deeds alive, not merely as a passive memory, but as a source of God's continuing favor, whether in battle or in the all-important quest for male heirs. Simon Ushakov's famous painting of Tsar Aleskei Mikhailovich watering the "Blessed Tree of the Muscovite Tsardom," painted in the 1660s, makes this point beautifully, though it was painted well beyond the bounds of the sixteenth century. The right branches of the tree (from the viewer's point of view) are occupied by Russian saints, especially monastic saints, with Saint Sergius in a most prominent place. The memory of these saints, symbolically cultivated by the tsar and his family, is depicted as part of the very foundation of the Russian state.[21]

One final means of commemorating Saint Sergius should be mentioned, though only in passing. The Holy Trinity Monastery not only served as a pilgrimage site in times of peace, but also played an important role during the Time of Troubles, in times of war. The monastery was never conquered by the Poles, who occupied most of central Russia, including the Kremlin. As the last remaining unconquered outpost of Orthodoxy amid a sea of occupying Catholic Poles, the monastery played a crucial role in arousing the country to resistance, and directly inspired the two national militias that eventually freed Moscow and much of the Muscovite state from Polish troops. I will not go into detail about these events, which are in any case fairly well known. Here I only mention that this direct political activity by the monks of the monastery illustrates another important way in which Saint Sergius was memorialized. His memory gave authority to the letters sent around by the monastery, and, after the election of Mikhail Romanov in 1613, Sergius and his monastery gained in stature and influence because of their role in the dramatic events at the close of the Troubles.

This brief discussion of the ways in which the memory of Saint Sergius was used during the sixteenth and early seventeenth centuries allows us a glimpse into some of the uses of memory in Muscovite Russia. The memory of Saint Sergius was not merely a passive remembrance of his holy life, though that memory, enshrined in Epiphanius's famous *Life*, was also important to generations of Russian monks and perhaps laymen as well. The memory of Sergius, encapsulated in a variety of *lieux de memoire*, was an active force in early modern Russia, constantly recreated to suit new circumstances, including the battle for Kazan´, the founding of Sviiazhsk, the need for spiritual and material security under the protection of the Mother of God in many corners of Muscovy, prayers for a new heir, the display of the piety of a ruler, or the projection of the power of the tsardom outward from Moscow into the provinces. This list represents no doubt only a small portion of the uses to which the memory of the saint was put by resourceful Muscovites, lay as well as clerical. Through the many memory devices available within Orthodox culture and beyond, Saint Sergius was conceived in sixteenth-century Russia as a living, vital force who affected events large and small on a daily basis.

Notes

1. *Kazanskaia istoriia*, ed. G. N. Moiseeva (Moscow-Leningrad: Izd. Akademii nauk, 1954), 139–140.

2. *Kazanskaia istoriia*, 88.

3. *Kazanskaia istoriia*, 88.

4. *Kazanskaia istoriia*, 140.

5. These stories are related in Jaroslaw Pelenski, *Russia and Kazan: Conquest and Imperial Ideology (1438–1560s)* (The Hague: Mouton, 1974), 229.

6. The dating of the *Kazanskaia istoriia* is disputed. Most scholars suggest a date in the 1560s, but Edward L. Keenan has argued that the first version of the text was not composed until early in the seventeenth century. See Pelenski, *Russia and Kazan*, 124–135; Keenan, "Coming to Grips with the *Kazanskaya Istoriya*: Some Observations on Old Answers and New Questions," *Annals of the Ukrainian Academy of Arts and Sciences in the United States* 9, nos. 1–2 (1964–1968): 146–160, 183. If Keenan is right, then the title of this chapter should refer to the memory of Saint Sergius in the sixteenth and early seventeenth centuries. The fact that most manuscripts of the text date to the seventeenth century shows that the saint's memory was alive and well in that century.

7. For a neurological and philosophical discussion of a man who, from alcohol abuse, lost many years of memory and the capacity to create new memories, and thus much of his identity, see Oliver Sacks, "The Lost Mariner," in Sacks, *The Man Who Mistook His Wife for a Hat* (New York: Touchstone Books, 1998), 23–42.

8. See, for example, Eviator Zarubavel, *Time Maps: Memory and the Social Shape of the Past* (Chicago: Chicago University Press, 2003).

9. For the nineteenth-century memory crisis, see Richard Terdiman, *Present Past: Modernity and the Memory Crisis* (Ithaca, NY: Cornell University Press, 1993). For the concept of memory sites, see Pierre Nora, "Between Memory and History: Les Lieux de Memoire," *Representations* 26 (1989): 7–25; the list of memory sites here comes from 22–23.

10. Mary Nooter Roberts, Allen F. Roberts, and S. Terry Childs, eds., *Memory: Luba Art and the Making of History* (New York: The Museum of African Art, 1996).

11. *Kazanskaia istoriia*, 87–88.

12. *Polnoe sobranie russkikh letopisei*, 34 vols. (Moscow-Saint Petersburg-Leningrad, 1846–1978), vol. 6, 150–151; vol. 20, part 1, 240–244; Pelenski, *Russia and Kazan*, 179.

13. *Kazanskaia istoriia*, 87–88.

14. *Kazanskaia istoriia*, 139.

15. *The "Vita" of St. Sergii of Radonezh*, trans. and ed. Michael Klimenko (Boston: Nordland, 1980), 174–175.

16. V. I. Antonova and N. E. Mneva, *Katalog drevnerusskoi zhivopisi XI–nachala XVII vv.*, 2 vols. (Moscow: Iskusstvo, 1963) 2:118, item 507.

17. Institute of Russian History, Saint Petersburg, Collection 2, *opis'* 1, *delo* 130. I am extremely grateful to Spock for this reference.

18. Nancy Shields Kollmann, "Pilgrimage, Procession, and Symbolic Space in Sixteenth-Century Russian Politics," in *Medieval Russian Culture*, vol. 2, ed. Michael Flier and Daniel Rowland (Berkeley: University of California Press, 1994), 163–181.

19. Kollmann, "Pilgrimage, Procession, and Symbolic Space," 170–171.

20. For a list of Ivan's pilgrimages, see Kollmann, "Pilgramage," 171–175.

21. See Antonova and Mneva, *Katalog* 2: 411–413. For beautiful full-color images of the icon, see Engelina S. Smirnova, *Moskovskaia ikona XIV–XVI vekov* (Leningrad: Avrora, 1988), plates 199–200, with clear explanation on p. 308. Showing the current tsar and his family watering the tree of state behind the Kremlin walls and underneath an image of the Dormition Cathedral, the most sacred site in the Kremlin, the icon can be seen as a celebration of the Kremlin as a national memory site, with a prominent place given to Sergius and his monastic associates.

Adding the Visual
Investigating Art and Architecture

Chapter 6

Biblical Military Imagery in the Political Culture of Early Modern Russia
The Blessed Host of the Heavenly Tsar

> "He deemed us soldiers of the Christian Faith
> Willing to die for God. The hour of proof
> Is come. The foes of Charles and God are here
> Before you. Now confess your sins, and pray
> God's bounteous mercy. Then shall I absolve you,
> And if you die, the crown of martyrdom
> Is yours, and yours great Paradise." He spoke,
> And so the Franks, dismounting, knelt them down,
> And Turpin signed them with the cross of God,
> And for a penance bade them deal stout blows.
>
> —Archbishop Turpin's sermon, *The Song of Roland*
>
> But the fight for our planet, physical and spiritual, a fight of cosmic proportions, is not a vague matter of the future; it has already started. The forces of Evil have begun their decisive offensive.
>
> —Aleksandr Solzhenitsyn, Harvard speech, 1978
>
> What a foolish notion
> That killing is devotion
>
> —Holly Near

In a recent review in *The Atlantic*, Neil Postman described the importance of mutually shared stories in the lives of nations, disciplines, and people:

> Human beings require stories to give meaning to the facts of their existence. I am not talking here about those specialized stories that we call novels, plays, and epic poems. I am talking about the more profound

---

This essay originally appeared in *Medieval Russian Culture*, vol. 2, ed. Michael Flier and Daniel Rowland (Berkeley: University of California Press, 1994), 182–212. The author gratefully acknowledges the publisher for permission to reprint this essay. The author would like to thank all the participants of the First Summer Workshop in Medieval Slavic Culture held at UCLA in June of 1990. He owes a special debt to Nancy Sevcenko, who expended a lot of her valuable time helping a neophyte art historian.

stories that people, nations, religions, and disciplines unfold in order to make sense out of the world. For example, ever since we can remember all of us have been telling ourselves stories about ourselves, composing life-giving autobiographies in which we are the heroes and heroines.[1]

What stories did early modern Russians tell themselves about their state, why it existed and why it deserved their allegiance? What image or images did Muscovites have of themselves as a political entity? What story did they see in history, and what role did they envision for themselves? These are some questions to which I hope this essay will provide a partial answer by briefly examining one set of overlapping biblical images. These images depicted the Muscovite state as a re-embodiment of the ancient Israelite army and simultaneously as what the Israelites themselves thought their own army to have been—an earthly representation of the forces of God engaged in a cosmic struggle against the forces of evil.

In states as diverse as medieval Java, Elizabethan England, and nineteenth-century Morocco, commonly believed stories about the state were of enormous political importance because they helped to generate a consensus that made government possible.[2] In Muscovy, the need for such a consensus was particularly urgent because the government, like that of an early medieval Western European state, was relatively weak. In 1450, 1500, or even 1600, Muscovy was economically poorer than most other contemporary European states, had a more rudimentary bureaucratic system, and yet succeeded remarkably well in expanding both its borders and its influence. Faced with relatively slender economic resources and an inability to compel obedience through brute force alone (though brute force was relied upon often enough), Muscovite rulers were of necessity dependent on shared stories, on the "symbolics of power," in Clifford Geertz's phrase, to maintain and expand their power. The idea of heavenly host was, at least potentially, an important source of Russian political loyalty because it was framed in military images that would have been immediately accessible to the most powerful group outside of the tsar himself—the military elite who formed the core of both the court and the army. It also gave this class a divinely sanctioned role to play in world history and God's invincible protection while they were playing it.

Most of the abundant evidence I discuss is located in the Moscow Kremlin, the social, political, and symbolic center of the Muscovite state. The Kremlin seems to fit perfectly Geertz's definition of a "glowing center." Such centers are "essentially concentrated loci of serious acts; they consist in the point or points in a society where its leading ideas come together with its leading institutions to create an arena in which the events that most vitally affect its members' lives take place."³ Such centers convey particular importance to the symbolic events that occur in them and charisma to the people who frequent them. The placement in the Kremlin of multiple images depicting the theme of the host of the heavenly tsar suggests that this idea was of exceptional importance.

The very abundance of evidence on this theme presents a methodological problem: Space limitations here require me to deal briefly with a large number of works on a general level. The biggest danger inherent in this approach is that future research may (and probably will) result in the redating of some of the works I describe. Although many of the works themselves were painted in the seventeenth century, they seem to have been carefully based on earlier paintings that had deteriorated or been destroyed. The date and nature of the earliest iconographical programs and their relationship to what we now see or what was described in the 1670s may never be known with certainty. In theory, all general overviews should await the completion of careful and skeptical investigations into the authenticity and dating of each of the monuments concerned. Since in the case of biblical military imagery in Muscovy, this point will probably never be reached to everyone's satisfaction, I have decided simply to proceed on the basis of present knowledge and to warn my readers of the danger that some pieces of evidence could turn out to come from the seventeenth rather than from the sixteenth century. I hope that this analysis demonstrates that the main ingredients of the idea of the Muscovite army as the "host of the Heavenly Tsar" were already present in Moscow by 1500. The dating of the murals in the Archangel Michael Cathedral remains uncertain, for example, but most of the scenes from the "life" of Michael, discussed below, can already be found in the same church's Saint Michael icon that scholars believe was painted around 1400. These scenes were described in the twelfth century by a Byzantine writer, as we will discuss below.

Limitations of both space and knowledge prevent me from following the traditional path of explaining this theme by tracing in detail the origins of each of its constituent parts. This traditional method would set Muscovite works of art produced at a given moment against earlier examples of the same tradition, and, by throwing into relief what was new, would show the intention of the painter or program designer. Earlier developments are important to show that the basic ingredients of the theme of the blessed host of the Heavenly Tsar had been around for some time, that they were commonplaces in the Orthodox world, both within the cultural sphere of Rus' and outside of it, and that these ideas would have therefore been easily accessible to most people, lay as well as clerical. By design as well as necessity, therefore, I have concentrated below on establishing a plausible reading of several visual texts in the light of Muscovite cultural ideas of the period roughly from 1550 to

1630. In spite of uncertainties of dating, I believe that this reading provides evidence of an important and powerful idea, of a story that, although it has been relatively ignored in recent times, may have given meaning to the lives of many Muscovites.

An emphasis on audience leads to a study of visual rather than textual evidence. In a society that was overwhelmingly illiterate, images were accessible to many more people than written texts were, and there were many more of them. As objects, they were also more powerful. M. T. Clanchy tells the fascinating story of an oral tradition from the reign of Edward I of England in which the Earl of Warenne shows a rusty sword in court to demonstrate the feudal rights acquired by his ancestors at the Norman Conquest. For the earl, the sword was worth much more than words on a paper. Painted or embroidered images were narrative objects whose meaning did not depend on literacy. On a wall they were passive, but as battle standards like the sword of the Earl of Warenne, they became active symbols.[4]

Historians have paid remarkably little attention to this visual evidence. Although both Michael Cherniavsky and David Miller, among American historians, have pointed to a virtual explosion of building and decorating in early modern Russia, conclusions drawn from this material have yet to enter the mainstream of our conceptions about Muscovy.[5] There are other reasons more compelling than the possibly provincial American views of Muscovy. One of the striking features of Muscovite literary life is that much more energy was spent on editing and compiling previously existing works than was expended on the composition of original works.[6] Original texts on general or abstract political subjects are particularly hard to find. Under these circumstances, the mural cycles in the Kremlin and the increasingly complex and didactic icons that were closely related to them may represent the best evidence we have of Muscovy's historical imagination and her political image of herself. Further, it was far harder to copy a mural cycle from another time and place than it was to copy a text, which could be easily transported.

Three sixteenth-century visual works serve admirably to illustrate the range of meanings conveyed in the theme of the blessed host of the Heavenly Tsar and provide evidence for the particular reading of other works that forms the basis of this essay. The most fully investigated is the *Church Militant* icon (figure 6.1), which provides the title for this essay. This icon, measuring seven feet in length, was given its current name, the *Church Militant*, only in the eighteenth century. It was painted apparently to commemorate Ivan IV's victory over Kazan′ in 1552 and to memorialize the holy martyrs who fell during the victorious campaign. Thereafter it was placed prominently near the tsar's place in the Kremlin's Dormition Cathedral, and was listed in an

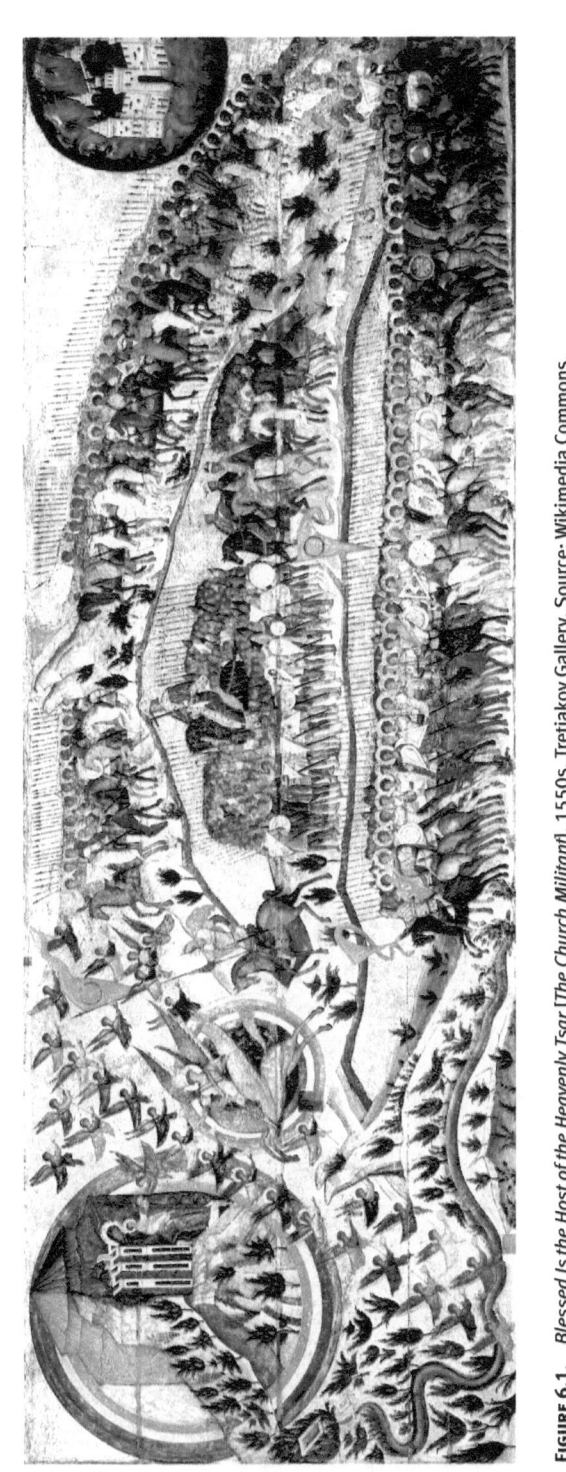

FIGURE 6.1. *Blessed Is the Host of the Heavenly Tsar* [*The Church Militant*], 1550s, Tretiakov Gallery. Source: Wikimedia Commons.

early seventeenth-century description under the title *Blessed Is the Host of the Heavenly Tsar*.

V. I. Antonova made the important discovery that this title comes from a liturgical text commemorating holy martyrs (a point to which we will return), but the icon is also closely linked to two biblical chapters, Daniel 12 and Revelation 19.[7] In Daniel's vision, the Archangel Michael leads the heavenly host against an unnamed northern king in the last days:

> And at that time shall Michael stand up, the great prince [*kniaz' velikii* in the Ostrih Bible] who standeth for the children of thy people, and there shall be a time of trouble such as never was since there was a nation even to that same time; and at that time thy people shall be delivered, every one that shall be found written in the book. (Dan. 12:1)

(Notice here how the language of the Slavonic Bible facilitates the transfer of meaning to a Muscovite military and political context. Moscow had long had its own *velikii kniaz'* standing for the children of God's people.)

In Revelation 19, Christ on a white horse leads an army, conventionally interpreted as an army of martyrs, against the forces of evil at Armageddon:

> 11. And I saw heaven opened and, behold, a white horse; and he that sat on him was called Faithful and True, and in righteousness he doth judge and make war . . .
> 14. And the armies that were in heaven followed him upon white horses, clothed in fine linen, white and clean.
> 15. And out of his mouth goeth a sharp sword, that with it he should smite the nations, and he shall rule them with a rod of iron; and he treadeth the winepress of the fierceness and wrath of Almighty God.
> 16. And he hath on his vesture and on his thigh a name written, KING OF KINGS AND LORD OF LORDS.

In the icon, Ivan IV follows the Archangel Michael in leading the troops of Muscovy as the heavenly host back from Kazan'. Angels fly to those fallen in battle, bringing martyrs' crowns. All are seen returning from Kazan'/Sodom? (Jericho?) to Moscow/Jerusalem in the three-column formation typical of the main part of the Muscovite army in the sixteenth century.

Generations of scholars have argued about the identity of the various figures in the three columns, seeing there Saints Vladimir, Boris, and Gleb, Dmitrii Donskoi, and so forth. A recent and persuasive reinterpretation by I. A. Kochetkov, however, argues from the absence of princely insignia on almost all of these figures and from other evidence that the identification with historical figures beyond Ivan (and possibly three others) was not intended.[8] What

BIBLICAL MILITARY IMAGERY 133

FIGURE 6.2. *Blessed Is the Host of the Heavenly Tsar*, late sixteenth-century copy of the icon in figure 6.1. Museum of the Moscow Kremlin. Source: Wikimedia Commons.

we have then is a straightforward depiction of a contemporary event, Ivan's return from Kazan´, in which the story of the Muscovite conquest of Kazan´ is told in terms of imagery borrowed from the books of Daniel and Revelation as a type of the cosmic struggle of good against evil in the last days.

In her admirably thorough discussion of this icon in the Tretiakov Gallery catalog, Antonova mentions several similar compositions created within the fifty years or so following the painting of this icon.[9] Two of these compositions illustrate important variations on the theme of *The Church Militant*. The first is a smaller, later, and cruder version of *The Church Militant* icon (figure 6.2), which has the same basic features: an army in three columns led by the Archangel Michael on a winged horse moving toward a heavenly Jerusalem on the left from some city on the right, with angels bringing crowns.[10] A crucial difference, however, is that many of the members of the host of the Heavenly Tsar are identified by inscriptions: the Byzantine emperors Leo and Constantine, plus David and Solomon and Saints Vladimir, Boris, and Gleb. A badly damaged inscription appears to take us back again to Revelation 19 (but this time verse 18) as well as to the *stikhira* for martyrs in the fifth tone to be sung in the morning service on Saturdays.[11]

A second example adduced by Antonova is the battle standard of Ivan IV of 1560 (of which I have not found an illustration). Here the Archangel Michael on a winged horse is followed by Christ leading a heavenly host of angels.

An inscription on the banner, from Revelation 19:11–14, shows this to be the Second Coming of Christ, although the Revelation text, of course, makes no mention of Michael.

Biblical references help to explain the meaning of these images. Although there is no biblical equivalent to the phrase "the host of the Heavenly Tsar," rough synonyms like "the host of the Lord" or "His host" do occur. In some passages, particularly in Daniel and Revelation, these expressions refer to a heavenly host in the literal sense of the forces of God or Christ arrayed in a cosmic battle in heaven against the forces of Satan at the end of time (see Dan. 12:1; Rev. 12:7 and 19:11–21, for example). In other passages, they refer to the army of Israel, or, by extension, to Israel as a whole. The Chosen People (or their army) were thus seen as the embodiment of the heavenly host at a given time and place (see Exod. 7:4; 1 Sam. 17:26, 45). The above three works show how the Muscovites understood and appropriated this imagery. The battle standard was meant to invoke the aid of the heavenly host in the cosmic sense during very real earthly battles. The *Church Militant* icon shows the Muscovite army returning from an actual battle (against Kazan´) as the embodiment of the heavenly host, led and aided by the Archangel Michael. In the third example, the icon with identified figures, historical personages from David and Solomon to Boris and Gleb have ascended to join the heavenly host in the battle against evil, possibly understood in this instance as the Tatars of Kazan´. (Note how well this last image coincides with the Muscovite rulers' well-documented desire to emphasize their dynastic links to earlier, particularly Kievan, members of the Riurikovich clan and their political links to Byzantium.)

This interpretation is supported by official pronouncements, particularly by Metropolitan Makarii. Perhaps the best example is his letter to Ivan and his "Christ-loving host" in Sviiazhsk on the eve of the conquest of Kazan´.[12] Makarii states that the Tatars were agents of "the dragon [*zmii*], the cunning enemy, the devil [*diavol*]" and asks that God send the Archangel Michael and other "incorporeal powers" to help the Muscovite army in its fight against Kazan´, just as Michael helped Abraham against the king of Sodom, Joshua against the Canaanites at Jericho, Gideon against the Midianites, and Hezekiah against Sennacherib. The Muscovite host will be strengthened by the prayers of the Theotokos (or Virgin), the Apostles, the Church Fathers, and various Rus´ saints, including Alexander Nevskii, and helped by the aid (*pomoshchiiu i pospesheniem*) of Michael together with four military saints ("passion-sufferers")—George, Dmitrij, Andrej, and Theodore Stratilates—together with Ivan's ancestors Vladimir, Boris, and Gleb. God will send his angels and all the holy martyrs as helpers (*posobniki*) to defeat the enemy. Those who shed their blood in the cause will have all of their sins forgiven, and those who die will go to heaven. Only the apocalyptic dimension of this theme is not explicitly mentioned.

The use that Muscovites made of these images depended on what we might call a typological sense of time, a view that may seem alien to us but would have been perfectly natural to anyone reared in an Orthodox liturgical culture. The same cosmic event—the struggle of God's forces against the forces of evil, surely one of the major preoccupations of the Muscovite historical imagination—was imagined as occurring many times: in the Old Testament, in Byzantium and Kiev, in the sixteenth-century "present," and at the Apocalypse. One version of this struggle was understood as implying the others. Given this typological sense of time, a military serviceman fighting in Kazan' or Livonia could easily imagine himself as part of a cosmic struggle lasting from the Old Testament to the Apocalypse.

These images had powerful resonances in other parts of Muscovite culture. The theme of holy martyrs is perhaps the best example. The veneration of martyrs plays a major role in Orthodox worship; liturgical texts about martyrs consistently use military imagery to describe them and thus reinforce the idea of an actual army of martyrs found in Muscovite sources and in Revelation 19. They are called "faithful soldiers" of Christ who "were not terrified by the threats of the tyrants," as "mighty defenders of the inhabited earth" who gave us "a rampart which cannot be destroyed."[13] A single martyr is called a *muchenik voinstva Khristovi* (a martyr of Christ's army).[14] Note the irony here: A military metaphor to express spiritual strength (martyrs obviously lacked military strength) is taken so literally that it becomes a potent inspiration for military conquest.[15] The recurrent theme of a battle against "tyrants" brings up an interesting linguistic point: The Slavic word *muchitel'* signified both one who torments martyrs (*mucheniki*) and a tyrant, an illegitimate, Godless ruler.[16] Since the persecutors of the early martyrs were usually pagans, this military martyr imagery could naturally be applied to a struggle against the Muslim Tatars, as in fact was done by Metropolitan Makarii just before the battle for Kazan'.[17] The role of martyrs thus links the Muscovite present to the Apocalypse of Revelation 19.

The "King of Kings" who will lead the army of martyrs in Revelation 19 was also an important image in Muscovy. The central prayer of Ivan the Terrible's coronation service was addressed to the "King of Kings and Lord of Lords."[18] The God invoked in the coronation service is thus the commander of the heavenly host. Further, there was in Muscovy an icon type called "the King of Kings" (*tsar' tsarem*). The psalm that serves as the scriptural basis for this type (in the Septuagint 44, in RSV 45) seems to be an ode for a royal wedding in which David and "the queen in gold of Ophir" foreshadow Jesus and

Mary.[19] Verses of the psalm specifically invoke earthly kingship and extend the typological reference to a contemporary ruler and his queen:

> Gird thy sword upon thy thigh, O most Mighty, with thy glory and thy majesty.... Thine arrows are sharp in the heart of the King's enemies; whereby the people fall under thee.... Thou lovest righteousness, and hatest wickedness: therefore God, thy God, hath anointed thee with the oil of gladness above thy fellows. (Ps. 45:3, 5, 7)

The King of Kings was thus a common link connecting the Old Testament, Muscovy, and the Apocalypse; Christ as the commander of the heavenly host was prefigured by David and represented in the "present" by the Muscovite tsar. This identity in turn activated a number of biblical texts like Psalm 45 or Revelation 19 and gave them current political significance.

The idea of a contemporary ruler and his army as a counterpart to Michael and the heavenly host was found well beyond the limits of the *Church Militant* icon. Both canonical and apocryphal biblical texts supported the conviction that each nation had an angel as its heavenly protector. The Archangel Michael became the first of the angels and their general in the battle against Satan and was appointed by God to protect Israel. From the time of Constantine, Michael's cult was associated with the imperial family. The archangel's presence in imperial triumphal iconography may have been connected with the need to replace the pagan Nike, or winged victory, with a Christian counterpart. That the Byzantine court reflected the heavenly court of Jesus and his angels in the heavenly Jerusalem was an idea developed in this early period, with archangels appearing in the dress of Byzantine court officials. Churches were dedicated to Michael from the fourth century on. The earliest known example of an entire mural cycle dedicated to the archangel is in the Hagia Sophia in Kiev, with similar cycles appearing in the Mirozh Monastery in Pskov (founded 1156) and, in a very full set of images, on the south doors of the nativity cathedral at Suzdal' (executed in the 1230s). Impressive murals about Michael can be found in the Balkans, particularly in Lesnovo.[20]

The fully developed idea of a Rus' army as a heavenly host first appears, as far as I know, in the thirteenth-century *Vita* of Alexander Nevskii. Just before the battle with the Swedes, Archbishop Spiridon reminds Alexander of the military value of God's help: "God is not in military power but in truth [*ne v silakh Bog a v pravde*]. Let us remember the psalmist who said: 'Some came with weapons and some came with horses, but we called the Lord God to our help and they were defeated and fell, but we got up and stood straight.'"[21] Spiridon's argument is practical and simple. God's help can give victory even to those at a military disadvantage. This promise is amplified when one of Alexander's men has a vision in which Boris, in a heavenly ship with his brother, says to the latter, "Brother Gleb, order them [the heavenly oarsmen] to row so that we can help our clansman [*srodniku svoemu*] Prince Alexander." This is followed by a marvelous miracle similar [to the one that occurred] in olden times during the reign of King Hezekiah. When Sennacherib, king of Assyria, approached Jerusalem, wishing to plunder the holy city of Jerusalem, suddenly there appeared the angel of the Lord, who killed 185,000 [Assyrian soldiers] and when the next morning came, the bodies were found there. The same occurred during the victory of Alexander, when he defeated the king. On the other shore of the River Izhora, which Alexander's troops did not reach, there were found a very large number [of enemy corpses] killed by the angel of the Lord.[22]

Here we have all the basic features of the iconography of the heavenly host: a contemporary battle seen as an analogue of an Old Testament conflict, help from an angel of the Lord, the protection of deceased princely clansmen (who were also martyrs), victory achieved by means of divine intervention. We saw earlier how military metaphors used to describe the spiritual strength of martyrs were taken literally in Muscovy. A few centuries after the death of the two brothers who peacefully accepted death rather than offer violent resistance, they were themselves turned into warrior-saints whose major function was to fight for the Rus′ land.

Figure 6.3, a thirteenth-century illustration of the Archangel Michael's visit to Joshua on the eve of the battle of Jericho, presents a slightly different Old Testament aspect of this theme. Significant here is the fact that Michael has been read into the story in place of "the *voevoda* of the host of the Lord" in the Ostrih Bible version of the story (Josh. 5:14).

I would argue that this insertion of Michael into biblical stories where he is absent in the relevant canonical texts shows a desire to strengthen and clarify the theme, though whether this addition occurred in Byzantium, in Rus′, or in both is not yet clear. Notice also here the tiny size of Joshua groveling at the feet of Michael.

A large icon of Michael with scenes from his life dating apparently from around the year 1400 contains further evidence for the development of this theme.[23] The border scenes include the meeting with Joshua (figure 6.4) and Michael's slaughtering the 185,000 Assyrian troops to help Hezekiah (figure 6.5), as described in the Nevskii *Vita*. The famous fifteenth-century Novgorod icon of *The Battle of the Novgorodians against the Suzdalians* (currently dated to the 1460s) brings the heavenly host theme into Rus′ history.

Michael in the bottom register (figure 6.6) leads the victorious Novgorodians against the Suzdalians. Notice the anticipation of the *Church Militant*

Figure 6.3. *Joshua and the Archangel Michael before the Battle of Jericho*, thirteenth century, Dormition Cathedral of the Moscow Kremlin. Source: Wikimedia Commons.

FIGURE 6.4. *Joshua and the Archangel Michael before the Battle of Jericho*. Border scene from the icon *The Archangel Michael with Scenes from his Life*, ca. 1400, Museum of the Moscow Kremlin (The Cathedral of the Archangel Michael). Source: V. Mashnina, *Arkhangel Mikhail: ikona "Arkhangela Mikhaila s deianiami" iz Arkhangelskogo Sobora Moskovskogo Kremlia*, Publikatsiia odnogo pamiatnika, no. 1 (Leningrad: Aurora, 1968), plate 19.

iconography in the depiction of Saints Boris, Gleb, George, and Alexander Nevskii, who lead the Novgorodian host.[24] Figure 6.7 shows an early sixteenth-century icon of Saints Vladimir, Boris, and Gleb. In the bottom register, Michael helps the forces of Iaroslav defeat the army of Sviatopolk.[25]

The theme of the host of the Heavenly Tsar appeared frequently in the mural cycles in the Moscow Kremlin, at least after 1547. The destruction wrought by the Moscow fire of that year makes it hard to say what importance the original wall paintings in the Kremlin churches gave to this theme. Some early murals may survive, however. In 1508, Feodosii, the son of the famous icon

140 CHAPTER 6

Figure 6.5. *The Archangel Michael Helps Hezekiah Defeat 185,000 Assyrian Troops*. Border scene from the icon *The Archangel Michael with Scenes from his Life*, ca. 1400, Museum of the Moscow Kremlin (The Cathedral of the Archangel Michael). Source: Mashnina, *Arkhangel Mikhail*, plate 12.

painter Dionisii, painted Michael and Joshua just before the battle of Jericho (figure 6.8) as part of the decoration of the Annunciation Cathedral.[26] The importance of the scene is emphasized by its position next to the door through which Vasilii III entered and left his family church, on the west wall of the choir gallery where the princely family sat. Is it too much to suggest that the author

FIGURE 6.6. *The Battle between the Novgorodians and the Suzdalians*, 1460s, Novgorod Architectural-Historical Museum. Source: Wikimedia Commons.

Figure 6.7. Saints Boris, Vladimir, and Gleb with scenes from the lives of Saints Boris and Gleb, early sixteenth century, Tretiakov Gallery. Source: Wikimedia Commons.

of the program for this church wanted Vasilii to see himself as (among other things) a new Joshua?

Comparisons of Rus´ princes with Old Testament military heroes were literary commonplaces of the time, and this interpretation would have been a natural one. The significance of Joshua and Michael as prototypes and protectors of Muscovite military leaders is illustrated in two later battle standards. The first is an early seventeenth-century banner showing Joshua and Michael under the protection of the God of Sabaoth (figure 6.9). The second (figure 6.10) is a much less elaborate banner painted on linen. It apparently

BIBLICAL MILITARY IMAGERY   143

FIGURE 6.8. *Joshua and the Archangel Michael before the Battle of Jericho*, sixteenth century, Annunciation Cathedral of the Moscow Kremlin. Source: G. Sokolova, *Rospis' Blagoveshchenskogo sobora* (Leningrad: Aurora, 1969), plate 22.

belonged to Ermak, the conqueror of Siberia, and shows him in his late sixteenth-century battle gear being blessed by Michael, as Joshua was blessed by Michael in the previous banner and in the Annunciation Cathedral mural.

On the vault beneath the gallery in the Annunciation Cathedral the Second Coming (figure 6.11) was painted with an inscription condensed from the crucial Revelation 19:11, the first verse of the passage quoted on the battle standard of 1560. Notice the similarity of images to those found on the *Church Militant*

FIGURE 6.9. Battle standard with images of Joshua, the Archangel Michael, and the Lord Sabaoth (known as "the Standard of Sapiega"), early seventeenth century, Tretiakov Gallery. Source: N. Maiasova, *Drevnerusskoe shit'e* (Moscow: Iskusstvo, 1971), plate 54.

icon—the mounted warriors with nimbi, the archangels (but this time two in number), the central figure on a horse. From the point of view of someone standing on the floor below the gallery, directly over this image of Christ as the leader of the heavenly host sat the grand prince, the current embodiment (if my hypothesis is correct) of that ideal. If the apocalyptic dimension of the *Church Militant* iconography needs further illustration, then a late sixteenth-century icon of the Last Judgment from Stockholm (figure 6.12) provides it, with its three columns of holy warriors led by the Archangel Michael.[27]

One might expect this theme of the host of the Heavenly Tsar to appear in the Golden Hall (Zolotaia palata), which served as the chief reception room for Ivan IV and which was decorated sometime between the 1547 fire and 1553–1554, when several of the murals were mentioned in documents connected with the so-called Viskovatyi Affair.[28] We do not find images of the

FIGURE 6.10. Battle standard with images of the Archangel Michael and Ermak, late sixteenth century, Armory Palace of the Moscow Kremlin. Source: *Oruzheinnaia palata,* ed. V. N. Ivanov (Moscow: Moskovskii rabochii, 1964), 68.

Church Militant type, but there were a large number of scenes depicting the victories of the "armies of the Lord" under Moses, Joshua, and Gideon over their various enemies. If the hypothesis about the overlapping ideas that constituted the theme of the host of the Heavenly Tsar is correct (and Makarii's letter to Ivan IV and his troops indicates that it is), these images may be treated as part of the theme. This hypothesis is strengthened by the placement of the Joshua scenes on the walls of the anteroom (*seni*), parallel with a series of scenes from the history of Rus' (the Christianization, transfer of regalia to Vladimir Monomakh) on the walls of the main room. Figure 6.13 shows a reconstruction of two of the Joshua scenes.[29] We see not the Archangel Michael, but God Himself directing military operations. The inscription of the

FIGURE 6.11. *And I Saw Heaven Opened, and Behold a White Horse, and He that Sat Upon Him was Called Faithful and True, and in Righteousness He Doth Judge and Make War*, sixteenth century, Annunciation Cathedral of the Moscow Kremlin. Source: G. Sokolova, *Rospis' Blagoveshchenskogo sobora* (Leningrad: Aurora, 1969), plate 3.

left-hand scene—"the Lord gave Akhil into the hand of Joshua, and Joshua seized him and killed him" (a reference to Josh. 10:30?) emphasizes this divine intervention.[30]

These graphic depictions of the bloody destruction of Israel's enemies would have been entirely accessible to the boyars who frequented the room and were probably far more meaningful to them than was the elaborate Holy Wisdom iconography on the vaults. These military scenes were not repeated when the Palace of Facets, the other main reception hall in the Kremlin, was furnished with an elaborate cycle of wall paintings in the late sixteenth century under Tsar Fedor Ivanovich and his regent Boris Godunov. (They were replaced by a large series of scenes of the life of Joseph, seemingly to illustrate the importance of Godunov's position as regent.) The vault of the chamber, repainted in the nineteenth century according to a detailed description compiled in 1672 by Simon Ushakov, may still contain some material on this theme, but in a surprising form.[31] In depicting the days of creation, the artists inserted a noncanonical (but iconographically traditional) preliminary moment when the nine angelic ranks of the heavenly hierarchy were created. In this scene and two subsequent ones—the Fourth Day with the creation of the sun and moon, and the Seventh Day when God rested—the artist takes the opportunity to go

BIBLICAL MILITARY IMAGERY

FIGURE 6.12. Top register of an icon of the Apocalypse, c. 1550–1575, National Museum, Stockholm, inventory number NMI 271. Photo: Erik Cornelius/National Museum.

well beyond the Genesis account to show the host of the Heavenly Tsar as a heavenly court, which I suggest was meant and taken as a heavenly archetype for the actual court of the earthly tsar of Muscovy, which met in the space immediately below and which was depicted on an adjacent wall. As in Muscovy, the chief warriors of the heavenly host were also counselors of the heavenly court. Comparisons between the Heavenly Tsar and Tsardom and the earthly tsar and tsardom were commonplaces in Muscovite literature, particularly in the works of Joseph Volotskii.[32]

The Palace of Facets murals tempt us toward the civil side of this imagery, though the scene of the Fourth Day does have an archangel gracefully spearing Satan and thus maintains a military action. The murals in the Archangel Michael Cathedral, however, bring us firmly back to the military theme and form a fitting conclusion to this discussion.[33] The north and especially the south walls contained a virtual compendium of Old Testament military stories into which Michael was inserted if the canonical books of the Bible did not already give him a place. On the north wall we find David and the Archangel Michael, the episode of Michael's killing the Assyrian troops mentioned in the Nevskii *Vita*, and Michael showing Daniel the four kingdoms of Daniel's famous vision (Dan. 8:16). On the south wall we see, in descending order: Abraham fighting his enemies with the help of Michael, The Archangel Michael Appoints Moses Prince(!) (figure 6.14), Michael and Joshua, and Michael appearing to Gideon and the subsequent routing of the Midianites.[34] The presence of Michael in stories where the canonical biblical texts give him no

Победы Иисуса Навина. Реконструкция росписи Переходной палаты. Нижний ярус.

FIGURE 6.13. *Joshua Conquering the Promised Land*, reconstruction of lost murals in the Golden Hall of the Moscow Kremlin by K. K. Lopialo. Source: O. A. Podobedova, *Moskovskaia shkola zhivopisi pri Ivane IV* (Moscow: Nauka, 1972).

role emphasizes the idea of the Israelite army as the host of the Heavenly Tsar. In fact, the two walls taken together constitute a sustained hymn to the blessed host of the Heavenly Tsar in its Old Testament guise, made recognizable by the unifying presence of Michael.

The contemporary Muscovite or Rus´ dimension of this theme was provided immediately below these murals. The Cathedral of the Archangel Michael served as the necropolis of the house of Moscow, and the tombs of the members of the Riurikovich clan line the walls, particularly the southern wall. They are accompanied by portraits of the most important clan members. Since these images and tombs have been discussed at length, most recently by Sizov and Cherniavsky, I do not need to list them here.[35] What has not been discussed as far as I know is the connection between these images and tombs on the ground level of the cathedral and the Old Testament scenes above them. This connection is precisely the theme of the heavenly host. In the more sacred space of the upper walls, in the sacred time of the Old Testament, a victorious and sacred battle between the forces of good and evil is proceeding. Again and again, the Israelite armies triumph through the intervention of the Archangel Michael, against whom no enemy can stand. The Old Testament heroes have as their earthly counterparts on the ground level of the cathedral the present embodiment of the blessed host of the Heavenly Tsar: the members of the house of

FIGURE 6.14. *The Archangel Michael Appoints Moses Prince*, seventeenth century, based on sixteenth-century scheme, the Archangel Michael Cathedral of the Moscow Kremlin. Source: Iu. N. Dmitriev, "Stenopis' Arkhangel'skogo sobora Moskovskogo Kremlia," *Drevnerusskoe iskusstvo. XVII vek* (Moscow: Nauka, 1964), plate facing page 150.

Moscow and their ancestors. Thus the Riurikovich clan is shown as the collective descendant of Abraham, Moses, Joshua, Gideon, David, and Hezekiah, as the inheritor of God's protection and the military advantages that that protection brings, advantages graphically symbolized by the Archangel Michael.

This point could be put in terms closer to the Muscovites' own political vocabulary. If we think of the Archangel Michael Cathedral as a kind of giant genealogical book, or *rodoslovnaia kniga* (genealogical book), of the grand princely clan, with both the tombs and portraits in place on the lower parts of the cathedral, then the genealogy is extended by implication as one ascends to the upper walls to include such Old Testament figures as Abraham, Moses, and David. This interpretation coincides with the program of the late sixteenth-century *Church Militant* icon where David and Solomon join Vladimir, Boris, and Gleb in the ranks of the heavenly host, as well as with Makarii's ideas as expressed in his letter to Ivan and his troops.

I have offered considerable evidence to demonstrate the importance of the theme of the host of the Heavenly Tsar in Muscovy in general, and in the Kremlin, the symbolic center of the state, in particular. From the point of view of the creators of the images and texts surveyed, the theme had clear advantages. For the ruler, it provided an image of invincible power under God's protection and glorified the royal clan both politically and genealogically. It thus builds on a well-known motif in Muscovite literature—the glorification of the ruler. What is of particular interest is that these images also provide a crucial role to the Muscovite army. The army is the center of attention in several of these image types (the *Church Militant* and the Old Testament scenes where the Israelite troops are depicted) and is implied in the other images, such as those depicting the Archangel Michael and Joshua. The theme of the host of the Heavenly Tsar thus provides a role in sacred history not only for the ruler but also for his military elite. As they battle against their enemies, the boyars and their subordinates are cast in the role of God's own warriors, aided by the unconquerable sword of the Archangel Michael and assured of martyrs' crowns should they fall in battle.

The theme of the heavenly host fit well with the Orthodox culture of Muscovy. Its striking historical sweep, from the Old Testament to the Apocalypse, accorded well with the historical cast of the Rus' imagination. It mined a very rich vein of liturgical literature on martyrs, and a long tradition, stretching back to Byzantium, venerating Michael as the protector of princes and their armies. It also drew on a plentiful but little-examined group of biblical texts that appear to have taken on political significance in Muscovy. Finally, the use of common terms—*tsar'*, *voevoda*, *velikii kniaz'*, *voinstvo*—facilitated the transfer of meaning from the sacred to the secular realms.

We can say, then, that the theme of the host of the Heavenly Tsar was intended by the framers of official ideology to strengthen the state by giving a sacred role to both the ruler and his nobility. The really tantalizing question is whether the hard-bitten military men of Muscovy took these images seriously or even understood them. As they prepared to attack Kazan´ or slogged through the endless campaigns of the Livonian War, did they really see themselves as the embodiment of the heavenly host?

Because the men concerned were for the most part illiterate, we have little or no direct evidence on this point. Yet I believe that various pieces of indirect evidence suggest that they might well have. The battle standards we have discussed must surely have been chosen because they had at least some meaning for the troops. The touching depictions of Ermak and the Archangel Michael on a simple linen banner in particular seem to reflect the personal sentiment of the Siberian explorer and conqueror. There seems to be a fairly good fit between the little we know of the culture of the military elite and this theme. Two major components of that theme—fighting and clan honor—were also the principal preoccupations of the Muscovite aristocracy. We have discussed common vocabulary, but visual representations of Christ's army or the Israelite army in the Old Testament *looked like* the Muscovite army. And of course all these armies were imagined as doing the same thing: They slaughtered ungodly enemies with fire and sword. The idea of receiving help from one's clan had pagan roots and had been a motif in East Slavic literature since the composition of the *Primary Chronicle*.[36]

Seeing oneself as a member of God's army would surely have provided spiritual comfort amid the violence and danger of war. Almost all Christian states since the time of Christ have attempted to convey this message in one form or another. Perhaps the best analogy to the great boyars who formed the backbone of the Muscovite army is the aristocracy of early medieval Europe. The *chansons de geste* provide useful evidence on the views of this class, since these songs were performed at the pleasure of, and for pay by, the secular courts of Europe. A thoroughly militarized version of Christianity quite similar to the Muscovite idea of the host of the Heavenly Tsar (but admittedly less well developed) can be found in the *Song of Roland*, for example, particularly in Archbishop Turpin's sermon before the battle of Roncevaux.

No doubt secular and even pagan ideas played their part in military minds, but there is no reason to suppose that military men could not have been part of both cultures, religious and secular. Aristocrats, after all, did sometimes become important churchmen. The slender evidence at our disposal thus tends to indicate that the theme of the host of the Heavenly Tsar constitutes a successful symbol. It may well have provided a most useful story for members of the

Russian elite to tell themselves to justify their sacrifices and strengthen their courage. If so, we are entitled to see in this powerful symbol an important political force strengthening the cohesion and military might of the Muscovite state.

Notes

1. Neil Postman, "Learning by Story," *The Atlantic*, December 1989, 122.

2. Clifford Geertz, "Centers, Kings, and Charisma: Reflections on the Symbolics of Power," in *The Rites of Power*, ed. Sean Wilentz (Philadelphia: University of Pennsylvania Press, 1985), 13–38.

3. Geertz, "Centers, Kings, and Charisma," 14, with further references to the work of Edward Shills.

4. M. T. Clanchy, *From Memory to Written Record: England: 1066–1307* (Cambridge, MA: Harvard University Press, 1979), 21–28.

5. Michael Cherniavsky, "Ivan the Terrible and the Iconography of the Kremlin Cathedral of the Archangel Michael," *Russian History/Histoire Russe* 2, no. 1 (1975): 3–28; David Miller, "The Viskovatyi Affair of 1553–1554: The Emergence of Autocracy and the Disintegration of Medieval Russian Culture," *Russian History/Histoire Russe* 8, no. 3 (1981): 293–332.

6. A. I. Sobolevskii, *Perevodnaia literatura Moskovskoi Rusi XlV–XVII vekov* (Saint Petersburg: Imp. Akademiia nauk, 1903), vi.

7. V. I. Antonova and N. E. Mneva, *Katalog drevnerusskoi zhivopisi X–nachala XVII vv.*, 2 vols. (Moscow: Iskusstvo, 1963), 2:131.

8. I. A. Kochetkov, "K istolkovanii ikony 'Tserkov' voinstvuiushchaia' (Blagoslovenno voinstvo nebesnogo tsaria)," *TODRL* 38 (1985): 185–209.

9. Antonova and Mneva, *Katalog*, 2:128–134.

10. M. P. Stepanov, *Khram usypal'nitsa Velikago Kniazia Sergiia Aleksandrovicha vo imia Prepodobnago Sergiia Radonezhskago v Chudovom monastyre v Moskve* (Moscow: Sinodal'naia tip., 1909), 104–105, plate 36.

11. Kochetkov, "K istolkovanii," 209.

12. The letter is found in *Akty istoricheskie, sobrannye i izdannye Arkheograficheskoi kommissiei*, 5 vols. (Saint Petersburg, 1836–1842), 1:290–296; it was incorporated in the *Letopisets nachala tsarstva* published in *Polnoe sobranie Russkikh letopisei* (hereafter *PSRL*), vol. 29 (Moscow, 1965): 86–90. Other documents associated with the metropolitan are described in Jaroslaw Pelenski, *Russia and Kazan: Conquest and Imperial Ideology (1438–1560s)* (The Hague: Mouton, 1974), 194–213.

13. Kochetkov, "K istolkovanii," 204–206; Mother Mary and Archimandrite Kallistos Ware, *The Lenten Triodion* (London: Faber and Faber, 1978), 669, 686, 685, 668–699.

14. *Mineia obshchaia* (Moscow: Patriarchal Press, 1649), f. 71.

15. For an excellent discussion of the militarization of martyr images in Serbia and the development of this theme in Rus' (particularly in Novgorod) at the turn of the fifteenth century when conflict with the Tatars was also a major concern, see O. A. Podobedova, "Voinskaia tema i ee znachenie v sisteme rospisej tserkvi Spasa na Kovaleve v Novgorode," *Drevnerusskoe iskusstvo. Monumental'naia zhivopis' XI–XVII vv.* (Moscow: Nauka,1980), 196–209.

16. See Daniel Rowland, "Did Muscovite Literary Ideology Place Limits on the Power of the Tsar (1540s–1660s)?," *Russian Review* 49 (April 1990): 125–155 (chapter 4 of this volume).

17. *PSRL* 29:89–90; Kochetkov, "K istolkovanii," 190.

18. E. V. Barsov, *Drevne-russkie pamiatniki sviashchennago venchanniia na tsarstvo, v sviazi s grecheskimi ikh originalami*, ChOIDR 1883, bk. 1 (repr., The Hague: Mouton, 1969), 51, 76.

19. Antonova and Mneva, *Katalog*, 1:135–136. For further discussion of this icon type, see E. Ia. Ostashenko, "Ob ikonografii tipa ikony 'Predsta tsaritsa' Uspenskogo sobora Moskovskogo Kremlia," *Drevnerusskoe iskusstvo. Problemy i atributsii* (Moscow: Nauka, 1977), 175–187.

20. The literature on the cult of the Archangel Michael, East and West, is extensive. I have based my brief comments on an excellent recent summary with ample references to other sources: Mina Martens, Andre Vanrie, and Michel de Waha, *Saint Michel et sa Symbolique* (Brussels: Lucien De Meyer, 1979). The classic account of Lesnovo and its predecessors is N. L. Okunev, "Lesnovo," *L'Art byzantin chez les Slavs: Les Balkans*, 2 vols. (Paris: Librairie Orientaliste Paul Guenther, 1930), vol. 1, part 2, 222–259, though later issues of *Zograf* have important supplementary information. V. I. Sventsitskaia has written an excellent brief history of the cult and early images of the archangel in Rus´ as part of a description of a fourteenth-century icon of Michael: "Master ikony 'Arkhangel Mikhail s deianiiami' vtoroi poloviny XIV v. iz sela Storonna na Boikovshchine," *Pamiatniki cultury. Novye otkrytiia* (Moscow: Nauka, 1989), 192–209. A crucial literary source for mural cycles and icons is an account of Michael's miracles by the late twelfth-century deacon Pantoleon of Constantinople, found in J.-P. Migne, "Patrologiae cursus completes ... Series Graeca," 161 vols. (Paris: Migne, 1857–1899), 140 (1887), 574–591. Pantoleon explicitly locates Michael in many scenes that became traditional in Michael's iconography but where canonical texts omit him. I have so far not been able to find evidence of a Slavic translation of this work that was available in Muscovy.

21. "Zhitie Aleksandra Nevskogo," *Pamiatniki literatury drevnei Rusi: XIII vek* (Moscow: Khudozhestvennaia literatura, 1981), 428. A thirteenth-century chronicle source credits Michael and other angels with helping Vladimir Monomakh against the Polovtsians. See Sventsitskaia, "Master ikony 'Arkhangel Mikhail,'" 193, 207.

22. *Pamiatniki literatury drevnei Rusi: XIII vek*, 430–432.

23. For a good description of this icon with excellent plates, see V. Mashnina, *Arkhangel Mikhail: ikona "Arkhangela Mikhaila s deianiiam" iz Arkhangelskogo Sobora Moskovskogo Kremlia*, Publikatsiia odnogo pamiatnika, no. 1 (Leningrad: Aurora, 1968).

24. I follow the identification of the haloed figures made in E. S. Smirnova, V. K. Lauriria, and E. A. Gordienko, *Zhivopis' Velikogo Novogoroda. XV vek* (Moscow: Nauka, 1982), 229.

25. Antonova and Mneva, *Katalog*, 2:60.

26. My description is based on G. Sokolova's *Rospis' Blagoveshchenskogo sobora. Freski Feodosiia (1508) i khudozhnikov serediny XVI v. v Moskovskom Kremle* (Leningrad: Aurora, 1969). I. Ia. Kachalova, N. A. Maiasova, and L. A. Shchennikova, *The Annunciation Cathedral of the Moscow Kremlin* (Moscow: Iskusstvo, 1990), apparently redates the "Feodosii" murals to the middle of the sixteenth century.

27. Helge Kjellin, *Ryska Ikoner* (Stockholm: Svensk literature, 1956), 298–312.

28. The murals were painted over in the 1670s and destroyed when the Golden Hall was pulled down in 1752. We know them from a very careful description compiled by the icon painters Simon Ushakov and Nikita Klement′ev and twice published: see S. P. Bartenev, *Moskovskii kreml ′v starinu i teper′* (Moscow: Sinodal′naia tip., 1916), 183–193; and I. E. Zabelin, *Materialy dlia istorii, arkheologii, i statistiki goroda Moskvy*, 2 vols. (Moscow: Moskovskaia gorodskaia tip., 1884), 1:1238–1255. The dating of the murals Ushakov and Klement′ev described is a complicated question, too complicated to be resolved here. Watermark analysis most kindly carried out by D. M. Bulanin has shown that an early manuscript (GPB, Pogodin Collection, n.1564) containing the Viskovatyi documents dates from the 1550s or the 1560s. This evidence suggests that most or all of the iconographical scheme described by Ushakov and Klement′ev was already in place by 1553–1554, although it may have been repainted one or more times as a result of fires or natural deterioration.

29. O. A. Podobedova, *Moskovskaia shkola zhivopisi pri Ivane IV: Raboty v Moskovskom kremle 40-kh–70-kh godov XVI v.* (Moscow: Nauka, 1972), appendix by K. K. Lopialo.

30. Bartenev, *Moskovskii kreml′*, 192.

31. Zabelin, *Materialy*, 1255–1271; Aida Nasibova, *The Faceted Chamber in the Moscow Kremlin* (Leningrad: Aurora, 1978), 11–12.

32. David Goldfrank, ed. and trans., *The Monastic Rule of Iosif Volotsky* (Kalamazoo, MI: Cistercian Publications, 1983), 71–72, with further references.

33. The dating of these murals presents problems similar to those presented by the two Kremlin palaces just discussed. Most of the images now visible were painted in 1666 when the cathedral was redecorated on orders from Tsar Aleksei Mikhailovich. Both Iu. N. Dmitriev and E. S. Sizov have concluded for several reasons that in 1666 the painters were quite careful to replicate the sixteenth-century images they were "repairing." First, it was standard practice at the time to make a careful written description of the murals to be repainted so that the new should follow the old as closely as possible. Second, the tsar himself ordered that the new painting be done *"protiv prezhnego"* (according to the earlier image). Third, two restorations and investigations carried out since World War II reveal that surviving fragments of pre-1666 painting coincide very well with adjoining 1666 sections. Sizov suggests a date of 1564–1565 for the original decoration of the cathedral. See E. S. Sizov, "Datirovka rospisi Arkhangel′skogo sobora i istoricheskaia osnova ee siuzhetov," *Drevnerusskoe iskusstvo. XVII vek* (Moscow: Nauka, 1964), 160–174; Iu. N. Dmitriev, "Stenopis′ Arkhangel′skogo sobora," *Drevnerusskoe iskusstvo. XVII vek* (Moscow: Nauka, 1964), 138–159. The latter article has useful diagrams of the iconographic program on the walls of the cathedral at 158–159.

34. For a beautiful reproduction of the Midianite image, see Jiri Burian and Oleg Shvidkovksy, *The Kremlin of Moscow* (New York: St. Martin's Press, 1975), plate 91.

35. Sizov, "Datirovka"; Cherniavsky, "Ivan the Terrible."

36. Gail Lenhoff, *The Martyred Princes Boris and Gleb: A Socio-cultural Study of the Cult and the Texts* (Columbus, OH: Slavica, 1989), 34–37; Helen Y. Prochazka, "On Concepts of Patriotism, Loyalty, and Honour in the Old Russian Military Accounts," *Slavonic and East European Review* 63, no. 4 (1985): 492.

CHAPTER 7

Moscow—The Third Rome or the New Israel?

Recent events in the former Soviet Union have stimulated the rethinking of many previously axiomatic notions about the past and present of Russia. This situation creates a propitious environment for the reexamination of received views of the Russian past, including the famous idea that sixteenth-century Russians thought of themselves as inhabitants of "The Third Rome." This idea, which sometimes seems like the only idea that the general public knows about Muscovite Russia apart from the imagined character and reign of Ivan the Terrible, has helped to create the impression that Muscovite Russia was exotic and expansionist, a worthy predecessor of the "evil empire" that occupied people's attention in the 1980s and before. This image of Muscovy, in turn, promotes the notion in the minds of Russians and foreigners alike that Russia is destined by her Muscovite past to behave in certain ways.

Most specialists in the Muscovite period of Russian history are already aware that the conventional notion of the Third Rome theory as an early justification for Russian expansionism is badly flawed; the idea continues nevertheless to

---

This essay originally appeared in *The Russian Review* 55, no. 4 (Fall 1996): 591–614. The author gratefully acknowledges the publisher for permission to reprint this essay. The author is grateful to Don Ostrowski, Samuel Baron, Valerie Kivlson and his anonymous reviewers (for the Russian Review) for their many helpful comments. He also thanks the Russian Research Center at Harvard University for providing an extraordinarily rich and supportive environment for research.

remain popular among nonspecialist writers. This essay points out briefly the relative scarcity of evidence for the Third Rome theme in Muscovite sources, especially in sources that originated before the 1590s. Most of our attention, however, is devoted to exploring a complementary theme, a theme that is overwhelmingly better represented in the source base than the Third Rome idea, but that answers the same basic question about the self-image of the Muscovite state: the idea of Russia as a New Israel. Both themes were products of the Muscovite perception of history as a succession of chosen peoples: Israel to Roman Empire to Eastern Roman Empire (Byzantium) to Muscovy. (Other lists of chosen peoples were also available, as we shall see, but all lists had to begin with Israel.) Russians in the sixteenth century, like early medieval Western Europeans, imagined themselves as part of a historical process stretching from the creation of the world to the Apocalypse, and were certainly aware of the prestige and importance of Rome as part of this divinely guided process. Yet the evidence overwhelmingly indicates that the Bible in general, and the Old Testament in particular, loomed far larger in the historical imagination of Muscovites than did any image of Rome. This correction in turn implies a common Christian ideological heritage shared by both Russia and Western Europe instead of an exotic Russian ideology that drove the Russian state in peculiar (and largely undesirable) directions. After reviewing a portion of the very large amount of evidence of Old Testament images in Rus' culture, we therefore conclude by briefly comparing the use of Old Testament models in Muscovy and Western Europe.

Several pitfalls await us at the outset. First, we must be careful not to substitute one oversimplification for another by exclusively emphasizing Old Testament models when Muscovite churchmen drew also on Byzantine history, the Church Fathers, liturgical texts, and so on. Yet in what we would call the political sphere, the influence of the Old Testament seems to have been exceptionally strong, at least in part because it was so often reworked in these later sources. Liturgical texts in particular, saturated as they are with typological analogies (Old Testament prefiguration, New Testament fulfillment), are full of Old Testament references. Second, the historical accounts that survive both from Kiev and Muscovy were remarkably factual when compared with their medieval or early modern West European counterparts, in which allegory and analogy often flourished much more lushly. I am therefore arguing not that Muscovites saw an Old Testament parallel whenever they contemplated some historical event or figure, but that, when they chose to compare that event or figure with a historical precedent, their choice more often than not involved the Old Testament, either by itself or as part of a more general scheme involving the New Testament and/or later events. Sometimes the comparison is an equal one ("X is a second Moses"); sometimes it implies the superiority of the current figure ("X is a second Moses, only better"). While bearing in mind this distinction, we include both types in our investigation.

Our common assumptions about the theme of the Third Rome raise another question, a question that is much harder to answer than that of the relative importance of one theme or another in the sources. The vast majority of the surviving evidence, literary and artistic, was generated within the church, within what we might call the literary-ecclesiastical establishment. Were these ideas important beyond the church circles that developed them? Did they influence foreign policy decisions? Did they affect domestic politics? Edward Keenan has argued that this church culture had little effect outside the church. More recently, however, scholars have found convincing evidence of close links between this church culture and society at large. Although this argument is beyond the bounds of the present discussion, there is considerable evidence that, although the Third Rome idea did not have the pernicious effects often ascribed to it, Moscow's self-image as a New Israel did have important effects both in generating internal support for the regime and its policies and perhaps in influencing some foreign policy decisions.[1]

In order to establish the relationship between the Third Rome and the New Israel themes and gain some idea of the relative importance of each theme in the sources, we need to begin by reviewing briefly the importance of the Third Rome theme in Muscovite sources. The idea of Moscow as the Third Rome, first worked out in the first half of the sixteenth century by the monk Filofei of Pskov, has had an irresistible attraction for historians. It has been the subject of numerous books and articles over the past century.[2] It is also discussed in every Russian history textbook that I have seen, in one case as a "monstrous fiction" that "twisted history" to fit Moscow's new pretensions to universal empire.[3]

Yet scholars have long since pointed out the limits of this theory as a satisfactory answer to the question of Muscovy's self-image.[4] For one thing, it arose relatively late in Muscovy's history, some three centuries after the beginning of her rise to power. For another, it gained currency (and a limited currency at that) even later, in the 1590s. Such an idea could spread in Moscow's literary culture in two ways, by the direct copying of one or more of the three "letters" ascribed to Filofei that refer to the doctrine, and by the indirect spread of the concept into other texts, historical, polemical, or even diplomatic.[5] A. L. Gol'dberg provides a list of some 104 manuscripts that contain one or more of the three relevant letters (often only as fragments), together with approximate dates of compilation.[6] If we tabulate the dates in very rough fashion (the dating of the manuscripts is necessarily vague), we find that seven were written in the sixteenth century, twenty-one in the late sixteenth and/or early seventeenth centuries, thirty in the seventeenth century (either "middle," "first half," or unspecified), eighteen in the late seventeenth century, and twenty-eight in the two centuries after 1700. Although the rise of printing casts doubt on manuscript evidence after the late seventeenth century, these figures show that the theory was significantly popular only from the late sixteenth century on. They also indicate that, even during that time, the original texts were nowhere near numerous enough to constitute evidence of a national myth.

As to the second, indirect, method of dispersal, the evidence about the limits of the theory's influence is just as clear. First, the concept of Moscow the Third Rome moved into other sources only in the second half of the sixteenth century at the earliest. Its first official use came in 1589 in the document establishing the Moscow patriarchate, and its new popularity seems to be closely linked to that event and the ensuing Time of Troubles.[7] Thereafter, aside from a handful of references in various less widespread sources, it appeared only in what was probably a 1590s redaction of the "Povest' o belom klobuke," in a probable insertion into the "Kazanskaia istoriia," in the "Povest' o zachale Moskvy," and in Old Believer literature after the 1660s. By the second half of the seventeenth century, the idea was under attack (at least by Iurii Krizhanich), and by 1700 was discarded by everyone except the Old Believers, who of course used it to undermine the state rather than to strengthen it.[8] Finally, Gol'dberg, Donald Ostrowski and others have convincingly shown that the Third Rome theory was mainly an ecclesiastical idea whose primary use came after 1589 as a means to buttress the position of the Moscow patriarchate within the Eastern Orthodox world. Within Muscovy, it was used more to limit than to expand the power of the ruler, and seems originally to have been aimed at increasing the independence of the church in Novgorod at the expense of Moscow.[9] There is no evidence to show that either Ivan the Terrible or any other alleged architect of Muscovite expansion was influenced by the idea. Indeed, Muscovite diplomats spent a good deal of time rebuffing papal attempts to persuade them to try to reclaim their "Byzantine heritage" from the Turks.[10]

If the Third Rome idea did not serve as a major source of Muscovy's image of itself, what did? The answer, it seems to me, lies not in the Roman middle of the series of chosen people that so interested literary Muscovites, but at its beginning. When we look for the context within which Muscovite events were seen, the "mother myth" as it were, the soil within which other ideas could grow, the most obvious answer from virtually every point of view is that Muscovy (or at least its artistic and literary culture) saw itself as the reembodiment of the Old Testament kingdom of David and Solomon, as a completion or fulfillment of biblical events, as a "New Israel." Marked biblical references and comparisons abound, and unlabeled references to scriptural passages are probably many times as common. The Bible, directly or indirectly, provided the chief reference point for understanding the meaning of passing events. In other words, it was part of the medium as well as part of the message. No one has ever thought of counting these references, but they undoubtedly outnumber references to Moscow as a parallel to Rome by many hundreds, if not thousands, of times. It is difficult to explain why scholars have paid so little explicit attention to this dominant pattern of references to the Bible, and particularly to the Old Testament.[11]

One reason may lie in the very abundance and relative formlessness of the evidence. The Third Rome theory is easily recognizable, among other ways by the presence of the words *"tretii Rim."* It can be broken down into a number of constituent parts and was given a classic statement in three relatively short letters. It provided an apparent explanation for Russia's differences with the West. The idea of Moscow as a New Israel has few of these advantages for the historian beyond its overwhelming presence in the sources. It is more diffuse and more difficult to define, sending few unambiguous political messages and operating at the level of an assumption rather than as an explicit "theory." Unlike the Third Rome theory, moreover, this theme is not so much a Muscovite innovation as an inheritance from Kievan Rus′ and Byzantium, which the Muscovites simply made more explicit. Since the same idea was very popular in the early medieval West, the New Israel theme constitutes rather a common inheritance than a sign of Russia's special destiny (or political pathology). A further reason for this neglect may be sought in changes in what historians know. Biblical references may have been so obvious to many historians and philologists, especially to those trained before the Russian Revolution of 1917, that they did not think them worthy of comment. Since the death of many scholars in the last prerevolutionary generation, however, we have become deaf to these scriptural references because our knowledge of Church Slavic biblical texts is so weak.[12] Thus the importance of the Bible went from assumption to relative oblivion in a generation or two, just at the time when interest in the Bible as a subtext for European culture was increasing.[13]

Societies—even badly documented societies like that of Muscovy—leave evidence about their image of themselves in a wide variety of sources: ideological tracts, history writing, art and architecture, folk literature, and diplomatic documents. For reasons both of space and coherence, we omit consideration of the last two (without in the least denying their importance) and concentrate on the "literary" culture of Muscovy. Within this culture and outside it, a central piece of evidence is surely the coronation service of Ivan IV, the occasion above all others on which the ideologues of the state, particularly Metropolitan Makarii, had to find an appropriate way to express their ideas on the power of the ruler and his duties and responsibilities toward the people. The entire court was assembled—boyars as well as church dignitaries. At the most solemn moment of the service, after Ivan had asked to be crowned as his father had wished, the metropolitan intoned a prayer that explicitly invoked the Old Testament kingship of David as the model for Ivan's rule, following which he bestowed the regalia upon the young prince:

> King of Kings and Lord of Lords, Who by Samuel the Prophet didst choose Thy servant David and anoint him to be king (*tsar'*) over Thy people Israel, . . . look down from Thy sanctuary upon Thy faithful servant the Great Prince Ivan Vasilievich whom Thou hast deigned to raise up as tsar over Thy people [*v iazytse tvoem*], whom Thou hast redeemed with the precious blood of Thine only-begotten Son.[14]

At the very heart of the coronation, then, Ivan is declared to be the heir to David, and Muscovy to be God's new chosen people. Each side of this equation deserves our attention. David was appointed king directly by God via the agency of Samuel, just as Ivan was divinely appointed through the agency of Metropolitan Makarii. The dominant and powerful message, clearly, is that Ivan rules by God's will. As the preceding story of Saul (1 Sam. 15) shows, however, God could and did reject rulers who had sinned against Him, a point not lost on Muscovite observers. The stories of Saul and David also suggest a greater power for the church (as represented by the figure of Samuel) than the actual church in Muscovy was accustomed to enjoy, for Samuel was God's direct agent in choosing (and judging) a king. Finally, we should note here that the Slavic word *tsar'* is a translation not only of the Byzantine title *basileus* and the Tatar title *khan*, as has been emphatically pointed out; it also is a translation of the Old Testament title of *melech* (king).[15] The conflation of the Old Testament "king" with *basileus* had already occurred in Byzantium, where the "King of Kings" prayer had long been a central feature of the coronation service of the emperor.[16]

Old Testament models of kingship were extremely important in the early medieval West as well. The formula that led up to the anointing of the monarch (the *unguantur* formula) specifically cites the Old Testament examples of Moses and Joshua (for military triumphs), David (for humility), and Solomon (for wisdom).[17] In the West, the unction ceremony served to emphasize the special position and power of the clergy as opposed to the rest of the Christian laity.[18]

The "King of Kings" prayer not only suggested a model of rulership; it also defined a "holy people" to be ruled over. In the context of Muscovy, which still consisted of a number of recently acquired, previously independent principalities, this aspect must have had considerable importance. In the same way that Christian texts on rulership envisaged for Charlemagne a "Christian people" to rule over instead of the miscellaneous set of warring tribes that he actually saw around him, so this prayer created a literary image of Muscovy as a single entity—"Thy people, whom Thou hast redeemed by the precious blood of Thine only-begotten Son"—for Ivan to rule over.

The Old Testament idea of Israel had three dimensions, each of which fitted the self-image and aspirations of Muscovite Rus' remarkably well—far better than the claim to universal empire implied by the Third Rome idea. Most obviously, Israel was a religious unit under the direct protection (and direction) of God and His appointed ruler. Literary Muscovites, like the ancient Israelites, saw their political and military history as a series of punishments and rewards sent by God. Second, Israel, like Rus', was also an ethnic unit with a strong emphasis on family and clan. The use of the *iazyk* in the prayer is significant, since that term meant "tribe" as well as "people." This dimension of the idea accorded well with Moscow's rulers' desire to emphasize their lineal descent from the Kievan princes and the ethnic and dynastic continuity between Kievan and Muscovite Rus'. Finally, Israel, like Rus', denoted a piece of territory. In neither case did the vagueness of the geographic boundaries concerned (or past struggles over those boundaries) prevent the terms from generating strong emotional attachments.

Of course, one might object that the Byzantine origin of the "King of Kings" prayer invalidates it as evidence to answer our question, since the prayer was not composed by a Muscovite. But to establish a Byzantine origin is not to deny the meaning of the prayer. We will never know how many people at the coronation service were aware of the prayer's Byzantine source. The prayer was probably even more moving for those who recognized its prestigious Byzantine origin, but even those who did not could take the text at its face value, as yet another of the many references that connected Muscovite political life with Old Testament (and other pre-Muscovite) events in a literary pattern that by this time had become utterly familiar. To understand this pattern and thus the literary context within which the prayer was understood and from which it derived its power and authority, we must pause for a moment to consider in the simplest terms the rules for understanding history that the Muscovites inherited from Kievan Rus'.[19]

When he incorporated this Byzantine prayer, Makarii placed himself among the many authors from both halves of the old Roman Empire who believed in the idea of historical recurrence, a tradition rooted both in the scriptures and in the culture of Ancient Greece.[20] Within the Christian tradition, the pattern of Old Testament prefiguration and New Testament fulfillment is already abundantly clear in the New Testament, beginning with the words of Jesus Himself as reported in the Gospels. An oft-quoted example is Matthew 12:40–41, where Jesus referred to Jonah's three days in the belly of a whale as a prefiguration of the three days he would spend "in the heart of the earth" before His resurrection. This correlation of Old and New Testaments became a central method of scriptural exegesis from the earliest Christian writers on. As the New Testament period itself receded into history, a third dimension of sacred or salvation history was needed for the present. The result was a three-part structure: Old Testament/New Testament/Now; any two elements were sufficient to establish the meaning of an event, but all three were often used.[21] It is obvious that early East Slavic history writing lacks the exclusive concern with secular, linear causation that lies at the base of all modern history writing. If we take East Slavic authors at their word that God causes everything, then this relative lack of concern with secular causation is perfectly understandable. The East Slavs saw history as much more than just one thing after another. Rather, they sought to find God's intention in a given recent event by searching for a parallel in sacred history. Since God's intention in the earlier event is explained in scripture, chronicle, and/or exegesis, the parallel signals a similar intention in God's mind and allows the interpretation of the earlier event to be applied to the more recent one. (It is this idea of recurrence, of course, that lies at the heart of both the Third Rome and the New Israel images.)

In the introduction to the *Primary Chronicle*, for example, the chronicle that was copied into the beginning of most Muscovite chronicles, the author explains an event like the Polianians' humiliating tribute to the Khazars by comparing it to an Old Testament event. The Khazars had taken tribute from the Polianians, but the Khazar elders protested that the tribute was evil and prophesied the Polianians would exact tribute from the Khazars.

> All this has come to pass, for they spoke thus not of their own will but by God's commandment. The outcome was the same in the time of Pharaoh, King of Egypt, when Moses was led before him, and the elders of Pharaoh foretold that he should subjugate Egypt. For the Egyptians perished at the hands of Moses, though the Jews were previously their slaves. Just as the Egyptians ruled supreme but were subsequently ruled over, so it has also come to pass that the Rus' rule over the Khazars even to this day.[22]

Shortly thereafter, in the guise of a visiting philosopher's speech to Vladimir in answer to his question about why God should have descended to earth and endured the crucifixion, the author inserts much of the story of both the Old and New Testaments, the latter serving as the fulfillment of carefully enumerated prophecies in the former.²³ No other non–East Slavic history is described in anything like the detail used for biblical history. Byzantine events are in general mentioned only if they affect the East Slavs or concern heresies, although Byzantine historical parallels are occasionally drawn, as when Vladimir is called "the new Constantine of mighty Rome."²⁴ The chronicler makes much of Israel's falling away from God in the reign of Rehoboam, after the death of Solomon, and cites a number of prophecies expressing God's anger with Israel. "Many prophesied of their [the Israelites'] rejection [by God], and to such prophets God gave His commandments to foretell the *calling of other nations in their stead*."²⁵ Rus' seems to have been such a nation. This implication is made clearer in another passage, where the Kievan Rus' are called "[God's] new people, enlightened by His Holy Spirit." The idea of Rus' as a New Israel is thus implied at the very beginning of the *Primary Chronicle*.²⁶

In addition to these only slightly veiled references to Rus' as a new chosen people, the *Primary Chronicle* provides a constant stream of Old Testament "thematic clues" that explain the meaning of contemporary events by providing scriptural parallels to those events. If the parallel is persuasive, the interpretation of the scriptural event is transferred to the contemporary event. The story of the Khazar elders is a good example: The prophecy by pagan advisers is seen as a recurrence or repetition of an event in sacred history. The Old Testament parallel gives the recent event intelligibility. This historical method is both more important and more common than specific references to the East Slavs as chosen people. It establishes the Old Testament as the dominant historical context within which East Slavic history was understood, and the method of explanation by historical analogy as the chief tool of historical understanding, a tool that led to the description of Vladimir as "the new Constantine."²⁷

Ilarion's famous "Sermon on Law and Grace" (which was also known in Muscovy) is based in part on an elaborate comparison between Old Testament law and New Testament grace as embodied, respectively, in Hagar and Sarah. The ideas of prefiguration and fulfillment lie at the core of the work, and Old Testament references abound. Ilarion compares Saint Vladimir to David, Iaroslav the Wise to Solomon, and the Hagia Sophia in Kiev to the Temple in Jerusalem. The calling of other nations in Israel's place is a major theme. Ilarion stated clearly that Kievan Rus' was superior to ancient Israel as the "font of the Gospel" is superior to the "lake of the law" that has now dried up. This view, stressing the superiority of Rus' over Israel, constitutes an important variant of our theme, a variant that continued to develop in Muscovy.²⁸

The example of biblical parallelism provided by the *Primary Chronicle* and by Ilarion was followed by virtually every writer in Kievan and Appanage Rus'.

I will not discuss their works in detail, but I cannot restrain myself from mentioning in passing one example that has received little attention. The author of the *Vita* of Alexander Nevskii rather surprisingly tells us that Nevskii had a face like the face of Joseph.[29] In so doing, he provides both an explanation and a justification for Nevskii's policy of reconciliation with the Mongols. As Joseph's friendship with Pharaoh (a figure frequently used as a symbol for a Mongol or Tatar Khan) justifiably protected Israel, so Nevskii's friendship with the Khan justifiably protected Novgorod and Rus'.

As integral parts of the historical self-image of Rus', these Old Testament images were naturally adopted by historians in Moscow. They were richly used by those authors, partly under South Slavic influence, who lauded Dmitrii Donskoi's victory at Kulikovo in 1380 in a whole cycle of literary works. The author of the "Tale about the Life and Death of Grand Prince Dmitrii Ivanovich, Tsar of Rus'," for example, devoted about 7 percent of his text to an extended favorable comparison of Dmitrii with the founders of the Israelite people from Adam to Moses and elsewhere likens Dmitrii to Moses and David, Khan Mamai to Og, King of Bashan, and the Tatars to the Amalekites.[30] The political and cultural events of the fifteenth and early sixteenth centuries that produced the various explicit ideological works about the Third Rome and about dynastic and religious links between Rome, Constantinople, and Moscow also led to a more intensive use of Old Testament parallels and images. This can be seen most clearly in Bishop Vassian Rylo's famous letter to Ivan III on the Ugra, in which God's liberation of Muscovy from the Tatars is compared to His liberation of the Israelites from the Egyptians, and in which Muscovy is called explicitly "the New Israel" for the first time, as far as I know.[31]

One of the most important, and certainly the most compendious, sources of official ideological thought in Moscow is Metropolitan Makarii's *Velikie Chetii Minei*, or *Great Menology*. If one can divine a consistent pattern, if not a philosophy, from the enormous volume of materials that make up the *Menology*, or at least those parts of it that deal with political themes, that pattern would center on the passing of God's protection and covenant, God's "choice," as in the expression "the chosen people," from one people and state to another people and state. This concept, as we have seen, was already established in the *Primary Chronicle* and was developed extensively in Ilarion's "Sermon on Law and Grace," the third edition of which was included in the *Menology*. In a synaxary *Life of Vladimir* and a eulogy to him that accompanied Ilarion's "Sermon" under July 15 in the *Menology*, Vladimir was called not only a "New Constantine" but also a "Second Moses," while his realm was referred to as "the newly chosen people, the Rus' land," and Kiev was named a "new Constantinople" and a "new Jerusalem."[32] By including as many sources as he did, Makarii did not force a choice among these titles, but included miscellaneous evidence for a bewildering variety of successions of chosen people and states. From the apocryphal vision of Daniel, for example, came the succession of Babylon, Persia, and Rome, as symbolized in Daniel's vision of a succession of beasts. Imperial regalia had been taken not only from Constantinople to Kiev to Moscow, as told in the well-known "Tale of the Vladimir Princes," but also from Babylon to Constantinople, as told in the "The Tale of Babylon." This preoccupation with successions of chosen empires was common in the medieval West; indeed, Isidore of Seville's treatment of this subject was translated especially on Makarii's orders.[33]

The evidence suggests that Makarii did not insist on any one particular list of chosen people and states, so long as the list began with Israel and ended with Muscovite Russia. While Filofei's letter explaining the doctrine of Moscow the Third Rome is included in the *Menology*, it occupies an exceptional place in that collection according to David Miller, who has investigated the *Menology* with great care. In the vast majority of texts that deal with the subject, Moscow's claim to be a chosen people goes back through Kievan Rus' and is not dependent on the Council of Florence, the fall of Byzantium, or the end of the sixth millennium from creation, all crucial ingredients of the Third Rome theory, although these events were sometimes mentioned to confirm Moscow's status.[34] It is for this reason that so many monuments of Kievan literature, including Ilarion's "Sermon," could be included in the *Menology*. The concept of Rus' in the *Menology* provided a vague but compelling territorial dimension to the discussion, just as the concept of Israel functioned in the Old Testament. No text makes any claim to a universal empire.

When we turn from Makarii's *Menology* to chronicles and other types of history writing, we find that the image of Moscow as the New Israel, as God's chosen people, is again a dominant theme. The chronicle format discouraged the elaboration of theories, but there can be no doubt that the conception of Muscovite-Rus' history as a continuation and even a repetition of Old Testament history remained central to all Muscovite history writing. Within the chronicle tradition, the *Primary Chronicle* established this conception at the beginning of many texts. The compendium (*khronograf*) tradition contained a variety of other texts dealing directly with the history of Israel, including full or partial texts of all the books of the Pentateuch, Joshua, Ruth, 1 and 2 Samuel, 1 and 2 Kings, Tobit, Esther, Jeremiah, and Daniel. (These naturally occur with wide variations in frequency.) At least two compiled works, the *Khronograf of Judah* and the *Tale about the Three Sackings of Jerusalem*, were included. These works combined Old Testament information with material from Josephus's *Jewish Wars* (itself well known in a Slavic translation) and Old Testament material from the *Chronicle of John Malalas*.³⁵ The Book of Jubilees was also an important source, as we have seen.

In addition to introducing a large number of texts concerning Old Testament history directly into chronicles and chronographs, Muscovite history writers, like their Kievan counterparts, used Old Testament parallels to bring meaning to their texts. Very often this took the form of direct quotations, especially from the Psalms or Proverbs, to comment on the historical situation being described. In the *Nikon Chronicle*, to take one example of many, verse 16 of Psalm 33 is used to portray the "humility" of the Muscovites and the "pride" of the Riazanians as reasons why God gave victory to the former.³⁶ Here the device is purely rhetorical or even propagandistic, since we have no reason to assume that the Riazanians were any more proud than the Muscovites. In addition, the Old Testament is used a source of types that again explain and justify events. Before the battle of Kulikovo field, Dmitrii Donskoi in the *Nikon Chronicle* asks God's help for the Muscovite champion Peresvet as God helped Israel's champion David against Goliath. The metropolitan blessed Ivan III before his battle with Novgorod, "just as Samuel blessed David when he fought against Goliath." The sickness of the Tatar Khan Temir Aksak is compared to the plague that God sent to the Egyptians.³⁷ In the *Stepennaia kniga*, the Bishop of Smolensk Varsonofii greets Vasilii III after his conquest of that town by comparing him to Moses who saved Israel from Pharaoh.³⁸ Muscovite rulers are thus identified with the heroes of the Old Testament, while their enemies, whether Tatar, Polish, Lithuanian, or even Rus´ian, are equated with Israel's enemies, Canaanites, Philistines, Egyptians, and so on. Often, the exact characteristics of these enemies and their similarity (or lack thereof) to the enemies of Moscow seem not to have been matters of concern.³⁹ They were seen as negative types, and their identity often consisted only in their being enemies of Israel or Muscovy and not in any shared qualities.

The Time of Troubles saw a further development of Old Testament parallels and the skill with which they were deployed. Ivan Timofeev, one of the most thoughtful historians of the Troubles, relied heavily on biblical narratives to bring meaning to his text. His method looks at first like standard scriptural window-dressing, but more is going on than may strike the modern eye. When he describes the murder of the Tsarevich Dmitrii by Boris Godunov, for example, he mentions two biblical parallels in which innocent victims are slaughtered by wicked murderers: Abel's murder by Cain (Gen. 4:1–15) and the slaughter of the innocents by Herod (Matt. 2:16).⁴⁰ In portraying Godunov, Timofeev faced a dilemma because none of the obvious literary images of a ruler fit Timofeev's vision of him as a tsar who appeared highly effective and capable but who nonetheless was spiritually flawed (by ambition) and of doubtful legitimacy. With elegant efficiency, Timofeev was able to create a remarkably subtle portrait by means of these seemingly decorative biblical comparisons. Cain and Abel both offered sacrifices to God, but only Abel's was accepted because he alone had faith. After he murdered Abel, Cain was driven east of Eden and lost his legitimacy, a vital point for Timofeev, for whom the legitimacy of Godunov was a central question. (This same comparison had already been used in the Kievan texts about Saints Boris and Gleb to undermine the legitimacy of Sviatopolk.[41]) Saint Paul's interpretation of this Genesis story (Heb. 9:4) is remarkably similar to Timofeev's description of Godunov's plan to build an imitation of Solomon's temple in the Kremlin (a matter to which we shall return) and other projects that, although ostensibly worthy acts, were done for reasons of vainglory rather than faith and thus, like Cain's sacrifice, were rejected by God. If we assume that Timofeev conflated the various rulers whom the New Testament refers to as "Herod," then "Herod" was not only the slaughterer of innocents, he was a symbol of vainglory who was finally killed by an angel of the Lord because "he gave not God the glory" (Acts 12:20–23). Timofeev thus breaks out of the standard binary characterization typical of Muscovite literature and shows Godunov as an overly ambitious usurper who seemed externally virtuous but who lacked faith.

Although there had been occasional explicit references to Muscovy as "the New Israel" or "the Lord's people" or "Zion" scattered throughout earlier texts, these expressions became more common during and after the Troubles. Ivan Timofeev calls Muscovy "the New Israel" three times, once in the title to his *Vremennik*. Patriarch Iov compared a church in a movable wooden tower set up by Boris Godunov for defense against the Tatars to "the ancient Israelite tabernacle [which promoted] the preservation and salvation of the city from the invasion of pagan barbarians," and Fedor Ivanovich to "the God-seer Moses who, having drawn up the chosen army of Israel, sent them against the Godless Amalekites."[42] Note the appropriateness of this latter comparison, for neither Fedor nor Moses took part in the actual fighting, but each guaranteed victory by interceding with God. Fedor's effectiveness as an intercessor was of course one of the main points that Iov was trying to make. In other tales about the Time of Troubles we find Muscovy referred to as "the New Zion," "the New Israel," "the remnant of the Christian tribe," and the Muscovites as the "People of the Lord," "Your [God's] People," or "the Sheep of the Word." "In truth," exclaimed Prince Ivan Khvorostinin, "we are called the newly enlightened Israelites." Conrad

Bussow even reported that the Second False Dmitrii included a reference to Muscovy as a "second Israel" in his formal title.⁴³

When we raise the question of how Muscovites imagined themselves and their history, we should bear in mind that, unlike texts, visual evidence (painting and architecture) was accessible to the vast majority of Muscovites who could not read. Visual media thus had a unique ability to cross the boundary from the literary-ecclesiastical establishment to secular society as a whole. Images in and around the sacred space of the Kremlin, though inaccessible to most people, were, of course, particularly well placed to influence the secular as well the ecclesiastical elite. Some examples from sixteenth-century art and architecture strongly suggest that Old Testament images were at least as important in the visual sphere as they were in the literary. Muscovite artists, both icon and wall painters, were explicit in their use of Old Testament themes.

The Golden Hall (*zolotaia palata*) of the Kremlin, newly decorated by Ivan IV after the Kremlin fire of 1547 and a main state apartment where foreign ambassadors were received, is perhaps the best example.⁴⁴ On the walls of the anteroom (*seni*) were ten scenes depicting the battles and victories of Joshua. These were counterparts to a series on the walls of the main room (the *zolotaia palata* itself) of scenes from Rus' history showing Vladimir's conversion to Christianity, his marriage to a Byzantine princess, the sending of gifts to Vladimir Monomakh by the Byzantine emperor Constantine, and so forth. Joshua was an excellent symbol for Muscovite rulers (as for Byzantine rulers before them) because he was both a political ruler and the mouthpiece for God's will. To use the epithet usually applied to David, he was both tsar and prophet; his political power derived from his direct link to God. He was in constant communication with God and displayed the attributes of kingship in his division of the land, in his calling of the people of Israel together for the making of the covenant, and, most importantly, in his military leadership. The scenes chosen for illustration were drawn from the brief (and seemingly unedifying) descriptions in chapters 10 and 11 of the book of Joshua, where Joshua brutally destroys various enemies as he conquers the Promised Land. Elsewhere, the victories of Moses and Gideon are depicted, including the victory of Israel over the Amalekites produced by Moses's intercession, the biblical scene that, as we have seen, Patriarch Iov referred to in his *Vita* of Fedor Ivanovich.⁴⁵ As in the depictions of Joshua, the direct protection and direction of God in all of these military scenes were emphasized pictorially by depicting God Himself in many of the episodes. The juxtaposition of the conquests of Joshua with the baptism of Vladimir and other events of Rus' history may also have implied the idea of Rus' as a new Promised Land. As Joshua conquered the land of the Old Israel, the rulers of Rus' from Vladimir to Ivan brought Christianity, Christian government, and military victory to the new Promised Land, the New Israel.[46] Lest the viewer miss these Old Testament roots of Muscovite kingship, a series of ruler portraits in the pendentives beneath the domes of the two chambers made them clear. In the main room were depicted eight "Grand Princes" of Rus', from Saint Vladimir to "Ivan Vasil'evich" (III?), while in the anteroom appeared Old Testament kings: the "Prophet and Tsar" David, plus "Tsars" Solomon and his descendants Rehoboam, Abijah, Asa, and Jehosephat. Note that this list of sometimes unremarkable Old Testament rulers was chosen to emphasize the dynastic theme that was so important in Muscovy. Old Testament themes on political subjects also seem to have been prominent in the Palace of Facets, decorated under Fedor Ivanovich.[47]

The Old Testament also played a crucial role in a set of images and texts that elaborated the theme of "Blessed Is the Host of the Heavenly Tsar."[48] This title is the original name of the famous large icon (often called *The Church Militant*) that hung near the tsar's throne in the Dormition Cathedral of the Moscow Kremlin. In the icon, Ivan the Terrible on a white horse follows the Archangel Michael in leading the troops of Muscovy as the heavenly host back from their victory over Kazan' to Moscow (depicted as a New Jerusalem).[49] The roots of this idea go back to Byzantium, and complementary images were found in the necropolis church of the Archangel Michael in the Kremlin, on various battle standards, and in several texts composed by Metropolitan Makarii in connection with the campaign against Kazan'. These images depicted the Muscovite army as the sixteenth-century embodiment of both the army of ancient Israel and the army of God or Christ engaged in a cosmic battle against the forces of Satan at the end of time (see Dan. 12:1 and Rev. 12:7; 19:11–21). This story, based heavily (but not completely, of course) on the Old Testament, provided a divine role not only for the tsar but also for his military elite, the boyars who formed his court. Both the tsar and his military retainers were assured of God's protection and military help while they fought, and martyrs' crowns should they fall in battle. And since the term "King of King and Lord of Lords" is taken from the crucial nineteenth chapter of Revelation describing the battle of Armageddon, the "King of Kings" of the coronation prayer with which we began our discussion refers to the leader of the "blessed host of the Heavenly Tsar."

Closely connected to the victory over Kazan' (and also sharing the sacred space of the Kremlin and its immediate surrounding area) was the Cathedral of the Intercession on the Moat (commonly known as Saint Basil's), which was built just outside the Kremlin as a votive church commemorating that victory. Scholars have produced varied interpretations of the theological program behind what has surely become one of the main symbols of Russian national culture, but its connection with the image of Jerusalem is not in doubt. The west (and largest) chapel of the ensemble, dedicated to the Entry into Jerusalem, served as a focal point of the elaborate Palm Sunday ritual, during which, in Michael Flier's description, "the tsar walked on foot from the Kremlin to Red Square, pulling a horse disguised as an ass at the end of a long rein, with the metropolitan seated sidesaddle in imitation of Christ at the center of a huge cross procession. By leading the metropolitan's horse on foot to the Jerusalem Chapel on Palm Sunday, Ivan recalled his own entry into Moscow on foot after his victory over Kazan."[50] Since, in the Gospel accounts (Mark 11:1–11; Luke 19:28–38), Christ traveled from Bethany to Jerusalem, the whole ensemble of the Cathedral of the Intercession on the Moat served in the ceremony as a symbolic representation of Jerusalem. The testimony of many contemporary observers tells us that, in the sixteenth and seventeenth centuries, the people referred to the cathedral as "Jerusalem" and believed that it was modeled on the Church of the Holy Sepulchre in that city. The square immediately adjacent was called the Lobnoe mesto, or "place of the skull," a clear reference to Golgotha in Jerusalem. The seven chapels that were originally intended to surround the central church (an eighth was added almost immediately) may have been meant to symbolize the seven pillars of the house of wisdom (Prov. 9:1), a reference to Solomon's temple (and to the Christian Church as well as to the Mother of God Herself).[51] Finally, the cathedral was built on raised ground and, with its surrounding chapels, resembled a walled city with towers, a reference not to any particular church but to Jerusalem as a whole, and particularly to the idea of the heavenly Jerusalem of the Apocalypse (Rev. 21). (Incidentally, the famous Russian onion dome may well have had its origins in "Zions," liturgical implements whose upper sections were meant to represent the cupola of the Church of the Holy Sepulchre in Jerusalem.[52])

Under the influence of the same forces, particularly the establishment of the patriarchate, which made the idea of Rus' as a New Israel so popular among the authors of tales about the Time of Troubles, Boris Godunov planned further elaborations on the idea of Moscow as a New Jerusalem. According to the testimony of both native sources and foreigners' accounts, Godunov planned to build a new church in the Kremlin that would eclipse all others in richness of decoration as well as in size, a church meant to be modeled both on Solomon's Temple in ancient Jerusalem (it was referred to as the "Holy of Holies") and on the Church of the Holy Sepulchre in contemporary Jerusalem. All sources agree in stressing Godunov's personal involvement in the project (and in condemning Godunov for vainglory, as we have seen in the

MOSCOW—THE THIRD ROME OR THE NEW ISRAEL? 171

case of Ivan Timofeev). According to the Dutchman Elias Herckman, Godunov asked his assistants to search for evidence of this "Holy of Holies" in scripture and in the works of Flavius Josephus and other authors, and then proceeded to order an elaborate model, encrusted with precious stones, of the proposed church. The only survival of this grandiose plan now is Godunov's reconstruction, with additional stories, of Ivan III's bell tower in the Kremlin, capped by a golden onion dome and encircled by a golden inscription proclaiming the tower as the work of Godunov and his son Fedor. The reconstructed tower made a strong impression on contemporaries and remained the chief vertical element in Moscow's architecture down to the beginning of the twentieth century.

Boris Godunov was also the first to construct a fortified wall around the entire territory of Moscow. On a map (the so-called *Petrovskii chertezh*), the original of which was apparently drawn up on his orders, the city is represented as a rounded square, with twelve gates leading in, three on each side, an apparent symbolic reference to the idea of Moscow as a heavenly Jerusalem (see Rev. 21:10–21).[53] Note that Godunov apparently conflated three images of Jerusalem: the Old Testament Jerusalem symbolized by Solomon's Temple, the (sixteenth-century) present Jerusalem symbolized by the Church of the Holy Sepulchre, and the Heavenly Jerusalem of the Apocalypse, with its twelve gates and precious stones. This conflation, characteristic of typological thinking, is very similar to the three-layered perception of the "Blessed Is the Host of the Heavenly Tsar," with its Old Testament, contemporary, and apocalyptic dimensions.

The culmination of the theme of the New Jerusalem in Muscovite architecture was of course Patriarch Nikon's careful reconstruction of Jerusalem's Church of the Holy Sepulchre and surrounding holy places at his New Jerusalem Monastery on the Istra River northwest of Moscow. Nikon continued to overlay the three images of Jerusalem, but, with his increasing awareness of and admiration for the non-Russian Orthodox world and its religious values, he placed a much greater emphasis on an attempt to create archaeologically correct versions of buildings existing in contemporary Jerusalem. To this end, he obtained extensive drawings of several Jerusalem holy places that had recently been published in Florence by Bernardino Amico, requested information (and possibly a model or drawing) from Patriarch Paisios of Jerusalem, and asked Arsenii Sukhanov for yet more information. On the Istra River he constructed his own Holy Land, including features named for the Jordan River, Golgotha, Bethlehem, Nazareth, the Mount of Olives, and, most important, the Church of the Holy Sepulchre. In plan there is indeed a very striking

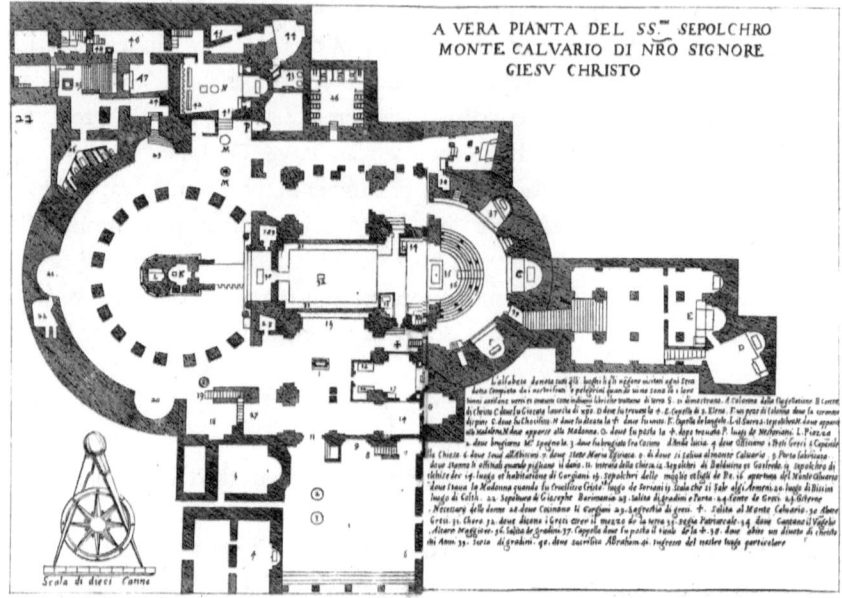

FIGURE 7.1. Plan of the Church of the Holy Sepulchre in Jerusalem by Bernardino Amico, from *Trattato delle piante & immagini de sacri edfizi di Terra Santa* (1620), 22. Source: British Museum.

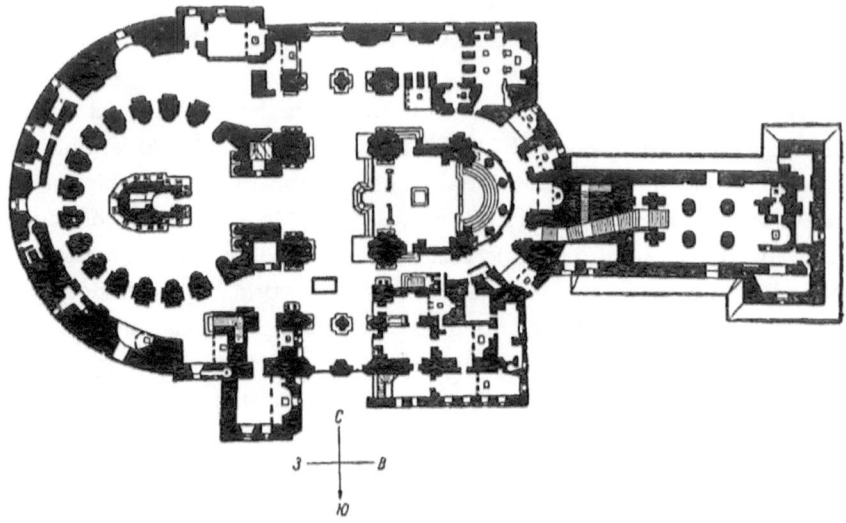

FIGURE 7.2. Plan of the Cathedral of the Resurrection, the New Jerusalem Monastery near Moscow. Source: M. I. Rzianin, *Pamiatniki russkogo zodchestva* (Moscow: Izd. Gosudarstvennoe, 1950), 64, figure 36.

MOSCOW—THE THIRD ROME OR THE NEW ISRAEL?   173

FIGURE 7.3. Early twentieth-century postcard of the Mount of Olives Chapel, the New Jerusalem Monastery near Moscow. Source: Resurrection New Jerusalem Stauropegial Monastery, http://www.n-jerusalem.ru/treasures/eleonskaya_gora.html.

resemblance between Amico's drawings and Nikon's buildings (the Cathedral of the Resurrection/Holy Sepulchre and the Mount of Olives Chapel [see figures 7.1, 7.2, and 7.3]), a reflection of the new, more self-conscious historicism typical of Nikon and his court.

Yet the buildings so carefully placed on the historical footprints indicated in Amico's drawings were based in elevation detail primarily on Russian architectural precedents. In the Mount of Olives Chapel, for example, Nikon kept the simple octagonal plan found in Amico's book, but completely changed the appearance of the roof of the octagon to reflect contemporary Russian tastes by replacing Amico's octagonal drum and hemispherical dome with a tent roof (see figures 7.3 and 7.4). The Cathedral of the Resurrection, although

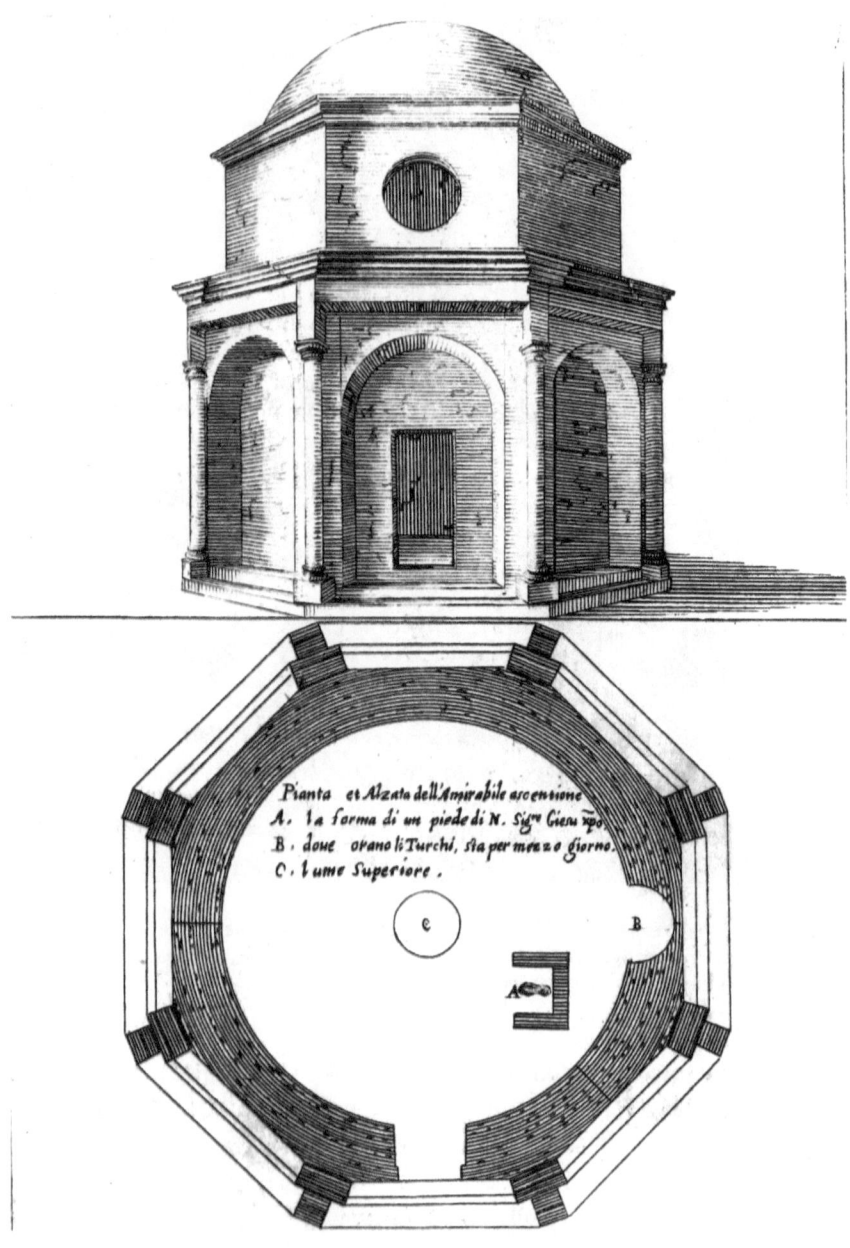

FIGURE 7.4. Plan and elevation view of the Church of the Admirable Ascension on the Mount of Olives, Jerusalem, by Amico, *Trattato delle piante*, 34. Source: British Museum.

quite faithful to Amico's drawing in plan, makes use of intense decorative elements, especially the plentiful use of colorful ceramic tiles depicting luxuriously growing plant forms, and the creation, as in Saint Basil's, of a multipartite form with numerous drums and domes on several levels (see figures 7.5 and 7.6), seem to indicate that Nikon continued to draw on the theme of the heavenly Jerusalem, now understood as a kind of Russian Big Rock Candy Mountain. This theme of New Jerusalem as fruitful paradise, according to M. A. Il′in, was popular in Russian culture of the seventeenth century, and was attested in literary texts, in icon painting, and in mural cycles.

Why would Nikon place obviously Russian decorative elements (onion domes, ceramic tiles, tent roofs) on buildings whose plan and massing were carefully based on contemporary buildings in Jerusalem? The answer, in part, may be that Nikon chose to follow the Jerusalem plans, not visible except from above, from God's perspective, as it were, to reflect the "real" eternal nature of his buildings, as opposed to their outward appearance, the buildings as they appear, with all their Russian decorative elements. The addition of these Russian elements in turn indicates Nikon's confidence in the importance of Russia within the Orthodox world at his own particular historical moment. In connection with the official proceedings against him in the 1660s, Nikon defended both his choice of the name "New Jerusalem" and his copying of the Jerusalem Church of the Holy Sepulchre as following a prototype in the same way that an icon painter follows his prototype. Since all Christian churches, in Nikon's opinion, follow the prototype of the Church of the Holy Sepulchre, and since all who follow Christian laws are Jerusalemites, then both monastery name and church design are validated by the most ancient patterns of Christian thought that regularly use prototypes (*pervoobraznye*) that originate in the Holy Land. "I cast no reproach on the old-new [*staronovogo*] Jerusalem," Nikon (with probable help from his assistants) stated, "[if I call the Monastery of the Resurrection New Jerusalem], since it is written in the prophets, 'Out of Sion shall go forth the law, and the word of the Lord from Jerusalem'" (Isa. 2:3). Significantly, he did not mention any changes made relative to the prototype, nor did he refer to the millennial New Jerusalem, though he discussed the last days at some length. In any case, the New Jerusalem Cathedral of the Resurrection itself exerted a major influence on Russian architecture both in its Jerusalem-derived centralizing plan and in its native exuberant decorative details, especially through the buildings commissioned by V. V. Golitsyn, and thus played an important role in establishing the style known as the "Moscow Baroque."[54]

Although this brief essay cannot hope to exhaust the evidence for this exceptionally rich subject, I hope that enough has been said to illustrate the importance

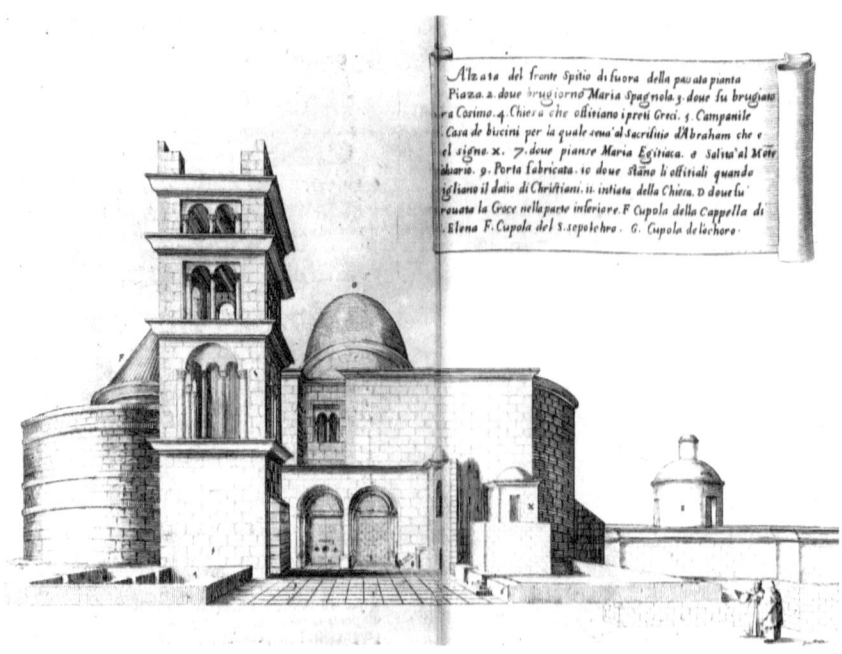

Figure 7.5. Elevation of the Church of the Holy Sepulchre in Jerusalem by Amico, *Trattato delle piante*, 23. Source: British Museum.

Figure 7.6. Cathedral of the Resurrection, New Jerusalem (Resurrection) Monastery on the Istra River. Photo by Vladimir Sklyarov, reproduced with permission from Getty Images.

of Muscovy's vision of itself as a chosen people in Old Testament terms, a religious and political community under the hand of God. The Bible in general, and the Old Testament in particular, dominated the historical imagination of Muscovites, providing not only the language of historical discussion but also the historical archetypes on which historical understanding of many later events, from Byzantine to Muscovite, was based. This dominance is not at all surprising when we consider how biblical and Old Testament texts saturated the culture of both Kiev and Muscovy. Translated works were overwhelmingly more common than original compositions, and biblical translations occupied "a central position" among all the translations.[55] These literal translations were supplemented, as we have seen, by Old Testament material in chronicles and historical compendiums. Old Testament information appeared even more commonly in lectionaries, in translated texts like "The Tale of Barlaam and Josephat," which is densely packed with scriptural references, and, most important, in liturgical texts themselves. To have imagined their history without the Old Testament would have been an astonishing feat for early modern Russians.

The opposition implied in the title to this essay is, as we have seen, a false one. Muscovites would have seen the Third Rome and New Israel images as complementary rather than contradictory; indeed, they are both part of the same idea of a series of Christian empires succeeding each other as prefiguration and fulfillment down to the Apocalypse. And the very historical forces in the two centuries after the Council of Florence that led to the evolution of the Third Rome theory and other fictions linking Moscow's dynasty to Caesar Augustus or describing the transfer of emblems of sanctity to Moscow also led to an increase in the explicitness of Old Testament parallels. The image of Muscovy as the New Israel, however, seems to have remained primary. The Old Testament lent to Muscovy not a claim to universal empire and a drive to rule the world, but a sense of being under a special divine protection or dispensation and a role in sacred history for both the tsar and his elite. More speculatively, one might even say the close connection with the Old Testament pattern of God's punishment of His chosen people to induce obedience led Muscovites to emphasize the strict judgmental qualities of God rather than His mercy and grace, to insist on order and obedience rather than on spontaneity and spiritual freedom.[56] The Third Rome theory, moreover, has often been used by Western historians and others, especially those not particularly conversant with other aspects of Muscovite history, as evidence of Muscovy's "Eastern" and exotic nature and as a prefiguration of later, especially Soviet, designs on world empire (the Third Rome, the Third International, and so on). The New Israel theme, on the other hand, links Muscovite culture both with

Western Europe and with America. The ideas of typology and historical recurrence, which figured so prominently in Muscovite historiography, received great elaboration in the West both in the Middle Ages and later. The Reformation in particular gave rise to the idea of a national covenant by which a particular ethnic group such as the English could see itself as the New Israel that would fulfill New Testament prophecies and usher in the Last Days.[57] The New England Puritans believed in a similar covenant between themselves and God. William Bradford as well as Saint Vladimir and Ivan III were seen as the "New Moses" by their contemporaries.[58] Although biblical allegory and typology developed perhaps more lushly in the West than in Muscovy, the tradition is a common one.

There seem to have been two chief differences between the Muscovite and the New World Puritan uses of Old Testament parallels. First, Muscovite thought gave an increasingly essential role to the state. Although some people other than grand princes or tsars were equated with Old Testament heroes, the overwhelming majority of these images, at least in historical sources, was focused on the state or its representatives. When, during the Troubles, both faith in the state and the state itself almost disappeared, the reaction was apocalypticism and despair rather than continued faith in the future of the New Israel. In this sense, the Muscovites were similar to those English Puritans who believed in a national covenant between God and England. These people were enthusiastic supporters of Oliver Cromwell, especially during the early years of his power, but the movement collapsed and disappeared as the rule of "the Saints" in the Barebones Parliament failed and was replaced by the Protectorate and ultimately by the restoration of Charles II. The New England Puritans, on the other hand, although they believed in a strong union between church and state, were not wedded to any particular political form. Their mythology could and did survive political change. This dissimilarity led to another, namely, the greater optimism of the New Englanders. No matter how great their difficulties, however heavy the rod with which God chastised His errant children, the Puritans believed in the absolute unchangeability and indissolubility of the covenant between God and the New Israel, including even the visible saints' unregenerate children.[59] The Muscovites' focus on the state made their ideology vulnerable to political change. During the darkest days of the Time of Troubles, a priest had a vision in the Dormition Cathedral (later duly written down) in which the Mother of God was seen interceding with Her Son to persuade Him to continue His mercy toward Muscovy and the Muscovite people. The message of the vision was clear: If the Muscovites did not reform their ways, Christ would wash His hands of them once and for all.[60]

We might finally note that there is nothing particularly exotic or Eastern about "New Rome" theories, either. In the Middle Ages, at least six West European towns—Aix-la-Chapelle, Tournai, Reims, Treves, Milan, and Pavia—were glorified by their chroniclers as "Second Romes."[61] As Americans know (and as our coins would tell us if we forget), our own Founding Fathers were preoccupied by the image of Rome. In 1803, the Irish poet Thomas Moore wrote mockingly of the pretensions of Washington, then a town barely and badly built, to be a "second Rome":

> In fancy now, beneath the twilight gloom,
> Come, let me lead thee o'er this "second Rome"
> Where tribunes rule, where dusky Davy bows,
> And what was Goose-creek once is Tiber now.[62]

Notes

1. Edward Keenan, "Muscovite Political Folkways," *Russian Review* 45 (April 1986): 138–148. See also Valerie Kivelson, "The Devil Stole His Mind: The Tsar and the 1648 Moscow Uprising," *American Historical Review* 98 (June 1993): 733–764; Daniel Rowland, "Did Russian Literary Ideology Place Limits on the Power of the Tsar (1540s–1660s)?," *Russian Review* 49 (April 1990): 125–155 (chapter 4 of this volume), "Biblical Military Imagery in the Political Culture of Early Modem Russia: The Blessed Host of the Heavenly Tsar" (chapter 6 of this volume), and Nancy Shields Kollmann, "Pilgrimage, Procession, and Symbolic Space in Sixteenth-Century Russian Politics," in *Medieval Russian Culture*, ed. Michael Flier and Daniel Rowland (Berkeley: University of California Press, 1994), 2:182–212, and 163–181, respectively. For the influence of religious and cultural ideas on the conquest of Kazan', see Jaroslaw Pelenski, *Russia and Kazan: Conquest and Imperial Ideology (1438–1560s)* (The Hague: Mouton, 1974), esp. chap. 9.

2. The Third Rome idea has been so popular in every genre of works on Russia that a full list of references has never been compiled. For an excellent brief survey of this literature, see George Majeska, "The Moscow Coronation of 1498 Reconsidered," *Jahrbucher fur Geschichte Osteuropas* 26, no. 3 (1978): 353–356. A more detailed evaluation is A. L. Gold'berg, "Historishce Wirklichkeit und Falschung der Idee 'Moskau-das dritte Rom,'" *Jahrbuch fur Geschichte der sozialistichen Lander Europas* 15, no. 2 (1975): 123–141. See also *Roma, Costantinopoli, Mosca: Seminario 21 Aprile 1981* (Naples, c. 1983). One of the most revealing features of the historiography on this issue is that the importance of the idea seems to grow in proportion to the generality and scope of the work concerned. For the importance of the Third Rome idea to one of the founders of modern art, see Marit Werenskiold, "Kandinsky's Moscow," *Art in America* 77 (March 1989): 97–111. Her discussion centers as much on the idea of Moscow as the New Jerusalem as on the Third Rome idea, but she repeats much of the old historiography on the latter theme, including the contention that Filofei's ideas led Ivan IV to assume the title of tsar (98). She also briefly discusses interest in that theme among contemporary Russian artists and in the organization "Pamiat'" (107).

3. Melvin Wren, *A Course of Russian History*, 4th ed. (New York: Macmillan, 1979), 98. Even the noted Russian specialist in the Muscovite period, R. G. Skrynnikov, chose

the title *The Third Rome* for a popular version of his earlier scholarly text on church-state relations (*Tretii Rim* [Saint Petersburg: Dmitrii Bulanin, 1994]), although neither text really discusses the subject.

4. See, in addition to the works cited in note 1, G. Olsr, "Gli ultimi Rurikidi e le basi ideologiche della sovranita dello Stato russo," *Orientalia Christiana Periodica* 12 (1946): 322–373; Nikolay Andreyev, "Filofey and His Epistle to Ivan Vasilyevich," *Slavonic and East European Review* 38 (1959): 1–31; A. L. Gol′dberg, "Istoriko-politicheskie idei russkoi knizhnosti XV–XVII vekov," *Istoriia SSSR*, no. 4 (1975): 59–77; and Paul Bushkovitch, "The Formation of National Consciousness in Early Modern Russia," *Harvard Ukrainian Studies* 10, nos. 3/4 (1986): 356–363. The most thorough evaluation of the evidence on the Third Rome theme is Donald Ostrowski, "Third Rome—Delimiting the Ruler's Power and Authority," *Muscovy and the Mongols: Cross-Cultural Influences on the Steppe Frontier, 1304–1589* (Cambridge: Cambridge University Press, 1998), 219–243.

5. See the letters to Misiur′ Munekhin (about astrology) and to Grand Prince Vasilii Ivanovich and Tsar Ivan Vasil′evich in V. I. Malinin, *Starets Eleazarova monastyria Filofei i ego poslanie* (Kiev: Tip. Kievo-Pecherskoi Uspenskoi lavry, 1901), 37–47, 49–56, and 57–66, respectively.

6. A. L. Gol′dberg, "Tri 'poslaniia Filofeia' (Opyt tekstologicheskogo analiza)," *Trudy Otdela drevnerusskoi literatury* (hereafter *TODRL*) 29 (1974): 93–97. He lists ten more manuscripts that contain other works ascribed to Filofei, but none of the three above letters.

7. *Sobranie gosudarstvennykh gramot i dogovorov* (Saint Petersburg, 1819), 2:97.

8. Gol′dberg, "Istoriko-politicheskie idei," 71–73; Bushkovitch, "National Consciousness," 358–359; Ostrowski, "Third Rome." Ostrowski gives a careful summary of the evidence for the Third Rome idea both in Filofei's letters and in other texts. The dating of the particular redactions of these other texts containing the Third Rome idea is often difficult to establish with precision. One frequently cited early locus for the Third Rome idea is the 1492 paschal canon by Metropolitan Zosima. In 1986, I. A. Tikhoniuk pointed out that three of the four earliest copies of the canon (the copies closest to the archetype) have the reading "New Jerusalem" instead of "New Rome" in a crucial passage. "'Izlozhenie paskhalii' Moskovskogo mitropolita Zosimy," in *Issledovaniia po istochnikovedeniiu SSSR XIII–XVII vv.: Sbornik statei*, ed. V. I. Buganov, V. A. Kuchkin, and V. G. Litvak (Moscow: Akademiia nauk, 1986), 53–54, quoted in Ostrowski, "Third Rome," 221.

9. Gol′dberg, "Istoriko-politicheskie idei," 71–73; Ostrowski, "Third Rome."

10. N. S. Chaev, "'Moskva-tretii Rim' v politicheskoi praktike moskovskogo pravitel′stva XVI v.," *Istoricheskie zapiski* 17 (1945): 1–23.

11. The only monograph dealing directly with the subject, as far as I know, is the rare N. I. Efimov, *Rus′-novyi Israel: Teokraticheskaia ideologiia svoezemnago Pravoslaviia v do-Petrovskoi pis′mennosti* (Kazan, 1912). See also G. P. Fedotov's still classic work, *The Russian Religious Mind* (1946; repr. New York: n.p., 1960), 1:63–93, 380–385. Most welcome recent additions to this literature are Joel Raba, "The Biblical Tradition in Old Russian Chronicles," *Forschungen zur osteuropaischen Geschichte* 46 (1992): 9–20; and Andrei Batalov and Aleksei Lidov, eds., *Ierusalim v russkoi kul′ture* (Moscow: Nauka, 1994). (An expanded English version of this collection is available: *Jerusalem in Russian Culture* [New York: A. D. Carattzas, 1994].) For some recent general arguments that

biblical references are crucial to understanding East Slavic texts, see Riccardo Picchio, "The Function of Biblical Thematic Clues in the Literary Code of 'Slavia Orthodoxa,'" *Slavica Hierosolymitana* 1 (1977): 1–32; Walter K. Hanak, "The Nature and Image of Grand Princely Power in Kievan Russia: 980–1054" (PhD diss., Indiana University, 1973); G. Stokl, "Die zweite Solomon," *Canadian-American Slavic Studies* 13, nos. 1–2 (1979): 23–31; Daniel Rowland, "Toward an Understanding of the Political Ideas in Ivan Timofeyev's *Vremennik*," *Slavonic and East European Review* 62 (July 1984): 379–384 (chapter 2 of this volume); Marilyn Nelson, "The Structure and Exegesis in 'Jaroslav Founded the Great City Kiev . . .' from the Primary Chronicle," *James Daniel Armstrong: In Memoriam* (Bloomington, IN: Slavica, 1994), 143–154; and Hugh Olmstead, "A Learned Greek Monk in Muscovite Exile: Maksim Grek and Old Testament Prophets," *Modern Greek Studies Yearbook* 3 (1987): 1–73. Almost every editor of a Muscovite text has pointed out at least some scriptural references (I. N. Lebedeva, ed., *Povest' o Varlaame i Ioasafe* [Moscow: Nauka, 1985], is particularly impressive in this regard), and discussions of biblical themes as developed in particular contexts are relatively common.

12. Horace Lunt points out in the preface to his *Concise Dictionary of Old Russian* (Munich: Wilhelm Fink, 1970) that "Soviet studies have neglected this sort of problem [of Biblical references] entirely, while Sreznevskij and other prerevolutionary scholars failed to point out such details because it all seemed so obvious to them" (vi).

13. The literature on this theme is vast. See, for example, the bibliography in Sacvan Bercovitch, ed., *Typology and Early American Literature* (Amherst, MA: University of Massachusetts Press, 1972), 245–337.

14. The text history of this service remains a little unclear. This quotation agrees with copy P of the *Nikon Chronicle* (*Polnoe sobranie russkikh letopisei* [hereafter, PSRL], vol. 13 [1904; repr., Moscow, 1965], 150), which B. M. Kloss considers was written in the late 1550s (*Nikonovskii svod i russkie letopisi XVI–XVII vekov* [Moscow: Nauka, 1980], 202–203). The coronation text in a much fuller version is found in a *tipikion* that E. V. Barsov claimed was contemporary with the service itself, but the text of this prayer is substantially the same in both the chronicle and liturgical versions (*Drevnerusskie pamiatniki venchaniia tsarei na tsarstvo* [Moscow: n.p., 1883], 42, 51, also 76). The inclusion of this prayer in the chronicle tradition testifies to its importance. See also the *L'vov Chronicle*, PSRL, vol. 20, part 2 (1914; repr., Dusseldorf, 1971), 468. For an excellent survey of the relevant literature, see David B. Miller, "The Coronation of Ivan IV of Moscow," *Jahrbucher fur Geschichte Osteuropas*, N.F. 15, part 4 (December 1967): 559–574.

15. Michael Cherniavsky, "Khan or Basileus: An Aspect of Russian Mediaeval Political Theory," *Journal of the History of Ideas* 20 (1959): 459–476, reprinted in Michael Cherniavsky, ed., *The Structure of Russian History* (New York: Random House, 1970), 65–79.

16. For the "King of Kings" prayer, see, among other references, Barsov, *Drevnerusskie pamiatniki*, 27; and N. H. Baynes, "The Thought World of East Rome," *Byzantine Studies and Other Essays* (London: Athlone, 1955), 33–34. So prominent is the model of David in imperial iconography that Christopher Walter has called him "the paragon of Byzantine Emperors." See Walter, "Raising on a Shield in Byzantine Iconography," *Revue des Etudes Byzantines* 33 (1975): 168. Old Testament themes in Byzantine imperial iconography are reviewed in Andre Grabar, *L'Empereur dans l'Art Byzantin* (Paris:

Les Belles lettres, 1936), 95–97; and in Paul Magdalino and Robert Nelson, "The Emperor in Byzantine Art of the Twelfth Century," *Byzantinische Forschungen* 8 (1982): 136, 139, 144–145, and figure 6.

17. C. A. Bouman, *Sacring and Crowning: The Development of the Latin Ritual for the Anointing of Kings and the Coronation of an Emperor before the Eleventh Century* (Groningen: Wolters, 1957), 107–126.

18. Janet Nelson, "Symbols in Context: Rulers' Inauguration Rituals in Byzantium and in the West in the Early Middle Ages," *Studies in Church History* 11 (1975): 97–119. The same may be true for the Muscovite coronation ceremony, or at least the anointing part of it, which was added in 1547 to the earlier ceremony used to crown Ivan III's grandson Dmitrii in 1498. In both 1547 and 1498 the government was in a weak position. In 1498 an heir who was not the eldest surviving son of the ruler was inserted into the succession by means of an extraordinary service (see Majeska, "The Moscow Coronation"). Note that the precedent was not followed in the case of Vasilii III, who succeeded in the normal fashion, with no recorded coronation ceremony. In 1547 the ruler was a young boy, and the service seemed to have been compiled by the powerful and widely read Metropolitan Makarii, who may well have been limiting the authority of the state in the ceremony rather than expanding it, as has often been thought. Certainly the speeches of the metropolitan and the young tsar show two seemingly opposed concepts of rulership, Makarii enunciating the biblical idea of the kingdom as a divine trust and Ivan simply stating that the kingdom was his because his father had given it to him. See Barsov, *Drevnerusskie pamiatniki*, 56–60, 80–84, 48, 73–74. Common sense would dictate that the tough and capable men of the Muscovite court, who apparently thought of the tsardom as the personal property of the ruler, would have looked askance at the idea of the state as a divine gift that brought with it certain obligations, however ill-defined. See Richard Pipes, *Russia under the Old Regime* (New York: Charles Scribner's Sons, 1974), 64; and Nancy Shields Kollmann, *Kinship and Politics: The Making of the Muscovite Political System* (Stanford, CA: Stanford University Press, 1987), 3.

19. I am not referring here to any explicit, written rules found in contemporary sources; rather, my comments are based on my analysis of the way East Slavic historians wrote history. For authors who share this general view, see note 11. For a parallel interpretation in which God's intention or will is revealed in events commemorated in both side altars of churches and in border scenes in icons, with citations to Orthodox writers who support this interpretation, see A. L. Batalov, "K interpretatsii arkhitektury sobora Pokrova na Rvu," in *Ikonografiia arkhitektury*, ed. A. L. Batalov (Moscow: VNIITAG, 1990), 28–29, passim.

20. G. W. Trompf, *The Idea of Historical Recurrence in Western Thought from Antiquity to the Reformation* (Berkeley: University of California Press, 1979). Trompf argues that the idea of recurrence played only "a secondary role" in the Middle Ages (208–209). I would suggest that recurrence remained more important in the Orthodox world, in part at least because of liturgical texts that consistently emphasized the pattern of recurrence to be found between New Testament and Old Testament events—manna, the Incarnation, the Eucharist, to give one example, or the tree of the Garden of Eden and the cross of the Crucifixion. In the first example we see a parallel relationship; the second illustrates a more reciprocal one. For types of recurrence, see 2–3.

21. For an excellent brief overview of this tradition of exegesis within the East Slavic context, see Marilyn Nelson, "Biblical Typology," in *Modern Encyclopedia of Religions in Russia and the Soviet Union*, ed. Paul Steeves (Gulf Breeze, FL: Academic International Press, 1991), 4:90–97.

22. D. S. Likhachev and V. P. Adrianova-Peretts, eds., *Povest' vremennykh let* (Moscow-Leningrad, 1950), 16–17; S. H. Cross and O. P. Sherbowitz-Wetzor, trans. and eds., *The Russian Primary Chronicle* (Cambridge, MA: Medieval Academy of America, 1953), 58.

23. *Povest' vremennykh let*, 61–74; *Russian Primary Chronicle*, 98–109. For a most useful discussion of the sources of the "philosopher's speech," with references to earlier discussions of this important passage, see Simon Franklin, "Some Apocryphal Sources of Kievan Russian Historiography," *Oxford Slavonic Papers* 15 (1982): 1–27. Franklin shows the importance of the pseudoepigraphical "Book of Jubilees" (which retells the story of mankind from the creation to the Exodus in a kind of partial paraphrase of the canonical books of Genesis and Exodus) to the *Primary Chronicle*, to the various historical compendiums (*khronografy*) that circulated in Kievan Rus' and to Kievan historical consciousness in general. Raba, in "The Biblical Tradition," traces Old Testament references in the *Primary Chronicle* in general, as does A. Shakhmatov, "Povest' vremennykh let i ee istochniki," *TODRL* 4 (1940): 38–41.

24. On the surprising lack of attention paid to Byzantine political affairs in Kievan historical works, both chronicles and historical compendiums, see Simon Franklin, "The Empire of the Rhomaioi as Viewed from Kievan Russia: Aspects of Byzantino-Russian Cultural Relations," *Byzantion* 53, no. 2 (1983): 507–537.

25. *Povest' vremennykh let*, 89, 68–69; *Russian Primary Chronicle*, 124, 104–105 (emphasis added).

26. *Povest' vremennykh let*, 289; *Russian Primary Chronicle*, 125–126.

27. See the typological interpretation of the story of Gideon and the fleece (Judges 6:36–40) as foreshadowing the sacrament of baptism and God's favoring of Gentiles over Jews (*Povest' vremennykh let*, 272; *Russian Primary Chronicle*, 109).

28. Ludolf Müller, ed., *Des Metropoliten Ilarion Lobrede auf Vladimir den Heiiigen und Glaubensbekenntnis* (Wiesbaden: n.p., 1962), 121–122, 69, 85–87, passim.

29. *Pamiatniki literatury drevnei Rusi: XII vek* (Moscow: Khdozhestvennaia literatura, 1981), 426.

30. *PSRL*, vol. 6 (Saint Petersburg, 1853), 110, 105, 106. M. A. Salmina gives a thorough discussion of the dating and text history of this tale in "Slovo o zhitii i o prestavlenii velikogo kniazia Dmitriia Ivanovicha, tsaria Rus'skago," *TODRL* 25 (1970): 81–104. For a survey of the entire cycle, see Charles Halperin, "The Russian Land and the Russian Tsar: The Emergence of Muscovite Ideology, 1380–1408," *Forschungen zur osteuropaischen Geschichte* 23 (1976): 7–103. For the dating of these texts, see Ia. S. Lur'e, *Dve istorii Rusi XV veka* (Saint Petersburg: Dmitrii Bulanin, 1994), 23–31.

31. *PSRL*, 6:228–229.

32. David Miller has written a careful survey of the contents of the *Menology* based on manuscripts of both the Novgorod and Moscow redactions. See his "The *Velikie Minei Chetii* and the *Stepennaia Kniga* of Metropolitan Makarii and the Origins of Russian National Consciousness," *Forschungen zur osteuropaischen Geschichte* 26 (1979): 263–313. The quoted expressions are at 276.

33. Miller, "The *Velikie Minei Chetii*," 270–273.

34. Miller, "The *Velikie Minei Chetii*," 274, 308. Although, as Miller asserts (272–273), most of the Octateuch was lacking in the *Menology*, some thirty-one Old Testament or Apocryphal books (or large parts of them) were present in the *Menology*, while "in place of the Octateuch there were large excerpts from a Palaea" (Robert Mathiesen, "Handlist of Manuscripts Containing Church Slavonic Translations from the Old Testament," *Polata knigopisnaja* 7 [March 1983]: 7). Much Old Testament information, moreover, was included in other sources, such as the "Golden Chain," excerpts from Flavius Josephus, and the "Tale of Barlaam and Josephat," to name only a few.

35. O. V. Tvorogov, *Drevnerusskie khronografy* (Leningrad: Nauka, 1975), 120n34.

36. *PSRL*, vol. 11 (Saint Petersburg, 1897), 17.

37. *PSRL*, 11:60; *PSRL*, vol. 12 (1901; repr., Moscow, 1965), 131; *PSRL*, 11:254. There was a separate tale about David and Goliath. A. I. Sobolevskii, *Perevodnaia literatura Moskovskoi Rusi XIV–XVII vekov* (Saint Petersburg: Tip. Imp. Akademii nauk, 1903), 278.

38. *PSRL*, vol. 21, pt. 2 (Saint Petersburg, 1913), 590, cited in Miller, "The Velikie Minei Chetii," 359.

39. Simon Schama finds evidence that the writers and painters of the early modern Netherlands used Old Testament terminology to signify gradations of badness among its enemies, calling those enemies Amalekites who were "so evil that extermination was called for." See his *The Embarrassment of Riches: An Interpretation of Dutch Culture in the Golden Age* (New York: Knopf, 1987), 95. I have not noticed this device in Muscovite usage of these terms, but the question of its use remains an open one.

40. *Vremennik Ivana Timofeeva*, ed. O. A. Derzhavina (Moscow: Izd. Akademii Nauk, 1951), 29–30. For a further discussion of this passage and a lengthy but still partial list of Old Testament comparisons in the *Vremennik*, see Rowland, "Toward an Understanding," 380–382 (chapter 2 of this volume).

41. Timofeev added Sviatopolk to his list of slayers of innocents (*Vremennik*, 29–30). On the use of the Cain comparison in the Boris and Gleb texts, see Picchio, "The Function of Biblical Thematic Clues." Timofeev's discussion of Godunov's building projects is in *Vremennik*, 64–65.

42. *Vremennik*, 10, 136, 150; *PSRL*, vol. 14 (1910; repr., Moscow, 1965), 11–13.

43. *Russkaia istoricheskaia biblioteka*, 2nd ed., vol. 13 (Saint Petersburg, 1909), cols. 224, 230, 234, 179, 181, 183, 1317, and 1540; N. F. Droblenkova, *Novaia povest' o preslavnom rossiiskom tsarstve* (Moscow-Leningrad: Akademiia nauk), 198; Conrad Bussow, *Moskovskaia khronika, 1584–1613*, ed. I. I. Smirnov (Moscow-Leningrad: Akademiia nauk, 1961), 159. I am grateful to Chester Dunning for the reference to Bussow.

44. The paintings were painted over in the 1670s, and the building itself was demolished in the eighteenth century, but a careful description made in 1672 by the icon painter Simon Ushakov and the scribe Nikita Klement'ev survives and has been twice published. See I. E. Zabelin, *Materialy dlia istorii, arkheologii i statistiki goroda Moskvy*, 2 vols. (Moscow: Moskovskaia gorodskaia tip., 1884), 1:1238–1255; and S. P. Bartenev, *Moskovskii kreml' v starinu i teper'*, 2 vols. (Moscow: Sinodal'naia tip., 1916), 2:183–193. The fullest analysis, together with an artist's reconstruction of the wall paintings, can be found in O. I. Podobedova, *Moskovskaia shkola zhivopisi pri Ivane IV: Raboty v Moskovskom Kremle 40-kh–70-kh godov XVI v.* (Moscow: Nauka, 1972), 59–68, and illustrations at the end of the book. Note that the dating of these paintings is disputed by

MOSCOW—THE THIRD ROME OR THE NEW ISRAEL?   185

K. K. Lopialo, the artist of the reconstructions (see Podobedova, *Moskovskaia shkola*, 194–196), among others. For paleographic evidence tending to confirm the mid-sixteenth-century dating of at least some details of the murals, see Rowland, "Biblical Military Imagery," 194n29 (chapter 6 of this volume). It is impossible finally to resolve the question of the dating of all the images described by Ushakov and Klenent'ev, many of which may well have been painted (or painted over) in the seventeenth century.

45. On the history of the depiction of Moses's raised hands at this moment, see Meyer Schapiro, *Words and Pictures: On the Literal and Symbolic in the Illustration of a Text* (The Hague: Mouton, 1973).

46. For a Byzantine example of imagery showing Joshua as the prototype of the Byzantine emperor Constantine Porphyrogenitus, see Kurt Wietzmann, *The Joshua Roll: A Work of the Macedonian Renaissance* (Princeton, NJ: Princeton University Press, 1948).

47. The original paintings from the Palace of Facets no longer exist, but a description of them by Ushakov and Klement'ev is printed in Zabelin, *Materialy*, cols. 1255–1271. The multiple scenes from Joseph's life probably were meant to emphasize the importance of Boris Godunov as chief adviser of Tsar Fedor Ivanovich. I thank Michael Flier for the identification of Jehosephat in the Zolotaia palata.

48. This theme is described in more detail in Rowland, "Biblical Military Imagery."

49. V. I. Antonova and N. E. Mneva, *Katalog drevnerusskoi zhivopisi XI–XVII vv.* (Moscow: Iskusstvo, 1963), 2 vols. 2:130–131, identify the figures in the army as Saints Vladimir, Boris, Gleb, and Alexander Nevskii, together with Dmitrii Donskoi and other rulers of Rus´, but I. A. Kochetkov brings convincing reasons to disagree. See his "K istolkovaniiu ikony 'Tserkov' voinstvuiushchaia' ('Blagoslovenno voinstvo nebesnogo tsaria')," *TODRL* 38 (1985): 186–209.

50. For recent surveys of the extensive literature on this subject, see Batalov, "K interpretatsii"; N. I. Brunov, *Pokrovskii sobor* (Moscow: Iskusstvo, 1988), esp. 216–236; and Frank Kampfer, "Uber die theologische und architektonische Konzeption der Vasilij-Blazennyj-Kathedrale in Moskau," *Jahrbiicher fur Geschichte Osteuropas* 24, no. 4 (1976): 481–498. The most convincing interpretation of the complex meaning of the architectural ensemble is Michael Flier, "Filling in the Blanks: The Church of the Intercession and the Architectonics of Medieval Muscovite Ritual," in *Kamen´ kraeug"l´n": Rhetoric of the Medieval Slavic World*, vol. 19, nos. 1–4, ed. Nancy S. Kollmann et al. (Cambridge, MA: Harvard Ukrainian Studies, 1995), 120–137. The quotation about the chapel, dedicated to the Entry into Jerusalem, is on 125.

51. Kampfer, "Uber die theologische," 493–494. For the importance of the wisdom theme in mid-sixteenth-century Muscovy, particularly in the Golden Hall, see Podobedova, *Moskovskaia shkola*, 59–68.

52. A. M. Lidov, "Ierusalimskii kuvuklii: O proiskhozhdenii lukovichnykh glav," in *Ikonografiia arkhitektury*, ed. A. L. Batalov (Moscow: VNIITAG, 1992), 57–68.

53. The most detailed discussion of Godunov's proposed radical changes to the Kremlin is M. A. Il'in, "Proekt perestroiki tsentra Moskovskogo Kremlia pri Borise Godunove," *Soobshcheniia instituta istorii iskusstv* 1 (1951): 79–83. See also M. A. Il'in, *Kamennaia letopis' moskovskoi Rusi* (Moscow: Izd. Moskovksogo universiteta, 1966), 56–58; and N. L. Batalov and T. N. Viatchinina, "Ob ideinom znachenii i interpretatsii Ierusalimskogo obraza v russkoi arkhitekture XVI–XVII vv.," *Arkhitekturnoe nasledstvo*

36 (1988): 22–28. On Godunov's larger urban designs, see N. E. Gulianitskii, ed., *Drevnerusskoe gradostroitel'stvo X–XV vekov* (Moscow: Stroiizdat, 1993), 329–339. The *Petrovskii chertezh* is reproduced in Gulianitskii, *Drevnerusskoe gradostroitel'stvo*, 246–247, but the history of this map requires further research. (Note that the legend of the *Petrovskii chertezh* points out that the Church of the Intercession on the Moat was called "Jerusalem" [*etiam Hierusalem dicitur*].) The best discussion of early maps of Moscow is M. V. Posokhin, ed., *Pamiatniki arkhitektury Moskvy: Kreml', Kitai-gorod, Tsentral'nye ploshchadi* (Moscow: Iskusstvo, 1982), 35–81. The precious gems with which Boris encrusted his model of the "Holy of Holies" may also have been meant as a reference to the heavenly Jerusalem (Rev. 21:18–21; Isa. 54:11–14). After this article was completed I was able to examine quickly M. P. Kudriavtsev's *Moskva-Tretii Rim: Istoriko-gradostroitel'noe issledovanie* (Moscow: Sol Sistem, 1994). In spite of the title, the book contains extensive comparisons of Jerusalem, either heavenly or real, to Moscow and to other Rus' towns. The chapter entitled "Tretii Rim" deals more with parallels with Jerusalem than with comparisons to Rome.

54. See Batalov and Viatchinina, "Ob ideinnom znachenii," 36–42; Il'in, *Kamennaia letopis'*, 176–204, particularly for discussions of the Mount of Olives Chapel and the theme of the heavenly Jerusalem in seventeenth-century Russian culture; James Cracraft, *The Petrine Revolution in Architecture* (Chicago: University of Chicago Press, 1988), 70–73; G. V. Alferova, "K voprosu o stroitel'noi deiatel'nosti Patriarkha Nikona," *Arkhitekturnoe nasledstvo* 18 (1969): 30–44. The history of the New Jerusalem Monastery should make us cautious when describing what was done (or intended) in Nikon's time. Construction remained unfinished at Nikon's death, but resumed in the 1680s and later; the masonry conical dome over the great rotunda of the Resurrection Cathedral collapsed in 1723, and a fire in 1726 caused further damage; the building was rebuilt in 1752–1759 from designs by Rastrelli; the Nazis inflicted tremendous damage on the whole monastery complex in 1941; and the complex has undergone extensive restoration since the war. Nikon's revealing defense of the name and Jerusalem-inspired designs for his monastery has been twice published from different manuscripts: in English by William Palmer, *The Patriarch and the Tsar*, 6 vols. (London, 1871–1876), 1:67–78; and in Russian by Valerie Tumins and George Vernadsky, eds., *Patriarch Nikon on Church and State* (Berlin, 1982), 149–158. The quoted words in square brackets are in Palmer's version, but not in Tumins and Vernadsky's.

55. Mathiesen, "Handlist of Manuscripts," 3–5.

56. "The commentaries found in Muscovite chronicles concerning the crucial events and developments in the relations between Muscovy and the Kazan Khanate were based on a simple moral formula. Muscovite defeats and misfortunes were explained by the sins of Christian Russians, and Russian victories and successes by God's grace and his positive intervention in a just cause." Pelenski, *Russia and Kazan*, 179. See alos Georges Florovsky, "The Problem of Old Russian Culture," *Slavic Review* 21 (March 1962): 115, reprinted in Cherniavsky, *Structure*, 126–139.

57. Harold Fisch, *Jerusalem and Albion: The Hebraic Theme in Seventeenth-Century Literature* (New York: Schocken, 1964). For the Dutch, Old Testament imagery helped to create a sense of national identity even in the absence of clear ethnic or linguistic links. See Schama, *Embarrassment of Riches*, chap. 2.

58. For a superb essay on the Old Testament roots of American culture, see Sacvan Bercovitch, *The American Jeremiad* (Cambridge: Cambridge University Press, 1974).

59. Bercovitch, *The American Jeremiad*, esp. chap. 3.
60. *Russkaia istoricheskaia biblioteka* 13, cols. 177–184.
61. William Hammer, "The Concept of the New or Second Rome in the Middle Ages," *Speculum* 19 (January 1944): 50–62.
62. Thomas Moore, *The Complete Poetical Works* (London: Longmans, Green, Reader, and Dyer, 1869), 100. I thank my colleague Mark Summers for this reference.

Chapter 8

Architecture and Dynasty
Boris Godunov's Uses of Architecture, 1584–1605

The political and geographic environment in pre-Petrine Rus´ favored architecture as a major but little-investigated arena for symbolic action by the ruler. Although conditions obviously varied from time to time and place to place, there were four overlapping characteristics of all of the various states of Rus´ before Peter that made architecture particularly useful as a tool of state-building: territories that were very large by European standards, the presence of multiple political and cultural units within those territories, relatively weak governmental structures, and almost entirely illiterate populations. Under these conditions, rulers from Saint Vladimir to Peter the Great used architecture both to demonstrate their power and to define their image. Texts could be read only by a tiny minority; the largest pictures could be seen by but a few. Buildings, on the other hand, were large and tangible; they were visible from a distance over the consistently open Russian landscape, and, though they may have communicated a sophisticated meaning to the learned observer, they required little or no special knowledge to understand at a basic level. They could mark various points distributed over the

---

This essay originally appeared in *Architectures of Russian Identity, 1500–Present*, ed. James Cracraft and Daniel Rowland (Ithaca, NY: Cornell University Press, 2003), 34–47. The author gratefully acknowledges the publisher for permission reprint this essay.

whole territory of a state, and thus create in real space visual symbols of the unity of that state.

This was so at least from the conversion to Christianity, for Vladimir, Yaroslav, and their successors effectively used architecture, in the form of new Christian churches, to create the image of a single Christian people and state in place of the fragmented tribal territories that existed on the ground. Architecture was working in harmony with the other arts in this case: chronicles, saints' lives, sermons, and monumental painting were all making the same point. For most of this period, it is difficult to document the people's reaction to architecture, but we do know that architectural construction, whether of churches, fortifications, or palaces, was avidly noted in chronicles from the *Primary Chronicle* to the *Nikon Chronicle* and beyond.

Rulers or elites who were rich enough to afford it used architecture to define and justify their rule as well as to demonstrate their wealth and power: Saint Vladimir and Yaroslav the Wise, Andrei Bogoliubskii, the merchants of Novgorod, and Ivan III, to say nothing of Peter and Catherine, Stalin, and our contemporary, Mayor Luzhkov of Moscow—all expended great personal effort, considerable bureaucratic resources, and a lot of money on buildings. Scholars, especially historians, have yet to match their effort: At least in relation to the pre-Petrine period, architecture finds too little place in discussions of political history, and is too often sequestered (and in a way trivialized) in chapters (or books) dealing with "the arts."

A brief discussion of the ways that Boris Godunov used architecture makes a useful case study of this issue for several reasons. First, although the architectural efforts of Ivan III (in the Kremlin) and Ivan IV (in the construction of Saint Basil's) have received due attention from historians, Godunov's architectural activities have not been widely discussed, particularly in relation to his other activities as a ruler or to the symbolism of political power in Muscovy. Second, we have a small but tantalizing amount of evidence about Godunov's own intentions, plus the comments of a number of contemporaries, native and foreign, on his architectural enterprises. These latter materials allow us access to some perceptions of Godunov's architectural efforts, and thus enable us to gauge how successful those efforts were. To this information may be added excellent studies, particularly of church architecture, by Russian architectural historians who have studied not only the buildings as they currently exist but such documentary evidence of their past states as can be found. They have also examined the results of "above-ground archaeology," the study of a building's history as revealed in its surviving fabric, a study that is often carried out in the process of restoration work and reported in restoration reports.

CHAPTER 8

Finally, a brief survey of all of the uses of architecture made by one ruler serves as a starting point for further discussions of architecture as a tool of government and state building.

When, after a good deal of maneuvering, Boris Godunov finally managed to arrange his own coronation in 1598, he faced the enormous problem of establishing his legitimacy as tsar and the legitimacy of the Godunov clan as the new ruling dynasty. This problem was unprecedented. In the past there had been disputed successions and rulers too young to really rule, but past difficulties had centered around too many heirs rather than too few. The dynasty, even in the form of a powerless boy such as the young Ivan IV, was the slender thread that kept the political system from sliding into chaos. The accession of Ivan's son, the mentally handicapped Fedor Ivanovich, in 1584 (under whom Godunov as royal brother-in-law exerted the real power) still left room to hope for a new heir, but the death of Fedor in 1598 snapped the thread and ended the dynasty.[1]

The selection of a new ruling dynasty was thus the most pressing political problem that Muscovy faced at the end of the sixteenth century, and it had two obvious components. First, a political consensus at court had to be found (or forged) around a new ruler and his clan. Here Godunov faced a major difficulty because his own clan was less prestigious in terms of origins and service than its main rivals, the Romanovs and the Shuiskies. Second, since the political culture of Muscovy was built around the idea that God alone chose the tsar, this political process had to be concealed under a myth of divine choice. Given his weak genealogical position at court, Godunov needed especially to rely on the public propagation of his and his family's image as embodying accepted ideals of Christian rulership and thus demonstrating God's choice of them. This symbolic side of his actions has received much less attention than his political efforts.

The sheer amount of building that Godunov either planned or carried out, the remarkable amount of obviously scarce resources that he devoted to his various architectural projects, and the comments of native and foreign observers at the time all testify to the emphasis that Godunov placed on architecture as a means to establish his legitimacy and that of his clan. His choice is hardly surprising. Ivan III had expended great effort and money in his campaign to rebuild the Moscow Kremlin, carried on largely through the efforts of his Italian architects and engineers. Vasilii III had commissioned the dramatic, tent-roofed Church of the Ascension at Kolomenskoe to commemorate the birth of his young son. That son, Ivan IV, in turn built the Cathedral of the Intercession on the Moat, popularly known as Saint Basil's, to commemorate not only his conquest of Kazan′, but also, as Michael Flier has recently shown, his success in producing a male heir.[2] The connections of architecture with both dynasty and military victory in sixteenth-century Muscovy were thus established as a subset of the relationship, common in virtually all states, between architecture and state power. From Godunov's point of view, architecture had the advantage over painting or texts. Here architecture operated in tandem with the growing reach of the governmental apparatus. In earlier years, when he stood looking at a church or fortification, the Russian peasant was probably having a rare direct encounter with the government under which he lived. Now the very bureaucratic forces that enabled Godunov to carry out his comprehensive architectural program also brought his government into closer contact with his subjects on a wide variety of social levels. These contacts reflected several areas of governmental concern, particularly the collection of taxes, the performance of military service, and the apparatus of justice.

Historians of Muscovite Russia might well be alarmed by my promiscuous use of the word "people" in connection with Godunov's ambition to become and remain tsar. Surely, they might say, it was the boyars who made and unmade tsars. The answer to this question reveals an important reason why architecture was so important to Godunov. It was in the Boyar Duma that Godunov had the most enemies, or so the traditional scholarship tells us.[3] During his campaign to become tsar, he successfully used the Assembly of the Land and the Sacred Council to bolster his position in the Duma. His strenuous staging of rituals of popular acclaim demonstrates his desire to appeal to an audience wider than the Boyar Duma.[4]

Architecture, as we have seen, had a better ability to communicate with people geographically and socially outside the elite than any other weapon in the cultural arsenal of Muscovite rulership. And indeed, the presumed audience for Godunov's projects was remarkably wide. The elite, both secular and ecclesiastic, would have been powerfully impressed by his planned transformation of Cathedral Square in the Kremlin. His fortified trading towns like Astrakhan′ and Archangel were of great benefit to merchants; his towns to the south and east provided protection and land to members of the middle and lower service classes, and new military positions for an expanding service elite. His building projects, whether on frontiers or in the central regions, provided employment. The great visibility of many projects made them accessible to anyone who passed through the wide Russian landscape. Finally, traditional Christian ideals of rulership stressed the tsar's obligations to the Christian people as a whole, not just to the elite. Architecture, of all the arts, allowed Godunov to be perceived as fulfilling these obligations.

From a practical point of view, surely the most important of Godunov's architectural activities was his construction or renovation of fortresses. The scale of Godunov's fortress building in virtually every section of the country is staggering. It required the mobilization of enormous resources, human and material, and was probably not equaled again until the building campaigns of Peter the Great. (When we consider that Godunov mounted this effort after the many disruptions of the latter part of Ivan the Terrible's reign, his achievement becomes even more remarkable.) The most recent scholar of his work has estimated that the state built or rebuilt more than fifty fortresses during the twenty-one years (1584–1605) that he ruled either directly or indirectly.[5] In the south, Boris extended and strengthened the "abatis lines" (*zasechnye cherty*), which consisted of natural features (rivers, forests, and so on) joined by either wooden walls or, more usually, rows of felled trees, linking fortified towns that were the administrative as well as the military centers of their regions. These towns were built according to detailed instructions containing maps and drawings (*chertezhi*), worked out on the basis of continuing exchanges between local agents and the central bureaucratic apparatus in Moscow, in this case usually the Military Chancellery (the Razriadnyi prikaz).[6] Towns founded in the south by Godunov included Voronezh and Livny (1585–1586); Novyi Elets (1592); Belgorod, Kromy, Valuiki, and Staryi Oskol (1596); and Kursk (1597), as well as Tsarev-Borisov (1597) and Borisov Gorodok (1600), whose names reflect Godunov's desire to connect these construction projects with himself and his dynasty. Godunov was similarly active on the western frontier, where his greatest achievement was the construction of 6.5 kilometers of massive stone fortifications around Smolensk, built under his personal supervision by Fedor Kon'. These fortifications enabled its defenders to resist for many months an intense Polish siege before their final defeat in June 1611, and turned its defenders into national heroes, celebrated in numerous patriotic circular letters in 1610 and 1611. He also repaired (or continued repairing) fortifications in Ladoga, Orekhov, and Pskov (1584–1585), and improved the defenses around several strategically placed monasteries, finishing the new masonry walls of the Cyril-White Lake Monastery (1580–1590) and building stone fortifications around the Ipat'ev Monastery (1586).

In the east, Godunov established defensive points all along the crucial Volga trade route, beginning with the replacement of the wooden fortifications in Astrakhan' with new masonry walls between 7 and 11 meters tall. Between Kazan' and Astrakhan', Godunov founded three major fortress towns, Samara, Tsaritsyn, and Saratov, and, in addition, built smaller intermediate forts between these major points. He thus created a defensive line along the middle and lower reaches of the Volga, effectively protecting the crucial trade route between Muscovy and the great markets of the Middle East.⁷ On the middle Volga, on the territory of the old Khanate of Kazan', Godunov built a series of fortified towns, one after the other: Kokshaisk (1585), Sanchursk (1586), Tsivil'sk (1590), Iaransk (1591), and Urzhum (1595), not to mention his continued work on the fortifications of Kazan' itself. Slightly further east, Ufa was established in Bashkiria. Further east still, in Siberia, the list of towns established during the period under consideration is equally impressive: Tiumen' (1586), Tobol'sk (1586), Surgut (1594), Tara (1594), Verkhotur'e (1598); along the Ob, Berezov (1593), Obdorsk (1595), and Narym (1596); Mangazeia on the Enesiey River (1601); and, further south, Tomsk (1604). While the earliest town foundations may have been carried out by the Stroganovs and their Cossacks with little direction from Moscow, soon Godunov's *prikazy* (chanceries) were bringing their formidable organizational and design skills to the task.⁸

In the north he improved fortifications along the White Sea, establishing in 1584 an *ostrog*, or wooden fortress, at Archangel, complete with musketeers, and soon furnished with many new buildings for trade. By the late 1580s, the government was reaping rich financial rewards from the taxes collected from the Archangel trade. Major fortifications were built around the Solovetskii Monastery, and a smaller fort was constructed in Kem'. In Moscow itself, Godunov built 9 kilometers of massive new masonry walls around Belgorod and completed an oak wall around all of Moscow in less than two years (1591–1592) (aptly named *skorodom* or *skorodum* ["quickly built"]), with fifty-seven towers and twelve gates, an astonishing 16 kilometers in length.⁹

As the above brief (and probably incomplete) account indicates, there were several motives, practical as well as symbolic, for the building of these fortresses. The expansion of the state and the defense of newly conquered territories depended on these structures, as did the growing (and increasingly profitable) trade through Archangel, down the Volga, in Siberia, and elsewhere. In these newly conquered territories, fortress towns, usually constructed on a bluff or high point near a river, established a visual dominance (see figure 8.1) over the surrounding countryside that was the counterpart and visual reinforcer of the military dominance exercised by the fortress and its garrison. In many of these territories, trade was constantly threatened by bands of Nogais, Crimeans, Cossacks, or other raiders; in the south, raiders regularly carried off massive numbers of Slavic slaves. In this context, Godunov's fortresses can be seen as potent visual symbols of government strength: Under their walls trade could flourish, and the military servicemen could cultivate their small estates.

Astrakhan' can serve as an example.¹⁰ Refounded in 1558, two years after its conquest, at an elevated site downstream and on the other side of the Volga

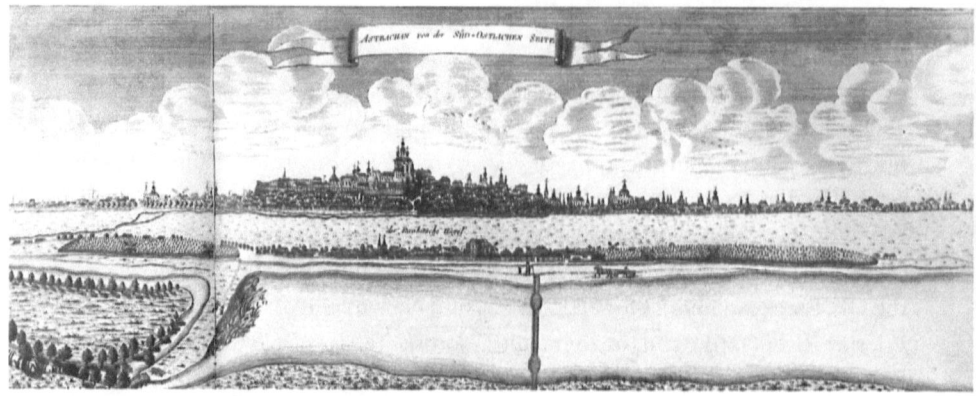

Figure 8.1. Early eighteenth-century view of Astrakhan' by Cornelius de Bruyn. Source: *Gradostroitel'stvo Moskovskogo gosudarstvo XVI–XVII vekov*, ed. N. F. Gulianitskii (Moscow: Stroiizdat, 1994), 90–91.

from the old Tatar town, the original wooden fortress was rebuilt in masonry in the 1580s. The result was impressive: The solid walls ranged in height (depending on the topography) from 7 to 11.3 meters, and were marked by eight towers. The site made the fortress the dominating feature of the landscape. The fortifications themselves were similar in style to two later fortresses built under Godunov (Smolensk and Belyi Gorod in Moscow). These similarities indicate more than a possible use of the same building personnel; by 1605, they created a visual link among major fortresses on the western and southern frontiers and the Moscow center. From a distance, the center of the town composition was the new stone Dormition Cathedral, built around 1600. The original church was pulled down and rebuilt at the end of the seventeenth century, but we may guess that the five-cupola design of the original church linked it with two pentacupolar Kremlin churches that had become canonic. The first of these was the Dormition Cathedral, which served as a model for many churches in the provinces during the sixteenth century in such towns as Rostov, the Sergius Holy Trinity Monastery, Vologda, and Kazan', usually under government sponsorship.[11] A stronger visual connection was made with the Archangel Michael Cathedral, which was an important model, as we shall see, for other Godunovian churches as well as for other sixteenth-century churches in general. Like the Astrakhan' fortress, then, its main cathedral was linked to other similar structures in widely scattered parts of the country and was further identified stylistically with the Godunov clan.

The commanding position of the Dormition Cathedral over the Astrakhan' landscape can be seen, like the Dormition Cathedral in Sviiazhsk (near Kazan', built under Ivan the Terrible), to symbolize Christian Moscow's conquest and domination of a Muslim people. The theme of Moscow's troops as a sacred army conquering the infidel was an important theme in Muscovite political culture.[12] This chauvinistic theme did not interfere, however, with Godunov's well-known desire to promote trade, in this case multiethnic trade. In the 1590s, two covered markets (the Bukhara and Persian markets) were built near the Astrakhan´ kremlin, and in the seventeenth century an Indian market, an Armenian *dvor*, and a Tatar bazaar were set up. Mosques and Armenian churches soon followed. This pattern is consistent with Boris Godunov's encouragement of the German Settlement (Nemetskaia sloboda) in Moscow, and his promotion of foreign trade through Archangel.[13]

Beyond these particular considerations, common sense would dictate that fortress architecture, by its bulk and obvious expense, served as a symbol of the wealth and power of a state, quite apart from the military or economic advantages it conveyed. A large scholarly literature on fortresses in Russia as well as in Western Europe confirms this view.[14] A revealing piece of evidence on this point is that, soon after the completion of the impressive (and expensive) walls surrounding Moscow's Belyi Gorod, Godunov rerouted the standard path followed by foreign ambassadors and their retainers so that diplomatic processions would pass by these walls.[15] Within Muscovite political culture, the image of the tsar as the figurative leader of the army in its struggle with foreign enemies occupied a central place. Literary sources and such visual monuments as the *Church Militant* icon and the murals in the Golden Hall throne room repeatedly emphasized the importance of the military strength of the monarch. Godunov's victory over the Tatars in 1598 was an important factor in persuading the Boyar Duma to support his candidacy for tsar. His use in the 1598 campaign of a *guliai gorod*, a kind of collapsible wooden fort on wheels, was remarked on by many Russian contemporaries. The *Piskarev Chronicle,* a semi-official chronicle apparently sponsored by the Printing Office (Pechatnyi dvor), enthusiastically listed Godunov's military and ecclesiastical building projects for those who had not noticed them. Godunov's military architecture, therefore, fit a well-defined cultural niche.[16]

Although by European standards Russia's wooden forts seemed primitive, and even the massive Smolensk fortress conservative, in the Russian context these structures were impressive, as chronicle accounts make clear. They were major improvements on what had existed earlier, and were a tangible and valuable sign of the growing power of the state, symbolizing both its geographical reach and, especially for the masonry fortifications, its physical strength and ability to marshal considerable resources. (The Smolensk fortress required some 100 million bricks and enormous quantities of other resources. Foreshadowing the measures of Peter the Great, Godunov's government prohibited on pain of death nonstate masonry construction while work on Smolensk proceeded.) As technology changed in succeeding centuries, the semiotic place of fortress architecture was taken in large part by military parades, but the need for the state to express its military might through symbols remained a major feature of Russian culture.

Godunov may also have had a more mundane (and more modern-sounding) motive for his vigorous program of military building. Contemporary opinion, according to Ivan Zabelin, held that Godunov's projects, particularly the construction of the *skorodom* in Moscow (1592), were aimed in part at providing work for the poorer people of Moscow, and thus securing their political support for him.[17] This motive would be consistent with his later coronation promise that he would abolish poverty and divide his last cloak with his subjects.[18] Events in the very near future were to demonstrate the political power of the people of Moscow.

Was this strategy successful? As usual, there is a frustrating lack of source testimony to help us answer this question. The behavior of the inhabitants of some of Godunov's new fortress towns during the Time of Troubles, however, may provide a clue. It turns out that many of these men deserted Godunov at the first opportunity. Oskol, Valuiki, Tsarev-Borisov, Voronezh, and Belgorod all acknowledged the First False Dmitrii in January and February of 1605 (well before Godunov's sudden death in April 13 [old style] of that year), followed shortly thereafter by Elets and Livny.[19]

Before leaving the subject of Godunov's military architecture, we should at least mention in passing a complementary achievement of his government that was crucial to his remarkable record of town building. I refer to the making of maps. We have already discussed the use of maps in the creation of these new towns. The personnel of the Military Chancellery (Razriadnyi prikaz) would prepare maps with instructions on the basis of preliminary investigations of the site. The local *voevoda* (governor) and his staff could alter the plan if they saw fit but otherwise (and this seems usually to have been the case) the town was constructed according to plans drawn up in Moscow. The planning, provisioning, construction, and staffing of a very large number of towns and fortresses spread over a space gigantic by European standards, from Smolensk in the west to Mangazeia in the east, must have required the ability to imagine fairly accurately the geography of Muscovy. It is not surprising, therefore, that the first map (or more likely collection of maps) that Russians ever made of their country, the famous Bol'shoi chertezh or Great Map, seems to have been made in the reign of Boris Godunov. The map or maps themselves have perished, but we have the accompanying text in a copy dating from the 1620s. Scholars are agreed that the original, whatever its form, dates to Godunov's time. In addition, an early and startlingly accurate map of Russia accompanied by an equally impressive map of Moscow (the so-called Petrovskii chertezh) (see figure 8.2) was also drawn up, surely by a foreigner, during Godunov's reign. We will have occasion to consider the Moscow map in another context, but for now we need only note that a very early version, published in Holland by Hessel Gerritsz in 1613 and provided to Gerritsz by Isaac Massa, is ascribed by Massa to Godunov's son, Fedor Borisovich.[20] These maps formed an important complement to Godunov's architectural projects. Just as those projects were designed to make the government and the Godunov family visible to the countryside, so Godunov's various maps made the countryside visible to the government. Indeed, the process of making the maps brought about over time sharp changes in the countryside being mapped. Empty spaces were filled with forts, armies, agriculture, and trade, first on paper and then, when circumstances permitted, in fact.[21] This double accomplishment was remarkable at any time, but has received only scant attention from historians of Godunov's reign.

The construction of churches and other religious buildings represents the other main arena of Godunov's architectural efforts. Here again, architecture answered requirements that were essential parts of the Muscovite ideology of rulership, in this case two closely connected requirements that were universally clear both in written texts and in painting. First, the tsar had to protect and support the Orthodox Church, an obligation that church construction

Figure 8.2. Plan of Moscow engraved before 1646 by Matthaus Merian (in his *Newe archontologia cosmica* [Frankfurt/Main, 1646]), based on the Petrov plan made in or before 1605 by order of Boris Godunov. Source: Wikimedia Commons.

obviously helped to fulfill. Second, and more important, the tsar had to be seen as being personally pious. As his piety alone insured that his will would reflect God's will, it was essential to the validation of the whole political system.[22] The piety of the tsar, a private virtue, was not easy to demonstrate to the general public, but architecture offered an important means of doing this. The tsar's piety was a constant theme in official history writing, in Kremlin art (especially in the halls of state), and even in royal titulature. The wider public in Moscow was shown royal piety during public rituals (Palm Sunday, Epiphany); pilgrimages, which by Ivan IV's reign used up a great deal of the ruler's time and put a considerable strain on the royal family, especially on the tsaritsa, accomplished the same goal in some central and northern districts.[23] Church building, though it was less personally linked to the ruler than pilgrimages or other ceremonies, was more visible, lasted much longer, and was capable of projecting an image of the ruler's piety into distant regions. Godunov had his name inscribed in a very conspicuous religious place: in the gold letters that still surround the golden dome of the Ivan the Great Bell Tower (see figure 8.3). This tower, due to Godunov's addition of two extra stories, was to dominate the Kremlin and even the Moscow skyline down to the twentieth

Figure 8.3. The Ivan the Great Bell Tower in the Moscow Kremlin. Photo by Dmitry Ivanov. Used according to the license agreement: https://commons.wikimedia.org/wiki/File:Ivan_the_Great _Bell_Tower_in_Moscow_Kremlin_1.jpg.

century.[24] Foreign visitors to Moscow in the seventeenth century frequently mentioned the bell tower and its visibility from great distances over the countryside.

This example of *superbia* (pride) was roundly condemned by contemporaries such as Isaac Massa and Ivan Timofeev. Timofeev, following the model of Paul's interpretation of the story of Cain and Abel, used this example of Godunov's pride to dismiss all of Godunov's church-building activities as praiseworthy acts that were vitiated by the motive (pride) that lay behind them.[25] This reaction shows how slippery were the slopes of Muscovite ideology. Since, following Christian tenets, contemporary writers focused on the motive as well as the act, even virtuous acts could be undermined in the public view if the motives for performing it were judged to be bad. This approach, which made the estimation of a ruler turn entirely on motives that could be only guessed at, allowed most commentators, especially those writing after the death of Godunov, to condemn Godunov's architectural achievements as vainglorious. Even these accusations, however, testify to the central place that church building occupied among the duties of a tsar: Building churches was seen as a great good even if Godunov's motives were suspect in this case.

Architectural historians in Russia, particularly A. L. Batalov, have investigated the churches built under Godunov with great care. In a short essay there is regrettably no space to go into much detail, but there seems to be a consensus about several features of Godunovian church architecture. First, in spite of the use of several church types ("columnless" churches with a single dome, five-dome churches, tent-roof churches), Godunov-era churches share more features than do churches built either under Ivan IV or in the first part of the seventeenth century. This sense of consistency has led E. G. Shcheboleva to suggest the existence of a "Godunov School" of architecture, including two major builders (or artels) that used common building techniques as well as common design features. She singles out a small group of churches closely connected with Boris Godunov and probably supervised by the Masonry Chancellery as being especially consistent. Though varying in type, they are characterized by compact massing of the central block, high pyramidal roofs with prominent rows of *kokoshniki* (small gables), and the careful use of Italian-inspired architectural "orders," based directly or indirectly on the Archangel Michael Cathedral in the Moscow Kremlin. The idea of a Godunov School of architecture and the governmental control implied by this research suggests that Godunov chose to identify himself and his dynasty with a particular set of architectural characteristics.[26]

What was the message that this architectural language conveyed to Godunov's contemporaries? Like almost all aspects of Orthodox Christian culture, church design was confined within narrow stylistic boundaries. Many viewers were likely sensitive to relatively small stylistic variations. One fairly obvious point is that the changes wrought by the "Godunov School" were quite conservative compared to those inspired by Ivan III or Ivan IV. No basic new forms were introduced, and the stylistic "signature," while recognizable, seems to have been aimed at conveying the message that Godunov's churches were securely anchored in traditional Russian architecture. In this context, the use of surface detailing based on Italian architectural orders, what Russian architectural historians refer to as "Italianisms," is meant to convey not an affinity with Italy or with foreign design principles, but a self-conscious, even archaizing, reference to one of the most influential buildings in the Kremlin, the Archangel Michael Cathedral, the burial place of Russian tsars.[27] Given Godunov's desire to establish a new dynasty, his choice of this building, with its explicit dynastic connections, can hardly have been accidental. The pyramidal mass-

FIGURE 8.4. The Old Cathedral of the Don. Photo by Ludvig14. Used according to the license agreement: https://commons.wikimedia.org/wiki/File:Small_Cathedral_of_the_Theotokos_of_the _Don_(Donskoy_Monastery)tim.jpg.

ARCHITECTURE AND DYNASTY

FIGURE 8.5. The Church of Boris and Gleb and the fortress in Borisov Gorodok, near Mozhaisk. View from the second half of the eighteenth century. Source: *Gradostroitel'stvo Moskovskogo gosudarstvo XVI–XVII vekov*, ed. N. F. Gulianitskii (Moscow: Stroiizdat, 1994), 168.

ing, created by more rows of higher *kokoshniki*, and, in pentacupolar churches, by the increasing height of the domes and their drums, and the placement of the four subsidiary domes closer to the central dome, is harder to decipher. If we take the single-domed Cathedral of the Don (figure 8.4) as typical, we can see a striking similarity between its pyramidal massing and "Zions," liturgical vessels that were meant to reflect the Church of the Holy Sepulchre in Jerusalem.[28]

For those less able to appreciate architectural subtlety, Godunov turned to that staple of architectural self-assertion, tall buildings. We have already briefly mentioned his additions to the Ivan the Great Bell Tower (figure 8.3). This building was 81 meters tall, and its golden dome (with its prominent mention of Boris and his son) was the first building in Moscow to be seen as a visitor approached the city. Equally impressive was the Church of Saints Boris and Gleb in Borisov Gorodok (figure 8.5), a personal estate that Godunov built near Mozhaisk. Some 74 meters tall without the cross, this was the highest church built in Russia up to that time. Set high on a riverbank, it could hardly have been better suited to proclaim the arrival of a new and powerful dynasty.

Can we discern an iconographical theme behind Godunov's works? One theme that powerfully linked Godunov's desire to portray himself both as a pious God-chosen ruler and the founder of a new dynasty was the idea of Moscow as a New Jerusalem. This idea had already taken form just outside the Kremlin in the Cathedral of the Intercession on the Moat (now usually referred to as Saint Basil's), which contemporaries routinely called "Jerusalem." Architectural historians have asserted that two images of Jerusalem were read into that building: Its design was believed to have been modeled on the Church of the Holy Sepulchre in contemporary Jerusalem, a church that figured prominently in pilgrims' accounts. At the same time, it was apparently seen as a reflection of the Heavenly or New Jerusalem of the Apocalypse (Rev. 21:18–21; Isa. 54:11–14), a golden city with walls in the form of a square, walls encrusted with precious stones and containing twelve gates, three on each side. According to the testimony of both native sources and foreign witnesses, Boris Godunov intended to develop this idea further by building a new church in the Kremlin that would eclipse all others in richness of decoration as well as in size. This church was to have been based simultaneously on Solomon's Temple in ancient Jerusalem (Godunov referred to the projected church as "the Holy of Holies") and on the Church of the Holy Sepulchre in contemporary Jerusalem. According to Elias Herckman, Boris asked his assistants to search for evidence of this "Holy of Holies" both in scripture and in the works of Flavius Josephus on Jewish history. On the other hand, Timofeev tells us that Godunov was equally intent on making an exact copy (*meroiu i podobiem*) of Jesus's tomb, or coffin (*grob*), in Jerusalem, which many historians have taken as a reference to the Church of the Holy Sepulchre there. A. L. Batalov, however, has persuasively argued that Timofeev and other contemporary authors were referring to "the Lord's coffin" (*grob Gospoden'*), a piece of liturgical furniture used in the Orthodox liturgy, especially during Friday and Saturday of Holy Week.[29] Godunov's opulent version was cast in gold and encrusted with precious stones, and that impressed Timofeev deeply. The image of Moscow as the New Jerusalem is suggested by the design of the oak wall (*skorodom*) with which Godunov surrounded Moscow. In a map of Moscow (the so-called Petrovskii chertezh) based, as we have seen, on a copy of a map drawn up under Godunov, the wall is represented as a square with rounded corners, with twelve gates, three on each side.[30]

There is a revealing piece of evidence about Godunov's architectural intentions that has been overlooked by historians. It is found in the murals in the throne room of the Palace of Facets, decorated under Tsar Fedor Ivanovich, but with the obvious participation of Godunov, who had himself depicted as Fedor's chief boyar on the south wall, directly next to the tsar's throne. (The entire north wall and one third of the east wall are devoted to the story of the Old Testament hero Joseph, a figure Godunov clearly saw as a symbol for himself.) On this same south wall, in addition to Fedor, Godunov, and the boyars, are a series of rulers meant to convey the message that divinely inspired leadership originated in the Old Testament and passed to Rus', leading directly to the living tsar, Fedor Ivanovich, and his adviser Boris Godunov. The series begins with Moses (who is shown before the Ark of the Covenant) and includes David (also shown worshipping before the Ark after repenting his sin with Bathsheba), Solomon, Vladimir Monomakh, and, finally, Fedor and his court. Solomon is shown before the Ark of the Covenant inside the Temple, specifically called in the inscription "the Holy of Holies," near which is a columnar cloud. Priests stand near Solomon, and the people of Israel stand behind Solomon. The inscription, carefully copied by Simon Ushakov and his assistant in 1672 and therefore probably an accurate version of the original, is worth quoting in full:

> And when Solomon finished [building] the Holy of Holies, the priests left the building, and a cloud filled the temple of the Lord, and the priests could not stand and serve before the face of the cloud, since the temple was full of the glory of God. Solomon, having come to the stairs, worshipped to the Lord, as did all the sons of Israel, who saw the cloud, fell down on the ground, and praised the Lord.[31]

The interpretation of this wall and its relation to Godunov's position seem clear. In each of the Old Testament scenes, the presence and protection of God, the covenant between God and His people, is symbolized by the Ark of the Covenant. In each case, the leader of Israel (including "Tsar" David and "Tsar" Solomon) affirms the covenant by his religious act. Moses places the Ten Commandments in the Ark; David worships God before the Ark after being punished for his sin by the death of his son; Solomon brings the Old Testament series to a climax by building a Temple (the Holy of Holies) for the Ark; in so doing, he earns God's favor, a favor not extended to the priests, and, through Solomon's architectural efforts, the people of Israel are brought to worship God.

These three scenes epitomize the link between religious and political leadership by illustrating three types of religious performance by the ruler: Moses gives the sacred law, David repents and then displays his personal piety by worshipping before the Ark, and Solomon builds the Temple.[32] No Ark of the Covenant is present in the last two, Rus′ian scenes, those depicting the courts of Vladimir Monomakh and Fedor Ivanovich. Its absence prompts the viewer to wonder where the Rus′ version of the Ark is, and what the religious *podvigi* (religious deeds) of Vladimir Monomakh and Fedor are. As the *Tale of the Vladimir Princes*, illustrated on the adjoining east wall, explains, Monomakh received charismatic regalia from Byzantium. What of Fedor and Godunov? Godunov's scheme to build a new and sumptuous "Holy of Holies" based on scriptural descriptions of Solomon's Temple would seem to supply both an

Ark (in the form of the Lord's tomb) and a *podvig*. Thus, by building a new version of the Temple in Moscow, Godunov casts himself as a new Solomon, reaffirming the covenant between God and His people through the architectural act of church construction. Note that in the scriptural description of the building of the Temple (1 Kings 6: 11–13), Solomon's building project was described as a sign of the continuing covenant between God and Solomon and between God and the people of Israel. Michael Flier has shown the Muscovite use of this idea in the 1550s, when a new prophet tier was added to the iconostasis in the Annunciation Cathedral. In the center of that tier was an image of the Mother of God with Christ on her knee, flanked on the left by David holding the Ark of the Covenant and on the right by Solomon holding his Temple. For Tsar Boris as for Tsar Ivan IV, the analogy with Solomon symbolized both divinely inspired kingship and the all-important dynastic theme, "the fertility and continuity enjoyed by Solomon and his progeny," as Flier puts it.[33]

This evidence about a project that would have transformed the very sacred center of the Muscovite state indicates how strong was the identity of Moscow and Jerusalem in the mind of Boris Godunov and how important were the twin images of God's houses in Jerusalem, Solomon's Temple and the Church of the Holy Sepulchre. To this evidence may be added the already-observed similarity in form between "Godunov School" churches and "Zions," liturgical implements that contemporaries believed reflected the design of the Jerusalem Church of the Holy Sepulchre, a similarity that takes on added meaning in this context.

This conflation of Jerusalem's two churches reminds us of Godunov's apparent confusion of three Jerusalems: Solomon's Jerusalem in the Old Testament, present-day (that is, sixteenth-century) Jerusalem, and the New Jerusalem of the Apocalypse, a conflation that has puzzled many commentators. I think that we see here an example of a typological sense of time that was characteristic of Orthodox culture generally.[34] It bears a striking resemblance in particular to the sense of time in the so-called *Church Militant* icon, in which an army is represented simultaneously as the Old Testament army of Israel, the present army of Muscovy under Ivan IV, and the army of the righteous led by Christ at the Apocalypse. Certainly, the theme of Russia as a New Israel was central in Russian culture of the time, and was richly represented both in the various tales about the Time of Troubles and, as we have seen, in such visual monuments as the mural cycle in the Palace of Facets.[35]

One last important (but less exalted) piece of evidence on Godunov's uses of architecture remains to be considered in our investigation: the *Piskarev Chronicle*. The section of this compiled chronicle dealing with the reign of Ivan

IV has been crucial to the interpretation of that period, but the section describing the reigns of Fedor and Godunov has received less attention. This section, which M. N. Tikhomirov believed was written by an employee of the Printing Office, is unique in the history of Russian chronicle writing for the proportion of space it devotes to architectural projects—mills, and bridges as well as fortresses and churches.[36] In several sections, the chronicle is nothing more than a listing of these projects, one after the other. Not surprisingly, the *Piskarev Chronicle* has been a basic source for the architectural history of the period. What interests us here, however, is the motive for compiling such a text. If Tikhomirov is right about the identity of the author, this section of the chronicle may have been a sketch compiled in the Printing Office for an official chronicle of Godunov's and Fedor's reigns, the completion (and dissemination) of which was cut short by Godunov's sudden death. If so, this text shows the extraordinary importance attached to architecture by Godunov's official publicists. Even if it was written under other circumstances, it indicates at the least what an important place Godunov's architectural projects occupied in one person's recollections of his reign.

Our brief investigation suggests several conclusions. First, Boris Godunov was an extremely active patron of architecture; his decision to devote so many scarce resources to buildings of various sorts, I would argue, was closely connected to his own insecure position at court and his need to accomplish the virtually unprecedented task of establishing a new dynasty. His attention to architecture in this context testified to the confidence Godunov had in this particular kind of symbolic action. Second, this survey of the scope of Godunov's architectural undertakings illustrates the extraordinary competence of his government in carrying out so many large-scale projects in widely separated geographical regions. Third, the uses that Godunov made of architecture showed him (or his helpers) to have been remarkably skillful in elaborating and manipulating the accepted political culture of the time, a culture that stressed the protective military abilities and the personal piety of the ruler. Fourth, the work that Russian architectural historians have done to establish both the generally high degree of similarity among churches of Godunov's time and, more particularly, the existence of a "Godunov School" closely connected with Godunov himself, may at least suggest that he imagined the idea of a kind of signature set of features that would visually connect buildings and embody both himself and his dynasty. Fifth, a good deal of evidence indicates that Godunov intended to rebuild Cathedral Square, the sacred center of the Muscovite state, to develop further the inherited idea of Moscow as a New Jerusalem, a component of the notion of Muscovy as a New Israel that seems to have been popular among many different groups at the end of the sixteenth century. All that survives of this grandiose scheme is the rebuilt Ivan the Great Bell Tower. Had Godunov survived to complete his scheme, his impact on Russian architecture would now be considered almost equal to that of Ivan III. Finally, the murals in the Palace of Facets explain why Godunov devoted so much energy to architecture, particularly church architecture. He felt that building was a sacred task of rulership, closely connected through Old Testament models to the establishment of a God-chosen dynasty.

Was Godunov's remarkable architectural campaign successful? His sudden and unexplained death in 1605 makes that question hard to answer. The ensuing Time of Troubles makes it difficult to see his reign in any light other than a tragic one. Yet Godunov's obvious skills in almost every sphere of government lead one to suspect that, had he survived, he might well have established a new and successful dynasty. At the same time, both domestic and foreign contemporaries wrote that Godunov's architectural projects, as admirable and impressive as they were, merely served to illustrate the measure of his pride. Although this judgment was usually made after Godunov's death rather than during his reign, it illustrates how subjective the criteria for rulership were in Muscovy and in Europe, since the tsar's (presumably unknowable) internal righteousness was the fundamental quality without which even the most praiseworthy deeds were useless or even harmful. Thus the interpretations of Godunov's architectural efforts by his contemporaries show how difficult, perhaps impossible, was his image-building task. As modern historians and Godunov's own contemporaries look back on his building campaign through the prism of the intervening Time of Troubles, what might have been regarded as one of his major accomplishments has been seen instead as evidence of his sinful nature.

Notes

After this essay was substantially complete, Andrei Batalov was kind enough to send me a copy of his excellent *Moskovskoe kamennoe zodchestvo kontsa XVI veka: problemy khodozhestvennogo myshleniia epokhi* (Moscow: Rossiiskaia akademiia khudozhestv, 1996).

Although his book arrived too late to be incorporated in this essay, the endnotes here reveal the extent of my debt to Andrei Batalov. His is one of the best books on Russian architecture to appear since World War II, and I recommend it warmly to all readers of this essay.

1. The most recent investigator of politics from 1584 to 1605 stresses Godunov's political skill and strength both before and after his election as tsar in 1598. In particular, he claims that Godunov was in control of the Military Chancellery (Razriadnyi

prikaz), the main organ entrusted with fortress construction, as discussed below. See A. P. Pavlov, *Gosudarev dvor i politecheskaia bor'ba pri Borise Godunove* (Moscow: Nauka, 1992), esp. 55–56.

2. For a recent survey of these projects, see William C. Brumfield, *A History of Russian Architecture* (Cambridge: Cambridge University Press, 1993), 89–106, 114–119, 122–129, with further references. For the dynastic connections of the Cathedral of the Intercession (Saint Basil's), see Michael Flier, "Filling in the Blanks: The Church of the Intercession and the Architectonics of Medieval Muscovite Ritual," *Harvard Ukrainian Studies* 19 (1995): 120–137.

3. Pavlov convincingly argues that Godunov had clearly established his dominance even in the Duma by the 1590s, after his victory over the Shuiskies. For his arguments and references to his predecessors (especially S. F. Platonov and R. G. Skrynnikov), who stressed Godunov's weak position in the Duma, see Pavlov, *Gosudarev dvor*, 50–85.

4. For a description of these efforts, see R. G. Skrynnikov, *Boris Godunov* (Moscow: Nauka, 1978), 112–116. Valerie Kivelson makes this point in her *Autocracy in the Provinces: The Muscovite Gentry and Political Culture in the Seventeenth Century* (Stanford, CA: Stanford University Press, 1996), 213–214.

5. E. G. Shcheboleva, "K voprosu o 'godunovskoi shkole' v drevnerusskoi arkhitekture kontsa XVI—nachala XVII v.," *Pamiatniki russkoi arkhitektury i monumental'nogo isskustva*, ed. V. P. Vygolov et al. (Moscow: Nauka, 1991), 28. V. V. Kirillov estimates that, while lack of evidence permits only an estimated range of new towns founded "in the sixteenth century" of 45 to 70, by 1620 there were 180 new towns. Given the disruptions of the Time of Troubles and the following years, it seems likely that the large majority of these 110 to 135 towns were built under Boris Godunov. See V. V. Kirillov, "Organizovannoe stroitel'stvo gorordov v Moskovskom gosudarstve," in *Gradostroitel'stvo Moskovskogo gosudarstva XVI–XVII vekov*, ed. N. F. Gulianitskii (Moscow: Stroiizdat, 1994), 7. The list of fortified towns founded between 1584 and 1605 found in the text below is based on the Kirillov article and also based in part on V. V. Kostochkin, *Gosudarev master Fedor Kon'* (Moscow: Nauka, 1964), 9–33, and on what is still the most reliable source on this subject: A. A. Zimin, "Sostav russkikh gorodov," *Istoricheskie zapiski* 52 (1955): 336–347. As Zimin's notes make clear, the sources sometimes offer conflicting dates for the founding of towns; my dates should be taken as approximate.

6. G. V. Alferova, *Russkie Goroda XVI–XVII vekov* (Moscow: Stroiizdat, 1989); Kirillov ("Organizovannoe," 43) also discusses the dominant role of the central chancelleries in producing sketches (*chertezhi*) and precise instructions for the construction of new towns. An excellent example of a published documentary record of the process is found in D. I. Bagalei, *Materialy dlia istorii kolonizatsii i byta stepnoi okrainy Moskovskogo gosudarstva*, 2 parts (Khar'kov: Tip. K. P. Schasni, 1886, 1890), 1:5–13. I gladly thank Edward Keenan for this last reference.

7. M. B. Mikhailova and A. P. Osiatinskii, "Goroda Srednego i Nizhnego Povolzh'e," in Gulianitskii, *Gradostroitel'stvo*, 87–102.

8. T. S. Proskuriakova, "Goroda Sibiri i Priural'ia," in Gulianitskii, *Gradostroitel'stvo*, 103–140.

9. Gulianitskii, *Gradostroitel'stvo*, 59–60, 160–163, 168–169, 243–244; N. F. Gulianitskii, ed., *Drevnerusskoe gradostroitel'stvo X–XV vekov* (Moscow: Stroiizdat, 1993), 329–330.

10. The information on Astrakhan' below is based chiefly on Mikhailova and Osiatinskii, "Goroda Srednego," 87–92. These authors refer (88) to a five-domed cathedral built "on the border of the sixteenth and seventeenth centuries," but then state that the builder was Dorofei Mineevich Miakishev. Since Miakishev was the builder of the late seventeenth-century church, there seems to be some confusion here. On Miakishev's church, see A. V. Vorob'ev, *Astrakhanskii kreml'* (Astrakhan': Volga, 1958), 20–23. I have been unable to find any other independent information on Godunov's church in Astrakhan'.

11. Brumfield, *A History of Russian Architecture*, 109–113; N. I. Brunov, A. I. Vlasiuk, and A. G. Chiniakov, *Istoriia russkoi arkhitektury* (Moscow: Gosstroiizdat, 1956), 145.

12. See Daniel Rowland, "Biblical Military Imagery in the Political Culture of Early Modern Russia: The Blessed Host of the Heavenly Tsar," in *Medieval Russian Culture*, vol. 2, ed. Michael S. Flier and Daniel Rowland (Berkeley: University of California Press, 1994), 182–212 (chapter 6 of this volume).

13. On Godunov's generosity to, and patronage of, Moscow's German Settlement, see Francine-Dominique Leichtenhan, "Les Etrangers a Moscou aux XVI–XXVII siedes," *Revue de la Biblioteque Nationale* 40 (1991): 13–14. (I am glad to thank John LeDonne for this reference.) Isaac Massa tells us how avid Godunov was to make connections (presumably including trade connections) with the natives of the Russian north: *Detectio Preti Hudsoni, or Hessel Gerritsz's Collection of Tracts by Himself, Massa, and de Quir*, ed. Fred John Millard (Amsterdam: Frederik Muller, 1878), 9–15.

14. On this theme, see Stanislaus von Moos, *Turm und Bollwerk: Beitrage zu einer politischen Ikonographie der italienschen Renaissancearchitektur* (Zurich: Atlantis, 1974); James Cracraft, *The Petrine Revolution in Russian Architecture* (Chicago: University of Chicago Press, 1997), 56–66; Aleksei Ivanovich Nekrasov, *Ocherki po istorii drevnerusskogo zodchestva X I–XVII veka* (Moscow: Izd. Vsesoiuznoi akademii arkhitektury, 1936), 325–331; and Christopher Duffy, *Siege Warfare: The Fortress in the Early Modern World*, 2 vols. (London: Routledge and Kegan Paul, 1979–1985), 1:173.

15. L. A. Iuzefovich, *Kak v posol'skikh obychaiakh vedetsia* (Moscow: Mezhdunarodnye otnosheniia, 1988), 73. I am grateful to Maria Salomon Arel for reminding me of the location of this reference.

16. See chapters 4 and 6 of this volume. For the Piskarev Chronicle, see note 38 below.

17. I. Zabelin, *Istoriia goroda Moskvy* (Moscow, 1902), 1:160–61. A. P. Pavlov (*Gosudarev dvor*, 54) describes Godunov's successful efforts to persuade the commercial-artisanal population of Moscow to switch their support from the Shuiskies to the Godunovs.

18. Palitsyn reports that Godunov announced loudly during the liturgy, "O Father and Great Patriarch Iov, let God be a witness to this: no-one in my kingdom will be poor or destitute [*nishch ili beden*]." Godunov then removed his shirt, and promised that he would divide his last shirt with everyone. Palitsyn called these words "loathsome to God [*bogomerzosten*]." *Skazanie Avraamiia Palitsyna*, ed. O. A. Derzhavina and E. V. Kolosova (Moscow-Leningrad: Izd. Akademii nauk, 1955), 252.

19. Maureen Perrie, *Pretenders and Popular Monarchism in Early Modern Russia: The False Tsars of the Time of Troubles* (Cambridge: Cambridge University Press, 1995), 63. The Pretender also claimed the support of the Volga towns, with some (but not full)

justification (73). This resistance to Godunov may have been resistance to the Moscow center rather than to Godunov personally, since these towns continued to oppose the government in Moscow well after Godunov had left the scene (117, 135–136).

20. Boris Polevoi has provided a useful survey of the history of both the Gerritsz maps and the Bol'shoi chertezh, with citations to other literature. See Boris Polevoi, "Concerning the Origin of the Maps of Russia of 1613–1614 of Hessel Gerritsz," in *New Perspectives on Muscovite History*, ed. Lindsey Hughes (London: Palgrave Macmillan, 1993), 14–21.

21. On maps and map making as a state-building enterprise, see Benedict Anderson, "Census, Map, Museum," chap. 10 in *Imagined Communities*, 2nd ed. (London: Verso, 1991), 163–185. James C. Scott described the power of maps to transform the countryside they describe in "State Simplifications: Nature, Space, and People," a talk delivered at Harvard University on March 14, 1996. Perrie (*Pretenders*, 63) points out that by the time of Godunov's death, many southern border towns still consisted almost entirely of military servitors. Agriculture and trade had not yet followed.

22. On the religious (and other) obligations of the tsar, see Daniel Rowland, "Did Muscovite Literary Ideology Place Limits on the Power of the Tsar (1540s–1660s)?" *Russian Review* 49 (1990): 125–155, here esp. 131ff. (chapter 4 of this volume). This essay provides references to the rich literature on the subject.

23. On pilgrimages, see Nancy S. Kollmann, "Pilgrimage, Procession, and Symbolic Space in Sixteenth-Century Russian Politics," in Flier and Rowland, *Medieval Russian Culture*, 163–181.

24. Godunov also had his name inscribed on the top of the Holy Trinity Cathedral in Pskov, the domes of which he had had gilded. See the *Piskarev Chronicle*, in *Polnoe sobranie russkikh letopisei* (hereafter, *PSRL*), vol. 34 (Moscow, 1978), 202.

25. *Vremennik Ivan Timofeeva*, ed. O. A. Derzhavina (Moscow-Leningrad: Izd. Akademii nauk, 1951), 64–65.

26. On a "Godunov School" of architecture, see E. G. Shcheboleva, "K voprosu," and the seminal P. A. Rappaport, "Zodchii Borisa Godunova," *Kul'tura drevnei Rusi: posviashchaetsia 40-letiiu nauchnoi deiatel'nosti Nikolaia Nikolaievicha Voronina* (Moscow: Nauka, 1966), 215–221.

27. See especially A. L. Batalov, "Osobennosti 'Italianizmov' v Moskovskom kamennom zodchestve rubezha XVI–XVII vv.," *Arkhitekturnoe nasledstvo* 34 (1986): 238–245. Batalov distinguishes between two groups of late sixteenth-century churches, one directly and consciously influenced by the Archangel Michael Cathedral, a group he associates particularly with the Godunovs, and the other based on the intermediate influence of Ivan IV's constructions at Aleksandrovskaia Sloboda and additions to the Kremlin Annunciation Cathedral.

28. A. M. Lidov, "Ierusalimskii kuvuklii: O proiskhozhdenii lukovichnykh glav," *Ikongrafiia arkhitektury*, ed. A. L. Batalov (Moscow: VNIITAG, 1992), 57–68.

29. A. L. Batalov, "Grob Gospoden' v zamysle 'Sviataia Sviatykh' Borisa Godunova," *Ierusalim v russkoi kul'ture*, ed. A. Batalov and A. Lidov (Moscow: Nauka, 1994), 154–173. This article is a model of painstaking scholarship. Its conclusions seem particularly consonant with Timofeev's thought and word usage, both of which emphasized liturgical matters. I gladly thank Marina Swoboda, who has just completed an excellent dissertation on Timofeev, for her cogent opinions on this subject expressed in private communications with the author.

30. The argument that the Petrovskii chertezh map resembles the New Jerusalem of the Apocalypse is also made by M. P. Kudriavtsev, *Moskva-Tretii Rim: istoriko gradostroitel'noe issledovanie* (Moscow: Sol Sistem, 1994), 135–140; 205–207. Kudriavtsev also points out the remarkable similarity between the Ivan III Bell Tower as rebuilt by Godunov and contemporary representations of the Church of the Holy Sepulchre in Jerusalem (200–201). There is a problem with the first argument, however, at least as it relates to Godunov's reign. The Petrovskii chertezh itself, which does clearly show a square, twelve-gate pattern reminiscent of the New Jerusalem, is a later version of the map of Moscow published by Gerritsz in 1613. This earlier map, and still earlier versions published as early as 1610, bear a slighter resemblance to the Heavenly Jerusalem. For reproductions of these maps, with illuminating discussion, see M. V. Posokhin et al., *Pamiatniki arkhitektury Moskvy: Kreml', Kitai Gorod, Tsentral'nye ploshchadi* (Moscow: Iskusstvo, 1982), 51–59.

31. Simon Ushakov and Nikita Klement'ev's careful description is printed in I. E. Zabelin, *Materialy istorii, arkheologii, i statistiki goroda Moskvy*, 2 vols. (Moscow: Moskovskaia gorodskaia tip., 1884), 1:1255–1271. The quoted passage is in col. 1262. On the Palace of Facets in general, with full reproductions of the currently visible murals that were painted in the 1880s following the 1672 description, see Aida Nasibova, *The Faceted Chamber in the Moscow Kremlin* (Leningrad: Aurora, 1978).

32. Note the connection between Temple building and a God-chosen dynasty: When David was informed by Nathan the prophet that he would not be able to build the Temple, Nathan also announced God's choice of David's dynasty as the vessel of godly rule (2 Samuel 7). The term "Holy of Holies" technically refers to the innermost room or sanctuary of the Temple, where the Ark of the Covenant was kept (1 Kings 6:23–28; 8:6–7).

33. See Michael S. Flier, "The Throne of Monomakh: Ivan the Terrible and the Architectonics of Destiny," in Cracraft and Rowland, *Architectures of Russian Identity*, 21–33, here 32.

34. A. L. Batalov and T. N. Viatchanina, in "Ob ideinom znachenii i interpretatsii Ierusaminskogo obraztsa v Russkoi arkhitekture XVI–XVII vv.," *Arkhitekturnoe nasledstvo* 36 (1988): 25 make the point that liturgical texts connect Solomon's Temple with the Church of the Holy Sepulchre in contemporary Jerusalem as prefiguration and fulfillment.

35. See Daniel Rowland, "Moscow—The Third Rome or the New Israel?," *Russian Review* 55, no. 4 (October 1996): 591–614 (chapter 7 of this volume).

36. The last sections of the *Piskarev Chronicle* were first published by O. A. Iakovleva in "Piskarevskii letopisets," *Materialy po istorii SSSR, II, Dokumenty po istorii XV–XVII vv*, (Moscow, 1955), 5–210; the text was published in full in *PSRL*, vol. 34 (Moscow, 1978), 31–220. The section on the reigns of Fedor and Boris is found on pages 194–205. On the nature and authorship of various parts of the chronicle, see M. N. Tikhomirov, "Piskarevskii letopisets kak istoricheskii istochnik o sobytiiakh XVI-nachala XVII v.," *Russkoe letopisanie* (Moscow, 1979), 232–247.

CHAPTER 9

Two Cultures, One Throne Room
Secular Courtiers and Orthodox Culture in the Golden Hall of the Moscow Kremlin

Many of the most distinguished American historians of Muscovite Russia have come to believe that the health, prosperity, even the survival of the Muscovite state throughout all of its life depended on the maintenance of a consensus among members of the ruling elite and the monarch. Robert Crummey, Edward Keenan, Nancy Shields Kollmann, and Valerie Kivelson have all helped to explain how this consensus was developed and maintained.[1] Since, like many premodern states, the Muscovite state lacked the wealth, the bureaucratic reach, and the military power to compel obedience from all its subjects, it had to rely on symbolic action to maintain this consensus. From the moment of the conversion of Kievan Rus´, ecclesiastics had been working to piece together an ideology of state power, expressing their ideas in images and architecture as well as in texts. In the second half of the fifteenth century, and especially in the sixteenth century, the Muscovite church expended a considerable amount of intellectual energy on this task. In the middle of the sixteenth century in particular, the church sponsored a number of works in various media on subjects that we would call political. These works took many forms, including literary texts, orations, buildings,

---

This essay originally appeared in *Orthodox Russia: Belief and Practice under the Tsars*, ed. Valerie A. Kivelson and Robert H. Greene (University Park: Pennsylvania State University Press, 2003), 33–57. The author gratefully acknowledges the publisher for permission to reprint this essay.

icons, mural cycles, thrones, battle standards, and a coronation service. But for these ideas to work in the political sphere to produce a consensus, they needed to be understood outside the narrow group of elite churchmen who conceived and executed them. Were lay members of the court able to understand these impressive products of Orthodox culture, or did they remain chiefly the preoccupation of the narrow circles that produced them?

In this essay, I examine the Golden Hall, one of the two main throne rooms of Muscovite Russia, and in particular the murals there, as one site where ideas may have passed between the educated church elite and the far less educated secular elite that frequented these important spaces.[2] As we shall see at the end of this essay, the murals were most probably painted after the great Moscow fire of 1547. We know from the accounts of numerous foreign ambassadors that courtiers spent a good deal of time there. And, as we shall see, the murals illustrated most if not all of the major themes current in ecclesiastical thinking about politics. Although these ecclesiastical "literary" ideas were separated from the elite by the barrier of literacy, were they accessible nonetheless through the medium of painting? To state the problem in a more general way, were the secular elite of early modern Russia Orthodox to any meaningful extent? Could visual means, including not only painting but architecture, have educated illiterate courtiers to the fundamental tenets of Orthodox political culture worked out within the literate and relatively well-educated circles of the church hierarchy? The murals of the Golden Hall can serve as one example that might suggest an answer to this important question.

Our task is an unusual one, then. We need to divine not the overall meaning of the murals in the Golden Hall (a task already well carried out by Michael Flier[3]) but the meaning(s) that may have been seen in these murals by a particular audience, the boyars (the highest members of the court elite) and other secular members of the court.[4]

I raise this question in part as a response to a powerful and eloquent argument stated some time ago by Edward Keenan: his theory of two separate cultures in Muscovy, one clerical and one lay, with few connections between them. In 1971, he wrote in The *Kurbskii-Groznyi Apocrypha*, his book about a correspondence conventionally attributed to Ivan the Terrible (reigned 1547–1584) and Prince Andrei Kurbskii, one of Ivan's courtiers who deserted to Lithuania:

> One of the distinctive features of Muscovite cultural life in the mid-sixteenth century is a rather sharp contrast between secular and religious cultures. Muscovite monastic culture, having inherited traditions and techniques familiar to students of medieval Western literature and philosophy, remained relatively free, during the sixteenth century, of out-

side influence, while the traditions and techniques of the court and counting house continued, by and large, the practices evolved by the great states that had preceded Muscovy as lords of the East European plain. There are very limited interchange and interaction between these [secular and lay] cultures: no strong traditions of formal education in the essentially religious formal culture were developed by the ruling dynasty or the warrior class; few if any princes of the Church succumbed to the lure of secular culture which so compromised Western clerics.[5]

Keenan then goes on to note the linguistic differences found in texts produced by clerical writers on one hand and lay writers on the other.

To understand Keenan's argument accurately, a couple of comments may be in order here. First, the two-culture hypothesis was invoked primarily in a linguistic context, to argue how unlikely it was that either Prince Kurbskii or Tsar Ivan the Terrible could have been the authors of the letters or other texts traditionally ascribed to them. In a recent restatement of his case, Keenan again emphasized the linguistic issue.[6] Second, Keenan sharply limits the duration of this cultural separation between the two cultures to the sixteenth and earlier centuries. These differences, in his opinion, became "less rigid" in the seventeenth century.[7]

This hypothesis and the rhetorical skill of its author have dampened enthusiasm for investigating Orthodox culture and have made it difficult to propose schemes of historical causation in which this culture plays a major part. I would like to argue against the two-culture hypothesis as a general proposition, and to argue in favor of the robust historical role played by culture in general, and Orthodox culture in particular, in the way the secular elite and the court behaved.

I also believe that Keenan's thesis has played a most useful role, since it has made impossible the innocent, Neoslavophile assumption, often cloaked in references to "the Russian soul," that all Russians were knowledgeable and committed Orthodox Christians and that interpretative methods from Orthodox culture from any time or place could be applied to the understanding of evidence from Muscovite Rus'. We cannot now posit the existence, to say nothing of the importance, of a religious idea in Muscovy without demonstrating the presence of texts or other sources through which Muscovites could have learned that idea and providing either direct evidence or a reasonable hypothesis that a certain person or group of people knew about the idea. In other words, Keenan has reminded us of our duties as careful historians or responsible literary critics. Yet the two-culture hypothesis has blocked important avenues of investigation and has made us perhaps too skeptical of the importance of Orthodoxy within the culture and history of Muscovy.

To start, it may be useful to talk about the assumptions that we bring to the question. These assumptions play an especially large role because the amount of direct evidence we have about the worldviews of laymen before 1600 is so small. First, and most obvious, it is as much an assumption that *no one* outside the church hierarchy knew anything about Orthodoxy as it is that *everyone* did. For the period before 1600, we know little about the frequency or quality of church services or other religious rituals, but we do know that members of the court spent a lot of time in the Kremlin churches and in the throne rooms. The state spent a great deal of scarce resources to make these spaces, and the ceremonies in them, as impressive as possible. Can we assume that the elaborate rituals, the singing, images, the liturgical or other texts left all laymen cold and unmoved? Given the evidence brought forward in the volume in which this essay originally appeared (see unnumbered note of this chapter), it seems likely that major events in the lives of lay courtiers—baptism, marriage, death— were all accompanied by Orthodox rituals. If we know so little about the opinions of lay sixteenth-century Muscovites, is it not just as arbitrary to assume that Russians were all self-serving cynics as to argue that they were all Father Zosimas in training?[8] Certainly Church Slavonic was not immediately intelligible to everyone, but neither is the sixteenth-century English of the Book of Common Prayer, which has so many fans among contemporary Episcopalians. The popularity of Latin within the Catholic Church in the era of Vatican II is an even better example. Another conception that bears examination is the notion that certain ways of thinking that were basic to Orthodox culture were too sophisticated to have been understood by most ordinary people. Who might have understood, for example, the idea that the army depicted in the icon *Blessed Is the Host of the Heavenly Tsar* (better known as the *Church Militant*) represented at once the contemporary army of Muscovy, the army of Israel in Old Testament times, and the army of God at Armageddon?[9] To the twentieth-century historian, this idea seems complex and far-fetched, yet the pattern of biblical typology and historical recurrence that underlie it were absolutely basic to Orthodox culture, embedded as they were in virtually all liturgical texts. Our modern progressive linear concept of time, by contrast, was largely absent. We need to examine the notion of what is, and what is not, a complex theological idea in the context of the culture of the period we are discussing.

Not being a linguist, I cannot dispute Keenan's point about the linguistic separation of the two cultures. And I am more convinced than ever that he is right about the origins of the famous correspondence ascribed to Kurbskii and Ivan the Terrible. Further, he is surely right to concentrate on education and the transfer of ideas as a key point in discovering what Muscovite laymen actually knew. The introduction of visual evidence, however, changes the equation somewhat, since acquaintance with high-style Slavonic texts, or even the ability to read, were not prerequisites for understanding ideas presented in visual form. Let us then turn to our example, the murals in the Golden Hall, one of the most important political spaces in early modern Russia.

As the places where the Boyar Duma met and the tsar and his court received foreign ambassadors, Muscovy's two throne rooms, the Golden Hall and the Hall of Facets, were places of extraordinary importance. Both are surely examples of what Clifford Geertz called a "glowing center." Such centers are, according to Geertz, "essentially concentrated loci of serious acts; they consist in the point or points in a society where its leading ideas come together with its leading institutions to create an arena in which the events that most vitally affect its members' lives take place."[10] The entire Kremlin was such a center, but the throne rooms occupied a special place even within the rarefied and sacred space of the Kremlin as a whole.

One reason, then, for using this mural cycle as a location where ideas could flow from the ecclesiastical, literary culture to the secular culture is that the Golden Hall was at the center of a nested set of hierarchical spaces.[11] As Geertz put it, the Golden Hall was of central importance as a place where society's important ideas (as represented in the murals, as well as by the architecture of the hall and rituals that took place there) and its important people (the tsar and his courtiers, lay and clerical) came together to do important things. This importance was underlined both architecturally and ritually. The Golden Hall was at the end of a sequence of hierarchically arranged spaces that began in Red Square outside the Kremlin and ended in the throne rooms. The courtier or visitor would typically pass through the massive masonry walls of the Kremlin via the Spasskii Gates, then proceed down a narrow street next to the Voznesenskii Monastery to Cathedral Square. From the square one climbed one of three staircases to the so-called Boyars' Porch; only from there could one enter either of the throne rooms (figure 9.1). Access to these spaces was progressively restricted, from the general populace in Red Square, to the highly select courtiers who were allowed into the vestibules of the throne rooms, to the even smaller number of courtiers admitted to the throne rooms themselves. This spatial hierarchy was reinforced by the rituals used in the reception of foreign diplomats. Here the spatial sequence began at the border of the state and continued by carefully detailed stages to Moscow, then to the Kremlin, to Cathedral Square, and finally to the throne rooms.[12] Thus architecture and ritual made the throne rooms the political center of the Kremlin, which was in turn the center of the Muscovite state. The space of the Golden Hall, therefore, was especially potent as a locus for the communication of ideas.

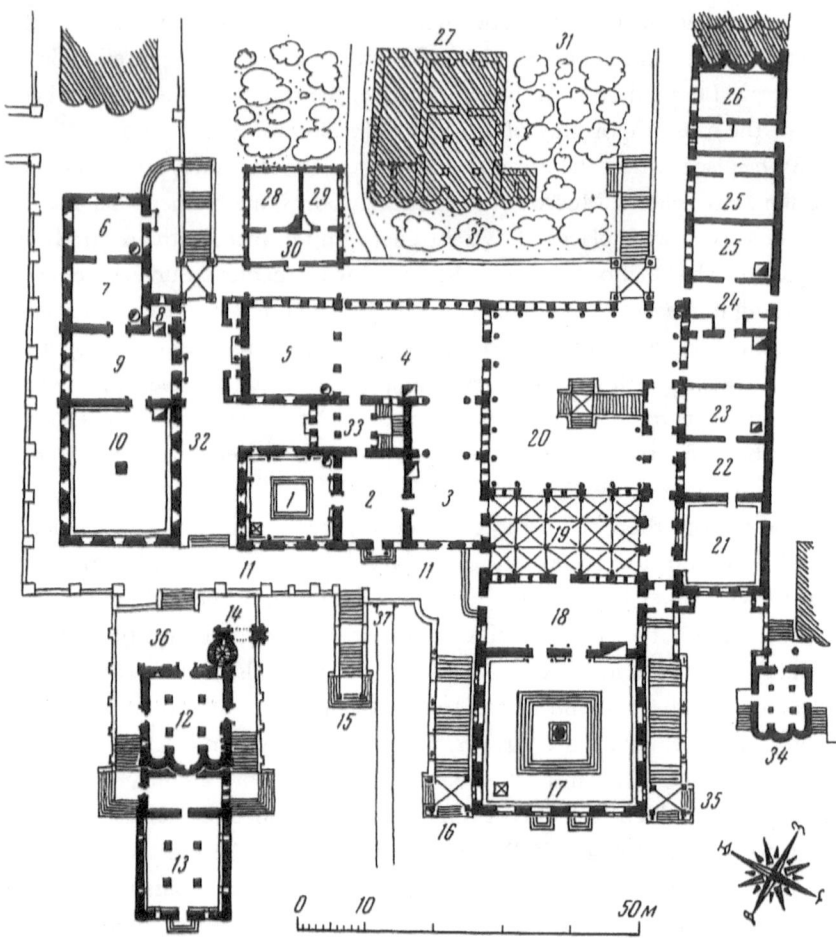

FIGURE 9.1. Map of the central portion of the royal palace in the Moscow Kremlin. The space below the diagram represents Cathedral Square. From there, diplomats and courtiers would climb to the Splendid Upper Porch or Boyars' Porch (11) via the stairs next to the Annunciation Cathedral (12), the Central Golden Stair (15), or the Great Splendid Golden Stair (16). From the Boyars' Porch, one entered the vestibule (2) and throne room (1) of the Golden Hall. Further along the balcony was the entrance to the vestibule (18) and throne room (17) of the Faceted Hall, the other main throne room in the Kremlin. Reconstruction by K. K. Lopialo, from an appendix in O. I. Podobedova's *Moskovskaia shkola zhivopisi* (Moscow: Izdatel'stvo Nauka, 1972).

I have also been inspired by reading the work of Valerie Kivelson to ask an important question to which the Golden Hall murals seem to provide at least a partial answer.[13] This question leads me to approach the murals from an angle that is a bit different from that used in earlier scholarship. By examining a large number of gentry petitions and other documents from the seventeenth century, Kivelson has shown that military servitors of all ranks used the ideas that can be found in historical and polemical texts from Ivan's reign as well as in the tales written about the Time of Troubles (a period of civil war and foreign intervention from 1598 to 1613), as the basis of their own political views. How did the servitor class, from boyar to provincial gentryman, learn this basic vocabulary of political ideas?

While most provincial noblemen probably never set foot inside the Golden Hall, members of boyar clans and the upper ranks of the Moscow gentry spent time, in many cases a lot of time, in the throne room and its adjacent vestibule. Lengthy court rituals, like the exchange of gifts with foreign ambassadors and the ceremonial meals that are well documented in foreigners' accounts, would have left ample time to examine, or at least glance at, the rich golden murals that surrounded the visitor on all sides.[14] Even for the disinterested, the murals could have served as the sixteenth-century equivalent of magazines in a doctor's office. Moreover, the medium of a monumental mural program, so unfamiliar to most modern viewers, was an ordinary part of the experience of most of those who populated the Golden Hall on important court occasions. The presentation of ideas in the form of murals arranged on the walls and vaults of a church structure was a standard experience within at least metropolitan churches since Kievan times. In fact, the arrangement of image-ideas on the interior surfaces of a church was better suited to the organization and presentation of political ideas than were any textual models available in Muscovy. The literary tradition of Rus' offered no models for sustained textual political discussion in which ideas were organized logically, but the traditional arrangement of images within an Orthodox church described in principle by Otto Demus some years ago gave painters a means to organize political ideas in space.[15] Spatial relations rather than Aristotelian logic thus became the glue that held together and organized discreet political ideas.

Further, the murals in the Golden Hall may have been more accessible to the eye than church murals for the simple reason that they were easier to see. In many churches, important scenes were placed in difficult-to-see spots at a great height. Others were hidden behind the iconostasis. The modest dimensions of the Golden Hall (the throne room was about 12 meters square, the vestibule, about 12 by 8 meters) and its open plan would have made the murals fairly easy to see from almost any vantage point. For those who could read fairly simple Church Slavonic, extensive inscriptions explained the meaning of the images. For those who could not, the images were in many cases self-explanatory, as we shall see. Finally, as teaching experience shows, repetition reinforces understanding. Important texts (like the crucial "Wisdom has built a house" from Proverbs 9) and figures (God, Solomon, the Mother of God) appear in many places. More important, many of the themes and scenes in the palace (like the Old Testament scenes of Israel's military defeat of its enemies under Moses, Joshua, and Gideon) were found over and over again both in other mural cycles elsewhere in the Kremlin and in various texts.[16] The habit of Metropolitan Makarii and his cultural helpers of repeating the same themes has been remarked on by many commentators; this repetition must have helped to drum these themes into even those heads that otherwise might have been hard to penetrate.[17] It seems fair to conclude, therefore, that the murals in the Golden Hall were potentially potent tools for communicating ideas to the lay elite of Moscow directly, and indirectly, to the rest of the servitor class.

What ideas were conveyed to these military-minded lay courtiers? Any means of communication creates some slippage between the intent of the communicator and the person or persons who get (or fail to get) the message. My question, therefore, is, "What political messages might a typical courtier have taken away from the repeated visits that we know he must have made to the Golden Hall?" This question is obviously different from the more usual, "What do the murals in the Golden Hall mean?" It is by now a truism that the meaning a person receives from a work of art depends on a variety of factors: the education and life experiences of the viewer, the time spent in viewing (a glance or a measured view), the year or even month in which the viewing takes place and thus the immediate context of events that could be associated with the images and texts, the place of the viewer within the room, and the visual accessibility of the images in question.[18] Available evidence does not allow us to define each of these variables accurately, but I think we can make a fairly shrewd guess, given the consistency of visual political messages at Ivan's court, that several points would strike our imagined military servitor with little or no theological education. I have selected seven themes that I believe resonate with other roughly contemporary monuments of culture, literary or artistic; most of these themes seem also to crop up both in various tales about the Time of Troubles and in Kivelson's gentry petitions. These themes are (1) the descent of political power from God, (2) the protection of Rus' (the name commonly used by the medieval East Slavs to describe themselves) by the Mother of God, (3) the importance of the clan of the ruler, (4) God's protection of the Muscovite army and its role in sacred history, (5) the good order of the realm, (6) the piety and moral behavior of the tsar, and (7) advice and the relationship of the ruler with his courtiers. My hypothesis is that the members of the court absorbed these ideas at least in part through the Golden Hall murals. In later generations, when the need to defend the interests of secular courtiers in the context of a set of political beliefs arose, these themes reappeared.

In order to understand the context of these ideas, a quick overview of the murals is essential. These images are not easy to describe in a few words. They covered the walls both of the vestibule and the throne room itself (nos. 1 and 2 on figure 9.1). The vestibule was devoted largely to Old Testament themes. At the center of the ceiling vault was an image of the Trinity, under which were spread seven scenes of godly governance. In the squinches were depicted the kings of ancient Israel, starting with David and Solomon (figure 9.3). On the walls and adjoining vaults was shown the military conquests of Israel's armies under Moses, Joshua, and in the throne room, Gideon.[19] In the throne room itself, God as Sabaoth (Lord of Armies) was shown in the center of the dome, surrounded by complex images connected to the themes of Divine Wisdom, the creation of the world, and the choice between the broad path of sin and the narrow path of righteousness. In the squinches were depicted members of the Riurikovich dynasty, starting with Saint Vladimir and ending with "Ivan Vasilevich" (Ivan III?). On the wall were depicted a series of scenes from Rus' history, including the conversion of Rus' to Christianity and the transfer

FIGURE 9.2. Reconstruction drawing of the sanctuary mural over the tsar's throne in the throne room of the Golden Hall. Note here the presence of the Mother of God as part of the theme of Divine Wisdom, but giving the impression of her as protectress of the tsar and his kingdom by her position right over the tsar's throne. Reconstruction by K. K. Lopialo, from an appendix in O. I. Podobedova's *Moskovskaia shkola zhivopisi* (Moscow: Izdatel'stvo Nauka, 1972).

FIGURE 9.3. Reconstruction drawing of the upper murals of the vestibule of the Golden Hall. In the middle is *Fatherhood* (*Otechestvo*, which can also be referred to as the Ancient of Days) surrounded by seven moralizing scenes about divinely inspired rulership. In the squinches are Old Testament rulers of Israel, while around the walls are scenes of the conquests by Israelite armies under Moses and Joshua. In general, the vestibule murals show Old Testament rulership, military and political, as a prefiguration of and model for rulership in Rus'. Reconstruction by K. K. Lopialo, from an appendix in O. I. Podobedova's *Moskovskaia shkola zhivopisi* (Moscow: Izdatel'stvo Nauka, 1972).

of charismatic regalia from Byzantium to Rus' in the reign of Grand Prince Vladimir Monomakh (Bartenev, 183–190).[20]

Complicating our task further is the fact that the Golden Hall and its murals were pulled down in 1752 to make room for the Kremlin Palace built for the Empress Elizabeth by the architect Rastrelli. We know the murals from a very careful description made in 1672 by the noted icon painter Simon Ushakov and an associate, Nikita Klement'ev[21] This description is almost the sole evidence we have for the murals. Most scholars assume that the murals were painted after the great Moscow fire in 1547, but this date has been contested, as we shall see in our conclusion.

The most obvious political idea in the Golden Hall, and also the most important political idea in Muscovite Russia, is the descent of the tsar's power from God. This point is made over and over again. Most potently, each room had a picture of God at the center of its domed ceiling, surrounded with more or less abstract theological or moral subjects. On the walls were depicted historical events from the history of Old Testament Israel (in the vestibule) and Rus' (in the throne room). Architecture and image worked powerfully together in the Golden Hall to illustrate this most important of themes. Rulers—Old Testament "tsars" in the vestibule and Rus' princes in the throne room—were placed in squinches or pendentives that structurally and visually linked the round dome above with the rectangular walls below. Set in their V-shaped squinches, these rulers stretched like God's fingers from the heavenly into the earthly realm (figure 9.4), thus linking spatially and architecturally the world of historical events in sacred states with the power and authority of God.[22] It is hard to imagine how this point would not come across to a viewer.

At the level of individual scenes, God was shown blessing, guiding, and helping rulers in their quotidian life in a straightforward way. In the many Old Testament battle scenes, for example, God as Sabaoth was explicitly shown helping Israelite leaders the way that the Archangel Michael helps the Muscovite troops in the so-called *Church Militant* icon. As courtiers and foreigners cooled their heels in the vestibule, they would have seen above them, in the seven moralizing scenes surrounding the Fatherhood (*Otechestvo*, or New Testament Trinity) composition in the center of the dome, God or an angel blessing the tsar. In scene 2, inscribed "the heart of the tsar is in the hands of God," a tsar enthroned, holding an orb and scepter, is shown next to God as Pantocrator ("Ruler of All"), who is holding out His left hand in a gesture of blessing and has placed His right hand on the orb that the tsar holds (Bartenev, 190). In scenes 4, 5, and 6, angels directly crown the ruler (note that Lopialo erroneously omits the crown in the angel's left hand in scene 4) or hold the scales of justice (scene 6) (Bartenev, 190). In the throne room, the crowning of Vladimir Monomakh is presided over by God as *Otechestvo* (Bartenev, 189). These images were all very direct and did not depend on knowledge of complex theological notions to be understood.

Far more difficult for our typical courtier to understand was the theme of Holy Wisdom (*Sofiia, premudrost' Bozhiia*), a theme that was perhaps the

Figure 9.4. Reconstruction drawing of the upper murals of the throne room of the Golden Hall. Beneath the complex iconography centering on Divine Wisdom in the dome are the rulers of Rus', arranged to parallel the Old Testament rulers in the vestibule. In the walls and lower vaults are scenes of Gideon's military victories, the conversion of Rus' to Christianity under Saint Vladimir, and the transfer of charismatic regalia from Byzantium to Rus' in the reign of Vladimir Monomakh, as well as depictions of several parables and historical episodes. The scenes about Saint Vladimir and Vladimir Monomakh show the importance of advisers, while the parables and historical scenes emphasize the moral responsibilities of earthly life in general and rulership in particular. Reconstruction by K. K. Lopialo, from an appendix in O. I. Podobedova's *Moskovskaia shkola zhivopisi* (Moscow: Izdatel'stvo Nauka, 1972).

dominant idea of the Golden Hall murals from a theological point of view. The complex iconography of Holy Wisdom occupies the northeast half of the throne room dome and was based largely on ideas that had come to Moscow at that time fairly recently from Novgorod. This theme was based on a mystical reading of the ninth chapter of Proverbs, beginning with the sentence, "Wisdom has built a house for herself." Briefly, the House of Wisdom symbolized the church and its seven ecumenical councils, the Mother of God as the "house" of the incarnated God, the altar during the Eucharist, and the Muscovite kingdom itself. This deeply layered interpretation must surely have seemed opaque to all but the most sophisticated courtiers, though an ability to read the inscriptions and an acquaintance with the Orthodox liturgy would have helped. My argument that Holy Wisdom was not all that well understood rests on two points. First, secular courtiers would have had little other experience of this abstract concept. Although Holy Wisdom is a prominent idea in Orthodox liturgical texts, its complex development as a political theme would not have been obvious from common liturgical experience. Second, the theme of Holy Wisdom was not used extensively in other parts of Moscow's court culture and was not included as a main theme in the decoration of the Hall of Facets done later, during the reign of Ivan the Terrible's son, Fedor Ivanovich (reigned 1584–1598). A likely reason for this latter omission is that the theme of Holy Wisdom had not by then entered the common vocabulary of political ideas. Similarly, Holy Wisdom plays no role in the various tales about the Time of Troubles.

A theme that was a cornerstone of Rus' culture over many centuries and would surely have been familiar to most courtiers is the protection of the Rus' state by the Mother of God. This theme might well have been read into the murals even though, in a strict interpretation, it was relatively unimportant there. She appears unambiguously in this role in the final scene of the Vladimir Monomakh cycle (V7 in figure 9.5; Bartenev, 189), where she blesses the coronation of Vladimir Monomakh with the regalia recently received from Byzantium and imagined by Ivan IV's contemporaries to be the same as that worn by Ivan himself. She also appears prominently in the throne room in a position close to the throne as the New Testament fulfillment of the House of Wisdom prophecy in Proverbs 9. An untutored viewer, however, might well have seen her presiding with Christ Emmanuel over the entire throne room, and thus understand her as a protectress of the Muscovite *tsarstvo*. This impression would have been strengthened by the composition (see figure 9.2; "Sanctuary" in figure 9.5) in which the Mother of God is directly over the throne and the tsar, with Solomon, David, and Saint Peter in the space between her and the tsar. A learned viewer would be informed by the inscription in Solomon's scroll, "Wisdom has built her house," and by the inscription above the whole composition, "The house of the Lord is a holy sanctuary [*sviataia ograda*]," that the Mother of God is again here as part of the Holy Wisdom iconography (as the "house" of the incarnate God). Our uneducated viewer may well have taken the "holy sanctuary" (if he could read the inscription) to refer to the Russian state (as symbolized by the tsar himself on his throne) under the protection of the Mother of God. Indeed, the composition and

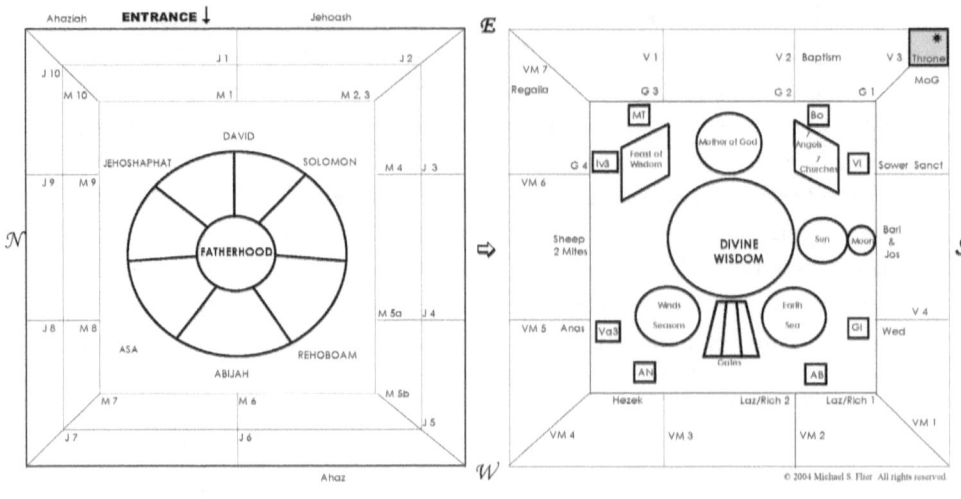

FIGURE 9.5. Diagram of the overall scheme of the murals of the Golden Hall. In the vestibule around *Fatherhood* (*Otechestvo*) are seven scenes of rulership. Below are the cycles about Moses (M 1–10) and Joshua (J 1–10). In the throne room itself (on the right), we see among the rulers of Rus', Boris (Bo) and Gleb (Gl), on either side of Saint Vladimir (Vl). Following clockwise from Gleb are Andrei Bogoliubskii (AB), Aleksandr Nevskii (AN), and Vasilii III (Va3). Following counterclockwise from Boris are Michael of Tver (MT) and "Grand Prince Ivan Vasil'evich" (probably Ivan III) (Iv3). In the outside part of the diagram, reflecting the lower vaults and walls, are scenes devoted to Gideon (Gid 1–4), Saint Vladimir (Vl 1–4), and Vladimir Monomakh (VM 1–7), as well as parables and historical scenes. Reconstruction by Michael S. Flier and reproduced with his permission.

placement of this "sanctuary" scene makes one suspect that both interpretations may have been intended (Bartenev, 188–189).

It is not necessary to engage in speculative misinterpretation of the murals in order to describe a number of themes that resonated with other parts of Muscovite culture and had close connections with the lives of lay courtiers. The importance of the ruler's clan is such a theme, for it was a major preoccupation of the court and a matter of great concern in their own sphere to the boyars who frequented the Golden Hall. This theme was emphasized in the two throne-room cycles on the baptism of the first Prince Vladimir (ca. 980–1015) and the transfer of regalia from Byzantium later, under Grand Prince Vladimir Monomakh (1113–1125). The clan theme was underlined in the placement of various Riurikovich rulers in the squinches in the throne room and the parallel selection of the lineal descendants of "Tsar and Prophet David" for the same position in the vestibule.

Another theme that would have been obvious to an illiterate lay courtier is the military one. Fighting would have been the main occupation of such a person. Numerous battle scenes appeared in the three cycles describing the liberation of the people of Israel from Egypt by Moses and the conquest of the Promised Land by Joshua and Gideon. These scenes echoed a number of other roughly contemporary cultural artifacts emphasizing the theme of "Blessed is the host of the Heavenly Tsar."[23] The point of these images was to suggest that the army of Muscovy (including the courtiers present in the throne room) played a vital role in salvation history, a role *prefigured* by the armies of Israel in the Old Testament, and *prefiguring* the troops of Christ at Armageddon. Again I want to emphasize the physical accessibility of many of these pictures on the walls or vaults close to the level of the lay courtiers who were lucky enough to get into the palace and the utter familiarity of the activity depicted (fighting) in the lives of these military servitors. If the *Church Militant* icon and the murals of the Archangel Michael Cathedral were typical, then these Old Testament warriors were clothed in contemporary Muscovite military dress, thus increasing the accessibility of these images still further.

The duty of the tsar to preserve the good order of the realm, to rule justly, and to protect the poor is a theme that was prominent in the tales about the Time of Troubles and also in many earlier literary texts. The ideal of the good order of the realm was certainly implied on the dome of the throne room, where depictions of the winds and seasons and the creation of the universe (sun, moon, stars, land, sea) shows God through Holy Wisdom ordering the universe as (it is implied) the tsar orders his *tsarstvo*. The inscription around the central figure of Christ Emmanuel, here signifying Holy Wisdom as the inscription makes clear, strengthens this implication (I use Michael Flier's translation), though whether an illiterate courtier would have gotten the point is unclear: "God the Father has through His Wisdom founded the earth and fixed the ages. O paternal Logos beyond eternity, who in God's image is and constitutes creation from non-being into being, who by his authority [*oblastiiu svoeiu*] has set the seasons and the years, bless the crown [or circle?] of time [*venets letu*] with thy beneficence, grant peace to thy churches, victories to the true tsar, fruitfulness to the land, and great mercy to us" (Bartenev, 183).

The correspondence between God's orderly creation of the world and the ruler's imposition of order in his realm was a commonplace in halls of state in Western and Eastern Europe. This correspondence seems to explain the even greater emphasis given to the creation in the Hall of Facets murals, although the role of Holy Wisdom there is much diminished.[24] A few other scenes in the Golden Hall murals emphasize good governance in a more practical sense. In the moralizing scenes around the Ancient of Days (*Otechestvo*) in the vestibule (see figure 9.3), Solomon gives money to the poor, seemingly as a sign of his fear of the Lord (scene 4), and in the adjoining fifth scene, an angel with scales and a sword clearly symbolizes royal justice, an attribute of the godly ruler (Bartenev, 190).

I conclude with two themes in the Golden Hall murals that had much in common with contemporary political discourse, one of which has been often referred to and the other, much less often: the personal piety and moral behavior of the tsar and the question of advice. Almost all commentators have remarked on the striking attempt in the murals to give moral/religious instruction to the tsar (and presumably, to everyone else in the palace). The seven Proverbs-inspired scenes in the vestibule arranged around the Ancient of Days like seven pillars stress the good deeds of a tsar that are a sign of the presence in him of Holy Wisdom. The ruler (sometimes depicted as Solomon) is shown not only being endowed by God or an angel with the symbols of office as we have already discussed, but worshipping (scene 3), giving money to the poor (scene 4), judging justly (scene 5), teaching his subjects (scene 6), and teaching his son with a book (scene 7) (Bartenev, 190). The New Testament counterparts to these scenes are Jesus's parables, shown in the vaults of the throne room itself. These include, starting at the tsar's throne, the parables of the sower, the wedding guests, the rich man and Lazarus, the lost sheep, and the lost coins. In the corner just opposite the tsar are added scenes of two rulers who foresee their own death: Hezekiah who repents and survives for fifteen more years, blessed by the Lord (2 Kings 20:1–6; Isa. 38:1–6), and the Emperor Anastasios, who does not, and dies condemned by his sins (Bartenev, 186–187). Many commentators have seen in the selection of these scenes specific references to the life of the young Ivan IV.[25] Whether or not those specific references were intended, this part of the mural program seems to emphasize the desire of God to pardon sinners, but his harsh judgment and punishment of those who refuse to repent. The parables of the wedding feast and the rich man and Lazarus single out greed as especially effective in separating the sinner from God's mercy. Taken together, these scenes imply the free will of a person before the choice between good and evil. This theme of a moral choice is amplified on the dome above, where two gates, one adorned with virtues and the other with vices, symbolize the choice between the "narrow path" of good and the "broad way" of evil. These moralizing scenes not only urge the tsar to choose good; they also by implication underline the conditionality of royal power: If a tsar chooses the broad way of sin, then he separates himself from God. The salvation of the tsar and God's blessing on the *tsarstvo* depend upon the "good soil" of the tsar's soul. (Incidentally, if indeed this part of the mural program does date from the 1550s, these scenes are evidence of a moralizing tendency in Russian Orthodoxy that Paul Bushkovitch has recently dated mostly to the second half of the seventeenth century.)[26]

Our last subject is the theme of advice. By itself, this theme is not the direct subject of any scene and has not been much noticed before. Yet a courtier approaching the palace with an interest in the relationship between the ruler and himself and his colleagues or advisers would have found considerable material to ponder. Ushakov's (and Klement'ev's) careful description of 1672 notes the existence of "boyars" or "grandees" (*vel'mozhi*) in a large number of scenes in both the vestibule and the throne room (see figures 9.3 and 9.4). They were shown prominently in the vestibule in the seven scenes around the Ancient of Days figure in the dome. They appeared in scene 1 in front of the God-crowned tsar, in the scene 2 (as "Israelites") assisting Solomon in the performance of his religious duties, in the scene 3 (as *vel'mozhi*) accompanying Solomon as he distributes alms, in scene 6 witnessing the tsar teaching the people, and in scene 7 observing the tsar teach his son. Advisers/courtiers are thus specifically mentioned in five of the seven scenes (Bartenev, 190). Ushakov specifies "boyars" as present in all four scenes in the cycle devoted to the conversion of Rus' under Prince Vladimir. In scene 1, they listen with the tsar as representatives from various faiths describe their beliefs; in scene 2, boyars are mentioned among the Byzantine emperor's retinue in church; in scene 3, boyars stand behind Vladimir holding his crown and royal vestments; in scene 4, four boyars are specified as present at the overthrowing of the idols (Bartenev, 188–189). In the Vladimir Monomakh cycle, boyars are present every time that the Rus' court is depicted. Monomakh consults his boyars about a military expedition to Constantinople (scene 1), collects and organizes his troops with the help of boyars (scene 2), receives the regalia in the presence of clergymen and boyars (scene 6), and is triumphantly crowned, also in the presence of his boyars (scene 7) (Bartenev, 189). The murals clearly depict boyars or grandees as standard parts of the royal court and show them consulting with and supporting their ruler in a wide variety of situations. (In military scenes, the same boyars would presumably be depicted as part of the army.) Whereas in the tales about the Time of Troubles, advisers were important chiefly as the most convenient means to correct an erring or sinful tsar, in the Golden Hall wise advisers are shown as part of the normal running of a pious tsar's court.[27] The consistency with which Ushakov and Klement'ev mention them indicates that the designers of the Golden Hall mural program considered boyar advisers an essential part of the tsar's court and made a point of including them in the murals' depiction of Christian governance. Indeed, "advice" may not be the right rubric for our discussion here; "boyars" or "grandees" are more accurately depicted as partners of the tsar in governance. Perhaps the modern viewer is too influenced here by a Whig view of history, which posited a constant and inevitable conflict between the ruler and his nobles: the designers of the Golden Hall murals seem to have regarded a ruler surrounded by powerful boyars as more powerful than one who rules by himself.

What can we conclude from this excursion into the meaning of some long-lost murals? The irony from the point of view of Keenan is that there is room for serious debate on the dating of the murals in the Golden Hall, and thus the dating question makes it unclear whether or not the murals disprove his two-culture hypothesis. We know that some murals were painted in the Golden Hall after the Moscow fire of 1547. As mentioned previously, virtually all of our evidence about the murals comes from a detailed description compiled by Simon Ushakov and his assistant in 1672, in connection with a proposed repainting of the Golden Hall. In between, Moscow suffered from the disastrous invasion of the Tatars in 1571, which severely damaged many buildings in the Kremlin, and from the depredations of the Time of Troubles. How old were the murals that Ushakov described? There is no evidence clear enough to resolve this question to everyone's satisfaction, at least for the moment. If, as some scholars think, the murals date from early in the seventeenth century, then they would neither confirm or contradict Keenan's thesis, that the secular world was not enlightened in most matters of religious culture until around 1600. My own judgment is that the mural program, if not the murals themselves, dates from the 1540s. The chief evidence is the surviving documentation on the "Viskovatyi affair," a dispute over developments at that time in iconography between a prominent courtier, Ivan Viskovatyi, and Metropolitan Macarii, in which the theological content of some of the most innovative sections of the murals was discussed in some detail. A manuscript containing this evidence, apparently dating from the 1560s, survives. There is also the habit, well documented in the seventeenth century, of repainting old murals according to the program that was there before. Even if the murals themselves were destroyed in one or more catastrophes, the program would most probably have been preserved. And, of course, it is the program, not the images themselves, which concerns us.[28] If the mural program does date from the middle of the sixteenth century, the Golden Hall, by virtue of its central role spatially and politically, would have endowed its murals with a high degree of political influence in the age of Ivan the Terrible. Other Kremlin locations, especially churches, were also well furnished with murals. It is precisely in these spaces, where we know courtiers spent a great deal of time, that an effective education in basic political values may well have taken place. We need not assume that a courtier would become so transformed by the throne-room murals that he would be able to translate Cicero, as Prince Kurbskii is alleged to have done. If the key question is one of education, as Keenan has stated, surely the Golden Hall murals, and the many other images that an average courtier encountered, were potential sources of education. Images could move more easily between the two cultures than texts could, simply because they bypassed the linguistic boundaries that Keenan drew to our attention. Each of the seven themes in the murals that we have discussed should have been transparent to this average courtier, whether or not he was literate in Church Slavonic or conversant with sophisticated theology. If so, the Golden Hall murals would surely have conveyed, over a long period of time from the 1550s to the 1670s, a series of important political messages that fit reasonably well with what servitors seemed actually to have believed in the seventeenth century.

Reception theory teaches us that a text or a work of art represents only one side of a kind of conversation that takes place between a particular viewer or reader (or a group of viewers or readers) and any given image or text. In order to understand the viewing experience of an audience, the historian needs to try to understand the socially determined values, concerns, and questions that a particular audience brought to an image, since these expectations formed the complement to the picture, the part of the viewing experience that now has to be reconstituted. As Michael Baxendall wrote in describing the experience of a fifteenth-century Italian audience to Bellini's *Transfiguration*, "The painting is a relic of a cooperation between Bellini and his public: the fifteenth-century experience of the *Transfiguration* was an interaction between the painting, the configuration on the wall, and the visualizing activity of the public mind—a public mind with different furniture and dispositions from ours."[29]

How can we recreate the conversations between the images of the Golden Hall and the boyars and other courtiers who frequented it? At the least, we can say that the choice of meanings of any text, performance, film, and so on, is not a binary one. We are not faced with the question of whether boyars understood the murals or not. They must have understood the mural program in some way, even if they saw only a confused jumble of images. Each courtier brought to his encounter with the murals his own experiences and interests, and each took away slightly different messages. As we try to locate each boyar along a continuum of understanding, with an almost infinite variety of choices along this spectrum, it would therefore be extremely unwise to suggest that all boyars occupied only one position in this possible spectrum of understanding, at either end or in the middle. A more likely argument is that, given the little that we can guess about the interests and knowledge of lay courtiers, the perceptions of the court as a whole fell within a range of understandings that would have enabled most people, most of the time, to understand the basic messages we have been discussing.

Court life in Russia, as elsewhere, offered many lessons about politics, in many formats. Courtiers went on military campaigns, took part in precedence disputes, did their best to forward the interests of themselves and their clans, attended lengthy ceremonies at court. Each of these activities produced its own lessons, many brutally practical. Among the many ways in which the political culture of the court took shape, the Golden Hall murals, and associated images elsewhere, may well have played an important role, since, by casting political relations in the language and rich context of Orthodox political culture, they provided answers to a level of question quite different from the other, more practical, lessons offered by court life. By emphasizing the divine purpose of the state, they strengthened the power of the tsar and made the growing political structure of the realm seem as if it were a part of the natural order of things, as inescapable as the turning of the seasons. The protection of the Mother of God strengthened the idea of divine support for the state while drawing on a long tradition of Marian veneration among a wide variety of inhabitants of Rus'. The celebration of the clan of the ruler echoed the clan concerns that occupied so much of the attention of the boyars, while the military theme of God's protection of the Russian army gave spiritual comfort to those on campaign and a role in salvation history not only to the tsar but to his nobles.[30] The active participation of the court came out even more clearly in the various scenes involving advice. The scenes dealing with moral choice served not only to edify the court but at the least to imply the conditionality of royal power.

These beliefs, couched entirely within the context of Orthodox culture, were surely of great importance to the political history of Russia. If we assume, as Keenan does, that the Muscovite state until the second half of the seventeenth century was too weak economically, bureaucratically, and militarily to enforce its will on all its subjects all the time, then these murals (and other images) may have been a particularly cost-effective way to hold the country together. This goal was achieved by giving members of the elite good reasons why, under normal circumstances, they should serve the tsar and support the state. Each of the religious ideas we have discussed worked powerfully toward this end. Each also depended on the kind of crossover of religious ideas into the secular culture that form such an important theme to the collection of essays in which this essay first appeared.[31]

Instead of relying on brute force, the ruler persuaded his courtiers that they were an important part of God's plan, that their work as warriors and advisers was crucial to salvation history. At the same time, and using the same religious vocabulary, the murals emphasized that the tsar was to govern with the advice of his nobles, and implied that the power of the tsar was conditional on the tsar's personal piety and morality and on his defense of the Orthodox faith. The Orthodox Church thus not only provided a language for the understanding of political relations, it also provided religious reasons for opposing the tsar. During the Time of Troubles, when a succession crisis led to civil war and an abundance of pretenders of doubtful lineage and questionable religious and moral credentials, the importance of these limitations was to become all too apparent.

Notes

I would like to thank participants in conferences held at the University of Michigan on the theme of "Russian Orthodoxy in Lived Historical Experience." In particular I am grateful to Valerie Kivelson and Robert Greene, for many helpful suggestions. I am also grateful to Sandy Isenstadt of the University of Kentucky College of Architecture and other members of the College's Seminar on Critical Issues for clarifying several points connected with reception theory.

1. Robert O. Crummey, *Aristocrats and Servitors: The Boyar Elite in Russia, 1613–1689* (Princeton, NJ: Princeton University Press, 1983); Edward L. Keenan, "Muscovite Political Folkways," *Russian Review* 45 (1986): 138–148; Nancy Shields Kollmann, *Kinship and Politics: The Making of the Muscovite Political System, 1345–1547* (Stanford, CA: Stanford University Press, 1987); Valerie A. Kivelson, *Autocracy in the Provinces: The Muscovite Gentry and Political Culture in the Seventeenth Century* (Stanford, CA: Stanford University Press, 1996).

2. The most important published accounts of the Golden Hall murals are O. I. Podobedova, *Moskovskaia shkola zhivopisi pri Ivane IV* (Moscow: Izdatel'stvo Nauka, 1972), 59–68, and the most useful appendix, with reconstructions of the murals, by K. K. Lopialo, in the same volume, 193–198; and Frank Kampfer, "'Russland an der Schwelle zur Neuzeit': Kunst, Ideologie und Bewusstsein unter Ivan Groznyj," *Jahrbücher für Geschichte Osteuropas* 23 (1975): 504–524. The most thorough and most convincing interpretation of the overall meaning of the murals is Michael Flier, "Putting the Tsar in His Place: The Apocalyptic Dimension of the Golden Hall Throne Room" (paper delivered at the annual convention of the American Association for the Advancement of Slavic Studies [AAASS], 1991). I have also given two papers at the AAASS relating to the murals: "The Artist's View of Politics: The Golden Palace" (1990), and "Political Messages in the Golden Palace Murals" (1995). The second of these papers forms the basis for this article. I would like to take this opportunity to thank Michael Flier for his help and advice over the many years we have both been thinking about these murals.

3. See, in addition to the Flier reference in footnote 2, his "K semioticheskomu analizu Zolotoi palaty Moskovskogo Kremlia," *Drevnerusskoe iskusstvo. Russkoe iskusstvo pozdnego Srednevekov'ia. XVI vek*, ed. Andrei Batalov et al. (Saint Petersburg: Dmitrij Bulanin, 2003), 178–187.

4. See Flier, "Putting the Tsar in His Place."

5. Edward L. Keenan, *The Kurbskii-Groznyi Apocrypha: The Seventeenth-Century Genesis of the "Correspondence" Attributed to Prince A. M. Kurbskii and Tsar Ivan IV*, with an appendix by Daniel C. Waugh (Cambridge, MA: Harvard University Press, 1971), 53–54.

6. Edward L. Keenan, "Response to Halperin, 'Edward Keenan and the Kurbskii-Groznyi Correspondence in Hindsight,'" *Jahrbücher für Geschichte Osteuropas* 46 (1998): 404–418, esp. 413–414.

7. Keenan, *The Kurbskii-Groznyi Apocrypha*, 54.

8. Father Zosima is a charismatic monk and elder (*starets*) in Dostoevsky's *Brothers Karamazov* and one of the most memorable religious figures in all of literature.

9. On this icon and its meaning for mid-sixteenth-century Russians, see Daniel Rowland, "Biblical Military Imagery in the Political Culture of Early Modern Russia: The Blessed Host of the Heavenly Tsar," in *Medieval Russian Culture*, vol. 2, ed. Michael S. Flier and Daniel Rowland, California Slavic Studies 19 (Berkeley: University of California Press, 1994), 163–181 (chapter 6 of this volume).

10. See Clifford Geertz, "Centers, Kings, and Charisma: Reflections on the Symbolics of Power," in *Rites of Power: Symbolism, Ritual, and Politics Since the Middle Ages*, ed. Sean Wilentz (Philadelphia: University of Pennsylvania Press, 1985), 13–38.

11. For a perceptive discussion of a similar nesting of architectural and social hierarchies, see Dell Upton, *Holy Things and Profane: Anglican Parish Churches in Colonial Virginia* (New Haven, CT: Yale University Press, 1997), esp. 199–218. I am indebted to Julie Riesenweber for this reference.

12. I have discussed both architecture and ritual in greater detail in Daniel Rowland, "Architecture, Image and Ritual in the Throne Rooms of Muscovy, 1550 to 1650" (chapter 10 of this volume). On the diplomatic rituals, see also L. A. Iusefovich, "*Kak v posol'skikh obychaiakh vedetsia*" (Moscow: Mezhdunatodnye otnosheniia, 1988), and the excellent paper by Maria Solomon Arel, "Muscovite Diplomatic Practice as a Prism through Which to View Tsarish Power: Encounter with the English" (paper presented at the American Association for the Advancement of Slavic Studies, Boca Raton, Florida, September 1998).

13. Valerie Kivelson, "'The Devil Stole His Mind': The Tsar and the 1648 Moscow Uprising," *American Historical Review* 98 (1993): 733–756; and Kivelson, *Autocracy in the Provinces*.

14. For example, see Richard Chancellor's description of the lavish state dinner in the Golden Hall ("golden court"), with mountains of golden serving vessels and "one hundred and forty servitors arrayed in cloth of gold that in the dinner time changed thrice their habit and apparel," to which Ivan IV invited him and his men. Chancellor was mightily impressed. Lloyd E. Berry and Robert O. Crummey, eds., *Rude and Barbarous Kingdom: Russia in the Accounts of Sixteenth-Century English Voyagers* (Madison: University of Wisconsin Press, 1968), 25–27. For similar receptions, see, in the same collection, the accounts of Anthony Jenkinson (who describes what is probably the Hall of Facets with its central pillar) and Sir Thomas Randolph.

15. Otto Demus, *Byzantine Mosaic Decoration: Aspects of Monumental Art in Byzantium* (London: Routledge and Kegan Paul, 1953).

16. These connections are particularly well laid out by Podobedova in *Moskovskaia shkola*.

17. For example, see Robert Crummey, *The Formation of Muscovy, 1304–1613* (London: Longman, 1987), 199–200, and Podobedova, *Moskovskaia shkola*.

18. Randolph Starn, "Seeing Culture in a Room for a Renaissance Prince," in *The New Cultural History*, ed. Lynn Hunt (Berkeley: University of California Press, 1989), 205–232; Randolph Starn and Loren Partridge, *Arts of Power: Three Halls of State in Italy, 1300–1600* (Berkeley: University of California Press, 1992), 118–131. Art historians have recently devoted a lot of attention to the viewing public. Thomas Crow's works are especially relevant in this respect. See his *Painters in Public Life in Eighteenth-Century Paris* (New Haven, CT: Yale University Press, 1985).

19. S. P. Bartenev, *Moskovskii kreml' v starinu i teper'* (Moscow: Sinodal'naia tip., 1916), 183–193, provides a full description of the murals made in 1672. References to this description, which is the clearest evidence we have about the murals, will be made parenthetically in the text.

20. See figures 3 and 4 for a reconstruction of the murals of each room by K. K. Lopialo. Figure 5 is a diagram by my colleague Michael Flier of the overall scheme of the murals.

21. Ushakov's description can be found in Bartenev, *Moskovskii kreml'*, 183–193; and I. E. Zabelin, *Materialy dlia istorii, arkheologii, i statistiki goroda Moskvy*, 2 vols. (Moscow: Moskovskaia gorodskaia tip., 1884), 1:1238–35.

22. See the sketches of the Golden Hall architecture and murals by K. K. Lopialo in Podobedova, *Moskovskaia shkola*, appendix.

23. See Rowland, "Biblical Military Imagery," 163–181, for further references to other works on this important theme. An important new work is N.V. Kvlividze, "Ikona 'Blagoslovenno voinstvo nebesnogo tsaria' i ee literaturnye paralleli," *Iskusstvo Khristianskogo mira. Sbornik statei*, vol. 2 (Moscow: Pravoslavnyi Sviato-Tikhonovskii Bogoslovskii Institut, 1997).

24. Aida Nasibova, *The Faceted Chamber in the Moscow Kremlin* (Leningrad: Aurora Art Publishers, 1978).

25. Ivan Zabelin, *Domashnii byt Russkikh tsarei v XVI i XVII st.* (Moscow: Tipografiia A. I. Mamontova, 1895), 166–167; Podobedova, *Moskovskaia shkola*, 61–62.

26. Paul Bushkovitch, *Religion and Society in Russia: The Sixteenth and Seventeenth Centuries* (New York: Oxford University Press, 1992).

27. Daniel Rowland, "The Problem of Advice in Muscovite Tales about the Time of Troubles," *Russian History* 6 (1979): 259–283 (chapter 3 of this volume).

28. On the dating of the Golden Hall murals, see my "Biblical Military Imagery," 194n29, with further references on the opinions of earlier art historians. Podobedova believed that the murals were painted in the 1540s; Lopialo, in the seventeenth century. See Podobedova, *Moskovskaia shkola*, 59, 194–198.

29. Michael Baxendall, *Painting and Experience in Fifteenth-Century Italy* (Oxford: Oxford University Press, 1972), 48. Baxendall, investigating a society with far more surviving documentation than sixteenth-century Russia, was nevertheless pessimistic about the force of his own ingenious arguments. At the end of his chapter "The Period Eye," he concluded ruefully, "It is proper to end this chapter on a faltering note." On the complex matter of reception theory, I have found helpful the following works: Terry Eagleton, *Literary Theory: An Introduction* (Minneapolis: University of Minnesota Press, 1983), 54–90; Eric Fernie, ed., *Art History and Its Methods: A Critical Anthology* (London: Phaidon Press, 1995), 357–358; and Ann Jefferson and David Robey, eds., *Modern Literary Criticism: A Comparative Introduction*, 2nd ed. (Totowa, NJ: Barnes and Noble Books, 1986), 138–144. For a wonderful example of reading architecture in the context of its contemporary society and geography, see Upton, *Holy Things and Profane*.

30. See here especially Kollmann, *Kinship and Politics*, and her recent book on precedence: Nancy Shields Kollmann, *By Honor Bound: State and Society in Early Modern Russia* (Ithaca, NY: Cornell University Press, 1999).

31. See unnumbered notes of this chapter.

CHAPTER 10

Architecture, Image, and Ritual in the Throne Rooms of Muscovite Russia

This essay attempts to build on Robert Crummey's work by exploring two themes that he has written about: rituals and the secular elite of Muscovy.[1] As the title indicates, it is more of a quick survey than a scholarly discussion of a complex but important set of problems presented by Muscovy's two main throne rooms, the Hall of Facets (Granovitaia palata) and the Golden Hall. Crummey has examined in great detail the composition of the elite over time, and the various ties that bound elite and monarch together. Crummey and other scholars have argued that the health, prosperity, and even the very survival of the Muscovite state throughout all its life depended on the maintenance of a consensus among members of the elite and between the elite and the monarch, and have uncovered of the details of this relationship over both time and space.[2] Less attention has been paid to the symbolic expression of this consensus, to the images used to portray the state, its elite, and its ruler to the elite itself (the court), to other residents of Muscovy, and to foreigners. The history of other premodern states would lead us to believe that this type of symbolic action could serve as a powerful

---

This essay, originally titled "Architecture, Image and Ritual in the Throne Rooms of Muscovy, 1550–1650: A Preliminary Survey," appeared in *Rude and Barbarous Kingdom Revisited: Essays in Russian History and Culture in Honor of Robert O. Crummey*, ed. Chester S. L. Dunning, Russell E. Martin, and Daniel Rowland (Bloomington, IN: Slavica, 2008), 53–71. The author gratefully acknowledges the publisher for permission to reprint this essay.

cohesive force for political organisms like the Muscovite state that lacked the wealth, bureaucratic reach, and military power to compel obedience from all subjects. This essay concentrates on two places where this symbolic action was especially densely concentrated: the two throne rooms of the Moscow Kremlin.

These two halls of state are ideal examples of "glowing centers" as defined by Clifford Geertz. According to Geertz, such centers are "concentrated loci of serious acts; they consist in the point or points in a society where the leading ideas come together with the leading institutions to create an arena in which the events that most vitally affect its members' lives take place."[3] It is precisely this coincidence of political institutions and symbolic display that gave these throne rooms their power for contemporaries then and constitute their importance for historians now. The tsar and the members of his court spent many hours in these chambers, making (or enunciating) important decisions or, through their persons and their dress, the costly furnishings of the rooms and rituals of unity and devotion, displaying to foreign visitors the power and wealth of the state and the unanimity of the court. The walls of each hall were covered with elaborate murals, those in the Golden Hall originating in the period right after the Moscow fire of 1547, and those in the Hall of Facets in the reign of Boris Godunov. More than any text, these mural cycles displayed the basic ideology of rulership in Muscovy. By depicting the governance of state in the context of Christian salvation history, they elevated the tsar and courtiers sitting immediately below to world historical significance and connected their decisions to the will of God. This conviction that the tsar's will reflected God's will, reinforced in countless other ways and attested by the observations of many foreign observers, was surely as vital a tool of statecraft as the army or the bureaucracy, and was, besides, a whole lot cheaper.

The mural cycles are important to the historian for another reason. In the West, there was a long tradition of sustained, disciplined discussion of politics and political theory that went back at least to Aristotle's *Politics* and was structured according to the rules of Aristotle's logic. This tradition was vigorous in the Middle Ages and flourished even more robustly in the early modem period. In Muscovy, this tradition was almost completely absent. This relative absence of formal political discourse is not surprising when we realize that the works translated from Greek that made their way into Kiev or Moscow offered no literary models for political philosophizing that went much beyond the tags and aphorisms of Agapetus or the Pseudo-Basil, texts that Ihor Sevcenko has aptly called "rather second-rate compendia."[4] No serious classical works of political theory were known in Rus´, and Aristotle's *Logic* was not available until the end of the seventeenth century to provide the intellectual

236   CHAPTER 10

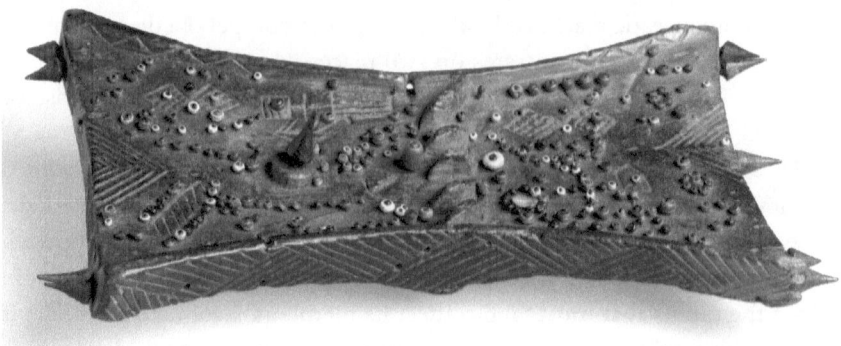

FIGURE 10.1. Luba. Lukasa Memory Board, late nineteenth or early twentieth century. Wood, metal, beads, 10 × 5-3/4 × 2-1/4 in. (25.4 × 14.6 × 5.7 cm). Brooklyn Museum, Gift of Marcia and John Friede, 76.20.4. Creative Commons-BY. Photo: Brooklyn Museum, 76.20.4_view2_PS9.jpg. Typically, various beads, nails, and cowrie shells represent a number of complex ideas, including in some boards, the royal residence with its court and the residence of the first king. Also represented are proverbs about kingship, spirit capitals of several types, and various sites related to the *Mbudye*, an elite group of royal advisers.

framework that supported much of Western political theorizing. Political ideas are certainly present in many kinds of Muscovite texts, but they are not connected through logic into a coherent set of principles; rather they lie as unconnected distinct ideas in various historical, polemical, or other texts. Architecture and painting together address, if not solve, this problem, since they operated in a quite distinct tradition that provided an organizational principle based, as we will see, on space rather than logic.

If we are to capture within the short compass of an essay the significance of these throne rooms and the rituals that took place within them, we must at least attempt to bring all three elements into focus—architecture, images, and ritual.

A useful, if unconventional, place to begin our discussion is with a memory board (*lukasa*) from the Luba people of central Africa, in present-day Zaire (see figure 10.1). A recent exhibit of Luba political art at the Museum for African Art in New York and the excellent catalog produced in connection with it show that the *lukasa* stands simultaneously (among other things) for the body of the tortoise, the animal form of the founding ancestress of the society of historians (and royal advisers) whose job it is to "read" the *lukasa*, and for the territory of the kingdom, with sacred sites and rulers represented by beads, shells, and nails. Created specifically for a particular ruler, the *lukasa* conveys in esoteric signs the principles on which Luba politics are founded. The Luba are useful to our inquiry because they have little connection with the tradition of Christian rulership of which the Muscovite throne rooms are part. Nevertheless, their "memory" art—memory boards, and closely related objects like staffs, stools, statues, and murals, together with dances, songs, and body decoration, which together constitute "the theater of Luba royal experience"— asks many of the same basic questions that the art and rituals of our throne rooms do. These ceremonial objects tell the history of Luba kings against the background of Luba geography, epic tales, and spirit worship; they are produced by a society of court historians/advisers (the Mbudye) whose job it is to interpret their multilayered and ambiguous symbols to suit the present time and place. They provide legitimacy for the monarch, but at the same time furnish standards for proper etiquette and behavior by which the monarch's actions may be (and are) judged. Used together, they explain the history of Luba kings starting with the legendary founder of kingship (appointed by a goddess or spirit in the form of a turtle); they describe the special divine wisdom by which the king and his advisers make judgments (spirit possession by Mbudye members); they map the social hierarchy of the society, they demonstrate the solidarity of the state; and they associate the power of the king with the forces of nature, the sun, moon, stars, trees, and so on.[5] These functions are strikingly similar to the functions performed, as we shall see, by Russian throne rooms. This similarity, in turn, underlines the basic nature of the questions that Muscovy's throne rooms set out to answer and helps us put the Muscovite answers in a comparative perspective.

There are three differences that stand out, however. The first is that knowledge of political principles is for the Luba esoteric knowledge, available to a few initiates and accessed by spirit possession; for early modern Russians, the principles of Christian rulership were at least in theory available to the public, though of course the way those principles were applied in practice was not. In both cultures, however, the production of state ideology was a monopoly of the court. A second difference is that the Luba have a more richly complex ideology of rulership than the Musocvites had, more ambiguous because unwritten, more coherently described in a variety of media from body decoration to implements to statues to dance to architecture to murals. The other difference revealed by the comparison is the comparative lack of concern with geography in Muscovite ideology; the Luba, like the Balinese of Clifford Geertz's descriptions, saw the landscape as inhabited by spirits that embodied the state on the spiritual level in the way that local officials embodied the state on a mundane level, so that the landscape in potential form *was* the state, even if no governing apparatus existed. Christianity obviously did not permit the veneration of local spirits. In Muscovite ideology, therefore, the geographical dimension in the core definition of the state was left largely blank; this disadvantage made it both all the more difficult and all the more imperative to extend the symbolic reach of the state out into the rapidly growing provinces.

The churchmen who developed and elaborated the image of rulership in Muscovy, like contemporary Luba historians, were working in a well-developed tradition whose general precepts had to be interpreted for specific circumstances. In both the Christian East and the Christian West, there was a long tradition of palace architecture and art that provided the basic vocabulary within which the Muscovites could work. The prototype of the imperial palace seems to have been the residence (*palatium*) of the Emperor Domitian (AD 81–96) on the Palatine Hill. This residence was approached across an open square, had an impressive façade with colonnades and pediment, and contained three separate halls for audiences, justice, and eating. In the West, Charlemagne built a Sacrum Palatium in Aachen, which in turn served as the prototype for a whole series of medieval halls of state, some, like the gigantic hall built by William II at Westminster (20 by 72 meters), were created for monarchs, some, especially in Italy, for republican regimes.[6] In the East, important palaces were built both in Constantinople and in the provinces. Typically, they contained images of the current ruler and/or his ancestors, and depictions of their victories. In individual palaces, images of the personified virtues, the Genesis creation story, or images of the Mother of God as guardian were also included.[7] The epic of Digenes Akritas contains a fairly lengthy description of Digenes's palace, "a big square house of cut stone, having stately columns and windows up above," containing halls whose ceilings were decorated with gold mosaics depicting Old Testament heroes, Samson, David, Moses, and Joshua, together with other heroes from Greek classical history.[8] Rus´ chronicles frequently mention royal palaces, but we know almost nothing about their decoration. They probably followed Byzantine models, at least at first. Theophanes the Greek apparently executed paintings in both the residence of the grand prince in Moscow and in the palace of Prince Vladimir Andreevich of Serpukhov.[9]

Architecture

Compared to the complex source problems relating to the murals in Muscovy's throne rooms, their architectural history is relatively straightforward. Figure 10.2 shows the two throne rooms as they appeared in the 1672–1673 *Book about the Election of Mikhail Fedorovich*. (For full title, see caption to figure 10.2.) On the right (nos. 17 and 18 on the plan in figure 9.1) is the Hall of Facets, begun in 1487 by Marco Friazin ("the Italian"), who laid out the basic plan of the building, including its main hall (22.1 by 22.4 by 9 meters), supported by

ARCHITECTURE, IMAGE, AND RITUAL 239

FIGURE 10.2. Colored drawing of the royal palace seen from Cathedral Square taken from the manuscript book *On the Election to the Most High Throne of the Great Russian Realm of the Great Lord, Tsar and Grand Prince Michael Romanov, Autocrat of All Rus'*, created 1672–1673. This manuscript book is particularly valuable in that it shows in several colored drawings the royal palace as it appeared before its destruction in the eighteenth century. On the far right is the Dormition Cathedral, with the Hall of Facets projecting into the square. On the viewer's left of the Hall of Facets is the Great Beautiful Golden Stair, one of three stairs leading up to the Boyars' Porch. The Golden Hall and its vestibule are seen immediately behind the Boyars' Porch. A corner of the Annunciation Cathedral, containing the third stair to the Boyars' Porch, is visible on the right. For a reconstruction of the original plan of palace, see fig. 9.1 Source: Wikipedia, https://ru.wikipedia.org/wiki/Файл:Соборная_площадь_Московского_Кремля_1672-1673.jpg.

one massive central pillar. The Milanese Pietro Antonio Solari, who was also active in the design of parts of the Kremlin wall, took over the project in 1490, and may have added the finishing details, especially the faceted limestone façade that gave the building its name, and the original paired gothic windows clearly seen in this drawing. Note the "Great Beautiful Golden Stair," the elaborate entrance stair with two landings (no. 16 in figure 9.1). Recent scholarship indicates that it was originally open, but at some point before the date of this drawing, an elaborate copper tent roof was added with a gilded grille to guard the entry. Some sources say that the roof was also gilded. An elaborate portal, possibly designed by Alevisio Novyi, led from the "Boyars' Porch" at the top of the stair into the vestibule of the Hall of Facets (no. 11 in figure 9.1). Note also that the faceted limestone blocks originally covered the whole façade, and the first story was considerably higher. During the restoration of the building that was carried out in 1968, traces of colored paint (red, yellow, light blue, green) were found on pieces of limestone from the building's exterior. Exactly where these pieces came from and what color patterns they imply has not been discussed in print, as far as I know. I also cannot find any clear evidence of when this color was first applied, though documentary evidence from 1667 indicates that the building was *repainted* at that time, and that a considerable amount of paint was used. We do know that the building's side walls were painted a dark red.[10] At least by the middle of the seventeenth century, then, the hall's exterior was characterized by considerable color contrasts: the red side wall with the white limestone of the façade and the original window frames, the other colors, wherever they were, and the steep copper roof, possibly gilded. Considerable evidence also exists that up until 1684 an inscription ran around the building just below the cornice.[11]

The history of the Golden Hall is a little simpler, largely because it is (unfortunately) shorter. The two rooms (vestibule and throne room, nos. 1 and 2 on the plan in figure 9.1) were built as part of the royal residence from 1499–1508 by Alevisio Novyi. Figure 10.2 shows what seems to have been the basic form of the façade, approached by three sets of stairs leading to a balcony (the Boyars' Porch, or Front Passages, no. 11 in figure 9.1), from which in turn one entered through a portal into the vestibule and finally into the throne room. Barberino states that the palace had a golden roof; around the cornice ran an inscription (dated 1561 and seemingly proclaiming the palace built by order of Ivan IV and his sons!) that survived until the building was pulled down in 1752, to be replaced by Rastrelli's Kremlin palace. Inside, the dimensions of both the throne room (12 meters square and about 12 meters in height) and the vestibule (about 12 by 8 meters) were quite modest, compared to either the Hall of Facets or to Western European palaces. Like the floor of the Hall of Facets, the floor of the Golden Hall was stepped down near the middle, leaving an elevated platform around the wall for benches from which courtiers could watch various court rituals, including the reception of foreigner diplomats, from above (figure 10.3). Unless the lower center space was very small, this platform would probably have been about 2 meters wide.[12]

These two throne rooms present a fascinating contrast, one with the other. The Faceted Hall projected out into Cathedral Square, where it boldly took its place among the other, largely religious, buildings there. Like them, its placement and design ensured that it would be seen as a three-dimensional object standing in space. It loudly proclaims its Italian origins, as can be seen by a quick comparison with Ferrara's Palazzo dei Diamanti (figure 10.4), and its placement in Cathedral Square is, at least to some extent, typical of how a Renaissance palace might be placed in a piazza.

FIGURE 10.3. Engraving by Adam Olearius of an audience granted to the Holstein embassy in the 1630s by Tsar Mikhail Romanov in an unidentified throne room, probably a badly remembered Golden Hall. Note the fairly narrow raised platform around the outside of the room, and the intimidating effect (at least in Olearius's memory) of the assembled notables in tall hats looming over the diplomats below. Illustration from *Offt begehrte Beschreibung der newen orientalischen Reise: so durch Gelegenheit einer holsteinischen Legation an den König in Persien geschehen* (Schlesswig: Jacob zur Glocken, 1647). Most of the illustrations were drawn by Olearius himself, the rest by another member of the Holstein embassy. Courtesy of the Beinecke Rare Book and Manuscript Library, Yale University.

As can be seen in figure 10.2, the Golden Hall, by contrast, was not really an independent structure, but rather a part of the royal residence as a whole. Seen from Cathedral Square, neither the hall nor the whole residence of which it was a part could be seen as clear and understandable three-dimensional objects. There was no attempt to create a front façade or to express the mass of the building. Rather, the front of the Golden Hall is concealed from an observer standing down at the level of Cathedral Square by the wide Boyars' Porch, revealing behind the balustrade only the roofs and tantalizing top parts of the building behind. If the Faceted Hall plainly represented an import from the Renaissance West, the Golden Hall and its surrounding palace harked back to an older and more complex ancestry going back both to the Great Palace of Constantinople and to a series of Islamic palaces. The central planning concept of these palaces originated with the placement of tents in the Mongol

Figure 10.4. Palazzo dei Diamanti, Ferrara, Italy, designed by Biagio Rossetti for Sigismondo d'Este, brother of the Duke, built ca. 1492–1495. Photo by Vanni Lazzari, used according to the license agreement: https://commons.wikimedia.org/wiki/File:Palazzo_dei_Diamanti_-_Ferrara.jpg.

court and reached its fullest development in the Topkapi Palace of Sultan Mehmed II, built about the same time as Ivan III carried out his rebuilding of the Kremlin. Like the Kremlin's builders, Topkapi's builders self-consciously used Italian architects (and, for the Ottomans, other foreign architects) in addition to the local talent. The tsar's palace had no apparent axial organization and consisted largely of comparatively low structures grouped around courtyards and passages. The verticality that was seen as appropriate for church architecture was here replaced by horizontal extension over space. Like the Topkapi as described by Gulru Necipoglu, the Kremlin was impressive as seen from a distance behind its walls and towers, but from inside the royal residence itself, the architecture appeared much more modest, and was characterized by "the repetitive use of elementary forms acting as surfaces for decoration applied with varying degrees of elaboration." The integration of nature in the form of gardens was also an important ingredient for both residences.[13]

The sprawling spaces of the Topkapi were held together by the "glue" of court ceremonies in which the official visitor was moved by carefully articulated stages through a series of ever more restricted spaces (restricted spatially and socially) toward the secluded monarch. Whether this is true of the entire royal palace within the Kremlin as a whole I do not know, but it seems to have been true, on a small scale at least, of our throne rooms. The Golden Hall is the most obvious example, since the visitor, after moving from the open spaces of Red Square through the massive Spasskii gates and the narrow street next to the Voznesenskii Monastery to Cathedral Square, experienced the building in stages, starting in the square, rising according to status on one of three stairways (14, 15, 16 in figure 9.1) to the porch (there were grilles protecting the stairways), from which the palace complex was much more visible, and proceeding to the vestibule and into the throne room itself. The same sequence also applied, surprisingly, to the Faceted Hall. Instead of entering the building directly from the square through a central doorway, as one would expect in an Italian *palazzo* (and as was done in the Palazzo dei Diamanti; the central door opens onto the street), the visitor climbed to the porch via one of the ceremonial staircases, and then entered the building from the back of the south wall, continuing on through the vestibule to the throne room. Thus the Faceted Hall, although it actually stood prominently in the square itself, was experienced ceremonially as if, like the Golden Hall, it receded away from the square into a hidden, privileged realm. The effect was to mark the space of the two halls off from the more public space of Cathedral Square, which itself was even more clearly separated from the truly public space of Red Square by the walls and intervening spaces of the Kremlin. Even a high-ranking boyar, who might live in the Kremlin and be familiar with most of its spaces, was made to feel the privileged nature of the throne halls and the exalted social status of those who frequented them. The space of the Kremlin as a whole, and the royal palace in particular, was thus encoded to display rank: the closer you got to the center of power, the tsar and his residence, the higher your rank. The distance from Red Square to the throne rooms mirrored the social distance from the lowliest commoner to the court, consisting of the highest nobles and ruler. Having access to "the bright eyes of the tsar" had a spatial as well as a symbolic meaning.

The increasing social restrictions of the Kremlin spaces were echoed by spaces that were meant to be experienced as increasingly restricted *physically*. Participants in throne-room ceremonies must have felt these restrictions bodily. This progressive tightening of spaces was felt as one progressed from the vast open space of Red Square and its bustling and freely moving market into the Kremlin and the more sedate and controlled space of Cathedral Square, up to the much smaller and narrower space of the Boyars' Porch. Spatial and physical restriction reached its height on the comparatively narrow steps on which courtiers sat on benches, restricted largely to movement in the two dimensions created by benches and the narrow space of the raised platform on which they sat (see figure 10.3.) This same progression of spaces reflected a sharply changing degree of freedom of action, from the freewheeling hurly-burly of Red Square to the carefully choreographed movements and stiff rituals of the two throne rooms.[14] This feeling of physical restriction would have been amplified by the heavy and elaborately embroidered costumes (with lavish use of gold thread) worn by courtiers on state occasions, discussed below.

The architecture of the two halls suggests two other points, one about the nature of the ruler and the other about Russia and the West. Necipoglu has perceptively observed that the architecture of the Topkapi, characterized by movement toward an aloof, receding ruler, implies just that: a ruler who is more icon than actor, a semidivine part of the natural order whose government governs but who personally is seldom or never seen to act. She sees this description as particularly appropriate to later sixteenth-century rulers, who were depicted by an increasingly ossified ceremonial in just this way. This image is the one conveyed by the Golden Hall. The Faceted Hall, on the other hand, implies just the opposite: the self-conscious active ruler who strides confidently into the public square and boldly governs. Literary portraits of Russian rulers reflect both types of ruler.[15] Tsar Fedor Ivanovich, mentally defective and almost totally inactive in government as far as we can tell, played the first role, and contemporary sources complimented him on his ritual success in interceding with God for Muscovy. Tsar Ivan IV might also fall into this category, particularly in his later years. Literary depictions of his son, Ivan Ivanovich, would place him in the second category; he was not shown as a Renaissance prince, certainly, but he was portrayed as forceful and active, both on the battlefield and off. Ivan III and Boris Godunov are two other rulers who could be put in this latter category. The fascinating thing is that, in throne-room architecture, in literary texts, and in political practice, both images of the ruler remained active and acceptable.

Another surprising point is that both throne rooms were built by Italian architects at roughly the same time for the same ruler (though Ivan III did not live to occupy his new palace). What we see here is something slightly more complex than the mere aping of Italian Renaissance forms. The interplay between the two throne rooms suggests the desire to incorporate the Italian technology and elegance that so captivated the rest of Europe, to integrate it into a larger vision of the state, but not to be overwhelmed by it. What now seems to us a balancing of native with foreign elements, so characteristic also of the Archangel Michael and the Dormition Cathedrals, bespeaks a surprising cultural self-confidence that inspired the sophisticated team of Italians to make their remarkable contributions to Russian culture, rather than making mere copies of what they had built at home. The best way to explain this evidence, it seems to me, is to suppose that neither the tsar nor his architects perceived the Russia-West dichotomy that so pervades our own view; rather, they held a premodern universalistic view that encouraged the borrowing of whatever was useful without worrying about its cultural identity.

Image

Architecturally, then, the Golden Hall and the Hall of Facets were based on very different, even opposing, principles, but the Faceted Hall was linked ceremonially and by the addition of decorative elements (colors, roofs, possibly an inscription) to the Golden Hall into one coherent system. The mural programs for the two halls were more closely related to start off with, and more explicit in their messages. But first, a few words about the sources. The Faceted Hall was first furnished with murals in the 1590s under Boris Godunov. The Golden Hall was decorated under Vasilii III, but these murals were apparently destroyed in the great fire of 1547, requiring the repainting of the hall shortly thereafter. The new murals were mentioned in a complaint by I. M. Viskovatyi, head of the Foreign Office, about new developments in iconography. Almost all of our information about the murals in both halls, however, comes from very detailed and systematic descriptions made in March 1672, by the famous icon painter Simon Ushakov and the *pod'iachii* (literally "underclerk" or scribe) Nikita Klement´ev.[16] To summarize a lot of confusing evidence, I think that the best we can do is to date the murals of Ushakov's description to the long period between 1547 and the 1630s. I am inclined toward the 1550s as the most likely date, however.

The diagrams in figures 9.5 (for the Golden Hall murals) and 10.5 (for the Hall of Facets murals) allow us an overview of the fairly complex set of images in each throne room and its associated vestibule.[17] To oversimplify considerably, the upper domed spaces in the Golden Hall are dominated by the theme of Holy Wisdom (throne room) and godly governance (vestibule), while the corresponding spaces in the Faceted Hall contain images of the creation of the universe (throne room) and miscellaneous scenes, some from the Old Testament (vestibule). Military and historical scenes from the Old Testament and from Rus´ history occupy the lower vaults and walls. In the Golden Hall, Old Testament scenes in the vestibule are seen as prefigurations of scenes from Rus´ history in the throne room.

There are plainly many levels on which these complex mural programs can be read. There is space here to touch on only a few of them. On a basic level, they answer many of the questions that Luba objects answered: They explain the founding of kingship in Christian terms by emphasizing the connection between the current ruler of Muscovy and Old Testament rulers, who, in the Christian tradition, were the first rulers to be chosen and protected by God. Both halls trace the ancestors of the current ruler in some detail; in the Faceted Hall, a long list of ancestor portraits were found, starting with the illustrations from the Tale of the Vladimir Princes on the east wall and then continuing in the window embrasures of the east, south, and north walls. In the Golden Hall, Riurikovich ancestors were placed in the squinches of the throne room in parallel with the Old Testament rulers on the squinches of the vestibule. Royal ancestors also appeared in illustrations to the Tale of Vladimir Princes and in the window embrasures. As the Luba associated the ruler with the natural order of the universe, the throne rooms of Muscovy (like many of their predecessors and successors) made the creation of the world a major theme, complete with the sun, moon, stars, and other natural features of the universe. The theme of the creation was found on the southern section of the dome of the Golden Hall throne room, as part of the larger theme of Holy Wisdom, through which God created the universe and the tsar then ruled his *tsarstvo*. In the Faceted Hall, the creation of the world occupies virtually the entire ceiling surface of the throne room. It begins with an impressive composition (Cr. 0 in figure 10.5) above the southern wall depicting the creation of the heavenly host as a kind of heavenly court, arranged in nine ranks, reflecting the social hierarchy of the court below, and continues with the seven days of creation followed by the Fall and the Expulsion from Eden. In both halls, as for the Luba, kingship is associated with the established order of the universe and thus imagined as both natural and immutable. On an even larger scale, the purpose of the murals in both halls is to place the Muscovite state within salvation history, starting with the creation and stretching out to the Apocalypse, an event very present in the Golden Hall but largely absent in the Hall of Facets.

Within this larger context, there are a number of themes common to both halls, most of which would have been quite understandable, because of their straightforward presentation, to an illiterate courtier or a foreigner. In an earlier article (chapter 9), I listed seven themes that were elaborated in the Golden Hall, all of which in slightly variant forms can also be found in the Hall of Facets.[18] These themes included (1) the descent of political power from God, (2) Holy Wisdom (largely absent in the Hall of Facets), (3) the protection of Rus' by the Mother of God, (4) the glorification of the clan of the ruler, (5) the maintenance of the good social order of the realm, (6) the obligations of the ruler to be merciful and just and to maintain his own piety and righ-

ARCHITECTURE, IMAGE, AND RITUAL 247

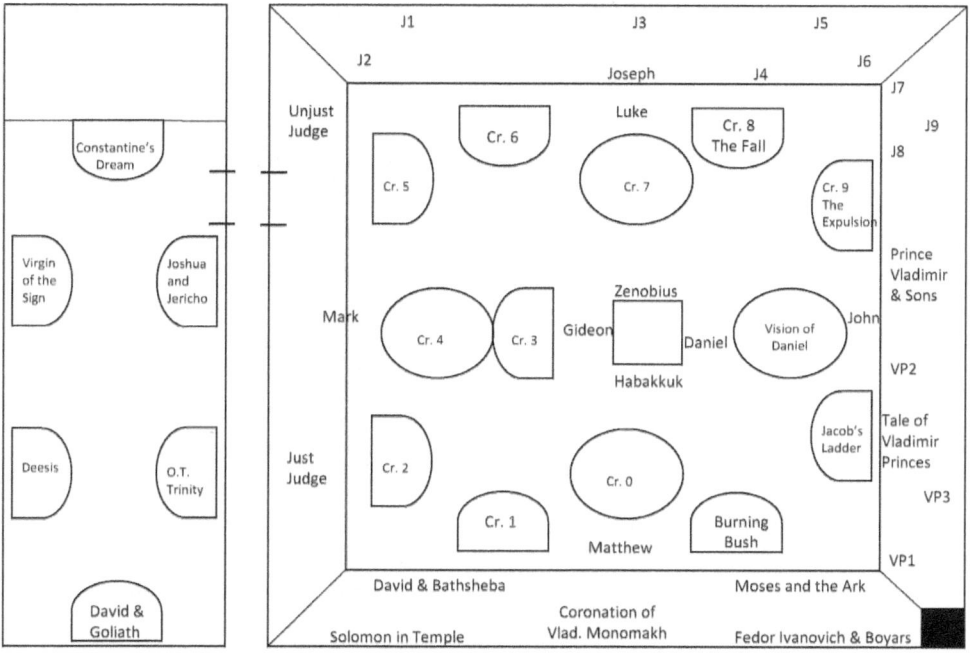

FIGURE 10.5. Simplified diagram of the scheme of murals in the Hall of Facets. The north sides of the rooms are at the top of the diagram. The lunettes in the vestibule, on the left of the diagram, are the only surfaces decorated with murals; the subjects are indicated in the diagram. The larger diagram on the right represents the throne room, with the large central column shown by the square in the middle, and the royal throne by the black square in the lower right. On the lunettes and vaults are ten scenes representing the creation story (Cr. 0–9); on the north and east walls are scenes from the life of Joseph (J 1–9), with Joseph's position as chief royal adviser of the Pharaoh presumably an echo of Boris Godunov's position at the Court of Fedor Ivanovich, which is illustrated on the south wall. The Tale of the Vladimir Princes is found on the east wall (VP 1–3). Diagram by the author.

teousness, and (7) advice and the relationship between the ruler and his courtiers. Particularly striking is the emphasis on the ruler's obligations and the importance of royal advisers. ("Boyars," *vel'mozhi*, and *mudrye skazateli* were listed by Ushakov and his assistant in almost every image of godly rule.)

This emphasis on the tsar's obligation to choose the righteous path is significant. If for the general public the identity of God's will with the tsar's will was, it was hoped, axiomatic, for the elite in the throne rooms, it was conditional. The great emphasis on moral choice, especially in the Golden Hall, clearly brought with it the possibility of a wrong choice. Not only the salvation of the tsar, but God's blessing on the *tsarstvo* and, ultimately, the legitimacy of the whole political system depended on the "good soil" of the tsar's soul. This evidence shows how far Russia was from the automatic and unquestionable identification of the ruler's will with God's will that was such an important part of Western European absolutist thought in the seventeenth century.

The Hall of Facets, as well as the Golden Hall, placed a major emphasis on advisers, not surprisingly, in view of Boris Godunov's role as chief adviser to Tsar Fedor, and as chief patron, presumably, of the Hall of Facets murals. *Premudrye skazateli* appear as a part of Pharaoh's court in the story of Joseph, as *vel'mozhi* in the parables about just and unjust judges, and, most significantly, as part of Tsar Fedor Ivanovich's court with Boris Godunov prominently at their head on the south wall next to the throne. Of the nine creation scenes, three (Cr. 0, 4, and 7 in figure 10.5) show God with His heavenly court of angels and archangels, images that I believe were meant as heavenly analogues of the tsar's earthly court meeting immediately below.[19] Whereas in the tales about the Time of Troubles, advisers were important chiefly as the most convenient means to correct an erring or sinful tsar, in both throne rooms wise advisers are shown as part of the normal running of a pious tsar's court. The consistency with which Ushakov and Klement'ev mention them indicates that the authors of the mural programs in both throne rooms considered boyar advisers an essential part of the tsar's court and made a point of including them in the murals' depiction of Christian governance. Indeed, "advice" may not be the right rubric for our discussion here; "boyars" or "grandees" are more accurately depicted as "partners" of the tsar in governance.

Ritual

We now turn to the rituals that took place in and around the throne rooms, chiefly, for the purposes of this essay, the rituals connected with the greeting and feeding of foreign ambassadors. Ritual, of course, is what knit together architecture and image, activating each in the context of ceremonies in which the actors—tsar, court, and foreign visitors—were also the chief audience. This dual role was crucial in convincing those present of the power and glory of the kingdom, and the importance of their own role within it: A ritual may look impressive from the outside, but it is often far more moving for those who take part in it, because, by taking part, those involved affirm by their own bodily actions the values implicit in the ritual. There were two important audiences, then, for these rituals: the foreign outsiders and the court itself, including the tsar. Although ostensibly the rituals were designed to impress the first, I believe that they also had a powerful effect on the second.

There were three chief types of ceremony carefully reported on by foreign ambassadors: (1) the procession by which the foreign delegation and its presents were conveyed to the throne rooms; (2) the greeting of the delegation by the tsar and court and the accompanying exchange of gifts; and, finally (3) an elaborate and lengthy feast, which usually took place in the Hall of Facets, but which was sometimes replaced, probably to save time, by the sending of a large number of dishes to the ambassador's lodgings.[20]

Our sources for these rituals are remarkably rich and reliable. The most important by far are the accounts of foreign diplomats who took part in the ceremonies and whose official duties included reporting a description of them. These accounts present far fewer source problems than most of our other sources on Muscovite history; their publishing history and/or archival location usually make it clear by whom they were written and, roughly, when they were written. There are also substantial Russian records (the *posol'skie knigi* [diplomatic books]) about these ceremonies, well described recently by Iuzefovich.[21] A third type of record is far less reliable: the illustrations that sometimes graced the pages of the published versions of various foreigners' accounts (see figure 10.3). These images are compelling and are very useful in registering those things that the diplomat-authors thought were important, like the arrangement of the room and the placement of the various actors (tsar, courtiers, diplomats), but they were often drawn up after the event, in some cases after the author had returned home. For that reason, details in the images concerning subjects like architecture and painting, which were not of such interest to the diplomats, are far less reliable.

Read together, these accounts eloquently testify to the extraordinary effectiveness of Muscovite rituals in displaying the wealth and political power of the state. The sixteenth century was an age of great diplomatic display, as anyone familiar with the meeting between Henry VIII and Francis I on the "Field of the Cloth of Gold" will know.[22] Several of the diplomats who visited Russia were exceptionally experienced and sophisticated men, yet virtually everyone was impressed by Muscovite ritual. Richard Chancellor was typical when he worried about his audience with the tsar, that "this so honorable an assembly, so great a majesty of the emperor and the place, might very well have amazed our men and dashed them out of countenance."[23]

One major tool to this end was the lavish and unceasing use of luxury goods, descriptions of which appear in almost every foreign account. The gifts brought and received by the ambassadors, the clothing of the tsar and his court, the tsar's regalia—all were described with a kind of breathless materialist devotion worthy of voice-overs on *The Wheel of Fortune*. We unfortunately do not have the space to enumerate these splendors, but the mountains of plate and the endless cloth-of-gold costumes were clearly effective in impressing foreigners. They cannot have failed also to have impressed Muscovites. The gifts brought by ambassadors were carefully displayed during the initial procession to the Kremlin, and the foreigners tell us that the common people crowded around to look at them. More important, the courtiers cannot have been insensitive to the obvious message of wealth and power conveyed by all of these goods.[24]

These deluxe objects also reinforce our earlier impressions about the "Russia and the West" problem: They were not entirely or even mainly Russian, but were drawn freely from all of the countries with which Russia had relations. Textiles came from Russia, Poland, and Western Europe; of the hatchets that the tsar's ceremonial body guards (*ryndy*) carried, some were of Russian manufacture and others were made in Turkey. Even the thrones themselves were of international origin. Of surviving thrones of this period that I have run across, one was made in Western Europe, one was Russian, another was Persian, and yet another was a gift from Armenian merchants trading in Persia.[25] Olearius tells us of another that was being crafted jointly by Russian craftsmen and a German from Nuremberg named Esaias Zinkgraf.[26] Again, objects were acquired wherever necessary, without much trace of national or ethnic awareness.

A second effective element of ritual was the skillful use of space, sound, and personnel to impress the observer and to map out social divisions. In our discussion of architecture, we have already seen how visually impressive was the progression from Red Square to the throne rooms, and the social distinctions that were reflected in this progression of spaces, from public to highly restricted. The foreigners' accounts allow us to add more details. The ceremonial entrance really began while the envoys were still a short distance outside of Moscow, whence they were conducted to their residence by noble courtiers and a large procession. Long rows of musketeers are often mentioned, through whose serried ranks the procession wound its way both into Moscow and, later, from the ambassador's residence to the Kremlin. Behind and above the soldiers clamored the common people, anxious for a look at the spectacle. Olearius mentions the ringing of huge bell cast by Boris Godunov (356 hundredweight, requiring "24 or more" people standing below to ring it), which, when added to other Kremlin bells, must have made the air fairly vibrate as the party entered Cathedral Square, dismounted, and then proceeded up the appropriate set of stairs to the large porch giving onto the two throne rooms.[27] As the diplomats entered the vestibule of one of the throne rooms, they report seeing some one hundred or more courtiers lavishly dressed

FIGURE 10.6. Coronation feast for Mikhail Romanov in the Hall of Facets taken from the manuscript book *On the Election to the Most High Throne of the Great Russian Realm of the Great Lord, Tsar and Grand Prince Michael Romanov, Autocrat of All Rus'*, created 1672–1673. Note the lavish display of silver and golden serving vessels around the central column, the original paired gothic windows, and the relatively wide top step, allowing for two rows of seating with a substantial table in between. Used with permission from History and Art Collection/Alamy Stock Photo.

(in outfits borrowed from the royal treasury) to do honor to the occasion. They then progressed, sometimes after a delay, into the throne room itself, which was full of splendidly arrayed courtiers, carefully arranged, as we know, according to rank, with the tsar on his throne in the southeast corner. Here, the foreign diplomats were architecturally put on the defensive, since, as Olearius's drawing shows (figure 10.3), they stood below in the center, while the tsar and his court sat around the periphery of the room on benches elevated several steps above the diplomats.

The spatial mapping of social relations inherent in this progression of spaces was reinforced by a culinary mapping of society. (Figure 10.6 shows an illustration from 1672 of the coronation banquet of Mikhail Fedorovich in 1613.) The number and quality of dishes provided to diplomats, either in a throne room or later at their residences, was carefully recorded and seems now quite amazing, in the range of thirty to one hundred dishes, usually, starting, in the Kremlin at least, with roast swan. In the Faceted Palace, where banquets seem usually to have been held, the tsar himself took an active role as provider of nourishment, personally giving bread and other dishes both to diplomats and Russian courtiers, calling each by name, a feat that impressed several observers. The tsar was able to display a finely graduated scale of royal favor by the order of presentation and the dishes presented. He also emphasized the personal protective relationship that bound him to his courtiers. Then there were the toasts. Again, there is not space, and probably no need, to go into details. Herberstein was probably not the first foreigner, and certainly not the last, to pretend inebriation and exhaustion as a desperate excuse to avoid further toasts *do kontsa* (to the bottom of the glass). For our purposes, however, two points are important: The toasts gave another opportunity for the court system to express finely graduated preferences, and the process took up a lot of everyone's time, probably a reason for what seems to be a change over time from ceremonial dinners in the Faceted Hall to take-out dinners, also very elaborate, sent to the ambassadorial residence so that the diplomats and their Russian friends and caretakers could, like the hunters in court entertainments who killed a bear, drink "bravely" and "merrily" to the sovereign's health without keeping everyone else up all night.

Conclusion

So far, our attention has been fixed on the impressions made on foreign visitors. Here one has to admire the skill displayed by the Muscovite state, with very slender financial resources as compared to those of many Western European states and a culture that Western Europeans looked on as backward, in impressing its sometimes quite sophisticated visitors with its wealth and power. These ceremonies also conveyed a carefully calculated image of unity and social order by mapping out the social order spatially, gastronomically, and choreographically, and depicting the great boyars of the realm and the rest of the court as harmonious partners in godly governance. (Why many of these same visitors concluded that the government was "plain tyrannical" was not, I submit, the fault of these ceremonies.)

More important, however, was the effect made on the domestic audience, the courtiers of various ranks who were both the actors and a major audience for these dramas. These courtiers seem to have spent an inordinate amount of time at these diplomatic rituals, not counting weddings, church ceremonies, and trials.[28] The historical record (and Marshall Poe's excellent bibliography) has made the writings of Western travelers particularly accessible, but there were waves of other diplomats from virtually every point of the compass, each of whom had to be received and entertained by basically the same dramatis personae.[29] This meant that courtiers experienced these ceremonies over and over again, with what must have been a mind-numbing repetition. Forced to sit in their borrowed stiff cloth-of-gold court dress, perhaps with the added burden of wearing a tall fur hat, for hours on end while formal questions were asked and toasts proposed, even disinterested courtiers must have been forced to look at the surrounding mural cycles, if only the way one looks at *Reader's Digest* in the dentist's office. Others, it seems safe to assume, took a more genuine interest in court symbolism. Although both mural programs that we have briefly examined were subtle and designed to communicate some quite complex messages, a courtier need not have been a theological whiz kid to take away some basic messages. These messages were repeated many times in the murals, reinforced by the rituals we have discussed, and elaborated at some length in both texts and images unconnected with the throne rooms.

What were these messages? Basically, they answered the same questions that the Luba asked through their art and ritual. They explained the origin of Christian kingship in the Old Testament, and traced the connections of the current court back to those origins and forward to the Apocalypse. These historical connections gave people a reason to believe under normal circumstances that the tsar's will reflected God's will. They also made the welfare of the Muscovite state, at least by implication, crucial to salvation history. The architecture and the rituals within it served to mark off the social divisions of the realm, and so contributed to maintaining the social hierarchy, an essential goal for any premodern state. The pomp and circumstance that so impressed foreigners must also have impressed the locals with the wealth and power of the state. More important, the very courtiers on whose consensus and cooperation the realm depended were forced to act out over and over again rituals of agreement and unity under the gaze of the monarch. These rituals gave an important role to the court as a whole and to occasional individual courtiers, a message reinforced by the strong emphasis on courtier-advisers in both cycles of murals. These benefits came with a cost, however; the logic of Christian rulership meant that the ruler had to be perceived as personally pious and as following God's will in order for his power to be valid. The Golden Hall murals in particular emphasized these responsibilities of the tsar.

Richard Wortman has recently argued that the monarch was presented in Muscovite "scenarios of power" as a foreign, here Byzantine, hero ruling a Slavic state.[30] The evidence of the throne rooms indicates that this assertion rests on an anachronistic ethnic orientation to a later question of national identity. The Muscovites, with their willingness happily to borrow architecture or luxury goods from any source available seem not to have been overly worried about such things. In the Kremlin, the nation-state was obviously not relevant, and notions of "foreign" may have been only marginally more useful. Instead, Muscovites borrowed the best from the world of jewelers, silversmiths, armorers, and other international professions, regardless of national origin. Similarly, as the artists who designed the program for the Hall of Facets represented history, God's choice of sacred states jumped over ethnic boundaries, starting with Moses and the burning bush, passing through Byzantium, and ending with Tsar Fedor Ivanovich and Boris Godunov.

A more useful approach to understanding our throne rooms was suggested by Dell Upton on the occasion of the twenty-fifth anniversary of the Vernacular Architecture Forum. In urging his listeners to consider new approaches to the interpretation of architecture, he proposed thinking of a given building as reflecting a number of "circles of knowledge," each of which contributed to the creation and the meaning of a particular building: the architect(s) and their design philosophy and vision, the craftsmen who constructed the building, other buildings with similar programs and uses, the engineers who made the building stand up, and so on. To this we might add the human actions and rituals performed in the building, performances that "create shared meaning through use."[31] The Kremlin throne rooms reflected widely different circles of knowledge: Italian architectural practice; Byzantine and Rus' (even Ottoman?) traditions of throne rooms; the rituals of diplomatic practice, borrowed both from Western Europe and the Eurasian steppe; and international connoisseurship of the individual arts so necessary for throne-room rituals: jewelry, armor, gold- and silver-smithing, and textiles, to name a few. The mural programs brought in a further circle: the long tradition of monumental mural painting, secular as well as religious, again going back to Byzantium, and practiced by Greek and Armenian as well as Rus' painters. All of these were brought into focus by the political and social structure of the Muscovite state. The rulers who paid the not inconsiderable sums to keep these theaters of Muscovite political culture running, together with the powerful courtiers who spent so much time there, fashioned spaces, images, and rituals to reflect their values. The finely graded social divisions, marked spatially and ritually, reflected the preoccupation with rank embodied legally in the *mestnichestvo* (precedence) system as well as in literary texts that placed a high value on the ruler's maintenance of the social order. The power of the ruler was shown as derived both from God and from powerful ancestors. Courtiers as symbolic advisers were given a prominent role, but were severely restricted by the architectural spaces of the throne rooms in the way that they could give it. In these ways, the throne rooms reflected many of the themes and tensions in Muscovite political culture uncovered or elaborated on by the pioneering work of Robert Crummey.

Notes

1. See Robert O. Crummey, *Aristocrats and Servitors: The Boyar Elite in Russia, 1613–1689* (Princeton, NJ: Princeton University Press, 1983). On rituals, see Robert O. Crummey, "Court Spectacles in Seventeenth-Century Russia: Illusion and Reality," in *Essays in Honor of A. A. Zimin*, ed. Daniel C. Waugh (Columbus, OH: Slavica Publishers, 1985), 130–158.

2. In addition to the works cited in note 1 above, see Edward L. Keenan, "Muscovite Political Folkways," *Russian Review* 45 (1986): 115–181; Nancy Shields Kollmann, *Kinship and Politics: The Making of the Muscovite Political System, 1345–1547* (Stanford, CA: Stanford University Press, 1987); Valerie A. Kivelson, *Autocracy in the Provinces: The Muscovite Gentry and Political Culture in the Seventeenth Century* (Stanford, CA: Stanford University Press, 1996).

3. Clifford Geertz, "Centers, Kings, and Charisma: Reflections on the Symbolics of Power," in *Rites of Power: Symbolism, Ritual, and Politics since the Middle Ages*, ed. Sean Wilentz (Philadelphia: University of Pennsylvania Press, 1985), 14.

4. Ihor Sevcenko, "A Neglected Source of Muscovite Political Ideology," *Harvard Slavic Studies* 2 (1954), reprinted in Michael Cherniavsky, ed., *The Structure of Russian History* (New York: Random House, 1970), 99.

5. Mary Nooter Roberts and Allen F. Roberts, eds., *Memory: Luba Art and the Making of History* (Munich: Prestel, for the Museum for African Art, New York, 1996), esp. chap. 4.

6. This brief discussion is based on Randolph Starn and Loren Partridge's inspiring *Arts of Power: Three Halls of State in Italy, 1300–1600* (Berkeley: University of California Press, 1992), 1–3.

7. Cyril Mango, *The Art of the Byzantine Empire, 312–1453* (Englewood Cliffs, NJ: Prentice-Hall, 1972), 15, 224, 197, 184, 247, 235, 252–253. The acts of the Seventh Ecumenical Council condemn emperors for being depicted with the attributes of Christ: "They ought instead to have recounted their manly deeds, their victories over the foe, the subjugation of barbarians which many have portrayed on panels and on walls so as to consign their narration to memory and to arouse the love and zeal of spectators" (154).

8. Mango, *The Art of the Byzantine Empire*, 215–216.

9. The evidence comes from a letter from Epiphanius the Wise to Kiril of Tver': O. I. Podobedova, *Moskovskaia shkola zhivopisi* (Mosc Nauka, 1972), 59–60; I. Grabar', "Feofan Grek," in *O drevnerusskom iskusstve*, ed. O. I. Podobedova (Moscow: Nauka, 1972), 78.

10. The best straightforward description of the Hall of Facets is A. I. Komech and V. I. Pluzhnikov, eds., *Pamiatniki arkhitektury Moskvy: Kreml', Kitai-gorod, Tsentral'nye ploshchadi* (Moscow: Iskusstvo, 1982), 330–331. Vital documentary evidence is discussed by E. M. Kozlitina, "Dokumenty XVII veka po isotorii Granovitoi Palaty Moskovskogo Kremlia," *Gosudarstvennye muzei Moskovskogo Kremlia: Materialy i issledovaniia* 1 (1973): 95–110.

11. Major renovations carried out by Osip Startsev in 1682 substituted large baroque windows for Solari's late Gothic paired openings. A fire in 1696 caused the original copper peaked roof to be replaced by a flatter roof. The removal of the first-floor limestone blocks on the main façade to create a smooth stuccoed surface and the alteration of the original first-floor openings were carried out in the eighteenth and nineteenth centuries. The elaborate entrance stair that, with its original three landings, was an essential part of the approach to the throne hall has also been removed, replaced in the 1930s by the low building seen to the viewer's left in most contemporary photographs.

12. K. K. Lopialo, "K primernoi rekonstruktsii Zolotoi palaty Kremlevskogo dvortsa i ee monumental'noi zhivopisi," in Podobedova, *Moskovskaia shkola*, 193–198.

13. Gulru Necipoglu, *Architecture, Ceremonial, and Power: The Topkapi Palace in the Fifteenth and Sixteenth Centuries* (Cambridge, MA: MIT Press, 1991), quotation on 243.

14. These comments were inspired in part by reading the stimulating essay by Dell Upton on the occasion of the twenty-fifth anniversary of the Vernacular Architecture Forum, an American organization devoted to the study and interpretation of vernacular buildings, Dell Upton, "The VAF at 25: What Now?," *Perspectives in Vernacular Architecture* 13, no. 2 (2007): 7–13, and derive from the work of LeFebvre, de Certeau, Gibson, and Bordieu. The work of these seminal theoreticians is clearly relevant to our study, and could be applied profitably in much greater detail than is possible here.

15. On these portraits, see Daniel Rowland, "Did Muscovite Literary Ideology Place Limits on the Power of the Tsar (1540s–1660s)?," *Russian Review* 49 (1990): 125–155, esp. 131–142 (chapter 4 of this volume). On Topkapi, see Necipoglu, *Architecture, Ceremonial, and Power*.

16. The question is: What precisely were the murals that Ushakov and Klement'ev described? The answer for the Hall of Facets now seems fairly straightforward. The murals described were old enough that the need for their repair had been clear for some time. They might well have been repainted in the early decades of the century, but the presence of Fedor Ivanovich and Boris Godunov in a mural immediately next the throne suggests that later painters tried hard to follow the original program, as was the custom at least from the 1630s on. The question of the origin of the Golden Hall murals described in 1672 is so murky that I am not sure it can ever be resolved. For further information on the Golden Hall, see Lopialo, "K premernoi rekonstruktsii"; Michael Flier, "K semioticheskomu analizu Zolotoi palaty Moskovskogo Kremlia," in *Drevnerusskoe iskusstvo: Russkoe iskusstvo pozdnego Srednevekov'ia. Shestnadtsatyi vek*, ed. Andrei Batalov et al. (Saint Petersburg: Dmitrii Bulanin, 2003), 178–187 (by far the best analysis of the meaning of the murals); and Daniel Rowland, "Biblical Military Imagery in the Political Culture of Early Modern Russia: The Blessed Host of the Heavenly Tsar," in *Medieval Russian Culture*, vol. 2, ed. Michael Flier and Daniel Rowland (Berkeley: University of California Press, 1994), 194–195, and 194n29 (chapter 6 of this volume). The Ushakov and Klement'ev descriptions have been twice published: S. P. Bartenev, *Moskovskii kreml' v starinu i teper'* (Moscow: Sinodal'naia tip., 1916), 183–193; and I. E. Zabelin, *Materialy dlia istorii, arkheologii, i statistiki goroda Moskvy*, 2 vols. (Moscow: Moskovskaia gorodovaia tip., 1884), 1:1238–1255. The Hall of Facets murals were redone in the late nineteenth century, closely following the notes of Ushakov, and were recently restored, with impressive results. See Aida Nasibova and B. Grosh-

ARCHITECTURE, IMAGE, AND RITUAL

nikov, *Granovitaia palata Moskovskogo Kremlia* (Leningrad: Aurora, 1978) for color illustrations and full information on the mural scheme.

17. I am deeply grateful, as always, to Michael Flier for permission to reproduce the diagram in figure 9.5.

18. Daniel Rowland, "Two Cultures, One Throne Room: Secular Courtiers and Orthodox Culture in the Golden Hall of the Moscow Kremlin," in *Orthodox Russia: Belief and Practice under the Tsars*, ed. Valerie A. Kivelson and Robert H. Greene (University Park: Pennsylvania State University Press, 2003), 32–57 (chapter 9 of this volume).

19. On Joseph, see Zabelin, *Materialy*, cols. 1265–1266; on parables, cols. 1269–1271. On other scenes with "boyars": Saint Vladimir and sons, east wall, col. 1266; Constantine Monomakh and his *sanovniki*, south wall, cols. 1266–1267.

20. Michael S. Flier, "Political Ideas and Rituals," in *The Cambridge History of Russia*, vol. 1, *From Early Rus' to 1689*, ed. Maureen Perrie (Cambridge: Cambridge University Press, 2006), 387–408.

21. L. A. Iuzefovich, *Kak v posol'skikh obychaiakh vedetsia* (Moscow: Mezhdunarodnye otnosheniia, 1988).

22. See, for example, Joycelyne Gledhill Russell, *The Field of Cloth of Gold: Men and Manners in 1520* (New York: Barnes and Noble, 1969). I gladly thank Marshall Poe for this reference.

23. Quoted in Lloyd E. Berry and Robert O. Crummey, eds., *Rude and Barbarous Kingdom: Russia in the Accounts of Sixteenth-Century English Voyagers* (Madison: University of Wisconsin, 1968), 25.

24. See the display of silver and gold plate around the central pillar in the Hall of Facets in figure 10.6. For the unique collection of pre–Civil War English silver still preserved in the Kremlin, see the remarkable *Britannia & Muscovy: English Silver at the Court of the Tsars*, ed. Ol'ga Dmitrievna and Natalya Abramova (New Haven, CT: Yale University Press, 2006).

25. For Russian hatchets, see *Gosudarstvennaia Oruzheinaia Palata* (Moscow: Gosudarstvennoe izdatel'stvo izobrazitel'nogo iskusstva, 1958), plates 98–99; on hatchets likely manufactured in Turkey, see *Treasures of the Czars from the State Museums of the Moscow Kremlin*, ed. A. F. Boldov and N. S. Vladimirskaia (London: Booth-Clibborn Editions, 1995), 117. For textiles, see Tsar Peter's caftan, made in Kremlin workshops with materials from Venice and Western Europe: Irina Polynina, N. N. Rakhmanov, and G. Mekhova, *The Regalia of the Russian Empire* (Moscow: Red Square, 1994), 100, plate 81. On caftans of Italian velvet, see *Treasures*, 114; formal caftan *terlik* made from Polish and Italian velvet, 115. On thrones, see *Regalia*, 38, plate 25 (Western Europe); 71, plate 56 (Russia and "Orient"); 46, plate 32 (Iran); 84, plate 69 (Armenian merchants).

26. Samuel H. Baron, ed. and trans., *The Travels of Olearius in Seventeenth-Century Russia* (Stanford, CA: Stanford University Press, 1967), 62.

27. Baron, *The Travels of Olearius*, 144.

28. Valerie Kivelson mentions a trial in the Golden Hall: "What was *Chernoknizhestvo*? Black Books, Foreign Writing, and Literacy in Muscovite Magic," in Dunning et al., *Rude and Barbarous Kingdom*, 459–472, Golden Hall trial on 464. On royal weddings, see Russell Edward Martin, "Dynastic Marriage in Muscovy" (PhD diss., Harvard University, 1996) and his *A Bride for the Tsar: Bride-Shows and Marriage Politics in Early Modern Russia* (DeKalb IL: Northern Illinois University Press, 2012).

29. Marshall Poe, ed., *Foreign Descriptions of Muscovy: An Analytic Bibliography of Primary and Secondary Sources* (Columbus, OH: Slavica Publishers, 1995). I am indebted to Marshall Poe for excellent and painstaking advice on these sources, the results of which, for the most part, await further publication.

30. Richard S. Wortman, *Scenarios of Power: Myth and Ceremony in Russian Monarchy* (Princeton, NJ: Princeton University Press, 1995), chap. 1.

31. Upton, "What Now?," esp. 10–11. On performance, see Susan Garfinkel, "Recovering Performance for Vernacular Architecture Studies," *Perspectives in Vernacular Architecture* 13, no. 2 (2007): 100–114, quotation on 106.

Chapter 11

Advice, Advisers, and Courtiers
Decision Making and Advice in the Royal Book of the Illustrated Chronicle Compilation

One of the interests that Nancy Shields Kollmann and I have shared over the years is the problem of advice and advisers in the political culture of Muscovy. In my doctoral dissertation, I found that this theme was vitally important to the various authors of the tales about the Time of Troubles (Timofeev, Shakhovskoi, Palitsyn, and others) as an explanation of how the God-protected *tsarstvo* collapsed and fell victim to a host of foreign invaders.[1] In this investigation, I was inspired by the work of the prerevolutionary scholars V. E. Val´denberg and M. D´iakonov, and much encouraged by Kollmann's interest in and enthusiasm for my early publications.[2] Since then, I have tried to widen my view to include evidence for the roughly one hundred years after 1550. More recently, in tracing this theme in the visual culture of Muscovy within this timeframe, I have joined historian Sergei Bogatyrev: In his study of royal counselors, he found that advisers were prominently visible in the illustrated *Radziwiłł Chronicle* (1490s), in the carvings on the Tsar's Pew in the Dormition Cathedral of the Moscow Kremlin (1551), and in the *Illustrated Chronicle Compilation* (*Litsevoi letopisnyi svod*, late 1560s–1570s, hereafter *ICC*), as well as, of course, in various literary and documentary

---

This essay originally appeared in *Seeing Muscovy Anew: Politics—Institutions—Culture: Essays in Honor of Nancy Shields Kollmann*, ed. Michael S. Flier, Valerie A. Kivelson, Erika Monahan, and Daniel Rowland (Bloomington, IN: Slavica Publishers, 2017), 159–171. The author gratefully acknowledges the publisher for permission to reprint this essay.

sources.³ Simon Ushakov and Nikita Klement'ev specified high-ranking courtiers (*vel'mozhi*, boyars, and so on) over and over again in their careful 1672 descriptions of the murals of the Golden Hall in the Moscow Kremlin, and advisers were similarly prominent in their descriptions of the murals in the Faceted Hall.⁴ In the images of the Great Entrance from the recently restored murals in the Dormition Cathedral in Sviiazhsk, Ivan IV is accompanied by men in fur coats, while Metropolitan Makarii has his advisers in the garb of monks.⁵ In succeeding versions of the Pokrov icon, the ruler, a standard feature of the iconography, is increasingly accompanied over time by a group of courtiers.⁶

A particularly fine essay by Kollman shows that consultation with advisers, together with other legitimizing factors like scepters and pillows, was a crucial ingredient in the *ICC* when depicting proper judicial procedure prior to punishment.⁷ The *ICC* artists were careful to represent the legitimating features of legal procedure (consultation, judgment by the ruler holding—and sitting on—the symbols of royal power, royal orders to officials, and supervision by those officials of the actual judicial punishment), while these very features were notably absent in cases of violence processed outside the official legal system. I would like to think that this short essay, focusing on the imagery in the *ICC* depicting crucial moments in the succession from Vasilii III to Ivan IV, as well as in diplomatic ceremonies, forms a complement to Kollmann's valuable article.

There is already considerable evidence, then, that when Muscovites imagined their ruler, they saw him as surrounded by a group of laymen, who seem to be courtiers and/or advisers. Identifying the largely unidentified figures in diplomatic ceremonies as courtiers/advisers is a reasonable assumption, given the description of events, both diplomatic and others, where courtiers are recorded as present. In addition, the supporting figures present were sometimes identified by rank as boyars, or even by name, as we see below.

In other words, Muscovites imagined the monarchy as much a corporate enterprise as a personal one. My question, in this article, is whether this pattern of presenting the monarch together with his advisers holds true for the *ICC*, an astonishing history of the world from the creation down to the sixteenth-century present, with some 16,000 illustrations. (The recent lavish facsimile publication of the sections dealing with Rus' and Russia has inspired and made possible much new scholarship.⁸) Since the ICC was composed in the late 1560s and 1570s,⁹ roughly the era of the *oprichnina*, when the normal relations between Ivan and the Boyar Duma were, to put it mildly, interrupted, I wondered whether the theme of advisers with monarchs might have gone into something of an eclipse.

ADVICE, ADVISERS, AND COURTIERS

To make my task more manageable, I have concentrated on two sections of the volume of the *ICC* containing the *Tsarstvennaia kniga* (or Royal Book), largely because this text does not derive from earlier sources, and, as far as I know, came into the *ICC* scriptorium with no history of illuminations. One section concerns the events around the death of Grand Prince Vasilii III, and the other depicts a large number of diplomatic events. For comparative purposes, the corresponding images of diplomatic receptions from the Synod volume, the last volume of the *ICC*, are examined as well.

We begin with the Royal Book's version of events at a perilous moment for the monarchy, when the reigning monarch, Vasilii III, was on his deathbed, and his heir, the future Ivan IV, was only three years old. This moment, when the monarch was either on his deathbed (Vasilii), or a small child (Ivan), did in fact require extensive consultation with the court elite, and the collaboration of that elite to prevent chaos. The active participation of courtier advisers is depicted clearly in a whole series of illuminations with accompanying texts. The *ICC* artists developed an ingenious way to depict the active participation of Vasilii's wife (and Ivan's mother), Elena Glinskaia, who dominated the court during these years.

The interactive nature of the relationship between courtiers acting as advisers and the ruler is apparent from the first image of this series: The ailing grand prince is persuading his boyars to guard the kingdom during the minority of his three-year-old son, Ivan (see figure 11.1). Here the text tells us that "The grand prince began to take counsel with his boyars [*dumati z boiary*]" (the boyars are named) about his will and the fate of his young son and wife, who both appear in the upper left. The image gives the impression that the courtiers are not only grieving but taking part in a discussion. In this case, the text names Mikhail Iur'evich, Vasilii's cousin, two boyars, and two state secretaries (*d'iaki*); the image corresponds quite exactly with the text, with Vasilii and his cousin (wearing distinctive caps) conversing with pointed fingers, the boyars taking part in the conversation with open palms, and one of the state secretaries holding a scroll, presumably containing Vasilii's will.[10] This case also suggests a hypothesis about hand gestures: Vasilii and his cousin are depicted as pointing (the former with one figure and the latter with two), while the boyars have open palms. This evidence indicates that hierarchy is preserved (royals ordering, boyars agreeing) within the structure of consultation. The significance of one versus two fingers remains obscure, at least to me.

In a following image (figure 11.2), Vasilii then addresses his boyars with a remarkable speech, reminding them that "we have been your born lords [since the time of Saint Vladimir] and you have been our boyars from ancient times. And you, my brothers, stand firmly, so that my son can become lord of the

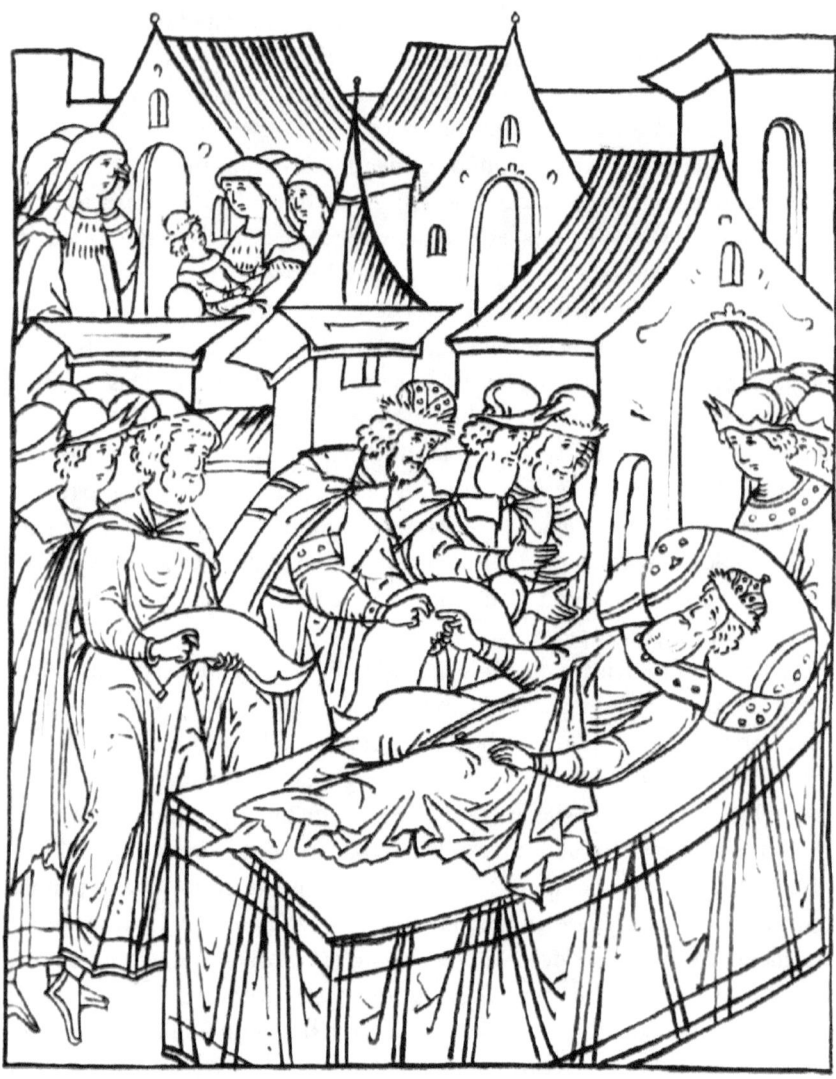

Figure 11.1. Vasilii III consults with his boyars. *Litsevoi letopisnyi svod*, *Russkaia letopisnaia istoriia* (hereafter, *LLS*) (Moscow: AKTEON, 2009–2010), bk. 19:297, f. 36. All the images in this chapter are published by the generous permission of AKTEON.

kingdom, and so that there will be truth and justice [*pravda*] in the land." Note in this last image the parallel gestures, using open palms, of Vasilii and one of his boyars, again indicating open consultation in both directions, rather than just one.

Of course, this set of images describes a real situation where, with Vasilii impotent on his deathbed and the kingdom about to fall into the hands of the

ADVICE, ADVISERS, AND COURTIERS 263

FIGURE 11.2. Vasilii's speech to his boyars. *LLS* 19:297, f. 36. Courtesy of AKTEON.

boyars and Vasilii's wife, the power relationship between monarch and boyars was exceptionally tilted toward the latter.

Note also in all of these images, the depiction of Princess Elena Glinskaia, here wiping her eye in a gesture of mourning, backed up by her courtiers, her ladies-in-waiting. In virtually every image in this series, Elena, who in fact exercised great power, was represented in an upper corner, necessarily separated from the male court, but always with her own female court, who, when they are named, seem to consist mostly of boyars' wives. These images give a double description of Elena, both as the grieving wife of the current ruler, and, as ruler with her ladies, crucial participants in the decisions being enacted.

After Vasilii's death, as Elena in fact took charge of the situation, she is shown (figure 11.3) as doing just that. This remarkable series of depictions of Elena's rule is outside our subject, but they show the more prominent and active role given to the princess, visually as well as textually, which Isolde Thyrêt sees as the beginning of the cult of royal wives.[11] In a remarkable series of images describing negotiations between Elena and the Kazanian "Tsar" Shah Ali and his "Tsaritsa" Fatima, the Royal Book artists took care to show an all-female diplomatic exchange, in which both Elena and Fatima were accompanied by their courtiers.

Our first image (figure 11.3) shows Ivan giving a fur coat to Shah Ali as a token of his good will. Elena consults with her ladies-in-waiting in the upper left, although the text does not mention them. Note the open palm of the lead boyar, denoting consultation. Next (figure 11.4), we see a crowned Elena consulting with the male boyars, asking them to consider her as tsar, at least temporarily *(chto progozhe u nee byti tsariu)*,[12] again backed by her ladies-in-waiting, who are not mentioned in the text, and the young grand prince. The young Ivan holds his legitimating staff, while the lead boyar extends his open right hand, toward Elena and Ivan, in agreement, and his pointing left, to the other boyars, in command. In the bottom register, this news is presumably conveyed to Shah Ali, with all figures displaying open palms. The diplomacy then shifts to a female plane, when (figure 11.5) Fatima arrives at the palace, and, at the wish of Elena and her *boyaryni*, she is met at her sled by Agrofena Ivanovna Volynskaia and junior boyars' wives *(s neiu molodym boyaryniam)*. Elena is surprisingly given a crown, while the open palm of the lead *boyarynia* again signals consultation. Elena, arranging a ritual of welcome with her outstretched finger, is again given a crown, while the lead lady-in-waiting gestures with open palm. Later, there is a feast (figure 11.6), where both Elena and her ladies-in-waiting, and Fatima with her attendants, are shown in the foreground, while the men, young Ivan and his courtiers, celebrate above and behind. This series of images shows that, in the highly unusual conditions of Ivan's minority and Elena Glinskaia's leadership, both Elena and Fatima are consistently represented as crowned,[13] and surrounded by female courtiers, thus complying with the mental image that rulers be represented as consulting with their courtiers. (This new emphasis on female rulers and their courtiers may explain the appearance in the Russian Museum Pokrov icon of

ADVICE, ADVISERS, AND COURTIERS 265

FIGURE 11.3. Ivan IV gives a fur coat to Shah Ali; Princess Elena and female advisers look on. *LLS* 19:468, f. 1220b. Courtesy of AKTEON.

Empress Theophano and her ladies-in-waiting accompanying Emperor Leo VI, in the place of the usual male attendants who accompany the ruler in earlier Pokrov icons, as discussed in an article by Michael Flier.[14]) Note also that the male banquet is represented as above and behind the female banquet, making the female banquet the most important scene.[15]

Figure 11.4. Elena's speech to the boyars. Note her female courtiers and the open palm of the lead boyar. *LLS* 19:469, f. 122. Courtesy of AKTEON.

On rare occasions, the court is shown together for a ceremonial occasion or to demonstrate unity. One such image (figure 11.7) occurs in the account of Vasilii's death, where a large crowd of courtiers surrounds the very young Ivan to show the solidarity of the powerful boyar elite, and thus the stability of the realm under precarious circumstances. The presence of these numerous courtiers is essential to convey this basic message. Note the image of Elena

ADVICE, ADVISERS, AND COURTIERS

FIGURE 11.5. Elena sends her young *boyaryni* to greet Fatima, tsaritsa of Kazan´, in her sledge. *LLS* 19:479, f. 127. Courtesy of AKTEON.

and one lady-in-waiting in the upper left corner. Interestingly, the text here does not mention this gathering but merely describes the time of Vasilii's death, his age, and his burial in the Archangel Cathedral, shown on the upper right of this image.

Years later, when Ivan is older, he is depicted in an unusual double-page image (figure 11.8) celebrating the court as a collective and used to illustrate a

268 CHAPTER 11

FIGURE 11.6. Princess Elena hosts a female banquet for Tsaritsa Fatima (below); Ivan IV's male banquet (above). *LLS* 19:484, f. 129ob. Courtesy of AKTEON.

ceremony in the Hall of Facets, when Ivan (appearing twice) distributed gifts to his courtiers, both clerical and lay, to celebrate his victory over Kazan´. Metropolitan Makarii heads the list of honored churchmen shown on our left, Ivan's right, while Ivan's brother and cousin head the list of laymen, shown on our right. (The Dormition Cathedral, mentioned in the text, is shown on

ADVICE, ADVISERS, AND COURTIERS 269

FIGURE 11.7. Ivan IV and his court at the death of his father. *LLS* 19:372, f. 73ob. Courtesy of AKTEON.

the upper left and repeated on the upper right, but the defining central pillar in the Faceted Hall is not shown.) This image seems to resemble closely the ceremonial meals held in this hall for visiting ambassadors, when the tsar gave food to each of his courtiers, addressing each by name. The purpose of this image, like the purpose of ceremonial meals in this hall, is to show the ruler as the supplier and donor to his courtiers, and to illustrate his ability to provide

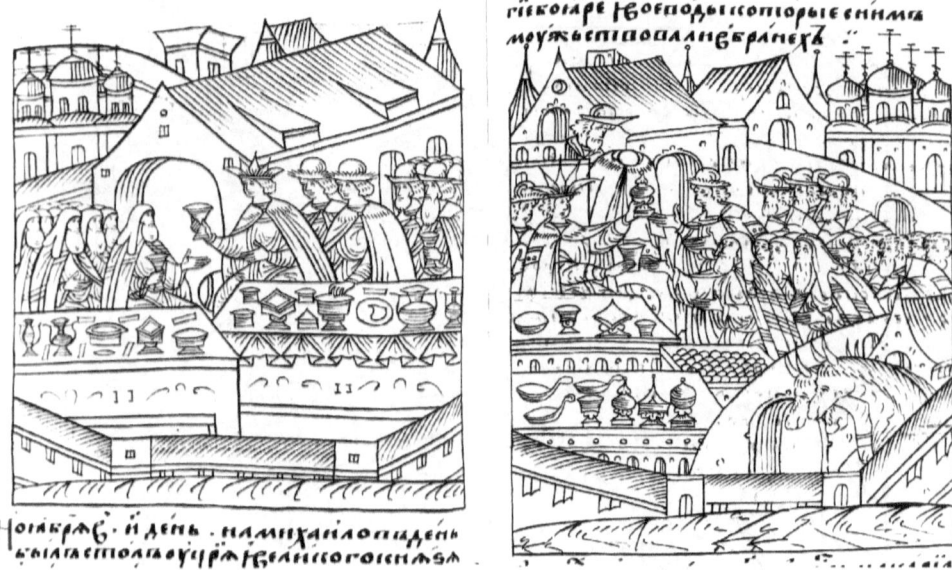

Figure 11.8. Ivan gives his courtiers gifts in the Hall of Facets after his victory in Kazan´. *LLS* 21:502–503, ff. 649ob.–650. Courtesy of AKTEON.

by listing and showing some of the gifts, including a fur coat, precious vessels, and horses.[16]

To end our discussion of depictions of actual consultations of various sorts, we should note the extraordinary place given to Metropolitan Makarii among Ivan's advisers. We have already seen him in many images. I'd like to add three. Makarii repeatedly blesses Ivan and his courtiers before battles, often sending messages to them with spiritual encouragement. The *ICC* artists begin (figure 11.9) by showing Makarii, accompanied by a number of monks, blessing Ivan in the presence of numerous other lay courtiers. But blessing the tsar is not enough, since the next image (figure 11.10) shows Makarii blessing the courtiers, with Ivan in the background. (The text of the blessing is provided.) My last image (figure 11.11) in this series is, for me, the most touching. It shows Ivan consulting with Makarii about his upcoming marriage. Yet again, courtiers are shown witnessing and approving the conversation, with the lead (unnamed) boyar gesturing with two open palms. While Ivan is pointing, and thus shown as the dominant partner, and Makarii shows an open palm, the text describes Ivan as taking counsel (*sovetoval*) with "his father, with Metropolitan Makarii of all Rus´." They sit together on the same throne with the same cushions (Makarii has a slightly lower footstool), and both hold identical staffs. Most moving to me, however, is the way that each inclines toward the other

Figure 11.9. Metropolitan Makarii blesses Ivan on the eve of the Kazan' campaign. *LLS* 21:409, f. 336. Courtesy of AKTEON.

in a gentle rhythm, an image that seems to imply a much closer relationship, even an emotional one, than that shown with any other adviser. One wonders if, from the perspective of the chaotic and violent events of the *oprichnina*, and particularly the then recent murder of Metropolitan Filipp, the relationship between Ivan and Makarii, and indeed the depiction of a harmonious, united court, was a perhaps unconscious attempt to convey the idea of these years as a kind of earlier constituent golden age.

Figure 11.10. Makarii blesses "the boyars, *voevodas*, princes, and all the people of the royal army." *LLS* 21:410, f. 336ob. Courtesy of AKTEON.

We might imagine three levels of meaning in the images discussed here. First, they depict an actual situation when consultation with the elite was essential to create a consensus among the major boyars, without which the country could all too easily have descended into chaos. Second, by carefully highlighting the consultations that were imagined to have taken place, the images and accompanying texts legitimated the many important decisions that

ADVICE, ADVISERS, AND COURTIERS 273

FIGURE 11.11. Ivan consults Metropolitan Makarii about his marriage. *LLS* 20:293, f. 278. Courtesy of AKTEON.

were taken when Ivan was too young to participate actively. Thus they were seen as laying a firm foundation for the rest of the reign. Finally, the images create a *model for* the way political decisions should be made, by a ruler literally (and visually) surrounded by wise advisers, all working to maintain truth and justice in the realm. And we might add a fourth level: the *ICC* artists seem to have had a baseline understanding that rulers normally function with advisers. It would be a mistake, however, to interpret this evidence in an excessively democratic way. Hierarchy and precedent were always carefully maintained: Ivan (or Elena) are usually depicted ordering with pointing fingers, while boyars or other courtiers respond with open palms, presumably agreeing with the order and starting to carrying it out.

If the images we have been considering so far dealt with situations where the actual context made consultation and collaboration essential, we can now consider a series of images from the Royal Book depicting the court at diplomatic events where actual consultation was a rarity, and courtiers were not usually even mentioned in the accompanying texts. The number of images depicting these diplomatic receptions is sufficient to permit some rough arithmetic calculations to answer the question of how often courtiers or advisers were depicted as present at these events.

I have chosen to count these images, chiefly the sending and receiving of ambassadors, as listed in the subject index of volume 24 of the *ICC*.[17] This decision provided me with an "objective" list of images to examine as a control group in considering which images belonged to my theme and which did not. The first part of my argument, therefore, could hardly be more straightforward: How many of the diplomatic scenes listed in the index showed the ruler with courtiers or advisers, and how many did not? The result of my quick tabulation is that, of a total of fifty-nine images listed in the index under ambassadorial customs (*posol'skii obychai*), forty-eight had one or more courtiers or companions shown, while eleven showed the monarch alone. In other words, slightly fewer than one image in four showed the monarch conducting diplomacy by himself. (Figure 11.12 shows Ivan IV receiving an embassy from Kazan' in 1541. The lower register shows the Kazanian "tsarevna" Kovgorshad sending a document, which Ivan receives with a pointing gesture, while a group of courtiers, led by a lead courtier [appearing twice?] with an open palm, legitimizes and carries out the tsar's order.)

Since the Royal Book deals so much with Ivan as a youth, and thus might be biased in favor of showing advisers at diplomatic functions to give authority to the young monarch, I did a check of similar images in the Synod volume. There, I found some forty-six entries under the category of "the arrival [*priezd*] of ambassadors." Of that number, a surprising forty-four images, or about 95 percent, showed the monarch with one or more courtiers, while only two showed him alone. (I did not tabulate images of other diplomatic functions.)

Thus it seems reasonable to conclude that, when the artists of the *ICC* imagined these diplomatic activities, they imagined them taking place in the presence of courtiers or advisers. This is noteworthy, because, although we know from many other sources that Duma members and others were almost always present at diplomatic gatherings, the texts associated with these

ADVICE, ADVISERS, AND COURTIERS   275

FIGURE 11.12.   Ivan receives ambassadors from Kazan' in 1541. *LLS* 20:23, f. 230. Courtesy of AKTEON.

images almost never mentioned them. Thus their presence is a reflection of the artists' own image of what these scenarios would have (and should have) looked like.

If the numbers convince us that these artists imagined the monarchy presented to outsiders as a corporate entity, the many images on this subject do not convey the idea of real consultation. In both the Royal Book and the Synod volume, the tsar and his courtiers are usually presented in a quite formulaic way, all facing in the same direction, the tsar often making a gesture of command with his right hand. The courtiers are represented in the Royal Book often by very simple profiles, while in the Synod volume, they are given more space and more three-dimensional bodies. Figure 11.13 shows Ivan receiving an embassy from Bukhara. The lower register shows the ambassadors, with their non-Russian headgear, en route to Moscow, where, in the upper register, Ivan receives them with a pointing gesture, while a courtier at the head of four other courtiers, carries out and validates Ivan's decision with an open palm.

Among the many images of diplomatic events in both volumes, however, the upturned palms of advisers or boyars occur from time to time. It is hard to say precisely what these gestures mean. Perhaps in this case, the adviser with upturned palms is an official of the Foreign Office (*posol'skii prikaz*), which generally organized and conducted these ceremonies. In such a circumstance, the tsar is seen issuing an order and the official carrying it out. Or they could illustrate the idea of moral norms and best practices, including consultation. When other sources mention such consultation, which in practice was a crucial ingredient of virtually all of these negotiations, it generally occurred out of sight, behind closed doors. Thus the seeming contradiction of courtiers' open palms during diplomatic rituals when actual consultation did not regularly occur can be explained by the perceived ritual necessity of consultation, in the *ICC* images during diplomatic receptions and in fact behind closed doors with Foreign Office officials.

There are many other types of relationships between monarch and his courtiers or advisers shown in the Royal Book, to say nothing of the other volumes of the *Litsevoi letopisnyi svod*. But I hope I have presented enough evidence to show that the presence of courtiers or advisers was a constant part of the imagined scenario of rulership in Muscovy. Not surprisingly, then, advisers are present at the series of scenes when Vasilii III, at the end of his life, consults with his boyars to ensure the safety of his three-year-old son and his wife, and the continued good order of the realm. But they populate images of rulership even more plentifully in the Synod volume, which deals with the mature period of Ivan's life. Advisers or courtiers are imagined as essential parts of the female court of Elena Glinskaia, of her Kazanian counterpart, Fatima (an early image of a court where women are shown to play a major role), and of the Kazanian male court as well.

But should we call these figures in the *ICC* advisers or courtiers? The answer would seem to depend on the context. In descriptions of diplomatic receptions, their presence is often recorded by simple profiles behind a gesturing

Figure 11.13. Ivan receives ambassadors from Bukhara in 1558. *LLS* 23:98, f. 409ob. Courtesy of AKTEON.

ruler. In certain instances more complex communication is indicated, but in a great majority of the diplomatic cases, words and power seem to flow in one direction, downward from the tsar to his courtiers. The situation is quite different when the real-life political power of the monarch was weak, as in the last days of Vasilii III, or when an adviser was depicted as having exceptional influence, as in the case of Metropolitan Makarii. In some cases, then, the advice is real and important, while in others the advice is more a ritual, that, as in Kollmann's legal examples, is inserted to give legitimacy to a given decision.

The evidence concerning our theme is so plentiful that I have done little more than scratch the surface. Indeed, I can justly be accused of stating the obvious. Courtiers seem to be shown in most cases when the monarch is acting in any situation, whether or not they are mentioned in the written text.

As in the other evidence briefly mentioned at the start of this essay, especially the ruler images in the two throne rooms of Muscovy, the Golden and Faceted Halls, and like the rituals of harmony and agreement enacted in those spaces on a regular basis by Ivan and his courtiers, the *ICC* images we have examined reflect an imagined harmony between the ruler and his elites, a harmony that modeled the real-life harmony and agreement so essential to the political health, even the survival, of the Russian *tsarstvo*. All of this evidence reveals a rich imaginative culture that created in image, word, and ritual models of government that were, in Clifford Geertz's famous phrase, both descriptive models *of* and prescriptive models *for* specific symbolic behavior.[18] Of course, the reality of court politics was not as harmonious as the images of ideal concord would suggest, but the ideal surely influenced the actual. As such, this evidence fits nicely with the work of a growing number of scholars, especially in the United States, and especially that of Kollmann together with Edward Keenan, Robert Crummey, Donald Ostrowski, Valerie Kivelson, and Russell Martin, to name a few, all of whom have concluded that Muscovy was ruled by the court as a whole, rather than by the ruler alone.[19] Their research has indicated that Muscovy was not "plaine tyrannical" as Giles Fletcher so famously put it, but was closer to an oligarchy than a tyranny. The visual evidence we have seen strengthens this hypothesis. The research of these scholars has also shown that communication between government and subjects involved constant negotiation and interaction, including interaction not only with the court elite but with provincial gentrymen and even peasants—in other words, the type of two-way communication that seems fairly often represented in the *ICC* scenes we have been looking at.

But to what extent was real consultation, advice giving and advice getting, going on in these images? What can we say about the figures depicted with the ruler? Were they just courtiers? Bureaucrats? Advisers? And what do the *ICC* images tell us in general about advice and advisers? The answer seems a very straightforward one. The conclusion would seem to be that, when actual consultation with advisers took place, it was shown; the participants were often identified in the text, sometimes by name, more often by rank; and the pictorial language clearly and sometimes poignantly indicated consultation. This is the case in most of the images we have examined concerning the period just before and after the death of Vasilii III. But in routine diplomatic encounters, where the major discussions were held by Foreign Office officials out of sight, courtiers would have been commanded to attend public encounters to give legitimacy to diplomatic agreements. And to show the strength and unity of the court to outside observers, the tsar was shown ordering in the legitimating presence of one or more courtiers, more or less as happened in real life. The courtier/adviser distinction may even have been less important to Ivan's contemporaries than it seems to us. In some cases the consultation was real and necessary; in others it was ritualized and merely confirmed decisions taken earlier, by the tsar himself, or, more likely, by members of his bureaucratic apparatus. But the boundary between these two models was surely fluid, since the ideal model of seeking and getting advice was the common denominator of both scenarios. Perhaps, as I would argue, the "ritual" examples are even more powerful evidence for the importance of advice in the minds of the *ICC* artists, especially when the accompanying text does not even mention courtiers or advisers. Thus, although there is a vast amount of evidence concerning this model still to be investigated in the *ICC*, the evidence examined so far, like the visual and textual evidence mentioned briefly at the beginning of this essay, testifies to the strong and lasting importance of this ideal in the minds of early modern Muscovites.

Whatever the case, the *ICC* gives us a wonderful glimpse into the imaginations of the team of artists, who, with huge labor, compiled this history, which spanned the periods from the creation of the universe to their sixteenth-century present. As we place this evidence into the larger context of its time, I like to think that the culture of which it bears eloquent testimony was important in shaping political action.[20] It is hard to say whose thoughts are embodied in these images. Such a large project must have been created with the sponsorship of the ruler, at least nominally. But it would seem that the collection of artists who carried out this vast task under the direct patronage of the Foreign Office were representing these events both as what they imagined actually happened, and as what should have happened in order to give legitimacy to the diplomatic and political accords being created. What we are seeing, then, is a set of norms of behavior, which, like the murals in the Golden Hall, may or may not have always reflected actual practice. But they do suggest the strong expectation that, in diplomatic ceremonies and crucial negotiations about domestic politics, as in Kollmann's judicial proceedings, consultation with advisers was a vital ingredient in giving legitimacy to the acts of the government. This contradicts the picture of arbitrary despotism conveyed by the travel texts of European visitors, and shows, again as Kollmann has demonstrated, the failure of these visitors to understand the careful scaffold of legitimizing acts and settings that were so important to the Muscovite government that it invested major amounts of elite time and considerable financial expense to mount them. This is no small point. In the absence of explicit texts on political theory, historians have often accepted the views of early modern visitors from the West that the tsar's power was unlimited. But the evidence of the *ICC* and the other visual sources mentioned at the start of this essay, added to the considerable evidence gleaned from careful reading of historical and other texts, indicates that advice and advisers were critical ingredients in the image of good governance in the minds of early modern Russians.

One final thought: Thyrêt and Flier[21] have shown us how Muscovite literary and visual culture, which we have often imagined as rigid, even unchanging, could in practice be manipulated by the *ICC* artists to change the meaning of a set of historical events in a quite radical way. When we consider that the *ICC* was compiled just after the worst excesses of the *oprichnina*—when Ivan not only did not consult with his boyars but frequently exiled or killed them by barbaric methods—why did the *ICC* artists emphasize the harmony and unity of the court in an earlier time? In the context of the *oprichnina*, were these images an attempt to criticize the *oprichnina* by implication? If, as we've argued above, the default assumption of these artists was that the ruler functioned normally with courtiers or advisers, that the images represented "widely accepted notions of what constituted legal and moral best practices,"[22] then these images would appear to send some sort of message. Possibly, they were merely a nostalgic look backward at periods imagined to have been more peaceful and harmonious. They may also have been seen to strike a subtle dissident note, thus throwing into question another common assumption: that texts and images, especially if they were created in a government office, were tightly controlled by the central government.

Notes

1. Daniel B. Rowland, "Muscovite Political Attitudes as Reflected in Early Seventeenth-Century Tales about the Time of Troubles" (PhD diss., Yale University,

1976); Rowland, "The Problem of Advice in Muscovite Tales about the Time of Troubles," *Russian History/Histoire Russe* 6, no. 2 (1979): 259–283 (chapter 3 of this volume).

2. V. E. Val´denberg, *Drevnerusskie ucheniia o predelakh tsarskoi vlasti* (Petrograd, 1916; repr., Moscow: Territoriia budushchego, 2006); M. D´iakonov, *Vlast´ Moskovskikh godudarei* (Saint Petersburg, 1889).

3. Sergei Bogaryrev, *The Sovereign and His Counsellors: Ritualized Consultations in Muscovite Political Culture, 1350s–1570s* (Helsinki: Finnish Academy of Science and Letters, 2000), esp. 69–77, 92–98, and plates 1–10.

4. On the Ushakov and Klement´ev descriptions of the Golden Hall murals, see S. P. Bartenev, *Moskovskii kreml´v starinu i teper´* (Moscow: Sinodal´naia tip., 1916), 188–190, and for a discussion of the theme of advice there, Daniel Rowland, "Two Cultures, One Throne Room: Secular Courtiers and Orthodox Culture in the Golden Hall of the Moscow Kremlin," in *Orthodox Russia: Belief and Practice under the Tsars*, ed. Valerie A. Kivelson and Robert H. Greene (University Park: Pennsylvania State University Press, 2003), 52–53 (chapter 9 of this volume). On the Faceted Hall murals, see Aida Nasibova, *The Faceted Chamber in the Moscow Kremlin* (Leningrad: Aurora Art Publishers, 1978); I. E. Zabelin, *Materialy dlia istorii, arkheologii, i statistiki goroda Moskvy*, 2 vols. (Moscow: Moskovskaia gorodskaia tip., 1916), 1:1265–1271; and specifically on the theme of advice there, Daniel Rowland, "Architecture, Image, and Ritual in the Throne Rooms of Muscovy, 1550–1650: A Preliminary Survey," in *Rude and Barbarous Kingdom Revisited: Essays in Russian History and Culture in Honor of Robert O. Crummey*, ed. Chester S. L. Dunning, Russell E. Martin, and Daniel Rowland (Bloomington, IN: Slavica, 2008), 65 (chapter 10 of this volume).

5. The best discussion of these images is still M. K. Karger, "Les portraits des fondateurs dans les peintures murales du Monastère de Svijažsk," *L'Art Byzantin chez les Slavs: L'Ancienne Russie, les Slaves, les Slaves Catholiques* 2, part 1 (Paris: Paul Guenther, 1932): 135–149.

6. Michael Flier, "Putting Novgorod to Work: Muscovite Intercession as Symbolic Succession" (paper delivered at the annual convention of the Association for Slavic, East European, and Eurasian Studies, Washington, DC, November, 17–20, 2011).

7. Nancy Shields Kollmann, "Representing Legitimacy in Early Modern Russia," *The Russian Review* 76, no.1 (2017): 7–21. See also the excellent analysis of visual images in the *ICC* and the work of the late seventeenth-century Siberian writer (and illustrator) Semyon Remezov in Valerie Kivelson, "Rivers of Blood: Illustrating Violence and Virtue in Russia's Early Modern Empire," *Journal of the British Academy* 3 (2015): 69–105, https://doi.org/10.85871/jba/003.0069.

8. E. N. Kazakova et al., eds., *Litsevoi letopisnyi svod XVI veka: Russkaia letopisnaia istoriia*, 38 vols. (Moscow: AKTEON, 2009–2014).

9. B. M. Kloss dates the compilation to the period 1568–1576 in *Nikonovskii letopisnyi svod i russkie letopisi XVI–XVII vekov* (Moscow: Nauka, 1980), 249–261.

10. On open palms as representing legitimating consultation, see Kollmann, "Representing Legitimacy."

11. Isolde Thyrêt, "The *Tale of the Death of Vasilii Ivanovich* and the Evolution of the Muscovite Tsaritsa's Role in Sixteenth-Century Russia," in *Dubitando: Studies in History and Culture in Honor of Donald Ostrowski*, ed. Brian Boeck, Russell E. Martin, and Daniel Rowland (Bloomington, IN: Slavica Publishers, 2012), 209–224.

12. This remarkable claim is further justified: "Since the great prince is young, and the status [*polozhenie*] of the royal scepter of all the great Russian kingdom is placed on her by God, and given to her by God for the preservation and the maintenance of all the piety of Orthodoxy and [for the giving of] mercy to the blessed and vengeance to the evil [ones]" (Kazakova, *Litsevoi letopisnyi svod*, 19:469).

13. Sergei Bogatyrev has commented in a personal e-mail communication that "royal women appeared in pointed crowns regardless of their title, age, or ethnicity. I went through the whole Russian part of *ICC* and found only a couple of images of female royalty depicted in princely hats (with fur brim), apparently the artist's error. On some occasions female members of Rus′ royalty could also appear in kerchiefs." This is the case with earlier images of Elena discussed above. He also cites Artsikhovskii's discussion of the headgear of royal women in miniatures: A. V. Artsikhovskii, *Drevnerusskie miniatiury kak istoricheskii istochnik* (Tomsk: Vodolei, 2004), 170–173.

14. Michael Flier, "Envisioning the Ruler in Medieval Rus′: The Iconography of Intercession and Architecture," in Boeck, Martin, and Rowland, *Dubitando*, 181–192.

15. See Michael Flier, "Murder Most Foul: Picturing the Death of Andrei Bogoliubskii," in Flier et al., *Picturing Muscovy Anew*, 143–157 for a discussion of the visual structure of images in the *ICC*.

16. For a fuller description of these throne room rituals in their architectural and visual contexts, see Rowland, "Architecture, Image, and Ritual." On gift giving as a crucial social bond, obligating both the giver and the receiver, based on the pioneering gift theory of Marcel Mauss and followers, see Russell E. Martin, "Gifts for Kith and Kin: Gift Exchanges and Social Integration in Muscovite Royal Weddings," in Dunning, Martin, and Rowland, *Rude and Barbarous Kingdom Revisited*, 89–108; Russell E. Martin, "Gifts and Commemoration: Donations to Monasteries, Dynastic Legitimacy, and Remembering the Royal Dead in Muscovy (1597/1659)," *Forschungen zur Osteuropaischen Geschichte* 76 (2010): 499–525; Russell E. Martin, "Praying for Health, Heirs, Victory over Enemies, and Prosperity: Projecting the Image of Dynasty through Gifts at Muscovite Royal Weddings," in *Everyday Life in Russian History: Quotidian Studies in Honor of Daniel Kaiser*, ed. Gary Marker, Joan Neuberger, Marshall Poe, and Susan Rupp (Bloomington, IN: Slavica Publishers, 2010), 23–42.

17. Kazakova, *Litsevoi letopisnyi svod*, 24:368.

18. "Unlike genes, and other nonsymbolic information sources, which are only models *for*, not models *of*, culture patterns have an intrinsic double aspect: they give meaning, that is, objective conceptual form, to social and psychological reality both by shaping themselves to it and by shaping it to themselves." Clifford Geertz, "Religion as a Culture System," in *The Interpretations of Cultures* (New York: Basic Books, 1973), 93.

19. See Edward L. Keenan, "Russian Political Folkways," *Russian Review* 45, no. 2 (1986): 115–181; Robert O. Crummey, *Aristocrats and Servitors: The Boyar Elite in Russia, 1613–1689* (Princeton, NJ: Princeton University Press, 1989); Donald Ostrowski, "The Façade of Legitimacy: Exchange of Power and Authority in Early Modern Russia," *Comparative Studies in Society and History* 44, no. 3 (2002): 534–563; Nancy Shields Kollmann, *Kinship and Politics: The Making of the Muscovite Political System* (Stanford, CA: Stanford University Press, 1987); Valerie A. Kivelson, *Autocracy in the Provinces: The*

Muscovite Gentry and Political Culture in the Seventeenth Century (Stanford, CA: Stanford University Press, 1996); Russell E. Martin, *A Bride for the Tsar: Bride-Shows and Marriage Politics in Early Modern Russia* (DeKalb: Northern Illinois University Press, 2012).

20. Kivelson, "Rivers of Blood," makes a convincing case that the ideal scenarios conveyed in the *ICC* and Remezov's work had real-world echoes in the surprisingly generous treatment that the government usually ordered its Siberian officials to carry out in regard to native populations once the period of conquest was over.

21. Isolde Thyret, "Saint Stephen of Perm' and the Dual Faith Phenomenon in Muscovite Texts and Images," in Flier at al., *Seeing Muscovy Anew*, 189–205; Michael Flier, "Murder Most Foul."

22. Kivelson, "Rivers of Blood," 79.

Appendix
The Presentation of Monarchs in the *Illustrated Chronicle Compilation*

Part 2: Scenes from the Old Testament and Rus´

This short unannotated paper was given at the 2017 annual meeting of the Association for Slavic, East European, and Eurasian Studies. I am particularly glad to thank Mary-Allen Johnson and the Hilandar Room at the Ohio State University for supporting the research on which both images and text are based. Its images and text form a natural complement to this chapter.

This appendix brings together two important themes in this collection, the issue of advice in Russian political ideology, and the place of the Israel of the Old Testament as the most important historical precedent in the minds of early modern Muscovites.

In the first part of this essay, I summarized examples of the presence of advisers or courtiers in visual sources as varied as the Radziwill Chronicle and the Tsar's Pew, the murals of the Golden Hall, the murals in the Dormition Cathedral in Sviiazhsk, and the Royal Book volume of the *Illustrated Chronicle Compilation* (hereafter *ICC*). Earlier chapters argue that authors writing about the Time of Troubles (Palitsyn, Timofeev, Shakhovskoi) had given advice and advisers a crucial role in correcting rulers whose actions were not perceived as following the will of God, obviously a crucial problem for those writing about the reign of Ivan IV and the following Time of Troubles.

Much of our discussion here centers on images from the *ICC* devoted to the Old Testament. The role of the Old Testament in Muscovite political thought

---

This appendix was completed and did not appear with it in the Kollmann festschrift. It provides further important evidence for the interpretation offered in that chapter.

has also been a rich source of evidence, a largely undiscovered continent of information, both for me and for a host of other scholars. The idea that Rus'/Muscovy/Russia was a new chosen people, and successor to the Israel of the Old Testament was a bedrock idea, perhaps *the* bedrock idea, of political thinking from Kievan Rus' to Peter the Great and beyond. One crucial example: Ivan's coronation service made explicit the comparison between the anointing of King David by Samuel the Prophet (1 Sam. 16:1–13) and the coronation of Ivan by Metropolitan Makarii. Thus, the depictions of David and Solomon in the *ICC* are good places to seek images of ideal rulers and rulership, though both rulers sinned and incurred Jehovah's wrath. At the end of this essay, I briefly discuss *ICC* images of Vladimir Monomakh and Dmitrii Donskoi, two Rus' rulers who loomed large in the Muscovite historical imagination.

My reading of the section of the *ICC* devoted to David and Solomon (and Jereboam and Rehoboam, for that matter) leaves the overwhelming impression that these rulers were depicted with an entourage of figures virtually every time they appeared. As in chapter 11, I tried to quantify this impression by checking every page listed under "Solomon" in the index book of the Khronograf volume of the biblical section of the *ICC* (bk. 4, 109). The results are impressive. Of the seventy-eight images of Solomon, including often multiple images in one illumination, seventy-one, or roughly 91 percent, showed Solomon surrounded by or backed by a group of figures, figures who are seldom identified in the text. (I did not count images where Solomon does not appear or pages with no images.) There are good explanations for the few instances where Solomon appears without retainers: Solomon is depicted alone while praying to God, or conversing with his mother or wife—in other words, when he was not ruling his kingdom.

Figure A.1 shows Samuel anointing David, a constituent event both for the kingdom of ancient Israel, and, through Ivan IV's coronation service, for the new *tsarstvo* of Muscovy. The *ICC* text tells us that God would tell Samuel which of Jesse's sons he should choose as king. After rejecting all the older sons, Samuel asks for David, the youngest, who is keeping sheep, here on our upper left, with a figure, representing, I believe, one of Jesse's other sons, bringing him from pasturing his sheep to the anointing ceremony in the foreground, while our upper right shows Samuel by himself, presumably getting his instructions from God. The anointing scene contains all the basic elements of Muscovite political theory. God is depicted as an old man pointing, and thus directing, with His right hand, and wearing, in His halo, the eight-pointed star of Divine Wisdom. Lest the viewer miss the point, the *ICC* artist connects God with Samuel with three lines, showing that Samuel's act reflects God's will, and, with another three lines, with the young David, shown here and after-

APPENDIX 285

FIGURE A.1. Samuel anoints David king. *LLS, Bibleiskaia istoriia*, bk. 3 (Moscow: AKTEON, 2011), 71, f. 85. Courtesy of AKTEON.

ward with a nimbus, illustrating the connection between the king ("tsar" in the *ICC*) and God, between God's will and David's will. This beautifully illustrates what historians of early medieval political thought call "the descending theme" of political theory, where authority descends directly from God to the ruler, and through him to the people.

But David and Samuel are not alone at this crucial moment: To their right (our left) are shown six young men and an older man, with a seventh young man summoning David, with open palm, and inviting him, with pointing left hand, to the anointing scene below. Who are these figures? The text makes clear that they are Jesse's other seven sons, but I would argue that the artist included them here as an essential symbol of legitimacy. As in the images surrounding the death of Vasilii III and his conversations with his boyars in the Royal Book that I discuss in in this chapter, the presence of the brothers represents their politically essential assent, visually signaled by their open palms, to the choice of their *youngest* brother to become the new king of Israel, thus repeating a well-known earlier instance in Rus' history, the accession of the younger Yaroslav the Wise over his elder brother Sviatopolk. In view of the almost universal presence of other supporting figures of David and Solomon in the *ICC*, however, the brothers' presence also serves as a kind portrait of David's royal court, his first retainers. Their presence visually supplements and strengthens the explicit link with God's will so clearly laid out to our right.

God's choice of David did not automatically provide the real-world political support he needed. This task took many years of civil war, with David battling against the house of Saul. A crucial event in this process is shown in figure A.2, where a much older David is anointed by the "men of Judah" to rule over them after the death of Saul, whose tomb, with mourners, is shown at the bottom of the image. (Saul's son Ishbosheth was anointed king over the rest of Israel in the following verses.) Here, in the upper register, we see the men of Judah on both sides, but on one side bearing a crown, while a figure that looks suspiciously like the image of Samuel in other *ICC* images anoints David with oil from a horn. (David on the lower right is informed of Saul's death.) The presence of the Samuel-like figure, not mentioned in the text, shows, I think, the discomfort of the *ICC* artist with the purely secular decision described in the text.

Figure A.3 is the final image in this series, showing the last anointing of David, over Israel as well as Judah. The *ICC* text says that "the elders of Israel [*startsy Israelevi*]" anointed David, after making a compact (*zavet*) with him. In the upper register, we see the bareheaded elders and David making the compact, while signaling mutual agreement with outstretched hands. David, as usual, is backed by his retainers. Below, Samuel, not mentioned at all in the text, but clearly identified by both physiognomy and nimbus, is deliberately inserted anointing David as the elders look on. Again, the *ICC* artist adds a religious ingredient not found in the text. On the lower right, we see a standard depiction of David, enthroned with staff, surrounded by the bareheaded elders of Israel, signaling their assent with the open palm of one figure. In all these cases, the figures surrounding David visually present the appearance of his entourage, and thus echo the many other royal Old Testament images in the *ICC*. Yet, in each case, the figures are identified as crucial participants in important political decisions, legitimizing by their presence the various constituent moments in David's kingship.

Retainers, usually unidentified, are also included in images of a ruler carrying out daily tasks, where their participation is not required by the situation. In these many, many cases, the *ICC* artists included them seemingly as part of

Figure A.2. The men of Judah anoint David king. *LLS, Bibleiskaia istoriia,* 3:160, f. 38v. Courtesy of AKTEON.

a visual formula of depicting a ruler at work ruling. This point is clear in four images of Solomon building his Temple, one of his most important tasks in both the Old Testament and in the Muscovite historical imagination. In the first (figure A.4), we see Solomon ordering Hiram, the king of Tyre, to gather building materials for the Temple. The figures of both Solomon and Hiram are in dynamic poses, expressing the amazing energy required for the construction of this impressive building. Figure A.5 shows Solomon gathering materials, particularly cedars of Lebanon, for the Temple. In figure A.6, the Temple

288　CHAPTER 11

FIGURE A.3. The elders of Israel anoint David king. *LLS, Bibleiskaia istoriia*, 3:180, f. 300v. Courtesy of AKTEON.

is almost complete, and Solomon is shown with attendants supervising the last details. Note the onion dome at the top, and the *kokoshnik*-like porches on the Temple, reminiscent of both Muscovite liturgical implements called "Jerusalems," or "Zions," meant to replicate in part Solomon's Temple, and actual churches of roughly the same time, like the Old Cathedral of the Don, built under Boris Godunov (figure 8.4). Our final Temple image (figure A.7) shows the triumphant completion of Solomon's *podvig* (or religious feat), with Solomon shown formally with his courtiers while God looks on from above.

I'll conclude this brief appendix with two examples from the history of Rus'. The Rus' section of the *ICC* begins with a brief mention of the reign of Vladimir Monomakh (reigned 1113–1125), who is shown in figure A.8 arriv-

FIGURE A.4. Solomon instructs Hiram to gather building materials for his Temple. *LLS, Bibleiskaia istoriia*, 3:366, f. 202v. Courtesy of AKTEON.

ing *with his retainers* in Kiev, and being greeted with joy by the Kievans. In figure A.9 the accompanying text describes Vladimir's ascent to the throne, and the image shows a formal portrait of the enthroned Vladimir with staff, surrounded by his courtiers, all with open palms signifying mutual acceptance and, as the text tells us, joy. Thus we have seen in both chapter 11 and this appendix a series of set pieces, across time and space: enthroned ruler with courtiers, deathbed scenes, consultation and advice from courtiers, politically important consent from surrounding figures.

Not surprisingly, by this point, Dmitrii Ivanovich Donskoi (reigned 1359–1389) is also presented in ways that echo our other ruler images. The *ICC*

290   CHAPTER 11

Figure A.5. Gathering cedars from Lebanon and other materials for Solomon's Temple. *LLS, Bibleiskaia istoriia*, 3:365, f. 202. Courtesy of AKTEON.

contains a version of the well-known and extensive text of Dmitrii's life and death accompanied by only a few images. The *ICC* artists chose to emphasize particularly scenes from the end of his life. In figure A.10, he gathers his court around him to bid them farewell, saying a final word and making final divisions of his lands to his widow and sons. Figure A.11 shows Dmitrii, after speaking with his sons, calling his boyars to him in order to deliver a remarkable speech about his lifelong love and collaboration with them. This speech

Figure A.6. Solomon's Temple nearing completion. *LLS, Bibleiskaia istoriia*, 3:367, f. 203. Courtesy of AKTEON.

and its depiction are remarkably similar both in text and image to the speech given to his boyars on his deathbed by Vasilii III in the Royal Book as discussed in this chapter. Finally, in figure A.12, Dmitrii is shown signing his will, a charter with a golden seal (*zlatopechatanoiu gramotoiu*), thus completing a crucial legal deathbed task witnessed by his wife, sons, and boyars.

Figure A.7. God approves of Solomon's Temple and moves in. *LLS*, *Bibleiskaia istoriia*, 3:369, f. 204. Courtesy of AKTEON.

What then can we make of these figures surrounding rulers, in the *ICC*, the Tsar's Pew, both throne rooms and elsewhere? Why are they there, and what are they doing?

As we've seen here, there seem to be two possibilities, or perhaps a range of possibilities between two poles. In some cases, made explicit in the accompanying texts, actual advice is being sought and given. Obvious examples in-

Figure A.8. Vladimir Monomakh enters Kiev with retainers. *LLS*, *Russkaia letopisnaia istoriia*, bk. 1 (1114–1151) (Moscow: AKTEON, 2009), 1, f. 1. Courtesy of AKTEON.

clude events surrounding the death of Dmitrii Donskoi and the "election" of David by the elders of Israel. At the other end of the spectrum, you have the simple profiles of figures in the Royal Book, with no action implied. I would argue that even these simple outlines hark back to images of rulers whose power is enhanced visually by the presence of impressive retainers. Within Byzantine iconography, the standard is surely the famous mosaic of Justinian and his court, including representatives of the army, the church, and the bureaucracy,

Figure A.9. Vladimir Monomakh ascends the throne surrounded by retainers. *LLS, Russkaia letopisnaia istoriia*, 1:2, f. 1v. Courtesy of AKTEON.

in San Vitale in Ravenna; another is its predecessor, the depiction of Constantine and his court in the Arch of Constantine in Rome. Although these images themselves were unknown in Muscovy, they were powerful influences on Byzantine iconography of rulership, which in turn influenced ruler images in Rus´ and Muscovy. The point, condensed to a tiny trope in the profiles of the

APPENDIX 295

FIGURE A.10. Dmitrii Donskoi on his deathbed with wife, Evdokiia, her ladies, and his sons, with his retainers on our lower right. *LLS, Russkaia letopisnaia istoriia*, bk. 10 (1381–1392) (Moscow: AKTEON, 2010), 398, f. 328v. Courtesy of AKTEON.

Royal Book of the *ICC*, is that great rulers have, should have, and must be depicted as having retinues: Rulers depicted acting alone are rarities in all of these traditions.

So, what do these images represent? In a word: legitimacy. This is true for our evidence as well, whether the figures are mere profiles, retainers signifying

Figure A.11. Dmitrii Donskoi's speech to his boyars. *LLS, Russkaia letopisnaia istoriia*, 10:401, f. 330. Courtesy of AKTEON.

agreement with open palms, or advisers engaged in giving advice on crucial questions, and thus legitimizing the decisions being taken. They are thus essential ingredients of the iconography of rulership.

This iconography, echoing the theme of advice in literary texts, leaves intellectual space most obviously for the robust development of representative institutions like Assemblies of the Land, but also for virtually all of the other

Figure A.12. Dmitrii Donskoi signs his will. *LLS, Russkaia letopisnaia istoriia*, 10:411, f. 335. Courtesy of AKTEON.

institutions in Muscovy, like the law and the system of precedence, in all of which legitimating procedures were essential. Thus the visual ambiguity of the actual function of these figures, echoing the feature in written texts where wise advisers were not usually identified as belonging to a specific institution like the Boyar Duma, was an inexplicit but effective complement to the institutional development of Muscovite society, and a crucial ingredient in any image of royal authority.

One last thought: The transmission of political ideas took place by means of both written texts *and* visual documents, often quite independent of each other. In the images we've seen, the *ICC* artists did their best to follow the biblical texts they inherited, with editing of course, but they also felt free to embellish the texts with new details, like the onion domes on Solomon's Temple, or, more radically, the presence of Samuel in some anointing scenes where he was entirely absent in the text. I would argue that the presence of retainers at virtually every depiction of an Old Testament or Rus´ ruler seems to have been a result of transmission by visual rather than textual means. These retainers thus convey visually a point largely absent in more theoretical texts on political theory: That good rulers rule not alone, but always in the presence of, and sometimes with the advice of, their retainers. They become thus an essential ingredient of rulership.

CHAPTER 12

Ivan the Terrible as a Carolingian Renaissance Prince

The history of comparisons of Russia with Western Europe is a long and somewhat discouraging one. Too often, this sort of exercise has resulted in the conclusion that Russia was inferior to Western Europe because it lacked certain features that European society or culture possessed. Partly for this reason, Edward Keenan wrote in 1974 that "repeated attempts to align Muscovite institutions with those of the West, to bring her developments into 'phase' with Western cultural history, have been at best brilliant and appealing hypotheses and more commonly hindrances to the progress of historical understanding." The title for this essay is a not overly subtle reference to one such attempt, Michael Cherniavsky's imaginative and original but—I think most historians would agree—ultimately unconvincing attempt to align the image of Ivan the Terrible, both in his own alleged "correspondence" with Prince Kurbskii and in other Muscovite sources, with literary ruler images and some actual rulers in contemporary, sixteenth-century Western Europe. I mean this text as a contribution to the discussion of how to align Muscovy with European history, and I would like to suggest, as Keenan did (though for different reasons), that the most appropriate comparison for

---

This essay originally appeared in *Harvard Ukrainian Studies* 19 (1995): 594–606. The author gratefully acknowledges the publisher for permission to reprint this essay.

The author would like to express his gratitude to Donald Ostrowski for his patient and perceptive comments on several drafts of this article.

the Muscovy of Ivan IV is early medieval, rather than early modern, Western Europe.

I do not believe that there is much to be gained by a detailed discussion of Cherniavsky's essay, but I do think it makes a useful starting point for several reasons. First, I would like to center my discussion on the type of evidence that Cherniavsky used, that is, what are generally called "literary" texts from Ivan's reign and the period immediately following. Second, I would like to raise some of the same questions that Cherniavsky raised, but, obviously, to suggest different answers. In particular, I believe that his assertion that Muscovite political ideas were independent of religion in the way that they were for Machiavelli is erroneous—indeed it contradicts many of Cherniavsky's own conclusions in *Tsar and People*—and that the acceptance of this assertion leads to a very distorted view of early modern Russian political culture.

I would like to insert at the outset a few cautionary words about the nature of the footnote-less essay on a large subject, a type of academic expression that has become rarer as American specialist knowledge of Russian affairs has grown, but one used most effectively by Keenan. One reason for treading on this dangerous ground is that implicit comparisons with Western Europe are almost impossible to avoid, given the training of most Western historians of Russia and the context of historical debate in America in the late twentieth century. Explicit comparisons between periods and places have the advantage of forcing us to examine our assumptions, but they require us to discuss a number of large historical questions in a short space, and thus lead us to the medium of the essay. Keenan's seminal essay "Russian Political Folkways" shows how effective this format can be in raising broad questions and suggesting challenging answers. The purpose of the exercise is to suggest broad lines of thought rather than to "prove" something, in this case the identity of the periods compared, an obviously impossible task. My goal, therefore, is to make a contribution to the discussion of some general questions; I hope to suggest some useful parallels and contrasts rather than to offer historical proof as usually conceived. I should admit at the start that my knowledge of Carolingian and post-Carolingian Europe is derived mainly from secondary sources. The situation is better for Muscovite texts, but there are obviously many texts that I have not read, including Makarii's *Great Menology*, for which I rely on David Miller's careful descriptions. Further, comparisons of Carolingian Europe and Muscovy inevitably produce the impression that Muscovy was "backward." Although a major point in what follows will be to stress the differences between political discourse in sixteenth-century Russia and that in sixteenth-century Europe, and thus to challenge Cherniavsky's thesis, I do not mean to

IVAN THE TERRIBLE AS A CAROLINGIAN RENAISSANCE PRINCE

imply that Europe was more advanced or better. The interlocking political and cultural systems of Muscovy worked remarkably well for a long period of time.

There are further difficulties if one is arguing, as I am, that the political discourse in a country in Eastern Europe was six or seven hundred years "out of phase" with Western Europe in the sixteenth century and roughly "in phase" by the eighteenth. The pace of change alone makes generalizations dangerous. The astonishing growth of the state apparatus from Ivan's reign through the end of the seventeenth century means that, at least in that field, Moscow was a fast-moving target that recapitulated centuries of European development in a matter of decades. Below, however, I discuss for the most part only a narrow aspect of Muscovite politics and society, that is, political ideas found in chiefly literary and artistic sources—ecclesiastical and publicistic works, histories, wall paintings, and the like. This aspect of Muscovite development changed slowly in spite of the availability of Western political culture both before and after the reign of Ivan the Terrible. Other types of evidence and other aspects of life pose different problems of alignment: Ivan's relations with his court, the evolution of the Muscovite bureaucracy, or the legal system may suggest other European parallels or none at all. At the end of this essay, I suggest, following Valerie Kivelson, that at least by the middle of the seventeenth century, there was a quite sharp disjuncture between the still medieval personal and moral nature of political discourse and the increasingly impersonal and legal nature of the tsarist administrative apparatus, best symbolized, perhaps, by the *Ulozhenie* (law code) of 1649.

In spite of these caveats, I still believe that, if one took a hypothetical European from each of the various periods into which historians have traditionally divided European history and set each of them down in mid-sixteenth-century Muscovy, the person from Carolingian Europe would feel most at home. He or she would have been used to living in a sparsely settled countryside, with enormous empty spaces of forest or wasteland. He or she would find a level of agricultural technology approximately that of home. No city in Carolingian Europe could have compared in size to sixteenth-century Moscow, but elsewhere, in the countryside where the vast bulk of the population had to farm and gather in order to support, by a very narrow margin of agriculture above subsistence, the few who did something else, life surely would have seemed similar. Only in Charlemagne's time did Europe have a state that could compare in size with Ivan's Muscovy, and both states therefore had to face similar problems, physical, administrative, and cultural, in administering an enormously large territory. Indeed, both sixteenth-century Muscovy and the Empire of Charlemagne combined great size with relatively weak state apparatuses, and therefore had to rely extensively on cultural constructs to hold their far-flung and diverse populations together.

Chief among these cultural constructs were the complementary images of ruler and people, images that seem to have been remarkably successful in persuading subjects of both of these large empires to obey the state and even to identify with it. In Russia, these ideas were assembled for Ivan—most or all of them were already available in literary sources—into something approaching a systematic whole by a group of ecclesiastical writers under the leadership of Metropolitan Makarii. The work of these writers can be seen as an answer to the question, What ideological clothes should the emperor and his people wear? As the size and pretensions of the state grew, this question became ever more pressing. An answer similar to or even the same in outline as that elaborated by Makarii and his colleagues may already have been worked out by the reign of Ivan's father, Vasilii III, or even earlier. Conveniently for the purposes of this essay, most of the ideas were much older yet. The achievement of the writers of Ivan's time is that, by dint mostly of repetition, they fused these ideas together into what modern historians of political thought would call "a universe of discourse": a group of ideas expressed in commonly understood language that enabled people to understand each other when they wrote (and perhaps spoke) about what we would call "political affairs." Given the increasing availability, by the late sixteenth century, of Western literature written from a very different point of view, it is a remarkable testimony to the conservatism of Muscovite literary culture that this universe of discourse remained the dominant one for so long—at least up to the middle of the seventeenth century.

Keenan has already pointed out the similarity of Muscovite historical thought to historical thought in the West in the early Middle Ages (before ca. 1100) by concentrating on the restrictions that the very narrow range of available literary genres imposed on that thought. Both cultures were just emerging from a period in which annalistic chronicles and saints' lives had held undisputed sway. It seems to me that the content of that thought, the ideas themselves, are also surprisingly similar—and therefore have telling dissimilarities—to the ideas expressed by Carolingian image makers, and that the images of the ruler were put together by a similar group of people using similar tools. Let us turn first, then, to the environment in which these ideas were put together, and then attempt a comparison of the ideas themselves.

First, the ideas appropriate for discussions of political affairs in a literary format were established for Charlemagne and his immediate predecessors and successors, as for Ivan and his family through time, by a group of learned clergymen closely connected with the court. (Both courts looked back to a tradition dating to the fourth century of the church as the chief definer of imperial power in the newly Christianized Roman Empire.) It is not clear in either case if the actual ruler played any important part in this process beyond a vague sponsorship, though scholars are more inclined to assign to Charlemagne personally a greater role than I think is safe to assign to Ivan. Under these circumstances, it is not surprising that we find the protection of the church and its members among the prominent obligations of the monarch in each case. Note the contrast to the lay identities of many of the most important Renaissance writers on political subjects, even profoundly Christian writers like Erasmus and Thomas More, and the secular environments within which they worked. Note also the lack at the courts of Ivan or Charlemagne of any literary genre that would permit the sustained discussion of political ideas or theories. Second, the language in which these ecclesiastical writers expressed themselves was a literary language quite separate from the ordinary vernacular of the day. This meant that political discussion was carried on in a stylistically rarified atmosphere that insulated it linguistically from day-to-day concerns and everyday problems, and placed a heavy emphasis on theological matters, since most of the other highly valued works in that language dealt with religious questions. To have written about politics in the spoken vernacular as Machiavelli did would have been as radical a departure at Ivan's court as at Charlemagne's. Indeed, in spite of the use of a nonecclesiastical language for administrative purposes in Muscovy, there was no written vernacular available at either court.

Yet a comparison of Latin and Church Slavonic, and the works available in those languages to writers in the respective courts, at once reveals how much narrower was the range of subjects, styles, and ideas available in Church Slavonic as opposed to Latin, even the comparatively restricted list of texts available to Carolingian scholars. First, Latin was the administrative language of Charlemagne's court and empire, and there were apparently considerable connections between the publicistic works of ecclesiastical writers and the Capitularia, the laws and administrative regulations by means of which the country was actually governed. In Muscovy, such connections are hard to find, in part because the two activities were carried on in different languages, the plain style of the chancellery and the Slavonic of the church. More important still was the access that Latin gave not only to Christian classical writers such as Augustine and Ambrose but to Roman imperial ideas, and, crucially, to Roman law. Even pagan poets were studied as examples of Latin style, though any sensuality in their poems was discreetly covered with allegorical interpretations. The contrast with the narrow range and small number of works available in Slavonic is clear.

This difference becomes even clearer when we examine one of the most striking similarities of Carolingian and Muscovite political thought—the central importance of the Bible as the primary source of political images and analogies. Carolingian texts, like their Muscovite counterparts, are dense with biblical material, whether as direct references or simply as phrases or even single words that had known biblical overtones. Yet because of the languages involved, the Bible was experienced differently in each place. When the Vulgate Bible, translated by Jerome into a fourth-century Latin saturated with terms drawn from Roman civil law, was read by a medieval jurist or even a well-educated clerical writer, it could yield legal meanings and associations that would not have been apparent to Muscovite readers at all. Thus, whereas in Muscovy the Bible served primarily as a source of political images by analogy, in the West, especially under the gaze of generations of jurists, it could yield rather precise legal precepts. Here lies one reason why it is precisely the early Middle Ages, when this development had not proceeded very far (though it was certainly well under way), that yields the closest parallels to Muscovite political thinking.

Let us now turn to the ideas themselves that were clustered around the dual images of ruler and people in Muscovy and in Carolingian Europe. In both cultures, the most important of these by far was the idea that all political power came from God. This powerful idea, termed "the descending theme of government" by Walter Ullmann, was articulated in similar ways in both cultures and had somewhat similar results. A careful reading of historical and publicistic texts from both cultures reveals that, if one were to ask (anachronistically) who the sovereign was in the state, the only accurate answer would be God Himself, an answer that would have seemed hopelessly naive to virtually everyone thinking about politics in Renaissance Europe. For Muscovites and Carolingians alike, the state was seen as a means to the end of carrying out God's will, and the ruler received his power because he was perceived as the divinely chosen agent for that purpose. This idea was expressed, apparently by Charlemagne himself, in the formula "King (or Emperor) by the Grace of God," a formula that Ullmann argues perfectly encapsulates Carolingian ideas on rulership and even on society. This theme dominated the coronation ceremonies of the Carolingian period, in which rulership was conceived as a revival of the biblical kingship of David, who was of course chosen by God. The Old Testament theme was carried further: Charlemagne's throne was modeled on Solomon's throne, and Aachen was called a New Jerusalem. Christian and imperial themes were added to this revival of the Old Testament kingdom by Pope Adrian I, who called Charlemagne the New Constantine. Within a generation of Charlemagne's death, Hincmar, archbishop of Reims and a crucial figure in the development of the Carolingian ceremony, introduced the idea of anointing the ruler with so-called Clovis oil, allegedly preserved from the baptism of Clovis, whom he referred to as the New Constantine.

The similarity of all of this to Muscovite ideas is striking. Although the Russians used the Dei Gratia formula (*Bozh'eiu milost'iu*) (by the grace of God), the more common (and more explicit) form was the epithet "chosen by God" (*Bogom izbrannyi*), encountered countless times in Muscovite texts and expanded in the coronation service of Ivan IV to "beloved by God, chosen by God, and honored by God." Before the bestowal of the regalia, Metropolitan Makarii intoned a prayer that explicitly invoked the kingship of David:

> King of Kings and Lord of Lords, who by Samuel the Prophet didst choose thy servant David and anoint him to be King over thy people Israel, ... look down from thy sanctuary ... upon thy faithful servant Ivan, whom Thou hast blessed and raised up as Tsar of thy holy people.

References to Saint Vladimir as the New Constantine were commonplaces in Muscovite literary sources, and the fuss over Monomakh's cap parallels the fuss over Clovis's oil. (Note, however, the dynastic connection with Saint Vladimir as opposed to the territorial and tribal connection with Clovis.) Moscow as well as Aachen was seen by contemporaries as a New Jerusalem.

If this descending theme powerfully enhanced the ruler's power by linking his will to the will of God, it also irresistibly brought with it the obligation to obey God's law and God's will, however those concepts were understood. Both Ivan and Charlemagne undertook royally sponsored reforms of the church, and each held a unique place within the church granted to no other layman. In his coronation ceremony, Charlemagne promised to obey God's laws and protect the church before he was crowned. At Ivan's coronation, the metropolitan admonished Ivan that his realm was a sacred trust for which he would be held responsible at the Last Judgment. Significantly, this admonition occurred after the bestowing of the regalia (but before the unction), and Ivan made no promises in reply.

I should emphasize again that the ideological wardrobes chosen by their clerical image makers for Ivan and Charlemagne were in neither case original creations, but they were remarkably similar, had similar sources (the Bible, Byzantium, and the Roman Empire), and were assembled as part of larger cultural programs, which in turn were also quite similar. Although the changes wrought by the "Carolingian Renaissance" were both more rapid and more radical than the corresponding changes in Muscovy (in part because the territories that constituted Muscovy, unlike many of Charlemagne's territories, had been at least nominally Christianized for centuries), the task for both courts was to overlay the existing layers of political thought and practice, particularly unwritten and customary layers, with a thoroughly Christian concept of rulership in which the power of the ruler came exclusively from above. The image of the people had simultaneously to be changed from the independent political and semi-independent cultural units that they had been in their recent past to a single Christian people united by a common Christian culture. From a functional point of view, the work of Makarii and his colleagues paralleled that of the writers and artists of the Carolingian Renaissance. Makarii's *Great Menology* collected and arranged the common store of liturgical and religious materials, particularly saints' lives; the *Book of Degrees*, composed in the latter part of the reign of Ivan the Terrible, attempted to create a common historical tradition based on the dynasty; in art and architecture, provincial styles and craftsmen were brought to Moscow to create a visual culture common to the whole Muscovite realm. A common iconography with common themes could be found in the Kremlin churches and in the Golden Hall (Many of the same themes were taken up again by the artists who decorated the Hall of Facets under the patronage of Boris Godunov.) In each of these areas of activity, considerable originality was displayed in working out the symbols of this common Christian culture. The so-called *Church Militant* icon is perhaps the best summary of these ideas expressed in symbols that surely would have been understood by Charlemagne and his court. The *Church Militant* title, added in the eighteenth century, misleadingly recalls later medieval developments in the West under a revived papacy. What is militant in the icon is not a church but a sacred state led by Ivan below and the Archangel Michael above. The theological tone and highly personal nature of these texts and images in both cultures is light-years away from the self-interested statecraft of Machiavelli as well as from the rational Christian humanism of Thomas More.

One might argue, and with some justice, that these royal symbols and concepts could be found as easily in later medieval or even Renaissance coronation services or documents, that they were common to European ideas of kingship in general. There are two answers to this argument. One is that they never occupied as much of stage center as they did in the Carolingian period. The other is that, though symbols and even texts may have survived, especially in a liturgical setting, three European developments that did not occur in Muscovy and had not begun or were only beginning under Charlemagne decisively changed the course of all political discussion, and in particular the ways in which these very symbols and concepts were understood. These developments were: (1) the enormous growth of legal thought in both royal and ecclesiastical chanceries, (2) the introduction of Aristotelian logic and the growth of scholasticism, and (3) the continuing physical isolation of the papacy, with its vast array of canon lawyers and theologians, from the political and intellectual control of any monarchy. Under both Charlemagne and Ivan IV, legal codes and practices were primitive when compared to Renaissance Europe, the habit of extended and logical analysis of abstract concepts was almost entirely absent, and the interests of the church were felt by almost everyone to coincide with the interests of the state, except in very exceptional circumstances. In any case, the church lacked the political, economic, and military strength to resist the state.

These very general statements can be illustrated at an only slightly lower level of generalization if we briefly consider from the perspective of later European history a central paradox inherent in the descending theme of government and if we also consider the Muscovite and Carolingian responses to that paradox. Simply stated, the paradox is this: The descending theme presupposes, for what might be called ritual reasons, an ideal ruler who can perfectly transmit God's will to the earthly realm. Few if any rulers were perfect; most were far from it. What do you do with a bad king? My verb "do" here conceals three paths that Europeans followed in their efforts to resolve this paradox, though by the Renaissance they had by no means reached the end of any path: (a) the working out of a definition of the law so that at least some people could agree when the ruler broke it; (b) the working out of concepts and terminology so that the ruler could be criticized (or merely described) without overthrowing the whole idea of legitimate government; and (e) the gradual evolution of machinery that could, short of civil war, constrain the ruler to obey the law as defined in (a) and thus obey God's will. The Muscovites did make considerable progress on path (a), especially during the Time of Troubles and during the long campaign of gentry petitions in the seventeenth century, but the personal and religious nature of political discussion prevented, for better or worse, much movement before about 1650 along paths (b) or (c), except for the idea of criticizing the advisers of the ruler in place of the ruler himself, a habit that was frequently used in the Carolingian period, as is discussed immediately below.

This identification of the law with God's will may strike us as naive and may have seemed so to later Europeans, but it seems to have been an obvious one to Carolingian and Muscovite alike. The early medieval concept of law, like the meaning that we find attached to *zakon* and its derivatives in Muscovite literary sources, went far beyond "mere" written law. It encompassed a frustrating (for us) amalgam of what we would call moral or ethical law, religious law, and customary law, all of which taken together, or even separately, were more important than written positive law. In particular, Muscovite and Carolingian thought placed a heavy emphasis on custom, the importance of doing what was done in your father's and grandfather's time, of preserving the social hierarchy, an emphasis common to most traditional societies. Neither the Muscovite nor the Carolingian literary culture seems to have differentiated public from private rights, laws from morals, or positive law from ideal law. This characteristic may have been at least as much an asset as a defect in Ivan's or Charlemagne's kingdoms, but it hampered the movement of political thought in the direction that Europe happened to take because, although both cultures agreed that the ruler had a primary obligation to uphold the law, each had to go through a painful period of trial and error in order to arrive at even a general sense of what the law was or was not.

Muscovite and Carolingian alike found it difficult to criticize the ruler within the accepted terms of political discussion. Both cultures placed a heavy emphasis, in coronation rituals and other texts, on the piety and wisdom of the ruler, but neither provided an effective conceptual framework for describing or correcting an erring ruler short of declaring him king no longer. In the West, the long and complicated evolution of the idea of the king's two bodies eventually provided an effective theoretical way of dealing with this question, since the ruler could be criticized as a person while his office remained unblemished, but this evolution had not begun in Carolingian Europe. I know of only one attempt (by Ivan Timofeev) in Muscovite sources before 1630 to separate the corrupted person of the ruler from his incorruptible throne, and this suggestion was not pursued. One suspects that the great popularity in Muscovy of Agapetus's "Hortatory Chapters" was largely due to his discussion of the two natures of the ruler, God-like and man-like, but Agapetus, like the texts available to the Carolingians, never succeeded in resolving the paradox or in separating the body politic from the body natural, so that the personal and political aspects of the ruler remained intertwined. For this reason, it was difficult to criticize the policies of a ruler without criticizing his personal piety and wisdom, and so making him an ineffective mirror of God's will.

Another solution to the problem, one that was frequently used by both Carolingian and Muscovite writers, was to focus on the ruler's advisers: The advisers of a ruler could be criticized without touching the ritually necessary perfection of the ruler. In Muscovy, the role of advice giving received more and more emphasis. The role of wise advisers was repeatedly emphasized in the murals in the Golden Hall. In contemporary sources, evil advice and the "foolish silence" (*bezumnoe molchanie*) of the righteous, who should have served as wise advisers, were described as major reasons for the evils of Ivan's reign and the coming of the Time of Troubles. In the purely practical realm, the creation of a political consensus was an essential step in driving out the foreign invaders and re-establishing the tsardom. After the Troubles, the gentry were more and more accustomed to being consulted, and firmly believed in their right to present petitions and grievances to the tsar. Post-Troubles coronation ceremonies added a popular acclaim—a part of the coronation service that included a ceremonial acclimation of the alleged public support of the coronation—that had been absent in Ivan IV's days. Yet in both cultures, Carolingian and Muscovite, the role of the wise adviser remained defined by personal qualities rather than institutional affiliation and remained in effect an aspect of the mercy of the ruler. Even when, in seventeenth-century Russia, advice was conveyed through quasi-institutional forms, it was seen as a manifestation of God's will rather than an expression of popular will that had legitimacy in its own right. And, as the gentry petitions of the mid-seventeenth century showed, if a ruler persisted in surrounding himself with scoundrels even after petitions and good advice, then criticism of the ruler himself was hard to avoid. Ultimately then, the brittle logic of political discourse in both cultures left little choice between accepting the will of the ruler as the will of God, or rejecting it as the prattling of a usurper or, worse, the poisonous message of the Antichrist himself or of his forerunner.

The practical result of this King–No King dualism was that, in the case of the breakdown of the informal mechanisms of consultation and negotiation that were the basis of government in both societies (and in Renaissance Europe), there was no clear institutional framework to resolve conflict. In later medieval and Renaissance Europe, however, the function of advice giving was progressively institutionalized and hedged around by legal formulations. Attempts in this direction were made both in countries like England, where representative institutions ultimately triumphed, and in countries like France, where they did not. In Carolingian Europe and in sixteenth-century Russia, by contrast, this pattern of representing conflict in constitutional or institutional terms seems not to have had much appeal. This feature of public political discourse in Russia seems largely responsible for the fact that, although the gathering of advice and political support from a fairly wide range of Muscovite society during and after the Time of Troubles was crucial to the survival of the state and the conduct of business, this function of advice giving found no long-term place in the structure of the government. Instead, the government of a "God-chosen" tsar as it was imagined to have existed in the sixteenth century was carefully reconstructed.

I hope that this survey, brief and undocumented as it has been, has illustrated some fundamental similarities between Muscovite and Carolingian political ideas. In both places, these ideas were assembled by clerics attached to the court drawing on imperial and Christian traditions, particularly the Bible. In both places, the central political idea was the descent of all political power from God alone, with the people seen as God's chosen people, the successors to Israel, ruled by God's will as transmitted by His chosen ruler. Around this central idea were arrayed similar notions of advice, of law and the ruler's obligation to govern in accord with it, and of the responsibility of the ruler to preserve Christian doctrine and the church. Russian ideology, therefore, has roots very similar to the roots of Western European ideology and is neither bizarre nor exotic in the European context.

Within this context of similarity, we have discussed a number of important dissimilarities. Almost all of these differences—in language, in concepts of law, in literary traditions governing the discussion of politics, in the relative power of church and state—worked to inhibit the Russians from following the path of establishing institutional or constitutional limits on the monarch's power that some Western countries followed. Although Muscovy had, by the seventeenth century, institutions like a powerful Boyar Duma and a wealthy church that might have acted as institutional checks on the power of the monarch, neither in fact played this role. This situation can surely be explained in part by the continuing medieval, noninstitutional nature of the political discourse that seventeenth-century Russians inherited from their sixteenth-century ancestors and in part by the differences between Carolingian and Muscovite political culture that we have just outlined. Moreover, before the ambiguities in Muscovite political culture had had a chance to work themselves out (scant progress was made in this direction), they were replaced, starting in the late seventeenth century, by Western European absolutist ideas that had been specifically designed to resolve those very ambiguities (in their Western medieval form) in favor of monarchical power. The Russian redaction of the medieval ideal of Christian rulership was thus both less hospitable to the evolution of constitutional or institutional limits on the monarch's power than was the Carolingian and was in any case replaced by a much more modern ideological system imported from the West designed to deny such limits.

How do these observations fit in with our knowledge of other aspects of Muscovite society? Many aspects of that society—the size of the state, its relatively primitive administrative apparatus (at least in the sixteenth century), the power of the boyars both relative to the ruler and to everyone else in the realm, the development of what Keenan has called "the land-for-service paradigm" of land held in return for military service to the state—had a strong resemblance to similar features of the early medieval Western European landscape. Yet, as we observed earlier, Muscovy was a fast-moving target. In particular, we have seen a number of impressive studies of the rapid growth and bureaucratic evolution of the administrative apparatus, which inevitably tended to substitute abstract legal norms and routine procedures for the personal contact and religious orientation of the political discourse we have been discussing. As Valerie Kivelson has argued, the tension between these two kinds of political discussion (and political action) became acute over the course of the seventeenth century, with first the bureaucracy, then the ruler, and finally the service aristocracy at all levels gradually abandoning the old way of looking at things.

The bureaucracy found the old personal and religious discourse impractical and difficult to accommodate in administrative procedure. The ruler was dismayed by the theoretical door left open to rebellion by those who disagreed with the religious policies of the church. The service aristocracy simply found it advantageous to adapt to the new circumstances for a variety of practical reasons. Thus, by the accession of Peter I, the most active parts of Russian society had begun to question the traditional way of representing political power. It remained for that energetic monarch finally to sweep away the traditional images and replace them with the image of a European-style *Rechtsstaat* based in theory (if not always in practice) on the impersonal rule of law, an ideal based on early modern, rather than early medieval, European models.

In spite of the illusion created by this ideological change of a revolution imposed from above, practical political life went on much as before, with the retention of everything from the land-for-service paradigm to an informal court politics based more on clan and patronage than on European-style laws. Whether or not these features deserve the name "medieval" or coincided with political practice further west are questions beyond the bounds of this essay. I think that Keenan would agree, however, that many of these "old-fashioned" features gave the Russian political system, surrounded by enemies and short of resources, its peculiar strength and durability, at least in the short and middle terms. Perhaps the same can be said for Muscovite political ideas in the years before 1650.

Summing Up
What Our Work Means

CHAPTER 13

Autocracy

Autocracy is perhaps the concept most widely used to describe the political culture of the Russian state before 1917. Indeed, autocracy, understood as the unlimited rule of the monarch over his subjects, is often taken as the signature characteristic of Russian political culture in general. "Autocracy" is also the term used to describe early modern Russia by many professional historians, especially in the United States, but their understanding is far more nuanced. These historians see the political structure of Russia as essentially oligarchical, with power shared in a mutually beneficial way among various layers of the nobility and the government. In this article I present autocracy in the relatively stable political culture from 1450 to 1650 and then discuss the changes wrought in that culture by massive influences from Western Europe under Peter I the Great (reigned 1682–1725) and his immediate predecessors.

Most responsible for the trope of total power of the Russian ruler over his subjects are the accounts of Western European visitors to Russia from the fifteenth to the seventeenth centuries. They developed a fairly simple picture of Russian political life, positing a ruler with total power over his subjects, helped

---

This essay originally appeared in *Europe, 1450–1789: Encyclopedia of the Early Modern World*, ed. Jonathan Dewald (New York: Charles Scribner's Sons, 2004), 1:182–184. The author gratefully acknowledges the publisher for permission to reprint this essay.

in his oppressive rule by his subjects' ignorance, a subservient church, and an ideology that made his orders the equivalent of God's will.

When we turn to evidence that reflects the way Russians themselves thought about politics, however, we find a slightly different picture. Lacking a literary model of abstract political theorizing, Muscovites expressed their political ideas in a wide variety of genres in various media, including saints' lives, chronicles, and other historical texts; icons, mural cycles, and even church building and other types of architecture. This varied body of evidence presents a fairly consistent set of interrelated political ideas. The ruler (grand prince until 1547, tsar thereafter) was understood to derive his political power directly from God. Russians saw their state as a kind of reincarnation of the ancient state of Israel, guided and protected by God so long as the people kept their faith in God. The Russians' picture of the tsar resembled his picture of God himself: a stern but merciful ruler whose relationship to his subjects was essentially personal.

If the ruler was seen as "chosen by God," was he then free to rule utterly as he saw fit, with no restraints to his power? The answer, not surprising within the context of Christian doctrines of rulership, was "no." Texts, court rituals, and images alike agree that rulers had clear obligations: to be personally pious (and thus open to receive God's will), to preserve the institution and doctrines of the Orthodox Church, and to preserve the social hierarchy while protecting the innocent and vulnerable and punishing wrongdoers.

But what of a ruler who willfully disregarded these obligations? Unlike their counterparts in early modern Europe, Russian thinkers had not worked out an answer to this problem. Even advocates of royal power admitted that subjects had not only the right but the obligation to resist an evil ruler, whom they called a "tormentor" (*muchitel'*), the Slavonic translation of the Greek *tyrannos*. There is considerable evidence that Ivan IV (the Terrible, reigned 1533–1584) was regarded as a tormentor by the end of his reign. Several rulers during the Time of Troubles (a period of civil wars and foreign intervention, 1598–1613) were regarded in the same way. The problem was that, since there was no organized mechanism for replacing a God-defying monarch with another, more godly ruler, the declaration that the current ruler was a tormentor could easily lead to the destruction of legitimate government altogether, and thus to chaos.

The monarch's advisers were the main mechanism for preventing this disastrous situation. Advisers were a standard attribute of good rulers in both literary and visual representations of monarchs. They were there to give godly advice to wise rulers or to correct sinful rulers through their counsel. But this theoretical function of providing wise advice remained a personal matter and was never given a legal or constitutional form. It was not firmly attached to the Boyar Duma, a consultative body of representatives of the most prominent aristocratic families and church hierarchs, which met frequently to advise the ruler throughout the early modern period up until the era of Peter the Great. Although consultative assemblies played a major and necessary role in the seventeenth century, in effect ruling the country on the eve of the election of Michael Romanov as tsar in 1613, the dominance of a personalized, God-dependent theory of governance prevented these assemblies from having a permanent, legitimate role in Muscovite affairs.

Discussion of assemblies brings us into the realm of practical politics. How was real political power distributed in Muscovy? Again, the foreigners' trope of the unlimited power of the monarch has had to be modified. Although there is disagreement among historians, most experts take the view that the successful ruler ruled with and through his boyars and with members of the provincial gentry, and not in opposition to them. Whereas previous historians emphasized the horizontal, corporate divisions in Muscovite society, with power flowing downward from the ruler through a growing bureaucracy, many more recent historians have emphasized a different overlapping structure. Here the great aristocratic families surround the ruler like the protons around the nucleus of an atom, with vertical patronage networks connecting the court with distant corners of the realm. Thus society was bound by the horizontal ties of a hierarchical precedence system (*mestnichestvo*) and by a growing body of law enforced by a bureaucratic apparatus, as well as by vertical and personal patronage connections across the boundaries of these groupings. Most importantly, the crown and the nobles were more allies than rivals: The crown depended on nobles at all levels to run affairs in the countryside, while the nobles depended on the crown to run national affairs and to protect noble interests in the localities.

Thus, the political culture of Russia on the eve of the eighteenth century had serious vulnerabilities. The legitimacy of any ruler could be challenged (and was challenged, for example, by the Old Believers) on the grounds of failing to carry out God's will, however the latter was interpreted. The ruler was bound by the vaguely defined theoretical obligation to consult with wise advisers and by the very real and growing power of the great aristocratic clans, as well as by a provincial gentry whose power and self-confidence were also growing. Peter tried, with limited success, to resolve these questions.

Borrowing from Western theorists of absolutism and from limited changes in Muscovite political culture at the end of the seventeenth century, Peter and his political assistants substituted reason of state and the common good, as defined by the will of the monarch, for the all-too-vague will of God as the source of legitimate authority in Russia. To be sure, the monarch still claimed to be God's chosen ruler, but to question or even discuss the link between God and the actual ruler became a treasonous act. In spite of the continued use of religious rhetoric, the state changed from an imagined revival of the ancient Israelite theocracy into a self-contained secular system, in which the good order of the state—its military successes and its cultural and social reforms—became the goals of political action.

The relationship of the monarch to the aristocracy was not resolved with similar clarity, perhaps because it did not need resolution. Though he exercised great personal power, used the title "emperor" rather than "tsar" after his victory over the Swedes in 1721, replaced the Boyar Duma with a Senate (1711), and attempted to create an aristocracy of merit through a new Table of Ranks (1722), Peter did not resolve the relationship of the crown to its nobles. Indeed, the power of the aristocracy of birth continued to grow throughout the eighteenth century as it had in the seventeenth. Russian nobles continued to find it advantageous to support the "autocracy" of the ruler at the center, while the ruler gave the nobles ever widening powers in the localities and, in many cases, great informal influence at the center. Thus the contradiction between a rhetoric of "autocratic" rule by one person and an oligarchical political structure, which had misled foreign observers in the pre-Petrine era, continued to characterize the political culture of Russia.

Bibliography

Kivelson, Valerie A. *Autocracy in the Provinces: The Muscovite Gentry and Political Culture in the Seventeenth Century.* Stanford, CA: Stanford University Press, 1996.

Kollmann, Nancy Shields. *Kinship and Politics: The Making of the Muscovite Political System, 1345–1547.* Stanford, CA: Stanford University Press, 1987.

LeDonne, John P. *Absolutism and Ruling Class: The Formation of the Russian Political Order, 1700–1825.* New York: Oxford University Press, 1991.

Rowland, Daniel. "Did Muscovite Literary Ideology Place Limits on the Power of the Tsar (1540s–1660s)?" *Russian Review* 49, no. 2 (1990): 125–155 (chapter 4 in this volume).

Chapter 14

Muscovy

There is little agreement among scholars on the nature of the Russian polity in the early modern period or on the nature and function of political thought within that polity. At a time of intense revisionist work by many historians, however, the moment is propitious to examine the history of political thought anew. Twentieth-century historians inherited from the nineteenth century chiefly the work of the dominant "state-juridical" school, which, in masterful and influential multivolume narratives, gave the state a dominant role in politics, and considered political thought, chiefly, either as weakening or as strengthening state power. Two late imperial studies offered a balanced view of these forces.[1] Following the 1917 Revolution, interpretations of the early modern period became the subject of government supervision. This had the effect of imposing a crude Marxist framework on interpretations of Muscovite history and Muscovite political thought alike. Most texts on political subjects were seen as products of a class war, chiefly between proponents of the centralizing government and supporters of a conservative "boyar opposition" that looked back nostalgically to an earlier period of aristocratic independence. There were also a few representatives of a

---

This essay originally appeared in *European Political Thought, 1450–1700: Religion, Law and Philosophy*, ed. Howell A. Lloyd, Glenn Burgess, and Simon Hodson (New Haven, CT: Yale University Press, 2007), 267–299. The author gratefully acknowledges the publisher for permission to reprint this essay.

peasant point of view, aiming to overthrow the "feudal" order altogether. Many scholars, discouraged from speculating about large historical questions, concentrated on careful textual studies. Meanwhile, historians in the West spent much time searching for the early modern roots of Soviet "totalitarianism." There has been a remarkable flowering of Muscovite studies since the Second World War, but before about 1980 much of this work concentrated on social history, consisting particularly of investigations of the Muscovite elite.

No comprehensive description, in English, of Russian political thought in this period has appeared since S. V. Utechin and Thornton Anderson published their excellent histories, in 1963 and 1967, respectively.[2] Since then, and particularly after 1980, the way scholars look at political thought has been transformed. Principally, the meager role historians once allocated to culture in general and to political thought in particular in explaining early modern civilization has been greatly magnified. Instead of merely examining texts in chronological order and relating them to each other and to political thinking in the West, historians are now more inclined to examine political ideas as forming a kind of culture system, in which relationships among ideas receive as much scrutiny as the ideas themselves. This approach has proved to be fruitful and has resulted in the increasingly successful integration of the history of political thought with new ideas about political history. Political thinking is becoming a major explanation of why people acted as they did at a given time.

Many of these new directions in writing the history of political thought relate to the issue of context. As I discuss below, many historians in the West now oppose the formerly dominant image of an all-powerful government commanding a powerless, supine society. Instead, they have discovered myriad ways in which members at least of the landholding classes negotiated with the government to produce outcomes advantageous to all parties. Further, the most important cultural context for political thinking in Muscovy—the culture of the Orthodox Church—neglected by political necessity in the Soviet Union and largely by inclination in the West—has been illuminated in pioneering studies by Russian and Western scholars alike.

Amid continuing debates about the nature of the Muscovite state and its relation to Muscovite society, scholars have grown skeptical of existing opinions as to when and by whom various texts were produced. While much of this discussion has focused on the well-known *Correspondence* ascribed to Ivan the Terrible and his courtier Prince Andrei Kurbskii, the authenticity of other texts has also been questioned.[3] The use of images, particularly paintings, as evidence for political thought is in its relative infancy. And visual evidence, of course, has its own problems of dating and attribution.

The present essay aims to place early modern Russian thought within the context of European thought and within a comparable academic discourse. And this is where the "fit" has always been difficult and where the inclusion of visual evidence becomes crucial to a better understanding. Prior to the 1650s, early modern Russian political thought appears to have had more in common with early *medieval* than with early *modern* Western Europe. Among the shared characteristics are: the relative paucity of written literary or documentary sources, the almost complete absence of literacy among laymen, the importance of visual evidence to a largely illiterate society, and the very narrow selection of genres available to writers or painters. After 1650, changes in both the political and the intellectual contexts created a shift in political thought from the personal tsardom of traditional Muscovite thought toward a more impersonal mode of rule, one that concentrated on the welfare rather than the salvation of the tsar's subjects. An excellent recent study places two of these changes, the new humanism of Ukrainian immigrants and the influence of Polish court culture in Russia at the end of the seventeenth century, into a comparative European context, and shows how resistant Russians, especially Russian aristocrats, were until 1800 and beyond, toward imported European humanism, defined chiefly as the study of pagan classical authors.[4] Apart from these immigrants and a very narrow class of educated Russians, traditional Muscovite ideas maintained their sway over the minds of most literate Russians until the end of the eighteenth century and beyond.

We have therefore to consider two centuries of relatively stable discourse after 1450, with a kind of postscript to describe the changes to that discourse that occurred in the last half of the seventeenth century. Hence this essay's organization by topic. Instead of examining authors and texts chronologically, I examine all of them, visual and written, as parts of (or exceptions to) a dominant intellectual paradigm. While the approach risks being less sensitive to change over time, it enables us to examine Muscovite political thought as a culture system embracing the numerous and important ideas that thinkers shared, as well as those on which they differed.

The volume in which this essay first appeared (*European Political Thought, 1450–1700*, see note above) aims to discuss evidence of political thought under three general rubrics: religion, law, and philosophy. But the balance among these elements in early modern Russia is necessarily different from the balance discernible in the countries of Western Europe, and more akin to my colleagues' findings for neighboring countries in the north and east. Here, the religious side of political thought was hypertrophied, while the law was important but far less developed, both intellectually and institutionally, than in the

West. And, before the last years of the seventeenth century, there were no institutions of higher learning, and few native practitioners of philosophy.

Russian Political Thought, 1450–1700: Context and Sources

The Reigns of Ivan III and Vasilii III, 1462–1533

In 1450 Russia was racked by civil war, and Moscow was setting the stage to emerge in the following centuries as the victor in a struggle for supremacy, both over other Russian towns and over regional rivals such as Lithuania in the west and the various Muslim Khanates that succeeded to the Qipchaq Khanate in the east.

The skillful leadership of Grand Prince Ivan III, son of the victorious Vasilii II, enabled Moscow to give form to its domestic political establishment by laying the foundations for a professional corps of literate bureaucrats to help in administering the state and by regularly consulting with the Boyar Duma, an assembly of representatives of the most prestigious aristocratic clans.

This growing political strength found a parallel in the increasing independence and self-confidence of the church in Russia, a phenomenon owing to three crucial events. The first was the Council of Ferrara–Florence (1437–1439), where Byzantine churchmen, their capital under tremendous pressure from Turkish forces, agreed to a union with the Roman Catholic Church almost completely on Catholic terms. The second was the fall of Constantinople in 1453, an event widely interpreted in Russia as God's punishment for the Byzantine Church's apostasy at Ferrara–Florence. The third was the arrival of the millennial year of 1492, the end of the seventh millennium according to the Orthodox calendar. No paschal tables had been compiled for the period after the year 7000 from creation, and, when new tables were issued, the accompanying text, discussed below, referred to Muscovy as the last Orthodox kingdom.

Thus, during the reigns of Ivan III and his successor, Vasilii III, Muscovite rulers and thinkers developed both the political strength of their state and an increasingly self-confident image of themselves and of their role in the economy of Christian salvation. Perhaps the greatest symbol (and engine) of this new confidence was the rebuilding of the Kremlin, initiated by Ivan III and carried out with the help of foreign architects, mostly Italians. This rebuilding, which extended into the reign of Ivan's successor, included the walls of the Kremlin, three new cathedrals, and a new palace for Ivan with two principal throne rooms of the realm, the Hall of Facets and the Golden Hall. These impressive buildings gave tangible form to Moscow's pretensions as a New Jerusalem. During the next century they were decorated with mural cycles that constituted the most important set of political texts available to the largely illiterate Russian society. This work in the Kremlin gave Moscow's "glowing center" a brilliance unmatched elsewhere on the western steppe and comparable with royal palace/church ensembles in Central and Eastern Europe.[5]

Two native religious thinkers emerged during these reigns who deserve mention here. Nil Sorskii was deeply influenced by the spirituality of hesychasm, a contemplative strain of Orthodox Christianity developed in fourteenth-century Byzantium. His pupil, Vassian Patrikeev, had been an important courtier and became a friend of Maksim the Greek, discussed below. Joseph Volotskii was a prolific writer on political and other subjects who stressed the organizational aspects of monastic life, particularly the maintenance of discipline and the good order of the monastery. The monastery he started, the Volokolamsk monastery, became known for the discipline of its rule, for its accumulation of landed wealth, and for the social and political activism of its monks, many of whom occupied high positions in the Church throughout the century.

The Era of Ivan IV, the Terrible, 1533–1584

The figure of Ivan IV, or Ivan the Terrible (*Groznyi*, or "awe-inspiring"), is commonly seen as the epitome of Russian governmental traditions of tyranny and violence. Coming to the throne in 1533, at the age of three, Ivan was officially crowned tsar in 1547 after a childhood dominated by a series of bloody struggles among various boyar clans. The initial part of his reign, until the early 1560s, saw a number of reforms, including the issuance of a new law code approved by the first Assembly of the Land (1550), the Church Council of 100 Chapters (1551), the reorganization of the central bureaucracy, the creation of a number of new ministries, and several other important administrative developments. The latter part of his reign took a distinctly different tone. Suffering from an increasingly painful spinal condition and poisoned by the mercury that his doctors used to treat him, Ivan unleashed against his own subjects a campaign of violence that seriously disrupted the political system so carefully built up by his grandfather and father. In a move unprecedented in the rest of Europe or elsewhere, he created a separate kingdom within his state, the *oprichnina*, in which his will alone, and not the will of the Boyar Duma, held sway. Waves of violence carried off elite courtiers, churchmen, chancellery officials, and simple peasants. Ivan's rule in the latter part of his reign deviated in almost every respect from the mainstream of Russian political development and created the conditions—including the murder of his eldest son and heir—which were to plunge the country into anarchy in the years after his death.

The tendency to consolidate earlier practice, so conspicuous in the early part of Ivan's reign, was evident also in the realm of political thought, where Metropolitan Makarii, Ivan's tutor and an important adviser, sponsored major ideological works that summed up and codified earlier thought rather than striking out in new directions. Makarii commissioned the important murals in the Golden Hall, one of the two main throne rooms of the Russian state, after the original murals had been destroyed by fire in 1547. Using the system of organizing images on the walls of Orthodox churches, the mural painters pulled together the most important political ideas of the time into a coherent spatial relationship, with more abstract or theological themes illustrated on the elevated spaces of the domes, while the walls and lower vaults were filled largely with historical scenes either from the Old Testament or from Rus' history.[6] Makarii probably commissioned the decoration (or redecoration) of parts or all of other Kremlin churches after the Moscow fire. The commissioning included the decoration of the Cathedral of the Archangel Michael, which served as the burying place for members of the royal family and thus as a site for the celebration of the ruling dynasty and its role in Christian history.[7]

Makarii also sponsored some large-scale literary works on political themes, including the innovative *Book of Degrees of the Imperial Genealogy*, which was organized by the reigns of various rulers instead of by year, and emphasized the dynastic as well as the divine origins of political power. In addition to compiling the *Lives* of various Rus' saints, and thus magnifying the sanctity of the Muscovite realm, Makarii sponsored new rituals, which emphasized the Christian source of the tsar's power—particularly the famous Palm Sunday ritual, in which the tsar led the Metropolitan (representing Christ), on a horse (disguised as an ass) into the Kremlin. They thus re-enacted Christ's entry into Jerusalem.[8] He probably had a major role in the construction of the Cathedral of the Intercession on the Moat, popularly known as Saint Basil's Cathedral. Like the rituals he initiated, this dramatic building brought out of the Kremlin and into the popular space of Beautiful (later, Red) Square the image of a sacred realm guiding the faithful until the last days.[9]

Lack of evidence on the personal beliefs of individuals, laymen or ecclesiastics, makes it hard to assess the effectiveness of this campaign of political education with its multiple vehicles of dissemination. But the basic ideas that Makarii and his circle worked so hard to publicize appeared again and again, with only slight variations, in the numerous texts about the Time of Troubles by authors of widely varied backgrounds, roughly between 1600 and 1630; in petitions by gentry militiamen throughout the seventeenth century; and in the extensive literature generated by the Old Believers in the second half of that century. In this sense, they constituted the dominant political discourse down to the time of Peter the Great.

At the same time there were, if not radically dissenting voices, at least voices speaking from different perspectives. In addition to Ivan Peresvetov, discussed below, these included the monk Artemii, former head of the Holy Trinity–Saint Sergius monastery, the most powerful monastic foundation in Russia. Artemii found it necessary to write a letter to Ivan IV denying that he had suggested that Ivan should take away monastic lands. Accused of holding unspecified "Lutheran schismatic views," he was excommunicated by a church council in 1554. Ermolai Erasm, a clerical writer, wrote with sympathy of the plight of the peasantry and criticized the abuses of the powerful, a stance not infrequently met in other Muscovite sources of the time. In more radical terms, Matvei Bashkin, a minor nobleman, questioned the institution of slavery. Feodosii Kosoi was even more radical, apparently condemning all social inequality and all political authority. Kosoi and Bashkin were arrested for heresy—and in Kosoi's case, accused of rejecting the authority of the church. But these divergent voices did not reach many listeners. And the heresy trials, of Kosoi, Bashkin and others, effectively eliminated the diversity of voices that had existed in Muscovy for a century.

The Time of Troubles and Its Aftermath: 1580–1645

Ivan the Terrible left Russia in a condition far worse than the one he had inherited. Years of exhausting wars in the Baltic and the depredations of his *oprichniki* thugs yielded little except economic collapse and political confusion. He was succeeded by his feeble-minded son Fedor, but the real power was quickly seized by Boris Godunov, Fedor's brother-in-law. Godunov was able to consolidate his power during several struggles with rival aristocratic clans.

When Fedor died in 1598, Godunov was elected tsar by an Assembly of the Land. In terms of ideology, the moment was important: The lack of a legitimate heir was unprecedented in the history of the Riurikovich dynasty. Godunov's legitimacy had to be created rather than assumed through inheritance. His death in 1605 ushered in a disastrous period of civil wars and foreign invasions. Eventually, at the end of 1612, a militia governed by an assembly of representatives from various towns drove out the Polish invaders who had occupied Moscow in 1610. And, after intense internal debate, a new Assembly of the Land elected Michael Romanov as tsar in 1613.

The new government's fragility and poverty forced it to rely on a series of Assemblies of the Land to generate support for itself and for extraordinary taxes. Michael Romanov was apparently chosen for his youth and pliability, but the return in 1619 of his father Filaret, the powerful former head of the Romanov clan and now patriarch, placed effective power in the hands of the father-patriarch rather than of the son-tsar. Assemblies of the Land were seldom called while Filaret was alive, but met sporadically later in the century. Filaret died in 1631, and his son fourteen years later.

These tumultuous events caused Russians to think intensely about political matters. Yet, despite the presence in Moscow of foreigners and foreign ideas on many subjects, the results of their thinking were conservative: a determination to return as closely as possible to the state of things, religious and political, before the Troubles began.

Although the militias that ultimately liberated Russia from the Poles operated under a representative assembly in the name of "the land" (a term that denoted Russia in the absence of a monarch), Russians raced to reestablish the monarchy; Assemblies of the Land continued to meet until the early 1680s. This defense of the imagined sacred kingdom of the sixteenth century is perhaps the best available evidence of the success of Metropolitan Makarii and his predecessors and successors in creating and promoting precisely this image of an Old Testament–style kingdom, where political reverses were explained by the sins of both the people and their rulers.

The sources of political thought during this period fall into several categories. First, Boris Godunov, his relatives, and his government officials proved to be excellent royal image makers. Though far less active on the literary plane than Makarii, Boris provided murals for the Hall of Facets, Moscow's other main throne room, still undecorated by the 1580s. He also sponsored an impressive amount of building, including fortresses and walls in locations all over Muscovy, many new churches (signs, visible to all, of the new ruler's piety), and a massive but largely unrealized scheme to rebuild Cathedral Square in the Kremlin.[10] During and after the Troubles, a large number of writers, laymen as well as clerics, aristocrats as well as bureaucrats, took up their pens to write about the disasters that befell Russia after Godunov's death. Some of this writing, the first of its kind in Russian history, was avowedly publicistic, and was pressed into use by one faction or another during the Troubles. Other texts were more private. The most thoughtful account of the Troubles is the *Vremennik* of Ivan Timofeev, some 312 manuscript folios in length. Yet it exists in only a single copy, which seems to come from a single earlier copy. So this highly innovative text was probably never seen by more than a handful of readers and never became part of ongoing thought about politics in Russia.

Ferment and Innovation, 1645–1700

For many reasons, the second half of the seventeenth century saw the breakup of the set of ideas that had previously held Muscovy together. First, learned clerics from Ukraine and Belarus began in the 1640s to come to Moscow. The Muscovite government's political acquisition of Ukraine in 1654 accelerated this process. Trained in some of the best academies and schools in Eastern Europe, over time these newcomers transformed the intellectual landscape in Russia and the methods used to discuss political ideas. They were soon joined by immigrants and visitors from Greece and other Orthodox communities around the Mediterranean.

At the same time a series of dramatic confrontations erupted within the church, and between the church and the realm. The chief polarizing figure here was Patriarch Nikon. Like many other churchmen at mid-century, Nikon had been anxious for reform, of church books and of the church's discipline and morals. Nikon and the young Tsar Alexis Mikhailovich agreed that the church needed an intellectual rebirth, and that this should come chiefly by bringing the Russian church more closely into contact with the rest of the Orthodox *ecumene*. This agenda was viewed with suspicion by another equally zealous group of reformers, largely drawn from the white or parish clergy and led by the Archpriests Avvakum and Ivan Neronov. Believing that Muscovy was indeed the last righteous kingdom, they felt that to imitate foreigners would lead to error and sin, and that the chief sources of religious truth should be sought in Russia's own past. The tsar's support for Nikon led to his appointment as patriarch in 1652.

Thus the stage was set for two historic contests, both involving Nikon and both generating an outpouring of political thought. As Nikon proceeded to publish new versions of liturgical texts based on Greek liturgical practice and on printed texts (many of them from Italy), he alienated the conservative party, some of whom, led by Avvakum, refused to accept the new changes. Hence the Old Believer schism. The number of people labeled by the government as Old Believers grew throughout the century, and soon approached one-fifth of the population. Recent research has convincingly shown that many so labeled in fact cared little or nothing about arcane religious matters, but simply opposed the political authority for any number of reasons, from those of mere brigands to those of monks trying to preserve their monasteries' independence from the growing bureaucratic reach of Nikon's church.[11] Traditional Muscovite ideology gave all such people a justification for resisting the government: If the tsar and his patriarch were in fact destroying the purity of the Orthodox faith and importing foreign errors, then the government had lost its legitimacy, and resistance was justified. Avvakum was exiled to Siberia, condemned by a church council in 1666, and finally executed in 1681. In 1685, the government decreed that unrepentant Old Believers should be burned at the stake.

Yet the same church council that condemned Avvakum also deposed Nikon—the result of a classic confrontation between church and realm, reminiscent of clashes in medieval Western Europe. Although in exile from 1658 onward, owing to tension with Alexis and the court, Nikon developed to an extreme the strain of political thought in Russia that gave the church independent authority over the tsar and his government. The controversy over the relationship between church and realm, which generated many texts, gravely weakened the former at the very time when its strength was being sapped by the exodus of adherents to old rituals and other dissenters.

At the same time that Nikon was pushing for a more robust and independent role for the church, bureaucrats in the rapidly growing government apparatus were developing an image of the tsar and his government based on impersonal procedures and bureaucratic routines very different from the personalized government envisioned by the dominant ideology that had held sway up to that point. This new vision of government was enshrined in the famous law code (*Ulozhenie*) enacted in 1649 by an Assembly of the Land, one of whose major achievements was the codification of serfdom.

All of these changes served to undermine a set of political ideas that seemed to have been generally held at least from the end of the fifteenth century. In the remaining years of the century, under the intellectual leadership of learned Ukrainians and Belarusians, new ideas appeared in Russia, but did not result in the creation of a Western-style discourse on political thought—a complex phenomenon that did not emerge until the reign of Catherine the Great, if then.

Religion as the Foundation of Russian Political Thought

The Ruler as God's Representative on Earth

The basis of all early modern Russian political thought was that the ruler, tsar or grand prince, was God's viceroy on earth, or even the image (or icon) of God on earth. The ruler's commandments were believed to reflect the will of God. This sentiment is found everywhere—even foreign observers routinely attributed it to all classes of Russians. Perhaps the most important statement of this point came in the coronation ceremony of Ivan IV in 1547. At the climax of the service, Metropolitan Makarii intoned the following prayer, based on good Byzantine precedent—the lesson of Basil of Macedonia for his son.[12]

> King of Kings and Lord of Lords, Who by Samuel the Prophet didst choose thy servant David and anoint him to be tsar over Thy people, Israel . . . look down from Thy sanctuary upon Thy faithful servant Great Prince Ivan Vasilievich whom Thou hast deigned to raise up as tsar over Thy people [*v iazytse tvoem*], whom Thou hast redeemed by the precious blood of Thine only-begotten son.[13]

Among several important political ideas expressed in this prayer, the most remarkable is that of political rule as a form of divine trust. God gave the kingdom to the ruler so long as the ruler obeyed God's will. Thus, God chose David as "tsar" over Israel.

While literate Russians were bombarded with this idea in texts of virtually all genres, the same theme was just as common and central to the experience of the illiterate majority. It was conveyed by numerous texts meant to be read aloud, by the placement of churches built under royal patronage that were visible over long distances in the Russian landscape, by royal titles stressing God's choice of the ruler, by pilgrimages that brought the piety of the ruler into the countryside, and in icons and mural programs, especially in the Kremlin.

The murals in the exclusive space of the Golden Hall offer the clearest example of this theme (see figures 9.3, 9.4, and 9.5 in chapter 9 of this volume). Both the vestibule and the throne room itself had an image of God at the very top of each vaulted ceiling, surrounded by more or less abstract political or theological subjects. On the walls were depicted historical events from ancient Israel (in the vestibule) and Rus' (in the throne room). Architecture and imagery worked powerfully together to show the divine basis of political power. Rulers—Old Testament "tsars" in the vestibule and Rus' princes in the throne room—were placed in squinches or pendentives that structurally and visually linked the curvilinear spaces above and their more abstract, theological themes with the rectilinear walls below, where God-chosen rulers guided their sacred kingdoms according to God's will. Thus the ruler images in both vestibule and throne room visually linked the divine world of the upper spaces with the day-to-day events of the history of Old Testament Israel and Rus'. God also appeared in a number of individual scenes directly guiding or helping rulers, both in battle and throughout the peacetime duties of rulership.[14]

Of course, conventional wisdom in all European countries linked the power of the ruler to the will of God. But Muscovite political thought remained

God-dependent in a very real sense, since the divinity was imagined to play a crucial and continuing role in Russian politics. Although Russian thinkers were ignorant of the concept of "sovereignty" as a term in formal political discourse, if we were to ask who was sovereign in the Russian state, the only correct answer from any abstract or theoretical point of view would be that God Himself was sovereign.[15]

The Duties of the Ruler

Metropolitan Makarii's prayer at Ivan IV's coronation does not imply that Ivan could treat the kingdom as he wished, or that Muscovy was his property. On the contrary, Russia, like ancient Israel in the Old Testament, was imagined in the ceremony to be ruled literally by God's will, as reflected in that of the tsar. The reference to Samuel reveals the conditional nature of God's trust. As the story of Saul shows (1 Sam. 15), God could and did reject rulers who failed to please Him—a point surely not lost on many of those present, especially the learned prelates who composed the service and may well have seen themselves as playing Samuel's role.

Given this strong Old Testament resonance, it is not surprising to find that many of the ruler's duties centered on religion. Perhaps the most important of these religious duties was to preserve his own piety, for piety alone could connect him with God and, thus, his commands with God's will. Accordingly, Fedor Ivanovich, Ivan the Terrible's mentally handicapped son, who ruled nominally from 1584 until his death in 1598, was described in very positive terms by all contemporary Russian sources. Although Boris Godunov exercised the real political power while Fedor spent most of his time in church, Russian writers ascribed much contemporary success, military as well as domestic, to Fedor's piety and to the power it gave him as intercessor for his kingdom before God. Patriarch Iov gave the clearest description of Fedor as an exemplary ruler:

> For this cross-bearing tsar was very pious, merciful to all, meek, gentle and compassionate [*krotok, nezlobiv i miloserd*]. He loved the humble and accepted suffering, and moreover was generous to widows and orphans, had mercy on all who grieved and helped those in misfortune. . . . He conquered all the neighboring countries of unbelieving nations that rebelled against the pious Christian faith and his God-preserved royal kingdom—not with military troops or with the sharpness of a sword but with the all-night vigil and ceaseless prayers to God did he finally conquer them.[16]

Royal wives were also given a crucial role as intercessors for the realm, as Isolde Thyret has effectively shown.[17]

Although the portraits of Fedor are the most striking example of the importance of the personal piety of a ruler, piety was an essential ingredient in all positive literary portraits of Russian rulers. The same emphasis appears in royal titulature, which, throughout our period, always included one or more words for "pious" (*blagovernyi, blagochestivyi*). The murals in the Golden Hall placed a similar emphasis on the ruler's piety, also stressing the importance of his moral choice between good and evil.[18]

If personal piety was such a weighty part of the ruler's duties, then demonstrating it became an important royal task. This task could be accomplished in several ways. One such way was public ritual, either in the capital—for instance, the Palm Sunday and Epiphany rituals, which brought the ruler out to the general public in a conspicuously pious context—or on pilgrimages, which made the piety of rulers visible in the provinces.[19] Or, like Boris Godunov, the ruler could display his piety by constructing churches throughout his realm and thereby portray himself as a new Solomon.[20]

The ruler had two other main obligations: to preserve the doctrinal purity and the institutional strength of the Orthodox Church and to maintain the social and political order of the realm. Though not as frequent as the comments on personal piety, protection of the church was a commonplace theme in literary descriptions of admired rulers. The idea of the tsar leading the Russian people to salvation is strikingly expressed in this comment on Tsar Vasilii Shuiskii— one of the rulers who reigned briefly during the Time of Troubles—from one of his apologists: "And now he observes the true Orthodox faith ... and corrects us, and sets each [of us] and the path of salvation so that after his departure, all would be inheritors of the paradise of life; he does not lead us into evil but [into] goodness, and, again I say, turns us from the path of perdition."[21]

It was when rulers failed to protect the church that this obligation was most clearly expressed. Most authors of texts about the Time of Troubles felt that the so-called First Pretender, a person of uncertain origin who claimed to be the youngest son of Ivan IV and ruled Moscow for about a year in 1605–1606, intended to convert Russia to Roman Catholicism. This intention, together with grave doubts surrounding his actual identity, moved writers to call him not a tsar, but a "tormentor" (*muchitel'*, the Slavic translation for the Greek *tyrannos*).[22] Like most of the Muscovite political vocabulary, this image of a ruler as a tyrant or tormentor was derived from Byzantium. Even Joseph of Volokolamsk, who is often seen (quite rightly) as an extravagant apologist for royal power, warned his readers early in the sixteenth century against such a ruler: "Such a tsar is not a servant of God but a devil, not a tsar but a tormentor. Our

Lord Jesus Christ did not call such a person a tsar but a fox; you should not heed such a person who leads you into dishonor and cunning."[23]

In the seventeenth century the Old Believers, convinced that the liturgical and other changes introduced by Patriarch Nikon and supported by Tsar Alexis Mikhailovich were destroying Orthodoxy, withdrew their allegiance from tsar and patriarch alike. In his petitions to the tsar, Avvakum compared Nikon to Julian the Apostate, Alexis to David and King Uzziah, and himself to Nathan and Azariah.[24]

The ruler's other, third, obligation was less contentious, but nonetheless important: to preserve the social and political order of the realm. Texts throughout most of our period are almost unanimous in implying that the role of the monarch was to conserve the God-given social order, and not to change society in any radical way. All of the authors from the early seventeenth century who wrote about Ivan IV's *oprichnina*, for example, condemned it as a gross violation of the natural order of society. Timofeev reported that Ivan "divided one people into two separate halves, creating as it were two faiths." He added that God would have permitted Ivan's murder.[25] Ivan was likewise condemned by more secular writers after 1650.

Rulers also had a fourth obligation, discussed below—the obligation to consult with pious wise advisers, who could correct erring monarchs. If this mechanism failed and the ruler was perceived to have violated God's law, then the language inherited from Byzantium could come into play and not only permit but require resistance. During the Time of Troubles, such rulers were overthrown. Otherwise they were not, though many Old Believers deserted the monarchy in large numbers during the late seventeenth and eighteenth centuries. The problem lay with the binary nature of Russian political thought. Like their counterparts in early medieval Western Europe and Byzantium, Russian thinkers had not worked out an answer to the problem of what to do with a bad king. There was no enforcement mechanism beyond advisers and the church to restrain a ruler from his evil ways. Worse, if a ruler were to be seen as a tormentor or anti-tsar and overthrown, there was no way to replace him with another ruler. This absence of a replacement mechanism made the political cost of declaring a given ruler to be a tormentor very high, as the civil wars of the Time of Troubles all too clearly illustrated. The image of a ruler as tormentor thus remained a potent source of instability.

The Tsar's "Slaves" and the Problem of Advice

The relationship of ruler and subject was one to which Russians devoted much thought. Several contemporary scholars agree with the judgment of Western

European visitors to Russia during our period, to the effect that the tsar's control over his subjects was unlimited both in theory and in fact.[26] There is considerable evidence for this view. The Russian word for "subject"—*poddannyi*, an abstract legal term—did not exist in the vocabulary of literate Muscovites until the latter part of the seventeenth century. The words commonly used to denote a person subjected to the ruler were *rab* (servant, or slave), or *kholop* (slave, or bondsman). Both words imply a relationship in which the ruler and his agents commanded and the "slaves" obeyed. (Scholars have recently explored the subtle meanings of these terms; to be the "slave" of the ruler elevated one's status in society by establishing a prestigious vertical link to the ruler himself.)[27]

Ivan Timofeev, pondering the causes of the Troubles, looked back to a golden age when "our own autocrats . . . kept the commandments given by God" and the people obeyed them "like voiceless fish." He continued: "When the years came to an end [i.e., in 1492], the more our rulers changed the old blessed lawful regulations [*blagoustavleniia zakonnaia*] passed on by our fathers, and changed the good customs into new opposing customs, the more in their obeying servants the natural fear of obedience to a master began to diminish."[28]

Western Europeans might reflect nostalgically on a golden age of ancient liberties. By contrast, for Timofeev at least, the golden age was a period when subjects followed the ruler like voiceless fish, or, as he also said, like animals being led to the slaughter. In Timofeev's view, as in the view of most Russian theorists, the people were sinful: They needed the strong hand of the monarch to restrain them from evil.

Yet the relationship is more complex than one of commanding rulers and obedient slaves. Almost all Russian thinkers believed that the monarch had certain obligations: Terms existed to describe rulers who persistently failed to carry out these obligations, and most thinkers recognized the duty to resist such "tsar-tormentors." One way of correcting an erring or sinful monarch was through wise advisers. In every kind of literary source—chronicles, sermons, lives of saints or saintly princes, virtually from the time of the conversion of Rus' to Christianity—rulers were depicted as consulting their retinues or advisers. In our period, these earlier literary depictions were supplemented by visual evidence. Royal advisers figure in a variety of medieval and early modern texts, and in such visual sources as the late fifteenth-century miniatures of the Radziwill Chronicle, produced in the late fifteenth century; the carvings on the Tsar's Pew in the Dormition Cathedral, executed in the 1550s; and the *Book of Tsardom* (*tsarstvennaia kniga*), executed about twenty years later.²⁹ In the two main throne rooms of Russia, the Golden Hall (painted in the 1550s, we think) and the Hall of Facets (painted in the 1590s), rulers, whether from the Old Testament, Byzantine history, or Rus´ history, or simply as generic images, such as in the seven moralizing scenes in the vestibule of the Golden Hall, were almost always depicted in the company of advisers as they acted and made decisions. In throne-room ceremonies, foreign ambassadors were presented to the ruler together with his chief courtiers, who sat on ledges raised two steps above the central space of the throne rooms where the ambassadors were placed. In all media, then, the ruler appeared with his chief courtiers, as part of a group, and not as a solitary figure.

The question of advice was approached from two angles: the duty of the ruler to consult with wise advisers, and the duty of the righteous subjects to give good advice. In literary texts, policies condemned by a given author were often ascribed to evil advisers, inspired by the devil. Conversely, virtuous rulers were depicted as being surrounded by wise advisers, and consulting them on important decisions. Those who wrote about the Time of Troubles were preoccupied with the issue of advice—predictably enough, when the theoretically perfect political system failed. The disasters of the time were persistently blamed on the influence of evil or foolish advisers.³⁰ But much earlier texts, from more settled times, emphasized the same theme. The late fifteenth-century *Orison on the Life and Death of Grand Prince Dmitrii Ivanovich* opens with a description of Dmitrii's childhood, when he "shunned evil people, and consorted always with honorable people." When the Tatar ruler Mamai attacked Dmitrii's forces, he was advised to do so "by evil counselors who were of the Christian faith, but who acted as pagans."³¹ Wise advisers were seen as a remedy for the problem of a bad king, since wise advice could restore the spiritual health of the ruler, and thus reconnect him with God's will.

Who were these wise advisers? Here the evidence points to contrary conclusions. The general assumption seems to have been that the ruler's chief courtiers would perform this duty. This assumption was based on the desirability of maintaining the social hierarchy, so that the important function of advising the ruler would naturally fall on those at its highest levels. And indeed, in the visual representations of the ruler with his advisers, the latter are often labeled "boyars" or "grandees." Nevertheless, the function of giving advice never gained the constitutional overtones that it acquired in the medieval West. As this function was primarily spiritual, the chief qualification for performing it was moral and spiritual authority rather than political position. In texts of all periods, the distinction lay between good and evil advisers, not between members and nonmembers of a particular institution. In Russia, there were in fact two institutions whose function was to advise the ruler: the Boyar

Duma, which existed from the beginning of our period, and the Assembly of the Land. This latter institution started meeting in the middle of the sixteenth century, voted on the election of tsars on a regular basis, including the election of Michael Romanov in 1613, played a very large role in governing the country from that election to about 1619, and then was called to discuss and approve the great law code (*Ulozhenie*) of 1649 and continued meeting until the early 1680s. Further, from 1610 to 1613, when there was no effective Russian ruler, representative assemblies financed and ran the military campaign to drive the Poles away from Moscow and governed the territories thereby controlled. Thus advice-giving institutions played a major role *in practical politics* throughout our period. Yet the connection between these institutions and the function of advice getting *in political thought* seems to have been weak at best.

The literature about Assemblies of the Land is very large, and debate shrouds everything in it, from the number and dates of meetings to the criteria by which a gathering could be properly designated as such. Recent research has demonstrated that an Assembly of the Land required the presence of the Boyar Duma, the Holy Synod, and representatives of the lower service or landholding classes, sometimes augmented by representatives from Moscow and other towns. It appears that this institution had its origins in the steppe *quriltai* and functioned to choose tsars, depose tsars, and provide advice on important matters. It did not exercise a legislative function, nor was its approval required for taxation. Instead, "the Assemblies of the Land brought to the attention of the upper ruling class the opinions of members of the lower ruling class," as well as of some urban representatives. As circumstances permitted, delegates were either selected by local government officials or simply drafted from among military servitors and townsmen who happened to be present in Moscow at the time.[32]

Important as they were in lending legitimacy to the choice of a ruler or to a new law code, Assemblies of the Land played almost no role in native Russian political thought. One looks in vain for some theoretical explanation of this institution, even in the preamble of the 1649 *Ulozhenie*. This absence may well have been dictated by the origin of the institution in the steppe or by the nature of prevailing political thought, in which legitimate power was seen as flowing downward through the ruler to the people, and not upward from the people, seen as sinful. The need to seek advice was never understood as a Western-style constraint on the power of the monarch.

The experience of the Troubles furnished another corollary to this theme—namely, the duty of subjects to advise the ruler if his policies were against the will of God. Avraamii Palitsyn famously attributed the disasters of the Time of Troubles to "the foolish silence [*bezumnoe molchanie*] of the whole community, when no one dared to speak the truth to the tsar about the destruction of the guiltless ones [i.e., members of the Romanov clan and others falsely accused by Boris Godunov]." Similar passages about the benefits of good advice or the harm caused by silence can be found in many other texts about the Troubles. However, the function of advice giving was assigned not to constitutional institutions but to subjects acting like Old Testament prophets correcting sinful rulers.[33]

Church and Realm

An obvious source of such prophet-like figures was the Russian Orthodox Church. Many commentators have noted the Russian Church's lack of political power when compared with the medieval papacy. There is much evidence for this view. Especially in the sixteenth century, rulers deposed church leaders with alarming frequency. In spite of its great landed wealth, it is obvious that the Russian Church lacked the independent geographical, financial, and political base that underpinned medieval papal power. And yet, heads of the church were remarkably powerful figures throughout our period. Metropolitan Makarii was a prolific political thinker and an influential royal adviser. Iov became the first Russian patriarch in 1589, making the Russian autocephalous church the equal of the patriarchates of Antioch, Alexandria, and Jerusalem, and enhancing the status both of the Muscovite church and of the Muscovite realm. Patriarch Germogen inspired the national revival that eventually led to the expulsion of the Poles from Moscow and the reestablishment of the Russian monarchy. Patriarch Filaret, on his return from Polish exile in 1619, rapidly took real control of the government, and even styled himself "Great Lord" (*Velikii Gosudar'*), a term previously reserved for the tsar alone. The precedent of Filaret's high standing was exploited by Patriarch Nikon, who developed theories about the superiority of the ecclesiastical power to the royal. Nikon overplayed his hand, but even after his deposition in 1666, the patriarchs remained formidable figures, until Peter the Great abolished the office of Patriarch altogether.

When we turn to texts concerning political thought, which were written overwhelmingly by churchmen, we find that the ideal was in the concept of harmony (*symphonia*) inherited from Byzantium. As in Byzantium, the concept entailed much tugging and pulling, but some balance of power between church and realm was largely maintained until the reign of Peter the Great. In the fifteenth and sixteenth centuries, issues of church power relative to the realm occurred most often in connection with two specific matters: the duty of the realm to punish heretics, and the defense of church property against royal limitations or even confiscations. In 1490, Archbishop Gennadii of Novgorod urged Grand Prince Ivan III to persecute heretics by approvingly citing the example of Spain's Inquisition. Joseph of Volokolamsk, advocate of a strong princely role in church matters, argued that princes had a solemn duty to hand over heretics for judgment by a church council and then to punish those found guilty. In a letter from the early part of the reign of Ivan IV, the priest Syl'vestr, or someone connected with him, wrote a fiery letter of advice to Ivan IV urging him to punish sinners, especially sodomites. If Ivan rooted out sin—and the suggested tortures are clearly described—then not only would he be saved, seemingly by this one act alone, but "by God's grace . . . all your enemies will fall beneath your feet and will be unable to rise."[34] Far from limiting the power of the tsar on earth, such sources affirm that great power and harsh punishment are needed to root out sinful behavior. But such power is always a means and never an end; for the end is nothing less than the salvation of the Russian people, given to the ruler by God.

While the question of heresy led to arguments for strong government, discussions of church property prompted writers to limit the ruler's power. On the issue of church land, Metropolitan Makarii himself wrote in defense of the church's position, quoting for the purpose a number of authorities, including the Donation of Constantine. According to Makarii, "Since the priesthood and the power and the glory of Christian piety were established by the Heavenly Tsar, it is unrighteous for an earthly tsar to rule over [the church]." He concludes by warning Ivan directly: "Even if I am constrained by the tsar himself and by his grandees, if they order me to do something contrary to divine rules, I will not obey them—even if they threaten me with death, I will not obey them in any way."[35] Metropolitan Daniel made similar statements earlier in the century. Yet this opinion was not universally held. A mid-sixteenth-century text connected to those who opposed church landholding and titled *The Conversation of the Miracle-Workers of Valaam* argued against the participation of churchmen in government and suggested that the ruler should not grant land to monasteries but should give them a yearly stipend, lest churchmen have civil jurisdiction over laymen, allegedly an abnegation of duty on the part of the tsar.

A real-life case of a metropolitan who lost his life for giving wise advice to a monarch is that of Metropolitan Filipp. Various sources record how he upbraided Ivan IV on several occasions for the excesses of the *oprichnina*, in terms strikingly similar to those used by the authors of texts about the Time of Troubles. Although Ivan did not agree with Filipp's judgments on his rule, he did guarantee the metropolitan's right to give advice, as had been done under his father and grandfather. The disagreement came to a dramatic head when, in the Dormition Cathedral itself, Filipp refused to bless Ivan, accusing him of spilling the blood of innocent Christians. According to the *Life of Metropolitan Filipp*, a text whose two redactions date, respectively, from the end of the sixteenth and the beginning of the seventeenth centuries, Filipp pronounced the tsar to be a mortal like any other man and equally subject to Christ's judgment. In November of 1567, Filipp was condemned and dethroned by a church council; a year later he was hauled out of church while officiating, and afterward murdered in his cell by one of Ivan's henchmen.

A more robust and radical assertion of church power was mounted by Patriarch Nikon a little less than a century later. Even before accepting the patriarchate, he declared before boyars and tsar, in the Dormition Cathedral, that he would take it only if the tsar and his assembled court vowed "to keep Christ's evangelical dogmas and the rules of the holy apostles and of the holy fathers and the laws of the pious [Byzantine] emperors intact . . . [and] if you also promise sincerely to obey us, as your superior and pastor and most esteemed father, in all that I shall make known to you of God's dogmas and of the laws."[36] After his elevation, he continued vigorously to defend the power of the church, and revived, from the time of Patriarch Filaret, the custom of the patriarch's use of the title Great Lord. Through his influence over the tsar, Nikon was able to prevent implementation of certain provisions of the *Ulozhenie* that limited the church's property rights. His statement that the *Ulozhenie* was "newly written, foreign to Orthodoxy and to the holy apostles and to the canon laws of the holy fathers and to the civil laws of the Orthodox Greek emperors," seems to imply that the law code, which was compiled through the efforts of an Assembly of the Land that included both the Boyar Duma and the Holy Synod, and was approved by the tsar, did not have to be obeyed unless it agreed with the authorities he vaguely cited. He thus challenged the legislative authority of the tsar and the Assembly of the Land. When Semen Streshnev, an important boyar, objected that Nikon derived from the tsar his power as patriarch, Nikon replied: "Hast thou not learned . . . that the highest authority of the priesthood is not received from tsars, but, contrariwise, it is by the priesthood that rulers are anointed to the empire? Therefore it is abundantly plain that priesthood is a very much greater thing than royalty."[37]

In due course a special synod of the Russian Church, convened by the tsar and supplemented by the patriarchs of Antioch and Alexandria and other prelates from abroad, solemnly condemned Nikon's assertion of the supremacy of church over realm. Nevertheless, the council kept in place Nikon's liturgical reforms, condemned Avvakum, the chief spokesman for the Old Believers, and reaffirmed the surprising principle that canon law had greater authority than either the secular law or the will of the tsar. This uneasy compromise lasted until the time of Peter the Great, who abolished the patriarchate altogether and turned the church into a branch of civil government.

Muslims, the Apocalypse, and Moscow As a Universal Monarchy

The idea of the realm as a vehicle for spiritual as well as economic or political salvation developed with particular richness in Muscovy, and accentuated the Muscovites' acute sense of the immediate and direct presence of the divine in terrestrial government and affairs. Two parallel developments in political thought at the outset of our period strengthened the role that Muscovy was thought to play in sacred history. The first was a change in the church's attitude toward neighboring Muslim steppe dwellers; the second, a growing awareness of the approaching Apocalypse.

For many centuries, since their emergence as a separate ethnic group, East Slavs (the common ancestors of Great Russians, Ukrainians, and Belarusians) had lived in close proximity to steppe nomads. The Mongol conquest brought the two groups closer together, although it also exacerbated tension between them. Scholarship has shown that Russian literary sources contain remarkably little anti-Muslim orientation until the middle of the fifteenth century, when texts with a strong anti-Tatar and anti-Muslim bias began to appear. Texts describing the so-called Stand on the Ugra by the troops of Ivan III transformed this apparently ordinary event into one of worldwide importance, in which, with God's help and in line with Israel's struggle against its Old Testament neighbors, the Christian forces of Rus' defeated the evil Tatars.[38]

A pervasive sense of the impending Apocalypse increased awareness of the Muscovite kingdom as a vehicle of salvation. This awareness took two forms: a predictive expectation of an impending end before 1492, the close of the seventh and final millennium, according to the Orthodox calendar; and a more optimistic, nonpredictive view that the exact date of the "end times" could not be known in advance. On this latter view, Russians, rather than concentrating on the cataclysm itself, imagined Moscow as a New Jerusalem, with the tsar or grand prince at its head, a sacred kingdom that would serve as the vessel for the salvation of the just in the eighth millennium preceding the End. While elite Muscovites were increasingly involved in this current of thought, as relevant texts, icons, and other information about the "Last Days" multiplied from the late fourteenth through to the late fifteenth centuries, linguistic and folkloric evidence discloses that their concern was shared by the common people.[39]

A new, optimistic vision was dramatically proclaimed by Metropolitan Zosima in paschal tables for the new millennium, which began on September 1,

1492. The text announced: "THE EIGHT MILLENNIUM IN WHICH WE EXPECT THE UNIVERSAL COMING OF CHRIST." Zosima writes that, since "we have reached the brink [*krai*] of seven thousand years," a new beginning is necessary at the end of the old order. He notes a succession of three rulers: the Emperor Constantine, who created the Christian Empire and the new city of Constantinople; Saint Vladimir (the Christianizer of Rus´), whom "the Lord chose for Himself from among the idolaters"; and Ivan III, whom Zosima calls "the new Emperor Constantine for the new city of Constantine, Moscow, and of all the Rus´ land, and many other lands."[40] This is the context of the unjustly famous "doctrine" of Moscow the "Third Rome," an idea responsible, in many people's minds, for Russian government expansionism in this period and later. In his *Letter against Astrologers*, the monk Filofei of Pskov argued, in the 1520s, that "all the Christian tsardoms have come to an end and gathered into one tsardom of our great lord, and this is the Roman [later reading: Russian] tsardom: for two Romes have fallen, a third stands, and a fourth will not be." Thus in this text, and in others often cited as examples of this "theory," the "Third Rome" was the Rus´ land or Rus´ tsardom, in many cases with its spiritual capital at Novgorod, not Moscow. The phrase "Moscow the Third Rome," first found in an inscription to a 1594 psalter, was never used to promote the expansion of Russian territory.[41] (Further, this idea is found only in a small number of manuscripts written before the 1590s, and was therefore not well known in Russia until the establishment of a Russian patriarchate in 1589.) Instead, the Third Rome theme was a subset of the belief that Rus´ was now the last remaining Orthodox kingdom, whose ruler had therefore a special responsibility to preserve the health and doctrinal purity of the Orthodox Church in Russia. Filofei's concluding phrase, "a fourth [Rome] will not be," invoked the coming Apocalypse.

A similar message is conveyed by an icon painted in the 1550s, named in an early seventeenth-century inventory as *Blessed Is the Host of the Heavenly Tsar*, but known in modern times as *The Church Militant* (see figure 6.1 in chapter 6 of this volume). Created to celebrate the victory of Ivan IV over the Tatar Khanate of Kazan´ in 1552, the icon shows three ranks of soldiers returning from a burning city, Kazan´, on the viewer's right, to Moscow, on the left, identified iconographically as the New Jerusalem, where the infant Christ, seated on the lap of the Mother of God, gives martyrs' crowns to those who fell in battle. Although the many figures in the icon are not labeled, the Archangel Michael leading the host is recognizable, a clear reference to the Apocalypse of Daniel. A similar icon from the end of the century, in which the figures are labeled, suggests that the upper row of troops was meant to include "tsars" David and Solomon, the Emperor Constantine, and Saint Vladimir, among other sacred rulers. Ivan IV himself is probably in the middle rank. The iconography and related texts make it clear that the army depicted on the icon represents, at once, the Muscovite army in the sixteenth-century present, the army of ancient Israel, and the army of God at the Apocalypse. In this case, of course, the theme of a sacred war against Muslim infidels has been added to the picture, and is thereby given a cosmic significance.[42]

This consciousness of the end times, expressed through a wide variety of media capable of reaching all levels of the population, lasted until the end of our period. The disasters of the Time of Troubles exacerbated it, since the God-established Muscovite monarchy seemed at various points to be on the brink of extinction. The thought of the Old Believers was similarly saturated with apocalyptic expectations. Believing that Nikon's liturgical changes had destroyed Orthodoxy, they concluded that tsar and government were the instruments of the Antichrist instead of being divinely appointed vessels of salvation.

The perception of a divine mission for the Muscovite realm, one crucial to salvation history, amplified the Muscovites' sense of God's direct and frequent intervention in Muscovite affairs—a parallel to His intervention in the affairs of ancient Israel in the Old Testament. This sense was reinforced by the idea of the ruler as an icon of God, an idea that implied the presence of God in the person of the ruler. These distinctive features of Muscovite political thought, added to the absence in Muscovy of the analytical tools provided by humanism, by European legal culture, or even by Scholasticism, gave Muscovite ideas of divine right a more literal, direct tone than conventional ideas of divine right had in Western Europe.

The Law and Political Thought in Muscovy

Muscovy had a surprisingly robust legal culture, and many groups of the population participated energetically in legal proceedings. Nevertheless, the law was seldom seen as restraining the monarch and did not usually need to dampen the effects of religious strife, as it often did in the West. All texts agreed on the ruler's obligation to provide effective and uncorrupt justice to his people. In literary texts, however, references to the law were often vague, based on biblical uses of the term, often meaning "God's law" or even "Christianity." Thus, such terms as "lawbreaker," "unlawful," and "according to the law" were used in general contexts where it is very difficult to tell which specific law, if any, was meant.

Administrative or legal texts perforce dealt with actual laws, but these laws were seldom discussed in literary works. A major reason for this absence was the linguistic and social separation between churchmen, the usual authors of literary texts and of canon law texts in the literary language of Church Slavic, and chancellery officials who compiled and enforced civil law codes written in a distinctive chancellery language.

As in the West, there were two types of law, each copied and interpreted by one of these two groups, though at the very beginning of our period churchmen, enjoying a virtual monopoly on literacy, controlled the texts of both types. Amid a variety of canon law texts, most of them deriving directly or indirectly from Byzantium, the most commonly cited was the *Kormchaia kniga* (*Book of the pilot*), a complex compendium of church canon, epistles, sermons, Byzantine secular legislation, and various legal sources from Rus′, such as the *Russkaia Pravda*. Similar compilations existed, as well as manuscript miscellanies. These heterogeneous texts were supplemented by the decisions of Muscovite church councils and interpreted by church courts staffed by clerics. In the absence of any institutions that could teach church law, however, it would be misleading to call such clerics canon lawyers.

Early princely statutes, such as the *Russkaia Pravda*, or "Russian justice," were essentially horizontal and dyadic. According to the law texts, plaintiff and defendant were merely required to meet in order to work out compensation, usually a fine, for injury. The rise of Muscovy and of the merchant republics of Novgorod and Pskov signaled a gradual change towards a triadic, vertical process, whereby the government, through its judicial officers, played a major role in the investigation and trial of defendants and then exacted punishment. Traces of this new system can be found in the earliest Muscovite legal charter, of 1397 to the Dvina Lands, and become much stronger in the law code (*Sudebnik*) of 1497 passed by Ivan III. Later law codes, of 1550 and 1649, greatly expanded the role of public authority and the number and power of these judicial officers.[43] Yet, outside these formal codes, legal proceedings involved negotiation and orderly participation by community members of virtually all ranks, a system reliant on ritual in a largely unlettered society and recently shown to have been remarkably effective.[44]

To what extent did the law and legal thinking, then, impinge on political thought? The answer must surely be: far less than in the West. Church law as found in the various collections had not been systematized and organized as had the work of generations of Western canon lawyers. Moreover, in Byzantium and Rus′, church law compendia contained few general statements of principle, but concentrated largely on procedure.

Nonetheless, Russia had a growing legal culture, and legal officials were increasingly active in government at all levels. Although there exist no explicit discussions of this issue dating from our period, the wording of the law codes leaves the impression that laws, beyond procedural questions, were considered to have been discovered rather than made. The preamble of the *Ulozhenie* of 1649, for example, stressed the process of surveying existing sources of the law: examination of "the canons of the holy apostles and holy fathers and the laws of Byzantine emperors in the *Prochieros Nomos* . . . [and] the decrees of former [rulers of Russia] and also boyar decisions on various state and civilian matters," and the search for "those laws . . . which were not inserted as a decree . . . [and] which were not [further enacted] as boyar decisions." As the preamble also states, the proposed law code was then compiled with the advice of the patriarch, metropolitans, archbishops, and bishops as well as members of the Boyar Duma, and read out to these officials with members of the Assembly of the Land, all of whom then signed a written version.[45] Thus in 1648–1649, the law was imagined as preexisting, although only parts of it had been written down in authoritative sources. The preamble also lists by name the groups who approved the new code, though without claiming that they had the power to make law. The list of legal sources consulted does not seem to differentiate between laws made as decrees by previous rulers and those strengthened through Duma approval. Grigorii Kotoshikhin, in his description of Russia written in 1666–1667, discusses the Duma as an integral part of government, but does not even mention the Assembly of the Land.[46] Thus representative institutions were denied the recognition often accorded them in the West.

The difference cannot be explained by Russian ignorance or lack of political imagination. Several incidents show that Russian thinkers were perfectly capable of envisaging institutional and/or legal restraints on the monarch. The most striking example occurred during the Time of Troubles in 1610, when a group of Russians led by Filaret/Fedor Romanov proposed constitutional limits on Władysław, the son of the Polish king, whom they invited to become tsar, provided he would agree to the conditions proposed and convert to Orthodoxy. The agreement stipulated that the Orthodox Church should not be harmed, that Władysław, having converted to Orthodoxy, should govern according to the *Sudebnik* of 1550, and that any changes from the norms specified in the *Sudebnik* be carried out only "at the discretion of the boyars and the entire land" (probably meaning the Assembly of the Land). It also stipulated that the monarch could punish offenders against the sovereign and the land only "after first holding a fair trial with the boyars and [other] Duma members." No landed property could be confiscated without a trial by the boyars, nor could a person's rank be lowered without trial.[47] Thus, when inviting a foreign prince to rule over them, these Russians were fully capable of setting constitutional limits on his rule—though no enforcement clause was added to deal with possible violations of the agreement.

The king of Poland ended the negotiations by arresting the Russian envoys, and this agreement never took effect. Even so, it may seem curious that, in offering the throne to Michael Romanov, the Assembly of the Land did not try to impose similar conditions.[48] However, in 1613 the Russians were not just electing a ruler, but reestablishing the God-chosen *tsarstvo*, with all of its millennial and other religious implications. Institutionalized consultation would be superfluous for a tsar leading his people to salvation at the end of time. It is revealing that Russian literary texts about the selection of Michael Romanov say almost nothing about the complex political negotiations that in fact took place before the final choice. Instead, the *Skazanie* of Avraamii Palitsyn, the most frequently copied text about the Troubles, argued that Michael had been chosen by God in his mother's womb.[49] In the sixteenth century, Russians looked down on a ruler who had come to power through an agreement or contract with his or her subjects—a creature of arrangements (*uriadnik*), as opposed to an unlimited lord (*gosudar'*).[50]

The ideology that pervaded the tales about the Time of Troubles continued to dominate political discourse. Gentry petitions throughout the first half of the seventeenth century appealed to the merciful tsar to redress their grievances, but to little avail. Matters came to a head in 1648, when the young Tsar Alexis was intercepted on his return from a hunting trip by a group of petitioners complaining about corrupt royal officials. Using traditional royal images, they termed themselves the "slaves and orphans" of a tsar regarded as fully legitimate and God-chosen. Yet as they enumerated the officials' abuses they clearly implied that, if these continued, God would send another Time of Troubles to punish Russia, and that the tsar would be responsible. When Alexis refused both to meet the petitioners and to accept their petitions, ten days of rioting broke out and the mob executed several major royal officials.[51]

This crisis led Alexis to summon a special Assembly of the Land. Its task was to debate and approve the last great Muscovite law code, the *Ulozhenie* of 1649. Huge by comparison with previous codes, it attached private peasants to the land forever, and thus codified serfdom. From the perspective of political thought, the *Ulozhenie* went far toward completing a revolution that had been long in the making. Traditional political thought, as we have seen, envisaged a personal monarchy where the monarch's decisions were above the law, reflecting God's will through his personal piety and righteousness. Gentry petitions from the first part of the seventeenth century show the importance of this sense of personal connection to the tsar. When bureaucratic procedures denied them such connection, the result was a sense of outrage. But a personal monarchy was no longer feasible. Muscovy had been growing at an extraordinarily rapid rate since the time of Ivan III. It now stretched into Siberia, virtually to the Pacific. At the same time, the military arm and the bureaucracy alike were expanding apace. The *Ulozhenie* codified what had gradually been happening in any case: Another long-held goal of Muscovite political thinkers, the duty of the monarch to provide justice, replaced the personal monarchy of traditional thought. The *Ulozhenie* rejected the wish of the gentry to have the tsar sit as the court of last resort; the boyars in council would serve this purpose. Individuals were specifically prohibited from presenting petitions directly to the tsar. Instead, detailed procedures were specified for dealing through the proper channels with every conceivable situation. The transition from the rule of a person to the rule of law, taken dramatically further by Peter the Great, was well under way after 1649. This goal is made clear in the preamble of the code: "So that for the people of all ranks, from the highest to the lowest rank, of the Muscovite realm, the law and justice will be equal for all in all cases."[52]

As the government and realm continued to grow, regularized procedures steadily replaced direct monarchical intervention, and thus had the effect of making the royal government, if not the ruler himself, subject to the law. On crucial matters, the tsar did not hesitate to intervene personally: Witness the affair of Patriarch Nikon. Meanwhile, gentry petitions gradually adapted themselves to the new order, requesting rather than rejecting investigations by the central authorities. Thus, slowly and hesitantly, new processes informed by a new political awareness and new ideas penetrated the provinces of Russia well in advance of Peter the Great.

The Realm as Dynastic Property?

In the 1547 coronation service, the young Ivan IV stated bluntly that the kingdom was his because his father had given it to him. Since genealogy was a crucial ingredient of noble identity, it was obvious that royal genealogy should occupy a central place in Russian political thought. The most important text stressing the dynastic origin of political power was *The Tale of the Vladimir Princes*, written early in the sixteenth century by an eminent churchman, Spiridon Savva. He strove to improve the status of the ruling dynasty by genealogically connecting Riurik, the eighth-century founder of the dynasty, with Prus, a fictional brother of Caesar Augustus, and by recounting the sending of sacred regalia (symbolizing God's favor) from Byzantium to the Rus′ian Grand Prince Vladimir Monomakh. Paralleling similar efforts to find impressive, if mythical, ancestors in the Ottoman Empire and in other parts of Europe, the argument was used in diplomacy with those countries, and variants of it figured in a wide range of domestic media, visual as well as literary.[53] The prestige of the royal dynasty was also stressed in royal titulature, and in chancery documents. Although the dynastic argument for the legitimacy of the regime was in theory a nonreligious one, an examination of the *Tale* itself and of its usage in other sources shows that dynastic and religious arguments were seen as complementary.[54]

The widespread presence of the dynastic theme has prompted the view that Russian rulers saw their kingdom as their own property, to do with as they pleased, regardless of legal restraints. Such a view challenges the existence of private property in Muscovite Russia. Its proponents often stress the unlimited power of the ruler and describe Russians as abjectly subservient, "a people born to slavery." Statements by early modern European observers and the use of the term *kholop* (slave) by even the highest nobles in petitions to the ruler are used to buttress this view. The example of a comment made during a fight in 1627 has often been cited: "Don't bother me. I am the great lord's man, and my beard is also the great lord's."[55]

However, recent research has demonstrated that, although Russian rulers had in theory the right to confiscate property, they rarely used this power and usually only in cases of treason. Further, the day-to-day practice of landholding indicated de facto private ownership.[56] In other words, private property rights in Muscovy were not as extensive as those granted by Roman law in the West, but were similar to concepts there deriving from feudal law (like that of "eminent domain"), which implied theoretical but seldom used ownership by the monarch.

A provocative essay attempts to reconcile these contradictory "hard" and "soft" views of realm-society relations through the concept of "subjecthood," or unfree citizenship. Surprisingly, Muscovites enjoyed many privileges of citizenship, including a right to political participation that was recognized and defended by both ruler and subject, and the right to be judged according to universal legal norms, as we have seen. What was missing from a comparative European point of view was the right to, or even enthusiasm for, personal freedom. Indeed, in a society where many obligations (particularly taxes) were collectively imposed and identity was framed in terms of belonging to various communities, the very adjective "free," expressed by the Russian word *vol'nyi*, had a negative connotation, similar to that of the English words "willful," or even "irresponsible." Political participation was also understood differently: Representative institutions, as we have seen, had less power than in the West, while alternative forms of political expression—supplication, petition, consultation, and riot—played a larger role. Political theory does not appear to have a single word to describe these seemingly contradictory characteristics.⁵⁷

Political Philosophy

Little formal political thought existed in Russia until the last half of the seventeenth century. There were several reasons for this: a lack of philosophical or analytical models in the Greek texts that were chosen for translation into Church Slavic; the absence of any educational institution that could train political philosophers or host visiting scholars; fear of foreign influences on the part of Russian Orthodox scholars; and a powerful ideology of rulership as a divine mission, which seemed to make philosophical speculation superfluous.

The works of the great fathers of the Eastern Orthodox Church were chiefly known through fragments, aphorisms, and sermons. Political thought was often conveyed in narrative mode, through saints' lives or chronicles. Pseudo-Aristotle's *Secret of Secrets* was known in a few manuscripts, and provided a mirror of princes for some readers.⁵⁸ Far more popular were the "Hortatory Chapters" of Deacon Agapetus, the sixth-century Byzantine writer and a major source for Russian political thought in the sixteenth and seventeenth centuries. His impact derived from his clear delineation of the central paradox of Muscovite political thought: the dual natures of the ruler, divine and human. Agapetus most famously expressed this duality in his twenty-first chapter: "Though an emperor in body be like all other, yet in power of his office he is like God, master of all men. For on earth, he has no peer. Therefore as God, be he never chafed or angry; as man, be he never proud. For though he be like God in face, yet for all that he is but dust, which thing teaches him to be equal to every man." Apart from offering a few moralistic phrases, however, Agapetus states the paradox without resolving it. Offering no systematic analysis of public authority, his work would scarcely have aided Muscovites in developing a rational grasp of political theory.⁵⁹

Another Greek philosophical idea strongly influential on Russian thought was the Orthodox theory of icons, itself derived from Neoplatonism. The concept that one thing, usually an image, could stand for, and embody, something else saturated the culture of the Orthodox Church and informed reasoning by analogy, so prevalent in historical and other texts and images. An icon of a saint was more than a picture; in important ways, the saint was believed to be present in it. The Byzantines believed that the emperor was "an icon of God in the political sphere." Although I have not seen this exact phrase in Russian sources, the grand prince or tsar seems to have been understood as an image, or analogue, of God. The inscription at the center of the main vault of the Golden Hall made this implication clearer by comparing God's rule over the universe with the tsar's over his tsardom.[60] The idea of the ruler as *imago dei* was also current in the West, though there its implications would seem less mystically charged and more influenced by legal considerations. Yet any image has, in some degree, to reflect the essence of its original; and concrete identification of the monarch with the divinity's earthly manifestation entails a requirement at least of certain modes of behavior sufficient to give the image force and actuality.

Until the middle of the seventeenth century humanism had little influence on Russian historical writing: The chronicle format was dominant, and it remained popular thereafter. Native experiments in creating new genres of history writing under Ivan IV and during the Time of Troubles have not been traced to foreign models, either from classical antiquity or from Western Europe. However, a few sixteenth-century thinkers did discuss political issues from a nonreligious point of view.

Fedor Karpov, though a native Russian without a formal education, has a good claim to the title of political philosopher. A member of the Boyar Duma, Karpov knew Latin well through his extensive diplomatic experience. His main work is an epistle to Metropolitan Daniil in which he considers two civic virtues: forbearance (modern Russian *terpenie*) and justice (*pravda*). Using sources that include Ovid's *Ars amatoria* and Aristotle's *Nicomachean Ethics*, Karpov argues that forbearance on the part of citizens and rulers will ruin a kingdom, since "holy customs and good law codes will be destroyed," and "human society will be without structure." Further, the powerful will oppress the weak, and worthy men be impoverished. If rulers and subjects pursue justice, on the other hand, everyone benefits. Karpov praises laws "so that by the fear of them, human audacity would be forbidden . . . [and] so that no one could be stronger than all." Every realm needs a leader to compel "the harmful sinners into the harmony of the good by the majesty of the law and justice." Unfortunately, there is little evidence that other Russians read or understood Karpov's remarkable arguments. His letter survives in a unique manuscript dating from the 1560s.[61]

Karpov's slightly younger contemporary, Maksim the Greek, had an amazingly sophisticated education, given the Russian context in which he spent the latter part of his life. Born Michael Trivoles in Arta, Greece, he went in 1492 to Italy, where he worked with or for John Lascaris, Marsilio Ficino, and Pico della Mirandola, among others. After a religious conversion, he entered a Dominican Monastery, and then returned to Greece to the Vatopedi monastery on Mount Athos. In 1516 he was sent to Moscow to help with the translation of church books, but was soon embroiled in local political disputes, particularly concerning the power of the realm over the church. He wrote biting satires about the abuse of royal power, including an allegory in which he described the Muscovite kingdom as a widow (*basilea*) surrounded by wild beasts. As she explains to Maksim, she weeps because she is surrounded by power lovers, slaves to their lower passions, and persecutors of the defenseless and innocent. This is one of the harshest condemnations of the government found in domestic sources of our period, and is typical of Maksim's critiques of the powerful and wealthy. He also condemned monastic ownership of large estates. Not surprisingly, Maksim fell foul of public authority. Twice convicted of heresy and treason, he remained in prison from 1524 until ca. 1548, died in 1555, and was canonized in 1988. Unlike in the case of Karpov, manuscript collections of Maksim's many works remained popular throughout the seventeenth century. In spite of his remarkable education, Maksim remained primarily a religious writer. He agreed with other Russians that rulers are appointed by God and must be obeyed. His Platonic background showed in his view that the social and political hierarchy reflected the hierarchy of the universe, and in his insistence, similar to Karpov's, that justice was the major goal of ruling.[62]

Finally, Ivan Peresvetov has some claim to be called a political philosopher, since he based his recommendations about political rule not on God's will, but on the goal of strengthening the realm. In two works, a *Petition* and a text about the Turkish sultan, both seemingly written in the late 1540s but surviving only in seventeenth-century manuscripts, this immigrant from western Rus´ urged Ivan IV to follow the example of the Turkish sultan by disciplining his nobles and extirpating corruption, thus improving the army and strengthening the kingdom. Constantine, the last Byzantine ruler, was merciful, but his boyars' abuses led to Byzantium's end. Sultan Mohammad was stern but just and did not hesitate to use the harshest methods to punish wrongdoers, saying that "like a horse without a bridle beneath an emperor, so is an empire ruled without terror" (*groza*, a noun which shares a common root with Ivan the IV's epithet, "Terrible" [*Groznyi*]).[63] There is no direct evidence that Ivan read Peresvetov's works, or that they were used by later writers.

The creation of a firmer base for political philosophy began with the establishment of the patriarchate in 1589, an event that brought into Russia a number of learned Greeks. Next came the fruits of closer connections between Muscovy and Ukraine, which was quickly becoming a major center of Orthodox learning in the early seventeenth century. Peter Mogila's founding of the Kievan Academy in 1630 was crucial, for this institution produced a steady stream of pupils educated in Scholastic philosophy as well as in Orthodox theology, individuals with a fully European humanistic education. Its curriculum included Latin and Greek as well as Church Slavic. Philosophy (logic, physics, and metaphysics) was taught from Aristotle as well as Thomist theology. In the 1640s some graduates made their way to Moscow, set themselves up in monasteries, and so were able to teach a few Russian pupils and to have a significant influence on the country's religious life. Their numbers gradually increased: By the time of the accession of Peter the Great (1682), Ukrainians occupied most of the bishoprics in Russia and dominated the educational institutions that had just sprung up. In fact, the first "academy" was started by the Belarusian Simeon Polotskii, a graduate of the Kiev Academy (and of a Jesuit academy in Vilnius) and, later, tutor to the royal children. Several experimental educational institutions were subsumed under the new Slavic-Greek-Latin Academy founded by the Likhudes brothers in 1687, the first substantial institution of higher learning in Russia. Between them, the Likhudes brothers and Polotskii and his pupil, the native Russian Sil'vestr Medvedev, laid the educational foundation for the achievements of the next generation of political thinkers under Peter the Great.

Yet the second half of the seventeenth century did see, if not the development of rational political philosophy, then at least some dramatic shifts in how elite Russians thought about politics.[64] The most potent evidence for this is, as we have seen, the *Ulozhenie* of 1649, which explicitly claimed to provide justice and good order on earth rather than salvation in heaven. Simeon Polotskii, who had a far deeper education than the framers of the law code, came to similar conclusions. Although he did not compose a formal work of political philosophy, he did publish in 1678 a collection of verses on various subjects arranged alphabetically (rather than logically) and titled *The Many-Flowered Garden*. In it, he echoes many traditional Muscovite ideas, such as the duty of subjects to obey the ruler and the latter's duty to seek good advice. But he places a much greater emphasis than was customary on the ruler's duty to follow the law (envisaged not as general religious law, but as particular laws of a kingdom) and to provide effective justice to his subjects. In spite of his religious vocation, he, like the framers of the law code, aimed in his political poems at good order in the realm rather than at salvation for its inhabitants. He even cites Aristotle in order to define the difference between a tsar and a tyrant: "The tsar wishes for and seeks benefits for his subjects / While the tyrant serves only himself, showing little concern for society."[65]

A third source for these ideas is a description of the government of Russia by Grigorii Kotoshikhin, a state secretary in the Foreign Chancellery who defected to the Swedes in 1664. At the request of the Swedes, he composed his description, known conventionally as *On Russia in the Reign of Alexei Mikhailov-*

ich, around 1666.⁶⁶ Kotoshikhin lacked Polotskii's sophisticated education and did not draw on Plutarch or Aristotle, but he came to many of the same conclusions, notably that the object of government should be the people's prosperity and happiness. He considered Ivan IV, like the rulers during the Time of Troubles, guilty of tormenting and oppressing his subjects. Most interesting is Kotoshikhin's contention that all rulers after Ivan IV and until Alexis Mikhailovich came to power only after signing an agreement to observe certain conditions. This contention implies a contractual view of royal power, although the idea is not stated as a general theory.

By far the most sophisticated political thinker in seventeenth-century Russia was not Russian at all, but a Croatian priest, Iurii Krizhanich (Juraj Krizanic), brilliantly educated in Graz and at the University of Bologna, among other places. He was familiar not only with classical writers on politics, notably Aristotle, whom he often quotes, but also with such early modern writers as Machiavelli and Lipsius. He had a life-long dream of helping to convert Russia to the Roman faith, and in 1659 at last succeeded in reaching Moscow. For unknown reasons he was soon exiled to Tobol'sk in Siberia, where he wrote a number of works, including his famous *Discourses on Government*, popularly known as *The Politika*. Although much of this text concerns the very practical goal of improving the economic health of Russia, Krizhanich engaged in political speculation of a general sort. More explicitly than Kotoshikhin, he uses the election of the Romanov dynasty in 1613 to postulate a contract theory of government, endowing members of that dynasty with a legitimacy based on the "contract" of 1613. He defends autocratic government as the form best suited to Russia, but, like Polotskii and Kotoshikhin, distinguishes between just rulers and tyrants. He repeatedly calls Ivan IV a tyrant, both as a corrupt ruler and as the issuer of unjust laws. Unjust laws, he argues, can turn even a well-meaning ruler into a tyrant. His defense of autocracy, therefore, does not permit the ruler to treat his kingdom as he will—a position he explicitly refutes. On the contrary, the purpose of the realm is, once more, the prosperity and happiness of its subjects. Like Polotskii, Krizhanich includes God in his discussions of politics, but his approach remains essentially secular and practical.⁶⁷

Thus, by the end of the century, several thinkers working largely in ignorance of each other arrived at similar conclusions: an increasingly secular view of government, a theory of the general good, an increased reliance on law to regulate society, and even a contract theory of government. The fate of Krizhanich, the most able political thinker in Russia, is instructive, however, and is reminiscent of the fate of Maksim the Greek over a century earlier. Most of his time in Russia was spent in exile, and so his influence in Moscow was limited during his lifetime. His work was not published until the nineteenth century, although manuscript copies existed in the libraries of important courtiers and of the tsar himself. Yet no other Russian author refers to him or to his ideas, and there is no evidence that any important people were influenced by him. Thus in another case, Russian political thought failed to be fertilized by the work of an innovative writer because of the suspicious attitude held by Muscovite ruling circles. The lack of a "Republic of Letters" or of even a printing press free of government influence meant that innovative minds remained isolated, without influence on the current and later generations of Russian thinkers.

Natural Law

Natural law played but a small role in Russian political thought during our period. Several writers mention it in passing, but, given the difficulty writers had in reading each others' work, the idea of natural law was never developed. Karpov describes the law of nature as the first in three stages of the evolution of the law, the others being Mosaic law and the law of Christ.[68] Krizhanich, surprisingly, mentions natural law in only a few instances, as when he cites "natural laws" as favoring men over women and older over younger brothers in succession laws, or when he vaguely mentions "divine or natural law" as limiting a monarch's power.[69] His primary authority in political matters is scripture, closely followed by examples from history.

Conclusion

The intellectual context of political thought in Russia differed profoundly from that of Western Europe. Based almost entirely on ideas inherited from Byzantium, the dominant ideology of the realm was skillfully elaborated in a variety of media for a variety of publics. Its success in winning the hearts and minds of many Muscovites can be shown in the monopoly that these ideas enjoyed in relatively spontaneous statements by laymen and clerics over two centuries. The paradigm of Christian rulership that they offered seems to have worked very well, despite its internal contradictions and ambiguities. However, by the second half of the seventeenth century, this body of ideas or ideology had become vulnerable in one respect: A ruler perceived as not following the will of God was pronounced a tormentor and thereby lost his legitimacy. Gentry petitioners and Old Believers alike used this idea, either explicitly or by implication, to undermine the legitimacy of reigning monarchs. Although some tentative steps were made to revise such traditional ideas in the late seventeenth century, a thoroughly new political philosophy, based on Western European concepts, had to await the reign of Peter the Great.

The present essay began by identifying a number of master narratives that have been used to explain early modern Russian political thought. It seems evident that none of these explanations will do. Definitive conclusions cannot be drawn from our currently unsettled grasp of government, society, and political thought in Russia. Even so, I would suggest that Russians saw themselves as inhabitants of an ideal Christian polity, destined by God to prevail until Christ's Second Coming. Strategies such as the use of wise advisers were deployed when the theoretical perfection expected of rulers failed to materialize. The complex of ideas available to buttress this ideal was used in various political situations, but did not essentially change until the consensus that had supported them broke down after 1650. At that point, a number of thinkers of varying backgrounds changed the traditional outlook in a decidedly secular direction, envisioning the realm as a mechanism for improving the lot of its subjects. These thinkers raised many of the same issues discussed by thinkers in the West: the source of governmental authority, limits to the power of rulers. But they lacked the social, institutional, and technical means to develop an independent political discourse or to deploy their arguments to challenge the Russian status quo. Indeed, classically educated political thinkers remained a tiny minority in Russia down to the end of the eighteenth century.

Notes

1. V. Val'denberg *Drevnerusskie ucheniia o predelaky tsarskoi vlasti* (Petrograd: n.p., 1916); M. D'iakonov, *Vlast' moskovskikh gosudarei* (Saint Petersburg: I. N. Skorokhodov, 1889).

2. S. V. Utechin, *Russian Political Thought: A Concise History* (New York and London: J. M. Dent and Sons, 1964); Thornton Anderson, *Russian Political Thought: An Introduction* (Ithaca, NY: Cornell University Press, 1967).

3. Edward L. Keenan, *The Kurbskii-Groznyi Apocrypha: The Seventeenth-Century Genesis of the "Correspondence" attributed to Prince A. M. Kurbskii and Tsar Ivan IV* (Cambridge, MA: Harvard University Press, 1971); Edward L. Keenan, "Response to Halperin, 'Edward L. Keenan and the Kurbskii-Groznyi Correspondence in Hindsight,'" *Jahrbucher fur Geschichte Osteuropas* 46 (1998): 404–418.

4. Max J. Okenfuss, *The Rise and Fall of Latin Humanism in Early Modern Russia: Pagan Authors, Ukrainians, and the Resiliency of Muscovy* (Leiden: Brill, 1995).

5. For "glowing center," see Clifford Geertz, "Centers, Kings, and Charisma: Reflections on the Symbolics of Power," in Sean Wilentz ed., *The Rites of Power* (Philadelphia, University of Pennsylvania Press, 1985), 14.

6. O. I. Podobedova, *Moskovskaia shkola zhivopisi: raboty v Moskovskom Kremle 40-kh–70-kh godov XVII veka* (Moscow: Nauka, 1972), 59–68, 193–198; Daniel Rowland,

"The Blessed Host of the Heavenly Tsar," in Michael Flier and Daniel Rowland, eds., *Medieval Russian Culture*, vol. 2 (Berkeley, Los Angeles and London: University of California Press, 1994), 194n29 on dating issues (chapter 6 of this volume); Daniel Rowland, "Two Cultures, One Throne Room," in Valerie Kivelson and Robert Greene, eds., *Orthodoxy in Russian History* (Philadelphia: University of Pennsylvania Press, 2003) (chapter 9 of this volume).

7. E, S, Sizov, "Datirovka rospisi Arkhangel'skogo sobora i istoricheskaia osnova ee siuzhetov," *Drevenrusskoi iskusstva. XVII vek* (Moscow: Nauka, 1964), 160–174.

8. Michael Flier, "Breaking the Code: The Image of the Tsar in the Muscovite Palm Sunday Ritual," in Flier and Rowland, eds., *Medieval Russian Culture*, 142–213.

9. Michael Flier, "Filling in the Blanks: The Church of the Intercession and the Architectonics of Medieval Muscovite Ritual," *Harvard Ukrainian Studies* 19, nos. 1–4 (1995): 120–137.

10. Andrei Batalov, *Moskovskoe kamennoe zodchestvo kontsa XVI veka: problemy khudozhestvennogo Myshleniia epokha* (Moscow: Rossiiskaia akademiiia khudozhestv, 1996); Daniel Rowland, "Architecture and Dynasty: Boris Godunov's Uses of Architecture, 1585–1606," in James Cracraft and Daniel Rowland, eds., *Architectures of Russian Identity, 1500–Present* (Ithaca, NY: Cornell University Press, 2003), 34–47 (chapter 8 of this volume).

11. Georg Michels, *At War with the Church: Religious Dissent in Seventeenth-Century Russia* (Stanford CA: Stanford University Press, 1999).

12. Kh. Loparev, "O chine venchaniia russkikh tsarei," *Zhurnal ministerstva narodnogo prosveshcheniia* (1887), 312–319.

13. E. V. Barsov, *Drevnerusskie pamiatniki venchaniia tsarei na tsarstvo* (Moscow: n.p., 1883), 42, 51, 76.

14. Rowland, "Two Cultures, One Throne Room."

15. The term most frequently used to refer to the ruler was *gosudar'*. This is routinely translated into English as "sovereign," but more accurately signifies "great or supreme lord, one who has no superior on earth." Since I am arguing that God was seen as playing such an active role in Russian political life, I have translated this term as "great lord." The related term *gosudarstvo*, meaning literally "the realm of the great lord," is usually translated as "state." To avoid confusion with more specialized senses of "state" considered in this volume, I translate *gosudarstvo* as "realm" or "kingdom."

16. *Polnoe sobranie russkikh letopisei* 14 (1910): 116.

17. Isolde Thyret, *Between God and the Tsar: Religious Symbolism and the Royal Women of Muscovite Russia* (DeKalb, IL: Northern Illinois University Press, 2001).

18. See Rowland, "Two Cultures, One Throne Room."

19. Flier, "Breaking the Code"; Nancy Kollmann, "Pilgrimage, Procession, and Symbolic Space in Sixteenth-Century Russian Politics," in Michael Flier and Daniel Rowland, eds., *Medieval Russian Culture*, vol. 2, 163–181.

20. Andrei Batalov, *Moskovskoe kamennoe zodchestvo kontsa XVI veka*. See also Daniel Rowland, "Architecture and Dynasty" (chapter 8 of this volume).

21. *Russkaia istoricheskaia biblioteka* 14, col. 173. Compare comment on *symphonia* below.

22. Daniel Rowland, "Did Muscovite Literary Ideology Place Limits on the Power of the Tsar (1540s-1660s)?" *The Russian Review* 49 (1990): 136–139 (chapter 4 of this volume).

23. Iosof Volotskii, *Prosvetitel'* (Kazan´: Tip. Imperatorskogo universiteta, 1896), 287. For an excellent discussion of the tsar/tormenter opposition in the works of Joseph, see David Goldfrank, "The Deep Origins of *Tsar-Muchitel'*," paper delivered at the American Association for Slavic Studies in 2003.

24. Rowland, "Limits," 149–151 (chapter 4 of this volume).

25. *Vremennik Ivana Timofeeva*, ed. O. A. Derzhavina (Moscow: Izd. Akademii nauk, 1951), 11, 15.

26. Marshall Poe, "What did the Russians Mean When They Called Themselves 'Slaves of the Tsar'?," *Slavic Review* 57 (1998): 585–608; Richard Hellie, "Why Did the Muscovite Elite Not Rebel?," *Russian History* 25 (1998): 155–162.

27. Valerie A. Kivelson, "Muscovite 'Citizenship': Rights Without Freedom," *Journal of Modern History* 74 (2002): 465–489.

28. *Vremennik Timofeeva*, 109–110.

29. Sergei Bogatyrev, *The Sovereign and his Counsellors: Ritualized Consultations in Muscovite Political Culture* (Helsinki: Suomalainen tiedeakatemia, 2000), 69–98.

30. Daniel Rowland, "The Problem of Advice in Muscovite Tales about the Time of Troubles," *Russian History/Histoire Russe* 6, part 2 (1979): 259–283 (chapter 3 of this volume).

31. *Pamiatniki literatury drevnei Rusi XIV–XV veka* (Moscow: Khodozhestvennaia literatura, 1981), 208, 210.

32. Donald Ostrowski, "The Assembly of the Land [*Zemskii Sobor*] as a Representative Institution," in Jarmo Kotilaine and Marshall Poe, eds., *Modernizing Muscovy: Reform and Social Change in Seventeenth-Century Russia* (London: Routledge Curzon, 2004), 117–142.

33. Rowland, "The Problem of Advice," 270–275 (chapter 3 of this volume). The quotation here is from Avraami Palitsym, *Skazanie Avraamiia Palitsyna*, ed. L. V. Cherepnin (Moscow: Izd. Akademii nauk, 1955), 252–253.

34. D. P. Golokhvastov and [Archimandrite] Leonid, "Blagoveshchenskii ierei Sil´vestr i ego pisaniia," *Chtenie v Imperatorskom Obsheshestvom istorii and i drevenosti rossiiskikh pri Moskovskom universiteta*, bk. 1, sec. 1 (1884): 82.

35. The best text is in Donald Ostrowski, "A 'Fontological' Investigation of the Church Council of 1503," PhD diss., Pennsylvania State University (1977), 426, 489.

36. Anderson, *Russian Political Thought*, 112.

37. Anderson, *Russian Political Thought*, 115–116; William Palmer, ed. and trans., *The Patriarch and the Tsar*, 6 vols. (London, 1871–1876), 189–190 in reference.

38. Donald Ostrowski, *Muscovy and the Mongols: Cross-Cultural Influences on the Steppe Frontier 1304–1789* (Cambridge: Cambridge University Press, 1998), 166; see also Ia. S. Lur´e, *Dve istorii Rusi XV veka: rannie and pozdnie, nezavisimye i ofitsial´nye letopisi o obrazovanii Moskovskogo gosudarstva* (Saint Petersburg: Dmitrii Bulanin, 1994), for examples of later revisions of early chronicle accounts.

39. Michael Flier, "Till the End of Time: The Apocalypse in Russian Historical Experience before 1500," in Kivelson and Greene, *Orthodox Russia*, 127–158.

40. Flier, "Till the End of Time," 153.

41. Donald Ostrowski, "Moscow the Third Rome as Historical Ghost," in Sarah Brooks, ed., *Byzantium: Faith and Power (1261–1557), The Symposium* (New York: The Metropolitan Museum of Art, 2007), 170–179.

42. Daniel Rowland, "Biblical Military Imagery in the Political Culture of Early Modern Russia," in Flier and Rowland, *Russian Culture*, 182–212 (chapter 6 of this volume, with further references).

43. Daniel Kaiser, *The Growth of the Law in Medieval Russia* (Princeton, NJ: Princeton University Press, 1980).

44. Nancy S. Kollmann, *By Honor Bound: State and Society in Early Modern Russia* (Ithaca, NY: Cornell University Press, 1999), 95–101 and passim.

45. *The Muscovite Law Code (Ulozhenie) of 1949*, ed. and trans. Richard Hellie, part 1 (Irvine CA: Schlacks, 1988), 1–3.

46. Benjamin Uroff, "Grigorii Karpovich Kotoshikhin, *On Russia in the Reign of Alexis Mikhailovich*," PhD diss., Columbia University (1970), 21–23, 232–235.

47. A. I. Iakovlev, *Pamiatniki istorii smutnogo vremeni* (Moscow: Izd. N. N. Klochkova, 1909), 47–49.

48. Kotoshikhin asserts that every tsar after Ivan IV was elected, and that each one signed a document promising "that they would not be cruel and wrathful, nor punish anyone for any reason without trial and without cause, and deliberate all matters together with the boyars and Duma men, and do nothing secretly or openly without their knowledge." He clearly meant to include Michael Romanov in this list: Uroff, "Kotoshikhin," 233.

49. Palitsyn, *Skazanie*, 231–233, 235, 238. Other accounts also stressed God's intervention in the choice of Michael.

50. Endre Sashalmi, "Contract Theory and the Westernization of Russian Ideology of Power under Peter the Great," *Dissertationes Historicae . . . Universitatis Quinqueecclesiensis* (Pecs: Pécsi Tudományegyetem Bölcsészettudományi Kar Középkori és Koraújkori Történeti Tanszék, 2003), 92; Richard Pipes, *Russia under the Old Regime* (London: Weidenfeld and Nicolson, 1974), 77, 323.

51. This important story is told and carefully analyzed in Valerie A. Kivelson, "The Devil Stole his Mind: the Tsar and the Moscow Uprising of 1648," *American Historical Review* 98 (1993): 733–356.

52. Valerie A. Kivelson, *Autocracy in the Provinces: The Muscovite Gentry and Political Culture in the Seventeenth Century* (Stanford, CA: Stanford University Press, 1996), passim, esp. 233–240.

53. R. P. Dmitrieva, *Skazanie o Kniaziakh Vladimirskikh* (Moscow: Izd. Akademii nauk, 1955), esp. chap. 3.

54. Michael Flier, "Who's Who, and Who's Not: The Culture of Genealogical Discontinuity in Muscovite Rus´," a paper delivered to the American Association for the Advancement of Slavic Studies (hereafter AAASS) in 2004; Daniel Rowland, "Genealogy in Sixteenth-Century Russian Political Thought," paper delivered to the AAASS in 2004.

55. Valerie A. Kivelson, "Muscovite 'Citizenship': Rights without Freedom," *Journal of Modern History* 74 (2002): 465–489, and 486, note 9.

56. Kollmann, *By Honor Bound*, 19–20, with further references. See especially two important essays by George Weickhardt: "The Pre-Petrine Law of Property," *Slavic Re-*

view 52, no. 4 (1993): 663–679 (with following reply to Richard Pipes, "Reply," 531–538); and "Due Process and Equal Justice in the Muscovite Codes," *The Russian Review* 51 (1992): 463–480.

57. Kivelson, "Muscovite 'Citizenship.'"

58. See M. A. Manzalaoui, ed., *Secreta Secretorum: Nine English Versions* (Oxford: Oxford University Press, 1977).

59. Ihor Sevcenko, "A Neglected Byzantine Source of Muscovite Ideology," *Harvard Slavic Studies* 2 (1954): 141–179.

60. See translation and discussion in Michael Flier, "The Throne of Monomakh: Ivan the Terrible and the Architectonics of Destiny," in Cracraft and Rowland, *Architectures of Russian Identity*, 23–33.

61. David Goldfrank, "Theology and Political Theory in Middle Muscovy: Abstracting the Abstract," paper delivered to the AAASS in 2004; E. H. Kimeeva, "Poslanie Metropolity Daniilu Fedora Karpova," *Trudy otdela drevnerusskoi literatury* 9 (1953): 221–234.

62. For basic information, see Dimitri Obolensky, "Italy, Mount Athos, and Muscovy: The Three Worlds of Maximos the Greek (c. 1470–1556)," *Proceedings of the British Academy* 67 (1981): 143–149; Maksim Grek, *Sochinenie prepodobnogo Maksima Greka*, 2nd ed., 3 vols. (Kazan´: Kazanskii universitet, 1894–1897). For updated information, see David Miller, "Orthodoxy," in *The Cambridge History of Russia. Volume I: From Early Rus´ to 1689*, ed. Maureen Perrie (Cambridge: Cambridge University Press, 2006), 352–354.

63. Ivan Peresvetov, *Sochineniia I. Peresvetova*, ed. A. A. Zimin and D. S. Likhachev (Moscow: Nauka, 1956), 153; also A. A. Zimin, *Peresvetov i ego sovremenniki: ocherki po istorii russkoi obshchestvenno-politicheskoi mysli serediny XVI veka* (Moscow: Izd. Akademii nauk, 1958).

64. Two excellent English-language surveys of political thought in this period are George Weickhardt, "Political Thought in Seventeenth-Century Russia," *Russian History/Histoire Russe* 21, no.3 (1994): 316–337; and Douglas J. Bennet Jr., "The Idea of Kingship in Seventeenth Century Russia," PhD diss., Harvard University (1967).

65. Bennet, "The Idea of Kingship," 239–242, 244.

66. For a complete English translation, with commentary, see Uroff, "Kotoshikhin."

67. Iurii Krizhanich, *Russian Statecraft; the Politika of Iurii Krizhanich: An Analysis and Translation of Iurii Krizhanich's Politika*, ed. and trans. John Letiche and Basil Dmytryshyn (Oxford: Basil Blackwell, 1985).

68. Goldfrank, "Theology and Political Theory."

69. Krizhanich, *Politika*, 246, 189.

CHAPTER 15

God, Tsar, and People
Some Further Thoughts

Introduction

In his recent popular book, *Sapiens*, Yuval Noah Harari makes a startling claim. Tracing the small number of major turning points in the history of our species, Harari singles out a development in *Homo sapiens*, sometime between seventy thousand and twenty thousand years ago, when we first invented fictions—the ability to imagine and describe, in texts, images, or sculpture, beings or concepts that we cannot perceive with our five senses. He calls this development, caused by genetic changes in our brains, the Cognitive Revolution. We could see and describe a wooly mammoth or a parrot, but, before this turning point, we could not make images of other things or beings; we could not describe or depict gods, or ideas, or limited stock companies. This new ability, not seen in any previous generations or in any other *Homo* species, opened the door to perhaps the most important moment in the evolution of humankind: the invention of culture. (This whole story bears an unsettling resemblance to the Garden of Eden story in Genesis: thus Harari's chapter title, "The Tree of Knowledge.")[1]

    This little-understood genetic mutation dramatically changed not only our ancestors but our world. It enabled Sapiens to invent boats, colonize places like Australia that were hitherto uninhabited by hominids, and to drive to extinction Australian marsupial megafauna like the *Diprotodon*, a two-and-a-half-ton wombat.[2]

GOD, TSAR, AND PEOPLE 359

Our fictions obviously play a crucial role both in history and in our current lives, a role arguably bigger than that played by any other force, human or even natural. Harari gives the example of the Peugeot automobile company, which grew from a hardware store making bicycles to a huge international corporation, vastly more powerful than M. Peugeot himself, on the basis of the fiction of a joint-stock company.[3] To Harari's list of economic fictions like Peugeot, we could add political fictions like Russia or the United States of America.

This addition takes us directly to our subject, and gives a powerful argument that culture can drive other historical forces as well as be driven by them. Harari goes on to argue that it was this new cultural skill that first allowed humans to organize themselves into political or social units larger than a few tens of individuals. Without cultural ideas to tie larger populations together, humans, like chimpanzees, could only form groups of individuals small enough that each person could know each other person well enough to trust him or her, and so create a bond that could hold the group together in the hunt or in warfare. With the new ability to imagine and deploy ideas of unseen things, much larger groups, thousands or even millions, could be held together in an organized mass through common cultural constructs, whether these ideas concerned mythic ancestors, cosmological forces, or, most effective, gods or goddesses. In short, it was the discovery of human culture that made possible human societies larger than a few dozen individuals.[4]

This breathtaking insight could not be more relevant to the essays in this collection. For I believe that it is precisely developments in Russian culture, largely Russian ecclesiastical culture, that made the creation and preservation of the Muscovite state possible, over a long period of time and against almost overwhelming odds. The ideas described in these essays, and many others besides, provided the indispensable cultural glue that held together this large and wildly growing assemblage of territories, aided by a bureaucratic and military structure that, until the middle of the sixteenth century at least, was woefully weak by the standards of surrounding states, whether in Western Europe, the Levant, or Asia.

The culture of Muscovite Russia seems to have been a very effective glue. Although the number of cultural genres was sharply limited in comparison to the genres available in the West, their restricted range and concentration of energies may well have made Muscovite culture more effective as social cement than the broader, more diffuse, and more divided cultures of the West. As we try to imagine the experience of a visitor to Moscow in, say, 1620, we are struck by the intense collaboration of many forms of art to produce what must have been an almost overwhelming effect. The architecture of the Kremlin—whether it was Italian designed, Italian influenced, or native—produced a series of impressive spaces, both external squares and internal domestic and ecclesiastical spaces, all arranged to dazzle and impress while at the same time defining the social divisions of the court. Much, even most, of the internal spaces of churches, throne rooms, and living quarters were covered with rich murals, often illustrating historical narratives foundational to the imagined origins and lineages of the Muscovite state. Churches all boasted elaborate icon screens, often stretching to the ceiling, with their theologically complex arrangement of sacred images. Choral music, which has survived, would have been performed in the excellent acoustic environments of the Kremlin churches by powerful male choirs. And outside, the air would literally vibrate with the ringing of hundreds of church bells, both in the Kremlin and around the city.

Until very recently, we could not know what most Russians thought about these cultural efforts. Without memoirs or any genres of literary fiction (except perhaps forgeries), the interior world of Muscovites, especially lay Muscovites, at least down to the middle of the seventeenth century, had remained largely mysterious to us. The few historical texts written by a wide variety of Russians about the Time of Troubles (1598–1613), to which several of the essays in this volume are devoted, do provide some useful clues, as does the body of petitions and legal cases that grew steadily in the course of the seventeenth century. Nevertheless, until the work of scholars like Valerie Kivelson and Nancy Shields Kollmann, discussed below, we could only guess at the reception of these ambitious efforts, whether by elite courtiers who populated the throne rooms and other rarified spaces of the Kremlin, or by more ordinary folk who watched diplomatic processions or royal pilgrimages both in Moscow and, importantly, in the provinces.

But we do have a lot of evidence about the cultural efforts exerted on the production side of culture, as it were, by government and ecclesiastical officials to define and celebrate matters that modern historians would call political. The essays in this volume explore some of the themes that Muscovite churchmen created and elaborated, like the importance of the Old Testament to the historical thinking of Muscovy, but they ignore many others, like the idea that Muscovy may have imagined itself as a "community of venerators" of Saint Sergius as a prelude to what modern historians call, in a vexed term, "national consciousness."[5]

The main conclusion of my efforts to understand these themes is to discover how little I know, and how much remains to be explored and explained. I go into this subject in more detail below, but for now I feel compelled to describe how often I have found one or another theme that was far too vast for me to fully explore, to say nothing of exhaust. The theme of the influence of the Old Testament on Russian historical thinking, for example, has proven an exceptionally fruitful field, explored with more skill and more evidence than I could ever hope to muster. Thus, I am ever aware of the contributions of my wonderful colleagues, both in Russia and in the West, from whom I have learned so much. Robert Crummey, in a private letter, justly referred to our little community of scholars of Muscovite Russia as a family. I thus beg the reader's pardon for beginning this short essay with a brief professional memoir, concentrating first on a few family elders, older historians who have had an outsized influence on me.

Famous Historians I Have Known

I was trained primarily as an historian, only learning Russian in graduate school. I earned "A" and "S" levels in history as a student at Shrewsbury School, one of England's top public schools, which I attended on an English Speaking Union Scholarship. My work there, with David Gee and Michael Hart, inspired me to aspire to become a member of the English community of historians, and to concentrate, as I was both forced and happy to do, on historiography—the study of what various historians at various times and places had written about one problem or another. I was fascinated in particular with the argument about the role of the gentry in early seventeenth-century England, carried on with typical wit bordering on the murderous. It was at Shrewsbury that I fell in love with the early modern period, an affection I have never lost. As an interdisciplinary student at Yale majoring in History, the Arts, and Letters, I wrote my senior thesis, published by Yale University Press in 1964, comparing Mannerist style in painting, poetry, and music. This training attracted me to the visual (and musical) in Muscovite culture, and, perhaps more important, gave me the courage to write about it.

My return to England, to Lincoln College, Oxford, as a Marshall Scholar to do a second undergraduate degree in "Modern History," marked the real beginning of my engagement with Russian history. I became an enthusiastic member of the local Orthodox church choir, and a close friend of Anne Pennington, a fellow chorister who taught me my first lessons in Russian. The eminent Byzantinist Dimitri Obolensky and John Fennell, the well-known historian of Muscovy, were both members of the small congregation of the Russian Orthodox Parish of the Annunciation, and both encouraged me in my fledgling interest in the history of early modern Russia.

Obolensky's lectures on the history of Muscovy provided my starting point. I had thought, rightly, that few of my fellow history undergraduates would attend a set of lectures on such an apparently obscure subject, and fewer still would choose to write an essay on that subject during the weeklong set of intimidating final exams I was facing in the near future, thus opening a path to a much-hoped-for "alpha" in one examination paper. I was fascinated by the dramatic events and outsized personalities described by Obolensky, but also struck by how similar the general structure of Muscovite political and social history that he described was to the way English historians had thought about English history in the early twentieth century. Politics was depicted as revolving around a conflict between a conservative boyar aristocracy yearning to retain their old medieval independence and privileges, and the encroachments of an increasingly centralized monarchy, aided by a growing bureaucracy and a rising middle class of "new men." My concurrent studies of the historians of Tudor and Stuart England had pointed out to me the difficulties of this oversimplified view of English history. If this view was inappropriate for early modern England, I reasoned, how much less appropriate would it be for early modern Russia, about which I knew little except that it must have been quite different from contemporary England.

My Oxford studies, like my preparation of "A" and "S" levels years earlier, had largely focused on the evolving views of particular historians. I had eagerly attended every lecture series by Hugh Trevor-Roper and other Oxford luminaries as they argued against the views of their colleagues about this or that historical interpretation. Intimidated by the generations of highly intelligent historians of early modern England, who seemed to have sifted through every available snippet of evidence, and the vigorous debates that had gone on for generations, I was looking for a new field of early modern history to pursue in graduate school. My historian heroes were revisionists: the more revisionist the better, I thought. And what better field for an aspiring revisionist than the history of early modern Russia, where progress seemed to have stopped not long after 1900?

I dimly understood at the time the reasons for this peculiar historiographic situation. Roughly a decade after the Russian Revolution and the rise of a genuinely Marxist school of history under the leadership of M. N. Pokrovskii, Stalin purged Pokrovskii and his followers, and rehabilitated the former students of V. O. Kliuchevskii, perhaps the greatest historian of Russia ever. But this unlikely turn of events resulted, to oversimplify greatly, in an uneasy marriage between the old historiography of the immediate prerevolutionary Kliuchevskii era and a crude form of Marxism that made independent investigations of cultural evidence difficult by assigning culture the role of a "mere" reflection of social and economic forces and conflicts. Under Stalin this new hybrid became enshrined as party doctrine, and thus largely frozen in place—in other words, a perfect arena for a would-be revisionist historian! I was still under the influence of this enthusiasm for heedless, youthful revisionism combined with an English, even Namier-inflected, historiography when I wrote the short essay at the beginning of this volume.

My return to the United States as a graduate student at Yale served as an introduction to contemporary work in Muscovite history by historians both Soviet and Western. As I read the sophisticated work of these historians, I was increasingly impressed and humbled by their work and intimidated to think of taking my place among them. My guide in this exploration was Bob Crummey, whose reading lists guided me, and whose carefully balanced and always erudite views have inspired me ever since. Bob was working on his history of the boyar aristocracy, and his conclusions, expressed first in a series articles and then in a masterful monograph, seemed to fit well with my growing unease with the view that Muscovite rulers had unlimited power to do absolutely as they chose. The boyar clans he described were clearly powerful in their own right, had massive wealth, and existed in some kind of uneasy political balance with the tsar. (Crummey's evidence forced him to concentrate in his monograph largely on the seventeenth century, though his articles dealt with earlier periods, as well.) Particularly striking was the longevity of the power of some of these clans, whose members populated the Boyar Duma for decades, even centuries, in spite of apparently catastrophic disruptions of the political order, like the Time of Troubles or the *oprichnina* of Ivan the Terrible. The attention Crummey paid to the visual culture of these boyar clans is still impressive.[6] We will return to the crucial question of the relationship between boyars and the crown below, but here I'd like to point out a theme to which we will also return: Crummey's emphasis on the paradoxical nature of that relationship. He wrote, "Aristocrats and servitors. Strength and insecurity. Such paradoxes shaped the lives of the members of the political and social elite of seventeenth-century Russia."[7] As I reread this sentence in the context of the essays in this volume, I am struck by how important the recognition of this paradoxical relationship is: Should we think of Muscovy as not *either* an oligarchy *or* a dictatorial monarchy, but perhaps both at once? This contradiction has been hard for me, and, I suspect, for many other historians to live with.

A second opinion that I shared with Crummey was a preoccupation in some of the early essays of this book: Soviet historians and many of their early Western colleagues had spoken of "politics" and "political parties" centered around policy issues that affected class interests. In his monograph, Crummey reminds us that such "court factions or parties" were necessarily small and unusual in the seventeenth century because such alliances around policy issues were "a poor risk. If the faction's leader won the struggle for power, his followers would gather the spoils; conversely, however, if he fell, they might well share in the catastrophe. Most men found it wiser to stay uncommitted."[8] Our own experiences in twentieth-century democracy made it hard for contemporary historians to understand court politics as largely devoid of groupings around one or another policy or intellectual issue. It was what appeared to me to be a gulf between the imagined political consciousness of early modern Russians and their nineteenth-century descendants that animated the first youthful essay in this volume, composed in my earliest days as a graduate student.

My first essay also owes a debt to another of my Yale teachers, Jack Hexter, a historian and writer whom I revered. Hexter sharpened my affection for the history of early modern Europe and taught me a number of lessons that I have tried, sometimes vainly, to follow. One was to let the evidence set the historian's agenda, not the preconceived questions suggested by either the historian's own environment, or by the reigning historiography. A second was Hexter's maxim that, once one had read the available primary sources, the job was only half done; the other half of the task was to write and rewrite the resulting story. Finally, and not coincidentally, Hexter's infectious, vigorous, and often humorous writing style became my goal. In class he told of his greatest compliment as an historian: While riding the Tube in London, the lady next to him was chortling away while reading a book. "Pardon me, Madam," asked Hexter, "but what is that book you are reading?" "*Reappraisals in History,*" replied the lady, referring to Hexter's own most famous book. For years, I would reread one of Hexter's essays to race my engines before embarking on my own writing tasks.

Whether or not my early essays could be termed Hexterian, I leave to the reader. In my memory, I wrote the Kurbskii and Timofeeev essays with Hexter most strongly in mind. I was reacting to the quite formal and often formulaic writing styles then still prevalent in Soviet historical writing, with high-style language and set lists of topics. All of my American colleagues have reacted against this type of writing, which was never popular in the West to begin with. But, when I search in my mind for the most "Hexterian" of these colleagues, Valerie Kivelson first comes first to mind. I have no idea if she has ever read a word by Hexter, but her writing has all the hallmarks of Hexter's. Her language is inflected with contemporary slang, echoing the language of her sources, particularly in her witchcraft trial records. She has a keen sense of humor, and her work has caused me both pleasure and many laughs. Most important, her work has the interpretative energy of Hexter's. One gets the feeling that, like Hexter, she pushes her evidence as far as it will take her, and is seldom content with one simple interpretation.[9]

The same interpretative energy and striking low-style expression can be found in the work of the third "great historian" that I worked with, Ned Keenan. I was most struck by this vigor in Ned's lectures, though the same style is evident in much of his writing. Leaving aside for now Keenan's scholarly views, I would be remiss if I did not mention the enormous influence Keenan had on me as a fledgling historian, largely through his lectures. As I mentioned above, I was itching for someone to dynamite the accepted view of Muscovite history. Ned's lectures scratched this itch, in almost every minute of every lecture. From the first lecture on the effect of the environment on Russian history and culture, through Ned's lectures on Kiev in the context of contemporary Central Asia and Europe, to his revolutionary ideas about Muscovy, I was spellbound. As in his famous "Russian Political Folkways" essay, Ned's lectures ranged from the peasant village to the court, and made reference to events as recent as yesterday.[10] Imagine hearing that the Scandinavian conquest of the river basins in East Slavic lands was planned at the court of King Alfred the Great of England! Or that the Mongols were not simply the vicious bringers of physical destruction and intellectual darkness that I had always heard about, but highly civilized nomads who, in addition to their obvious violence, connected the East Slavic territories with a vast commercial and cultural network stretching from China to Europe.

The attraction of these lectures for me was greatly increased by Keenan's rhetorical brilliance. Though a member of the History Department at Harvard, Ned had a life-long fascination with language, with its various registers, and with the always-changing vernacular of his students. When he compared Russian rulers' patronage of Italian architects to rebuild the Kremlin to the acquisition of Mercedes limousines by African statesmen, we all gained an intuitive understanding that otherwise would have eluded us. The same effect was produced when he equated desirable court fashions with desirable ice cream sold at Steve's Ice Cream in Somerville, Massachusetts, a beloved ice-cream palace that invented the idea of "mix-ins" and had around-the-block lines even in below-zero winter evenings. His uncanny skill in analogy was matched by a very canny use of linguistic registers to convey his revolutionary, but often abstract, ideas.

I should add here that Ned distrusted the sources that I was most interested in, particularly literary texts, whose authorship and dating he often questioned, and privileged instead documentary sources. Yet he could not have been more supportive of my work and its importance to our field, writing, like Crummey, countless letters for me as I made my academic way. I am grateful to Bob and Ned, my two most important "famous historians" for their genuine and faithful friendship, and for their unflagging support.

Let me add a final note of gratitude to Don Ostrowski, a contemporary of mine, and thus not a "famous historian" in my formative years as a historian, but a major influence on me at that time, and since. Ostrowski has been perhaps my closest friend in the field. He put me up on his floor in the early days when I was driving in a frigid VW Microbus in the depth of a Maine winter to work at the Harvard library. My wonderful and continuing conversations with him have been a major influence on me, both on my teaching and my views of Muscovy.

Political Culture, East and West

I would like to concentrate in this final essay not on a general summary, a task well beyond my capabilities, but on an attempt to fit the essays in this volume into the context of work by my colleagues, with particular emphasis on three American colleagues, Russell Martin (to be discussed a little later) Nancy Shields Kollmann, and Valerie Kivelson. I've chosen this trio because they have persistently asked the sort of questions that I have asked, but from sources very different from the ones I have used. I also discuss other valued colleagues, particularly Michael Flier, for the opposite reason: that he has used similar or the same sources as I have, but has sometimes come to quite different conclusions.

I need to say first how honored I am to be in this company. If there is ever a history of the historiography of Muscovy, these figures will each play a major role. Each study by these scholars is based on a huge base of archival evidence, carefully sifted and interpreted, most generally with colorful quotations from petitions or court records that report the words of Russians whose voices have seldom been taken into account by historians. They also have put their conclusions into a broad comparative perspective, comparing their conclusions most frequently with recent scholarship on the early modern West, but often using fruitful comparisons with scholarship about other parts of the globe. Finally, these scholars have been scrupulous in avoiding a Manichean, or binary, view of the questions they discuss. As we will see, this quality is crucial to our discussions.

Keenan in his undergraduate lectures often posed the question of why historians so often seemed to blame Muscovy for being unlike Western Europe. This question haunted my early work, as I sought to understand evidence from Muscovy on its own terms, particularly in my case the context of Eastern Orthodox culture, and not on the terms of nineteenth-century politics and political assumptions, such as political "parties" formed around one issue or another, monastic landholding, for example. I have tried to be wary of such terms as "politics," "parties," "council" (as opposed to counsel), and even "state," since each of these words bring with it assumptions and concepts that were common in nineteenth-century Europe, but, I argue, were largely absent in Muscovy.[11] Given that modern historians have quite different basic assumptions about what we call politics, it is not surprising that we have been irresistibly attracted to the travel accounts of visitors to Muscovy from the West, whose vocabulary and tools of analysis were so similar to our own. These visitors came from a highly articulated political culture deeply infused with Aristotelian categories and rational secular philosophy, though religion also played a major role. In that sense, they spoke a political language similar to our own, and asked (and answered) questions similar to those posed by modern historians.

Marshall Poe has discussed these Western travel accounts in great detail, and, unlike many of the scholars discussed in this essay, has decided that their conclusions about Muscovy were essentially correct, that, as Giles Fletcher put it, the typical Russian ruler was "plain tyrannical."[12] My own thought about these Western travel writers is that their comments about Russia need first to be placed into the context of contemporary political thought in the West. For a writer like Giles Fletcher, whose brother was a Calvinist bishop under Queen Elizabeth I, Muscovy was an emphatic "other" that embodied all the fears that Calvinists had of Roman Catholicism. Muscovy for him attracted evil features like nails to a magnet. (One wonders whether, in future investigations, the theories of Orientalism might be usefully applied in the interpretation of these still very influential sources.)

My point in several of my early essays was to stress the difference in the political cultures of Muscovy and the West. Politics as we understand it existed in Muscovy only rarely or not at all. Crummey made this point in his 1983 study of the boyar elite: "Detailed investigations of the political crises of 1648 and 1682 suggest that court parties in the seventeenth century were small and short-lived. Personal ties to a statesman or family held them together; as far as we can tell, their members did not share economic interest or political program."[13]

This battle has largely been won. In addition to Crummey, scholars like Kollmann, Kivelson, and Martin (and almost everyone else) have concentrated on understanding their evidence not as a sign of allegiance to one fictional party or another, as some kind of an unconscious echo of an outdated Western historiography, but in an operational sense: How did a given system such as the law or honor—each with its own procedures, bureaucratic apparatus, and language—*work in practice* to provide stability, financial strength, and reliable military service to a government that was, for most of the Muscovite centuries, sharply weaker than most of its contemporary states in the West. Though these scholars certainly recognize that decisions in cases of law, property, honor, or royal marriage had potentially grave consequences that we might call political, the systems themselves worked to avoid partisan conflict and seem to have benefited both the ruler and society at all levels. For this reason, as we will see, government efforts were supported and vigorously engaged by almost all segments of society. In the process of their investigations, contemporary historians of Muscovy, both in Russia and the West, have been extraordinarily sophisticated in comparing their findings about Muscovy with scholarship about other regions, carefully delineating both similarities and equally revealing differences.

Muscovite Theologies of "Political" Power

A theme that emerges from almost every one of the essays in this volume is the theoretical and practical importance of the concept of God as an active force in political life. This point is perhaps made most clearly in the essay about Ivan Timofeev, where I argue that the system of political thought, presented as a diagram, was God-dependent. In other words, Muscovites believed in ways that Western Europeans thinkers had not for many centuries, that God Himself was the ultimate political authority, and that the legitimacy of a ruler and his commands depended in no small part on the perception that his will reflected God's will. (This means, I believe, that terms like "state" and "sovereign" are misleading, terms which, after the Renaissance in Europe, denoted self-contained political systems in which reference to God's will independent of the ruler's will was systematically prohibited.)

Rulers spent large amounts of their time, and often very large amounts of precious financial resources, to demonstrate their piety, and, through good works, the connection between their will and God's will. The essay on Boris Godunov's construction projects documents a series of very expensive building projects, while the long habit of conducting lavish ceremonies in Muscovy's two throne rooms required both great expense and major amounts of time, both for the ruler and for his elite, including both bureaucrats and noble servitors. Kollmann's fine essay on royal pilgrimages documents the enormous amount of royal time spent to demonstrate the ruler's piety, as well, of course, as projecting the power of the court outward into the hinterland.[14]

On these themes of rituals, their architectural settings, and the theology of rulership in Russia, there has been a great deal of path-breaking work by scholars both in Russia and in the West. These scholars have dealt with evidence similar to or the same as the evidence used in the essays in this volume (but vastly greater in type and number), and so it is to them that I briefly turn. My colleague and most generous friend Michael Flier of Harvard must lead this list. In his numerous essays on Muscovite cultural artifacts, Flier displays both enormous erudition and exceptional interpretive skill. As a result, he has a good claim to have established the original intended meaning of a host of crucial cultural products, from Saint Basil's Cathedral, perhaps the most commonly recognized monument of all of Russian culture, to the Tsar's Pew in the Dormition Cathedral, to numerous important icons and icon types, and Muscovite rituals, both sacred and secular.[15] His work and our many discussions on the Golden Hall, in particular, have been crucial to my own investigations of this most important (but now destroyed) site of political images and rituals.[16]

There is not sufficient space here to summarize all of Flier's conclusions, but I need to point out that each of us has emphasized a different aspect of royal ideology. Flier, especially in his work on the Golden Hall, but elsewhere as well, has stressed the greatness of the ruler's power, while I have noted rather the limits to this power. My investigations of the related issues of advice, moral restraints on royal power, and procedural expectations explore largely informal boundaries to royal power. Flier, ever mindful of the apocalyptic dimension of Muscovite thought, has focused on the role of the tsar leading his people to salvation in the end times, and thus has stressed the greatness of royal power necessary to carry out this millennial task.[17] I have made a similar point in describing the "descending theme" of political power in Muscovite thought: that the purpose of political life is to transfer God's will *downward* to the people through the autocratic commands of the tsar. In the end, of course, we are both right, since we both have strong evidence for our points of view. We seem to be faced with one of the central conundrums—or better, contradictions—in the evidence: that Muscovite thought both exalted and limited royal power. Unlimited power was necessary to be persuasive in the structure of Russian political thought, while limits were essential both in describing actual rulers, and in the here-and-now process of actually governing. In other words, Muscovy was an oligarchy in terms of power relationships, but a pure autocracy in terms of its dominant theory.

Recent decades have seen the emergence of a remarkably rich and imaginative series of Russian publications on themes very closely related to those in this volume. Most closely related is the remarkable volume on architecture during the reigns of Fedor Ivanovich and Boris Godunov by Andrei Batalov, one of the very best books on the history of architecture that I have ever read.[18] Batalov brings to the table not only an unmatched and detailed knowledge of virtually every masonry church built during the period but also careful research into the history of liturgical practices in Muscovy as they evolved over time. His book combines the insights of architectural history, the latest discoveries from investigations and repairs on the relevant structures, and deep knowledge of the particular moment in Eastern Orthodox culture that provided the intellectual and spiritual context for his buildings. He has a particularly fine chapter on the image of the Holy Land in the architectural thought of Godunov.

In addition to major studies on other periods and monuments of Russian architecture, Batalov and his colleague Leonid Beliaev have published illuminating studies of how medieval Russians "designed the sacred space of the country and the city."[19] This idea of the sacralization of the Russian landscape and therefore of Russia itself was one of the most powerful cultural forces in Muscovy. It is only sketched briefly in several essays here, but has been developed richly by Batalov and his colleagues. The first volume (edited by Batalov and Beliaev) of the important series *The Papers of the Institute for Medieval Christian Culture* is suggestively entitled *The Sacral Topography of the Medieval Town*.[20] In addition to Flier's essay on Saint Basil's Cathedral mentioned above, it contains a wonderful series of studies describing in detail how Russians developed in various places and at various times rituals and ceremonies that sacralized the urban landscapes of Rus´, and of Moscow in particular. It includes a fine essay by Nina Kvlividze' on the relationship between the innovative Novgorod icon type depicting the Wisdom of God, and liturgical practices in Novgorod at the end of the fifteenth century. Kvlividze's deep knowledge of the history of the liturgy has been a great resource for the field. In an excellent introductory essay, the authors lay out their methodological principles: the rigorous analysis of sources (and a Keenanesque avoidance of nineteenth-century "fantasies"); the careful study of buildings themselves, including important archaeological data; an analysis of the creators of buildings or architectural ensembles (patrons and builders); and, emphatically, an exploration of the function of the built environment within the system of rituals used by the church at a particular time and place.[21] The beauty of this approach is that it allows conceptual space for the inclusion of many types of evidence largely absent from earlier Soviet-era (and Western) scholarship—not only icons and church architecture, but also liturgical history, liturgical objects and furnishings, and the ritual life that tied these materials together and vivified them for Muscovite contemporaries.

These advantages bear rich fruit in Batalov and Beliaev's masterful 2010 book on sacral space in medieval Moscow.[22] This ambitious book provides a provocative new look at many aspects of the urban history of medieval and early modern Moscow, including not only the evolution of ecclesiastical architecture and fortifications and the development of the Kremlin and its buildings but also the landscape of Moscow from a monk's point of view, and a remarkable chapter on the life of the dead in Moscow as shown in the history of Muscovite cemeteries and the rituals associated with them. The introduction describes the decades-long efforts, stretching back into the 1980s, that underlie this monumental research program, with particular emphasis on the painstaking study of the *sources* for the study of church topography, many, perhaps most, of them unpublished. They lay out a complex theory of research in various layers of meaning, and the sources for each, including the idea of two cities—the "real" city of bricks and mortar that existed at one point and changed over time, and the mental city of symbolic and mental models, also subject to change. They examine the complex and ever-changing interactions between these two cities. The authors also make clear how much work remains to be done on their fecund topic, so that we can anticipate new publications on this theme. Particularly impressive for me is their emphasis on how contemporaries might have perceived the ecclesiastical topography of Moscow. The work of Batalov, Beliaev, and their colleagues constitutes an exciting revolution in the study of the history of Russian architecture, one that combines an acute critique of primary sources with a highly sophisticated and imaginative methodology.

Aleksei Lidov, one of these colleagues, has edited two volumes (one with Batalov) on the theme of New Jerusalems and, in the process, has invented a new and important term, "hierotopia," to describe the process of creating sacred spaces.[23] "Hierotopia is the creation of sacred spaces regarded as a special form of creativity, and a field of historical research which reveals and analyzes particular examples of that creativity."[24] The beauty of this term is that it, like the closely associated work of Batalov and Beliaev, contains wide conceptual space for the consideration of many types of evidence, from icons, murals, and church architecture to liturgical ceremonies, including liturgical clothes and vestments, lighting effects, and fragrances, to symbolic understandings.[25] In his introduction to a collection of his essays on Byzantine subjects, Lidov gives an exciting theoretical discussion of this new term that is emphatically not the positivistic study of any class of objects or of symbolic meaning, but the investigation of the creative process that produced all of them. He cites the classic examples of rulers who were creators of hierotopic spaces going back to Solomon and Justinian, and, in Rus´, Yaroslav the Wise. I might add to this list Boris Godunov and his own Solomonic building projects. One senses in Lidov's words the same revolutionary excitement in discovering new methods and largely unexamined evidence that we see in the methodological statements of Batalov and Beliaev, the opening of an exciting new chapter in our understanding of sacred spaces in Rus'.[26]

Jerusalem, Lidov tells us, is a many-leveled sacred model (*obraz*) around which the basic ideas of Orthodox Christianity gather. International contributors to his second New Jerusalem volume document references in many forms to the idea of Jerusalem in late Rome, Aachen, Loreto, Rus', Serbia, Cyprus, Armenia, and Georgia, among other places. Perhaps the most remarkable of these is Nikon's New Jerusalem Monastery in Russia, which I describe briefly in my "New Israel" essay (chapter 7), but which is in Lidov's volume explored more fully, including his description of the New Jerusalem Monastery as a "spatial icon" of impressive dimensions (5×10 km).[27]

I could not welcome more warmly the work of this inspiring group of scholars, with its new energetic theorizing and radically widening array of evidence. I feel that I stumbled on a continent of important evidence in my "New Israel" essay, but this continent is now being imaginatively explored by these worthy successors of Pavel Florenskii and other members of the "Russian Religious Renaissance."[28]

I am happy to note here that Kollmann, in her 1994 book on honor disputes, points out the importance of the sacred spaces in the Kremlin, particularly the royal palace, and of the rituals held therein. In her typically concise and thorough fashion, she lists and analyzes important royal rituals, both inside and outside the Kremlin, and cites the work of earlier scholars who had discussed these rituals at length. These scholars include not only prerevolutionary scholars like Zabelin, but also Flier and Crummey. Thus the work of investigating the ritual life, particularly of the court, has a long history. Kollmann, Flier, and Crummey all consider the social implications of these extensive rituals, mostly as promoting social cohesion, and cite various contemporary social-science and culture theories to define and defend their interpretations.[29]

To conclude this section, I need to mention the recent relevant work of several scholars. Let me begin with a valued young American colleague, Kevin Kain. Kain has explored the theme of New Jerusalem and related topics with great energy and creativity, publishing one essay in a Lidov collection. In particular, he has concentrated on Patriarch Nikon as a creator of hierotopias, particularly (but not exclusively) the New Jerusalem Monastery. He has shown, using Richard Wortman's idea of a ruler's "scenario," that rulers from Aleksei Mikhailovich through Peter the Great relied on New Jerusalem and related scenarios to create and maintain their own image as God-chosen rulers. His essays are a major contribution to our field, and amplify several of the themes in this collection.[30]

Another scholar, Dmitrii Antonov, has examined the various historical texts about the Time of Troubles, which I have also discussed at some length. His book includes chapters on Palitsyn, Timofeev, and Khvorostinin, and the depictions of rulers considered of questionable legitimacy, Vasilii Shuiskii and the First False Dmitrii. The chapter "Excurses" discuss oaths on the cross, the depiction of angels and devils in contemporary images, and, most relevant, the problem of contradictions in our sources, an issue that I have wrestled with throughout this volume. Antonov stresses, with sound evidence, the revolutionary character of the historical thought in these sources, rather than their similarity to earlier historical texts, and emphasizes the loss of faith in the sanctity of all authorities, tsar and patriarch alike, and the later consequences of that loss. I continue to believe that the mainstream of Muscovite seventeenth- and eighteenth-century history shows that the Romanov effort to put the ideological Humpty-Dumpty together again worked surprisingly well, though the evidence of continued civil strife indicates a serious weakening of the old governing "myths." The final essay on contradictions lays out a crucial problem, and tries to solve it by reference to various "explanatory systems," perhaps a not dissimilar solution to the one I proposed in my "Limits" essay (chapter 4).[31] Most exciting for me was the discovery, through Antonov's bibliography, of what appears to be a post-Soviet cottage industry devoted to scholarship about this important group of sources.[32] After not thinking much about these texts for many years, I look forward to joining this scholarly conversation.

Finally, I need to discuss, again too briefly, the work of Ostrowski, a close friend and highly original scholar. The last two chapters of his book *Muscovy and the Mongols* discuss with typical thoroughness two themes relevant to this volume: the ways that Muscovite churchmen adopted and altered the cultural package that they inherited from Byzantium, and the history of the Third Rome theory.[33] The first chapter analyzes many of the same sources that I've used, but from a different, and very useful, perspective. Ostrowski is able to subtract, as it were, the Byzantine sources for Muscovite ideology, and thus separate out the uses that Muscovites made of Byzantine texts and the important changes that Muscovites made in the Byzantine inheritance. The second chapter makes a fine complement to my "New Israel" essay by exploring with exceptional clarity the uses of the Third Rome theory in Muscovy, its sources, and evolution. Ostrowski successfully explodes several common myths about this idea and its uses and abuses by later historians, while clarifying the importance of this idea in Muscovy.[34]

Two Cultures?

The theme of the importance of God in the political ideology of early modern Russia seems to run in opposition to a well-known "two-culture" theory that I discuss in chapter 9. This idea was championed by Keenan, as well as by a number of other scholars, and was based, perhaps primarily, on language issues. On one side was the Church Slavic of the churchmen who, before the beginning of the seventeenth century, commissioned and painted all the icons and murals and compiled virtually all literary works in Russia. On the other were the bureaucrats that wrote in a chancellery language quite different from Church Slavic, far lower in register, and filled with bureaucratic formulae and even boilerplate. The elegance of this theory rests on the correspondence between this clear *linguistic* division, and the corresponding *social* division, with clergy and bureaucrats each occupying a separate caste within Muscovite society. The landowning class, with the very wealthy boyars at their pinnacle, was presumed, by Keenan at least, to have been largely illiterate down to the end of the sixteenth century. To confuse the linguistic picture even further, there were one or more spoken dialects, mostly undocumented, that had an unknown relationship to written texts.

The two-culture theory presents a challenge to the arguments presented in the essays in this book. This theory seriously diminishes the importance of the ideas contained in the evidence, dating at least until the seventeenth century, on which most of this book is based, to say nothing of the brilliant work of historians like Lidov and his colleagues discussed above. Ecclesiastical sources, whether visual or textual, would then represent an unimportant, closed, even fringe conversation among members of a tiny literate elite of churchmen, aesthetically beautiful and intellectually fascinating for us moderns, but with little or no effect on Muscovite society at large.

At the heart of the problem is our almost-complete lack of evidence about the opinions of nonliterate laymen. The very limited genres available to Muscovite bookmen well into the seventeenth century did not include fictional or nonfictional choices for writers that explored the personalities and thoughts of individuals, the exception being saints as depicted in their *Lives*. And, of course, the absence of organized educational institutions for laymen until the very end of the seventeenth century makes it hard to imagine a laity with well-developed religious or political ideas. This lack of evidence has allowed historians and publicists either to romanticize early modern Russian laypeople as preternaturally wise and spiritual, or to condemn them as irretrievably ignorant, even stupid.

My "Two Cultures" essay in chapter 9 argues against this hypothesis by trying to recreate the experience of secular, even illiterate, courtiers in the Golden Hall of the Moscow Kremlin, a place where, we know, members of both bureaucratic and aristocratic elites spent a great deal of time. That hall, and the other main throne room, the Hall of Facets, served, I argue, as weepholes through which ideas from the ecclesiastical culture could seep into the secular culture at the highest social levels. The chapters here that discuss the various historical texts about the Time of Troubles make the same point: Authors from a quite wide variety of social backgrounds all seem to have shared a common set of assumptions remarkably similar to the political theology found in the Russian throne rooms and described both in my essays and in those of my colleagues.

The events of the Time of Troubles themselves and their immediate aftermath also offer important evidence. After the almost fatal failure of traditional Muscovite ideology to provide any answer to the question of who should succeed the last Riurikovich ruler, Fedor Ivanovich, who died in 1598, Muscovites seem to have preferred to return to the theology of a God-chosen and all-powerful tsar, rather than keeping representative institutions like Assemblies of the Land, that were required to perform basic governmental functions in the chaotic conditions of the Troubles. The government under Patriarch Filaret seems to have led in making this choice, but many Russians would seem to have agreed with it, at least by implication. Assemblies of the Land were used when necessary to solve fiscal, legal, and political problems, but there does not seem to have been any organized defense of them as an institution.

New research by my colleagues has continued to challenge this "two-cultures" hypothesis. Perhaps the best and most startling example of this recent research is Kivelson's work on property maps and property disputes.[35] Using largely nonelite sources, sources far removed from Kremlin ideologues, sources that would seem to be the last place to seek evidence of political thought, she shows the enthusiastic adoption by local laymen of a God-centered religious philosophy, and even parts of the particular ideology described in this collection and by the scholars referred to above.

Kivelson examined two major types of maps: intimate, hyperlocal maps connected with property disputes in the Muscovite heartland, and maps covering much larger territories in Siberia. Maps of the first type were drawn by a motley group of local bureaucrats, army men, and pretty much anyone who could draw one of the rough but quite beautiful maps that were produced in the process of resolving property disputes. A virtuosic example of cultural history, Kivelson's chapter entitled "'The Souls of the Righteous in a Bright

Place': Landscape and Orthodoxy in Seventeenth-Century Russian Maps," makes the case that these quotidian sketch maps created for entirely secular purposes were infused with Russian Orthodox values.[36] Orthodox churches (along with trees) were key orientation points in these maps, with other markers (secular buildings, rivers) oriented around churches. This point echoes the visual evidence of foreign depictions of the Russian landscape, as briefly discussed in chapter 8 about Godunov. Visually, the maps echo the visual language of icons. In Kivelson's analysis, the trees serve as signs of paradise, of the sacralization of the local Russian landscape as a divine creation for man's benefit and edification. This evidence, she argues, illuminates the interior spiritual life of the motley assortment of mapmakers, an interior life marked deeply by the values of the Orthodox Church and by the conviction, echoing, on a local level, official sources, that the Russian land, in all of its local specificity, was created by God for the delight and edification of its Russian inhabitants. The mapmakers' churches, their trees, the whole picture that they drew of their flowering neighborhoods—all reflect both the glory of God and His presence in this transfigured landscape.

Maps of Siberia, covering much larger areas, embodied many of the points in Muscovite ideology discussed in this volume, particularly the idea that Russia was a God-chosen kingdom presided over by His chosen tsar. In particular, these maps are important for understanding the reception of some of the themes related to the famous icon *Blessed Is the Host of the Heavenly Tsar*. In chapter 6, I pose the question of whether the stories implicit in this and related images became stories that Muscovite military men told themselves on campaign, and used the battle standard of the Cossack conqueror of Siberia, Ermak, as an example. Kivelson develops this theme with great richness, using both texts and images to show that, for her mapmakers and chroniclers, the conquest of Siberia was a fulfillment of God's plan, and therefore could be accomplished, like Hezekiah's victory over Nebuchadnezzar, against overwhelming odds. Kivelson relates that the late seventeenth-century mapmaker Semen Remezov, echoing earlier Muscovite descriptions of Moscow, described the city of Tobol'sk as "God-protected, God-chosen, radiant, supreme, and reigning (*tsarstvuiushchii*)."[37] A striking Remezov image showing that "Ermak's arrival in Siberia brought a 'light of inexpressible joy' to the land" uses the metaphor of a divine eagle whose radiating feathers bear miniature towns to the various corners of the newly conquered land, with Tobol'sk as a fortress city on a hill filled with church domes in the center of the foreground. Kivelson stresses that this vision, like the earlier property maps, is not purely, or even chiefly, an ecclesiastical project, but includes chancellery offices as part of the [divine] angel's right arm. Her most significant mapmaker, Semen

Remezov, was a chancellery official, not a churchman. And the emphasis she found in her sources on the construction of churches and the loud ringing of church bells as a symbol of divinely ordained conquest echoes texts about the conquest of Kazan′ described in chapter 5 on the memory of Saint Sergius.

One could go further. Let us recall the recent theoretical advances by Lidov and others around the idea of hierotopia. Kivelson's conclusions would seem to be related closely to the basic tenet of that theory, that holiness from one sacred place can be transferred to another, making it holy as well. Kivelson's interpretation of her maps argues that the entire Russian landscape, from the small domestic paradises in the central regions to the wild landscapes and exotic flora and fauna of Siberia—all of Russia—was sacralized, even transfigured in the imagination of her mapmakers.

This remarkable book by Kivelson serves as an example of how cultural history has expanded in recent years to include innovative and even daring use of evidence in unexpected places to trace the influence of official ideology over many nonelite and nonclerical people in the seventeenth century. In that way, it confirms some of the conclusions about the diverse authors of tales about the Time of Troubles included in this volume. Not only are her maps produced by wide variety of draftsmen from many places and social levels, but her interpretations allow us to penetrate the worldviews of these diverse mapmakers, both in the central regions and in Siberia. She has a fine appreciation of the visual beauty of her images, and her evocative language allows us not only to learn from her research but to accompany her on her voyages of intellectual discovery.

One more example shows how investigations into unexpected subjects have led to major advances in cultural history. Chapter 11 details the regular insertion in the images in the *Illustrated Chronicle Compilation* (*ICC*) of a figure or figures near the ruler when he is making important decisions, particularly at diplomatic events. Who precisely were these figures, and what did they represent? My essay agonizes over this question, but Kollmann, in a recent article about the representation of legal judgments in the *ICC* solves the problem, I believe.[38] She observes that these adviser figures were present as a sign of correct judicial procedure. They are shown when the chronicler was depicting just judgments, rendered with all the other visual signs of justice, with the ruler seated on a throne and holding a scepter. But in cases of unjust judgments, those signs, including consultation with other figures, are absent. Thus the figures may not represent any particular class of people at all, but merely serve as an essential symbol of legitimizing consultation, a theme that appears over and over again in recent scholarship, as we shall see.

In spite of this fascinating, and to me convincing, evidence, there remains a very serious problem of chronology. Much of Kivelson's evidence, in particular, comes from the second half of the seventeenth century, the period when such records apparently began to be kept. Can we read this testimony back into earlier centuries? At this point, we don't know. But the evidence of the historical texts about the Time of Troubles discussed in this book, many composed by bureaucrats and secular courtiers, also seems to indicate wide acceptance of the same basic concepts of what we might call normative Muscovite political ideology.

Finally, and perhaps most importantly, we have the large amount of new evidence and theories about sacred spaces and ritual discussed above. The scholars involved in this exciting enterprise have researched sacred sites and ceremonies in their fullness, and, for the attentive reader, have shown how powerful the experiences associated with these places and ceremonies might have been. These experiences were not dependent on literacy, and, in theory reached down to the level of parish churches. They surely were a major means of communicating across the imagined two-cultures barrier.

Keenan, in his undergraduate lectures at Harvard, used the metaphors of the relationship between the nucleus of an atom and the protons moving around it or the planets orbiting the sun to describe the carefully maintained and balanced relationship between the Muscovite ruler and the major boyar clans. At the moment when Sir Isaac Newton discovered gravity, neither he nor his contemporaries understood the mechanics of gravitation, since the force of gravity appeared to function across a huge void. As we search for the mechanisms that held the early modern Russian political systems together, the ceremonial life of the country, and particularly of the court, may have been a major part of this political gravitational force. What, if anything, happened in local parish churches in the fifteenth or even the sixteenth centuries is unclear, though, as we've seen, by the second half of the seventeenth century, local churches, presumably functioning as hierotopias, were given a central place in the imagined hyperlocal landscapes drawn by mostly secular mapmakers from a wide variety of social backgrounds. The case for the far more important elite members of the court is much easier to make. We know that they were present in various churches for great amounts of time, both for regular services, for the extensive ceremonies surrounding royal weddings, and for extraordinary events like coronations, not to mention pilgrimages, religious processions to local and distant sacred sites, and so on. But there were also extensive "secular" ceremonies held in the two Kremlin throne rooms, and elsewhere. I put "secular" in quotation marks because, although the function of throne-room ceremonies was formally secular (sessions of the Boyar Duma, lengthy diplomatic receptions, and so on), the throne rooms themselves surely qualify as hierotopias, with their highly religious mural cycles, carefully designed architectural settings, great attention to formal costumes, and so forth. And the sensibility developed by boyars, whether literate or not, in church ceremonies would have carried over into the more secular ceremonies of the Muscovite government.

Who Governed Russia Anyway, or to What Question Was the Government of Muscovy an Answer?

This question has been the focus of much of my work, but now seems largely to have been resolved. In reaction to a decades-long assumption that Muscovite Russia was a despotism or dictatorship,[39] almost all scholars now have a much more nuanced understanding that delineates both real and moral limits to the ruler's power without denying that he still had influence that was extraordinary, at least by the standards of his royal neighbors in Western Europe. Muscovy remained a service state, where all landowners owed service to the ruler, who could, until the middle of the seventeenth century, arrest anyone and take his property with little restraint. There was no constitutionally defined class of nobles with legal rights as there was in the West. Indeed, as the essays in this volume argue, there was little or no concept of "freedom" in the political vocabulary of Muscovy.[40] And of course, serfdom, which had largely disappeared in the West by 1500, was being created in Russia in the seventeenth century. These characteristics convinced many Western visitors to Russia in the early modern period to characterize the government and ruler there as "plain tyrannical," to use Giles Fletcher's famous phrase.[41]

This view has been seriously modified by much recent scholarship. There has been a change in the question the scholarly community is asking, from "Was Muscovy a despotism?" to "How did a relatively impoverished government ruling over a vast, rapidly growing, and increasingly multi-ethnic empire survive and even thrive?" The fascinating thing about this work is that many, perhaps all, of the devices that in theory magnified the ruler's power also simultaneously limited that power. A great example of this phenomenon is the vigorous growth of the administrative *prikaz* system, on which the American scholar Peter Brown has done a lot of important work.[42] However, Mikhail Krom's expert dissection of the administrative apparatus during the minority of Ivan IV (1533–1547) has the most telling evidence on this point. Obviously, the bureaucracy was an increasingly important tool of governance by the ruler, helping him gather money, conduct diplomacy, and other crucial tasks, but Krom explores what happened when a supposedly all-powerful monarch was far too young to take any real part in politics. Under these unusual circumstances, the government continued to function smoothly, making important decisions and keeping order. After a careful chronological account of the period and a painstaking study of all the sources, particularly documentary sources produced routinely by bureaucrats, Krom produced a picture of the day-to-day life of the bureaucracy. He examined how decisions were made and how the country was governed in the absence of an active monarch (and without the institution of a regency, which might have solved the problem of a too-young monarch). He concludes that "the ruler's prerogatives were confined to symbolic representation of the realm (especially in foreign policy) and control over the elite," while "the state apparatus functioned stably in spite of the factional rivalries at the court in the 1530s and 1540s." The bureaucratic system continued to function normally also when the monarch was absent from Moscow for extended periods.[43] A. P. Pavlov makes much the same arguments in describing the smooth functioning of the court during factional struggles under the feeble-minded Fedor Ivanovich and Boris Godunov.[44] And, a number of scholars have produced careful recent examinations of the bureaucratic apparatus over the entire Muscovite period, again documenting its relative independence, efficiency, and personnel.[45]

On the basis of the same careful analysis of documentary evidence Krom was able to come to some important conclusions about the role of advice and advisers, particularly boyar advisers, in governance during the minority of Ivan IV. His first point is that, even though the boyars had complete control of the government apparatus, they pointedly refused to infringe on the royal prerogatives of conducting foreign policy and dealing with the court elite. Instead, they carefully maintained the fiction of royal participation and proper court etiquette by having the monarch present, even if he was only four years old. But, by studying the formulae of bureaucratic documents, Krom was also able to tell which courtier or group of courtiers authorized a given decision. The second major conclusion was that getting some form of advice was essential. Although at the beginning of Ivan's minority individual boyars were consulted according to political power, the subject to be decided, or a particular boyar's presence (or absence) in Moscow, by the end of the reign the custom was established that most boyars would be present, and that all decisions would be unanimous, a tradition that was codified in the Law Code of 1550. What makes Krom's analysis so relevant here is that he is analyzing the very period described in the *ICC*, as discussed in chapter 11. Both the *ICC* and Krom place significant emphasis on the process of consultation and its importance in affirming the most important governmental decisions.

Yet the nature of Muscovite political thought as we've discussed it, with its formal reliance on the direct link from God's will to the people via the divinely inspired orders of a pious ruler, made it both difficult and undesirable for Muscovite thinkers to create theoretical limits to the ruler's power, whether by means of legal/constitutional institutions or by theoretical limits described in written or visual texts. This conjunction of an early medieval belief system and an early modern governmental structure also explains the determination of the boyars to maintain a fiction of royal participation in decision making, obviously fictional as any real participation was. For God's will to be seen as descending through the will of a pious ruler, the ruler had to seem to be making the most important decisions. This brittle theory of autocracy also left little or no conceptual space for the institution of a regency during Ivan's minority.

I'd like to conclude by briefly discussing further the highly relevant work of Martin and Kollmann. There is far too little space to do their work justice, so I will simply try to comment briefly on the ways their work intersects with the essays in this volume. There are other excellent colleagues whose work I am forced to ignore, for which I apologize.

Martin's work on royal marriages in his fine book *A Bride for the Tsar*, like Kivelson's work on property maps, provides surprising conclusions from largely untapped sources. Most obvious in the context of the current volume are his references to the elaborate, expensive, and time-consuming rituals surrounding royal marriages, arguably the most important events in the life of the court. In a forthcoming book, Martin gives a detailed account of these fascinating ceremonies.[46] Both books provide yet more evidence of the importance of the ritual life of the court and of the hierotopic nature of that court, evidence that can be added to further findings in this volume as well as information brought forward by Lidov, Batalov, Beliaev, and colleagues discussed above. Like the throne-room rituals, marriage ceremonies were another crossover between political thought and political action in which the political structure of the court was acted out and made visible.

Martin's book perfectly illustrates the paradoxical relationship between royal power and limits to that power. The royal bride shows, in which members of the elite apparently offered their maiden daughters to the tsarist gaze, had been traditionally interpreted as a vaguely erotic demonstration of royal power. In a wonderful transformation of this view, Martin sees royal marriages, the elaborate marriage ceremonies, and the bride shows themselves in the context of Muscovite court politics as a whole, and stresses the political meaning and function of these important rituals. On the basis of his unrivaled command of the documentary sources for royal weddings, he fits these ceremonies into what Keenan has called "the grammar of Muscovite court politics," showing how everything—from seating at wedding banquets to the elaborate prenuptial rituals—acted both to demonstrate royal power and, importantly, to give scope for rivalry and competition among aristocratic clans without resort to bloodshed or violence. He proves conclusively that the process of bride shows was actually run by the aristocratic clans, both in Moscow and in the provinces, to mediate the potentially fatal struggle among themselves to become royal in-laws. Again, we find a paradox: These elaborate ceremonies that provided extremely fine-grained social maps of the court elite both amplified royal power by limiting and regulating clan rivalry and casting the ruler at the ritual center, and limited it by placing control of ceremonies and bride shows in the hands of provincial and Moscow-based aristocrats. Beneath a façade of unlimited royal power stood the complex interaction of powerful boyar clans, all expressed through elaborate rituals.

Kollmann's magisterial books have provided perhaps the most thorough and thoughtful overall picture of Muscovite political culture in the broadest sense, based always on a dazzling command of immense quantities of archival evidence and all relevant scholarship, theoretical, comparative, and Muscovy-specific. Her first book, *Kinship and Politics*, asserts a patrimonial rather than a class basis for Muscovite political culture, arguing that, from the time of the civil wars in the fifteenth century, boyar clans and seniority both among and within these clans were the crucial building blocks of court politics. Like Crummey's findings about the seventeenth century, Kollmann argues that neither class, nor policy issues, nor ideological differences had important impacts on court life, the purpose of which was to provide stability by limiting potentially fatal conflicts within the court elite. This view, based on the earlier work of S. B. Veselovskii and Keenan, has long been part of my own imagined picture of Muscovy.[47]

Kollmann's 2012 book on the legal culture of early modern Russia makes similar points. She argues that Russian law was not the barbaric, cruel, and arbitrary instrument of unbridled state power that both Russian and Western stereotypes often depict. Instead, hobbled as it was by a bureaucratic apparatus far too small for its vast territories and thin populations, the government depended on local residents, from local gentrymen to village peasants, to staff courts and take part in investigations. Their energetic participation in legal cases both demonstrated their acceptance of the tsar's justice and gave them ample opportunity to manipulate that justice for their own ends.[48]

But I think Kollmann's 1999 book on honor and the Muscovite system of precedence might be the most directly relevant to this collection of essays, and a suitable place to end this concluding essay. In a brilliant chapter on "Strategies of Integration in an Autocracy," Kollmann beautifully summarizes scholarship on both Muscovite society and its culture in the context of social science theories about how societies may be held together by integrating all members, particularly elite members, into a perceived community in which they willingly participate. She wisely not only emphasizes the sorts of "limits" of royal power that I argue in the essays here but puts the cultural restraints imposed on rulers in the context of a number of social practices that helped to integrate the large and expanding, multifaith and multi-ethnic population of Muscovy into a state and empire that was, taken together, remarkably successful given its resource limitations. Indeed, Kollmann joins Martin in stressing the utility of seeing political culture in light of the goal of integration, rather than through the lens of a Whiggish, zero-sum question of who had more power, ruler or subject, tsar or boyar. This approach allows her to avoid any romanticism in her view of Muscovy; she stresses violence and coercion as well as strong traditions of consultation, but sees them as complimentary rather than contradictory. As she concludes: "Cohesion came from a combination of factors: coercive control; tolerance of local autonomies; distribution of awards; effective dissemination of unifying ideas in laws, texts, and ritual; and the ability of individuals to interpret and manipulate the dominant ideas and institutions to their own ends, within bounds acceptable to the state."[49]

I am happy to put the essays in this volume into this capacious and convincing framework. Instead of paying attention to pesky logicians, we can place the evidence considered in this volume in the context of how various aspects of Muscovite political culture worked in practice to enable the government to govern. The ideological contradictions that are so apparent to us may be seen as functioning like the apparent contradictions described by historians in the law or the honor system: Ideology was a tool of creating cohesion that both necessarily emphasizes the unrestrained power of the ruler as the essential legitimizing link to God's will and simultaneously provides a role for subjects, especially elite subjects, who could manipulate the ideology to promote their own interests. In that context of comparisons with other integrating aspects of political culture, political thought can be cheerfully contradictory: loose as well as tight, autocratic, even dictatorial, as well as consensual.

We began our discussion with Yuval Harari's description of the crucial role that culture played in helping to organize human society after the cognitive revolution. This function depended on a culture's ability to create a clear and widely accepted message. The idea that a ruler's will reflected God's will was such a message, a commonplace in medieval Christian states and perhaps, if we leave aside the specifically Christian content, in almost all premodern societies. It is probably the most powerful political idea in human history, reflected for Christians even in the Lord's Prayer: "Thy will be done on earth as it is in Heaven." In Russia, perhaps alone among European nations, the clarity of this idea had not been much clouded by later debates by philosophers and theologians, and thus retained greater strength. Muscovite ideology preserved this strength in its programmatic statements about a ruler's unlimited power, but left vital, but logically inconsistent, conceptual room for two tasks that cheerfully contradicted this ideal of pure autocracy: describing actual rulers and describing actual governance, particularly the importance of consultation. The façade of autocracy was indeed a fiction, but a necessary fiction.

As historians writing at this historical moment, when stereotypes of Russian despotism are still widespread both in Russia and in the West, and tensions between the two remain high, this ambiguity is important to convey to a broader audience. The early modern Russian past is often taken as the clear, unpolluted source for Russian culture and values before the advent of the Westernizing changes under Peter the Great. The essays in this book, plus what seems to me to be a pretty clear scholarly consensus among historians, will, I hope, help diminish the Russian version of exceptionalism, an idea that may take the form of predicting an authoritarian future based on Russia's uniquely authoritarian past. By stressing the complexity of Muscovite political culture and its similarities with the political cultures and states of the rest of Europe, I hope that, as historians, we may have an impact, however modest, on Russia's future.[50]

Notes

1. Yuval Noah Harari, *Sapiens: A Brief History of Mankind* (New York: HarperCollins, 2015), 20–39.
2. Harari, *Sapiens*, 65–69.
3. Harari, *Sapiens*, 25–31, 105, 117–18.
4. Harari, *Sapiens*, 33–59, and elsewhere.
5. See, for example, the excellent study by David B. Miller, *St. Sergius of Radonezh, His Trinity Monastery and the Formation of the Russian Identity* (DeKalb: Northern Illinois University Press, 2010).
6. Robert O. Crummey, *Aristocrats and Servitors: The Boyar Elite in Russia, 1613–1689* (Princeton, NJ: Princeton University Press, 1983). See also references to Crummey's articles in his bibliography, 279.
7. Crummey, *Aristocrats and Servitors*, 164.
8. Crummey, *Aristocrats and Servitors*, 167.
9. Valerie Kivelson, *Desperate Magic: The Moral Economy of Witchcraft in Seventeenth-Century Russia* (Ithaca, NY: Cornell University Press, 2013). See also Valerie Kivelson, *Cartographies of Tsardom: The Land and Its Meaning in Seventeenth-Century Russia* (Ithaca, NY: Cornell University Press, 2006).

10. Edward L. Keenan, "Muscovite Political Folkways," *Russian Review* 45, no. 2 (April 1986): 115–181. On Keenan as historian and teacher, see Russell Martin, "'To Stimulate and Provoke, Rather Than to Convince': Edward L. Keenan and the Teaching and Writing of Russian History," *Modern Greek Studies Yearbook* 32/33 (2016/2017): 117–132.

11. Claudio Sergio Ingerflom, "La historia conceptual y las distorsiones cognitivas del uso acrítico del concepto 'Estado,'" *J Prohistoria* 28 (December 2017).

12. Marshall Poe, *Foreign Descriptions of Muscovy: An Analytic Bibliography of Primary and Secondary Sources* (Columbus, OH: Slavica Publishers, 1995); Marshall Poe, *"A People Born to Slavery": Russia in Early Modern European Ethnography, 1476–1748* (Ithaca, NY: Cornell University Press, 2000).

13. Crummey, *Aristocrats and Servitors*, 10.

14. Nancy Shields Kollman, "Pilgrimage, Procession, and Symbolic Space in Sixteenth-Century Russian Politics," in *Medieval Russian Culture*, vol. 2, ed. Michael Flier and Daniel Rowland (Berkeley: University of California Press, 1994), 163–181.

15. Michael S. Flier, "Filling in the Blanks: the Church of the Intercession and the Architectonics of Medieval Muscovite Ritual," *Harvard Ukrainian Studies* 29, nos. 1–4 (1995): 120–137; Michael S. Flier, "The Throne of Monomakh: Ivan the Terrible and the Architectonics of Destiny," in *Architectures of Russian Identity, 1500–Present*, ed. James Cracraft and Daniel Rowland (Ithaca, NY: Cornell University Press, 2003), 21–33; Michael S. Flier, "Political Ideas and Rituals," in *The Cambridge History of Russia*, vol. 1, *From Early Rus' to 1689*, ed. Maureen Perrie (Cambridge: Cambridge University Press, 2006), 387–408.

16. See especially Michael S. Flier, "Golden Hall Iconography and the Makarian Initiative," in *The New Muscovite Cultural History: A Collection in Honor of Daniel B. Rowland*, ed. Valerie Kivelson, Karen Petrone, Nancy Shields Kollmann, and Michael S. Flier (Bloomington, IN: Slavica, 2009), 63–75; also Michael S. Flier, "Seeing Is Believing: The Semiotics of Dynasty and Destiny in Muscovite Rus'," in *Ceremonial Culture in Pre-Modern Europe*, ed. Nicholas Howe (Notre Dame, IN: Notre Dame University Press, 2006), 63–88; and Michael S. Flier, "K semioticheskomu analizu Zolotoi palaty Moskovskogo Kremlia," in *Drevnerusskoe iskusstvo. Russkoe iskusstvo pozdnego srednevekov'ia. XVI vek*, ed. Andrei Batalov et al. (Saint Petersburg: Dmitrii Bulanin, 2003), 178–187.

17. Michael S. Flier, "Till the End of Time: The Apocalypse in Russian Historical Experience before 1500," in *Orthodox Russia: Belief and Practice under the Tsars*, ed. Valerie A. Kivelson and Robert H. Greene (University Park: Pennsylvania State University Press, 2003), 127–158.

18. Andrei Batalov, *Moskovskoe kamennoe zodchestvo kontsa XVI veka: problemy khodozhestvennogo myshleniia epokhi* (Moscow: Rossiiskaia Akademiia Khudozhesv, 1996).

19. The phrase is from Batalov, *Moskovskoe kamennoe zodchestvo*, 290, referring to the foundational cultural work of Metropolitan Makarii. The works of Batalov and Beliaev are discussed immediately below.

20. *Sacral'naia topografiia srednevekovogo goroda* (Moscow: Izd. IKhKS, 1998).

21. Given the near impossibility of writing about Christian culture during the long Soviet period, this methodology could not be more welcome. Several volumes of institute papers are both impressive and inspiring, even revolutionary. Yet I would

venture here some modest suggestions. First, although Batalov and Beliaev have an impressive bibliography of Western scholarship (in English) on sacred topography in the medieval West, they understandably do not explore interpretations of more secular and later landscapes by scholars like Dell Upton and his quite relevant concept of the "processional landscape." Second, although the sacred was crucial in forming early Russian urban landscapes, there must have been other paths by other people that invested the built environment with meaning: merchants or peasants coming to Red Square to sell livestock or produce, for example, or bureaucrats moving among governmental spaces, including back stairs and interstitial spaces, in the Kremlin. The processional landscape experienced by foreign diplomats is another example, explored more fully by Michael Flier in an essay mentioned earlier, in some of my essays, as well as by L. A. Iusefovich. Except in the case of the diplomats, we lack much evidence for these secular processional spaces, but it may be possible to recreate them by studying circulation patterns of buildings or entire ensembles of buildings. See Dell Upton, *Holy Things and Profane: Anglican Parish Churches in Colonial Virginia* (New Haven, CT: Yale University Press, 1997); Flier, "Political Ideas and Rituals"; and L. A. Iusefovich, "Kak v posol'skikh obychaiakh vedetsia . . ." (Moscow: Mezhdunarodnye otnosheniia, 1988).

22. Andrei Batalov and Leonid Beliaev, *Sacral'noe prostranstvo srednevekovoi Moskvy* (Moscow: Dizain, informatsiia, kartografiia, 2010), esp. introduction, 6–11.

23. Andrei Batalov and Aleksei Lidov, eds., *Ierusalim v Russkoi kul'ture* (Moscow: Nauka, 1994); Aleksei Lidov, *Novye Ierusalimy: Ierotopiia i ikonografiia sakral'nykh prostranstv* (Moscow: Indrik, 2009). See also Michael Flier's particularly fine review of the latter, in which he classifies and lucidly explains the two types of Jerusalem references, one to the earth-bound Old Jerusalem (the actual city described in the Hebrew and Greek scriptures and in other sources), and the invisible New Jerusalem of the book of Revelation: *Jahrbucher fur Geschichte Osteuropas*, jgo.e-reviews, vol. 2/3 (2012): 4–6.

24. Aleksei Lidov, ed., *Ierotopiia. Prostranstvennye ikony i obrazy-paradigmy v vizantiskoi kul'ture* (Moscow: Feoria, 2009), English quotation in "Summary," 307. Since he has placed such an emphasis on his terminology, I have used Lidov's own translations into English where possible, with the one important exception of the word "Hierotopia" [*Ierotopiia*] where I have preferred "Hierotopia" to Lidov's "Hierotopy."

25. I am surprised by the relative lack of attention, at least theoretical attention, to music and other sounds, particularly bells. Choral singing surely was a crucial ingredient in the creation of hierotopias. Such singing played a major role in Sergei Eisenstein's recreation of Ivan the Terrible's coronation in the sacred space of Moscow's Dormition Cathedral.

26. Lidov, *Ierotopiia*, 11–38; "Summary," 306–337.

27. Lidov, *Novye Ierusalimy*, especially Lidov's introduction, "New Jerusalems: Transferring the Holy Land as a Generative Matrix [*parozhdaiushchaia matritsa*] of Christian Culture," 5–10; and Galina Zelenskaia, "New Jerusalem Near Moscow: Aspects of the Conception and New Discoveries," in Lidov, *Novye Ierusalimy*, 745–773.

28. Nicholas Zernov, *The Russian Religious Renaissance* (New York: Harper and Row, 1963); Judith Kornblatt and Richard Gustavsam, *Russian Religious Thought* (Madison: University of Wisconsin Press, 1996); Avril Pyman, *Pavel Florensky; A Quiet Genius: The Tragic and Extraordinary Life of Russia's Unknown Da Vinci* (New York: Continuum, 2010).

29. Nancy Shields Kollmann, *By Honor Bound: State and Society in Early Modern Russia* (Ithaca, NY: Cornell University Press, 1999), 186–199, with references particularly to Crummey (192n78) and Flier (193n85). Flier is in close contact with Lidov and colleagues, and their edited collections often include Russian versions of his English-language essays. See also Kollmann's superb discussion of "theoretical discussions about cohesion," both by Western theoreticians and Russian writers chiefly from the Muscovite period (169–180).

30. Kevin Kain, "New Jerusalem and the Politics of Byzantine Renewal in Russia: The Resurrection of the Resurrection 'New Jerusalem Monastery' in the Reign of Tsar Fedor Alekseevich (1676–1682)," *Canadian-American Slavic Studies*; Kevin Kain, "'New Jerusalem' in Seventeenth Century Russia: The Image of a New Orthodox Holy Land," *Cahiers du monde russe* 58, no. 3 (2017): 371–394; Kevin Kain, "The Sacred Waters of the 'Holy Lake' Valdai: A Wellspring of Hierotopic Activities in the Reign of Tsar Aleksei Mikhailovich," in *Zhivonosnyi istochnik: voda v ierotopii i ikonografii khristianskogo mira*, ed. Aleksei Lidov (Moscow: Filigran, 2014), 152–176; Kevin Kain, "Before New Jerusalem: Patriarch Nikon's Iverskii and Krestnyi Monasteries," *Russian History* 39, nos. 1–2 (2012): 173–223.

31. D. I. Antonov, *Smuta v kul'ture srednvekovoi Rusi: evolutsiia drevnerusskikh mifologem v knizhnosti nachala XVII veka* (Moscow: Rossiiskii gosudarstvennyi gumanitarnyi universitet, 2009), esp. chapter on contradictions, 259–271.

32. Antonov, *Smuta v kul'ture srednvekovoi Rusi*, 18–25.

33. Donald Ostrowski, *Muscovy and the Mongols: Cross-Cultural Influences on the Steppe Frontier, 1304–1589* (Cambridge: Cambridge University Press, 1998).

34. There is some important evidence about the Third Rome theory that I was unaware of. Agnes Kriza has recently pointed out clear references to that theory in images depicting a flying icon of the Mother of God, which traveled from Constantinople to Rome during the iconoclastic period in Byzantium, returned to Constantinople after icon veneration was restored, and was then imagined to reside in Russia, the Third Rome. "Now Moscow is the new dwelling place, which the Virgin chose as a Third and final Rome, after the first Rome and the second Rome." Agnes Kriza, "Icon, Empire, and Orthodoxy: Representations of Byzantine Iconoclasm during the Reign of Ivan the Terrible," paper presented at the American Society for Eastern European and Eurasian Studies annual conference, Boston, December 2018.

35. Kivelson, *Cartographies of Tsardom*.

36. Kivelson, *Cartographies of Tsardom*, 99–116.

37. Kivelson, *Cartographies of Tsardom*, 138.

38. Nancy Shields Kollmann, "Representing Legitimacy in Early Modern Russia," *Russian Review* 76, no.1 (2017): 7–21.

39. The classic statement is Richard Pipes, *Russia under the Old Regime* (New York: Charles Schribner's Sons, 1974).

40. See also Valerie Kivelson's provocative and wise "Muscovite 'Citizenship': Rights without Freedom," *Journal of Modern History* 74, no. 3 (September 2002): 465–489.

41. Lloyd E. Berry and Robert O. Crummey, eds., *Rude and Barbarous Kingdom: Russia and the Accounts of Sixteenth-Century English Voyagers* (Madison: University of Wisconsin Press, 1968), 132.

42. See, for example, Peter Brown, "How Muscovy Governed: Seventeenth-Century Russian Central Administration," *Russian History* 36, no. 4 (2009): 459–529.

43. Quotations in Mikhail M. Krom, "Recent Trends in the Russian Historiography of the Muscovite State," paper presented at the American Society for Eastern European and Eurasian Studies, Chicago, November 2017. See also the fuller analysis in Mikhail M. Krom, *"Vdovstvushchee tsarstvo": Politicheskii krizis v Rossii 30-40-x godov XVI veka* (Moscow: Novoe Literaturnoe Obozrenie, 2010), 412–438.

44. A. P. Pavlov, *Gosudarev dvor i politicheskaia bor'ba pri Borise Godunove: 1584–1605* (Saint Petersburg: Nauka, 1999). See also D. V. Liseitsev, *Prikaznaia sistema Moskovskogo gosudarstva v epokhu Smuty* (Moscow: Institut rossiiskoi istorii RAN, 2003).

45. See, for example, Peter Brown, "Guarding the Gate-Keepers: Punishing Errant Rank-and-File Officials in Seventeenth-Century Russia," *Jahrbücher für Geschichte Osteuropas* 50 (2002): 224–245; Iu. G. Alekseev, *U kormila Rossiiskogo gosudarsta: ocherki razvitiia apparata upravleniia XIV–XV vv.* (Saint Petersburg: Izdatel'stvo Sankt-Peterburgskogo Universiteta, 1998); A. L. Korzinin, *Gosudarev dvor Russkogo gosudarstva v dooprichnyi period, 1550–1565* (Mosocw-Saint Petersburg: Alians-Arkheo, 2016); P. V. Sedov, *Zakat Moskovskogo tsarstva: Tsarskii dvor kontsa XVII veka* (Saint Petersburg: Sankt Peterburgskii institut istorii, 2006). See also the pioneering article by Borivoj Plavsic, "Seventeenth-Century Chanceries and Their Staffs," in *Russian Officialdom: The Bureaucratization of Russian Society from the Seventeenth to the Twentieth Century*, ed. Walter Pintner and Don Rowney (Chapel Hill: University of North Carolina Press, 1980), 19–45.

46. Russell Martin, *The Tsar's Happy Occasion: Ritual and Dynasty in the Weddings of Russia's Rulers, 1495–1745* (Dekalb: Northern Illinois University Press, an imprint of Cornell University Press, 2021).

47. S. B. Velelovskii, *Issledovaniia po istorii klassa sluzhilykh zemlevladel'tsev* (Moscow: Nauka, 1969); Keenan, "Muscovite Political Folkways."

48. Nancy Shields Kollmann, *Crime and Punishment in Early Modern Russia* (Cambridge: Cambridge University Press, 2012), esp. 416–426.

49. Nancy Shields Kollmann, *By Honor Bound: State and Society in Early Modern Russia* (Ithaca, NY: Cornell University Press, 1999), 201, esp. chap. 5.

50. See Russell Martin, "The Uses of the Past: Political Culture in Early Modern Russia and the Problems of the Present," *The Sixteenth Century Journal* 50, no. 1 (Spring 2019): 196–204; Daniel Rowland, "Why Authoritarian Rule Is Not Russia's History—or Destiny," *Monkey Cage* (blog), *Washington Post*, March 6, 2018.

Index

Abel (biblical figure), 29–30, 40, 166–67, 199
absolutism, 28, 37, 51n47, 73, 82–83, 85–87, 90, 106, 248, 310, 317
Adam (biblical figure), 33–34, 36, 59–60, 164
Adashev, Aleksei, 4, 6–9, 13, 18, 21n35
Adrian I, Pope, 304
advice and advisers
    in Carolingian Europe, 308–9
    corrective, 104–5
    and declaration of ruler as tormentor, 316–17
    Duma and, 66–67
    evil, 62, 77n40
    Golden Hall murals and, 227–28
    ideology and, 98–99
    in *Illustrated Chronicle Companion*, 276–79
    as obligation of ruler, 332
    persons qualified to give, 63–64
    problem of, 57–63, 332–36
    and promotion of unworthy people, 61–62
    in Timofeev, 61–62
Afanasii, Metropolitan, 94, 97–98
Agapetus, 34–35, 38, 43, 52n56, 60, 88, 102, 111n64, 235, 308, 347
Ambrose, 303
Anderson, Thornton, 320
And I Saw Heaven Opened, and Behold a White Horse, and He that Sat Upon Him was Called Faithful and True, and in Righteousness He Doth Judge and Make War (Annunciation Cathedral), 143, 146
Angelov, Andrei, 116
Antonov, Dmitrii, 373
Antonova, V. I., 132–33
Apocalypse, 135–36, 147, 156, 170–71, 177, 204, 246, 253, 339–41
apocalypticism, 41, 110n54, 114n99, 178
Archangel Michael Appoints Moses Prince (Archangel Michael Cathedral), 149

Archangel Michael Cathedral, 129, 147–48, 150, 154n33, 200, 225
Archangel Michael Helps Hezekiah Defeat 185,000 Assyrian Troops, 137, 140
Archangel Michael with Scenes from his Life, 137, 139–40
architecture. *See also* Golden Hall; Kremlin (Moscow)
    Bible and, 203–4
    Godunov and, 171, 188–206, 306
    "Italianisms" in, 200
    maps and, 196–97
    New Israel concept and, 171–76, 186n54
    Peter the Great and, 188
    religious, 197–201
    Saint Sergius and, 120–21
aristocracy
    boyars as, 151
    in Crummey, 363
    in distribution of political power, 317
    Godunov and, 65, 71, 325
    humanism and, 321
    in Keenan, 382
    in Kliuchevskii, 56, 74n4
    opposition of, 44
    oprichnina and, 74n4, 98
    Peter the Great and, 318
    in Platonov, 74n4
    and power of tsar, 44–45
    service, 311
    sufferance and, 12
    in tales, 66
    in Timofeev, 32
Aristotle, 28, 86, 217, 235, 306, 347–48, 350–51, 367
Ars amatoria (Ovid), 348
Assembly of Land, 55, 66–67, 69, 93, 105, 191, 296, 323, 325–26, 328, 335, 338, 343–44, 375
Astrakhan', 191–95, 208n10
Auerbach, Inge, 108n24

INDEX

Augustine, 303
Avvakum, 87, 101–2, 114n99, 327–28, 332, 338

Barsov, E. V., 181n14
Bashkin, Matvei, 325
Basil of Macedonia, 329
Batalov, A. L, 199, 202, 209nn27,29, 370, 385n19
Battle between the Novgorodians and the Suzdalians, The, 137, 141
battle standards, 130, 133–34, 142–45, 151, 169, 212, 376
Baxendall, Michael, 229, 233n29
Bekbulatovich, Semen, 39, 89
Belarus, 327–28, 339, 350
Beliaev, Leonid, 370–72, 381, 385n19, 386n21
Bel′skii, Bogdan, 89
Bible
  advisers in, 101
  architecture and, 203–4
  in battle standard of Ivan IV, 133–34
  Church Militant icon and, 132–33
  correlation of Old and New Testaments in, 162–63
  in Golden Hall murals, 217–19, 221, 226
  in historical imagination, 156–57
  Illustrated Chronicle Companion and, 283–88
  Israel in, 161
  kingship in, 160
  in Makarii, 134–35
  martyrs in, 135–36
  New Israel concept and, 79n55, 158–59, 163–70
  as political source, 304
  tales and, 70n55
  in Timofeev, 17–18, 33–34, 36–37, 40, 49n29, 80n55
Blessed Be the Host of the King of Heaven, 133. *See also* Church Militant icon
Bogatyrev, Sergei, 259, 282n13
Boiarskaia Duma (Kliuchevskii), 18, 21n58
Book of Degrees of the Imperial Genealogy (Metropolitan Makarii), 324
Book of Tsardom, 333–34
Borisov Gorodok, 192, 201
Boyar Duma, 343, 378–79
  adviser role of, 317, 334–35
  Assembly of the Land and, 335, 338
  in Crummey, 363
  Godunov and, 191, 195, 207n3

  Illustrated Chronicle Companion and, 274–75
  Ivan III and, 322
  Ivan IV and, 260, 323
  replacement of, with Senate, 318
  in tales, 66–67, 69
  in Timofeev, 94
boyars
  as advisers, 334–35, 380
  as aristocracy, 151
  corruption of, 13
  as flatterers, 104
  Golden Hall murals and, 229, 260
  harmony with, 114n104
  and *Illustrated Chronicle Companion*, 261–64, 272, 274, 276, 280
  Ivan IV and, 122, 380
  in Kurbskii, 7, 13–19
  and Muscovy as Israel, 146, 150, 169
  and power of tsars, 44–45
  in tales, 61, 64, 69, 71–72
  in Timofeev, 50n34
  in Ushakov, 227
  Vasilii III and, 285, 291
Boyars' Porch, 215–16, 239–41, 243
Bride for the Tsar, A (Martin), 381–82
Bulanin, D. M., 154n28
bureaucracy, 25–26, 74n4, 103, 128, 191–92, 279, 293–94, 310–11, 317, 323, 344–45, 374–75, 378–80
Bushkovitch, Paul, 114n104, 226
Bussow, Conrad, 50n31, 168
Byzantium, 44, 87, 102, 134–35, 137, 150, 156, 159–60, 203, 220–24, 254, 323, 331–32, 336, 342, 345, 373, 387n34

Cain (biblical figure), 29–30, 40, 49n28, 166–67, 199
Carolingian Europe. *See also* Charlemagne
  advice and advisers in, 308–9
  Bible as political source in, 304
  Carolingian Renaissance and, 305–6
  custom in, 307–8
  Latin texts and, 303
  power in, 304–7
Cathedral of the Don, 200–201, 288
Cathedral of the Intercession on the Moat, 169–70, 186n53, 190–91, 201–2, 324, 369
Chancellor, Richard, 232n14, 249
Charlemagne, 161, 238, 301–8. *See also* Carolingian Europe

Cherniavsky, Michael, 35, 37–40, 52nn53,56, 106n4, 114n99, 130, 148, 299–300
"Chosen Council" of Ivan IV, The: A Reinterpretation (Grobovsky), 45n3
Church. See clergy; Orthodox Church
Church Council of 100 Chapters, 323
Church Militant icon, 49n30, 130–34, 143–44, 169, 214, 221, 306, 340–41
Church of Boris and Gleb, 201
Church Slavonic, 11, 72, 159, 214, 217, 229, 303, 342, 347, 350, 374
Clanchy, M. T., 130
clergy, 374. See also Orthodox Church
  royal absolutism and, 82
  in Timofeev, 36, 53n65
  unction ceremony and, 160
Clovis oil, 305
Cognitive Revolution, 358
Coke, Edward, 60
Constantine, 91, 101, 133, 136, 163, 168, 304–5, 337, 340, 349
Constantinople, 91, 164–65, 322, 340, 387n34
Conversation of the Miracle-Workers of Valaam, The, 337
Correspondence between Prince A. M. Kurbsky and Tsar Ivan IV of Russia 1564–1579, The (Kurbskii), 7–8, 13, 108n24, 320
corruption
  advice and, 67
  of boyars, 13
  Godunov and, 58, 111n60
  in Karamzin, 9
  in Kurbskii, 15–16
  subjects and, 77n39
  tales and, 68
  in Timofeev, 61–62
  Timofeev and, 32–42
Council of Ferrara-Florence, 322
Course in Russian History (Kliuchevskii), 54–55
Cromwell, Oliver, 178
Crummey, Robert O., 74n4, 86, 211, 278, 363–64
Cyril-White Lake Monastery, 192

Daniel (biblical figure), 132–34, 147, 165, 340
Daniil, Metropolitan, 337, 348
David (biblical figure), 11, 30, 52n56, 69, 80n55, 96, 100, 133–36, 147, 150, 158, 160, 166, 168, 181n16, 210n32, 219, 223, 284–88, 293, 304, 332, 340
Demus, Otto, 217
Derzhavina, O. A., 71, 76n21

despotism, 280, 379–80, 384
D'iakonov, M., 259
Discourses on Government (Krizhanich), 351
Dmitriev, Iu. N., 154n33
Dmitry of Uglich, 4, 8
Donskoi, Dmitrii, 115–16, 118, 284, 289–91, 293, 295–97
Dormition Cathedral (Astrakhan'), 194–95, 338
Dormition Cathedral (Moscow), 137–39, 259, 268–69, 333–34
Dormition Cathedral (Sviiazhsk), 260
Drevnernusskie skazaniia i povesti o smutnom vremeni XVII veka (Old Russian tales and stories about the time of troubles of the seventeenth century) (Platonov), 54
Duma. See Boyar Duma
duties of ruler, 330–32
duties of subject, 63–73

Earl of Warenne, 130
Eastern Orthodox. See Orthodox Church
Eden, 33–35, 61, 167, 182n20, 246, 358
Edward I of England, 130
Enlightener (Joseph of Volokolamsk), 84
Epiphanius the Wise, 118–19, 123, 198
Erasm, Ermolai, 325
Erasmus, 303
Eve (biblical figure), 33–34, 59, 61

Faceted Hall. See Palace of Facets
False Dmitrii. See First False Dmitrii; Second False Dmitrii
Fedor I, 203, 223
  piety of, 58, 330–31
  power of, 90–91
  in tales, 57–58
  in Timofeev, 30, 36–38, 51n48, 65–66
Fennell, John, 361
Feodosii (icon painter), 139–40
Ficino, Marsilio, 348
Filaret, Patriarch, 25, 47n11, 48n20, 64, 326, 336, 375
Filipp, Metropolitan, 96–98, 101–2, 111n64, 271, 337–38
Filofei of Pskov, 157, 180n8, 340
First False Dmitrii, 36, 38, 50n31, 52n62, 62, 79n50, 91–92, 196, 331, 373
First Pretender. See First False Dmitrii
Fletcher, Giles, 31, 50n31, 278, 367, 379
Flier, Michael, 170, 191, 212, 225, 265, 280, 370, 387n29
Florenskii, Pavel, 49n30, 372

Florovsky, Georges, 110n51
fortresses, 192–96, 201, 205, 326
Franklin, Simon, 183n23

Gee, David, 361
Geertz, Clifford, 46n3, 108n13, 128, 215, 278
Genesis, 33–36, 167. *See also* Adam (biblical figure); Eden; Eve (biblical figure)
Gennadii, Archbishop, 337
Germogen, Patriarch, 62, 64, 66–68, 77n40, 336
Gerritsz, Hessel, 197
Glinskaia, Elena, 261, 263–68, 276
Glinskii, Elena, 5–6
God. *See also* Bible; Orthodox Church
  in Golden Hall murals, 218, 221, 227
  Israel and, 161
  in Kurbskii, 7–9, 17–18
  and power of ruler, 33–34, 37, 86–88, 92, 99–100, 304–5, 307–8, 310, 316, 328–30, 368
  and righteousness of tsar, 67–68
  subjects and, 65
  in Timofeev, 29–30, 34–35, 37, 40–42, 59
Godunov, Boris, 50n31
  architecture and, 171, 188–206, 306
  Bible and, 166–67
  Duma and, 191, 207n3
  fortresses and, 192–96
  Ivan IV and, 89
  legitimacy of, 190
  maps and, 196–97
  New Israel concept and, 170–71, 201–2, 205–6, 210n30
  political thought and, 326
  power of, 92
  in Shakhovskoi, 88
  in tales, 58–59, 62
  in Timofeev, 25, 29, 37–38, 58, 65–66, 94, 110n60, 202
Gol´dberg, A. L., 157–58
Golden Hall, 144–45, 148, 154n28, 168–69, 212, 215–30, 232n14, 308, 324, 329, 331, 334
Golitsyn, V. V., 175
Great Menology (Metropolitan Makarii), 164–65, 300, 306
Grobovsky, Antony N., 20n15, 45n3
Gryazev, I. K., 25

Hall of Facets. *See* Palace of Facets
Harari, Yuval Noah, 358–59, 383
Hart, Michael, 361

Herckman, Elias, 171, 202
Hexter, J. H., 81n62, 364
hierotopia, 371–72, 377
Hincmar, 304–5
historiography, 3–5, 19, 20n11, 24, 90, 178, 179n2, 361–64, 366–67
History of Ivan IV (Kurbskii), 4–8, 13
History of the Russian State (Karamzin), 8
Holy Trinity Cathedral (Pskov), 209n24
Holy Trinity Monastery, 115, 117–23
Hortatory Chapters (Agapetus), 34–35, 308, 347
humanism, 306, 321, 341, 348, 350

Iakovlev, A., 78n42
ICC. *See Illustrated Chronicle Companion* (ICC)
icons, religious, 31, 49n30, 118–20, 124n21, 130–32, 137–47, 347–48. *See also* Church Militant icon
ideology
  advice and, 98–99
  defined, 85, 87, 108n13
  literary, 83
  as symbolic language, 85, 87
Ilarion of Kiev, 163–65
Illustrated Chronicle Companion (ICC), 259–80, 284–97, 377, 380
Iov, Patriarch, 48n20, 57–58, 90, 167–68, 208n18, 330
Ipat´ev Monastery, 192
Israel, 161, 163. *See also* New Israel, Muscovy as
Ivan III, 121, 164, 166, 171, 190, 219, 302, 322–23, 337, 342
Ivan IV. *See also* oprichnina
  architecture and, 190–91
  aristocracy and, 74n4
  battle standard of, 133–34
  Boyar Duma and, 260
  boyars and, 122, 186
  bureaucracy under, 379–80
  coronation of, 99, 101, 135, 159–61, 169, 181n14, 284, 305, 329–30
  David (biblical figure) and, 160
  Holy Trinity Monastery and, 122–23
  in *Illustrated Chronicle Companion*, 261, 264–65, 267–71, 273–77
  in Karamzin, 8–10
  Kazan´ and, 115–16, 118, 133
  in Kliuchevskii, 14–19
  in Kotoshikhin, 351
  Kurbskii and, 4, 7–8, 52n53, 88, 212–13

Metropolitan Filipp and, 96–98, 101
Peresvetov and, 349
political thought in era of, 323–25
power of, 88–90, 96–97
regarded as tormentor, 316
Saint Sergius and, 116, 118–19
in Shakhovskoi, 89
in Solov'ev, 10–14
in tales, 72
in Timofeev, 30, 36–37, 39–40, 53n65, 89, 91
as writer of tales, 58–59
Ivan the Great Bell Tower, 198, 201, 206
izbrannaia rada, 20n15, 45n3

Jeremiah, Patriarch, 91
Jerome, 304
Joseph (biblical figure), 164, 185n47, 202, 247, 248
Joseph of Volokolamsk, 83–85, 87, 100, 331, 337
Joshua (biblical figure), 137–43, 146, 168, 185n46, 219, 225
Joshua and the Archangel Michael before the Battle of Jericho (Annunciation Cathedral), 140, 143
Joshua and the Archangel Michael before the Battle of Jericho (Dormition Cathedral), 137–39

Kain, Kevin, 372
Karamzin, Nikolay, 5, 8–10
Karpov, Fedor, 348–49, 352
Katyrev-Rostovskii, I. M., 75n16
Kazan', 8, 13, 18, 31, 49n30, 115–19, 133–35, 151, 169–70, 191–94, 268, 274, 340, 377
Kazanskaia istoriia, 115, 117–19, 124n6, 158
Kazanskoe skazanie, 57, 64, 66
Keenan, Edward, 3, 20n11, 42–43, 48n17, 96, 124n6, 157, 211–13, 228, 230, 278, 299–300, 302, 365–67, 378–79, 382
Kern, Fritz, 110n53
Khazars, 162–63
Khronograf of 1617, 66, 70, 77n40, 88–89, 92, 111n60
Khvorostinin, Ivan, 24, 62, 66, 88, 92
Kievan Academy, 349
Kievan Rus', 159, 161, 163, 183n23, 211, 284
"King of Kings" prayer, 160–61, 169, 181n16, 305, 329
Kinship and Politics (Kollmann), 382
Kirillov, V. V., 207n3

Kivelson, Valerie, 211, 216–17, 278, 301, 311, 364–66, 375–78
Klement'ev, Nikita, 154n28, 184n44, 221, 260
Kliuchevskii, Vasilii, 5, 14–19, 21nn58, 60, 362
  aristocracy in, 74n4
  subjects in, 68–69
  tales in, 54–56, 63
Kloss, B. M., 181n14
Kobrin, V. B., 47n7, 84
Kochetkov, I. A., 132, 185n49
Kollmann, Nancy Shields, 103, 121–22, 211, 259–60, 278, 280, 366, 372, 381–83
Komilii of Rostov, 97
Kon', Fedor, 192
Kormchaia kniga (*Book of the pilot*), 342
Kosoi, Feodosii, 325
Kotoshikhin, Grigorii, 343, 350–51, 356n48
Kremlin (Moscow), 128–29, 139–40, 168–69, 190, 198–99, 215–16, 322–23, 326, 360, 378–79. *See also specific structures*
Kriza, Agnes, 387n34
Krizhanich, Iurii, 158, 351–52
Krom, Mikhail, 379–80
Kromy, 192
Kurbskii, Andrei Mikhailovich, 3–19, 212–13, 320
  background of, 3–4
  Ivan IV and, 4, 52n53, 88
  Karamzin and, 8–9
  Karamzin vs., 9–10
  in Kliuchevskii, 14–19, 21nn58,60
  in Solov'ev, 13–14
  Solov'ev vs., 11–12
  style of, 5–8
  tales and, 108n24
Kurbskii, Semen, 6
Kurbskii-Groznyi Apocrypha, The (Keenan), 3, 212–13
Kursk, 192
Kurs Russkoi Istorii (Kliuchevskii), 18, 21n58
Kvlvidze, Nina, 370

Lascaris, John, 348
Latin language, 214, 303–4, 348
law, 50n35, 60–61, 72–73, 76n25, 307, 317, 328, 335, 341–47, 350, 380
lawlessness, 55, 61, 92, 101
Letter against Astrologers (Filofei of Pskov), 340
Lidov, Aleksei, 371–72, 386n24, 387n29

Life of Sergius (Epiphanius the Wise), 119, 123
Likhachev, D. S., 51n44
Lithuania, 10, 30, 80n55, 212–13, 322
Livny, 192
Lopialo, K. K., 185n44
Louis XIV of France, 85–86
Lunt, Horace, 181n12

Makarii, Metropolitan, 98–99, 134, 159–61, 164–65, 181n18, 218, 228, 260, 268, 270–72, 278, 300, 302, 306, 324, 337
Maksim the Greek, 4, 6, 19n3, 83, 96, 323, 348–49
Mamai (Tatar ruler), 116, 118, 164, 334
maps, 196–97, 209n21
Martin, Russell, 278, 366, 381–82
martyrs, 49n30, 91–92, 130, 132, 135–36, 150, 152n15, 340
Marxism, 319, 362–63
Massa, Isaac, 197, 199, 208n13
Medvedev, Sil′vestr, 350
memory sites, 116–18
Merian, Matthaus, 197
Miakishev, Dorofei Mineevich, 208n10
Michael (archangel), 129, 132, 136–43, 145, 147–51, 153n20, 221
middle class, 74n4, 362
Mikhailovich, Aleksei, 101, 154n33, 332, 350–51, 372
Miller, David, 112n81, 130, 165, 300
Minin, Kuzma, 66
Mirandola, Pico della, 348
Mogila, Peter, 349
Moore, Thomas, 179
More, Thomas, 303, 306
murals, in Golden Hall, 212, 216–30, 308, 324, 329, 331
Muslims, 115, 118, 195, 339–41

Nathan (biblical figure), 96–97, 101, 210n32, 332
natural law, 352
Near, Holly, 127
Neoplatonism, 347
Neronov, Ivan, 327
Nevskii, Alexander, 134, 136–37, 139, 164, 185n49
New Israel, Muscovy as
  Bible and, 79n55, 158–59, 163–70
  chosen peoples and, 156
  in *Church Militant* icon, 49n30, 169
  Godunov and, 170–71, 201–2, 205–6, 210n30
  in Golden Hall at Kremlin, 168–69
  New Jerusalem Monastery and, 171–76
  in tales, 79n55
  Third Rome theory *vs.*, 159
  Time of Troubles and, 166–68
  Timofeev and, 30, 166–67
New Jerusalem Monastery, 171–76, 186n54, 372
Nicomachean Ethics (Aristotle), 348
Nikon, Patriarch, 101, 171–76, 327–28, 332, 338, 341, 372
Nikon Chronicle, 166, 189
"Non-possessors," 84, 100
Nora, Pierre, 116
"Novaia povest′," 64–66, 70, 93
Novyi Elets, 192

Obolensky, Dimitri, 361–62
Old Believers, 43, 70, 81n66, 101, 106, 110n54, 114n99, 158, 317, 327–28, 332, 341
On Russia in the Reign of Alexei Mikhailovich (Kotoshikhin), 350–51
oprichnina, 9, 72, 96, 105
  aristocracy and, 74n4, 98
  German Polev and, 97
  Illustrated Chronicle Companion and, 260, 280
  Ivan IV and, 323
  Kurbskii and, 13
  Metropolitan Filipp and, 96–97
  in tales, 93
  in Timofeev, 39, 40, 89, 110n54, 280
order
  as responsibility of tsar, 93–95, 332
Orthodox Church, 336–39. *See also* Bible; clergy; God
  architecture and, 197–201
  Mikhail Romanov and, 93
  political thought and, 327–41
  Psalm of David and, 69–70
  royal absolutism and, 82–83
  Third Rome concept and, 157
  in Timofeev, 36–37, 53n65
Orthodox culture, 211–14, 230
Ostrowski, Donald, 84, 158, 180n8, 278, 366, 373
Ovid, 348

Palace of Facets, 146–48, 169, 185n47, 202–3, 206, 215–16, 223, 225, 306, 334
Palitsyn, Avraamy, 24, 61, 66–67, 70–71, 78n44, 91, 95, 110n57, 208n18, 335–36, 344

Palm Sunday, 170, 198, 324
Patrikeev, Vassian, 6, 83, 323
patrimony, 74n4, 82–83, 93, 98, 104, 112n80, 382
Paul (biblical figure), 29, 117, 167, 199
Pavlov, A. P., 207n3, 380
Peresvetov, Ivan, 58–59, 325, 349
personalism, of Timofeev, 32
Peter (biblical figure), 223
Peter the Great, 188, 284, 311, 315, 317–18, 336, 350, 384
Petrovna, Elizabeth, 220
philosophy, political, 28, 86, 347–52
Picchio, Riccardo, 49n25
piety
   of Fedor I, 58, 90, 330–31
   as responsibility of tsar, 90–91, 105, 114n104, 331
pilgrimage, 4, 121–22, 202, 329, 331, 360, 368, 378
Pipes, Richard, 82–86, 96, 99, 106
Piskarev Chronicle, 195, 204–5
"Plach o plenenii," 62–63
Platonov, S. F., 46n5, 54, 74n4
Pocock, J. G. A., 23, 45n2
Poe, Marshall, 367
Pokrovskii, M. N., 362
Polev, German, 97, 100–101
Polevoi, Boris, 209n20
Polianians, 162
political philosophy, 28, 86, 347–52
Pollard, A. F., 74n4
Polosin, I. I., 26, 47n14, 48n15, 52n60
Polotskii, Simeon, 350
Pope Adrian I, 304
"Possessors," 82, 84, 100
Postman, Neil, 127–28
"Povest' kako," 66, 70
"Povest' knigi sea," 75n16
"Povest' o belom klobuke," 158
"Povest' o zachale Moskvy," 158
power, of rulers
   absolutist view of, 82–83, 85–87
   aristocracy and, 44–45
   Boris Godunov, 92
   in Carolingian Europe, 304–7
   clergy and, 82
   and duties of ruler, 330–32
   Fedor I, 90–91
   God and, 33–34, 37, 86–88, 92, 99–100, 304–5, 310, 316, 328–30, 368
   vs. human nature of tsar, 39–40
   Ivan IV, 88–90, 96–97

   limitations of, 69–70, 76n25, 87–102, 316
   order and, 95
   piety and, 90–91
   responsibility and, 103–4
   theologies of, 368–73
Primary Chronicle, 162–65, 183n23, 189
Prosvetitel' (Joseph of Volokolamsk), 100
Protopopov, Afanasii, 97
Psalm of David, 69–70
Puritanism, 178

Radziwiłł Chronicle, 259, 283, 333
Rastrelli, Bartolomeo, 186n54, 220, 240
Red Square, 170, 215, 243–44, 250, 324, 386n21
religion. *See* Bible; clergy; God; icons, religious; Orthodox Church
Remezov, Semen, 283n20, 376–77
"Reply of Makarii," 99
Roman Catholicism, 322, 331, 367
Romanov, Fedor. *See* Boyar Duma
Romanov, Mikhail, 317, 325–26, 335, 344
   in Kliuchevskii, 55
   Orthodox Church and, 93
   in Timofeev, 25, 30, 36–37, 52n55
Romanovna, Anastasia, 4, 9, 21n35, 89
Russian Orthodox Church. *See* Orthodox Church
Russian Revolution of 1917, 83, 159, 319, 362
Russkaia Pravda, 342
Rylo, Vassian, 164

Saburova, Solomonia, 6–7
Saint Basil's. *See* Cathedral of the Intercession on the Moat
Saint Sergius, 115–23
Samuel (biblical figure), 96–97, 160, 166, 284–85, 330
Sapiens (Harari), 358
Saul (biblical figure), 30, 69, 92, 96, 160, 286, 330
Savva, Spiridon, 345
Schama, Simon, 184n39
Schlichting, Albert, 98
Scott, James C., 209n21
Second False Dmitrii, 168
Sergius. *See* Saint Sergius
"Sermon on Law and Grace" (Ilarion), 163–64
Sevcenko, Ihor, 34–35, 76n17, 107n4, 235
Shah Ali, 264–65
Shakhovskoi, Semen, 24, 62, 66, 88–89, 92, 96

Shcheboleva, E. G., 199
Shuiskii, Vasilii, 25, 30, 62, 77n40, 88, 91, 93, 331
Siberia, 143, 151, 193, 283n20, 328, 345, 351, 375–77
Sidorka, 38, 52n62
Sigismund III of Poland, 30, 80n55
Sizov, E. S., 148, 154n33
Skazanie (Palitsyn), 61, 66, 70–71, 78n44, 91, 95, 110n57, 344
Skazanie I, 62, 79n50
Skopin-Shuyskii, Mikhail, 25, 30
Skrynikov, R. G., 98, 179n3
Smolensk, 192, 194–96
smuta tales. *See* tales, *smuta*
Solomon (biblical figure), 30, 133–34, 150, 158, 160, 203, 219, 223, 225–27, 284, 287–92, 304, 340
Solov'ev, Sergey, 5, 10–14
Solzhenitsyn, Aleksandr, 127
Song of Roland (Archbishop Turpin), 127, 151
Sorskii, Nil, 323
sources
    approaches to, 23–24
    lack of, 5
    tales as, 56–57
Soviet Union, 70, 73, 107n4, 155, 320
Spasskii Gates, 215, 243
Spiridon, Archbishop, 136–37
Stand on the Ugra, 339
Staritskii, Vladimir Andreievich, 4, 9
Staryi Oskol, 192
"state-juridical" school, 319
Stepennaia kniga (*Book of degrees*), 117, 166
Streshnev, Semen, 338
subject(s)
    duties of, 63–73
    God and, 65
    in Kliuchevskii, 68–69
    responsibility of, 64–65
    as slaves, 333–34
    terminology used for, 63
    in Timofeev, 77n39
    in *Vremennik*, 64
Sudebnik, 342–43
Sweden, 25, 76n28
Swoboda, Marina, 209n29
Syl'vestr, 6–9, 13, 18, 99–101, 113n82, 337

Tale of the Vladimir Princes, The (Savva), 345
tales, *smuta*
    advice to tsar in, as subject, 61–62

    advice to tsar in, persons giving, 63–64
    Assembly of the Land in, 66–67
    Bible and, 70n55
    Boris Godunov in, 58–59
    boyars in, 61, 64, 69, 71–72
    Duma in, 66–67, 69
    duties of subject in, 63–73
    Fedor I in, 57–58
    Ivan IV in, 72
    in Kliuchevskii, 54–56
    Kurbskii and, 108n24
    language in, 62
    limitations to power of tsar in, 85
    as sources, 56–57
Tatars, 7–8, 115, 118, 135, 152n15, 160, 164, 195, 228, 334, 339
Tatishchev, Mikhail, 47n11, 94
textology, 23–24, 54
Third Rome, Muscovy as, 340
    chosen peoples and, 156
    church and, 157
    false tsar and, 105
    Makarii and, 165
    New Israel concept *vs.*, 159
    in Ostrowski, 373
    power and, 103
    timeline of, 157–58
    Time of Troubles and, 158
Thyrêt, Isolde, 264, 280, 331
Tikhomirov, M. N., 205
Time of Troubles. *See also* tales, *smuta*
    historiography and, 24
    in Kliuchevskii, 55
    New Israel concept and, 166–68
    in "Plach o plenenii," 62–63
    political thought and, 325–26
    Third Rome concept and, 158
    in Timofeev, 32–35, 38–41, 51n44, 65–66, 79n50
    "tormentor" rulers in, 316
Timofeev, Ivan. *See also Vremennik* (Timofeev)
    background of, 25–26, 43, 47n7
    corruption and, 32–42
    as historian, methods of, 28–32
    historiography and, 24
    language of, 26, 44, 45n2
    New Israel concept and, 166–67
    personalism of, 32
    philosophy of, 28–29
    political thought of, 40–42, 44
    on *Vremennik*, 26
Toporkov, Vassian, 8, 11

tormentor, ruler as, 38, 83, 85, 92–93, 95, 105–6, 109n47, 114n99, 316–17, 331–33, 352
totalitarianism, 320
Transfiguration (Bellini), 229
Trevor-Roper, Hugh, 362
Tsar's Pew, 259, 283, 292, 333, 369
Turpin, Archbishop, 127

Ukraine, 327, 349–50
Ullmann, Walter, 304
Ulozhenie of 1649, 301, 328, 335, 343, 345, 350
Ushakov, Simon, 117, 122, 146, 154n28, 184n44, 220–21, 256n16, 260
Utechin, S. V., 320

Val'denberg, V. E., 259
Valuiki, 192, 196
Vasilii III, 5–6, 121, 140, 181n18, 190, 261–64, 276, 278–79, 285, 291, 302, 322–23
Velikie Chetii Minei (Great Menology) (Metropolitan Makarii), 164–65, 300, 306
Veselovskii, S. B., 382
Viskovatyi, Ivan, 228, 245
Viskovatyi Affair, 144, 228
Vita (Metropolitan Filipp), 97, 102, 111n64
Vita (Nevskii), 136–37, 164
Vita (Saint Sergius), 118
Vladimir Monomakh, 145, 168, 203, 220, 223–24, 227, 284, 288–89, 293–94, 345
Vladimir of Staritsa, 31–32
Vladimir of Staritskii, 89
Vlasov, Afanasii, 94
Volotskii, Joseph, 147, 323
Volynskaia, Agrofena Ivanovna, 264
Voronezh, 192, 196

Vremennik (Timofeev), 24–45. *See also* Timofeev, Ivan
  advice to Tsar in, as subject, 61–62, 64
  authorship of, 27–28
  Boris Godunov in, 29, 37–38, 58, 65–66, 94, 110n60, 166–67, 202
  clergy in, 36, 53n65
  corruption in, 61
  as diary, 24–25
  editions of, 46n4
  Fedor I in, 30, 36, 51n48, 65–66
  God in, 29–30, 34–35, 37, 40–42, 59
  Ivan IV in, 30, 36–37, 39–40, 53n65
  language of, 26
  legitimacy in, 38–39, 42
  New Israel concept in, 30, 167
  oprichnina in, 40
  order in, 94
  Orthodox faith in, 36–37, 53n65
  political thought and, 326
  structure of, 26–27
  subjects in, 64
  Time of Troubles in, 32–35, 38–41, 51n44, 65–66, 79n50
  Timofeev on, 26
  tsar-subject relation in, 59–60
  writing of, 26–28, 48n20

Walter, Christopher, 181n16
Wilson, John A., 78n42
Władysław, 343
World War II, 154n33, 320

Yaroslav the Wise, 189, 286, 371

Zabelin, Ivan, 196, 208n17, 372
Zimin, A. A., 100, 111n72, 113n87, 207n5
Zobninovskii, Dionisii, 71, 75n14
Zosima, Metropolitan, 180n8, 339–40

www.ingramcontent.com/pod-product-compliance
Lightning Source LLC
Chambersburg PA
CBHW020217240426
43672CB00006B/338